Lecture Notes in Computer Science

Lecture Notes in Artificial Intelligence   14120

Founding Editor

Jörg Siekmann

Series Editors

Randy Goebel, *University of Alberta, Edmonton, Canada*
Wolfgang Wahlster, *DFKI, Berlin, Germany*
Zhi-Hua Zhou, *Nanjing University, Nanjing, China*

The series Lecture Notes in Artificial Intelligence (LNAI) was established in 1988 as a topical subseries of LNCS devoted to artificial intelligence.

The series publishes state-of-the-art research results at a high level. As with the LNCS mother series, the mission of the series is to serve the international R & D community by providing an invaluable service, mainly focused on the publication of conference and workshop proceedings and postproceedings.

Zhi Jin · Yuncheng Jiang ·
Robert Andrei Buchmann · Yaxin Bi ·
Ana-Maria Ghiran · Wenjun Ma
Editors

Knowledge Science, Engineering and Management

16th International Conference, KSEM 2023
Guangzhou, China, August 16–18, 2023
Proceedings, Part IV

 Springer

Editors
Zhi Jin 🆔
Peking University
Beijing, China

Robert Andrei Buchmann 🆔
Babeş-Bolyai University
Cluj-Napoca, Romania

Ana-Maria Ghiran 🆔
Babeş-Bolyai University
Cluj-Napoca, Romania

Yuncheng Jiang 🆔
South China Normal University
Guangzhou, China

Yaxin Bi 🆔
Ulster University
Belfast, UK

Wenjun Ma 🆔
South China Normal University
Guangzhou, China

ISSN 0302-9743 ISSN 1611-3349 (electronic)
Lecture Notes in Artificial Intelligence
ISBN 978-3-031-40291-3 ISBN 978-3-031-40292-0 (eBook)
https://doi.org/10.1007/978-3-031-40292-0

LNCS Sublibrary: SL7 – Artificial Intelligence

This Springer imprint is published by the registered company Springer Nature Switzerland AG
The registered company address is: Gewerbestrasse 11, 6330 Cham, Switzerland

Preface

We are extremely pleased to introduce the Proceedings of the 16th International Conference on Knowledge Science, Engineering and Management (KSEM 2023), this is a four-volume set containing the papers accepted for this year's conference, which was organized by and hosted at the South China Normal University, Guangzhou, China during August 16–18, 2023.

Since its inaugural conference back in 2006, KSEM has accumulated great success under the immense efforts from each year's organizing committee and beyond. Previous years' events were held in Guilin, China (KSEM 2006); Melbourne, Australia (KSEM 2007); Vienna, Austria (KSEM 2009); Belfast, UK (KSEM 2010); Irvine, USA (KSEM 2011), Dalian, China (KSEM 2013); Sibiu, Romania (KSEM 2014); Chongqing, China (KSEM 2015); Passau, Germany (KSEM 2016); Melbourne, Australia (KSEM 2017); Changchun, China (KSEM 2018); Athens, Greece (KSEM 2019). Even during the COVID pandemic, KSEM was continued and held in Hangzhou, China (KSEM 2020); Tokyo, Japan (KSEM 2021) and Singapore (KSEM 2022), respectively.

The objective of KSEM is to create a forum that gathers researchers and practitioners from academia, industry, and government around the globe to present advancements in theories and state-of-the-art technologies in the field of knowledge science, engineering, and management. Attendees were encouraged to present prototypes and deploy knowledge-based systems, discuss and debate practical challenges as well as opportunities for the research community. With its interdisciplinary nature, KSEM 2023 focused on four broad areas: Knowledge Science with Learning and AI (KSLA), Knowledge Engineering Research and Applications (KERA), Knowledge Management Systems (KMS), and Emerging Technologies for Knowledge Science, Engineering and Management (ETKS).

In this year's conference, we received 395 submissions. Single-blind review was adopted for the conference review process. Each submission was peer reviewed by 2 to 4 reviewers from the program committee members and external reviewers. Among them, 114 regular papers (28.8% acceptance rate) and 30 short papers were selected, giving a total of 144 papers. We have separated the proceedings into four volumes: LNCS 14117, 14118, 14119, and 14120. The collection of papers represents a wide range of research activities, covering knowledge representation and reasoning, knowledge extraction, knowledge integration, data mining and knowledge discovery, and beyond.

In addition to the regular sessions, this year's event featured the following keynote speakers:

- Witold Pedrycz, University of Alberta, Canada, with the presentation titled *Credibility of Machine Learning Through Information Granularity*;
- Zhi-Ḥua Zhou, Nanjing University, China, with the presentation titled *A New Paradigm to Leverage Formalized Knowledge and Machine Learning*;

- Geoff Webb, Monash University, Australia, with the presentation titled *Recent Advances in Assessing Time Series Similarity Through Dynamic Time Warping*;
- Jie Tang, Tsinghua University, China, with the presentation titled *ChatGLM: Run Your Own "ChatGPT" on a Laptop.*

We would like to express our sincere gratitude to the many contributors who were steadfast supporters and made KSEM 2023 a great success. First of all, we would like to thank the KSEM 2023 Organizing Committee, the School of Computer Science at South China Normal University, Sun Yat-sen University, and our publisher Springer, without their crucial support the conference would not have been possible. Secondly, we would like to thank the members of our Steering Committee (Honorary General Chairs), Ruqian Lu from the Chinese Academy of Sciences, and Dimitris Karagiannis from the University of Vienna, Austria, for their invaluable guidance throughout the event; the General Co-chairs, Zhi Jin from Peking University, Christos Douligeris from the University of Piraeus, Daniel Neagu from the University of Bradford, and Weihua Ma from South China Normal University. They were involved in the whole process of the organization efforts, and provided various critical resources, including but not limited to connections to external reviewers and professional advice. Last but not least, we would like to thank the authors who submitted their papers to this year's conference, the Program Committee and the external reviewers, without whom the daunting tasks of paper reviews would not have been accomplished in time.

We hope that the reader finds the results of the conference program valuable and thought-provoking, and we hope attendees had a valuable opportunity to share ideas with other researchers and practitioners from institutions around the world.

August 2023

Zhi Jin
Yuncheng Jiang
Robert Andrei Buchmann
Yaxin Bi
Ana-Maria Ghiran
Wenjun Ma

Organization

Honorary General Chairs

Ruqian Lu   Chinese Academy of Sciences, China
Dimitris Karagiannis   University of Vienna, Austria

General Chairs

Zhi Jin   Peking University, China
Christos Douligeris   University of Piraeus, Greece
Daniel Neagu   University of Bradford, UK
Weihua Ma   South China Normal University, China

Program Chairs

Yuncheng Jiang   South China Normal University, China
Robert Buchmann   Babeş-Bolyai University, Romania
Yaxin Bi   Ulster University, UK

Publication Chairs

Ana-Maria Ghiran   Babeş-Bolyai University, Romania
Wenjun Ma   South China Normal University, China

Publicity Chairs

Ye Zhu   Deakin University, Australia
Jieyu Zhan   South China Normal University, China

Steering Committee

Ruqian Lu (Honorary Chair)   Chinese Academy of Sciences, China
Dimitris Karagiannis (Chair)   University of Vienna, Austria

Bo Yang	Jilin University, China
Chengqi Zhang	University of Technology, Sydney, Australia
Christos Douligeris	University of Piraeus, Greece
Claudiu Kifor	Lucian Blaga University of Sibiu, Romania
Gang Li	Deakin University, Australia
Hui Xiong	State University of New Jersey, USA
Jörg Siekmann	German Research Centre of Artificial Intelligence, Germany
Martin Wirsing	Ludwig-Maximilians-Universität München, Germany
Meikang Qiu	Texas A&M University-Commerce, USA
Xiaoyang Wang	Zhejiang Gongshang University, China
Yaxin Bi	Ulster University, UK
Yoshiteru Nakamori	Japan Advanced Institute of Science and Technology, Japan
Zhi Jin	Peking University, China
Zili Zhang	Southwest University, China

Technical Program Committee

Achim D. Brucker	University of Exeter, UK
Achim Hoffmann	University of New South Wales, Australia
Agostino Cortesi	Universita' Ca' Foscari di Venezia, Italy
Andrea Polini	University of Camerino, Italy
Ben Roelens	Open Universiteit, Netherlands
Bo Luo	University of Kansas, USA
Bowen Zhao	Singapore Management University, Singapore
Chaobo He	South China Normal University, China
Chenyou Fan	South China Normal University, China
Cheng Huang	Sichuan University, China
Chunxia Zhang	Beijing Institute of Technology, China
Claudiu Kifor	Lucian Blaga University of Sibiu, Romania
Cungen Cao	Chinese Academy of Sciences, Beijing, China
Dan Oleary	University of Southern California, USA
Daniel Volovici	Lucian Blaga University of Sibiu, Romania
Dantong Ouyang	Jilin University, China
Dimitris Apostolou	University of Piraeus, Greece
Dongning Liu	Guangdong University of Technology, China
Florin Leon	Gheorghe Asachi Technical University of Iasi, Romania
Haibo Zhang	University of Otago, New Zealand

Keynotes Abstracts

Credibility of Machine Learning Through Information Granularity

Witold Pedrycz[iD]

Department of Electrical and Computer Engineering, University of Alberta,
Edmonton, Canada
wpedrycz@ualberta.ca

Abstract. Over the recent years, we have been witnessing numerous and far-reaching developments and applications of Machine Learning (ML). Efficient and systematic design of their architectures is important. Equally important are comprehensive evaluation mechanisms aimed at the assessment of the quality of the obtained results. The credibility of ML models is also of concern to any application, especially the one exhibiting a high level of criticality commonly encountered in autonomous systems and critical processes of decision-making. With this regard, there are a number of burning questions: how to quantify the quality of a result produced by the ML model? What is its credibility? How to equip the models with some self-awareness mechanism so careful guidance for additional supportive experimental evidence could be triggered?

Proceeding with a conceptual and algorithmic pursuits, we advocate that these problems could be formalized in the settings of Granular Computing (GrC). We show that any numeric result be augmented by the associated information granules being viewed as an essential vehicle to quantify credibility. A number of key formalisms explored in GrC are explored, namely those involving probabilistic, interval, and fuzzy information granules. Depending on the formal settings, confidence levels and confidence intervals or coverage and specificity criteria are discussed in depth and we show their role as descriptors of credibility measures.

The general proposals of granular embedding and granular Gaussian Process models are discussed along with their ensemble architectures. In the sequel, several representative and direct applications arising in the realm of transfer learning, knowledge distillation, and federated learning are discussed.

A New Paradigm to Leverage Formalized Knowledge and Machine Learning

Zhi-Hua Zhou

Department of Computer Science and Technology, School of Artificial Intelligence,
Nanjing University, China
zhouzh@nju.edu.cn

Abstract. To develop a unified framework which accommodates and enables machine learning and logical knowledge reasoning to work together effectively is a well-known holy grail problem in artificial intelligence. It is often claimed that advanced intelligent technologies can emerge when machine learning and logical knowledge reasoning can be seamlessly integrated as human beings generally perform problem-solving based on the leverage of perception and reasoning, where perception corresponds to a data-driven process that can be realized by machine learning whereas reasoning corresponds to a knowledge-driven process that can be realized by formalized reasoning. This talk ill present a recent study in this line.

Recent Advances in Assessing Time Series Similarity Through Dynamic Time Warping

Geoff Webb

Department of Data Science and Artificial Intelligence, Monash Data Futures Institute,
Monash University, Australia
Geoff.Webb@monash.edu

Abstract. Time series are a ubiquitous data type that capture information as it evolves over time. Dynamic Time Warping is the classic technique for quantifying similarity between time series. This talk outlines our impactful program of research that has transformed the state of the art in practical application of Dynamic Time Warping to big data tasks. These include fast and effective lower bounds, fast dynamic programming methods for calculating Dynamic Time Warping, and intuitive and effective variants of Dynamic Time Warping that moderate its sometimes-excessive flexibility.

ChatGLM: Run Your Own "ChatGPT" on a Laptop

Jie Tang

Department of Computer Science, Tsinghua University, China
jietang@tsinghua.edu.cn

Abstract. Large language models have substantially advanced the state of the art in various AI tasks, such as natural language understanding and text generation, and image processing, multimodal modeling. In this talk, I am going to talk about how we build GLM-130B, a bilingual (English and Chinese) pre-trained language model with 130 billion parameters. It is an attempt to open-source a 100B-scale model at least as good as GPT-3 and unveil how models of such a scale can be successfully pre-trained. Based on GLM-130B, we have developed ChatGLM, an alternative to ChatGPT. A small version, ChatGLM-6B, is opened with weights and codes. It can be deployed with one RTX 2080 Ti (11G) GPU, which makes it possible for everyone to deploy a ChatGPT! It has attracted over 2,000,000 downloads on Hugging Face in one month, and won the trending #1 model for two weeks.

GLM-130B: https://github.com/THUDM/GLM-130B.
ChatGLM: https://github.com/THUDM/ChatGLM-6B.

1

Contents – Part IV

Emerging Technologies for Knowledge Science, Engineering and Management

Federated Prompting
and Chain-of-Thought Reasoning
for Improving LLMs Answering

Xiangyang Liu, Tianqi Pang, and Chenyou Fan[✉]

South China Normal University, Guangdong, China
{2022024952,2022024954}@m.scnu.edu.cn, fanchenyou@scnu.edu.cn

Abstract. We investigate how to enhance answer precision in frequently asked questions posed by distributed users using cloud-based Large Language Models (LLMs). Our study focuses on a typical situation where users ask similar queries that involve identical mathematical reasoning steps and problem-solving procedures. Due to the unsatisfactory accuracy of LLMs' zero-shot prompting with standalone questions, we propose to improve the distributed synonymous questions using Self-Consistency (SC) and Chain-of-Thought (CoT) techniques with a crowd-sourced federated question pool. Our methods can generate significantly more accurate answers for all user queries without requiring sophisticated model-tuning. Through extensive experiments, we demonstrate that our proposed methods can significantly enhance question accuracy by fully exploring the synonymous nature of the questions and the consistency of the answers.

Keywords: Synonymous Question-answering · Federated Learning · Large Language Model · Prompt Learning · Chain-of-Thought

1 Introduction

Recently, Large Language Models (LLMs) such as PaLM [2] and GPT family [1] have revolutionized the methodology of tackling natural language processing (NLP) tasks such as sentiment analysis [13], question answering [16], text summarization [15], and reasoning on arithmetic and common sense questions [17].

LLMs are usually cloud-deployed for solving customized tasks from distributed users. For example, more and more students use LLMs for solving mathematical problems. Primary school students may ask "How many chickens and rabbits are in the same cage with a total of 35 heads and 94 feet?". Due to the complexity in task understanding and reasoning, the LLMs often return the wrong answers.

One commonsense is that can we crowd-source many questions and aggregate those questions to better understand some common questions. A common question might be asked frequently as its variants in the concrete parameters or rephrased formulations. For example, the Chickens-and-rabbits questions can be asked with different number of heads and feet. Now we want to ask *Can we fully*

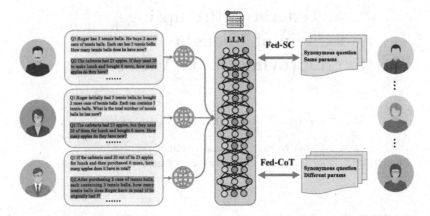

Fig. 1. An overview of our approach. We federate synonymous questions from distributed users and apply self-consistency and Chain-of-Thought techniques to improve answering from central LLMs.

utilize those similar questions to improve the question answering of the LLMs without tuning the model parameters or infringing user privacy?

Recent progressives in federated learning (**FL**) [8] have proved that utilizing distributed data sources can both preserve data privacy and enhance model training. In the FL paradigm, each client trains a local learning model with *own data*, while a central server regularly communicates with all agents to generate a better global model through the aggregation of the local models.

In this study, we consider improving the reasoning capacity of LLMs by better understanding crowd-sourced similar questions, from which we can explore the contextual information and improve the LLM answers substantially. Inspired by FL, we propose two typical scenarios when a user sends a QA request to the LLM and the LLM tries to answer with a collected question database.

The first is **Synonymous Questions with Same Parameters (SP-questions)**. The cloud-deployed system retrieves from the database and finds several synonymous but rephrased questions with exactly the same parameters. For SP-questions, we propose to leverage LLMs to directly generate answers first. Then we federate the answers and apply the self-consistency [12] technique to obtain the most voted answer for all synonymous questions in the federation. We call this method **Fed-SP-SC** (Fed-SP with Self-Consistency).

The second is **Synonymous Questions with Different Parameters (DP-questions)**, which is more general than SP-questions. We propose to leverage LLMs to generate consistent answers for each DP-questions first. As we cannot directly agglomerate the answers for questions of different parameters, we federate them by forming the Chain-of-Thought (CoT) to provide hints to the LLMs. We append the original query to the CoT as the full prompt to obtain improved final answer. We call this technique **Fed-DP-CoT**.

We extensively evaluate our methods on the GSM8K and SVAMP datasets and demonstrate that the Fed-SP-SC method achieves a notable improvement in accuracy of 13.9-18.1% over the standalone LLMs with Zero-Shot-CoT ("Let's think step by step"). Additionally, our Fed-DP-CoT method delivers an impressive increase of 9.2-14.2% over the standalone LLMs with Zero-Shot-CoT.

We summarize our contributions in this study as follows.

1) We consider a practical but under-studied scenario that the cloud-based LLMs are frequently asked synonymous questions from distributed users.
2) We identify two main user scenarios: synonymous questions are of same parameters (SP-questions) or of different parameters (DP-questions).
3) We design to federate synonymous questions first then utilize self-consistency to select the most voted answer to improve SP-question answering.
4) We also amalgamate consistent answers and create a chain-of-thought prompt to improve DP-questions answering. We design a simple disclaimer to handle noisy CoT generated from LLM answers better.
5) Inherited from FL, our methods can enhance the QA quality of LLMs while preserving the anonymity without data exchange among distributed users.

2 Related Work

Pre-trained Language Models (PLMs). Recent studies in Transformer-based language models such as ELMo [10] and BERT [4] have shown their capabilities in scaling up model sizes with pre-training methodology such as Masked Language Modeling [4]. Shortly after, several Large Language Models (LLMs), e.g., the GPTs [1], PaLM [2], LLaMA [11], have emerged with huge amount of parameters from 100B to 5000B. They have shown great advantages in language modeling tasks such as arithmetic reasoning and question answering.

Some recent studies made efforts towards unveiling the power of those LLMs. The *Chain-of-Thought* (CoT) [14] proposes to generate intermediate reasoning steps and obtain significant improvement in the performance of on reasoning tasks. The *Self-consistency* [12] suggests to aggregate multiple CoT paths, rather than relying on one greedy decoding path. This can lead to further improvements in the accuracy of models on reasoning tasks.

However, **it is unknown how to apply proper pre-training to distributed learning scenarios.** The recent popular *Federated Learning* [5,8,18] (FL) provides a way of learning models over a collection of distributed devices while keeping data locality. However, classical FL studies assumed the agents in FL can own copies of local models while receiving updates from centralized model. In contrast, we focus on a practical scenario that the clients can only query answers from centralized LLMs without owning any local model as LLMs are computational extensive to be deployed locally.

3 Scenarios and Approaches

In this section, we describe the federated scenarios that distributed users query the LLMs with synonymous questions. We first introduce some basic concepts.

Table 1. Examples of SP-questions and DP-questions. *Q1* and *Q2* are synonymous with same parameters. *Q1* and *Q3* are synonymous but with different parameters.

Q1: *"If a farmer has chickens and rabbits in a barn and there are a total of 32 heads and 100 feet, how many chickens and rabbits does the farmer have?"*

Q2: *"In a barn, there are a certain number of chickens and rabbits that have a total of 32 heads and 100 feet. how many of each animal are in the barn?"*

Q3: *"A farmer has a total of 20 chickens and rabbits in his barn. If the total number of legs is 56, how many chickens and how many rabbits?"*

Chain-of-Thought (CoT). [14] is a series of generated intermediate reasoning texts that can be added to the original prompts. CoT can enhance the capability of language models to perform various reasoning tasks by decomposing complex problems into intermediate steps that could be solved well step-by-step. Chain-of-thought prompting, i.e. prompting LLMs with CoT, is a simple and practical method for improving the reasoning tasks readily without tuning the LLMs.

Self-Consistency (SC). [12] is a decoding strategy that enhances language model reasoning with voting ensemble. SC first samples a diverse set of answers as reasoning paths of a question, rather than only the greedy path. By exploring multiple paths, SC is capable of identifying the most consist answer as the final answer by majority voting. Compared with a single-path reasoning, SC ensembles answers to improve accuracy and filters out noises or outliers. SC has also been widely explored in reasoning and QA tasks.

3.1   Synonymous Questions with Same Parameters (SP-Questions)

The first practical user scenario that we consider is as follows. Given a user query, we can retrieve from the cloud database several **synonymous questions with same parameters (SP-questions)**, as shown in Table 1. For complex reasoning tasks, the LLMs may provide unreliable answers to each standalone question, due to the zero-shot way of asking complex questions which may lack context or proper reasoning paths.

Thus, our task is to *fully explore the SP-questions as a federation to enhance their common answer collectively*, instead of dealing them separately. To this end, we propose a technique named **Fed-SP-SC** (Federated SP-questions with Self-Consistency) for answering the questions with the self-consistency technique mentioned above. Fed-SP-SC can improve the zero-shot accuracy of the answers by eliciting answers from multiple synonymous questions which are presumably the same. We ensure this self-consistency by making a majority vote and selecting the most voted answer as the final answer of all SP-questions. The most voted answer is the agreement of multiple reasoning paths from multiple rephrased SP-questions, thus is more likely to be better than a single prompted answer.

In our experiments, we demonstrate that Fed-SP-SC achieves a 18.1% improvement in accuracy on the GSM8K dataset and a 13.9% improvement on the SVAMP dataset in Table 2. In a practical system, we can further store these user prompts and the SC-selected answer back into the database.

3.2 Synonymous Questions with Different Parameters (DP-Questions)

We now describe the second scenario which is broader and more practical, named **synonymous questions with different parameters (DP-questions)**. Based on the user query question, the cloud-deployed system searches and retrieves questions with same meanings but may have different parameters.

DP-questions are more practical yet harder than SP-questions as the question parameters retrieved from the database are different. We show exemplary questions Q1 and Q3 above which have the same meaning yet with different parameters *heads* and *feet* in Table 1.

Note that tackling DP-questions would face all the difficulties of SP-questions, and would have additional obstacles. As there is no uniform ground-truth for DP-questions in the database, direct application of self-consistency is not possible. We propose the **Federated questions of Different Parameters with Chain-of-Thought** (Fed-DP-CoT) technique to leverage existing answers of DP-questions in CoT forms to improve new query answering.

When a user starts querying the cloud-based LLM service with a user query, the system matches several DP-questions with the highest similarity in the database. We assume they already have *pseudo-labels* with high-confidence generated by self-consistency in the Fed-SP-SC processes [6]. Then we use them as a CoT prompt for the original query-question. We also add an error disclaimer at the end of this prompt as the complete prompt. We found the disclaimer can boost performance by approximately 2%. Finally, we use the entire disclaimed CoT as a prefix to the user's query prompt for the LLMs to provide the final answer.

4   Experiment

We evaluate our proposed **Fed-SP-SC** and **Fed-DP-CoT** methods on benchmark datasets with simulated user scenarios such that SP- and DP-questions are retrieved to improve over standalone question answering. We compare our methods with *Zero-Shot-CoT* [1], which refers to adding *"Let's think step by step."* to prompt as a composite prompt, such as "[Question] A: Let's think step by step."

We describe two datasets that we use to compare our methods. **GSM8K** is a math dataset with 7,473 training and 1,319 testing examples of grade-school-level word problems [3]. GSM8K is widely used as a benchmark dataset for testing the arithmetic and commonsense reasoning capacities of LLMs [6,7]. **SVAMP** is a dataset of simple arithmetic math word problems [9] with around 6,000 samples. Each data instance has a short story and a question about unknown quantities. SVAMP provides a benchmark test set for comparing the textual understanding and reasoning abilities of LLMs, which is widely compared in recent studies [9,12,14].

We conduct our experiment on a subset of GSM8K and cv-mawps of SVAMP. In practice, we use GPT-3 and GPT-3.5 to generate synonymous questions. We selected OpenAI text-davinci-003 for the GSM8K dataset and text-davinci-002 for the SVAMP dataset so that the accuracy neither too high nor too low.

4.1   Results of Fed-SP-SC

The experiment of Fed-SP-SC contains five steps: (1) Load the GSM8K and SVAMP datasets as our benchmark and extract the questions and answers in the dataset; (2) Add each question a prompt prefix "Rephrase in 4 ways: [QUES-TION]" to generate SP-questions; (3) Prompt both the original and rewritten questions to the LLMs to obtain their respective answers; (4) Use the majority vote for self-consistency; (5) Get the answer generated by Fed-SP-SC and compare it with the answer in the dataset to determine the accuracy rate.

Table 2. Fed-SP-SC results

Data\Method	Zero-Shot-CoT	Fed-SP-SC (GPT-3 Gen.)	Fed-SP-SC (GPT-3.5 Gen.)
GSM8K	52.5%	62.7%	70.6%
SVAMP	77.2%	86.3%	91.1%

We show accuracy of self-consistency after obtaining results from different phrasings of the synonymous question on GSM8K and SVAMP in Table 2. We have the following observations. *Fed-SP-SC can improve answering accuracy* of LLMs by federating multiple SP-questions through self-consistency. *The quality of the synonymous questions can affect the accuracy significantly,* as seen in the larger improvement of using GPT-3.5 vs. GPT-3.

4.2   Results of Fed-DP-CoT

The experiment of Fed-DP-CoT contains five steps: (1) Extract consistent questions and answers in Fed-SP-SC. We use SP-questions with a confidence greater than 0.5; (2) Rephrase the questions using different parameters manually and providing answers; (3) Add a disclaimer to form the CoT prompt; (4) Add the rephrased questions after the CoT prompt; (5) Prompt LLMs with entire CoT prompt and compared the answers with the rephrased answers for evaluation.

Table 3. Fed-DP-CoT results.

Setting\Method	Zero-Shot-CoT	Fed-DP-CoT (GPT-3 Gen.)	Fed-DP-CoT (GPT-3.5 Gen.)
GSM8K	48.3%	59.2%	62.5%
SVAMP	76.5%	82.4%	85.7%

We report results of Fed-DP-CoT on GSM8K and SVAMP in Table 3, and compare with the baseline Zero-Shot-CoT. We observe that *Fed-DP-CoT outperforms Zero-Shot-CoT* by approximately 10.9%-14.2% and 5.9%-9.2% on the datasets GSM8K and SVAMP, respectively. *Fed-SP-SC performs better than Fed-DP-CoT.* The results of Fed-SP-SC on the GSM8K and SVAMP datasets are both higher than Fed-DP-CoT, with an approximate improvement of 5%. *There is less performance difference between GPT-3 and GPT-3.5 Gen., compared to Fed-SP-SC.* The reason is that the disparity in parameters reduces the difference of synonym usage in the CoT prompt.

4.3 Ablation Studies

The Number of Reasoning Paths for Self-Consistency. We study the effect of using different number of sampled reasoning paths for Fed-SP-SC (Sect. 4.1) to apply self-consistency. We conduct hyper-parameter search with a subset of the data for this ablation study due to the limits of accesses of the OpenAI API.

On the GSM8K dataset, GPT-3 Gen. achieved accuracy of 44.8%, 48.2%, 58.6%, 55.2%, and 51.7% for reasoning paths 1 (no SC), 3, 5, 7, and 9, respectively. GPT-3.5 Gen. achieved accuracy of 44.8%, 62.1%, 68.9%, 65.5%, and 66.7%. Similarly, on the SVAMP dataset, GPT-3 Gen. achieved accuracy of 73.5%, 79.4%, 88.2%, 89.7%, and 85.2%, while GPT-3.5 Gen. achieved accuracy of 73.5%, 82.3%, 91.2%, 91.4%, and 90.9%. This shows that the accuracy increases when the number of sampled reasoning paths increases from one to five. However, when the number exceeds five, the accuracy of the model starts to decrease. We speculate that introducing synonymous questions also brings noisy phrases, causing a deviation in the semantic meaning of the original questions. This deviation is particularly evident in synonymous questions generated by GPT-3.

Table 4. GSM8K disclaimer ablation.

Method\Setting	Zero-shot -CoT	Fed-DP-CoT (GPT-3 Gen.)	Fed-DP-CoT (GPT-3.5 Gen.)
w/o disclaimer	48.3%	57.7%	60.0%
w/ disclaimer	NA	59.2%	62.5%

Disclaimer. We investigate whether the disclaimer is effective of correcting noisy CoTs in this ablation experiment. As Zero-Shot-CoT does not employ pseudo-labels, we do not conduct disclaimer ablation on it. Table 4 compares the DP-questions answering accuracy with disclaimer and without disclaimer. We observe that the addition of a disclaimer in the questions and answers generated by GPT-3 resulted in an increase in accuracy from 57.7% to 59.2% for the

Fed-DP-CoT task. Similarly, in the case of questions and answers generated by GPT-3.5, the accuracy increase from 60.0% to 62.5%. These results indicate that the use of a simple disclaimer can potentially improve the accuracy of LLMs by approximately 2% for the Fed-DP-CoT task. We postulate that the improvement in accuracy may be attributed to the fact that the disclaimer prompts LLMs to be careful of the pseudo-labels and self-examine the reasoning steps.

5   Conclusion

We investigate the potential benefits of employing synonymous queries from distributed users to enhance question-answering beyond what is achievable by a single user. We extract SP- or DP-questions and apply self-consistency to identify the most consistent answers for SP-questions and utilize them as CoT to improve the answers provided for DP-questions. Our method yields a significant boost in performance compared to standalone zero-shot QA. Future research may implement more realistic systems that can efficiently retrieve federated questions while also improving CoT correctness to further advance reasoning capabilities. Future work can further extend to semi-supervised scenarios that part of the DP-questions have no answers or have only pseudo-answers.

References

1. Brown, T., et al.: Language models are few-shot learners. NeurIPS **33**, 1877–1901 (2020)
2. Chowdhery, A., et al.: PaLM: scaling language modeling with pathways. arXiv:2204.02311 (2022)
3. Cobbe, K., Kosaraju, V., et al.: Training verifiers to solve math word problems. arXiv:2110.14168 (2021)
4. Devlin, J., Chang, M.W., Lee, K., Toutanova, K.: BERT: pre-training of deep bidirectional transformers for language understanding. In: NAACL (2019)
5. Fan, C., Huang, J.: Federated few-shot learning with adversarial learning. In: WiOpt (2021)
6. Huang, J., et al.: Large language models can self-improve. arXiv:2210.11610 (2022)
7. Kojima, T., Gu, S.S., Reid, M., Matsuo, Y., Iwasawa, Y.: Large language models are zero-shot reasoners. arXiv:2205.11916 (2023)
8. McMahan, H.B., Moore, E., Ramage, D., Hampson, S., y Arcas, B.A.: Communication-efficient learning of deep networks from decentralized data. In: AISTATS (2017)
9. Patel, A., Bhattamishra, S., Goyal, N.: Are NLP models really able to solve simple math word problems? In: Proceedings of the 2021 Conference of the North American Chapter of the Association for Computational Linguistics: Human Language Technologies, pp. 2080–2094 (2021)
10. Peters, M.E., et al.: Deep contextualized word representations. In: ACL (2018)
11. Touvron, H., et al.: LLaMA: open and efficient foundation language models. arXiv:2302.13971 (2023)
12. Wang, X., et al.: Self-consistency improves chain of thought reasoning in language models. arXiv:2203.11171 (2022)

13. Wankhade, M., Rao, A.C.S., Kulkarni, C.: A survey on sentiment analysis methods, applications, and challenges. Artif. Intell. Rev. **55**(7), 5731–5780 (2022)
14. Wei, J., et al.: Chain of thought prompting elicits reasoning in large language models. arXiv:2201.11903 (2022)
15. Yadav, D., Desai, J., Yadav, A.K.: Automatic text summarization methods: a comprehensive review. arXiv:2204.01849 (2022)
16. Zaib, M., Zhang, W.E., Sheng, Q.Z., Mahmood, A., Zhang, Y.: Conversational question answering: a survey. Knowl. Inf. Syst. **64**(12), 3151–3195 (2022)
17. Zhao, W.X., Zhou, K., et al.: A survey of large language models. arXiv:2303.18223 (2023)
18. Zhao, Y., Li, M., Lai, L., Suda, N., Civin, D., Chandra, V.: Federated learning with non-IID data. arXiv preprint arXiv:1806.00582 (2018)

Advancing Domain Adaptation of BERT by Learning Domain Term Semantics

Jian Yang[1,2], Xinyu Hu[2,3], Weichun Huang[2], Hao Yuan[2], Yulong Shen[1(✉)], and Gang Xiao[2(✉)]

[1] School of Computer Science and Technology, Xidian University, Xi'an, China
ylshen@mail.xidian.edu.cn
[2] National Key Laboratory for Complex Systems Simulation, Beijing, China
[3] School of Systems Science and Engineering, Sun Yat-sen University, Guangzhou, China

Abstract. Pre-trained Language Models, such as BERT, have recently experienced a significant advancement, enhancing state-of-the-art performance across various Natural Language Processing (NLP) tasks. However, these models yield an unsatisfactory results in domain scenarios, particularly in specialized fields like biomedical contexts, where they cannot amass sufficient semantics of domain terms. To tackle this problem, we present a semantic learning method for BERT, focusing on the biomedical domain, to acquire and inject biomedical term semantics. Specifically, we first use BERT to encode the definitions of biomedical terms, acquiring their semantics and storing them as embeddings. Next, we design a contrastive learning task based on these embeddings to inject semantics, facilitating the transfer of domain term semantics from term embeddings to BERT's vocabulary. This process narrows the semantic gap between the original vocabulary and domain terms in the embedding space. We evaluate our method on both general and biomedical NLP tasks, and experimental results demonstrate a significant improvement in BERT's performance across all biomedical NLP tasks without affecting its performance on general tasks.

Keywords: pre-trained language models · biomedical domain adaption · knowledge representation learning

1 Introduction

Pre-trained language models (PLMs) [4,32–34] effectively capture rich semantic patterns via transferring general knowledge [30] and have achieved remarkable breakthroughs across a broad range of NLP tasks. BERT [7], a prominent example, acquires contextualized word representations using bidirectional information from a masked language model and can be fine-tuned for downstream tasks. However, these general-domain models, despite excelling in various general NLP tasks, face challenges in domain adaptation, particularly in specialized fields like

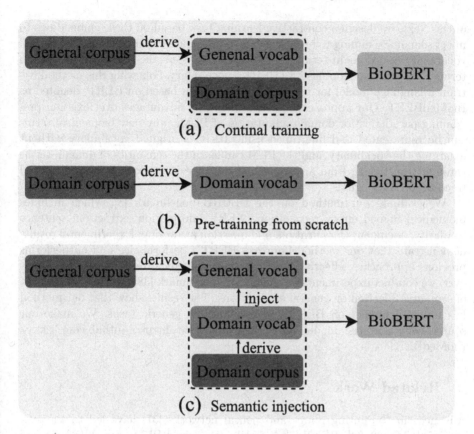

Fig. 1. Comparison of different pretraining paradigms for biomedical domain adaption of BERT.

biomedical contexts, where their vocabularies struggle to learn the semantics of domain-specific terms effectively [17].

To address this issue, some researchers have attempted to continue pre-training with biomedical corpora based on the original vocabulary [1,22], as illustrated in Fig. 1 (a). However, these approaches split biomedical terms into tokens and capture their semantics only from their co-occurrence signals, which leads to inadequate semantic learning due to sparsity. Gu et al. [8] instead propose deriving the vocabulary exclusively from in-domain text to preserve the completeness of biomedical terms and pre-training a domain language model from scratch, as shown in Fig. 1 (b). Although the model vocabulary treats biomedical terms as basic semantic units, training the model from scratch incurs substantial costs. To resolve this, we propose a two-phase method, semantic acquisition and injection, to complement the semantics of domain terms for the vocabulary of BERT. Specifically, we first use BERT to encode the context of biomedical terms, acquiring the semantics of domain terms and storing them as embeddings. Next, we design a contrastive learning task based on these embeddings to inject semantics, aiming to bring the embedding space closer between the original vocabulary and domain terms. This process transfers the semantics of domain terms from term embeddings into BERT's vocabulary. Following this method, we train a language model for the biomedical domain based on BERT, denoted as BioMedBERT. Our approach offers the following advantages over existing pre-training paradigms for domain adaptation of PLMs: any new biomedical terms can be represented and fine-tuned using BERT's original vocabulary without enlarging the vocabulary, and the PLM can learn the semantics of domain terms through transferring from any beneficial unsupervised texts, not being limited to co-occurrence signals.

We evaluate our method on the BLURB benchmark [8], which includes biomedical named entity recognition (NER), information extraction, sentence similarity, document classification, and question answering. Experimental results demonstrate that our method improves BERT's performance and outperforms previous approaches, effectively transferring biomedical term semantics. Moreover, we conduct experiments on the GLUE benchmark [38] to assess the impact of semantic injection on general applications. The results show that our method has minimal impact on BERT's performance in generic tasks. We make our source code and the model publicly available at https://github.com/jskxy/BioMedBERT.

2   Related Work

Advances in computing power and neural networks [37] have led to the success of PLMs [32–34]. BERT [7], a widely recognized PLM, introduced masked language model pre-training and bidirectional context for learning robust word representations. This architecture inspired extensions such as RoBERTa [24], which refined BERT's pre-training strategies, and ALBERT [21], which implemented parameter-reduction techniques for model scaling while maintaining performance. However, these models learn linguistic properties from general domain corpora, performing suboptimally in domain-specific scenarios.

To address this issue, one approach learns domain term semantics from word co-occurrence signals in specialty corpora. BioBERT [22] continues training BERT with a biomedical corpus without altering its architecture or vocabulary, improving performance in biomedical downstream tasks. Following BioBERT, models like RoBERTaNews [9], CodeGPTadapted [26], NetBERT [25], and ClinicalBERT [1] use continual pretraining. However, they do not treat domain terms as basic semantic units, and their split subwords lack specific domain semantics. Unlike them, our method introduces novel pretraining tasks to recognize complete domain terms and inject semantics into split subwords.

Another approach learns a new domain vocabulary from scratch or adds an extra vocabulary based on the original one. PubMedBERT [8], for example, customizes a biomedical-specific vocabulary and pretrains from scratch on specialty corpora. Various domains, such as finance [40], science [2], and law [5], have also

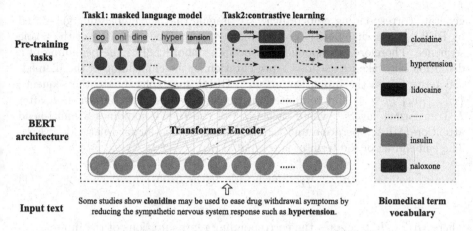

Fig. 2. The overall architecture of BioMedBRET. The entity embedding vocabulary is generated by the BERT and is used for semantic injection.

developed domain-specific PLMs. Some researches [15,19,36,41] instead introduce additive domain entity vocabularies to extend PLMs to specific domains. However, these methods require massive domain corpora and computing overhead for pre-training, or result in memory redundancy. Our method captures domain terms without increasing vocabulary or training from scratch.

Other studies attempt to learn domain term semantics based on external structured knowledge. Some [12,13,23,43] design entity-related classification tasks to incorporate triplet information, while [42] investigates structured dictionary information to inject entity knowledge. Despite their effectiveness, they rely on available structured knowledge. Our approach requires only unstructured text to achieve domain adaption of PLMs.

3 Methodology

In this section, we introduce the details of our proposed method. We first describe how to generate corresponding embeddings of domain terms based on their descriptions to acquire their semantics. Then we detail the process of semantic injection for PLMs with pre-constructed embeddings.

3.1 Semantic Acquisition

Since there are no available biomedical knowledge base, we first derive biomedical terms from the biomedical corpus via WordPiece [39] and then crwal their descriptions from Wikipedia. Concretely, we use the biomedical terms as entries to search their Wikipedia pages and crawl the first paragraph as their context given it usually define the terms. As BERT [7] is adept at learning the semantics of tokens from context, we utilize it to encode the context of domain terms and generate corresponding embeddings. We assume that the embedding generated by BERT at the first position of the input captures the semantics of the whole sequence. Therefore, we append the special symbol [CLS] at the beginning of a definition and take its encoded representation as the embedding of the biomedical term. Given the input $\{w_1, ..., w_n\}$, BERT first split it into the sequence $\{w_1', ..., w_j\}$ $(j > n)$ and computes their contextualized representations h after L Transformer layers , where each layer of the BERT combines a multi-head attention (MhA) operation and a fully connected feed-forward network (FFN). The embedding of the term e_i is computed as:

$$h_1, ..., h_j = FFN(MhA(\{w_1, ..., w_j\})), \tag{1}$$

$$e_i = h_1, \tag{2}$$

where $\{h_1, ..., h_j\}$ denotes the corresponding representations of the input.

3.2 Semantic Injection

With the domain entities and corresponding embeddings, the next critical step is to inject the semantics of biomedical terms to BERT. Inspired by Hadsell et al. [10], we employ contrastive learning that pulls the representations of domain mentions closer to aligned entities but pushes them away from irrelevant ones to achieve the objective.

We first travel the sequence and implement automatic annotation of biomedical mentions by string alignment of domain terms in the vocabulary. To construct triplet training samples, we treat the mention $\{m_i\}$ and aligned biomedical terms $\{e_{m_i}\}$ as a anchor and positive sample, respectively, and randomly select k terms $\{e_{\bar{m}_i}^1, ..., e_{\bar{m}_i}^k\}$ that do not align with mentions as negative samples. Given the split sequence $\{w_1, ..., w_j\}$, BERT encode and generate resultant representations $\{h_1, ..., h_j\}$. Then we calculate the representation h_{m_i} of mentions that made up of l tokens $\{w_s, ..., w_{s+l-1}\}$ $(1 < s < s + l < j)$ of the sequence through pooling strategy. For simplicity, the average pooling is used, which is denoted as follows,

$$h_{m_i} = (h_s + ... + h_{s+l})/l, \tag{3}$$

where the $\{h_s, ..., h_{s+l}\}$ denotes the representations of $\{w_s, ..., w_{s+l}\}$. Afterward, positive and negative samples are projected onto embeddings via the precomputed vocabulary as follows,

$$e_{m_i} = Embed(e_{m_i}), \tag{4}$$

$$\{e_{\bar{m}_i}^1, ..., e_{\bar{m}_i}^k\} = Embed(\{e_{\bar{m}_i}^1, ..., e_{\bar{m}_i}^k\}), \tag{5}$$

where e_m denotes the positive term, $e_{\bar{m}}$ denotes the negative term. With the training samples, we adopted InfoNCE (Oord et al., 2018) to achieve semantic injection, defined as,

$$\mathcal{L}_{con} = -\mathbb{E}[\sum_{i=1}^{n} \log \frac{\exp^{cos(h_{m_i}, e_{m_i})}}{\sum_{j=1}^{k} \exp^{cos(h_m, e^i_{\bar{m}_j})}}], \qquad (6)$$

where the cos denotes the cosine similarity, h_{m_i} denotes the representation of m_i, e_{m_i} and $e_{\bar{m}_i}$ denote the representation of positive and negative sample, respectively, and expectation is over n independent samples (h_m, e_m). The model should assign high values to the positive pair (h_m, e_m), and low values to all negative pairs. Notably, unlike conventional contrastive learning, the positive and negative samples from the pre-constructed vocabulary keep their embeddings fixed during training. Instead, they guide semantic space of the original vocabulary to move toward the one of pre-constructed vocabulary.

To avoid catastrophic forgetting [27] of general language generation ability, we still keep the masked language model as one of our pretraining tasks together with contrastive learning. However, we mask all subwords of a term at once instead of randomly selecting subwords to mask. As for the masking strategy, we follow the same operations as BERT. The whole term masking explicitly forces the model to recognize and recover the terms based on left and right context, which is much more challenging. Therefore, we modify the objective in Eq. 4 as,

$$\mathcal{L}_{total} = \lambda_1 \mathcal{L}_{con} + \lambda_2 \mathcal{L}_{mlm}, \qquad (7)$$

where λ_1, λ_2 are introduced as hyperparameters to control the importance of each task. The overall architecture is shown in Fig. 2.

4 Experiments

In this section, we introduce the experiment settings and results of the model on biomedical NLP tasks, including named entity recognition (NER), information extraction, relation extraction, sentence similarity, document classification, and question answering, along with some analyses of the results.

4.1 Experimental Setup

Pretraining. Following BioBERT [22], we utilize PubMed abstracts and PubMed Central full-text articles that contain 18B words in total as the pretraining corpus. We adopt BERT-base with 110M parameters as the basic PLM. BERT-base consists of 12 Transformer layers. For each layer, the hidden size is set to 768, and the number of attention heads is set to 12. Our model is pretrained for 460k steps with a batch size of 200 and a maximum sequence length of 512. The training uses Adam [18] as the optimizer (learning rate $= 1 \times 10^{-5}$, $\beta_1 = 0.9$, and $\beta_2 = 0.99$) on 2 A100 NVIDIA GPUs and takes more than 11 days.

Table 1. Comparison of pretrained language models on the BLURB biomedical NLP benchmark. The standard task-specific models are used in the same fine-tuning process for all models.

Dataset	BERT	RoBERTa	BioBERT	ClinicalBERT	BlueBERT	PubMedBERT	BioMedBERT
BC5-chem	89.89	89.39	92.87	90.82	91.21	93.28	**93.31**
BC5-disease	79.89	80.63	84.72	83.12	83.68	85.60	**85.65**
NCBI-disease	85.85	86.62	89.12	86.41	88.08	87.94	**89.60**
BC2GM	81.28	80.93	83.79	81.61	81.86	**84.50**	84.42
JNLPBA	77.55	77.89	78.56	78.17	77.68	79.05	**79.14**
EBM PICO	71.72	73.02	73.20	72.11	72.51	73.36	**73.52**
BIOSSES	81.42	81.27	89.55	91.18	85.40	**92.32**	92.18
ChemProt	71.64	72.97	76.32	72.15	71.38	77.15	**77.41**
DDI	79.57	79.71	81.26	78.72	77.98	82.19	**89.31**
GAD	79.79	80.91	82.44	80.62	79.21	83.89	**84.07**
HoC	80.32	79.85	81.62	80.64	80.51	82.34	**82.50**
PubMedQA	50.07	52.54	**60.19**	49.38	48.62	56.21	56.04
BioASQ	74.66	75.42	84.07	68.65	68.56	87.51	**87.88**

Fine-Tuning. For task-specific fine-tuning, we used a single A100 NVIDIA GPU to fine-tune BioMedBERT on each task. Similar to pretraining, we use Adam as the optimizer and adopt the standard slanted triangular learning rate schedule. Noticing that the development performance is not very sensitive to hyperparameter selection, we utilize the same setting for all tasks to fine-tune. Concretely, we set the learning rate to 1×10^{-5}, batch size to 16, and epoch number to 20.

4.2 Baselines

We use the public releases of BERT [7] and RoBERTa [24] as baselines to verify the validity of our approach. Since there are not available biomedical knowledge graphs, we compare the methods that use unstructured texts with ours. Specifically, we conducted experiments for BioBERT [22], BlueBERT [31], ClinicalBERT [1], and PubMedBERT [8] on the same benchmark to compare performance of different methods. BioBERT and BlueBERT conduct continual pretraining from BERT, whereas ClinicalBERT conducts continual pretraining from BioBERT. All the above models adopt the original vocabulary of BERT. PubMedBERT instead constructs a new biomedical vocabulary and pre-trains a domain language model from scratch.

4.3 Experimental Results

We compare BioMedBERT with baselines by applying them to the biomedical NLP tasks in BLURB [8]. For each task, we conduct fine-tuning following a general process as described in PubMedBERT. The results are show in Table 1.

Sequence Labeling Task. Given the sequence, the NER task seeks to recognize mentions of biomedical entities. For the sequence labeling task, we conduct evaluations on BC5-Chemical, BC5-Disease, NCBI-Disease, BC2GM, JNLPBA [6] and take F1 as primary metrics. Although Evidence-Based Medicine corpus (EBM PICO) [29] is an information extraction task conceptually, it can also be formulated as a sequential tagging task like NER. Therefore, we take the same fine-tuning process with NER. Concretely, we use a simple linear layer for classification and take BIO as the standard tagging scheme to classify the positions of subwords of a term. The experimental results show that our model outperforms BERT and RoBERTa by a large margin in all NER datasets, even if RoBERTa is pre-trained with the largest corpus. Besides, our method consistently outperforms BioBERT, BlueBERT, and ClinicalBERT, which proves semantic injection is superior to pure continual pretraining. Except for NCBI-Disease, our method is slightly better than PubMedBERT in the rest of the datasets.

Regression Task. The sentence similarity task aims to measure the similarity between two sentences and generate a reasonable score. For this task, we conduct fine-tuning on Sentence Similarity Estimation System (BIOSSES) [35] and take Pearson correlation as the evaluation metric. We add the special token [CLS] at the beginning of the sentence pair and utilize its representation to compute the score after a regression layer. Like sequence labeling tasks, BioMedBERT achieves over 10 points gain to BERT and RoBERTa and outperforms methods that adopt continual pretraining. Despite the slightly worse performance than PubMedBERT, our method is more efficient than training from scratch as the latter requires massive corpus and computing power.

Classification Task. The relation extraction task tends to judge if the text indicates a relation for the mention pair given a pair of entity mentions in a sentence. For this task, we conduct evaluations on Chemical Protein Interaction corpus (ChemProt) [20], Genetic Association Database corpus (GAD) [3] and Drug-Drug Interaction corpus (DDI) [14] and report F1. To prevent the model from memorizing the mention pair, we replace the entities with a dummy token and concatenate their encoded representations for prediction after the linear classification layer. Document Classification seeks to determine whether the text belongs to the category. For this task, we conduct fine-tuning on Hallmarks of Cancer corpus (HoC) [11] and report F1. Like sentence similarity, we adopt the representation of [CLS] for classification. The goal of the question answering is to judge whether the question and the answer match. For this task, we conduct evaluations on PubMedQA dataset [16] and BioASQ corpus [28] and take accuracy as the evaluation metric. We add [CLS] at the beginning of the input and insert [SEP] after the question and answer. Then we employ the representation of [CLS] as the feature to predict. Experimental results demonstrate that BioMedBERT achieves significant improvements over baselines, especially in the PubMedQA, BioASQ, and DDI, with an increase of nearly 10 points. Besides, our model consistently outperforms the continual pretraining models except for

Table 2. Performance of different models on GLUE tasks. Each configuration is run five times with different random seeds, and the average of these five results on the validation set is reported in the table.

Dataset	BERT	BioMedBERT	$\Delta_{\mathcal{L}_{joint}}$	BERT+$\mathcal{L}_{mlm}$	$\Delta_{\mathcal{L}_{mlm}}$	BERT+$\mathcal{L}_{con}$	$\Delta_{\mathcal{L}_{con}}$
MNLI	84.42	84.80	+0.38	**84.89**	+0.47	84.26	−0.16
QNLI	90.93	91.38	+0.45	**91.51**	+0.58	90.73	−0.20
QQP	90.45	90.76	+0.31	**90.82**	+0.37	90.35	−0.10
SST	92.67	92.90	+0.23	**92.98**	+0.32	92.61	−0.06
CoLA	58.64	59.48	+0.84	**59.75**	+1.11	58.40	−0.24
MRPC	86.82	86.95	+0.13	**87.18**	+0.36	86.64	−0.18
RTE	68.71	69.05	+0.34	**69.13**	+0.42	68.51	−0.20
STS-B	88.92	89.13	+0.21	**89.25**	+0.33	88.77	−0.15

Table 3. Results on the effects of different pre-training tasks on model performance.

Dataset	BERT	BERT+$\mathcal{L}_{mlm}$	$\Delta_{\mathcal{L}_{mlm}}$	BERT+$\mathcal{L}_{con}$	$\Delta_{\mathcal{L}_{con}}$	BioMedBERT
BC5-chem	89.89	91.43	+1.54	92.87	+2.98	93.31
BC5-disease	79.89	83.03	+3.14	85.12	+5.23	85.65
NCBI-disease	85.85	87.90	+2.05	89.13	+3.28	89.60
BC2GM	81.28	82.86	+1.58	83.91	+2.63	84.42
JNLPBA	77.55	78.27	+0.72	78.83	+1.28	79.14
EBM PICO	71.72	72.56	+0.84	73.21	+1.49	73.52
BIOSSES	81.42	86.27	+4.85	90.74	+9.32	92.18
ChemProt	71.64	74.76	+3.12	76.83	+5.19	77.41
DDI	79.57	84.20	+4.63	87.15	+7.58	89.31
GAD	79.79	82.12	+2.33	83.16	+3.37	84.07
HoC	80.32	81.63	+1.31	81.92	+1.60	82.50
PubMedQA	50.07	53.34	+3.27	54.88	+4.81	56.04
BioASQ	74.66	78.80	+4.14	86.79	+12.13	87.88

PubMedQA and obtains better or comparable performance than PubMedBERT. We assume that the exception resulted from the relatively high variances among runs.

To explore the effect on general applications after semantic injection of biomedical terms, we also conducted experiments on eight natural language understanding tasks in GLUE [38]. The results are show in Table 2. Experimental results illustrate that BioMedBERT outperforms BERT on all tasks, which proves our method does not influence the performance of BERT. In a word, the superior performance on two benchmarks proves that the our method can capture the semantics of the domain and the general words simultaneously.

4.4   Ablation

As shown in Eq. 8, BioMedBERT takes a multitask loss. To explore how pre-training tasks impact performance, we compare the joint training model with models trained with whole-term masked language model (BioMedBERT+$\mathcal{L}_{mlm}$) and contrastive learning (BioMedBERT+$\mathcal{L}_{con}$). As shown in Table 3, the consistent improvement of two ablations over all tasks shows that both pretraining tasks benefit learning the semantics of biomedical terms. Although both are necessary, contrastive learning contributes more to performance improvement than masked language modeling, which proves the former plays a critical role in the semantic transfer of biomedical terms.

Different from the case of biomedical applications, the ablation study in Table 2 shows that the masked language model is much more significant for general NLP tasks than contrastive learning. According to the results, the whole-term masked language model brings positive benefits to BioMedBERT in all tasks. Contrast learning, however, resulted in slightly lower performance on the tasks. For this phenomenon, we believe that adopting a different pretraining paradigm to the original PTM (e.g., BERT) will somewhat lead to catastrophic forgetting.

5   Conclusion

In this paper, we propose to capture the meaning of biomedical terms for BERT by semantic acquisition and injection. Following the method, we train the BioMedBERT based on BERT. The impressive performance on downstream tasks verifies that the original vocabulary of BERT can simultaneously learn general and biomedical terms semantics. Further analysis shows that two pretraining tasks are necessary to learn the representation of biomedical terms. Compared to the existing pretraining paradigms for the biomedical domain adaption of BERT, our method is more efficient since it acquires the semantics of biomedical terms without pretraining from scratch.

Considering that our model can flexibly transfer domain semantics from other sources, we will investigate how to encode and inject structural biomedical knowledge in future work. Besides, since we adopt the BERT as the basic PTM, the current method can only be applied to language understanding tasks. Therefore, we will further explore the semantic injection of autoregressive models such as the series of GPT to explore this method's performance on generation tasks.

Acknowledgements. This research was supported by grants from the National Key Laboratory for Complex Systems Simulation Foundation (No.6142006200406).

References

1. Alsentzer, E., et al.: Publicly available clinical BERT embeddings. In: Proceedings of the 2nd Clinical Natural Language Processing Workshop, pp. 72–78. Association for Computational Linguistics, Minneapolis, Minnesota, USA (2019)

2. Beltagy, I., Cohan, A., Lo, K.: SciBERT: pretrained contextualized embeddings for scientific text. CoRR abs/1903.10676 (2019). http://arxiv.org/abs/1903.10676
3. Bravo, A., González, J.P., Queralt-Rosinach, N., Rautschka, M., Furlong, L.I.: Extraction of relations between genes and diseases from text and large-scale data analysis: implications for translational research. BMC Bioinform. **16**, 1–17 (2015)
4. Brown, T.B., Mann, B., Ryder, N., Subbiah, M., Kaplan, J., Dhariwal, P., et al.: Language models are few-shot learners. In: Larochelle, H., Ranzato, M., Hadsell, R., Balcan, M.F., Lin, H.T. (eds.) Advances in Neural Information Processing Systems 33: Annual Conference on Neural Information Processing Systems 2020, NeurIPS, 6–12 December 2020, virtual (2020)
5. Chalkidis, I., Fergadiotis, M., Malakasiotis, P., Aletras, N., Androutsopoulos, I.: LEGAL-BERT: the muppets straight out of law school. arXiv preprint arXiv: arXiv: (2020)
6. Crichton, G.K.O., Pyysalo, S., Chiu, B., Korhonen, A.: A neural network multi-task learning approach to biomedical named entity recognition. BMC Bioinform. **18**(1), 1–14 (2017)
7. Devlin, J., Chang, M.W., Lee, K., Toutanova, K.: BERT: pre-training of deep bidirectional transformers for language understanding. In: Burstein, J., Doran, C., Solorio, T. (eds.) Proceedings of the 2019 Conference of the North American Chapter of the Association for Computational Linguistics: Human Language Technologies, NAACL-HLT 2019, vol. 1, pp. 4171–4186. Association for Computational Linguistics, Minneapolis, MN, USA (2019)
8. Gu, Y., Tinn, R., Cheng, H., Lucas, M., Usuyama, N., Liu, X., et al.: Domain-specific language model pretraining for biomedical natural language processing. ACM Trans. Comput. Healthcare **3**(1), 1–23 (2022)
9. Gururangan, S., Marasović, A., Swayamdipta, S., Lo, K., Beltagy, I., Downey, D., Smith, N.A.: Don't stop pretraining: adapt language models to domains and tasks. In: Proceedings of the 58th Annual Meeting of the Association for Computational Linguistics, pp. 8342–8360. Association for Computational Linguistics (2020)
10. Hadsell, R., Chopra, S., LeCun, Y.: Dimensionality reduction by learning an invariant mapping. In: 2006 IEEE Computer Society Conference on Computer Vision and Pattern Recognition (CVPR 2006), pp. 1735–1742. IEEE Computer Society, New York, NY, USA (2006)
11. Hanahan, D., Weinberg, R.A.: The hallmarks of cancer. Cell **100**(1), 57–70 (2000)
12. Hao, B., Zhu, H., Paschalidis, I.C.: Enhancing clinical BERT embedding using a biomedical knowledge base. In: Proceedings of the 28th International Conference on Computational Linguistics, COLING 2020, pp. 657–661. International Committee on Computational Linguistics (2020)
13. He, B., et al.: BERT-MK: integrating graph contextualized knowledge into pretrained language models. In: Findings of the Association for Computational Linguistics: EMNLP 2020, pp. 2281–2290. Association for Computational Linguistics (2020)
14. Herrero-Zazo, M., Segura-Bedmar, I., Martínez, P., Declerck, T.: The DDI corpus: an annotated corpus with pharmacological substances and drug-drug interactions. J. Biomed. Inform. **46**(5), 914–920 (2013)
15. Hong, J., Kim, T., Lim, H., Choo, J.: Avocado: strategy for adapting vocabulary to downstream domain. In: Proceedings of the 2021 Conference on Empirical Methods in Natural Language Processing, pp. 4692–4700. Association for Computational Linguistics, Online and Punta Cana, Dominican Republic (2021)

16. Jin, Q., Dhingra, B., Liu, Z., Cohen, W., Lu, X.: PubMedQA: a dataset for biomedical research question answering. In: Proceedings of the 2019 Conference on Empirical Methods in Natural Language Processing and the 9th International Joint Conference on Natural Language Processing (EMNLP-IJCNLP), pp. 2567–2577. Association for Computational Linguistics, Hong Kong, China (2019)
17. Kalyan, K.S., Rajasekharan, A., Sangeetha, S.: AMMUS: a survey of transformer-based pretrained models in natural language processing. arXiv preprint arXiv:2108.05542 (2021)
18. Kingma, D.P., Ba, J.: Adam: a method for stochastic optimization. In: Bengio, Y., LeCun, Y. (eds.) 3rd International Conference on Learning Representations, ICLR 2015. San Diego, CA, USA (2015)
19. Koto, F., Lau, J.H., Baldwin, T.: IndoBERTweet: a pretrained language model for Indonesian twitter with effective domain-specific vocabulary initialization. In: Proceedings of the 2021 Conference on Empirical Methods in Natural Language Processing, pp. 10660–10668. Association for Computational Linguistics, Online and Punta Cana, Dominican Republic (2021)
20. Krallinger, M., et al.: Overview of the BioCreative VI chemical-protein interaction track. In: Proceedings of the Sixth BioCreative Challenge Evaluation Workshop, vol. 1, pp. 141–146 (2017)
21. Lan, Z., Chen, M., Goodman, S., Gimpel, K., Sharma, P., Soricut, R.: ALBERT: a lite BERT for self-supervised learning of language representations. In: Proceedings of the 8th International Conference on Learning Representations, ICLR 2020. OpenReview.net, Addis Ababa, Ethiopia (2020)
22. Lee, J., et al.: BioBERT: a pre-trained biomedical language representation model for biomedical text mining. Bioinformatics 36(4), 1234–1240 (2020)
23. Liu, W., et al.: K-BERT: enabling language representation with knowledge graph. In: The Thirty-Fourth AAAI Conference on Artificial Intelligence, AAAI 2020, The Thirty-Second Innovative Applications of Artificial Intelligence Conference, IAAI 2020, The Tenth AAAI Symposium on Educational Advances in Artificial Intelligence, EAAI 2020, pp. 2901–2908. AAAI Press, New York, NY, USA (2020)
24. Liu, Y., Ott, M., Goyal, N., Du, J., Joshi, M., Chen, D., et al.: RoBERTa: a robustly optimized BERT pretraining approach (2019)
25. Louis, A.: NetBERT: a pre-trained language representation model for computer networking, Master's thesis, University of Liège, Liège, Belgium (2020)
26. Lu, S., Guo, D., Ren, S., Huang, J., Svyatkovskiy, A., Blanco, A., et al.: CodeXGLUE: a machine learning benchmark dataset for code understanding and generation. arXiv preprint arXiv:2102.04664 (2021)
27. McCloskey, M., Cohen, N.J.: Catastrophic interference in connectionist networks: the sequential learning problem. In: Psychology of Learning and Motivation, vol. 24, pp. 109–165 (1989)
28. Nentidis, A., Bougiatiotis, K., Krithara, A., Paliouras, G.: Results of the seventh edition of the BioASQ challenge. In: Machine Learning and Knowledge Discovery in Databases: International Workshops of ECML PKDD 2019, Würzburg, Germany, 16–20 September 2019, Proceedings, Part II, pp. 553–568 (2020)
29. Nye, B.E., et al.: A corpus with multi-level annotations of patients, interventions and outcomes to support language processing for medical literature. In: Gurevych, I., Miyao, Y. (eds.) Proceedings of the 56th Annual Meeting of the Association for Computational Linguistics, ACL 2018, Melbourne, Australia, July 15–20, 2018, Volume 1: Long Papers, pp. 197–207. Association for Computational Linguistics (2018)

30. Pan, S.J., Yang, Q.: A survey on transfer learning. IEEE Trans. Knowl. Data Eng. **22**(10), 1345–1359 (2010)
31. Peng, Y., Yan, S., Lu, Z.: Transfer learning in biomedical natural language processing: An evaluation of BERT and ELMO on ten benchmarking datasets. In: Proceedings of the 18th BioNLP Workshop and Shared Task, pp. 58–65. Association for Computational Linguistics, Florence, Italy (2019)
32. Radford, A., Narasimhan, K., Salimans, T., Sutskever, I., et al.: Improving language understanding by generative pre-training. Tech. rep, OpenAI (2018)
33. Radford, A., Wu, J., Child, R., Luan, D., Amodei, D., Sutskever, I.: Language models are unsupervised multitask learners. OpenAI Blog **1**(8), 9 (2019)
34. Raffel, C., Shazeer, N., Roberts, A., Lee, K., Narang, S., Matena, M., et al.: Exploring the limits of transfer learning with a unified text-to-text transformer. J. Mach. Learn. Res. **21**, 1–67 (2020)
35. Sogancioglu, G., Öztürk, H., Özgür, A.: BIOSSES: a semantic sentence similarity estimation system for the biomedical domain. Bioinformatics **33**(14), i49–i58 (2017)
36. Tai, W., Kung, H.T., Dong, X., Comiter, M., Kuo, C.F.: exBERT: extending pre-trained models with domain-specific vocabulary under constrained training resources. In: Findings of the Association for Computational Linguistics: EMNLP 2020, pp. 1433–1439. Association for Computational Linguistics (2020)
37. Vaswani, A., Shazeer, N., Parmar, N., Uszkoreit, J., Jones, L., Gomez, A.N., et al.: Attention is all you need. In: Guyon, I., et al. (eds.) Advances in Neural Information Processing Systems 30: Annual Conference on Neural Information Processing Systems 2017, pp. 5998–6008, 4–9 December 2017, Long Beach, CA, USA (2017)
38. Wang, A., Singh, A., Michael, J., Hill, F., Levy, O., Bowman, S.R.: GLUE: a multi-task benchmark and analysis platform for natural language understanding. In: 7th International Conference on Learning Representations, ICLR 2019. OpenReview.net, New Orleans, LA, USA (2019)
39. Wu, Y., Schuster, M., Chen, Z., Le, Q.V., Norouzi, M., Macherey, W., et al.: Google's neural machine translation system: bridging the gap between human and machine translation. arXiv preprint arXiv:1609.08144 (2016)
40. Yang, Y., Uy, M.C.S., Huang, A.: FinBERT: a pretrained language model for financial communications. arXiv preprint arXiv:2006.08097 (2020)
41. Yao, Y., Huang, S., Wang, W., Dong, L., Wei, F.: Adapt-and-distill: developing small, fast and effective pretrained language models for domains. In: Findings of the Association for Computational Linguistics: ACL-IJCNLP 2021, pp. 460–470. Association for Computational Linguistics (2021)
42. Yu, W., et al.: Dict-BERT: enhancing language model pre-training with dictionary. In: Findings of the Association for Computational Linguistics: ACL 2022, pp. 1907–1918. Association for Computational Linguistics, Dublin, Ireland (2022)
43. Zhu, H., Peng, H., Lyu, Z., Hou, L., Li, J., Xiao, J.: Pre-training language model incorporating domain-specific heterogeneous knowledge into a unified representation. Expert Systems with Applications, p. 119369 (2022)

Deep Reinforcement Learning
for Group-Aware Robot Navigation
in Crowds

Xianwei Zhou, Xin Ye, Kun Zhang, and Songsen Yu[✉]

South China Normal University, Guangzhou, Guangdong, China
{zhouxianwei,2021024177,2021024182}@m.scnu.edu.cn, yss8109@163.com

Abstract. Balancing safety, efficiency and social norms when robots navigate in crowded situations is a major challenge, as human intentions are variable and unpredictable. Previous research has addressed the problem of navigating in dense crowds by modelling the crowd and using a self-attention mechanism to assign different weights to each individual. However, in reality, crowds do not only consist of individuals, but more often appear as groups, so avoiding groups is also part of social etiquette. In particular, humans are aware of other groups and actively circumvent them when they keep a certain distance from others. Based on this, we proposes a deep reinforcement learning navigation method that incorporates group recognition. The proposed method distinguishes groups from individuals by behavioural similarity and designs a group space-based reward function in a reinforcement learning framework to encourage the robot to avoid group intrusion. According to the simulation experiments, the suggested method can produce navigation paths that are more group-friendly.

Keywords: Social navigation · Deep reinforcement learning · Group recognitio

1 Introduction

As artificial intelligence and robotics industry grow rapidly, more and more robots are emerging on the scene, such as hotels, airports, restaurants, and shopping malls. The expansion of robotic applications has forced robots and crowds to share the same environment, especially when robots are used in service scenarios. The challenge is to navigate safely and freely through the crowd, while remaining efficient and socially distant, as human intentions are variable and unknown.

Traditional approaches to robot navigation have focused on obstacle avoidance, treating humans as obstacles and ignoring human-robot interaction. Some of these approaches set the same rules of motion for humans and robots, such as RVO (Reciprocal Velocity Obstacles) [16] and SFM (Social Force Model) [8]. However, these artificially designed rules may lead to the freeze dilemma for the

Z. Jin et al. (Eds.): KSEM 2023, LNAI 14120, pp. 25–34, 2023.
https://doi.org/10.1007/978-3-031-40292-0_3

robots in face of crowded environments. And they are prone to inefficiencies in navigation due to the inability to understand dynamic groups.

The advent of deep reinforcement learning has enabled robots to navigate through crowds with perceptual capabilities. Examples include the use of attention mechanisms [4], graph convolutional networks [3], and structure-RNN [10]. Although these methods give the robot some perceptual capabilities, they do not clearly delineate groups from individuals in a crowded environment and may cause the robot to generate navigation paths that interfere with the direction of the group. As shown in Fig. 1, the focus of this paper is on how to generate polite and comfortable navigation paths (that do not infringe on the group space), rather than only considering social etiquette or navigation efficiency.

Fig. 1. Social bot navigation. Our approach (b) considers the group space to generate group-friendly navigation paths.

The main contributions are as follows: (1) Our approach uses behavioural similarity to identify groups and constructs a group space. (2) We set up a new reward function in conjunction with the group space to encourage the robot to learn more polite navigation strategies to reduce the impact on group travel. (3) The method outperforms other existing methods in generating more group-friendly navigation paths.

2   Related Work

2.1   Robots Navigating Through Crowds

Current research work on this problem can be broadly divided into two categories: approaches based on traditional methods and Deep Reinforcement Learning (DRL).

Traditional approaches to the above problem are based on mathematical models, with RVO [16], ERVO [18] and ORCA [15] implementing dynamic obstacle avoidance by setting up corresponding velocity geometry regions and steering rules, whereas SFM [8] uses attractive and repulsive forces to model crowd interaction. However, these methods are largely based on heuristics and they often lack foresight and encounter the issue of robot freezing, especially in more complicated situations.

Deep reinforcement learning-based approaches offer some solutions to the above problems. CADRL [6] and SACADRL [5] were among the first works to replace manual modelling with DRL and have had some improvement in navigating scenes containing two agents. However, their work is still based on certain behavioural assumptions and cannot handle scenarios with multi-agent. LSTM-RL [7] uses LSTM units to encode crowds' features and combine them with the state of the robot for planning. Chen et al. [4] proposed an attention-based mechanism approachSARL, which defines and calculates the environment's attention weights and scores for all robot-human interaction pairs, so that decisions are made based on the attention scores. Nishimura et al. [12] proposed a deep reinforcement learning framework named L2B for interactive navigation in crowded environments. However, these efforts neglect the fact that crowds often move in groups, so the robot path generated by the policy above may disturb the grouped pedestrians. A group-aware robot navigation scheme based on deep reinforcement learning approach that follows this insight is proposed in this paper to deal with the issues mentioned above.

2.2   Group Recognition in Crowded Environments

One branch of group recognition is static group detection, which is commonly implemented using F-formation detection [9], which detects groups by analysing the location and orientation of people in a scene, and finding regions that meet the F-formation criteria, but it cannot handle dynamically changing groups, such as when people are joining or leaving the group. Another branch is dynamic group detection, where a common approach is to treat groups as probabilistic processes, in which groups are a reflection of the probability that pedestrian trajectories are closely related [1,2]. Another common approach is clustering [13,14], which groups pedestrians with similar behavioural characteristics into the same group. The group identification method used in this paper is based on the work of Allan Wang [17]. In contrast, this paper focuses on the crowd comfort level during robot navigation and eventually generates an effective strategy. Specifically, our method identifies groups via HDBSCAN [11] and uses a convex packet algorithm to represent the group space. Finally, we use the constructed group space to set additional reward functions that encourage the robot to learn group-friendly navigation strategies.

3   Method

3.1   Problem Formulation

This paper is concerned with robots navigating in a crowded environment without disturbing the population. We simplify the problem by treating it as a sequential decision problem with partially observable states, where multiple agents have to avoid obstacles while considering groups. Suppose there are n agents in the environment, including robots and pedestrians. We denote the robot's state by S_r^t, containing the robot's observable states at time t: position (p_x, p_y), velocity (v_x, v_y), radius r and unobservable states: target point (g_x, g_y) and preferred velocity v_{pref}. S_i^t denotes the observable state of pedestrian i.S_g^t denotes the observable state of the group in the environment. The robot navigates from state S_r^0 to destination S_r^T by executing strategy $\pi(S_{jn}^t)$generating action a_t and the robot does not know the destination of other pedestrians and strategy $\pi_i(S_{jn}^t)$, so that we can define the states of all agents at time t as:

$$
\begin{aligned}
S_r^t &= \left[p_x, p_y, v_x, v_y, r, g_x, g_y, v_{pref}\right] \\
S_i^t &= \left[\tilde{p}_x^i, \tilde{p}_y^i, \tilde{v}_x^i, \tilde{v}_y^i, \tilde{r}^i, g_x^i, g_y^i, v_{pref}^i\right] \\
S_g^t &= \left[\tilde{p}_x^g, \tilde{p}_y^g, \tilde{v}_x^g, \tilde{v}_y^g, \tilde{r}^g\right] \\
S_{jn}^t &= \left[S_r^t, S_g^t, S_1^t, \ldots, S_n^t\right]^{\mathrm{T}}
\end{aligned}
\tag{1}
$$

where S_{jn}^t is the joint state of the environment consisting of S_r^t and S_i^t. Our ultimate goal is to learn a strategy $\pi(S_{jn}^t)$ that allows the robot to navigate safely to its destination while taking into account the comfort of the group.

3.2   Group Space Recognition

Group Clustering. To obtain group information from spatial similarities between humans, we used the unsupervised clustering algorithm HDBSCAN [11], which can adapt the density based on each cluster. The algorithm uses behavioural features to identify groups of humans, these features include the current position of the human (x_i, y_i) and the velocity (v, θ), where the magnitude v and the direction θ represent the velocity.

Individual Space. Previous research has proposed a two-dimensional asymmetric Gaussian distribution in the form of a mobile individual private space, and defined the parameters of the asymmetric Gaussian distribution, the front variance σ_h, the side variance σ_s, and the back variance σ_r, as follows:

$$
\sigma_h = \max(2v, 0.5), \sigma_s = \frac{2}{3}\sigma_h, \sigma_r = \frac{1}{2}\sigma_h
\tag{2}
$$

According to the human activity model, we denote the individual space $IS_i(\cdot)$ of the ith individual as:

$$
\begin{aligned}
&IS_i\left(x, y; x_i, y_i, v, \theta\right) \\
&= e^{-\left(A(x-x_i)^2 + 2B(x-x_i)(y-y_i) + C(y-y_i)^2\right)}
\end{aligned}
\tag{3}
$$

where the spatial shape of the individual is controlled by the coefficients A, B and C, depending on the speed of the agent(v, θ).

Group Space. With the results of group clustering and the construction of individual spaces, we can further construct group spaces that reflect group behaviour. Based on the work of Allan Wang [17], our method constructs the group space $GS_j(\cdot)$ for the jth group by means of the convex packet algorithm, formulated as follows:

$$GS_j(\cdot) = \text{ConvexHull}\left(IS_i(\cdot) \mid i \in G_j\right) \tag{4}$$

where $IS_i(\cdot)$ denotes the individual space of people clustered in the same group.

3.3 DRL Framework Combining Group Features

Based on the description in Sect. 3.1, the problem of finding the optimal value function in reinforcement learning is equivalent to the original problem.

$$V^*\left(s_{jn}^0\right) = \mathbb{E}\left[\sum_{t=1}^{T} \gamma^{t \cdot v_{\text{pref}}} R\left(s_{jn}^t, \pi^*\left(s_{jn}^t\right)\right) \mid s_{jn}^0\right] \tag{5}$$

Based on the optimal value function V^*, the optimal strategy π^* can be expressed as:

$$
\begin{aligned}
\pi^*\left(s_{jn}^{t+1}\right) = &\underset{a}{\text{argmax}} R\left(s_{jn}^t, a\right) \\
&+ \gamma^{\Delta t \cdot v_{\text{pref}}} \int_{s_{jn}^{t+1}} P\left(s_{jn}^t, s_{jn}^{t+1} \mid a_t\right) V^*\left(s_{jn}^{t+1}\right) ds_{jn}^{t+1}
\end{aligned}
\tag{6}
$$

where $\gamma \in (0,1)$ is the discount factor and v_{pref} is used for normalization. $R(s_{jn}^t, a)$ denotes the reward received for performing action a.

In order to guide the robot not to invade the group space on its way to the target, a new reward function was designed as follows:

$$R\left(s_{jn}^t, a_t\right) = R_P\left(s_{jn}^t, a_t\right) + R_g\left(s_{jn}^t, a_t\right) \tag{7}$$

One of the main purposes of R_P is to reward the robot for reaching its destination and acting positively, and to penalise situations such as collisions, uncomfortable social distances, timeouts and freezes. The details are as follows:

$$R_P\left(s_{jn}^t, a_t\right) = \begin{cases} -0.25 - 0.01 * t & \text{if } d_t = 0 \\ \frac{(d_t - 0.2)}{20} & \text{else if } d_t < 0.2 \\ 1 - 0.01 * t & \text{else if } p_t = p_g \\ -0.01 * t & \text{else if } t \geq t_{\max} \\ -0.01 & \text{else if } p_t = p_{t-1} \\ 0 & \text{otherwise} \end{cases} \tag{8}$$

where d_t is the minimum distance between the robot and its closest agent during the period $[t - \Delta t, t]$, t_{max} is the set maximum navigation time, p_t is the robot's current position, p_{t-1} is the robot's position at the previous time step, and p_g is the robot's navigation target.

Besides this, we introduce a new reward, R_g, to encourage robots to learn to avoid group space so as not to interfere with group actions. This is specifically defined as:

$$R_g\left(s_{jn}^t, a_t\right) = \lambda_1 \sum_{j=1}^{G} \min\left(0, d_g^j - d_s\right) \tag{9}$$

where d_g^j represents the minimum distance from the robot's position to the groups. and d_s is the safety threshold and λ_1 represents the reward function's hyper-parameter.

3.4 Network Architecture

Our network architecture is based on previous work [6] and is shown in Fig. 2. The entire network structure is divided into three parts: feature extraction, state aggregation, and value assessment.

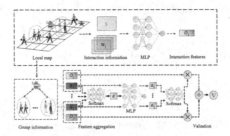

Fig. 2. Network structure. We use a multilayer perceptron to extract local features and group information. The extracted information is then aggregated to calculate the attention score α_i for the current state, and finally the value representation V of the current state is obtained by a softmax function. where g_i denotes the distance of the robot to the ith group.

The first step is to parameterize the input with the robot at the centre and the x-axis pointing to the robot's target. The transformed states of the robot and pedestrian are:

$$\begin{aligned} s &= \left[d_d, v_{\text{pref}}, v_x, v_y, r, d_r^j\right] \\ w_i &= \left[\tilde{p}_x^i, \tilde{p}_y^i, \tilde{v}_x^i, \tilde{v}_y^i, r_i, d_i, r_i + r, d_i^j\right] \end{aligned} \tag{10}$$

where s denotes the state of the robot and w_i denotes the state of the ith person. d_d denotes the distance of the robot to the target point, d_i denotes the distance of the robot to the ith person, and r and r_i denote the radius of both the robot and pedestrian i, respectively. In contrast to previous work, we additionally include group information d_r^j and d_i^j in the input to the network, where d_r^j denotes the distance of the robot from group j and d_i^j denotes the distance of pedestrian i from group j.

Subsequently, we put the defined human-robot interaction information $[s, w_i]$ into the network and extract the interaction features o_i using a multilayer perceptron (MLP). Next the attention score α_i is calculated and the state value V is further evaluated.

Finally, the DRL method can generate a trajectory to the target using the value network in equation (6). To improve the robot's navigation skills, we aim to train and fine-tune the value network with a strategy. We apply the Deep V-learning algorithm [4] for this purpose.

4 Experiments

4.1 Experimental Setup

We use python to build a simulation environment to simulate the navigation of a robot through a crowd. Where the simulated crowd is controlled by a social force model of movement. We use two scenarios in both training and testing, an open scene and a corridor scene respectively. The scenes contain a number of individual pedestrians and groups of people who are randomly given a state: stationary or moving. The starting positions of the robot and the moving pedestrians were placed at 0 and 10 on the y-axis respectively, while random perturbations were added to the x-axis to introduce behavioural diversity. The robot needs to reach y=10 from its starting point, while everyone else's destination is relative to their starting point, i.e. pedestrians and robots need to interleave to reach their destination.

We compared with two methods, CADRL [6] and SARL [4], and used the Deep V-learning algorithm to train all of the basic methods and our own method in two phases: imitating and reinforcing learning.

4.2 Results and Analysis

Figures 3 and 4 show the navigation results of our method with the SARL method and the CADRL method for the open and corridor scenes respectively.

As can be seen, in the open scene step-25, the SARL method does not change its direction when facing the group because it does not take into account the presence of the group space, and passes straight through the crowd, disrupting the crowd formation and affecting the group's travel despite the absence of collisions. On the other hand, our method observes the group and chooses to turn to avoid the human group and not to intrude the group's social space. Although this behaviour entails additional time and journey cost, our method reduces the robot's impact on other pedestrians and improves the comfort of the crowd in the environment compared to SARL, while ensuring a high success rate.

In the corridor scenario we set up additional static obstacles and it is worth noting that the CADRL approach, due to a lack of understanding of the groups

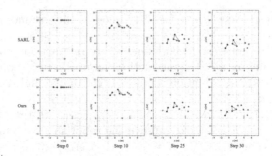

Fig. 3. Comparison of open scenes. Where the red pentagrams represent robots and the other coloured circles indicate other pedestrians in the environment, groups are connected by straight lines. Our approach shows group avoidance behaviour, while SARL invades the group space. (Color figure online)

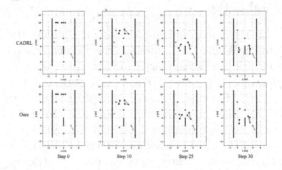

Fig. 4. Comparison of corridor scenes. The inability of the CADRL method to understand the group leads to unnecessary wandering and waiting in the face of the group, and it is clear at steps 25 and 30 that it lags behind our method in terms of distance travelled.

in the environment, takes too long to navigate around the groups and thus does not reach the destination at the required time. Our method, on the other hand, recognises groups quickly and changes direction and speed in advance, minimising interaction with the group space and thus ensuring a comfortable navigation experience and good navigation efficiency.

Table 1 shows quantitatively the performance metrics of each method in the comparison experiments. Where Success indicates the rate at which the robot reaches the target without collision, Collision indicates the rate at which the robot collides with other pedestrians, Time indicates the average navigation time consumed by the robot to reach the target, and Invasion indicates the rate at which the robot invades the group space during navigation.

The table shows that our method has a high success rate as well as a low collision rate in both open scenes and corridor scenes. At the same time, our method has a much lower group invasion rate and a longer average navigation

Table 1. Quantitative results. Each scene contains 500 cases to test the performance of all method, where time and invasion are counted in successful cases.

Environment	Method	Success	Collision	Time	Invasion
Open scenes	CADRL [6]	0.87	0.11	14.79	0.30
	SARL [4]	**0.93**	0.05	**14.58**	0.26
	Ours	0.92	**0.04**	15.72	**0.07**
Corridor scenes	CADRL [6]	0.74	0.21	23.84	0.46
	SARL [4]	0.85	0.13	**18.36**	0.28
	Ours	**0.89**	**0.10**	20.57	**0.09**

time compared to the SARL method, which means that we sacrifice time as well as distance travelled for the comfort of other pedestrians in the environment.

5   Summary

To improve the comfort of crowds during robot navigation, this paper proposes a deep reinforcement learning navigation method incorporating group recognition. The proposed method distinguishes groups from individuals by behavioural similarity and designs a reward function based on group space in a reinforcement learning framework to encourage the robot to avoid group space intrusion. We add group information to enrich the hierarchy of the neural network. Simulation experiments show that our approach is essentially equal to or better than the best baseline approach in terms of success rate and collision rate. Moreover, it outperforms all baseline methods in terms of comfort.

Future work will focus on optimising the navigation path and reducing the navigation time of the robot. Real-world deployment and generalisation issues will also need to be explored.

Acknowledgements. This work was supported by the Guangdong Provincial Fund for Basic and Applied Basic Research (2020A1515110783), the Guangdong Provincial Enterprise Science and Technology Specialists Project (GDKTP2020014000), and the Foshan City High-level Assigned Talents Project (Local-level Leading Talents 303475).

References

1. Bazzani, L., Cristani, M., Murino, V.: Decentralized particle filter for joint individual-group tracking. In: 2012 IEEE Conference on Computer Vision and Pattern Recognition, pp. 1886–1893. IEEE (2012)
2. Chang, M.C., Krahnstoever, N., Ge, W.: Probabilistic group-level motion analysis and scenario recognition. In: 2011 International Conference on Computer Vision, pp. 747–754. IEEE (2011)
3. Chen, C., Hu, S., Nikdel, P., Mori, G., Savva, M.: Relational graph learning for crowd navigation. In: 2020 IEEE/RSJ International Conference on Intelligent Robots and Systems (IROS), pp. 10007–10013. IEEE (2020)

4. Chen, C., Liu, Y., Kreiss, S., Alahi, A.: Crowd-robot interaction: crowd-aware robot navigation with attention-based deep reinforcement learning. In: 2019 international conference on robotics and automation (ICRA), pp. 6015–6022. IEEE (2019)

5. Chen, Y.F., Everett, M., Liu, M., How, J.P.: Socially aware motion planning with deep reinforcement learning. In: 2017 IEEE/RSJ International Conference on Intelligent Robots and Systems (IROS), pp. 1343–1350. IEEE (2017)

6. Chen, Y.F., Liu, M., Everett, M., How, J.P.: Decentralized non-communicating multiagent collision avoidance with deep reinforcement learning. In: 2017 IEEE International Conference on Robotics and Automation (ICRA), pp. 285–292. IEEE (2017)

7. Everett, M., Chen, Y.F., How, J.P.: Motion planning among dynamic, decision-making agents with deep reinforcement learning. In: 2018 IEEE/RSJ International Conference on Intelligent Robots and Systems (IROS), pp. 3052–3059. IEEE (2018)

8. Helbing, D., Molnar, P.: Social force model for pedestrian dynamics. Phys. Rev. E **51**(5), 4282 (1995)

9. Kendon, A.: Conducting interaction: patterns of behavior in focused encounters, vol. 7. CUP Archive (1990)

10. Liu, S., Chang, P., Liang, W., Chakraborty, N., Driggs-Campbell, K.: Decentralized structural-RNN for robot crowd navigation with deep reinforcement learning. In: 2021 IEEE International Conference on Robotics and Automation (ICRA), pp. 3517–3524. IEEE (2021)

11. McInnes, L., Healy, J.: Accelerated hierarchical density based clustering. In: 2017 IEEE International Conference on Data Mining Workshops (ICDMW), pp. 33–42. IEEE (2017)

12. Nishimura, M., Yonetani, R.: L2B: learning to balance the safety-efficiency trade-off in interactive crowd-aware robot navigation. In: 2020 IEEE/RSJ International Conference on Intelligent Robots and Systems (IROS), pp. 11004–11010. IEEE (2020)

13. Solera, F., Calderara, S., Cucchiara, R.: Socially constrained structural learning for groups detection in crowd. IEEE Trans. Pattern Anal. Mach. Intell. **38**(5), 995–1008 (2015)

14. Taylor, A., Chan, D.M., Riek, L.D.: Robot-centric perception of human groups. ACM Trans. Human-Robot Interact. (THRI) **9**(3), 1–21 (2020)

15. Van Den Berg, J., Guy, S.J., Lin, M., Manocha, D.: Reciprocal n-body collision avoidance. In: Pradalier, C., Siegwart, R., Hirzinger, G. (eds.) Robotics Research. Springer Tracts in Advanced Robotics, vol. 70, pp. 3–19. Springer, Berlin, Heidelberg (2011). https://doi.org/10.1007/978-3-642-19457-3_1

16. Van Den Berg, J., Lin, M., Manocha, D.: Reciprocal velocity obstacles for real-time multi-agent navigation. In: 2008 IEEE International Conference on Robotics and Automation, pp. 1928–1935 (2008). https://doi.org/10.1109/ROBOT.2008.4543489

17. Wang, A., Mavrogiannis, C., Steinfeld, A.: Group-based motion prediction for navigation in crowded environments. In: Conference on Robot Learning, pp. 871–882. PMLR (2022)

18. Xu, M., et al.: Crowd behavior simulation with emotional contagion in unexpected multihazard situations. IEEE Trans. Syst. Man Cybern. Syst. **51**(3), 1567–1581 (2019)

An Enhanced Distributed Algorithm for Area Skyline Computation Based on Apache Spark

Chen Li[1], Yang Cao[2(✉)], Ye Zhu[2], Jinli Zhang[3], Annisa Annisa[4], Debo Cheng[5], Huidong Tang[6], Shuai Jiang[6], Kenta Maruyama[6], and Yasuhiko Morimoto[6]

[1] Graduate School of Informatics, Nagoya University, Nagoya, Japan
[2] Centre for Cyber Resilience and Trust, Deakin University, Geelong, Australia
charles.cao@ieee.org
[3] Beijing University of Technology, Beijing, China
[4] Department of Computer Science, IPB University, Bogor, Indonesia
[5] STEM, University of South Australia, Adelaide, Australia
[6] Graduate School of Engineering, Hiroshima University, Hiroshima, Japan

Abstract. Skyline computations are a way of finding the best data points based on multiple criteria for location-based decision-making. However, as the input data grows larger, these computations become slower and more challenging. To address this issue, we propose an efficient algorithm that uses Apache Spark, a platform for distributed processing, to perform area skyline computations faster and more salable. Our algorithm consists of three main phases: calculating distances between data points, generating distance tuples, and computing the skyline. In the second phase, we apply a technique called local partial skyline extraction, which reduces the amount of data that needs to be sent from each executor (a parallel processing unit) to the driver (a central processing unit). The driver then computes the final skyline from the received data and creates filters to eliminate irrelevant points. Our experiments show that our algorithm can significantly reduce the data size and the computation time of the area skyline.

Keywords: Area skyline query · Distributed algorithm · Apache Spark

1 Introduction

Selecting good locations from a map is a crucial task for many applications such as trip planning [9], real estate [13], and business analysis. In recent years, map-based mobile applications have become more popular because they provide users with the ability to navigate maps and easily locate points of interest [1]. However, with the vast amount of information available on maps, selecting good locations can be challenging, and users feel overwhelmed by the available choices.

An area skyline query [19] is a type of query used in spatial databases for location-based decision-making. It can retrieve a set of objects that are not dominated by any other locations in a specific area. In other words, it aims to identify a subset of regions in a given area such that each identified region has

Z. Jin et al. (Eds.): KSEM 2023, LNAI 14120, pp. 35–43, 2023.
https://doi.org/10.1007/978-3-031-40292-0_4

at least one of attributes that are not worse than that of all other regions. To execute an area skyline query, the database first partitions the entire space into a grid of cells. The query then specifies the area of interest, which may span multiple cells. Within the specified area, the database retrieves all objects and compares them with each other. The objects that are not dominated by any other objects in the area are returned as the area skyline result. One of the challenges in performing area skyline queries is the high computational complexity of the operation. As the number of objects and the size of the query area increase, the time required to execute the query will significantly increase as well. To address this issue, parallel processing optimization algorithms such as MapReduce, can be used to improve the performance of area skyline queries.

MapReduce [2,16] is a popular programming model for processing large data sets in a distributed computing environment. It provides a scalable and fault-tolerant framework for parallel processing, making it an ideal choice for performing complex operations on large data sets. Area skyline query is one such complex operation, which can be implemented using MapReduce [12]. In a MapReduce-based area skyline query, the data is first partitioned and distributed across multiple nodes in a cluster. Then, the Map function is applied to each partition, which extracts the relevant attributes of the objects and identifies the local skyline of that partition. The local skylines will be combined using the Reduce function to obtain the global skyline of the entire data set [11]. One of the benefits of using MapReduce for area skyline queries is that it can scale to handle very large datasets. The parallel processing capabilities of MapReduce can be leveraged to speed up the computation time of the query. In addition, the fault-tolerant nature of MapReduce ensures that the query can continue to run even if one or more nodes in the cluster fail [3].

Apache Spark [14] is a distributed computing framework designed for large-scale data processing, which has gained popularity in recent years due to its performance and flexibility compared to MapReduce [8]. To the best of our knowledge, no algorithms have been developed for distance tuples and skyline calculation in such distributed frameworks. In this study, an enhanced algorithm based on the Spark framework is proposed to compute area skyline queries. The main contributions are as follows. I) Spark is a distributed framework for big data that provides better performance and flexibility than MapReduce; II) this study proposes a distributed algorithm for computing distance tuples and area skylines in the Spark framework. Unlike the previous MapReduce-based area skyline computation algorithm, skyline selecting and filtering is embedded in the proposed algorithm; III) experimental results show that the performance and calculation speed of our proposed algorithm outperforms the SOTA models.

2   Related Work

2.1   Skyline Query

Skyline computation for large databases is proposed for the first time in study [4]. Three algorithms (i.e., the Block Nested-Loop (BNL) algorithm, the Divide-

and-Conquer (D&C) algorithm, and the B-tree-based algorithm) are presented in their work. In [6], the Sort-Filter-Skyline (SFS) algorithm, which performs sorting before performing the skyline computation, is introduced. SFS algorithm, which performs sorting before the execution of the skyline computation, and suppresses the number of comparison operations duplicated in the BNL algorithm. In [17], two algorithms, i.e., the Bitmap algorithm and the Index algorithm are proposed. Among the algorithms for skyline computation, the Branch and Bound Skyline (BBS) algorithm proposed in [18] has the fastest computation time.

2.2 Skyline Computation with Distributed Framework

The first algorithm for skyline computation using MapReduce is proposed in [20]. Three algorithms, MR-BNL, MR-SFS, and MR-Bitmap, are introduced in that study. MR-NL and MR-SFS include three tasks: center value calculation for each dimension, local skyline computation, and global skyline calculation. However, two fundamental problems exist in MR-BNL and MR-SFS: (1) Only $2 *$ dimension tasks can be computed in parallel in the Reduce process of local skyline computation. As the number of nodes increases, the performance cannot be improved; (2) In the Reduce process of global skyline computation, the data is to be concentrated in one executor. Therefore, the load of the global skyline computation becomes extremely large. SKY-MR is a enhanced algorithm based on MapReduce, which can solve the issues of MR-BNL and MR-SFS [16].

In recent years, the superiority of the Apache Spark framework has attracted many researchers to use Spark to compute skyline objects [7,10,15]. SparkALS [15] is a divide-and-conquer-based approach, where the data is partitioned into smaller subsets and the skyline of each subset is computed in parallel. Spark-SQL [7] extends the Spark SQL engine to support skyline queries by defining new user-defined functions that implement the skyline computation. Senti-Spark [10] proposed a skyline query approach to build recommendations based on the Skyline Sort Filter algorithm in the Apache Spark cluster computing framework.

2.3 Area Skyline Computation with MapReduce

All algorithms of the above studies are for skyline calculations. An algorithm for computing area skyline with MapReduce is proposed in [11,12]. Based on the Euclidean distance transformation algorithm that exists as a problem in image analysis, the distance calculation algorithm is successfully integrated into the MapReduce framework. In the Map process, the shortest distance between the grid and the facility is calculated for each row on a map. In the subsequent Shuffle process, data are shuffled for the Reduce process. In the Reduce process, the distance between each grid and the facility is calculated by finding the grid with the closest distance to the facility based on the values of each grid.

However, although they focused on area skyline calculations, the above algorithms for distance tuples and skyline calculations are not developed. Moreover, the execution time cannot be effectively optimized when calculating distances

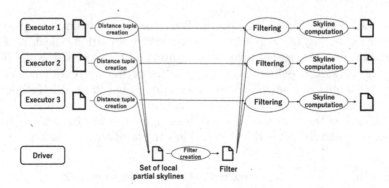

Fig. 1. Overview of the proposed Spark-based area skyline computation algorithm.

and local skylines in the Reduce process, which leads to an increase in the execution time of the whole computation process. Particularly, the execution time of the Reduce process for local skyline computation increases significantly with the growth of the number of grids and facilities. In this study, we improve the distributed algorithm based on the Spark framework for area skyline computation, as detailed in the following section.

3   Area Skyline Computation with Spark

Let A_{area} indicate a square area in a map and $F = \{F_1, F_2, \cdots\}$ is a set of facilities (e.g., stations, Warehouses, and landfills). A user aims to find an suitable region on the map that is close to some desirable facilities and away from some undesirable ones. The area skyline and area dominance can be defined as follows:

Definition 1. *A square area A_{area} can be divided into $k \times k$ grids and $A_{area} = \{a_1, a_2, \cdots, a_{k \times k}\}$. A grid a_i is said to be **an area skyline object** if there is no other grid a_j $(i \neq j)$ on a map that the distance of a_j to the closest desired facilities is smaller than that of a_i and the distance to the closest undesired facilities is larger than that of a_i.*

Definition 2. *If there exists a grid a_i that is a area skyline object, then a_i dominates $a_j (i \neq j)$ or a_j is dominated by a_i.*

Figure 1 demonstrates the overview architecture of the proposed algorithm. The proposed algorithm extracts a part of the local skylines when creating distance tuples. Then, our proposed algorithm creates a filter from the extracted tuples and performs filtering before the area skyline calculation. The algorithm can be divided into three processes, i.e., local partial skyline extraction at each executor, filter creation at the driver, and filtering in each executor.

3.1 Local Partial Skyline Extraction

In this process, each executor extracts a tuple with the minimum distance from the origin and a tuple with the minimum value in a dimension. The two types of tuples extracted from executors are local skyline points. Thus, the set containing both two types of tuples is a local skyline (a subset of the local skyline). In a set of tuples, the origin tuple is a tuple which can dominate all others. Therefore, more tuples can dominate if the distance becomes smaller from the origin. Furthermore, the tuples with a minimum value in a dimension can dominate other tuples that are not dominated by others. In the process of reducing the creation of distance tuples, the proposed algorithm not only output distance tuples, but also computes and extracts local partial skylines. Whenever a distance tuple is created, our algorithm requires checking the distance of the new tuple from the origin and the value of each dimension to determine whether it is included in the local partial skyline.

3.2 Filter Creation

In this process, the driver receives local partial skylines from each executor and performs the skyline calculation to create a filter. With n facilities on the map, the tuple is n-dimensional, and local partial skyline points obtained from each executor are $n + 1$. With m executors, the number of local partial skyline points obtained from all executors is $m * (n + 1)$. The driver performs a skyline calculation on $m * (n + 1)$ tuples. For example, a map with $1000 * 1000$ grids has 3 facilities and 32 executors. In this case, the number of local partial skyline points obtained from all executors is 128. When creating a filter, the driver of the proposed algorithm performs a skyline calculation for 128 tuples. In contrast, each executor of previous work performs $1000/32 \approx 32$ skyline computations for 1000 tuples during the Reduce process of local skyline computation. Compared with the Reduce process for local skyline computation, this filtering process is computationally low and is not a bottleneck for the whole skyline computation.

3.3 Filtering

In this process, each executor receives a filter from the driver and filters the tuples before skyline computation. First, the driver broadcasts the filter to each executor. Then, the executor receiving the filter checks the dominance of each tuple that is an input to the skyline calculation against the tuples in the filter. The tuple is removed if it is dominated by a tuple in the filter. While a tuple is not dominated by any of the tuples in the filter, the tuple is passed through the filter and becomes the input data for the skyline calculation.

4 Experiment

Since Azure HDInsight [5] is a cloud service provided by Microsoft that can create Hadoop and Spark clusters without any environment construction, we used it

Table 1. Configuration of Spark clusters.

Node type	RAM	The number of cores	The number of machines
Master node	64 GB	8	2
Worker node	64 GB	8	3

Table 2. Descriptions of the eight datasets.

	Set A	Set B	Set C	Set D
Facilities	3	3	3	3
Grids	1000 × 1000	2000 × 2000	3000 × 3000	4000 × 4000
	Set E	Set F	Set G	Set H
Facilities	3	4	5	6
Grids	5000 × 5000	3000 × 3000	3000 × 3000	3000 × 3000

to create Spark clusters in our experiments. Table 1 shows the configuration of clusters. Each distributed task is allocated 7GB of memory resources per core, and the Spark application is configured to have 24 parallel distributed executors.

Table 2 shows the properties of 8 datasets used in the experiments. Five datasets (i.e., Sets A–E) are used with three facility types to evaluate the scalability with an increasing number of grids. Additionally, four datasets (i.e., Sets C, F, G, and H) with 3000 × 3000 grids are used to evaluate the effects of the number of facilities. The facilities in each dataset are randomly scattered at a rate of one facility per row. When multiple facilities are on the same grid, the grid has a tuple close to the origin. Therefore, when filtering with the proposed algorithm, the tuple may remove many other tuples, which may improve the results of the proposed algorithm. This study sets the ratio to overlap to create a dataset to prevent such situations. Moreover, since the ratio of the number of facilities to the number of grids decreases as the number of grids increases when using the regional skyline calculation on the actual map, the dataset used is also designed so that the ratio of the number of facilities decreases as the number of grids increases.

4.1 Baselines

E-MR-BNL, E-MR-SFS, E-SKY-MR, P-MR-BNL, P-MR-SFS, and P-SKY-MR are used as baselines in the experiments, where E and P denote the existing and proposed algorithms, respectively. The area skyline computation consists of three parts: distance computation, distance tuple creation, and skyline computation. The algorithm of the previous study is used for the distance calculation. The algorithms of existing or proposed algorithms are used to create distance tuples. MR-BNL, MR-SFS, or SKY-MR is used for the skyline calculation.

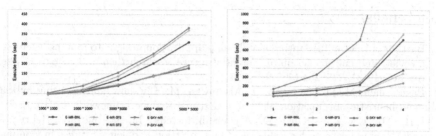

(a) Execution time with an increase in the number of grids.

(b) Execution time with an increase in the number of facilities.

Fig. 2. Effect of grids and facilities.

4.2 Effect of Grids and Facilities

Figure 2(a) shows the relationship between the increase in the number of grids and the execution time. When the number of grids is 1000 × 1000 and 2000 × 2000, there is little difference in the execution time between the existing and the proposed algorithms. However, for data with 3000 × 3000 or more grids, the execution time of the proposed algorithms is reduced. For 3000 × 3000 data, the proposed algorithms reduce the execution time to 62–75% of that of the existing algorithms. For 4000 × 4000 grids, the execution time of the proposed algorithms is reduced to 55–71% of that of the existing algorithms. When the number of grids is 5000 × 5000, the execution time is reduced to 48–60% of that of the existing algorithms. Overall, the execution time increases as the number of grids increases, but the time consumption of the proposed algorithm is lower than that of baseline algorithms.

Figure 2(b) depicts the relationship between the number of facilities and overall execution time. The execution time of our proposed algorithms reduces to 59 ~ 75% when the number of facilities is 3. Additionally, the execution time is reduced to 35 ~ 67% and 20 ~ 60% with four and five facilities, respectively. In summary, the execution time increases as the number of facilities increases, but the time consumption of the proposed algorithm is lower than that of baselines.

5 Conclusion

This study proposes a Spark-based distributed algorithm to reduce the execution time of area skyline computation. By creating a filter from the local partial skyline points at distance table creation and filtering before the skyline calculation, the load of the area skyline calculation and overall execution time are significantly reduced. The execution time in the proposed algorithm is proportional to the number of grids and the number of facilities.

References

1. Bartling, M., et al.: Adapting mobile map application designs to map use context: a review and call for action on potential future research themes. Cartogr. Geogr. Inf. Sci. **49**(3), 237–251 (2022)
2. Bashabsheh, M.Q., Abualigah, L., Alshinwan, M.: Big data analysis using hybrid meta-heuristic optimization algorithm and mapReduce framework. In: Houssein, E.H., Abd Elaziz, M., Oliva, D., Abualigah, L. (eds.) Integrating Meta-Heuristics and Machine Learning for Real-World Optimization Problems. Studies in Computational Intelligence, vol. 1038, pp. 181–223. Springer, Cham (2022). https://doi.org/10.1007/978-3-030-99079-4_8
3. Bessani, A.N., et al.: Making hadoop mapReduce byzantine fault-tolerant. DSN, Fast abstract (2010)
4. Borzsony, S., Kossmann, D., Stocker, K.: The skyline operator. In: Proceedings 17th International Conference on Data Engineering, pp. 421–430. IEEE (2001)
5. Chauhan, A., Fontama, V., Hart, M., Tok, W.H., Woody, B.: Introducing Microsoft Azure HDInsight. Microsoft press (2014)
6. Chomicki, J., Godfrey, P., Gryz, J., Liang, D.: Skyline with presorting. ICDE **3**, 717–719 (2003)
7. Grasmann, L., Pichler, R., Selzer, A.: Integration of skyline queries into spark sql. arXiv preprint arXiv:2210.03718 (2022)
8. Neogi, A.G., Eltaher, A., Sargsyan, A.: NGS data analysis with apache spark. In: Dorpinghaus, J., Weil, V., Schaaf, S., Apke, A. (eds.) Computational Life Sciences. Studies in Big Data, vol. 112, pp. 441–467. Springer, Cham (2023). https://doi.org/10.1007/978-3-031-08411-9_16
9. Kar, M., Sadhukhan, S., Parida, M.: Location planning of park-and-ride facilities around rapid transit systems in cities: a review. J. Urban Plann. Develop. **149**(1), 03122004 (2023)
10. Lapatta, N.T.: Ecotourism recommendations based on sentiments using skyline query and apache-spark. J. Soc. Sci. **3**(3), 534–546 (2022)
11. Li, C., Annisa, A., Zaman, A., Qaosar, M., Ahmed, S., Morimoto, Y.: MapReduce algorithm for location recommendation by using area skyline query. Algorithms **11**(12), 191 (2018)
12. Li, C., Zaman, A., Morimoto, Y., et al.: MapReduce-based computation of area skyline query for selecting good locations in a map. In: 2017 IEEE International Conference on Big Data (Big Data), pp. 4779–4782. IEEE (2017)
13. Li, H., Yu, L., Cheng, E.W.: A GIS-based site selection system for real estate projects. Constr. Innov. **5**(4), 231–241 (2005)
14. Pallamala, R.K., Rodrigues, P.: An investigative testing of structured and unstructured data formats in big data application using apache spark. Wireless Pers. Commun. **122**(1), 603–620 (2022)
15. Papanikolaou, I.: Distributed algorithms for skyline computation using apache spark (2020)
16. Park, Y., Min, J.K., Shim, K.: Parallel computation of skyline and reverse skyline queries using mapReduce. Proceed. VLDB Endow. **6**(14), 2002–2013 (2013)
17. Tan, K.L., Eng, P.K., Ooi, B.C., et al.: Efficient progressive skyline computation. VLDB **1**, 301–310 (2001)
18. Xia, T., Zhang, D., Tao, Y.: On skylining with flexible dominance relation. In: 2008 IEEE 24th International Conference on Data Engineering, pp. 1397–1399. IEEE (2008)

19. Zaman, A., Morimoto, Y., et al.: Area skyline query for selecting good locations in a map. J. Inf. Process. **24**(6), 946–955 (2016)
20. Zhang, B., Zhou, S., Guan, J.: Adapting skyline computation to the mapReduce framework: algorithms and experiments. In: Xu, J., Yu, G., Zhou, S., Unland, R. (eds.) DASFAA 2011. LNCS, vol. 6637, pp. 403–414. Springer, Heidelberg (2011). https://doi.org/10.1007/978-3-642-20244-5_39

TCMCoRep: Traditional Chinese Medicine Data Mining with Contrastive Graph Representation Learning

Zecheng Yin[1], Jinyuan Luo[1], Yuejun Tan[1], and Yanchun Zhang[1,2(✉)]

[1] Guangzhou University, Guangzhou, China
{yinzecheng,2112106041,2112233104}@e.gzhu.edu.cn, yzhangvu@gmail.com
[2] Pengcheng Lab, Shenzhen, China

Abstract. Traditional Chinese Medicine(TCM) is a highly empirical, subjective and practical discipline. One of the most realistic data mining tasks in TCM is prescription generation. While recommendation models could be applied to provide herb recommendation, they are limited to modeling only the interactions between herbs and symptoms, ignoring the intermediate process of syndrome induction, which betrays a main principle in real-world TCM diagnosis: doctors suggest herb based on the holism syndrome inducted from symptoms.

Targeting on this pain point, we proposed **TCMCoRep**, a novel graph contrastive representation learning framework with explicit syndrome awareness. For a given symptom set, predictive representation from TCMCoRep not only locates high quality prescription herbs but also explicitly detects corresponding syndrome via syndrome-aware prescription generation that follows the philosophy of TCM diagnosis in real life. Hybridization of homogeneous and heterogeneous graph convolutions is able to preserve graph heterogeneity preventing the possible damage from early augmentation, to convey strong samples for contrastive learning. Experiments conducted in practical datasets demonstrate our proposed model's competitive performance compared with existing state-of-the-art methods, revealing the great potential in real-world applications. Our source code is available at https://github.com/Yonggie/TCMCoRep.

Keywords: data mining · graph contrastive learning · traditional Chinese medicine · heterogeneous graph · syndrome-aware prescription generation

1 Introduction

Traditional Chinese Medicine (TCM) is a very ancient Chinese treatment system that has developed over thousands of years [1], which is listed as one of the patrimoine culturel immatériel. The World Health Organization (WHO) has proved that TCM is effective for COVID'19, which is very promising for medical development worldwide [2]. Doctors follow the TCM principles of holism thinking, which emphasizes the integrity of the human body and its interactions with

Z. Jin et al. (Eds.): KSEM 2023, LNAI 14120, pp. 44–55, 2023.
https://doi.org/10.1007/978-3-031-40292-0_5

the natural environment. TCM prescription is given by taking three steps: doctors first observe the symptoms of patient, then make an induction of syndromes that reflect the holism of body condition, finally prescribe herbs based on the syndromes. Figure 1 shows an example of TCM process.

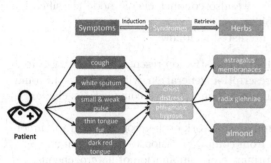

Fig. 1. An example of TCM process

As a domain-specific data, TCM data's own specialty makes it hard to conduct data mining. (1)Multiple relations with rich TCM knowledge. Numerous interaction relations are very commonly seen in the scenario of diagnosis. For example, doctors consider suitable herbs for symptoms and examine their compatibility to make them more effective with fewer side effects. Managing such complex structural information and preserving the various feature information are critical problems. (2)Skewed Data Distribution. As often faced in recommender problem, the interaction between herbs and symptoms usually follows a power-law distribution. Hence, models are easily biased towards highfrequent herbs, sacrificing the low-frequent (long-tail) ones. (3)Expensive Data Labeling. To label any prescription related data is time-consuming.

In TCM, prescription generation and syndrome detection are realistic tasks. Concretely, model takes symptoms as input and outputs the diagnosis syndrome and corresponding prescription. [3–6] are proposed for these tasks, yet most of them consider this task as a direct recommendation problem between symptom and herb, ignoring the syndrome, which betrays the philosophy of TCM.

A variety of graph convolution networks are proposed in recent years. Homogeneous graph convolutions [7–9] show promising performance in various kinds of tasks, but do not take semantic information of different types of nodes into consideration. Heterogeneous graph based supervised models [10,11], and unsupervised models [12,13], are proposed to handle heterogeneous graph, which greatly enriched graph convolution family. SMGCN [14] successfully integrates recommender system and graph convolution in TCM data to get a syndrome-aware herbal recommender, but cannot induct explicit syndromes. Besides, SMGCN cannot take in the syndrome information even if it is explicitly provided due to its methodology. Moreover, data must be preprocessed into herb-herb and symptom-symptom bipartite to fit in the model, which leads to expensive data labeling on herb and symptom relationship.

In this paper, to overcome multiple challenges (heterogeneous relation, skewed distribution, expensive labeling, explicit syndrome awareness) in TCM data mining, we propose **TCMCoRep**, a novel unsupervised contrastive learning framework. Different from recommender system, TCMCoRep is able to provide explicit syndrome node awareness. Moreover, momentum mechanism is applied to empower the contrastive learning framework, in order to generate better node representations.

To mimic TCM in the real-world scenario, following TCM 2-step philosophy, we designed Prescription Generation task and Syndrome Detection task. In addition to practical downstream tasks, we also conduct classic node classification task to represent our model capability.

To this end, our contributions are listed as follows:

- We proposed a novel unsupervised contrastive representation learning framework **TCMCoRep** for TCM prescription generation, with explicit syndrome-awareness and high prescription performance, to overcome various challenges faced in TCM data mining.
- We designed a contrastive learning framework on heterogeneous graph inheriting from SimCLR and MoCo from computer vision to graph domain.
- We explored the potential performance of combination of heterogeneous and homogeneous graph convolution in TCM dataset.

2   Related Work

2.1   Graph Convolution and Graph Neural Network

Convolution methods adopted for computer vision have been adapted to graph domain and achieved great success.

[8] takes 1-hop neighbor and linear transformation for massage passing and [7] added attention mechanism, however they could not capture abundant type information. However, most real systems consist of a large number of interacting components [15]. [11] follows [7] to extend attention mechanism to heterogeneous graph and [10] adopted a graph transformer for graph convolution, yet they are semi-supervised methods that require expensive labeled data.

2.2   Contrastive Learning

Various popular computer vision contrastive learning frameworks [16–18] are proposed recently. [19,20] are two important base branches with many other contrastive losses [21–24].

In graph contrastive learning, [25] extended [26] to graphs using node-global contrastive loss to maximize mutual information of node and whole graph, and [9] follows [19] conveys a graph version of SimCLR. [12]/ [13] following [25] convert multiplex graph into multiple homogeneous graphs using meta-path based graph decomposition, and aggregates embeddings, which succeeded in extending [26] series onto multiplex graph, but its data preprocessing requires metapath manual selection and leads to longer and heavier training.

3 Preliminary

TCM Heterogeneous Information Graph (THIG). THIG is domain specific heterogeneous graph composed of various TCM entities with rich relations, defined as $\mathcal{G} = (\mathcal{V}, \mathcal{E}, X)$ where $\mathcal{V}$ and $\mathcal{E}$ are the sets of nodes and edges respectively, and X is the node representation. Figure 2 shows an example of THIG, which describes 3 types of nodes and the relations among them.

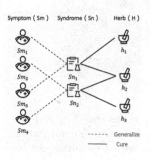

Fig. 2. Toy THIG.

Symptom-Syndrome edges represent the generalization of symptom to syndrome in a prescription. Syndrome-Herb edges indicate the therapeutic or palliative effect of prescribed herbs on specific symptoms.

THIG builds edge connection of the nodes only once no matter how many times this connection appears in the data. This way, the frequent and the less frequent share equal attention from the model, rather than skewed attention.

Following TCM philosophy, we restrict message flow by building connections only between herb and syndrome, and between symptom and syndrome, which means message passing between herb and symptom must go through syndrome. Syndrome node plays a holistic role in diagnosis. We wish that THIG topology could provide TCM prior in advance.

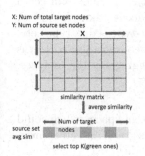

Fig. 3. The "find" process.

Real-World Based Prescription Generation. Real-world-based Prescription Generation is a 2-step retrieval process that follows TCM philosophy to mimic the real-world diagnosis process, with the thinking of holism.

In evaluation, symptoms(sm) firstly "find" the syndrome(sn) nodes (usually 1–3 nodes, much less than symptom), and then based on the syndrome nodes, find herb(h) nodes. Formally, for a given symptom node set $S_{sm} = (sm_1, sm_2, sm_3, ...sm_n)$, we firstly find the top nodes S_{sn}, then find top K herb nodes $S_h = (h_1, h_2, h_3, ..., h_n)$ according to S_{sn}, such that S_{sn} could represent the the holistic body condition of the patient, and the herb set S_h could relieve the symptoms in set S_{sm}. The detailed retrieval process,i.e. symptoms → syndromes or syndromes → herbs, is shown in Fig. 3, where s_{ij} means the similarity between source node i and target node j.

4 Framework

Our **TCMCoRep** overview is shown in Fig. 4.

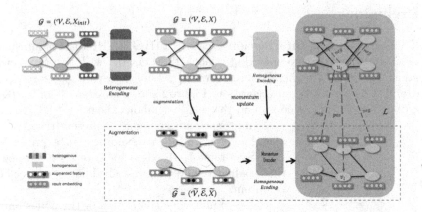

Fig. 4. TCMCoRep overview. THIG is encoded by heterogeneous encoding and projected into the same latent space with augmentation followed. After augmentation, both two views are then encoded by homogeneous encoders with momentum mechanism. Finally contrastive loss is calculated.

4.1 Heterogeneous Encoding

We adopted two sota heterogeneous convolutions HAN [11] and HGT [10], and take HAN as final encoder. Due to limited space, we explain it in a general simplified format.

For input $\mathcal{G}_{init} = (X_{init}, \mathcal{E})$, where $X = (X_{sn}, X_{sm}, X_h)$ and undirected edge $\mathcal{E} = (\mathcal{E}_{sn,h}, \mathcal{E}_{sm,h})$, heterogeneous encoder $HeteEncode$ takes X and $\mathcal{E}$, which contains heterogeneous information such as node type, edge type, etc. and outputs feature X'. For HAN, it splits the heterogeneous graph and learns attentions between different types of nodes, and then aggregates the features. This is formulated as:

$$X' = HeteEncode(X, \mathcal{E})$$

Heterogeneous encoding projects nodes into a same latent space, which could be regarded as a transformation that turns a heterogeneous graph into an approximately homogeneous graph, since they are fully interacted.

4.2 Graph Augmentation

We conduct augmentation in two aspects: attribution (node feature) and topology. By providing abundant samples, encoders could capture the essential features from THIG.

- Topology augmentation. We apply Edge Removing and Node Removing on topology augmentation. Edge Removing randomly drops edges of THIG with probability P_{er} using Bernoulli distribution. Node Removing deletes all edges related to the selected nodes with a probability of P_{nr} using Bernoulli distribution.

– Attribution augmentation. We apply Feature Masking in attribution augmentation, which randomly masks certain feature vector elements with zeros in node attribution. Formally, we generate a mask M with probability P_{fm} using Bernoulli distribution, then XOR the mask with feature matrix to get augmented feature $\widetilde{X}$.

By applying these augmentations in THIG $\mathcal{G} = (\mathcal{V}, \mathcal{E}, X)$, we generate a correlated graph views $\widetilde{\mathcal{G}} = (\widetilde{\mathcal{V}}, \widetilde{\mathcal{E}}, \widetilde{X})$, the contrastive learning will be conducted on these two views.

4.3 Homogeneous Encoding

We apply GCN [8] on homogeneous encoding. GCN layer takes node representation X and adjacent information A as input and outputs node representation X'. Formally, message passing of GCN layer is formulated as:

$$X' = f(H, A) = \sigma\left(\hat{D}^{-\frac{1}{2}}\hat{A}\hat{D}^{-\frac{1}{2}}XW\right) \tag{1}$$

where $\hat{A} = A + I$ is the adjacency matrix with self-loops, and $\hat{D}$ is degree matrix, W is a trainable weight, and σ is a nonlinear activation function.

4.4 Momentum Mechanism

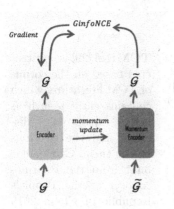

Fig. 5. Momentum mechanism.

Momentum encoder mechanism is a powerful component in contrastive learning with a wide use in many popular works [27].

In momentum framework, momentum mechanism stops negative encoder updating from backforward, and uses running mean to update θ_{neg} from positive encoder's parameter θ_{pos}. As shown in Fig. 5, we generalize the momentum mechanism into graph-structured data in the homogeneous encoding phase of TCMCoRep for better contrastive learning. The encoders in TCMCoRep are GCNs, where the augmented graph's encoder is the negative encoder, while original branch has the positive encoder. Formally, iteration equation of the parameter of momentum encoder updating is:

$$\theta_{neg} \leftarrow m\theta_{neg} + (1 - m)\theta_{pos} \tag{2}$$

where m controls the speed of updating, usually being $[0.9 - 1)$.

4.5 GinfoNCE Loss

Following [24,28], to maximize agreement of similar nodes, we generalize infoNCE loss to graph structured data, named Graph infoNCE (GinfoNCE). The sampling strategy of GinfoNCE is intuitive. For one node u_i in $\mathcal{G}$, we take the corresponding augmented node v_i as the positive sample, and any other nodes $v_{j[j\neq i]}$ as negative samples. Loss function $\mathcal{L}$ written as:

$$l(u_i, v_i) = -log\frac{e^{s(u_i,v_i)/\tau}}{\sum_{u\in\mathcal{G}\backslash\{u_i\}} e^{s(u_i,u)/\tau} + \sum_{v\in\tilde{\mathcal{G}}\backslash\{v_i\}} e^{s(u_i,v)/\tau}} \tag{3}$$

$$\mathcal{L} = \frac{1}{2N}\sum_{i=1}^{N}[l(u_i, v_i) + l(v_i, u_i)] \tag{4}$$

where s is dot product as a similarity function, N is the number of nodes in $\mathcal{G}$.

5 Experiments

We demonstrate the performance of TCMCoRep by conducting several real-world problems experiments, including herb prescription generation, syndrome detection and herb node classification, compared with 5 supervised and 4 unsupervised models. On top of that, we conducted extensive ablation study to explore the reasonality of TCMCoRep framework.

5.1 Datasets

Table 1. Syndrome detection on LuCa.

Method	hit@1	hit@2	hit@3	hit@5	hit@10
GCN	0.1323	0.2040	0.4057	0.4476	0.4689
GAT	0	0.3099	0.3577	0.4172	0.5849
HGT	0.1614	0.1697	0.4967	0.4967	1
HAN	0.0108	0.1252	0.1697	0.3998	0.5279
SMGCN	-	-	-	-	-
DGI	0	0.5258	0.8111	0.8319	0.9921
GRACE	0.0429	0.3261	0.8201	0.8299	0.9900
DMGI	0.1651	0.3973	0.5033	0.5035	0.505
Raw	0.0295	0.0695	0.1102	0.1968	0.4384
TCMCoRep	**0.2275**	**0.5923**	**0.9626**	**0.9971**	1

TCMRel [29] is constructed based on the corpus of TCM literature, which contains entities such as herbs, symptoms, diseases, and the relations among them. **ChP** [30] is built from the Pharmacopoeia of the People's Republic of China 2015 Edition, which contains various TCM information including formula, herb, symptom and function. **LuCa** is a real-world lung cancer clinical dataset, from our cooperative hospital, which includes symptom, syndrome and herb. Syndrome Detection and Prescription Generation performance are reported on this dataset.

5.2 Syndrome Detection

The holistic syndrome plays an important role in TCM therapeutic process. Syndrome detection explicitly predicts syndromes based on given symptoms, which provides interpretability and reliability for doctors in practice.

Syndrome Detection is a similarity-score-based retrieval described in Fig. 3, in this step source nodes are symptoms and target nodes are syndromes. We show the hit rate of syndrome detection.

In Table 1, *Raw* uses initial BOW representation. TCMCoRep is able to reach nearly 97% when K is just 3, which surpasses all baselines by large margins, demonstrating powerful feature representation ability of our model.

5.3 Prescription Generation

Table 2. Prescription generation on LuCa.

Method	r@10	r@20	p@10	p@20
GCN	0.1222	0.3036	0.2404	0.2969
GAT	0.0647	0.0651	0.1295	0.0647
HGT	0.0258	0.2493	0.0526	0.2513
HAN	0.0416	0.1090	0.0826	0.1095
SMGCN	0.0939	0.1203	0.0808	0.0537
DGI	0.2270	0.3708	0.2263	0.3693
GRACE	0.0522	0.0541	0.1036	0.0538
DMGI	0.0320	0.0517	0.0654	0.0521
Raw	0.0141	0.0586	0.0282	0.0273
TCMCoRep	**0.1360**	**0.3839**	**0.2730**	**0.3827**

Through Prescription Generation, model could retrieve accurate herb prescription for patience. Prescription Generation is the same similarity retrieval described in Fig. 3, while syndrome nodes given by Syndrome Detection as source node and herb nodes as target nodes. We show the prescription precision@K (p@K) and recall@K (r@K) .

In Table 2, *Raw* means uses initial BOW representation. As shown in Table 2, our model outperformed all baselines.

Among the baselines, SMGCN selects frequent relations of herb-herb and symptom-symptom over a threshold that the connections must appear multiple times as input, while TCMCoRep does not require any special selection yet still achieving high performance, demonstrating our superb feature representation ability.

5.4 Node Classification

We conduct classic graph downstream node classification on herb nodes according to herbal representation.

Specifically, we implement a logistic regression model to calculate the averaged Macro-F1, Micro-F1 on node embeddings with 8:2 of training and test, 10 repeats averaged.

As shown in Table 3, to demonstrate the representation capability of our model, The first 4 baselines are supervised model and the rest are unsupervised. Our model shows competitive performance among all models.

5.5   Ablation Study

Table 3. Herbal classification.

Method	Micro F1			Macro F1		
	TcmRel	ChP	LuCa	TcmRel	ChP	LuCa
GCN	0.1778	0.1549	0.1333	0.0684	0.0392	0.0288
GAT	0.2000	0.0423	0.1600	0.1099	0.0222	0.0302
HGT	0.1636	0.1398	0.1471	**0.1443**	0.0210	0.0160
HAN	0.2593	0.1684	0.1364	0.0453	0.0260	0.0306
DGI	0.1233	0.1382	0.1832	0.0292	0.0549	0.0415
GRACE	0.1644	0.1789	0.1679	0.0246	0.0164	0.0237
DMGI	0.2055	0.1301	0.1756	0.0921	0.0433	0.0236
ours	**0.2603**	**0.2033**	**0.2366**	0.0485	**0.0629**	**0.0417**

For the hybridization convolution ablation, as a 2-phrase encoding, we tried different combinations of heterogeneous (*hetero*) and homogeneous (*homo*) convolutions, reported in row 1–3 and 10. For example *homo-hetero* means we first apply homo-encoding then apply hetero-encoding and *none-hetero* means we do not apply any graph convolution and then apply hetero-encoding.

Different convolutions (row 4, 5), losses (row 6,7), augmentations (row 8) are compared. $ours_{jsd}$ [25] used loss from DGI, and $ours_{p.r.}$ [31] delete graph edges with edge weights. $ours_{no-mo}$ represents model with no momentum mechanism.

Table 4. Prescription generation of model variants

	Method	r@10	r@20	p@10	p@20
1	homo-hetero	0.0362	0.0389	0.0712	0.0384
2	none-homo	0.0463	0.1933	0.0372	0.0651
3	none-hetero	0.0284	0.0482	0.0895	0.0893
4	$ours_{gat}$	0.0070	0.1134	0.1388	0.1138
5	$ours_{hgt}$	0.1360	0.3288	0.2730	0.3277
6	$ours_{jsd}$	0.1292	0.3630	0.2586	0.3614
7	$ours_{grace}$	0.1355	0.3704	0.2699	0.3825
8	$ours_{p.r.}$	0.1369	0.2730	0.2731	0.2720
9	$ours_{no-mo}$	0.1251	0.3729	0.2632	0.3655
10	TCMCoRep	**0.1360**	**0.3839**	**0.2730**	**0.3827**

Hybridization of heterogeneous and homogeneous encoding preserves heterogenity compared with early augmentation and direct hetero-encoding. In the Table 4, *none-hetero*, THIG information is directly feed into heterogeneous convolution after augmentation and the performance is fairly unsatisfactory. Direct augmentation before hetero-encoding may corrupt too much to preserve certain heterogenity, leading to unqualified contrastive learning samples. THIG is not a web-scale heterogeneous graph with a large number of node types and massive noise. As heterogenity information is provided by different reorganization of edge connections, early augmentations could corrupt the THIG too much to be correlated with the original view. *none-homo* is higher than *homo-hetero* or *none-hetero* because the homogeneous graph convolution is not sensitive to the heterogenity. *homo-hetero* and *none-homo* perform poorly compared to TCMCoRep because they corrupt rich heterogeneous information in THIG. TCMCoRep (*hetero-homo*) properly handled this dilemma by using hetero-homo strategy.

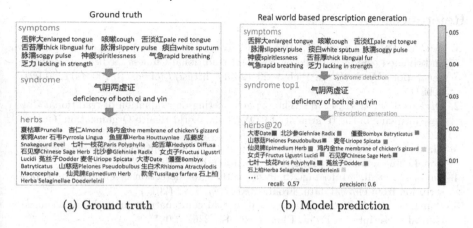

(a) Ground truth   (b) Model prediction

Fig. 6. Case study of TCMCoRep (Color figure online)

Different losses do not change much of the model performance. We see ours$_{p.r.}$ could provide competitive performance, but it's a computationally heavier augmentation compared with random augmentation. Ours$_{no-mo}$ indicates momentum mechanism does limited contribution and the main contribution comes from good feature and augmentation timing.

5.6 Case Study

To demonstrate in concrete examples, we conduct case study on the LuCa dataset. In Fig. 6, color represents frequency of the herb. Each true positive herb is matched with a color.

In Fig. 6(b), TCMCoRep generates a prescription with a total of 20 herbs, which contains 6 commonly used herbs (green), 2 frequently used herbs (yellow), and 3 long-tail herbs (dark blue) with 0.57 recall and 0.6 precision, even if certain nodes are not commonly seen. As shown above, our model is able to not only find prescription herb, but also explicitly infer the holistic syndrome.

6 Conclusion

We proposed a novel unsupervised contrastive learning framework, **TCM-CoRep**, and its corresponding evaluation and data structure, THIG, to deal with the lack of explicit syndrome detection in TCM models, as well as multiple challenges in TCM data mining, such as heterogeneous relations, skewed distribution, and expensive labeling. Our model adopted two contrastive learning frameworks MoCo and SimCLR from computer vision to graph contrastive learning and explored the hybridization of homogeneous and heterogeneous graph convolution on real-world datasets. Furthermore, we designed real-world-based downstream tasks of syndrome detection, prescription generation, as well as node classification evaluation to reveal that our scheme outperformed many state-of-the-art baselines on various datasets.

References

1. Wu, Y., Pei, C., Ruan, C., Wang, R., Yang, Y., Zhang, Y.: Bayesian networks and chained classifiers based on SVM for traditional Chinese medical prescription generation. World Wide Web 1–22 (2021). https://doi.org/10.1007/s11280-021-00981-5
2. Organization, W.H., et al.: Who expert meeting on evaluation of traditional Chinese medicine in the treatment of COVID-19. World Health Organization, Geneva (2022)
3. Li, C., et al.: Herb-know: Knowledge enhanced prescription generation for traditional chinese medicine. In: BIBM. pp. 1560–1567, IEEE (2020)
4. Yang, K., et al.: Multistage analysis method for detection of effective herb prescription from clinical data. Front. Med. 7(7), 1–12 (2017)
5. Wang, N., et al.: Network patterns of herbal combinations in traditional chinese clinical prescriptions. Front. Pharmacol. 11, 2367 (2021)
6. Ruan, C., Ma, J., Wang, Y., Zhang, Y., Yang, Y., S. Kraus, D.: Discovering regularities from traditional Chinese medicine prescriptions via bipartite embedding model. In IJCAI, pp. 3346–3352 (2019)
7. Veličković, P., Cucurull, G., Casanova, A., Romero, A., Lio, P., Bengio, Y.: Graph attention networks, arXiv preprint arXiv:1710.10903 (2017)
8. Kipf, T. N., Welling, M.: Semi-supervised classification with graph convolutional networks, In: 5th ICLR (2017)
9. Zhu, M., Xu, Y., Yu, F., Liu, Q., Wu, S., Wang, L.: Deep graph contrastive representation learning. arXiv preprint arXiv:2006.04131 (2020)
10. Hu, Z., Dong, Y., Wang, K., Sun, Y.: Heterogeneous graph transformer. Proc. Web Conf. 2020, 2704–2710 (2020)
11. Wang, X., et al.: Heterogeneous graph attention network. In: The World Wide Web Conference, ser. WWW '19. New York, NY, USA: Association for Computing Machinery, pp. 2022–2032 (2019). https://doi.org/10.1145/3308558.3313562
12. Park, C., Kim, D., Han, J., Yu, H.: Unsupervised attributed multiplex network embedding. AAAI 34(04), 5371–5378 (2020)
13. Ren, Y., Liu, Y., Huang, C., Dai, P., Bo, L., Zhang, J.: Heterogeneous deep graph infomax, CoRR, vol. abs/1911.08538 (2019). http://arxiv.org/abs/1911.08538
14. Jin, Y., Zhang, W., He, X., Wang, X., Wang, X.: Syndrome-aware herb recommendation with multi-graph convolution network, In: ICDE. IEEE, pp. 145–156 (2020)
15. Shi, C., Li, Y., Zhang, J., Sun, Y., Philip, S.Y.: A survey of heterogeneous information network analysis. IEEE Trans. Knowl. Data Eng. 29(1), 17–37 (2016)
16. Jaiswal, A., Babu, A. R., Zadeh, M. Z., Banerjee, D., Makedon, F.: A survey on contrastive self-supervised learning. CoRR, vol. abs/2011.00362 (2020). https://arxiv.org/abs/2011.00362
17. Grill, J.-B.: Bootstrap your own latent - a new approach to self-supervised learning, In: Advances in Neural Information Processing Systems, H. Larochelle, M. Ranzato, R. Hadsell, M. Balcan, and H. Lin, Eds., vol. 33. Curran Associates Inc, pp. 21 271–21 284 (2020)
18. Caron, M., Misra, I., Mairal, J., Goyal, P., Bojanowski, P., Joulin, A.: Unsupervised learning of visual features by contrasting cluster assignments, In: Advances in Neural Information Processing Systems, H. Larochelle, M. Ranzato, R. Hadsell, M. Balcan, and H. Lin, Eds., vol. 33. Curran Associates Inc, pp. 9912–9924(2020).https://proceedings.neurips.cc/paper/2020/file/70feb62b69f16e0238f741fab228fec2-Paper.pdf

19. Chen, T., Kornblith, S., Norouzi, M., Hinton, G.: A simple framework for contrastive learning of visual representations. In: International conference on machine learning. PMLR, pp. 1597–1607 (2020)
20. He, K., Fan, H., Wu, Y., Xie, S., Girshick, R.: Momentum contrast for unsupervised visual representation learning, In: CVPR, pp. 9729–9738 (2020)
21. Wu, Y., et al.: A hybrid-scales graph contrastive learning framework for discovering regularities in traditional Chinese medicine formula, In: BIBM, pp. 1104–1111 (2021)
22. Zbontar, J,. Jing, L,. Misra, I., LeCun, Y., Deny, S.: Barlow twins: Self-supervised learning via redundancy reduction, In: Proceedings of the 38th International Conference on Machine Learning, ser. Proceedings of Machine Learning Research, M. Meila and T. Zhang, Eds., vol. 139. PMLR, 18–24 pp. 12 310–12 320 (2021). https://proceedings.mlr.press/v139/zbontar21a.html
23. Liu, Y., et al.: Graph self-supervised learning: a survey (2021). https://arxiv.org/abs/2103.00111
24. Oord, A. v. d., Li, Y., Vinyals, O.: Representation learning with contrastive predictive coding, arXiv preprint arXiv:1807.03748 (2018)
25. Velickovic, P., Fedus, W., Hamilton, W. L., Liò, P., Bengio, Y., Hjelm, R. D.: Deep graph infomax. In: ICLR (Poster) (2019)
26. Hjelm, R. D. et al.: Learning deep representations by mutual information estimation and maximization, arXiv preprint arXiv:1808.06670 (2018)
27. Tao, C., et al.: Exploring the equivalence of siamese self-supervised learning via a unified gradient framework (2021). https://arxiv.org/abs/2112.05141
28. Wu, Z., Xiong, Y., et al.: Unsupervised feature learning via non-parametric instance discrimination, In: Proceedings of the IEEE conference on computer vision and pattern recognition, pp. 3733–3742 (2018)
29. Wan, H., et al.: Extracting relations from traditional Chinese medicine literature via heterogeneous entity networks. JAMIA **23**(2), 356–365 (2016)
30. Chen, X., Ruan, C., Zhang, Y., Chen, H.: Heterogeneous information network based clustering for categorizations of traditional Chinese medicine formula, In: BIBM. IEEE, pp. 839–846 (2018)
31. Page, L., Brin, S., Motwani, R., Winograd, T.: The PageRank citation ranking : bringing order to the web, In: WWW Conference (1999)

Local-Global Fusion Augmented Graph Contrastive Learning Based on Generative Models

Di Jin[1], Zhiqiang Wang[1], Cuiying Huo[1], Zhizhi Yu[1(✉)], Dongxiao He[1], and Yuxiao Huang[2]

[1] College of Intelligence and Computing, Tianjin University, Tianjin, China
{jindi,wzhiqiang,huocuiying,yuzhizhi,hedongxiao}@tju.edu.cn
[2] George Washington University, Washington, USA
yuxiaohuang@gwu.edu

Abstract. Recently, graph contrastive learning (GCL) has emerged as a dominant technique for unsupervised graph representation learning. Existing GCL-based approaches typically adopt data augmentation to generate two contrastive views, and maximize the similarity between representations that share the same semantics in these two views. However, there are two weaknesses in existing methods: 1) They are highly dependent on the selection of augmentation modes, such as random node and edge perturbation as well as node feature masking, which may lead to changes in the structure and semantic information of the graph. 2) Existing augmentation strategies fail to adequately model local and global information. Graph-based generative models can use graph topology and semantic information to reconstruct node features, so as to avoid random perturbation of features. Therefore, we design a novel graph contrastive learning approach based on generative model augmentation that minimizes damage to the original graph and incorporates local-global information into the augmented view. Specifically, we first obtain the diffusion graph with global information by diffusion method. Based on the structural and semantic information of the original graph and the diffused graph, local and global augmentations are performed using generative models respectively. Then, we fuse the local and global information into the final augmented view. Extensive experiments illustrate the superior performance of model over state-of-the-art methods.

Keywords: Contrastive learning · graph representation learning · unsupervised learning · generative model · graph neural network

1 Introduction

In the past few years, graph-structured data have been broadly studied in various fields, such as social sciences, computational biology and knowledge graphs. Graph representation learning presents powerful advantages as a method for analyzing graph data. In particular, Graph Neural Networks (GNNs) have received

Z. Jin et al. (Eds.): KSEM 2023, LNAI 14120, pp. 56–68, 2023.
https://doi.org/10.1007/978-3-031-40292-0_6

extensive attention to obtain graph representations, which aim to transform original node features into a low-dimensional space while maintaining the features and topology of the graph. Most existing GNNs are trained in a supervised manner, which means that the model needs labels from the data. However, obtaining labels for data is tedious and expensive.

To address this problem, tremendous effort has been put into self-supervised learning to learn unlabeled graph representations. As a form of self-supervision, contrastive learning, originated in computer vision, aims to generate effective representations by bringing semantically similar (positive) pairs closer and pushing semantically dissimilar (negative) pairs apart. Generally, the model augments the image, using methods such as rotation and cropping, to obtain two augmented views as positive sample pairs, the rest of the images are considered negative. Inspired by the success of contrastive learning in computer vision, attempts have been made to apply these methods to graphs [13].

As a contrastive learning method applied to graphs, Deep Graph InfoMax (DGI) [11] first generates an augmented graph by disturbing the nodes features. Then, an objective based on mutual information (MI) maximization is proposed to maximize the MI between node embeddings and a global summary embedding. Following DGI, GMI [9] measures the MI between input and output from the perspective of node features and topological structure respectively, without explicit data augmentation. GCA [18] proposes an adaptive augmentation method, which perturbs the connection structure based on the node centrality measure and breaks the node features based on its importance.

However, the augmentation-based graph contrastive learning method is highly dependent on the selection of augmentation modes, which may changes the structure and semantic information of the graph [4]. Taking GRACE [17] as an example, the model generates two correlated graph views by randomly corrupting the topology and node features, which changes the graph topology and node features. Furthermore, existing augmented view methods fail to adequately model local and global information. For example, MVGRL only considers global information but not local information. AFGRL constructs positive samples according to local structure and global semantics respectively, so the constructed positive samples do not contain local and global information simultaneously.

To make the augmented view fully model the local and global information of the graph under the premise of minimizing the damage to the original graph information, we design a novel graph contrastive learning approach (LGFA) based on generative model augmentation. We train a generative model using the features of anchor nodes and their first-order neighbors to obtain a graph-level distribution. Different neighbors are generated according to different anchor nodes, and then the generated neighbor features are used as the original features of the anchor nodes in the augmented view. In this way, the augmented view can be generated with full consideration of the topology and node features, thereby avoiding the change of graph structure and semantic information. In addition, we fuse local-global information in the augmentation process, so that the node features in the augmented view contain rich local-global information. Specifically, we first use graph diffusion to obtain the global information of the graph. Then, we utilize generative models to enhance local and global information according to the topological and semantic structures of the original and diffuse graphs. We fuse local and global information together as initial node features for the final enhanced view, which contains rich local-global information, and use the original graph as another view. Finally, we maximize the agreement between one view's node representation and another view's graph representation, and vice versa.

We summarize our main contributions as follows:

- We find that the augmentation strategies employed in previous work lead to changes in graph structure and semantics, and augmentation methods fail to adequately model local and global information of graphs.
- Different from previous stochastic augmentation strategies, we propose a new augmentation method based on structure and semantics from a generative perspective, to avoid the change of graph information. Meanwhile, we integrate local and global information into the augmented view, so that the augmented view contains rich local and global information.
- Extensive experiments across three public datasets demonstrate the superior performance of the new approach LGFA over state-of-the-art baselines.

2   Preliminaries

Notations. Let $\mathcal{G} = (V, E)$ be an undirected and unweighted graph, where $V = \{v_1, v_2, ..., v_n\}$ is a set of nodes, and $E \subseteq V \times V$ is a set of edges. $\mathbf{X} = \{x_1, x_2, ..., x_n\} \in \mathbb{R}^{n \times f}$ is a set of node features, where n represents the number of nodes and f represents the dimension of features. $\mathbf{A} \in \mathbb{R}^{n \times n}$ is an adjacency matrix, where $a_{ij} = 1$ if nodes v_i and v_j are connected, or $a_{ij} = 0$.

Problem Definition. Given a graph $\mathcal{G} = (V, E)$, the objective of graph representation learning is to learn a low-dimensional embedding matrix $\mathbf{Z} \in \mathbb{R}^{n \times d}$ using the topological structure $\mathbf{A}$ and feature matrix $\mathbf{X}$, whose formal format is $g : (\mathbf{A}, \mathbf{X}) \rightarrowtail \mathbf{Z}$, where d is the dimension of embeddings and $d \ll f$. In particular, the learned embedding $\mathbf{Z}$ should generalize well to various downstream tasks without class information.

3   Method

3.1   Overview

In order to make the augmented view fully model the local and global information of the graph under the premise of minimizing the damage to the original graph information, we design a novel graph contrastive learning approach based on generative model augmentation. First, we utilize a generative model to achieve local and global information augmentation based on the original graph and the diffusion graph, respectively. Then, local and global information augmentation are fused into the final augmented view. Next, we introduce two GNN encoders

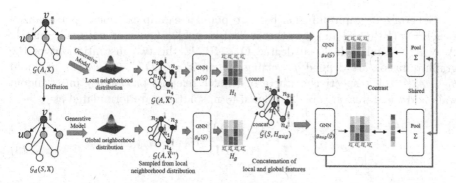

Fig. 1. The overall architecture of LGFA. Given a graph, a graph diffusion is used to generate a graph structure containing global information. The generative model is then trained separately based on the original and diffused graphs. Encoders g_l and g_g encode the augmented information to obtain node representations $\mathbf{H}_l$ and $\mathbf{H}_g$. We concatenate $\mathbf{H}_l$ and $\mathbf{H}_g$ to get $\mathbf{H}_{aug}$, and finally get the augmented view $\bar{\mathcal{G}}(\mathbf{S}, \mathbf{H}_{aug})$, where $\mathbf{S}$ stands for the diffusion matrix. Next, we encode both views to learn node representations. The learned features are then fed to a graph pooling layer to learn graph representations. Finally, we maximize the agreement between one view's node representation and another view's graph representation, and vice versa.

to learn node representations from these two views respectively, and use a graph pooling layer to learn graph representations. Finally, a discriminator is used to compute the consistency score between the node representation of one view and the graph representation of another view, and vice versa.

3.2 Graph Diffusion

We believe that the global information contained in the augmented view can enable the encoder to learn more essential semantic information in the process of contrastive learning [4]. In many GNN methods, the information of a larger field of view is often obtained by increasing the number of GNN layers. This often makes the representations between the nodes in the graph indistinguishable, that is, the problem of over-smoothing in the graph neural network. By transforming the adjacency matrix into a diffusion matrix, and obtaining global information only from the structural point of view, better results can be obtained [1].

Mathematically, the diffusion of generalized graphs can be defined by a diffusion matrix:

$$\mathbf{S} = \sum_{k=0}^{\infty} \theta_k \mathbf{T}^k \in \mathbb{R}^{n \times n}, \tag{1}$$

where $\mathbf{T} \in \mathbb{R}^{n \times n}$ is the generalized transition matrix and θ_k is the weighting coefficient which determines the ratio of information from different hops. To ensure Eq. 1 converges, we impose $\sum_{k=0}^{\infty} \theta_k = 1$, $\theta_k \in [0,1]$, and $\lambda_i \in [0,1]$ where λ_i is the eigenvalues of $\mathbf{T}$.

Generalized graph diffusion has two popular examples. One is personalized PageRank (PPR) [8] and the other is heat kernel [3]. Given an adjacency matrix $\mathbf{A} \in \mathbb{R}^{n \times n}$ and a diagonal degree $\mathbf{D} \in \mathbb{R}^{n \times n}$, the two instantiations of the graph diffusion are defined by setting matrix $\mathbf{T} = \mathbf{A}\mathbf{D}^{-1}$, $\theta_k = \alpha(1 - \alpha)^k$ and $\theta_k = e^{-t}t^k/k!$, respectively, where α denotes teleport probability in a random walk and t is diffusion time [2]. Closed-form solutions are formulated as:

$$\mathbf{S}^{heat} = exp(t\mathbf{A}\mathbf{D}^{-1} - t), \tag{2}$$

$$\mathbf{S}^{PPR} = \alpha(I_n - (1 - \alpha)\mathbf{D}^{-1/2}\mathbf{A}\mathbf{D}^{-1/2})^{-1}. \tag{3}$$

3.3   Pre-training Generative Models

Existing methods use random perturbation for augmentation, which may lead to changes in the structural and semantic information of the graph [4]. Graph-based generative models typically use graph topology and semantic information to reconstruct node features, so as to avoid random perturbation of features. We train a generative model using the features of anchor nodes and their first-order neighbors to obtain a graph-level distribution. Different neighbors are generated according to different anchor nodes, and then the generated neighbor features are used as the original features of the anchor nodes in the augmented view. In this way, the augmented view can be generated with full consideration of the topology and node features, thereby avoiding the change of the structure and semantic information of the graph by the random perturbation adopted in previous work.

Specifically, given an anchor node v, we exploit conditional variational auto-encoder (CVAE) [5] to learn the conditional distribution of neighbors $u(u \in \mathcal{N}_v)$. We let the representation $\mathbf{X}_v$ of the anchor node v as the condition for generating the model because the distribution of the neighbor nodes $\mathbf{X}_u(u \in \mathcal{N}_v)$ are related to $\mathbf{X}_v$. The latent variable $\mathbf{z}$ is obtained from the prior distribution $p_\eta(\mathbf{z}|\mathbf{X}_v)$, and then the conditional data $\mathbf{X}_u$ is generated by the generative distribution $p_\eta(\mathbf{X}|\mathbf{X}_v, \mathbf{z})$ conditioned on $\mathbf{z}$ and $\mathbf{X}_v : \mathbf{z} \sim p_\eta(\mathbf{z}|\mathbf{X}_v)$, $\mathbf{X}_u \sim p_\eta(\mathbf{X}|\mathbf{X}_v, \mathbf{z}_v)$. Let ϕ denote variational parameters and η denote generative parameters:

$$\log p_\eta(\mathbf{X}_u|\mathbf{X}_v) = \int q_\phi(\mathbf{z}|\mathbf{X}_u, \mathbf{X}_v) \log \frac{p_\eta(\mathbf{X}_u, \mathbf{z}|\mathbf{X}_v)}{q_\phi(\mathbf{z}|\mathbf{X}_u, \mathbf{X}_v)} d\mathbf{z}$$

$$+ KL(q_\phi(\mathbf{z}|\mathbf{X}_u, \mathbf{X}_v) \parallel p_\eta(\mathbf{z}|\mathbf{X}_u, \mathbf{X}_v)) \tag{4}$$

$$\geq \int q_\phi(\mathbf{z}|\mathbf{X}_u, \mathbf{X}_v) \log \frac{p_\eta(\mathbf{X}_u, \mathbf{z}|\mathbf{X}_v)}{q_\phi(\mathbf{z}|\mathbf{X}_u, \mathbf{X}_v)} d\mathbf{z},$$

and the evidence lower bound (ELBO) is shown as:

$$\mathcal{L}(\mathbf{X}_u, \mathbf{X}_v; \eta, \phi) = - KL(q_\phi(\mathbf{z}|\mathbf{X}_u, \mathbf{X}_v) \parallel p_\eta(\mathbf{z}|\mathbf{X}_v))$$

$$+ \frac{1}{L} \sum_{l=1}^{L} \log p_\eta(\mathbf{X}_u|\mathbf{X}_v, \mathbf{z}^{(l)}), \tag{5}$$

where $\mathbf{z}^{(l)} = g_\phi(\mathbf{X}_v, \mathbf{X}_u, \epsilon^{(l)})$, $\epsilon \sim \mathcal{N}(\mathbf{0}, \mathbf{I})$ and L is the number of neighbors of node v. A function $g_\phi(\cdot, \cdot)$ is used to reparameterize the recognition distribution $p_\eta(\mathbf{z}|\mathbf{X}_v)$, which allows error backpropagation. Note that we only train one CVAE for all nodes of the graph. In the stage of obtaining the latent variable, we expect to use the neighbor pair $(\mathbf{X}_v, \mathbf{X}_u, u \in \mathcal{N}_v)$ as input to maximize the ELBO, i.e., Eq. 5. During the augmentation process, we use the center node feature $\mathbf{X}_v$ as the condition and sample a latent variable $\mathbf{z} \sim \mathcal{N}(\mathbf{0}, \mathbf{I})$ as input for the decoder. Then we get the local enhancement information $\bar{\mathbf{X}}_v$ associated with node v.

The process includes two parts: 1) Local information augmentation based on the original graph structure, which does not change the graph structure. 2) Global augmentation is performed using the diffusion graph structure, which is performed after graph diffusion. Note that we trained the generative model separately for these two parts. Since the second part is local augmentation after global diffusion, the generative model contains not only rich local semantic information but also rich global information. In this way, we get the local augmented view and the global augmented view.

3.4 Encoders

Our framework places no restrictions on models. Here we adopt a simple and general graph convolutional network (GCN) as our base encoder.

Augmented Information Encoder. As shown in Fig. 1, during augmentation, we use two specialized L-GCN and G-GCN encoders to encode local and global information, i.e., $g_l(\cdot)$, $g_g(\cdot) : \mathbb{R}^{n \times n} \times \mathbb{R}^{n \times d_x} \longmapsto \mathbb{R}^{n \times d_{aug}}$, where d_x represents the original feature dimension of the node, d_{aug} represents the feature dimension of the augmented encoder output, and we set $d_{aug} = d_x$. Note that we define GCN layers as $\sigma(\tilde{\mathbf{A}} \mathbf{X}_l \mathbf{W}_l)$ to learn node representations with local information and $\sigma(\mathbf{S} \mathbf{X}_g \mathbf{W}_g)$ to learn node representations with global information. $\bar{\mathbf{A}} = \hat{\mathbf{D}}^{-1/2} \hat{\mathbf{A}} \hat{\mathbf{D}}^{-1/2} \in \mathbb{R}^{n \times n}$ is symmetrically normalized adjacency matrix, $\hat{\mathbf{D}} \in \mathbb{R}^{n \times n}$ is the degree matrix of $\hat{\mathbf{A}} = \mathbf{A} + \mathbf{I}_N$ where $\mathbf{I}_N$ is the identity matrix, $\mathbf{S} \in \mathbb{R}^{n \times n}$ is diffusion matrix, $\mathbf{X}_l, \mathbf{X}_g \in \mathbb{R}^{n \times d_x}$ represent locally enhanced sampled features and globally enhanced sampled features, respectively, $\mathbf{W} \in \mathbb{R}^{d_x \times d_{aug}}$ is network parameters, and σ is a parametric ReLU non-linearity. The obtained sets of two nodes representing $\mathbf{H}_l, \mathbf{H}_g \in \mathbb{R}^{n \times d_{aug}}$ correspond to the results of local augmentation and global augmentation, respectively. To fuse local and global information into the augmented view, we concatenate the local and global augmented features:

$$\mathbf{H}_{aug} = \text{CONCAT}(\mathbf{H}_l, \mathbf{H}_g) \in \mathbb{R}^{n \times 2d_x}, \tag{6}$$

where CONCAT is the concatenation operator. We take $\mathbf{H}_{aug}$ as the node representation for local-global information fusion.

View Encoder. As shown in Fig. 1, for original and augmented views, we use a dedicated graph encoder for each view, i.e., $g_\theta(\cdot) : \mathbb{R}^{n \times n} \times \mathbb{R}^{n \times d_x} \longmapsto \mathbb{R}^{n \times d_h}$

and $g_{aug}(\cdot) : \mathbb{R}^{n \times n} \times \mathbb{R}^{n \times 2d_x} \longmapsto \mathbb{R}^{n \times d_h}$. We define GCN layers as $\sigma(\widetilde{\mathbf{A}}\mathbf{X}\mathbf{W})$ and $\sigma(\widetilde{\mathbf{S}}\mathbf{H}_{aug}\Theta)$ to learn two sets of node representations each corresponding to one of the views, respectively, where $\Theta \in \mathbb{R}^{2d_x \times d_h}$. The obtained sets of two nodes representing $\mathbf{H}_\alpha, \mathbf{H}_\beta \in \mathbb{R}^{n \times d_h}$ correspond to two views.

Graph Pooling. For each view, we obtain the graph representation by feeding the resulting node representation into the graph pooling (readout) function: $\mathcal{P}(\cdot) : \mathbb{R}^{n \times d_h} \longmapsto \mathbb{R}^{d_h}$. We use a readout function similar to DGI where we use a simple averaging of all the nodes' features:

$$\mathcal{R}(\mathbf{H}) = \sigma \left(\frac{1}{N} \sum_{i=1}^{N} h_i \right), \tag{7}$$

where σ is the logistic sigmoid nonlinearity. Applying the readout function on the node representation set to obtain two graph representations $h_g^\alpha, h_g^\beta \in \mathbb{R}^{d_n}$. The graph representation will be used to calculate the contrastive loss. Finally, we concatenate the node representations: $\mathbf{H} = \mathrm{CONCAT}(\mathbf{H}_\alpha, \mathbf{H}_\beta) \in \mathbb{R}^{n \times 2d_x}$ and return it of the two views for the downstream tasks.

3.5 Training

For the learned node representation, we expect it to be rich in underlying semantic information and independent of downstream tasks. We utilize the deep Info-Max to maximize the MI between two views by contrasting the node representation of one view with the graph representation of the other, and vice versa. Formally, the objective function is defined as follows:

$$\max_{l,g,\theta,aug} \frac{1}{N} \sum_{i=1}^{N} \left[\mathcal{D}\left(h_i{}^\alpha, h_g^\beta\right) + \mathcal{D}\left(h_i{}^\beta, h_g^\alpha\right) \right], \tag{8}$$

where l, g, θ, aug are graph encoder parameters, n is the number of nodes in graph, and $h_i{}^\alpha, h_g^\beta$ are representations of node i and graph encoded from views α, β, respectively.

We implement the discriminator: $\mathcal{D}(\cdot : \cdot) : \mathbb{R}^{d_h} \times \mathbb{R}^{d_h} \longmapsto \mathbb{R}$ as the dot product between two representations:

$$\mathcal{D}(h_i, h_g) = h_i \cdot h_g, \tag{9}$$

where h_i is the node representation from one view and h_g is the graph representation from another view, the discriminator $\mathcal{D}$ scores the agreement between them. We obtain negative sampling by randomly shuffling the node features [11]. Finally, we optimize the model parameters for the objective using mini-batch stochastic gradient descent.

4   Experiments

We first introduce the experimental setup, then compare the new approach LGFA with state-of-the-arts on three graph analytical tasks, and finally perform an in-depth analysis of different components of LGFA.

Table 1. Mean node classification accuracy (%) for supervised and unsupervised models. The input column highlights the data available to each model during training (X: features, A: adjacency matrix, S: diffusion matrix, Y: labels).

Methods	Input	Cora	Citeseer	Pubmed
Raw features	X	47.90 ± 0.40	49.30 ± 0.20	69.10 ± 0.30
DeepWalk	A	67.20 ± 0.20	43.20 ± 0.40	65.30 ± 0.50
DeepWalk+features	X,A	70.70 ± 0.60	51.40 ± 0.50	74.30 ± 0.90
DGI	X,A	82.30 ± 0.60	71.80 ± 0.70	73.80 ± 0.60
GMI	X,A	83.00 ± 0.20	72.40 ± 0.20	79.90 ± 0.40
GRACE	X,A	80.70 ± 1.12	66.65 ± 0.33	78.74 ± 1.77
GCA	X,A	79.46 ± 0.00	66.59 ± 0.00	78.88 ± 1.38
SUGRL	X,A	82.40 ± 0.05	73.0 ± 0.40	79.70 ± 0.70
AFGRL	X,A	79.82 ± 0.17	69.29 ± 0.22	77.98 ± 0.13
MVGRL	X,A	81.65 ± 0.40	72.79 ± 0.17	75.96 ± 1.52
Ours	X,A	$\mathbf{83.30 \pm 0.36}$	$\mathbf{73.94 \pm 0.18}$	$\mathbf{80.00 \pm 0.90}$
LP	X,A,Y	68.00	45.30	63.00
Planetoid-T	X,A,Y	75.70	62.90	75.70
GCN	X,A,Y	81.50 ± 0.20	70.30 ± 0.40	79.00 ± 0.50
GAT	X,A,Y	83.00 ± 0.70	72.50 ± 0.70	79.00 ± 0.30

4.1 Experimental Setup

Datasets. We evaluate the performance of the proposed method LGFA and existing methods on three citation network datasets including Cora, Citeseer, and Pubmed, which are widely used to verify GNNs [7,10].

Baselines. We consider representative benchmarks that can be divided into the following three categories: 1) classical network embedding algorithms based on random walk DeepWalk; 2) unsupervised learning algorithms DGI, GMI, GRACE, GCA, SUGRL, AFGRL and MVGRL; and 3) semi-supervised learning algorithms GCN, GAT, LP [16] and Planetoid-T [14].

Implementation Details. All baselines are initialized with the same parameters suggested in their paper.

For LGFA, the parameters of the generative model are initialized with Local Augmentation for Graph Neural Networks [5]. Other parameters are initialized by the MVGRL's initialization and optimized by the Adam optimizer. We use $0.0001 \sim 0.001$ learning rate with Adam optimizer, and set the parameter k of k-means equal to the original number of categories in the data. We train four 1-layer GCN encoders, where the encoder g_l and g_g have the same hidden layer dimension (nhid_aug1) and the same output dimension (nhid_aug2), and the encoders g_θ and g_{aug} have the same hidden layer dimension (nhid1) and the same output dimension (nhid2). When the diffusion matrix is sparse, for Cora and Citeseer, we set the top-k to 32 and the threshold to 0.005. For Pubmed, we set top-k to 8 and threshold to 0.005. We sample four times from the generative model and then average as the final local information supplement. Besides, early stopping with a patience of 20 is also utilized.

4.2   Node Classification

In node classification, our goal is to classify nodes into one of several classes. We follow DGI and use a classifier, which consists of a fully connected layer and a sigmoid function. We report the average classification accuracy and standard deviation on the test nodes after training for 50 epochs.

Table 1 summarizes classification accuracy on three real graph-structured datasets. Specifically, in terms of accuracy, LGFA outperforms all self-supervised methods (i.e., DGI, GMI, GRACE, MVGRL, SUGRL, AFGRL, and GCA). On the one hand, it demonstrates that our augmentation method can obtain the original semantic information to the greatest extent. On the other hand, it demonstrates the importance of complementing local information and fusing local-global information in a generative manner. To be specific, compared with methods that focus on global information, such as MVGRL and AFGRL, the improvement of LGFA over the above baseline achieves 1.65% and 3.48%, 1.15% and 4.65%, and 2.02% and 4.04% on Cora, Citeseer and Pubmed, respectively. LGFA significantly outperforms the GCL method with perturbation strategy, i.e., DGI, GMI, GRACE, GCA and SUGRL, ranging from 0.9% to 3.84%, 0.94% to 7.35% and 0.1% to 6.2% on these three datasets, since they destroy the original features and structure of the graph. In addition, LGFA outperforms traditional supervised models such as LP, Planetoid-T, GCN, and GAT, ranging from 0.3% to 15.3%, 1.44% to 28.64% and 1.0% to 17.0% on Cora, Citeseer, and Pubmed,

Table 2. Performance on node clustering task in terms of NMI and ARI.

Methods	Cora		Citeseer		Pubmed	
	NMI	ARI	NMI	ARI	NMI	ARI
Raw Features	0.129	0.055	0.290	0.258	0.310	0.281
BigClam	0.007	0.001	0.036	0.007	0.006	0.003
GraphEnc	0.109	0.006	0.033	0.010	0.209	0.184
DeepWalk	0.327	0.243	0.088	0.092	0.279	0.299
GRACE	0.528	0.478	0.362	0.316	0.224	0.224
GCA	0.482	0.388	0.311	0.339	0.236	0.226
AFGRL	0.422	0.315	0.369	0.344	0.312	0.277
MVGRL	0.559	0.509	0.449	0.460	0.282	0.254
Ours	**0.561**	**0.517**	**0.462**	**0.474**	**0.321**	**0.282**

respectively. This further demonstrates that reasonable information augmentation and supplementation can help the encoder learn better node representations even without labels.

4.3 Node Clustering

In node clustering, our goal is to cluster nodes. After getting the node embeddings, we use the k-means algorithm to cluster the node embeddings. The performance is validated by measuring the NMI and ARI.

As shown in Table 2, our LGFA performs the best on the three datasets in terms of both NMI and ARI. On average, LGFA outperforms the best baseline method in node clustering by 1.8% in terms of NMI and 1.7% in terms of ARI, which further demonstrates the effectiveness of augmentation methods based on generative models and considering both local and global information.

4.4 Visualization of Embeddings

In order to illustrate more intuitively and further show the effectiveness of our proposed model, we use t-SNE [6], which projects the learned node representations onto a two-dimensional space, to visualize the derived representations.

As shown in Fig. 2, we can find that the visualization results of AFGRL and GRACE are not satisfactory, because the nodes with different labels are mixed together and the borders between different classes are still not so clear. Moreover, the visualization results of GCA and MVGRL are relatively better, but the intra-class similarity is low. Obviously, the visualization of our LGFA performs much better, where the representations have the highest intra-class similarity and form more discernible clusters. The results of this visualization demonstrate that our method outperforms other methods.

(a) AFGRL   (b) GCA   (c) GRACE   (d) MVGRL   (e) LGFA

Fig. 2. t-SNE embeddings of nodes in the Cora dataset.

4.5 Ablation Study

In this section, we perform ablation study on the four schemes for generating graph views, non-local enhancement, local enhancement based on original graph (LA), local enhancement based on global information (i.e., global augmentation) and local-global fusion enhancement (L-GA), to prove the effectiveness of simultaneously augmenting local and global information and fusing them in the augmented view. We report four augmentation schemes for node classification on all datasets under identical settings as previous, except for different enabled schemes. The results are presented in Table 3. It can be found that our proposed fusion local-global augmentation mode outperforms using only local or global alone. These results validate the effectiveness of our proposed augmentation model and further illustrate the necessity of fusing local and global information into the augmented view.

Table 3. Node classification (%) of different augmentation schemes.

Schemes	Cora	Citeseer	Pubmed
w/o LA	81.65 ± 0.40	72.79 ± 0.17	75.96 ± 1.52
+LA	81.77 ± 0.30	73.00 ± 1.03	78.60 ± 0.76
+GA	81.89 ± 0.60	72.90 ± 0.25	79.10 ± 0.50
+L-GA(Our)	$\mathbf{83.30 \pm 0.36}$	$\mathbf{73.94 \pm 0.18}$	$\mathbf{80.00 \pm 0.90}$

5   Related Work

5.1   Contrastive Representation Learning

With the rapid development of self-supervised learning, contrastive representation learning, as its main branch, has also been further studied. Inspired by DIM, DGI introduces its idea to the graph domain, training an encoder model to maximize the mutual information between a high-level "global" representation and "local" parts of the input. However, DGI cannot guarantee that graph embeddings extract useful information from nodes, and DGI fails to work well with sparse matrices. In order to provide different node contexts for contrastive objectives, GRACE proposes to generate two views via corruption from the graph structure and attribute levels, and learns node representations by maximizing the consistency of node representations in these two views. After that SimGRACE [12] tries to simplify graph contrastive learning via discarding the negatives, parameterized mutual information estimator, or even data augmentations. GCA proposes an adaptive augmented representation learning method based on prior knowledge of graph topology and semantics.

5.2   Graph Diffusion Network

Since the traditional GNN restricts the information of each layer to one-hop neighbors is arbitrary, and there will be a lot of noise in the graph, GDN [2] uses a generalized form of sparse graph diffusion for information transfer. Diffusion acts as a denoising filter to allow information to pass through higher-order neighborhoods. Graph Diffusion Convolution (GDC) utilizes generalized graph diffusion to expand the propagation neighborhood. However, the neighborhood size in GDC is manually tuned for each graph by grid search on the validation set, which makes its generalization practically limited. ADC [15] believes that all GNN layers and feature channels should use the same neighborhood size for propagation. Its strategy enables the ADC to learn a specialized propagation neighborhood for each GNN layer and each feature channel, making the GNN architecture fully coupled with the graph structure.

6   Conclusions

In order to avoid changes in graph information caused by random augmentation strategies, we implement graph augmentation from the perspective of generation based on graph topology and semantic information. Then, to better model local and global information, we use generative models to augment local and global augmentations based on the original and diffuse maps, respectively and then fuse the resulting information into the final augmented view. Finally, we encode both views and maximize the MI between two views by contrasting the node representation of one view with the graph representation of the other and vice versa. Expensive experiments demonstrate that our proposed augmentation method is effective and outperforms existing contrastive learning methods.

References

1. Hassani, K., Khasahmadi, A.H.: Contrastive multi-view representation learning on graphs. In: International Conference on Machine Learning, pp. 4116–4126. PMLR (2020)
2. Klicpera, J., Weißenberger, S., Günnemann, S.: Diffusion improves graph learning. arXiv preprint arXiv:1911.05485 (2019)
3. Kondor, R.I., Lafferty, J.: Diffusion kernels on graphs and other discrete structures. In: Proceedings of the 19th International Conference on Machine Learning. vol. 2002, pp. 315–322 (2002)
4. Lee, N., Lee, J., Park, C.: Augmentation-free self-supervised learning on graphs. In: Proceedings of the AAAI Conference on Artificial Intelligence. vol. 36, pp. 7372–7380 (2022)
5. Liu, S., et al.: Local augmentation for graph neural networks. In: International Conference on Machine Learning, pp. 14054–14072. PMLR (2022)
6. Van der Maaten, L., Hinton, G.: Visualizing data using t-sne. J. Mach. Learn. Res. 9(11) (2008)
7. Namata, G., London, B., Getoor, L., Huang, B., Edu, U.: Query-driven active surveying for collective classification. In: 10th International Workshop on Mining and Learning with Graphs. vol. 8, p. 1 (2012)
8. Page, L., Brin, S., Motwani, R., Winograd, T.: The Pagerank Citation Ranking: Bringing Order To The Web. Tech. rep, Stanford InfoLab (1999)
9. Peng, Z., et al.: Graph representation learning via graphical mutual information maximization. In: Proceedings of The Web Conference 2020, pp. 259–270 (2020)

10. Sen, P., Namata, G., Bilgic, M., Getoor, L., Galligher, B., Eliassi-Rad, T.: Collective classification in network data. AI Mag. **29**(3), 93–93 (2008)
11. Velickovic, P., Fedus, W., Hamilton, W.L., Liò, P., Bengio, Y., Hjelm, R.D.: Deep graph infomax. ICLR (Poster) **2**(3), 4 (2019)
12. Xia, J., Wu, L., Chen, J., Hu, B., Li, S.Z.: Simgrace: A simple framework for graph contrastive learning without data augmentation. In: Proceedings of the ACM Web Conference 2022. pp. 1070–1079 (2022)
13. Xie, Y., Xu, Z., Zhang, J., Wang, Z., Ji, S.: Self-supervised learning of graph neural networks: A unified review. IEEE Transactions on Pattern Analysis and Machine Intelligence (2022)
14. Yang, Z., Cohen, W., Salakhudinov, R.: Revisiting semi-supervised learning with graph embeddings. In: International Conference on Machine Learning, pp. 40–48. PMLR (2016)
15. Zhao, J., Dong, Y., Ding, M., Kharlamov, E., Tang, J.: Adaptive diffusion in graph neural networks. Adv. Neural. Inf. Process. Syst. **34**, 23321–23333 (2021)
16. Zhu, X., Ghahramani, Z., Lafferty, J.D.: Semi-supervised learning using gaussian fields and harmonic functions. In: Proceedings of the 20th International Conference on Machine learning (ICML-03), pp. 912–919 (2003)
17. Zhu, Y., Xu, Y., Yu, F., Liu, Q., Wu, S., Wang, L.: Deep graph contrastive representation learning. arXiv preprint arXiv:2006.04131 (2020)
18. Zhu, Y., Xu, Y., Yu, F., Liu, Q., Wu, S., Wang, L.: Graph contrastive learning with adaptive augmentation. In: Proceedings of the Web Conference 2021, pp. 2069–2080 (2021)

PRACM: Predictive Rewards for Actor-Critic with Mixing Function in Multi-Agent Reinforcement Learning

Sheng Yu, Bo Liu, Wei Zhu$^{(\boxtimes)}$, and Shuhong Liu

School of Information and Communication, National University of Defense
Technology, Wuhan 430014, China
yusheng17@nudt.edu.cn, zhuwei929@hotmail.com

Abstract. Inspired by the centralised training with decentralised execution (CTDE) paradigm, the field of multi-agent reinforcement learning (MARL) has made significant progress in tackling cooperative problems with discrete action spaces. Nevertheless, many existing algorithms suffer from significant performance degradation when faced with large numbers of agents or more challenging tasks. Furthermore, some specific scenarios, such as cooperative environments with penalties, pose significant challenges to these algorithms , which often lack sufficient cooperative behavior to converge successfully. A new approach, called PRACM, based on the Actor-Critic framework is proposed in this study to address these issues. PRACM employs a monotonic mixing function to generate a global action value function, Q_{tot}, which is used to compute the loss function for updating the critic network. To handle the discrete action space, PRACM uses Gumbel-Softmax. And to promote cooperation among agents and to adapt to cooperative environments with penalties, the predictive rewards is introduced. PRACM was evaluated against several baseline algorithms in "Cooperative Predator-Prey" and the challenging "SMAC" scenarios. The results of this study illustrate that PRACM scales well as the number of agents and task difficulty increase, and performs better in cooperative tasks with penalties, demonstrating its usefulness in promoting collaboration among agents.

Keywords: Multi-agent reinforcement learning · Discrete action · Collaborative task · Mixing function · Predictive reward

1 Introduction

The application of artificial intelligence (AI) technologies has been extended in recent years to tasks such as smart manufacturing [20,25], business siting [22,27], and path planning [17,30]. Cooperative tasks under discrete actions have emerged as a popular topic of research given their crucial role in these tasks. Leading by the centralised training with decentralised execution (CTDE) [7] paradigm, multi-agent reinforcement learning (MARL) techniques have made significant progress in solving cooperative tasks with discrete actions by centrally training agents and reconstructing the reward function [35]. However, as the number of agents involved in a task increases, many MARL methods, such as DOP [26], QPLEX [24] and MADDPG [10], suffer from dimensional catastrophe, resulting in degraded algorithm performance.

To address this issue, several approaches have been proposed, such as mixed Q-networks [15,36] and Actor-Critic frameworks [4,19]. While mixed Q-networks improve scalability to some extent by combining the Q-values of each agent, it remains a value-based approach. In this approach, agents compute the value function each time and choose the action with the largest value, making it difficult to enhance the performance of the algorithm and its scalability decreases significantly with changing scenarios. In contrast, the Actor-Critic framework-based method overcomes the value function problem by using the policy gradient and parameterizing for the policy representation, leading to better performance and scalability. However, the policy gradients are usually applicable to continuous action space while the policy gradients themselves are unable to handle the cooperation task under discrete actions.

Furthermore, the CTDE-based MARL approach primarily focuses on maximizing global rewards over time to improve algorithm performance, through sharing a value function [6,13] or factorizing it [23,37]. However, this approach assumes an ideal cooperative task where the global rewards can simply be combined and maximized by each agent without considering the cooperative rewards of the environment for multiple agents. Real-world environments often involve cooperative rewards, such as penalty-based cooperative environments where the rewards for agents completing a task together are greater than those for individual agents, but with a penalty imposed for failed tasks. When using the purely CTDE paradigm-based MARL method in such environments, the algorithm may converge slowly or even to a local optimal solution.

To tackle these challenges, researchers have proposed various approaches, such as safe exploration [3,31] and intrinsic reward [9,34]. Safe exploration involves introducing a safety probability into the action space and setting a safety threshold. Actions with a safety probability lower than the threshold are not executed, allowing agents to reselect their actions. However, this approach is highly conservative and does not necessarily promote cooperation between agents. Conversely, intrinsic rewards provide additional rewards for cooperation between agents, but distributed calculation of these rewards and the required parameters potentially lead to inaccurate estimates, resulting in cumulative errors that adversely affect performance.

In this study, we propose a novel method to solve cooperative tasks under discrete actions, called the Predictive Rewards for Actor-Critic framework with Mixing function (PRACM). The PRACM approach utilizes a monotonic mixing function to create a global value function Q_{tot} by combining the Q values generated by each critic network. The critic networks are updated by computing the loss value for each agent. Additionally, PRACM employs deterministic policy gradients to update the policies used by the agents and incorporates Gumbel-Softmax to handle the discrete action space. To enhance cooperation among agents and accommodate a cooperative environment with penalties, we introduce predictive rewards to the PRACM approach. The main contributions of our study are as follows:

- A novel MARL method, PRACM, is proposed which uses Actor-Critic networks and predictive rewards to address cooperative tasks in discrete action spaces.
- The Actor-Critic framework is improved in PRACM by adding Gumbel-Softmax to the network to handle the discrete action space, introducing a global joint value function Q_{tot}, and utilizing a linear mixing function for computation. This enhances the scalability of the algorithm and enables it to perform well when the scenario changes.
- Cooperative behavior is encouraged among agents in cooperative environments with penalties by introducing predictive rewards as a module of PRACM. Due to the global nature of the joint value function Q_{tot}, the predictive rewards become global rewards that help agents find the global optimal solution and perform excellently in cooperative tasks with penalties.

2   Background

2.1   Dec-POMDP

In a fully cooperative multi-agent task, the decentralized partially observable Markov decision process (Dec-POMDP) model is used to represent the task as a tuple $G = S, A, P, r, \gamma, N, \Omega, O$, where $N \equiv \{1, 2, ..., n\}$ is a finite set of agents. Each agent x derives its own observation $o_x \in O(s, x)$ from the state $s \in S$. At each time step t, each agent selects an action $a_i \in A$, resulting in a joint action selection a. A shared reward $r = R(s, a)$ is given, and each agent transitions to the next state s' with a probability function $P(s'|s, a) : S \times A \rightarrow [0, 1]$. Each agent maintains an action-observation history $\tau_i \in T \equiv \{\Omega \times A\}$ based on its local observations. The objective is to find a joint policy $\pi = \pi_1, ..., \pi_n$ that maximizes the joint action-value function $Q(s_t, a_t) = \mathbb{E}[R_t|s_t, a_t]$ and corresponds to the joint policy function $V(\tau, a) = \mathbb{E}_{s_{0:\infty}, a_{0:\infty}} [\sum_{t=0}^{\infty} \gamma^t r_t \mid s_0 = s, a_0 = a, \pi]$ with a discount factor $\gamma \in [0, 1)$. Similarly, the joint deterministic policy μ can be derived as a joint action value function $Q^{\mu}(s_t, a_t)$.

2.2   QMIX and QPLEX

Both QMIX [18] and QPLEX [24] are Q-learning algorithms that utilize the CTDE [7] paradigm to solve cooperative multi-agent tasks with discrete actions, and they both aim to learn a joint action value function, Q_{tot}. In order to balance scalability and stability in complex domains, QPLEX is based on the dueling decomposition structure $Q = V + A$ proposed by Dueling DQN [28]. This approach adopts a duplex dueling network structure to decompose the joint value function, which can be represented as follows:

$$Q_{tot}(\boldsymbol{\tau}, \boldsymbol{a}) = V_{tot}(\boldsymbol{\tau}) + A_{tot}(\boldsymbol{\tau}, \boldsymbol{a})$$
$$= \sum_{i=1}^{n} Q_i(\tau, a_i) + \sum_{i=1}^{n} (\lambda_i(\tau, a) - 1) A_i(\tau, a_i), \tag{1}$$

where A represents the action-dependent advantage term and V represents the state-value function.

In contrast, QMIX utilizes a linear monotonic mixing function to reflect the global nature of Q_{tot}, which combines the Q values of all the agents. Q_{tot} is denoted as:

$$Q_{tot}(\boldsymbol{\tau}, \boldsymbol{a}, s; \boldsymbol{\phi}, \omega) = f_\omega \left(s, Q_1(\tau_1, a_1; \phi_1), \dots, Q_n(\tau_n, a_n; \phi_n) \right), \tag{2}$$

where ω is the parameter of the monotonic mixing function f. By using a monotonic function, QMIX ensures that the maximum value of individual Q in all agents is the same as the maximum value of Q_{tot}. After each training step, QMIX updates the network parameters by minimizing the loss function, which is expressed as follows:

$$LOSS(\boldsymbol{\phi}, \omega) = \mathbb{E}_D[(y^{tot} - Q_{tot}(\boldsymbol{\tau}, \boldsymbol{a}, s; \boldsymbol{\phi}, \omega))^2], \tag{3}$$

where $y^{tot} = r + \gamma \max_{a'} Q_{tot}(\boldsymbol{\tau}', \boldsymbol{a}', s'; \boldsymbol{\phi}^-, \omega^-)$. r is the global reward, ϕ^- and ω^- are the parameters of the target Q function and the mixing function f, and all other values in the formula are sampled from the replay buffer D.

2.3   MADDPG and FACMAC

MADDPG [10] and FACMAC [14] are both multi-agent algorithms based on the Actor-Critic framework, and both are used to learn deterministic policies in the continuous action space; MADDPG uses the CTDE paradigm for learning, specifically each agent has an independent actor and critic and relies on itself to update them, so the joint action value function Q_i^μ of agent i is a set of Q values, i.e., $Q_i^\mu(s, a_1, \dots, a_n; \phi_i)$, and this joint action value function is private to agent i. During centralized training, agent i updates the critic network by minimizing the following loss:

$$LOSS(\phi_i) = \mathbb{E}_D[(y^i - Q_i^\mu(s, a_1, \dots, a_n; \phi_i))^2], \tag{4}$$

where $y^i = r_i + \gamma Q_i^\mu(s', a_1', \dots, a_n'; \phi_i^-), a_i' = \mu_i(\tau_i'; \theta_i^-)$, r_i is agent i's reward, $\{a_1', \dots, a_n'\}$ is the set of other agent actions, and ϕ_i^- is the parameter for the target critic of agent i, which are derived from sampling the replay buffer D.

FACMAC borrows from QMIX by introducing the mixing function into the Actor-Critic framework and using a nonlinear monotonic function to combine the Q values of each agent to obtain the joint action value function $Q_{tot}^\mu(\boldsymbol{\tau}, \boldsymbol{a}, s; \boldsymbol{\phi}, \omega) = g_\omega(s, \{Q_i^{\mu_i}(\tau_i, a_i; \phi_i)\}_{i=1}^n)$, ϕ and ϕ_i are the parameters of the joint action value function Q and the $Q_i^{\mu_i}$ of a single agent i, respectively. All agents update the critic network by minimizing the following loss:

$$LOSS(\phi, \omega) = \mathbb{E}_D[(y^{tot} - Q_{tot}^\mu(\tau, a, s; \phi, \omega))^2], \qquad (5)$$

where $y^{tot} = r + \gamma Q_{tot}^\mu(\tau', \mu(\tau'; \theta^-), s'; \phi^-, \omega^-)$, ω^-, θ^-, and ϕ^- are the parameters of the mixing functions, target actor and critic, respectively.

2.4 MACOPT and ELIGN

MACOPT [16] and ELIGN [11] are frameworks designed for multi-agent cooperative environments with penalties. MACOPT is based on the safe exploration approach, derived from the single-agent algorithm GOOSE [18]. It calculates all potential risks and all agents avoid potentially punishing actions as well as choose safe ones during greedy exploration.

In contrast, ELIGN offers a novel perspective for multi-agent cooperative tasks with penalties. Unlike MACOPT, it does not calculate potential risky actions. Instead, it enables agents to cooperate with each other through expectation alignment. Specifically, assuming agent i is adjacent to agent j, agent j generates an intrinsic reward for agent i. The size of the intrinsic reward depends on whether the observed value o_i' after agent i's next action satisfies agent j's expectation, and the intrinsic reward r_{in} is calculated as follows:

$$r_{in}(o_i, a_i, o_j) = -\left\| o_{i \cap j}' - f_{\theta_i}(o_{i \cap j}, a_i) \right\|, \qquad (6)$$

where $o_{i \cap j} = o_i \odot o_j$, and f_{θ_i} is the expectation function of agent j on agent i's next action after o_i' with parameter θ_i. In ELIGN, the cooperation among agents is not centralized, while each agent performs decentralized training to obtain its own expectation function f, and then trains based on the intrinsic reward of neighboring agents.

3 Method

This section describes the components and overall process of the PRACM method, the overview of PRACM is shown in Fig. 1.

3.1 Training Critic

The CTDE paradigm has gained popularity, and algorithms based on the Actor-Critic framework, such as MADDPG, are being used to efficiently obtain a global optimal solution by training centrally on the critic [32]. However, as the number of agents increases, obtaining a single value function with global states through critic centralized training becomes difficult. To address this issue, we introduce the mix network in the Actor-Critic framework [2]. The mix network factorizes the Q value of each agent, but unlike FACMAC, however, our value function decomposition is linear, which greatly enhances scalability.

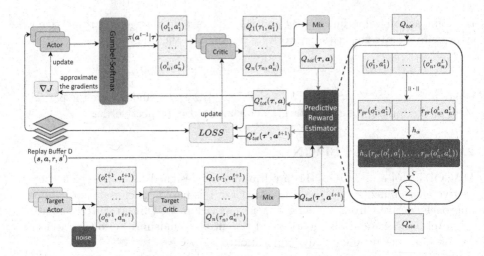

Fig. 1. Overview of the proposed method PRACM.

Specifically, in PRACM, critic is trained centrally using the value functions of all agents to obtain Q_{tot}:

$$Q_{tot}^{\pi}(\boldsymbol{\tau}, \boldsymbol{a}, s; \phi, \omega) = g_{\omega}(s, Q_1^{\pi_1}(\tau_1, a_1; \phi_1), ..., Q_n^{\pi_n}(\tau_n, a_n; \phi_n)), \qquad (7)$$

the joint action value function, Q_{tot}, depends on the parameters ϕ, while the single agent value function, Q_n, depends on ϕ_n. The mix network parameter is denoted by ψ, and the mixing function, g_{ψ}, is a linear function. Unlike MAD-DPG, the policies utilized in this study are discrete and represented by $\boldsymbol{\pi}$. Notably, the Gumbel-Softmax [5] is introduced to sample continuous policies to fit the discrete action space, and the output of the actor after sampling is $\pi(\boldsymbol{a}^{t-1}, \boldsymbol{\tau})$. During the training process, the critic network is updated by minimizing the loss function:

$$LOSS(\phi, \omega) = \mathbb{E}_D[(y^{tot} - Q_{tot}^{\pi}(\boldsymbol{\tau}, \boldsymbol{a}, s; \phi, \omega))^2], \qquad (8)$$

where $y^{tot} = r + \gamma Q_{tot}^{\pi}(\boldsymbol{\tau}', \boldsymbol{\pi}(\boldsymbol{a}, \boldsymbol{\tau}'; \psi^-), s'; \phi^-, \omega^-)$, and D represents the replay buffer. The parameters ψ^-, ϕ^-, and ω^- represent the target actor, target critic, and target mix network, respectively.

3.2 Policy Gradients

Actor networks typically employ deterministic policy gradients to update individual agent policies [26]. In the case of MADDPG, each agent's policy is updated separately via its own policy gradient. Nevertheless, this approach poses a challenge since each agent updates only its own policy, while the update parameters rely on the actions of other agents [29]. These fixed values are taken from the replay buffer D, which makes it difficult to update the policy globally for each iteration. Consequently, this convergence issue raises the probability of an agent's policy reaching a suboptimal solution.

In this research, we propose a novel policy gradient estimator in PRACM which enables global policy updates and enhances the chances of achieving a global optimal solution. Similar to FACMAC, we extract all agent actions from the current policy rather than the replay buffer D while computing the policy gradient. However, unlike FACMAC, we optimize each agent individually and combine them linearly. This significantly reduces the computational complexity and facilitates the attainment of a global optimal solution compared to the nonlinear combination,. The policy gradient of PRACM can be expressed as follows:

$$\nabla_\psi J(\boldsymbol{\pi}) = \mathbb{E}_D[\nabla_\psi \boldsymbol{\pi} \nabla_{\boldsymbol{\pi}} Q_{tot}^{\boldsymbol{\pi}}(\boldsymbol{\tau}, \pi_1(\tau_1, a_1), ..., \pi_n(\tau_n, a_n), s)], \tag{9}$$

where $\boldsymbol{\pi} = \{\pi_1(\tau_1, a_1|\psi_1), ..., \pi_n(\tau_n, a_n|\psi_n)\}$ is the set of current policies of all agents, ψ is the parameter of actor network, and D is the replay buffer.

To support the deterministic policies of the Actor-Critic framework, the Gumbel-Softmax technique [5] is incorporated after the actor network. This transformation changes the actor output's deterministic policy μ to a discrete policy π for action sampling. The sampling process is $\boldsymbol{a}^t = \mu(\boldsymbol{\tau}) \approx \pi(\boldsymbol{a}^{t-1}|\boldsymbol{\tau})$, in addition, the Gumbel-Softmax computes the policy gradient for the gradient approximation of discrete samples, with the gradient approximation process shown as follows:

$$\begin{aligned}\nabla_\psi J(\boldsymbol{\mu}) &= \mathbb{E}_D[\nabla_\psi \boldsymbol{\mu} \nabla_{\boldsymbol{\mu}} Q_{tot}^{\boldsymbol{\mu}}(\boldsymbol{\tau}, \mu_1(\tau_1), ..., \mu_n(\tau_n), s)] \\ &\approx \mathbb{E}_D[\nabla_\psi \boldsymbol{v} \nabla_{\boldsymbol{v}} Q_{tot}^{\boldsymbol{v}}(\boldsymbol{\tau}, v_1, ..., v_n, s)] = \nabla_\psi J(\boldsymbol{\pi}),\end{aligned} \tag{10}$$

where $\boldsymbol{v} = \boldsymbol{\pi}(\boldsymbol{a}|\boldsymbol{\tau})$, and $\boldsymbol{v} = \{v_1, ..., v_n\}$ is the action of performing continuous sampling.

3.3   Predictive Rewards

In some partially observable cooperative environments, such as Predator-Prey with Punish, the rewards for collaborative work among agents exceed those for individual task completion, and certain agent behaviors are penalized [8]. Utilizing a single Actor-Critic framework leads to a sparse reward environment during training, which can ultimately hinder convergence. A predictive rewards estimator is designed to solve the above problem, and the application of predictive rewards is shown in Fig. 2.

Like ELIGN, predictive rewards utilize expectation alignment [12], which draws from the concept of self-organization in animals and enables cooperation among diverse groups of animals to achieve a common goal. The alignment of expectations is realized by instructing agents to perform actions that align with the expectations of nearby agents. Nevertheless, PRACM differs from ELIGN in that it assigns rewards to a centralized Q_{tot} value to adapt to certain cooperative scenarios, such as the Predator-Prey with Punish environment.

To achieve expectation alignment, each agent in the predictive rewards approach learns a dynamics function expressed as $\hat{o}_i' = f_{\eta_j}(o_i, a_i)$, where $\hat{o}_i'$ is the

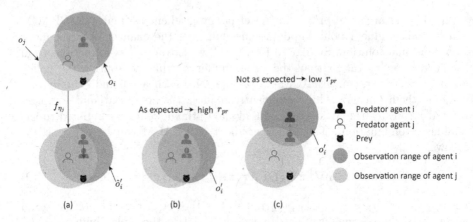

Fig. 2. Example of predictive rewards applied to the Predator-Prey environment. (a) predator agent i has to learn an action that matches predator agent j's predicted value oi for the next observation. In this example, i needs to move down to capture prey. (b) predator agent i's action is consistent with the expectation (e.g., moving down), obtaining high r_{pr}. (c) predator agent i's action is inconsistent with expectations (e.g., moving up), obtaining low r_{pr}.

next observation predicted by agent j, η is the parameter of the kinetic function f, and o_i and a_i are the observation and action of agent i, respectively. To achieve expectation alignment, predictive rewards are computed as:

$$r_{pr}(o_i, a_i) = -\frac{1}{|M(i)|} \sum_{j \in M(i)} \|o'_i - \hat{o}'_i\|, \tag{11}$$

where r_{pr} is the predictive rewards and $M(i)$ represents the set of all agents within agent i's observation range. In Eq. (11), the value of r_{pr} will be larger when the loss value is smaller (i.e., when the observation o'_i of agent i at the next moment is similar to the expectation $\hat{o}'_i$ of agent j), and when the loss value is larger (i.e., when the observation o'_i of agent i at the next moment is more different from the expectation $\hat{o}'_i$ of agent j). In ELIGN, it is necessary to approximate o'_i with $o'_{i \cap j}$ due to the decentralized training, while the o'_i used by PRACM is extracted from the replay buffer D, which can better exploit the advantages of centralized training.

After the predictive rewards r_{pr} are calculated, it needs to be put into the Q_{tot} generated by the critic network, but it is obviously unreasonable to add it directly, which will lead to an imbalance of the weights and thus reduce the training effect, therefor a linear combination of r_{pr} is used as follows:

$$\boldsymbol{r}^*_{pr} = h_\alpha(r_{pr}(o_1, a_1), ..., r_{pr}(o_n, a_n)), \tag{12}$$

where $\boldsymbol{r}^*_{pr}$ is the reward after the combination and α is the parameter of the combination function h. Once $\boldsymbol{r}^*_{pr}$ is obtained, it needs to be summed with Q_{tot}

to obtain Q_{tot}^* as follows:

$$Q_{tot}^* = Q_{tot} + \varsigma r_{pr}^*, \tag{13}$$

where $\varsigma \in [0,1]$ is the weight parameter of predictive rewards, reflecting how important cooperative training is to the agents. A larger ς value indicates that agents place more importance on cooperation with each other.

4 Experiments and Results

In this section, the experimental results of PRACM on various tasks in Cooperative Predator-Prey [1] and StarCraft Multi-Agent Challenge (SMAC) are presented. The Cooperative Predator-Prey tasks include Predator-Prey with Punish and Predator-Prey without Punish. To establish the effectiveness, RRACM was compared against state-of-the-art Actor-Critic framework algorithms such as FACMAC [14], MADDPG [10], DOP [26], FOP [33], as well as value-based algorithms QMIX [18] and QPLEX [24]. To evaluate the significance of predictive rewards, PRACM was introduced without predictive rewards and label it as PRACM-pr. An ε-greedy exploration strategy was used and given $\gamma = 0.85$ during the experiments. The training time for Cooperative Predator-Prey was set to 1 million, while for the challenging task of SMAC, the training time to 2 million was increased for better exploration. To ensure fairness among the algorithms, the size of the replay buffer D was set to 5000, and 5 random seeds were conducted for each experiment. The experimental results with the 95% confidence interval were presented.

4.1 Cooperative Predator-Prey

The experimental analysis began with "Predator-Prey", a partially observable experimental environment based on discrete actions. To verify the scalability and collaborative of the PRACM algorithm, two experimental scenarios were considered: a simple Predator-Prey without Punish and a more challenging Predator-Prey with Punish.

The Predator-Prey without Punish environment consists of n manipulable predators that capture n preys controlled by the built-in AI in a 10×10 grid world. Each agent's observation range is a 2×2 grid centered on itself. Three experiments were conducted with n values of 4, 6, and 8, and the results are illustrated in Fig. 3.

In the Predator-Prey with Punish environment, to intensify the task, n was set to 8, i.e., there were 8 predators and 8 preys. A successful capture is counted only when two or more predator agents surround and capture the same prey at the same time. A penalty reward of p is given when the capture fails. Three experiments were conducted with p values of –0.5, –1, and –2, and the results are presented in Fig. 4.

As demonstrated in Fig. 3, both PRACM and PRACM-pr outperform other algorithms in different numbers of Predator-Prey environments without punishment. When n is small, as shown in Fig. 3(a), all algorithms perform well.

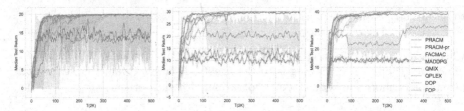

(a) 4 predators and 4 preys (b) 6 predators and 6 preys (c) 8 predators and 8 preys

Fig. 3. Median test returns for different numbers of Predator-Prey.

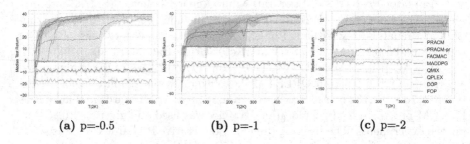

(a) p=-0.5   (b) p=-1   (c) p=-2

Fig. 4. Median test returns of Predator-Prey with Punish for different P values.

However, as the number of predators increases, as shown in Fig. 3(b) and 3(c), the performance of some baseline algorithms, such as FACMAC, MADDPG, and FOP, decreases significantly, indicating their poor scalability. In particular, PRACM-pr achieves the highest rewards when n=8, while another Actor-Critic-based algorithm, MADDPG, performs poorly, demonstrating the effectiveness of using a monotonic mixing function to increase scalability. Remarkably, the performance of PRACM decreases slightly compared to PRACM-pr, indicating that predictive rewards have a negative impact on the algorithm's scalability.

Figure 4 demonstrates that PRACM performs well for different p-values. When p is small, as shown in Fig. 4(a), PRACM, PRACM-pr, and the baseline algorithms QMIX, QPLEX, and FOP all achieve the highest rewards. However, as p increases, as illustrated in Fig. 4(b) and 4(c), the convergence rates of all algorithms decrease, with PRACM indicating the smallest decline and the best overall performance. Notably, , PRACM-pr performs poorly when p=-2, whereas PRACM achieves the highest reward, indicating that predictive rewards effectively facilitate agents' cooperation, enabling them to converge and obtain higher rewards. It is worth mentioning that the baseline algorithms FACMAC, MADDPG, and DOP performed poorly in the experiments, highlighting their difficulty in completing cooperative tasks with penalties under discrete actions.

4.2   SMAC

Subsequently, experiments were performed in the more challenging SMAC environment to demonstrate the transferability of PRACM in other environments. conducted total of three experiments were conducted, each using the maps and parameters detailed in Table 1, while other parameters remained the same as in the study of Samvelyan et al. [21]. The results of the experiments are presented in Fig. 5.

Table 1. The maps and parameters of the SMAC in experiment.

Map name	Difficulty	Ally	Opponent
3s5z	Easy	3 Stalkers & 5 Zealots	–
3s_vs_5z	Hard	3 Stalkers	5 Zealots
3s5z_vs_3s6z	Super hard	3 Stalkers & 5 Zealots	3 Stalkers & 6 Zealots

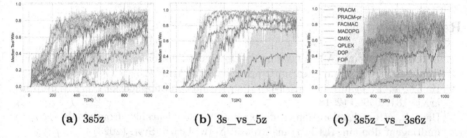

(a) 3s5z   (b) 3s_vs_5z   (c) 3s5z_vs_3s6z

Fig. 5. Median test win for easy(a), had(b) and super-hard (c) maps of SMAC.

As depicted in Fig. 5, both PRACM and PRACM-pr demonstrated strong performance in various difficulty levels in the challenging SAMC. In the simple tasks depicted in Fig. 5(a), the win rates of PRACM, PRACM-pr, and baseline algorithms FACMAC, MADDPG, QMIX, and DOP were all above 0.5. However, as the map complexity increased in Fig. 5(b), the win rate of MADDPG decreased significantly, indicating that the algorithm's scalability was insufficient to handle an increasing number of agents. When the map difficulty was super hard, only PRACM-pr, FACMAC, and QMIX performed well, with PRACM-pr achieving the highest win rate, demonstrating the scalability and transferability of the proposed algorithm.

Compared to PRACM-pr, the win rate of PRACM decreased significantly with increasing map difficulty, indicating that predictive rewards increases the algorithm's complexity and limits its scalability to some extent. This side effect is more pronounced with more hard tasks. Notably, the consistently low win rate of QPLEX proves that it is difficult to complete challenging tasks.

5 Conclusion

In this study, a novel approach , called PRACM, is proposed for addressing multi-agent cooperative tasks under discrete actions based on the Actor-Critic framework, to. The proposed method employs a monotonic mixing function to construct the global action value function Q_{tot} and incorporates Gumbel-Softmax to handle discrete actions. To address cooperative environments with penalties, predictive rewards to promote collaboration among agents is introduced. Through experiments in the "Cooperative Predator-Prey" and the challenging "SMAC" environments, PRACM can effectively enhance cooperation among agents in the presence of discrete actions, and outperforms other baseline algorithms in terms of scalability and transferability in multi-agent cooperation tasks. Also, PRACM facilitate collaboration among agents in a penalized environment. In future work, we plan to further optimize the algorithm to reduce the negative impact of predictive rewards on scalability and to consider more challenging continuous action spaces to expand the range of algorithm applications.

Acknowledgements. This work is sponsored by Equipment Advance Research Fund (NO.61406190118).

References

1. Böhmer, W., Kurin, V., Whiteson, S.: Deep coordination graphs. In: International Conference on Machine Learning. pp. 980–991. PMLR (2020)
2. Haarnoja, T., et al.: Soft actor-critic algorithms and applications. arXiv preprint arXiv:1812.05905 (2018)
3. Hao, J., et al.: Exploration in deep reinforcement learning: from single-agent to multiagent domain. IEEE Trans. Neural Netw. Learn. Syst. (2023)
4. He, W., Chen, T.: Scalable online disease diagnosis via multi-model-fused actor-critic reinforcement learning. arXiv preprint arXiv:2206.03659 (2022)
5. Jang, E., Gu, S., Poole, B.: Categorical reparameterization with gumbel-softmax. arXiv preprint arXiv:1611.01144 (2016)
6. Kim, D., et al.: Learning to schedule communication in multi-agent reinforcement learning. arXiv preprint arXiv:1902.01554 (2019)
7. Kraemer, L., Banerjee, B.: Multi-agent reinforcement learning as a rehearsal for decentralized planning. Neurocomputing **190**, 82–94 (2016)
8. Li, J., Wu, F., Shi, H., Hwang, K.S.: A collaboration of multi-agent model using an interactive interface. Inf. Sci. **611**, 349–363 (2022)
9. Li, W., Liu, W., Shao, S., Huang, S., Song, A.: Attention-based intrinsic reward mixing network for credit assignment in multi-agent reinforcement learning. IEEE Trans. Games (2023)
10. Lowe, R., Wu, Y.I., Tamar, A., Harb, J., Pieter Abbeel, O., Mordatch, I.: Multi-agent actor-critic for mixed cooperative-competitive environments. Adv. Inf. Process. Syst. **30** (2017)
11. Ma, Z., Wang, R., Li, F.F., Bernstein, M., Krishna, R.: Elign: Expectation alignment as a multi-agent intrinsic reward. Adv. Neural Inf. Process. Syst. **35**, 8304–8317 (2022)

12. Ndousse, K.K., Eck, D., Levine, S., Jaques, N.: Emergent social learning via multi-agent reinforcement learning. In: International Conference on Machine Learning. pp. 7991–8004. PMLR (2021)
13. Omidshafiei, S., et al.: Learning to teach in cooperative multiagent reinforcement learning. In: Proceedings of the AAAI Conference on Artificial Intelligence. vol. 33, pp. 6128–6136 (2019)
14. Peng, B., et al.: Facmac: Factored multi-agent centralised policy gradients. Adv. Neural Inf. Process. Syst. **34**, 12208–12221 (2021)
15. Pina, R., De Silva, V., Hook, J., Kondoz, A.: Residual q-networks for value function factorizing in multiagent reinforcement learning. IEEE Trans. Neural Netw. Learn. Syst. (2022)
16. Prajapat, M., Turchetta, M., Zeilinger, M., Krause, A.: Near-optimal multi-agent learning for safe coverage control. Adv. Neural Inf. Process. Syst. **35**, 14998–15012 (2022)
17. Puente-Castro, A., Rivero, D., Pazos, A., Fernandez-Blanco, E.: A review of artificial intelligence applied to path planning in UAV swarms. Neural Comput. Appl. **34**(1), 153–170 (2021). https://doi.org/10.1007/s00521-021-06569-4
18. Rashid, T., Samvelyan, M., De Witt, C.S., Farquhar, G., Foerster, J., Whiteson, S.: Monotonic value function factorisation for deep multi-agent reinforcement learning. J. Mach. Learn. Res. **21**(1), 7234–7284 (2020)
19. Ryu, H., Shin, H., Park, J.: Multi-agent actor-critic with hierarchical graph attention network. In: Proceedings of the AAAI Conference on Artificial Intelligence. vol. 34, pp. 7236–7243 (2020)
20. Sahoo, S., Lo, C.Y.: Smart manufacturing powered by recent technological advancements: a review. J. Manuf. Syst. **64**, 236–250 (2022)
21. Samvelyan, M., et al.: The starcraft multi-agent challenge. arXiv preprint arXiv:1902.04043 (2019)
22. Sharma, R., Shishodia, A., Gunasekaran, A., Min, H., Munim, Z.H.: The role of artificial intelligence in supply chain management: mapping the territory. Int. J. Prod. Res. **60**(24), 7527–7550 (2022)
23. Son, K., Kim, D., Kang, W.J., Hostallero, D.E., Yi, Y.: Qtran: Learning to factorize with transformation for cooperative multi-agent reinforcement learning. In: International conference on machine learning. pp. 5887–5896. PMLR (2019)
24. Wang, J., Ren, Z., Liu, T., Yu, Y., Zhang, C.: QPLEX: Duplex dueling multi-agent q-learning. arXiv preprint arXiv:2008.01062 (2020)
25. Wang, J., Li, Y., Gao, R.X., Zhang, F.: Hybrid physics-based and data-driven models for smart manufacturing: Modelling, simulation, and explainability. J. Manuf. Syst. **63**, 381–391 (2022)
26. Wang, Y., Han, B., Wang, T., Dong, H., Zhang, C.: Off-policy multi-agent decomposed policy gradients. arXiv preprint arXiv:2007.12322 (2020)
27. Wang, Z., Li, M., Lu, J., Cheng, X.: Business innovation based on artificial intelligence and blockchain technology. Inf. Process. Manag. **59**(1), 102759 (2022)
28. Wang, Z., Schaul, T., Hessel, M., Hasselt, H., Lanctot, M., Freitas, N.: Dueling network architectures for deep reinforcement learning. In: International conference on machine learning. pp. 1995–2003. PMLR (2016)
29. Wen, M., et al.: Multi-agent reinforcement learning is a sequence modeling problem. Adv. Neural Inf. Process. Syst. **35**, 16509–16521 (2022)
30. Yang, J., Ni, J., Li, Y., Wen, J., Chen, D.: The intelligent path planning system of agricultural robot via reinforcement learning. Sensors **22**(12), 4316 (2022)
31. Yang, T., et al.: Exploration in deep reinforcement learning: a comprehensive survey. arXiv preprint arXiv:2109.06668 (2021)

32. Ye, Z., Chen, Y., Jiang, X., Song, G., Yang, B., Fan, S.: Improving sample efficiency in Multi-Agent Actor-Critic methods. Appl. Intell. 1–14 (2021). https://doi.org/10.1007/s10489-021-02554-5
33. Zhang, T., Li, Y., Wang, C., Xie, G., Lu, Z.: Fop: Factorizing optimal joint policy of maximum-entropy multi-agent reinforcement learning. In: International Conference on Machine Learning. pp. 12491–12500. PMLR (2021)
34. Zhang, T., Liu, Z., Wu, S., Pu, Z., Yi, J.: Intrinsic reward with peer incentives for cooperative multi-agent reinforcement learning. In: 2022 International Joint Conference on Neural Networks (IJCNN). pp. 1–7. IEEE (2022)
35. Zhang, X., Liu, Y., Xu, X., Huang, Q., Mao, H., Carie, A.: Structural relational inference actor-critic for multi-agent reinforcement learning. Neurocomputing **459**, 383–394 (2021)
36. Zhou, D., Gayah, V.V.: Scalable multi-region perimeter metering control for urban networks: a multi-agent deep reinforcement learning approach. Transp. Res. Part C Emerg. Technol. **148**, 104033 (2023)
37. Zhou, M., Liu, Z., Sui, P., Li, Y., Chung, Y.Y.: Learning implicit credit assignment for cooperative multi-agent reinforcement learning. Adv. Neural Inf. Process. Syst. **33**, 11853–11864 (2020)

A Cybersecurity Knowledge Graph Completion Method for Scalable Scenarios

Peng Wang[1,2]([✉]), Jingju Liu[1,2], Qian Yao[1,2], and Xinli Xiong[1,2]

[1] College of Electronic Engineering, National University of Defense Technology,
Hefei 230037, China
{wangpeng21e,yaoqian21,xiongxinli_}@nudt.edu.cn, jingjul@aliyun.com
[2] Anhui Province Key Laboratory of Cyberspace Security Situation Awareness
and Evaluation, Hefei 230037, China

Abstract. Cybersecurity knowledge graph can well organize and manage cybersecurity data. However, there are still some challenges in the utilization of cybersecurity knowledge graph. Due to the limited cognitive ability and cyberspace exploration ability of human beings, the data in cybersecurity knowledge graph is incomplete. With the continuous changes of cyberspace, there are many unseen entities in the newly added data, and it is difficult to use this kind of data. In order to realize knowledge graph completion in scalable scenarios, we propose a knowledge graph completion method, which uses meta-learning to transfer knowledge from seen entities to unseen entities. It also utilizes a new scoring function to model the relationships between entities from multiple perspectives such as spatial rotation and angle transformation. For improving the robust expression of samples, it uses the correlation matrix and multi-head attention mechanism to explore the relationships between samples. To mitigate the catastrophic forgetting problem, a new self-distillation algorithm is designed to enhance the robustness of the trained model. We construct knowledge graph based on cybersecurity data, and conduct knowledge graph completion experiments. The experiments show that our method is effective in dealing with the problem of cybersecurity knowledge graph completion in scalable scenarios.

Keywords: Cybersecurity data · Knowledge graph completion · Scalable scenarios · Meta learning · Self-distillation

1 Introduction

With the wide application of the Internet in people's study and life, the cybersecurity risk has also increased. It seriously affects the economy, culture and other fields. There is a large amount of valuable information in cybersecurity data, which can better improve the intelligent level of cyberspace governance capabilities. At present, great progress has been made in characterizing hacker attack behaviors and formulating defense strategies based on cybersecurity threat intelligence and cybersecurity experience knowledge. For example, MITRE maintains

Z. Jin et al. (Eds.): KSEM 2023, LNAI 14120, pp. 83–98, 2023.
https://doi.org/10.1007/978-3-031-40292-0_8

cybersecurity knowledge bases such as CVE (Common Vulnerabilities and Exposures), CWE (Common Weakness Enumeration) and CAPEC (Common Attack Pattern Enumeration and Classification), which play an important role in maintaining cybersecurity. CVE helps defenders understand the basic status of vulnerabilities. CWE associates common weakness with vulnerabilities and attack patterns. CAPEC records a series of attack patterns, it helps people accurately identify the behaviors of hackers.

Traditional database storage is difficult to make full use of cybersecurity data. Knowledge graph is a semantic network composed of entities and relationships, which can effectively represent the things and relationships in the real world. Knowledge graph provides the possibility to maximize the value of cybersecurity data. In recent years, knowledge graphs have been widely used in medical care [4], education [11] and other fields [8,19]. However, due to the limited cognitive ability of people, most of the existing knowledge graphs are incomplete. And the knowledge graphs in the real world are usually dynamic. If new cybersecurity intelligence knowledge is acquired, new entities are likely to be added. According to the general practice, when the content of the knowledge graph changes, we will learn the entire knowledge graph again, and expand the entire knowledge graph. It will consume large amounts of computation and waste more time, which is obviously not well adapted to the rapidly changing cyberspace. However, for the newly added entity, it may have similar multi-hop neighborhood structures with the existing entities in the knowledge graph, and this information can form an effective knowledge transfer between the entities. For example, a vulnerability entity may be associated with some operating systems or software weaknesses. If a new vulnerability entity is added to the knowledge graph, it can be linked with some existing entities based on similar structures and other information.

Facing the phenomenon of missing information in cybersecurity knowledge graph, we propose a novel knowledge graph completion model called MCSD. Since the cybersecurity knowledge graph is dynamically changing, it uses Meta-learning to realize the rapid transfer of knowledge from seen entities to unseen entities. It also implements relational operations in the Complex number space to model the relationship between entities. In order to further improve the utilization of training samples, a robust deep representation can be formed by exploring the relationships between Samples. At the same time, a new knowledge Distillation strategy is designed to alleviate catastrophic forgetting problem during training.

In summary, our contributions are as follows:

1. We design a knowledge graph completion model called MCSD for scalable scenarios, which uses meta-learning to realize knowledge transfer from seen entities to unseen entities. It implements relational operations in the complex number space to model the relationships between entities from multiple perspectives such as spatial rotation and angle transformation. It uses the correlation matrix and multi-head attention mechanism to characterize the relationships between samples.
2. We design a SEMA (Sine Exponential Moving Average) self-distillation algorithm, which takes into account the constraints of exploration and global

experience. It effectively alleviates the catastrophic forgetting problem when the number of iterations is large.
3. We construct cybersecurity knowledge graph and conduct knowledge graph completion experiments on it. Experiments show that our method can be well applied to cybersecurity knowledge graph completion in scalable scenarios.

2 Related Work

2.1 Research on Knowledge Graph Completion

Beacuse of the limited information collection ability, the content of the knowledge graph is incomplete. Knowledge graph completion technology can effectively realize the completion and error correction of the content. The current mainstream completion techniques represent entities and relationships as low-dimensional vectors, and then perform relevant mathematical transformations. Due to the variety of entities and the complexity of relationships, we need to represent entities and relationships more accurately. TransE [1] uses word vector translation to model the relationships between entities. It uses a scoring function in the form of $h + r = t$ to evaluate whether a triple is true, where h is the head entity, r is the relationship and t is the tail entity. This method is simple in form and greatly reduces the amount of calculation, but this method still has some shortcomings. Therefore, many methods use spatial projection [20] and matrix mapping [10] to improve the simple word vector translation model, which makes the translation model can deal with more complex relation types. Simple Euclidean space is difficult to fully represent entities and relationships. Therefore, many researchers have extended the representation of knowledge graph to complex number space [15], quaternion space [23] and octonion space [22].

In addition to translation models, tensor decomposition models have also received more attention because they can better mine the potential semantic knowledge, such as RESCAL [12], DistMult [21] and ComplEx [17]. The above models can perform feature extraction and representation learning for entities and relationships in the knowledge graph. They obtain the score of the triple through matrix factorization, which is used to measure the rationality of the triple. The above two kinds of models can be applied to different application scenarios, we consider the combination of tensor decomposition model and translation model to enhance the interpretability and semantic mining ability.

Neural networks have made great progress in natural language processing, computer vision and other fields in recent years. Therefore, many researchers have designed knowledge graph completion models based on neural networks. ConvE [5] uses convolutional neural network to extract features of the encoded entities and relationships. It obtains the output vector through convolutional neural network, and multiplies the output vector with the vectors of all entities to determine whether the triple is true. Graph neural network has great advantages in processing graph data, many methods solve the knowledge graph completion problem from the perspective of graph structure. RGCN [13] is an earlier graph neural network method used for knowledge graph completion.

It effectively aggregates the surrounding information of entities to describe entities and relationships more accurately. Many methods [14,18] also consider using related auxiliary information for knowledge graph completion. For example, text descriptions are used to further model entities and relations, so that the meaning of entities and relations is richer. However, it is difficult to obtain a large amount of auxiliary information about entities and relationships in a short time, especially in scalable cyberspace scenarios.

2.2 Research on Meta-Learning

Supervised learning has achieved great success in recent years. However, the experimental results of supervised learning rely heavily on high-quality data. There is no enough data in the real world. Therefore, improving the model performance under the condition of limited sample data is an important research hotspot. Meta-learning is an important machine learning method, which can achieve fast learning on limited sample data. Unlike supervised learning, meta-learning divides tasks into training tasks and testing tasks. In the training task, there are support sets and query sets. Meta-learning approaches can be divided into metric-based, model-based and optimization-based approaches. The optimization-based approaches are the most widely used. MAML (Model-Agnostic Meta-Learning) [6] is the most classical optimization-based approach, which expects the model to have the ability of learning. MetaR [2] is an earlier meta-learning method for knowledge graph completion. It realizes the encoding of entities and relations by learning relation meta and gradient meta. GraIL [16] utilizes the graph structure for reasoning, which makes the method have better generalization ability. When new nodes and relationships are added to the knowledge graph, it can learn with less computation. MorsE [3] makes full use of meta-learning and spatial structure to realize knowledge graph completion. It generates entity embeddings from entity-independent information, and uses graph neural network to enhance the information interaction. Although MorsE provides a good framework for scalable scenarios, it still has shortcomings, such as catastrophic problems and insufficient exploration between samples.

3 Methodology

The cyberspace situation changes rapidly, which puts forward high requirements for the response speed of defenders. When a new foreign entity is added, a large number of repeated calculations are needed, which seriously reduces the efficiency of the model. It is difficult to deal with the rapidly changing cyberspace situation. We can formulate the scalability problem as the following form, given the source knowledge graph KG_1 and the target knowledge graph KG_2, where KG_1 is constructed from known data, mainly used for training, KG_2 is mainly used to simulate new foreign entities. E_1 and R_1 are the sets of entities and relationships in the source KG, E_2 and R_2 are the sets of entities and relationships in the target KG. T_1 is the set of triples in KG_1, and T_2 is the set of triples in KG_2. A triple is of the form (h, r, t), where h is the head entity, r is the relationship, and t is the tail entity. The above elements have the following relationships:

$$\begin{cases} KG_1 = \{E_1, R_1, T_1\} \\ KG_2 = \{E_2, R_2, T_2\} \\ E_1 \cap E_2 = \emptyset \\ R_2 \subseteq R_1 \\ T_1 \cap T_2 = \emptyset. \end{cases} \tag{1}$$

To this end, we design a knowledge graph completion method called MCSD based on meta-learning, which models entities and relationships from the perspective of inductive structures instead of directly learning specific embedded representations. By modeling the meta-knowledge learned from the source knowledge graph, effective entity independent information can be obtained, which helps to generate embedding representations for unseen entities. MCSD optimizes the score function for knowledge graph completion to be more expressive. At the same time, MCSD uses the correlation matrix and the multi-head attention mechanism to improve the robustness of knowledge representation. The catastrophic forgetting problem has always been a major difficulty faced by model training, the learning of later tasks may reduce the learning performance of previous tasks. Therefore, we design the SEMA self-distillation algorithm to fully retain the effective empirical knowledge of previous rounds. The overall architecture of knowledge graph completion in scalable scenarios is shown in Fig. 1.

3.1 Meta-Knowledge Learning

Traditional knowledge graph embedding methods need to define the entities in advance. For achieving entity-independent modeling, MCSD vectorizes entities by using spatial structure information. Inspired by MorsE [3], MCSD also uses two parts to form meta-knowledge, one is to use the relationships around the entity to initialize it, the second is to further generate the embedded representation of entities according to the subgraph of the knowledge graph. Graph neural networks can successfully encode the multi-hop neighborhood information of a node into the embedding representation. Through the message passing mechanism, the representation of nodes can be closely related to the spatial structure. The overall entity embedded expression formula is as follows:

$$\begin{cases} Ent_{ori} = \dfrac{\sum_{i=1}^{n} Rel_i}{n} \\ Ent_t = \dfrac{\sum_{(h,r) \in \mathcal{D}(t)} W_r \cdot Ent_h + W_0 \cdot Ent_{ori}}{|\mathcal{D}(t)|}, \end{cases} \tag{2}$$

where Rel_i is the vector of relationship around the entity t, n represents the sum of indegree and outdegree of the entity t, $\mathcal{D}(t)$ denotes the set of head entity and relation pair of immediate ingoing neighbor triples of entity t. W_r

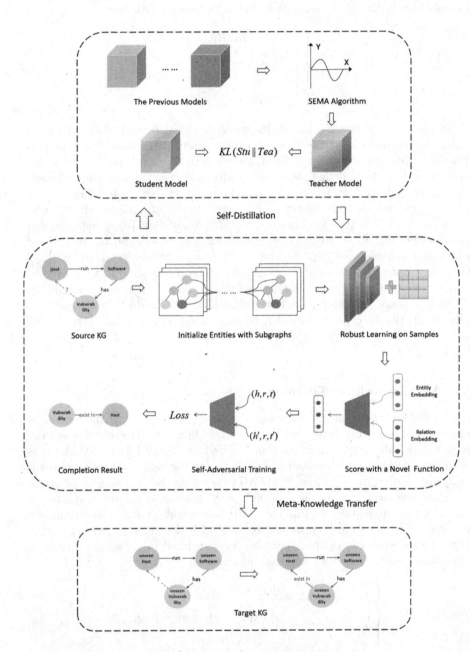

Fig. 1. The knowledge graph completion process of MCSD in scalable scenarios.

is the relation-specific transformation matrix for relation r and W_0 is a self-loop transformation matrix for entity. The training task of meta-learning usually contains many subtasks. In the subtask, it is divided into support set and query set. Similar to the meta-learning mechanism, we sample a series of subgraphs in the source knowledge graph, regard the entities in these subgraphs as unseen entities, and use them to simulate the target graph. At the same time, we regard each subgraph as a training task, a part of triples in each subgraph are regarded as the support set, and the remaining triples are regarded as the query set. The entity-independent modeling can be effectively achieved by meta-learning. For unseen entities, meta-knowledge can be used to generate entity embeddings, so that entities with similar relationships and multi-hop neighborhoods have more similar embedded expressions. We obtain the representations of entities on the support set, and compute the corresponding loss value on the query set to evaluate the quality of the embedded representation. The basic calculation of the meta-learning mechanism is as follows:

$$min \ L(Q_i|f_\theta(S_i), R), \tag{3}$$

where R is the relation matrix obtained by training, $R \in \mathbb{R}^{m \times d}$, m is the number of types of relation, d is the dimension of embedded expression, f is used to output the embedded expression of the entity based on the current task, θ is the training parameter, Q_i is the query set, S_i is the support set and $L(\cdot)$ represents the calculated loss. The details of loss calculation are described in Sect. 3.2.

3.2   Scoring Function

The calculation method of the loss value has an important impact on the model training, so the design of a reasonable scoring function is crucial in knowledge graph completion. Inspired by RotatE [15] and ComplEx [17], MCSD extends the representation of entities and relations to the space of complex numbers, not limited to the traditional Euclidean space. MCSD performs further computations on transitions between entities in complex number space.

Firstly, similar to the tensor decomposition model, it measured the product between the entity and the relationship vectors as the first part of the scoring function. The true triples tend to have higher scores. After that, the relationship vector is normalized and projected into the angle period $[0, 2\pi)$. Then, it realizes the spatial rotation of the head vector to the tail vector, and the gap between the rotated vector and the tail vector is used to measure whether the triple is true. The gap is used as the second part of the scoring function. The true triples tend to have smaller gaps. Finally, the entity vectors are also projected into the angle period $[0, 2\pi)$ by using a similar normalization operation. The angle gap is used to measure the true possibility of the triple. When the angle gap is small, the true possibility of the triple is high. The angle period can also be better used to distinguish entities at the same level [24], so it can be used as the third part of the scoring function. Based on the above steps, the scoring function is shown in the following equation:

$$score = h \times r \times t - (h \times p_r - t) - (p_h + p_r - p_t), \tag{4}$$

where h, r, t are the vector representations of head entity, relation and tail entity in complex number space respectively, $h, r, t \in \mathbb{C}^{2d}$, d is the dimension of the real and imaginary parts of a complex number, p_h, p_r and p_t are the angled representations of the head entity, relation and tail entity vectors after projection, $\|p_h\|_2 = \|p_r\|_2 = \|p_t\|_2 = 1$. Since most of the constructed knowledge graphs only contain correct triples, there is a high probability that the unobserved correct facts are judged as negative. The generalization of the trained model based only on positive triples is weak. In order to alleviate this phenomenon, the negative triples are constructed by randomly replacing the head entity or tail entity, the generalization ability of the model can be effectively improved by comprehensively training the positive triples and negative triples. The specific details of the self-adversarial training [15] are given below:

$$loss = - log\sigma(\mu - score(h, r, t))$$
$$- \sum_{i=1}^{l} p(h_i', r, t_i') log\sigma(score(h_i', r, t_i') - \mu), \tag{5}$$

where $\sigma(\cdot)$ is the sigmoid function, μ is a fixed margin, $score(\cdot)$ is the scoring function, (h, r, t) is a positive triple, (h_i', r, t_i') is the ith negative triple, and $p(\cdot)$ is the sampling weight. The training expectation of the whole expression is that the positive triple has a higher score and the negative triple has a lower score.

3.3   Robust Representation Learning on Samples

Although researchers have achieved great success in representation learning, it heavily relies on collecting large-scale training samples, which is not very straightforward in real-world applications. Therefore, in order to improve the utilization efficiency of samples, it is still a great challenge to find a flexible and powerful method to explore sample relationships for robust representation learning.

In linear algebra, the correlation matrix is an effective way to describe the correlation between variables, so we use correlation matrix to describe the correlation between samples, and its basic calculation is as follows:

$$corr(u, v) = \frac{Cov(u, v)}{\delta_u \delta_v} = \frac{\sum_{i=1}^{n} (u_i - u_{mean})(v_i - v_{mean})}{\sqrt{\sum_{i=1}^{n} (u_i - u_{mean})^2} \sqrt{\sum_{i=1}^{n} (v_i - v_{mean})^2}}, \tag{6}$$

where u and v are the two sample representation vectors, $Cov(u, v)$ is the covariance between u and v, δ_u and δ_v are the variances, u_{mean} and v_{mean} are the mean values of the two vectors, respectively. Attention mechanism is a module that is good at capturing the correlation of features. Due to the complexity of features, simple self-attention mechanisms are difficult to cope with it. The multi-head attention mechanism further expands the self-attention mechanism, which performs multiple groups of self-attention processing on the original input sequence. Finally, it concatenates each self-attention result and performs a linear transformation to obtain the final output result. The transformer encoder has powerful multihead self-attention blocks. Inspired by Batchformer [7], the relationship between samples can be effectively revealed by using the transformer encoder, the interaction between channels and spaces can be captured. At present, there are many methods that explore sample relationships from the input or output of deep neural networks, but there is no interaction from the perspective of batch dimension. Therefore, it can consider introducing a transformer encoder in the batch dimension of each mini-batch data to capture the sample relationships in each mini-batch training sample. In this way, it can effectively promote the information interaction between the features in the mini-batch samples [7].

MCSD fuses the eigenvalues of the correlation matrix with the embedding vectors enhanced by multihead self-attention blocks, which are jointly used for the generation of vectors. The generation of the vectors is shown in Fig. 2.

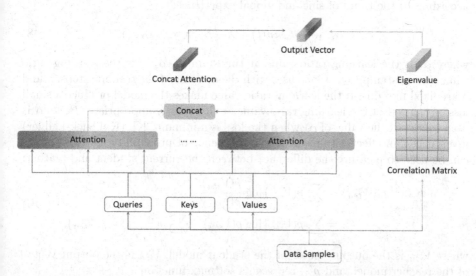

Fig. 2. The robust representation learning framework for the data samples. The multihead attention mechanism and the eigenvalues of the correlation matrix are used to generate vectors.

3.4   SEMA Self-distillation

For restraining the catastrophic forgetting phenomenon, we use knowledge distillation to optimize the training process. Knowledge distillation [9] usually uses knowledge from a larger and better performing teacher model to generate soft targets for a student network, and the student imitates the output of teacher. Considering further reduce the amount of computation, we use the self-distillation strategy to train the model. Most of the current knowledge distillation strategies often use only a single teacher model. However, the level of different teachers is uneven in real life. In order to enable students to learn accurate and rich knowledge, students can consider consulting multiple teachers. For the knowledge taught by each teacher, students can study selectively. In order to better simulate this actual process, we use the SEMA (Sine Exponential Moving Average) strategy to learn multiple teacher models. The teacher model can be expressed in the following form:

$$\theta_{tea} = \alpha_t \cdot \theta_{t-1} + (1 - \alpha_t) \cdot \theta_{t-2}, \tag{7}$$

where θ_{tea} denotes the parameters of the teacher model, θ_{t-1} denotes the parameters of the model at timestamp $t-1$, θ_{t-2} denotes the parameters of the model at timestamp $t-2$, and α_t is the learning ratio value. In order to enhance the exploratory ability of knowledge learning, we change the learning ratio value according to the trend of sine and global experience:

$$\alpha_t = \alpha_{t-1} + \gamma \cdot sin(t) + \lambda \cdot (Best\_\alpha - \alpha_{t-1}), \tag{8}$$

where α_t is the learning ratio value at timestamp t, α_{t-1} is the learning ratio value at timestamp $t-1$, t increases with the increase of the training steps, γ and λ are fixed margins. If the learning ratio value makes the model produce a small loss, it can reflect the learning ratio value at this time is appropriate. $Best\_\alpha$ is used to record the value of α_t when the loss is minimum. KL (Kullback-Leibler) divergence can effectively measure the difference of probability distribution. It can be used to measure the difference between the current student and teacher:

$$
\begin{aligned}
KL(V_{stu}||V_{tea}) &= \sum \rho(V_{stu}) \log \frac{\rho(V_{stu})}{\rho(V_{tea})} \\
&= \sum \rho(V_{stu}) \log \rho(V_{stu}) - \sum \rho(V_{stu}) \log \rho(V_{tea}),
\end{aligned}
\tag{9}
$$

where V_{stu} is the output vector of the student model, V_{tea} is the output vector of the teacher model, and $\rho(\cdot)$ represents softmax function.

4 Experiments

4.1 Dataset

In order to better apply the model to the field of cybersecurity and make it adapt to the continuous expansion of cybersecurity knowledge graph, we collected relevant data in the field of cybersecurity. The data mainly includes three categories: cyberspace detection intelligence, vulnerability exploitation tool, and cybersecurity experience knowledge. The cyberspace detection intelligence is mainly composed of IP address, subdomain and other elements. The data of vulnerability exploitation tool is mainly the built-in module data of metasploit, such as EXP, Post and AUX. The cybersecurity experience knowledge mainly comes from knowledge bases such as CVE, CWE and CAPEC. The details of the associations between entities are shown in the Table 1.

Table 1. The description of relationships in cybersecurity knowledge graph. SD denotes the subdomain, CAP denotes the CAPEC.

Relationships	Head→Tail	Relationships	Head→Tail
Address	DNS→IP,SD→IP	HasPost	EXP→Post
IsAddressOf	IP→DNS,IP→SD	LocArea	IP→Region
BePlatformOf	OS→EXP	OpenPort	IP→Port
AffectPlatform	EXP→OS	OpenedBy	Port→IP
BeAuxOf	AUX→EXP	RelatedTo	Port→Service,Service→Port
BeExpOf	EXP→CVE	InstanceOf	CVE→CWE
BePostOf	Post→EXP	ObservedExample	CWE→CVE
Connect	SD→SD	PeerOf	CWE→CWE,CAP→CAP
Control	DNS→SD	AttackTo	CAP→CWE
ControlledBy	SD→DNS	TargetOf	CWE→CAP
Exist	CVE→IP,CVE→SD	CanFollow	CWE→CWE,CAP→CAP
HasAux	EXP→AUX	CanPrecede	CWE→CWE,CAP→CAP
HasCve	IP→CVE,SD→CVE	Childof	CWE→CWE,CAP→CAP
HasExp	CVE→EXP	ParentOf	CWE→CWE,CAP→CAP

For the purpose of simulating the real scalable scenarios, we reconstruct two graphs based on the collected cybersecurity data, denoted as the source knowledge graph and the target knowledge graph. The source KG is used to help the model learn meta-knowledge, and the target KG is used to test the effectiveness of the learning. The newly constructed source KG and the target KG have the following characteristics: (1) there is no overlapping entity between them. (2) the set of relationships in the target KG is a subset of relationships in the source KG. In order to simulate the scene with increasing entities, we construct two groups of source knowledge graphs and target knowledge graphs with different proportions. In the first group $C1$, the number of triples in the source KG is roughly equal to that in the target KG. In the second group $C2$, the number of triples in the source KG is smaller than that in the target KG, which is used to verify the scalable knowledge graph completion under scarce training resources. The details of each group are shown in Table 2.

Table 2. The quantity statistics of each group in cybersecurity knowledge graph.

Group	Source KG			Target KG		
	Entities	Relationships	Triples	Entities	Relationships	Triples
C1	26526	28	29174	21866	28	29008
C2	21777	28	22791	26056	28	36032

4.2 Evaluation Metrics and Results

For demonstrating the effectiveness of our method, we compare our method with a variety of knowledge graph completion methods based on MorsE [3] to verify the experimental effect. TransE is an excellent distance-based knowledge graph completion method, DistMult uses tensor decomposition to mine the potential relationships between triples, and ComplEx further extends DistMult in the complex number space. RotatE effectively rotates in complex number space to measure whether the triple is true. The baseline methods include translation models, tensor decomposition models, etc., which are well representative.

The information in our cybersecurity knowledge graph is relatively complete, but it is intended to simulate the phenomenon of lack facts in the cybersecurity field. We remove the head entity or tail entity of the triples in the dataset to form the prediction task $(?, r, t)$ or $(h, r, ?)$. The removed head entity or tail entity can be used as the standard answer to test the completion performance of the model.

Our experimental metrics are MRR and Hits@K. MRR is the mean reciprocal ranking, Hits@K is the average proportion of triples whose rank is less than or equal to K in the completion results. Large MRR and Hits@K mean excellent experimental results. The experimental results of MCSD and various methods are shown in the Table 3.

Table 3. The experimental results on cybersecurity knowledge graph.

Method	C1				C2			
	MRR	Hits@1	Hits@5	Hits@10	MRR	Hits@1	Hits@5	Hits@10
MorsE-TransE	0.425	0.233	0.682	0.872	0.321	0.146	0.540	0.820
MorsE-DistMult	0.320	0.146	0.531	0.810	0.292	0.132	0.462	0.706
MorsE-ComplEx	0.398	0.213	0.649	0.854	0.308	0.159	0.462	0.677
MorsE-RotatE	0.410	0.220	0.679	0.866	0.348	0.171	0.568	0.816
MCSD	0.452	0.250	0.742	0.924	0.430	0.229	0.722	0.899

We can find that the performance of most experimental methods decreases when facing the situation that the data of source KG is less and the data of target KG is increasing. MCSD maintains the leading experimental effect in both groups of data. MCSD is higher than other methods in MRR and Hits@K, which means that it can more quickly complete cybersecurity knowledge and help users improve emergency response ability to cybersecurity situations. The reason is that MCSD enhances the utilization ability of samples, strengthens the robust expression of samples through the correlation matrix and the multi-head attention mechanism. The knowledge distillation is used to mitigate the catastrophic forgetting problem. And MCSD forms a more robust expression form in the complex space. Although MorsE has made great progress in inductive knowledge graph reasoning, it still has shortcomings in dealing with the relationship between data samples and solving the forgetting problem.

In order to verify the effectiveness of our design method, we also conduct ablation experiments on various parts of MCSD. We successively remove the new score function (NSF) part, the robust sample representation (RSR) part and the SEMA self-distillation part. In removing the new score function (NSF) part, we use the ComplEx instead of our new score function. The experimental results are shown in the Table 4.

Table 4. The ablation study of MCSD.

Method	$C1$				$C2$			
	MRR	Hits@1	Hits@5	Hits@10	MRR	Hits@1	Hits@5	Hits@10
w/o NSF	0.404	0.219	0.652	0.841	0.328	0.162	0.522	0.761
w/o RSR	0.425	0.226	0.706	0.931	0.375	0.197	0.594	0.828
w/o SEMA	0.434	0.233	0.713	0.927	0.399	0.208	0.668	0.865
MCSD	0.452	0.250	0.742	0.924	0.430	0.229	0.722	0.899

Through the ablation experiment, we can find that the scoring function has a great influence on the experimental effect, indicating that the new scoring function is accurate and effective in modeling the relationships between entities from multiple perspectives such as spatial rotation and angle transformation. We can also find that our exploration of the relationships between samples is also successful. Traditional training samples lack effective information interaction. By introducing attention mechanism and correlation matrix to model the relationships between different samples, it can promote information interaction to a certain extent and improve the efficiency of data utilization. The knowledge distillation strategy we designed can alleviate the catastrophic forgetting problem of the model and make the model achieve a continuous improvement in performance.

In the representation of entities, the embedding dimension is an important factor affecting the experimental effect. At the same time, too high embedding dimension often occupies a lot of computing resources and consumes more computing time. However, the cyberspace changes rapidly, requiring the defender to have a rapid emergency response ability, so it is also particularly important to use less training time and other resources to achieve the goal. Therefore, we conduct experiments on MCSD in a low embedding dimension space, and the experimental results are shown in the Table 5.

Although MorsE-RotatE achieves good results in the low-dimensional group $C1$, it is difficult to deal with the gradually increasing foreign entities only by rotation operation. The vector dimension still have an important effect on MCSD, which also provides us with further optimization direction. Higher MRR and Hits@1 mean that the model can complete the entity at a faster speed. This is critical for emergency response capabilities in cyberspace. In the group $C2$, when the number of samples in the source KG is small, MorsE-RotatE have

Table 5. The cybersecurity knowledge graph completion results in low-dimensional space.

Method	C1				C2			
	MRR	Hits@1	Hits@5	Hits@10	MRR	Hits@1	Hits@5	Hits@10
MorsE-TransE	0.309	0.134	0.517	0.749	0.270	0.117	0.416	0.724
MorsE-DistMult	0.298	0.132	0.471	0.751	0.268	0.108	0.429	0.729
MorsE-ComplEx	0.265	0.124	0.386	0.646	0.264	0.109	0.419	0.709
MorsE-RotatE	0.389	0.193	0.672	0.875	0.321	0.140	0.560	0.829
MCSD	0.366	0.178	0.618	0.828	0.335	0.162	0.547	0.802

certain difficulties in knowledge transfer. Because MCSD has excellent entity independent information and its utilization of samples is enhanced, so it has a better experimental effect in MRR and Hits@1.

5   Conclusion

This paper designs a cybersecurity knowledge graph completion model MCSD for scalable scenarios. It uses meta-learning to transfer knowledge from seen entities to unseen entities. MCSD uses a novel score function in complex number space to model the relationships between entities from multiple perspectives. At the same time, it uses the correlation matrix and the multi-head attention mechanism to characterize the relationships between samples. In order to mitigate the catastrophic forgetting problem, the SEMA self-distillation method is designed to improve the training effect through periodic exploration and the constraint of the global experience. In the future, we will further optimize our method to address the challenge of long-tailed distributions in cybersecurity data and mitigate the impact of vector dimensions on it, so that the method can continue to maintain excellent performance in cybersecurity knowledge graph completion.

References

1. Bordes, A., Usunier, N., García-Durán, A., Weston, J., Yakhnenko, O.: Translating embeddings for modeling multi-relational data. In: Advances in Neural Information Processing Systems, Lake Tahoe, Nevada, United States, pp. 2787–2795 (2013)
2. Chen, M., Zhang, W., Zhang, W., Chen, Q., Chen, H.: Meta relational learning for few-shot link prediction in knowledge graphs. In: Proceedings of the 2019 Conference on Empirical Methods in Natural Language Processing and the 9th International Joint Conference on Natural Language Processing, EMNLP-IJCNLP 2019, Hong Kong, China, November 3–7, 2019. pp. 4216–4225. Association for Computational Linguistics (2019). https://doi.org/10.18653/v1/D19-1431
3. Chen, M., et al.: Meta-knowledge transfer for inductive knowledge graph embedding. In: Proceedings of the 45th International ACM SIGIR Conference on Research and Development in Information Retrieval. pp. 927–937. SIGIR 2022, Association for Computing Machinery, New York, USA (2022). https://doi.org/10.1145/3477495.3531757

4. Cui, Z., Yuan, Z., Wu, Y., Sun, X., Yu, K.: Intelligent recommendation for departments based on medical knowledge graph. IEEE Access **11**, 25372–25385 (2023)
5. Dettmers, T., Minervini, P., Stenetorp, P., Riedel, S.: Convolutional 2d knowledge graph embeddings. In: Thirty-Second AAAI Conference on Artificial Intelligence, (AAAI-18), New Orleans, Louisiana, USA. pp. 1811–1818 (2018). https://www.aaai.org/ocs/index.php/AAAI/AAAI18/paper/view/17366
6. Finn, C., Abbeel, P., Levine, S.: Model-agnostic meta-learning for fast adaptation of deep networks. In: Proceedings of the 34th International Conference on Machine Learning, ICML 2017, Sydney, NSW, Australia, 6–11 August 2017. Proceedings of Machine Learning Research, vol. 70, pp. 1126–1135. PMLR (2017), http://proceedings.mlr.press/v70/finn17a.html
7. Hou, Z., Yu, B., Tao, D.: Batchformer: Learning to explore sample relationships for robust representation learning. In: IEEE/CVF Conference on Computer Vision and Pattern Recognition, CVPR 2022, New Orleans, LA, USA, June 18–24, 2022. pp. 7246–7256. IEEE (2022), https://doi.org/10.1109/CVPR52688.2022.00711
8. Jiao, Y., You, S.: Rescue decision via earthquake disaster knowledge graph reasoning. Multim. Syst. **29**(2), 605–614 (2023). https://doi.org/10.1007/s00530-022-01002-9
9. Kim, K., Ji, B., Yoon, D., Hwang, S.: Self-knowledge distillation with progressive refinement of targets. In: 2021 IEEE/CVF International Conference on Computer Vision, ICCV 2021, Montreal, QC, Canada, October 10–17, 2021. pp. 6547–6556. IEEE (2021), https://doi.org/10.1109/ICCV48922.2021.00650
10. Lin, Y., Liu, Z., Sun, M., Liu, Y., Zhu, X.: Learning entity and relation embeddings for knowledge graph completion. In: Twenty-Ninth AAAI Conference on Artificial Intelligence, Austin, Texas, USA. pp. 2181–2187 (25–30 January, 2015), http://www.aaai.org/ocs/index.php/AAAI/AAAI15/paper/view/9571
11. Ma, Y., Liu, B., Huang, W., Dan, F.: Knowledge graph based recommendation algorithm for educational resource. In: Proceedings of the 14th International Conference on Education Technology and Computers, ICETC 2022, Barcelona, Spain, October 28–30, 2022. pp. 436–441. ACM (2022), https://doi.org/10.1145/3572549.3572619
12. Nickel, M., Tresp, V., Kriegel, H.: A three-way model for collective learning on multi-relational data. In: 28th International Conference on Machine Learning, ICML 2011, Bellevue, Washington, USA. pp. 809–816 (28 June - 2 July, 2011), https://icml.cc/2011/papers/438_icmlpaper.pdf
13. Schlichtkrull, M.S., Kipf, T.N., Bloem, P., van den Berg, R., Titov, I., Welling, M.: Modeling relational data with graph convolutional networks. In: The Semantic Web - 15th International Conference, ESWC 2018, Heraklion, Crete, Greece. Lecture Notes in Computer Science, vol. 10843, pp. 593–607 (2018), https://doi.org/10.1007/978-3-319-93417-4_38
14. Shen, J., Wang, C., Gong, L., Song, D.: Joint language semantic and structure embedding for knowledge graph completion. In: Proceedings of the 29th International Conference on Computational Linguistics, COLING 2022, Gyeongju, Republic of Korea, October 12–17, 2022. pp. 1965–1978. International Committee on Computational Linguistics (2022), https://aclanthology.org/2022.coling-1.171
15. Sun, Z., Deng, Z., Nie, J., Tang, J.: Rotate: Knowledge graph embedding by relational rotation in complex space. In: 7th International Conference on Learning Representations, ICLR 2019, New Orleans, LA, USA, May 6–9, 2019. OpenReview.net (2019), https://openreview.net/forum?id=HkgEQnRqYQ

16. Teru, K.K., Denis, E.G., Hamilton, W.L.: Inductive relation prediction by sub-graph reasoning. In: Proceedings of the 37th International Conference on Machine Learning, ICML 2020, 13–18 July 2020, Virtual Event. Proceedings of Machine Learning Research, vol. 119, pp. 9448–9457. PMLR (2020), http://proceedings.mlr.press/v119/teru20a.html

17. Trouillon, T., Welbl, J., Riedel, S., Gaussier, É., Bouchard, G.: Complex embeddings for simple link prediction. In: 33nd International Conference on Machine Learning, ICML 2016, New York City, NY, USA. vol. 48, pp. 2071–2080 (2016), http://proceedings.mlr.press/v48/trouillon16.html

18. Wang, B., Shen, T., Long, G., Zhou, T., Wang, Y., Chang, Y.: Structure-augmented text representation learning for efficient knowledge graph completion. In: WWW '21: The Web Conference 2021, Virtual Event / Ljubljana, Slovenia, April 19–23, 2021. pp. 1737–1748. ACM / IW3C2 (2021), https://doi.org/10.1145/3442381.3450043

19. Wang, H., Wang, D., Xu, X.: Research on the construction method of rice knowledge graph. Autom. Control. Comput. Sci. 56(4), 291–299 (2022). https://doi.org/10.3103/S0146411622040095

20. Wang, Z., Zhang, J., Feng, J., Chen, Z.: Knowledge graph embedding by translating on hyperplanes. In: Twenty-Eighth AAAI Conference on Artificial Intelligence, Québec City, Québec, Canada. pp. 1112–1119 (2014), http://www.aaai.org/ocs/index.php/AAAI/AAAI14/paper/view/8531

21. Yang, B., Yih, W., He, X., Gao, J., Deng, L.: Embedding entities and relations for learning and inference in knowledge bases. In: 3rd International Conference on Learning Representations, ICLR 2015, San Diego, CA, USA (2015), http://arxiv.org/abs/1412.6575

22. Yu, M., et al.: Translation-based embeddings with octonion for knowledge graph completion. Appl. Sci. 12(8), 3935 (2022). https://doi.org/10.3390/app12083935

23. Zhang, S., Tay, Y., Yao, L., Liu, Q.: Quaternion knowledge graph embeddings. In: Advances in Neural Information Processing Systems, NeurIPS 2019, Vancouver, BC, Canada. pp. 2731–2741 (2019)

24. Zhang, Z., Cai, J., Zhang, Y., Wang, J.: Learning hierarchy-aware knowledge graph embeddings for link prediction. In: Thirty-Fourth AAAI Conference on Artificial Intelligence. pp. 3065–3072. AAAI Press (2020)

Research on Remote Sensing Image Classification Based on Transfer Learning and Data Augmentation

Liyuan Wang⬥, Yulong Chen(✉)⬥, Xiaoye Wang, Ruixing Wang, Hao Chen, and Yinhai Zhu

Hubei Normal University, Hubei, Huangshi 43500, China
ylchen0424@stu.hbnu.edu.cn

Abstract. Traditional algorithms are no longer effective in the context of the current proliferation of remote sensing image data and resolution, and the remote sensing image classification algorithm based on convolutional neural net-work architecture needs a significant amount of annotated datasets, and the creation of these training data is labor-intensive and time-consuming. Therefore, using a small sample dataset and a mix of transfer learning and data augmentation, this paper suggests a method for classifying remote sensing images. In this paper, the parameters from the Resnet50 model's pre-training on the Imagenet dataset are migrated to the Resnet50-TL model and ultimately classified using Log softmax. The NWPU-RESISC45 dataset is used in this study to train the model and for data Augmentation procedures. The experimental findings demonstrate that the ResNet50-TL model performs better than other popular network architectures currently in use. The model can classify objects with an accuracy of 96.11% using only 700 data points per class, resulting in a high accuracy rate in a limited amount of data. In the future, the dataset will be increased and the network architecture will be updated frequently to make remote sensing picture interpretation more intelligent and portable.

Keywords: ResNet50 · Image classification · Remote sensing imagery · Transfer learning · Data Augmentation

1 Introduction

Remote sensing image technology has advanced to a new level with the quickening pace of worldwide science and technology development, and China's remote sensing technology is also advancing. The accuracy of remote sensing pictures currently obtained in China has reached the sub-meter level. In addition to improving accuracy, remote sensing technology advancements have also resulted in a massive rise in data volume. A large number of details progressively emerge in the high-resolution remote sensing images, increasing their complexity, and statistics show that the number of these images grows at a terabyte level every

Z. Jin et al. (Eds.): KSEM 2023, LNAI 14120, pp. 99–111, 2023.
https://doi.org/10.1007/978-3-031-40292-0_9

day, and it is already challenging to manage such enormous and complex data using manual and machine learning interpretation techniques, leading to the development of efficient classifiers. High-performance methods for classifying and interpreting remote sensing images are therefore crucial for study [1].

The maximum likelihood method [2], the minimum distance method [3], K-means [4], and other traditional classification methods for remote sensing images have gradually lost accuracy as a result of the growth of data volume and image resolution, making it challenging to process these images effectively. Miller et al. used neural networks [5] to classify remote sensing images in 1995, expanding the area of machine learning. In 2011, Mountrakis used support vector ma-chines [6] to classify remote sensing images, demonstrating that machine learning algorithms based on image categorization can produce superior results to conventional statistical techniques. However, for sub-meter high-resolution images, the features that must be extracted and the expressions made up of the corresponding functions are more complex, and the shallow learning network only has a small number of computational units to effectively represent the complex functions. As a result, the shallow model gradually becomes unable to adapt to the complex samples as the number of samples and sample diversity increase. Deep learning networks, on the other hand, shine at complex classification thanks to their excellent features, including strong function representation and the capacity to extract high-level semantic features layer by layer, reflecting the intrinsic character of the data.

Since deep learning's rapid growth in 2010, the technology it represents has been gradually revealing its benefits. Deep learning is frequently used in remote sensing image analysis tasks [7], including scene classification [8], target detection [9], image fusion [10], and other uses. The image technology represented by convolutional neural network (CNN) [11] shows great advantages in scene classification and target detection. Compared with traditional machine learning algorithms and manual interpretation, CNN does not require manual processing of features, has high accuracy and strong generalization, and can mine deeper features to build an effective and accurate classification model, which solves the current problems in remote sensing image classification.

In recent years, a large number of CNN designs have emerged from convolutional neural networks. In 2012, Alex Krizhevsky et al. introduced Alexnet [12], which is the first deep learning computation on GPU and addresses the computational bottleneck of deep learning. Alexnet11 has a deeper network than Lenet and adds a dropout layer and activation function Relu. To create a very deep network, the Visual Geometry Group at Oxford University suggested VGG [13] in 2014. This innovation had a significant influence on the design of later CNN architectures. In 2014, Christian Szegedy et al. proposed the Googlenet [14] network, which is based on Inception modules. It addresses the issue of overfitting in deeper networks by superimposing multiple Inception modules and creates a sparse, high-performance network structure by integrating the processing of various filters. By introducing the design of residual blocks, the Resnet [15] network, proposed by Kaiming He et al. in 2015, greatly eliminated the issue of network degradation brought on by too many layers of the network. As a result, the "depth" of the neural network was able to surpass 100 layers for the first time, and the largest neural network even exceeded 1000 layers. However, since neural networks frequently have tens or even hundreds of layers, a lot of datasets are required for training, and most of the time, these datasets must be manually labeled. As a result, the focus of current research is on finding small sample datasets to train high-precision models [16]..Additionally, the data augmentation operation can create data actively to increase the dataset and aid in training the model using small batch samples, allowing the model to learn more details and features about the picture. In 2020, Shawky O. A. et al. suggested combining data augmentation and CNN, and they had success with remote sensing picture classification tasks [17].

Nowadays, using Transfer learning [18] to train on datasets has become the choice of many. Many pre-trained models can be used for prediction using Transfer learning, which can maximize training time, reduce model overfitting, and still have good accuracy in the case of small samples. The majority of commonly used CNN models have already trained weights on the dataset ImageNet.

To improve the accuracy of remote sensing image classification and reduce the workload of manual annotation of datasets, this paper proposes a Transfer learning model with ResNet50 as the architecture for the development characteristics of remote sensing images [19], combining deep learning techniques to obtain pre-trained models through Transfer learning, and adding a fully connected layer behind the ResNet50 network to fine-tune the model for the dataset, so as to achieve deep feature extraction of remote sensing images and obtain high prediction accuracy under the background of a small batch of data. This study also compares and contrasts experimental data from the VGG and Denesnet models, demonstrating that Resnet has the benefit of accuracy in this classification of species.

2   The Resnet50 Model Based on Transfer Learning

2.1   Analysis of the ResNet50 Model

As the neural network architecture becomes deeper and deeper, from a few layers at the beginning to more than 100 layers at present, we begin to find that as the network gets deeper and deeper, it will lead to a decline in accuracy, that is, the network degradation problem and the ResNet (residual neural network) pro-posed by Kai-Ming. His team at Microsoft Research solves this problem, the net-work uses the residual function to achieve a constant mapping, avoiding accuracy degradation. avoiding the degradation of accuracy.

The ResNet network structure is mainly composed of numerous residual blocks. As shown in Fig. 1, each residual block consists of two weight layers and a ReLu activation function.

ResNet residual block uses to provide a short circuit connection x to make the output become (f(x)-x)+x,where x is the output of the previous layer, f(x) is the total output of the residual block, (f(x)-x) is the output of x through the network.

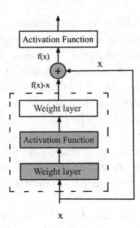

Fig. 1. ResNet residual blocks.

In this case if the network layer is too deep, resulting in a very small output f(x)-x when x enters the network, this will cause the gradient to disappear and thus lead to a loss of accuracy. The model uses a residual block in order to output (f(x)-x) + x after the residual block. Even though f(x)-x is very small, adding x is equivalent to the output of the previous layer, which avoids the disappearance of the gradient of the current layer and thus helps the neural network to become deeper without loss of accuracy.

The output of the fully-connected layer of the original ResNet50 model is a feature dimension vector of 1000, and since there are five classifiers in this case, a Log softmax classifier is added after the fully-connected layer to classify the output to complete our multi-classification task.

2.2 Log Softmax Classifier

To achieve the final output classification in this study, we add a fully connected layer and a Log softmax classifier at the end of the ResNet network. Log softmax will accept the feature matrix returned from the fully connected layer and obtain the probability value of each category by operation, and finally, the model outputs the classification results. In this paper, we classify five remote sensing images, where we are provided with M inputs (x_i, y_i), where x_i(i=1, 2, 3, 4, 5) is the output of the fully connected layer and y_i(i=1, 2, 3, 4, 5) is the corresponding category. i is the category of the output, our paper K is 5, K is the target number of categories, let the function $f(x_i)$ output the probability value of the category corresponding to each input as $P(y_i = j|x_i)$, the function is as follows:

$$f(x_i) = \begin{pmatrix} p(y_i = 1 \mid x_i) \\ p(y_i = 2 \mid x_i) \\ M \\ p(y_i = k \mid x_i) \end{pmatrix} = \frac{1}{\sum_{i=1}^{k} e^{x_i}} \begin{pmatrix} e^{x_i} \\ e^{x_i} \\ M \\ e^{x_i} \end{pmatrix} \tag{1}$$

Compared with ordinary softmax, Log softmax will penalize larger errors in the likelihood space more highly, and the computation process is smoother without overflow problems due to too large or too small x_i. The function is as follows:

$$
\begin{aligned}
\log_e [f(x_i)] &= \log_e \left(\frac{e^{x_i}}{e^{x_1} + e^{x_2} + L + e^{x_n}} \right) \\
&= \log_e \left(\frac{e^{(x_i - M)}}{\sum_j^n e^{(x_j - M)}} \right) \\
&= \log_e \left(e^{(x_i - M)} \right) - \log_e \left(\sum_j^n e^{(x_j - M)} \right) \\
&= (x_i - M) - \boxed{\log_e \left(\sum_j^n e^{(x_j - M)} \right)}
\end{aligned}
\tag{2}
$$

where M is the maximum of the input x_i. When x_i is a positive number, $x_i - M$ is always less than 0; when $x_i - M$ is a very large negative value, there must be an $x_i - M = 0$. This ensures that the result of the formula in the black box is equal to $log_e(x)$, where $x_i > 1$ is not a very large number, so that the problem of underflow is solved.

While in the image classification task, the values keep changing in the deep network may lead to too large or too small feature matrices in the final output, thus leading to errors in the softmax classifier, and the Log softmax classifier solves this situation by logarithmic operations, which can speed up the operation and improve data stability.

2.3 Classification Methods of Transfer Learning Models

Transfer learning is the transfer of knowledge from a model that has been trained and learned on other similar data sets to an existing problem to help solve the problem, where the most critical aspect is the transfer of knowledge, where the knowledge gained from training on other tasks is used to develop models for new tasks. [20]

Knowledge transfer between the source domain X and the target domain Y is really the foundation of transfer learning. When X≠Y and T1≠T2, the source domain X's knowledge of the task T1 solved is used to assist the target domain Y in solving the task T2.

This paper will examine how to train ResNet50 on small batch samples using Transfer [21] learning and apply it to remote sensing image classification in order to lessen the dependence of convolutional neural networks on datasets and to obtain models with higher accuracy.

2.4 Data Augmentation

Data augmentation is a method to fictitiously increase the amount of data by generating new data from existing data, as convolutional neural network (CNN) require a large data set for training and CNN are not well trained with small sample sizes. This involves conducting operations linked to image fusion as well as making minor changes to the data, such as flipping, cropping, changing the color, etc., or creating new data using deep learning models. The enhanced data sets have more features, allowing the model to extract features and magnify feature points more effectively. This enhances the deep learning model's performance and output [22].

The findings of the remote sensing images vary depending on the spectral range and contain complex data information. The model can adapt to remote sensing images with various resolutions and spectra by adding data augmentation operations, which can increase the accuracy of image classification.

2.5   ResNet50-TL

The block diagram of this study model is shown in Fig. 2.

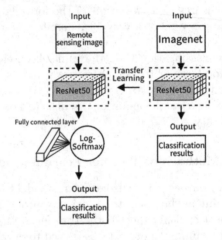

Fig. 2. Block diagram of ResNet50-TL model.

As the feature extraction layer of this model, we first take the pre-training model, which is the ResNet50 model trained on ImageNet. After that, we move the trained ResNet50 model's parameters to our ResNet50-TL model so that our model can pick up information from the previously trained large model. Finally, we add the fully connected layer and log softmax for classification after the neural network layer, and the output result is the ResNet50-TL model used in this experiment.

In order to maximize the knowledge and performance gained from Transfer learning, we first freeze the pre-trained layers during the training process. This prevents them from back propagating during the following training period. In order to obtain its own fully connected layer parameters and subsequently classify the dataset, we redefine the final fully connected layer and train it using our image dataset.

2.6 Evaluation Metrics

Accuracy was used to assess the outcomes of this experiment, where Accuracy is the proportion of correctly predicted outcomes across all samples.

$$Accuracy = \frac{number\ of\ correctly\ classified\ samples}{total\ number\ of\ samples} \quad (3)$$

We are able to determine the accurate rate of image classification using this evaluation metric.

3 Model Training and Validation

3.1 Experimental Dataset

The remote sensing image scene classification (RESISC) dataset used in this study is the NWPU-RESISC45 [23] dataset, which was produced by Northwestern Polytechnic University (NWPU). The dataset has a total of 403.74 MB in size and includes 31,500 images with 256*256 pixel resolution, 700 images per class. 45 scene classes are addressed, The 45 scene categories include aircraft, airports, baseball fields, basketball courts, beaches, bridges, jungles, etc. In terms of the quantity of images and the variety of classifications, the NWPU-RESISC45 dataset is one of the most intricate and significant remote sensing scene datasets. The data examples are shown in Fig. 3 below.

Fig. 3. Image of the dataset.

The aircraft, bridge, palace, building, and arena are chosen in this experiment. Additionally, the data set is split into three categories: the training set (70%), the confirmation set (10%), and the test set (20%).

Additionally, the RSSCN7 dataset, which consists of seven different categories of remote sensing photographs and 400 images in each category, was donated by Wuhan University in 2015 and is used in this study to assess how well the model performs when tested against other datasets.

3.2   Data Pre-processing

The experiments in this article were carried out using the pytorch-1.11.0 environment and jupyternotebook. Once we had the dataset, we used PyTorch's Image-Folder to import the images and resize them all to 254*254 before performing image Augmentation procedures on the dataset. After performing RandomResizedCrop and RandomHorizontalFlip, the data is finally converted to Tensor format.

3.3   Image Data Augmentation and Feature Extraction Figure

The deeper network levels and increased feature extraction of the Resnet network are one of its benefits. Under the assumption of small batch samples, this research conducts data Augmentation on the original dataset by cutting, cropping, flipping, changing the color of the data, and other operations to improve the dataset and assist the model in extracting more features. Figure 4 depicts the picture after a color change. Figure 5 shows the image with random flipping and cropping.

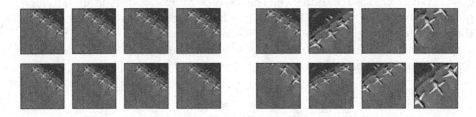

Fig. 4. Data augmentation image 1.   **Fig. 5.** Data augmentation image 2.

As can be seen, data augmentation procedures significantly increase the dataset, enabling the model to extract more features.

Based on the data Augmentation operation, this experiment employs ResNet50 to extract the image texture and shape features. After network computation, the feature map is visualized, and Fig. 5 shows that the features extracted by the network ignore the background and other redundant factors and only extract the essential information.

Figure 6 displays the outcomes of the second layer of convolutional rendering. Figure 7 displays the outcomes of the second convolutional layer's rendering component.

As can be seen, as the network's layer count rises, the shallow convolutional layer's feature information remains comparatively rich and the feature data is fairly similar to the original picture data. But as the number of layers increases, the obtained characteristics become less and less useful and more and more abstract. This is so because, while the deeper convolutional kernel begins to extract features like lines and edges, the shallower convolutional kernel prefers to learn basic features like points and colors. The learned characteristics become more precise and abstract as the layers are added to.

Fig. 6. Second layer feature map.   **Fig. 7.** Fifth layer feature map.

3.4 Training and Testing of Remote Sensing Picture Classifier Models

The pre-trained Resnet50 network architecture in Torchvision, which was trained on the imagenet competition dataset, is used in this exercise. We added a fully connected layer and a pooling layer to the end of the network design and set the number of outputs to 5 to create a classifier for remote sensing images. The original resnet50 parameters were then adjusted in accordance with the dataset's features.

The loss function used in this experiment in the model training is NLLLoss, the parameters are set as follows while the optimizer is used to Adam: Learning Rate = 0.03, Epochs = 10 and Batch size = 256.

The dataset is first trained without the Transfer learning model and Data Augmentation, and the findings are as Table 1 follows.

Table 1. Accuracy under no Transfer learning.

Model	Accuracy
SVM	72.23%
Alexnet	80.03%
VGG16	83.12%
GOOGleNet	90.21%
Denesnet121	91.03%
ResNet50	91.54%

Then we add the data augmentation operation to get the Table 2 result.

Table 2. Precision after Data Augmentation.

Data Augmentation Operation	Accuracy
Alexnet	83.13%
VGG16	85.33%
GOOGleNet	92.29%
Denesnet121	93.63%
ResNet50	93.74%

You can see that the data augmentation has improved the overall accuracy of the model. And the deep learning model has higher accuracy compared to the traditional machine learning model SVM.

For experimental comparison, we simultaneously trained VGG, SVM, and Denesnet using the Transfer learning model. The training set and test set errors are displayed in Table 3.

Table 3. Precision after Transfer learning.

Model	Accuracy
Alexnet	89.21%
VGG16	91.34%
GOOGleNet	93.06%
Denesnet121	94.71%
ResNet50	96.11%

It is clear that transfer learning has a significant positive impact on these models' accuracy, and by gaining knowledge of the source domain, the models are able to perform better in classification tasks even with small batch sizes.

And from among them, we have selected the ResNet50 architecture. Compared to other existing models, ResNet50-Tl model accuracy is more accurate than the conventional algorithm. It also runs more quickly and has a superior ability to extract features.

We also execute the code both before and after fine-tuning, and both times the accuracy is approximately 94% before and 96% after. The best accuracy was 96% with a learning rate of 0.03 after we tried the ac-curacy at various learning rates. Then, we evaluated the accuracy using various batch sizes and epochs, and the best accuracy was obtained with batch sizes of 256 and 10 respectively. The overall accuracy varied by about 3%. The accuracy varies by about 3% overall,and the findings are as Table 4 follows.

Table 4. Accuracy at different hyperparameters.

Learning Rate	Epochs	Batch size	Accuracy
0.03	10	256	96.11%
0.03	12	128	96.01%
0.03	8	64	93.22%
0.10	10	256	95.45%
0.10	12	128	95.44%
0.10	8	64	93.01%
0.07	10	256	95.18%
0.07	12	128	94.64%
0.07	8	64	93.22%

And we can see that changing hyperparameters like learning rate has little effect on the model. Ultimately, we select the collection of hyperparameters that has the highest accuracy.

We validated the experiments using the RSSCN7 dataset and only 400 photos per class, achieving 93.14% classification accuracy using the ResNet50 model. This was done to further confirm the validity of the experiments. This model's great accuracy in classifying images with few samples is further demonstrated.

In conclusion, Transfer learning based on the neural network achieved under the training of small batch samples gives the Resnet network a greater advantage in remote sensing image classification tasks. At the same time, Transfer learning based on the neural network is also able to have high accuracy under these conditions.

4 Conclusion

In light of the current rapid growth in the quantity and resolution of remote sensing data, this paper proposes a method of remote sensing image classification based on the combination of transfer learning and data augmentation. It does this by transferring the parameters obtained from the pre-training of the ResNet50 network on Imagenet to the ResNet50-Tl model, which significantly enhances the feature extraction ability and makes the model more general. The network's over-all accuracy eventually reaches about 96%, which is a significant improvement compared to other models, after the fully connected layer and Log softmax classifier are added to the network's back. This is followed by a data augmentation operation on a real dataset and the training prediction.By using transfer learning and data augmentation, this experiment accomplishes the classification of high-precision remote sensing images with small batch samples, thereby reducing the workload associated with manually labeling the dataset and achieving a high degree of accuracy. The number of network layers will be increased, more remote sensing image dataset types added, the accuracy and robustness of the model improved, high-precision and low-cost remote sensing image classification sought after, and the speed of light weight and intelligence of remote sensing image interpretation work accelerated in the ensuing research.

References

1. Zhu, X.X., et al.: Deep learning in remote sensing: a comprehensive review and list of resources. IEEE Geosci. Remote Sens. Mag. 5(4), 8–36 (2017)
2. Strahler, A.H.: The use of prior probabilities in maximum likelihood classification of remotely sensed data. Remote Sens. Environ. 10(2), 135–163 (1980)
3. Wacker, A., Landgrebe, D.: Minimum distance classification in remote sensing. LARS Technical Reports, p. 25 (1972)
4. Lv, Z., Hu, Y., Zhong, H., Wu, J., Li, B., Zhao, H.: Parallel K-means clustering of remote sensing images based on mapReduce. In: Wang, F.L., Gong, Z., Luo, X., Lei, J. (eds.) WISM 2010. LNCS, vol. 6318, pp. 162–170. Springer, Heidelberg (2010). https://doi.org/10.1007/978-3-642-16515-3_21
5. Miller, D.M., Kaminsky, E.J., Rana, S.: Neural network classification of remote-sensing data. Comput. Geosci. 21(3), 377–386 (1995)
6. Mountrakis, G., Im, J., Ogole, C.: Support vector machines in remote sensing: a review. ISPRS J. Photogramm. Remote. Sens. 66(3), 247–259 (2011)
7. Ma, L., Liu, Y., Zhang, X., Ye, Y., Yin, G., Johnson, B.A.: Deep learning in remote sensing applications: a meta-analysis and review. ISPRS J. Photogramm. Remote. Sens. 152, 166–177 (2019)
8. Zou, Q., Ni, L., Zhang, T., Wang, Q.: Deep learning based feature selection for remote sensing scene classification. IEEE Geosci. Remote Sens. Lett. 12(11), 2321–2325 (2015)
9. Chang, C.I., Heinz, D.C.: Constrained subpixel target detection for remotely sensed imagery. IEEE Trans. Geosci. Remote Sens. 38(3), 1144–1159 (2000)
10. Liu, Y., Chen, X., Wang, Z., Wang, Z.J., Ward, R.K., Wang, X.: Deep learning for pixel-level image fusion: recent advances and future prospects. Information Fusion 42, 158–173 (2018)
11. Zhang, W., Tang, P., Zhao, L.: Remote sensing image scene classification using CNN-CapsNet. Remote Sens. 11(5), 494 (2019)
12. Krizhevsky, A., Sutskever, I., Hinton, G.E.: ImageNet classification with deep convolutional neural networks. Commun. ACM 60(6), 84–90 (2017)
13. Simonyan, K., Zisserman, A.: Very deep convolutional networks for large-scale image recognition. arXiv preprint arXiv:1409.1556 (2014)
14. Szegedy, C., et al.: Going deeper with convolutions. In: Proceedings of the IEEE Conference on Computer Vision and Pattern Recognition, pp. 1–9 (2015)
15. He, K., Zhang, X., Ren, S., Sun, J.: Deep residual learning for image recognition. In: Proceedings of the IEEE Conference on Computer Vision and Pattern Recognition, pp. 770–778 (2016)
16. Zhang, H., Liu, Y., Fang, B., Li, Y., Liu, L., Reid, I.: Hyperspectral classification based on 3D asymmetric inception network with data fusion transfer learning. arXiv preprint arXiv:2002.04227 (2020)
17. Shawky, O.A., Hagag, A., El-Dahshan, E.S.A., Ismail, M.A.: Remote sensing image scene classification using CNN-MLP with data augmentation. Optik 221, 165356 (2020)

18. Alem, A., Kumar, S.: Transfer learning models for land cover and land use classification in remote sensing image. Appl. Artif. Intell. **36**(1), 2014192 (2022)
19. Shabbir, A., et al.: Satellite and scene image classification based on transfer learning and fine tuning of resnet50. Math. Probl. Eng. **2021**, 1–18 (2021)
20. Zhang, D., Liu, Z., Shi, X.: Transfer learning on efficientNet for remote sensing image classification. In: 2020 5th International Conference on Mechanical, Control and Computer Engineering (ICMCCE), pp. 2255–2258. IEEE (2020)
21. Xie, M., Jean, N., Burke, M., Lobell, D., Ermon, S.: Transfer learning from deep features for remote sensing and poverty mapping. In: Proceedings of the AAAI Conference on Artificial Intelligence, vol. 30 (2016)
22. Lv, N., et al.: Remote sensing data augmentation through adversarial training. IEEE J. Select. Top. Appl. Earth Observ. Remote Sens. **14**, 9318–9333 (2021)
23. Cheng, G., Han, J., Lu, X.: Remote sensing image scene classification: benchmark and state of the art. Proc. IEEE **105**(10), 1865–1883 (2017)

Multivariate Long-Term Traffic Forecasting with Graph Convolutional Network and Historical Attention Mechanism

Zhaohuan Wang⑩, Yi Xu⑩, Liangzhe Han⑩, Tongyu Zhu$^{(\boxtimes)}$⑩, and Leilei Sun⑩

State Key Laboratory of Software Development Environment, Beihang University, Beijing 100191, China
{zy2106134,xuyee,liangzhehan,zhutongyu,leileisun}@buaa.edu.cn

Abstract. Due to the complexity of the traffic system and the constantly changing characteristics of many influencing factors, long-term traffic forecasting is extremely challenging. Many existing methods based on deep learning perform well in short-term prediction, but do not perform well in Long-Term Time Series Forecasting (LTSF) tasks. These existing methods are difficult to capture the dependencies of long-term temporal sequences. To overcome these limitations, this paper introduces a new graph neural network architecture for spatial-temporal graph modeling. By using simple graph convolutional networks and developing novel spatial-temporal adaptive dependency matrices, our model can capture the hidden spatial-temporal internal dependency in the data. At the same time, we add external dependency to the model. We utilize the periodicity between long-term time series and historical data and introduce a Historical Attention Mechanism to capture historical dependencies in combination with historical data, which can expand the receptive field of the model from local relationships to historical relationships to help improve the prediction accuracy and avoid the problem of too long sequence and too much useless information caused by taking the entire historical sequence as input. Experimental results on two public traffic datasets, NYC-TLC and England-Highways, demonstrate the superior performance of our method.

Keywords: Traffic Forecasting · Deep Learning · Long-Term Time Series Forecasting · Graph Convolutional Network · Historical Attention Mechanism

1 Introduction

Traffic forecasting has mostly belonged to the category of multivariate time series prediction. There are various prediction methods in the academic community for the prediction of multivariate time series related to traffic forecasting.

Z. Jin et al. (Eds.): KSEM 2023, LNAI 14120, pp. 112–123, 2023.
https://doi.org/10.1007/978-3-031-40292-0_10

Statistical methods, such as Historical Average model (HA) and Vector Auto-Regressive model (VAR) [5], assume that there is a linear dependency between variables. The model complexity of statistical methods rapidly increases with the increase of the number of variables, and faces the limitation to handle a large number of variables. Recently developed methods based on deep learning such as DCRNN [6] and Graph WaveNet [11], have achieved relatively excellent results in the prediction of short-term time series. For the prediction of short-term time series, it mainly focuses on predicting the information in the next few minutes or hours. There are a lot of existing theoretical research in academia such as TCN(Temporal Convolutional Network) [1].

For the Long-Term Time Series Forecasting (LTSF) task, it mainly focuses on forecasting the information in the next few days or even weeks. There are few existing theoretical studies in academia. However, LTSF task has a wide range of practical applications. For example, the weekend traffic flow will be significantly different from the weekday traffic flow, resulting in the inability to predict the weekend traffic flow through short-term traffic conditions; Short-term forecast requires real-time data, while for long-term forecast such as holiday forecast, there is no real-time data to support the forecast when it needs to forecast the next holiday traffic for a period of time (such as a week) in advance.

Therefore, this paper will focus on the Long-Term Time Series Forecasting (LTSF) task, build a model named GCN-HAM, based on long-term spatial-temporal dependencies, introduce a Temporal Graph Convolutional Network for temporal processing and name it Temporal GCN, and introduce a Spatial Graph Convolutional Network for spatial processing and name it Spatial GCN. We also introduce a Historical Attention Mechanism to capture longer term historical dependencies, which has achieved good results on multiple traffic datasets.

The contributions of our work include:

- A Temporal Graph Convolutional Network is introduced to process long-term time series to capture temporal dependencies, which is based on the characteristic that long-term time series have internal periodicity.
- A completely new Historical Attention Mechanism is introduced to leverage the historical periodicity of long-term time series. By introducing similar historical series, the model integrates the information of historical series and current series, captures the external characteristics of time series, and expands the receptive field of the model from local relationships to overall historical relationships.
- Extensive experiments are conducted to compare and verify the effectiveness of Temporal GCN, Spatial GCN and Historical Attention Mechanism. The findings will benefit future research in the field of LTSF tasks.

2   Related Work

2.1   Traditional Time Series Forecasting

Time series prediction has a long history, and most traditional methods follow statistical methods. The Historical Average (HA) is a simple algorithm, which models the traffic flow as a seasonal process, and uses the weighted average of previous seasons as the prediction. The Auto-Regressive Integrated Moving Average (ARIMA) [2] summarizes a series of linear models, including Auto-Regressive (AR), Moving Average (MA) and Auto-Regressive Moving Average (ARMA). The Vector Auto-Regressive model (VAR) [5] extends the AR model to capture the linear correlation between multiple time series.

Although statistical models are widely used in time series prediction because of their simplicity, they make strong assumptions about stationary processes and cannot be well extended to multivariate time series data. The method based on deep learning is not affected by fixed assumptions, and is an effective method to capture the nonlinear interaction between multiple variables. In the early days, the Recurrent Neural Network (RNN) model was often used to model the time correlation of time series.

2.2   Multivariate Spatial-Temporal Short-Term Series Forecasting

For traffic flow prediction, it is a spatial-temporal task, with complex spatial and temporal dependencies as its challenges. The prediction of multivariate time series involves not only considered temporal relationships, but also spatial relationships between road segments or areas. Due to the popularity of graph convolution and its combination with road network structure, graph convolutional network has achieved good results in the application of traffic forecasting. Some LSTM-based models [4,7,12] and TCN-based models [10,11] simultaneously consider spatial dependencies and achieve good results on Short-Term Time Series Forecasting (STSF) tasks.

2.3   Multivariate Long-Term Time Series Forecasting

Compared to the Short-Term Time Series Forecasting (STSF) task, the Long-Term Time Series Forecasting (LTSF) task has a significant feature of longer time series and more input information. This characteristic has caused poor performance of TCN [1] in time series processing. Because TCN only focuses on local temporal relationships, when the model is transferred from an STSF task that requires less memory to an LTSF task that requires more memory, TCN may perform poorly because its receptive field is not large enough.

In recent years, a large number of Transformer-based [9] methods have also emerged in time series analysis. Most famous models focus on the less explored and challenging LTSF tasks, including Informer [13], FEDformer [14], and so on. The main capability of Transformer comes from its self-attention mechanism, which has the significant ability to extract semantic correlations between long sequence elements. However, to some extent, self-attention computing is permutation invariant and "anti-order". For time series analysis, numerical data itself often lacks semantics, and our main interest is to model the temporal changes among a continuous set of points, with the order itself often playing the most crucial role. Therefore, it is not difficult to doubt whether the Transformer-based model is truly effective in handling LTSF tasks.

3 Methodology

In this section, we first give the mathematical definition of the problem we are addressing in this paper. Next, we introduce a Historical Attention Mechanism, which is used to extract the historical dependency of long-term time series. Before that, we also have a Similarity Selection Module, which is mainly used to select some sequences more similar to the input sequence from the historical sequence, and input them into the Historical Attention Mechanism as Key and Value. Then we introduce two building blocks, the Temporal Graph Convolutional Network (Temporal GCN) and Spatial Graph Convolutional Network (Spatial GCN). They work together to capture the spatial-temporal dependencies. Finally, we outline the architecture of our framework. We present the framework of our model in Fig. 1.

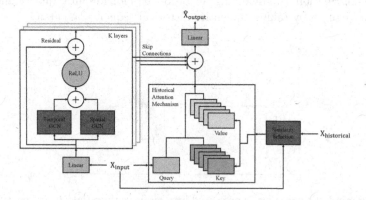

Fig. 1. The framework of GCN-HAM. It consists of K spatial-temporal layers and a Historical Attention Mechanism.

3.1 Problem Definition

For a long-term time series containing N variables, our task is to forecast future data $\widehat{\mathbf{X}}_{output} = \{\widehat{X}_1^t, ..., \widehat{X}_N^t\}_{t=h+L+1}^{h+L+T}$ based on input data $\mathbf{X}_{input} = \{X_1^t, ..., X_N^t\}_{t=h+1}^{h+L}$ and historical data $\mathbf{X}_{historical} = \{X_1^t, ..., X_N^t\}_{t=1}^{h}$, where X_i^t represents the value of the variable i in the time step t, and L and T are the length of historical time series and the length of future time series, and h is the end of the historical sequence. The mapping relation is represented as follows:

$$[\mathbf{X}^{1:h}, \mathbf{X}^{(h+1):(h+L)}] \xrightarrow{f} \widehat{\mathbf{X}}^{(h+L+1):(h+L+T)}, \tag{1}$$

where $\mathbf{X}^{1:h}$ represents $\mathbf{X}_{historical} = \{X_1^t, ..., X_N^t\}_{t=1}^{h}$ and $\mathbf{X}^{(h+1):(h+L)}$ represents $\mathbf{X}_{input} = \{X_1^t, ..., X_N^t\}_{t=h+1}^{h+L}$ and $\widehat{\mathbf{X}}^{(h+L+1):(h+L+T)}$ represents $\widehat{\mathbf{X}}_{output} = \{\widehat{X}_1^t, ..., \widehat{X}_N^t\}_{t=h+L+1}^{h+L+T}$.

3.2 Historical Attention Mechanism

The purpose of designing the Historical Attention Mechanism is to integrate the historical sequence and the current sequence information, in order to better capture the external characteristics of the sequence. For LTSF tasks, there is not only periodicity inside, but also periodicity between the current time series and the historical time series outside. For example, the New Year's Day holiday of a year will have a stronger similarity with the time series of the New Year's Day holiday of last year, while it will have a weaker similarity with other time series of the same length. This periodicity or similarity will become more obvious when the historical time series is longer. Figure 2 shows the similarity of time series. Therefore, this paper will introduce the Historical Attention Mechanism, slice the length of a certain period of time series, calculate the similarity according to the historical periodicity, and select the more noteworthy historical sequence information, thus avoiding the problem of long input sequence and high complexity caused by taking the entire historical sequence as input.

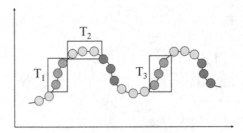

Fig. 2. A period of time series, represented by a circle as timesteps. It can be seen that the similarity between T_1 and T_3 is significantly higher than that between T_1 and T_2.

Before introducing the Historical Attention Mechanism, we will introduce a Similarity Selection Module to select some sequences similar to the input sequence from the historical sequence and input them into the Historical Attention Mechanism as Key and Value. There are many methods for calculating the similarity between two time series, and in this paper we use cosine similarity. Given two time series $P = (x_1, x_2, ..., x_n)$, $Q = (y_1, y_2, ..., y_n)$, the cosine similarity is as follows:

$$D_{cos}(P,Q) = \frac{\sum_{i=1}^{n} x_i y_i}{\sqrt{\sum_{i=1}^{n} x_i^2} \sqrt{\sum_{i=1}^{n} y_i^2}},
\tag{2}$$

where Fig. 3 shows the procedure of the Similarity Selection Module.

After selecting K most similar sequences of the current sequence, how to aggregate them for prediction is also important. As the importance of these sequences may be slightly different to the current prediction, an attention-based module is designed to aggregate them. Specifically, the embedding vector of

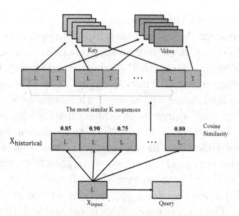

Fig. 3. The illustration of the Similarity Selection Module. After inputting the historical sequence into this module, Key and Value will be generated by calculating similarity.

time period $\mathbf{X}^{(t+1):(t+L)}$ is represented as $\mathbf{e}^t \in \mathbb{R}^D$ where $D = N \times L$. Taking the current time series $\mathbf{X}_{input}$ which means $\mathbf{X}^{(t+1):(t+L)}$ as the Query, the K most similar historical time series $\mathbf{X}^{(t_i+1):(t_i+L)}(i = 1, ..., K$ and $L \mid (t - t_i))$ in $\mathbf{X}_{historical}$ as the Key by calculating similarity and the future time series $\mathbf{X}^{(t_i+L+1):(t_i+L+T)}(i = 1, ..., K)$ of the subsequent T time steps of the above-mentioned K historical time series as the Value, so the correlation between time t and t_i is defined as:

$$\lambda_{t,t_i} = \frac{< \mathbf{e}^t, \mathbf{e}^{t_i} >}{\sqrt{D}}, \tag{3}$$

$$\alpha_{t,t_i} = \frac{exp(\lambda_{t,t_i})}{\sum_{i=1}^{K} exp(\lambda_{t,t_i})}, \tag{4}$$

where λ_{t,t_i} denotes the relevance between time step t and t_i, α_{t,t_i} is the attention score indicating the importance of time step t to t_i. Once the attention score is obtained, the state of embedding vectors e^t at time step t_i is updated as follows:

$$\widehat{\mathbf{X}}_{att} = \tilde{\mathbf{e}}^t = \sum_{i=1}^{K} \alpha_{t,t_i} \cdot (W_{t,t_i} \mathbf{e}^{t_i+L}), \tag{5}$$

where $\widehat{\mathbf{X}}_{att}$ is a four-dimension tensor with size [B,T,N,1].

3.3   Temporal Graph Convolutional Network

For LTSF tasks, our model did not adopt TCN-based or Transformer-based models, but innovatively introduced a simple graph convolutional network to handle temporal relationships. This is because long-term time series have certain internal patterns such as time periodicity. We name this graph convolutional network used to handle temporal relationships as Temporal GCN, which has good performance in terms of both performance and runtime.

In this section, we views time steps as nodes on graphs and propose a self-adaptive adjacency matrix $\mathbf{A}^T$ to handle temporal dependencies. This adaptive adjacency matrix does not need any prior knowledge and can be learned by stochastic gradient descent. Through the adaptive adjacency matrix, the model can find the connection between time steps by itself. The adaptive matrix is realized by randomly initializing two nodes with learnable parameters $\mathbf{E}_1^T, \mathbf{E}_2^T \in \mathbb{R}^{T \times c}$. We name $\mathbf{E}_1^T$ as the source node embedding and $\mathbf{E}_2^T$ as the target node embedding. $\mathbf{E}_1^T$ and $\mathbf{E}_2^T$ are used to represent the c-dimensional characteristics of T nodes as different time slices in the temporal dimension. By multiplying $\mathbf{E}_1^T$ and $\mathbf{E}_2^T$, we derive the temporal dependency weights between the source nodes and the target nodes. ReLU is to remove the values close to 0 in the adjacency matrix, which is to remove the weak connections in the graph and reduce the training parameters. Then a normalization is carried out through Softmax, so that the adaptive adjacency matrix can be regarded as the transfer matrix of the diffusion process. The generation method of adaptive adjacency matrix is as follows:

$$\mathbf{A}^T = Softmax(ReLU(\mathbf{E}_1^T \mathbf{E}_2^{T\top})), \mathbf{E}_1^T, \mathbf{E}_2^T \in \mathbb{R}^{T \times c}, \tag{6}$$

We use J finite steps diffusion convolution [6] to simulate the diffusion process of graphic signals, and conduct temporal modeling in a way of diffusion convolution layer. Therefore, the temporal dependency of Temporal GCN module obtained in this paper is:

$$\mathbf{H}^T = \sum_{j=0}^{J} \mathbf{A}_j^T \mathbf{X} \mathbf{W}_j^T, \tag{7}$$

where $\mathbf{X}$ is the $\mathbf{X}_{input}$ that has passed through a linear layer, $\mathbf{W}_j^T$ is parameters for depth j and J is max diffusion steps.

3.4   Spatial Graph Convolutional Network

For LTSF tasks, we also used a simple graph convolutional network to handle spatial relationships. Similarity, we propose a self-adaptive adjacency matrix $\mathbf{A}^N$ to handle spatial relationships, and we also have $\mathbf{E}_1^N$ as the source node embedding and $\mathbf{E}_2^N$ as the target node embedding to represent the c-dimensional characteristics of N nodes as different stations in the spatial dimension. We can obtain spatial dependency weights between the source nodes and the target nodes by multiplying $\mathbf{E}_1^N$ and $\mathbf{E}_2^N$. We name this method of using self-adaptive adjacency matrix to learn spatial relations Spatial GCN.

Spatial GCN and Temporal GCN have the same input but the self-adaptive adjacency matrix is different, corresponding to spatial dependence and temporal dependence respectively. Therefore, similarly we have:

$$\mathbf{A}^N = Softmax(ReLU(\mathbf{E}_1^N \mathbf{E}_2^{N\top})), \mathbf{E}_1^N, \mathbf{E}_2^N \in \mathbb{R}^{N \times c} \tag{8}$$

and

$$\mathbf{H}^N = \sum_{j=0}^{J} \mathbf{A}_j^N \mathbf{X} \mathbf{W}_j^N, \tag{9}$$

where $\mathbf{X}$ is the $\mathbf{X}_{input}$ that has passed through a linear layer, $\mathbf{W}_j^N$ is parameters for depth j and J is max diffusion steps.

3.5 Framework

We present the framework of our model in Fig. 1. It consists of stacked K spatial-temporal layers and a Historical Attention Mechanism. A spatial-temporal layer is constructed by a Spatial Graph Convolutional Network (Spatial GCN) and a Temporal Graph Convolutional Network (Temporal GCN) which respectively deal with the spatial-temporal relationship of the sequence. By stacking multiple spatial-temporal layers, our model can handle spatial-temporal dependencies at different levels. For each layer k, we have aggregated hidden states $\mathbf{H}_k^T$ and $\mathbf{H}_k^N$ and added residual links:

$$\mathbf{H}_k = ReLU(\mathbf{H}_k^T + \mathbf{H}_k^N) + \mathbf{H}_{k-1}, \qquad (10)$$

where $\mathbf{H}_0$ is the $\mathbf{X}_{input}$ that has passed through a linear layer. Moreover, skip-connection is added for spatial-temporal layers. Skip-connection $\mathbf{H}$ is a four-dimension tensor with size [B,C,N,L] as follows:

$$\mathbf{H} = ||_{k=1}^K reshape(\mathbf{H}_k), \qquad (11)$$

where $||$ is the concatenation operation, reshape($\cdot$) is the function to reshape hidden layer $\mathbf{H}_k$ for concatenation. The output $\widehat{\mathbf{X}}_{s-t}$ of spatial-temporal layers is a four-dimension tensor with size [B,T,N,1], which can be obtained by passing $\mathbf{H}$ through a series of linear layers [B,C,N,L] $\rightarrow$ [B,C $\times$ L,N,1] $\rightarrow$ [B,T,N,1].

The Historical Attention Mechanism is mainly used to fuse the information of the historical sequence and the current sequence. By introducing the concept of similarity, we can obtain the periodicity between the current sequence and the historical sequence over a long period of time, thereby obtaining the external dependencies of the current sequence. The final output of the model can be obtained by weighting the output $\widehat{\mathbf{X}}_{s-t}$ of the stacked spatial-temporal layers and the output $\widehat{\mathbf{X}}_{att}$ of the Historical Attention Mechanism as follows:

$$\widehat{\mathbf{X}}_{output} = \widehat{\mathbf{X}}_{s-t} + \widehat{\mathbf{X}}_{att}. \qquad (12)$$

We use Mean Absolute Error (MAE) as the training objective of our model, which is defined by

$$\mathcal{L} = \frac{1}{T \times N} \sum_{i=1}^{T} \sum_{j=1}^{N} \left| \widehat{\mathbf{X}}_j^{(t+i)} - \mathbf{X}_j^{(t+i)} \right|. \qquad (13)$$

4 Experiments

4.1 Baselines

We compare our model with the following baseline models: (1) HA: Historical Average, which models the traffic flow as a seasonal process, and uses weighted average of previous seasons as the prediction; (2) VAR: Vector Auto-Regression (Hamilton) [5]; (3) LSTM: Long Short-Term Memory (Hochreiter & Schmidhuber, 2012) [8]; (4) GRU: Gated Recurrent Unit (Kyunghyun Cho, et al. 2014) [3]; (5) Informer (Haoyi Zhou,et al. 2021) [13]; (6) FEDformer (Haoyi Zhou, et al. 2022) [14]; (7) DCRNN: Diffusion Convolution Recurrent Neural Network (Li et al. 2017) [6]; (8) Graph WaveNet: Spatial-Temporal Graph Convolutional Network (Wu et al. 2019) [11].

Among them, HA and VAR [5] are two statistics-based models, LSTM [8] and GRU [3] are two RNN-based models, Informer [13] and FEDformer [14] are two state-of-the-art Transformer-based models, DCRNN [6] and Graph WaveNet [11] are two GCN-based models.

4.2   Datasets

Table 1. The statistics for the two datasets for the LTSF tasks. The data in brackets refers to the Historical Input.

Datasets	NYC-TLC	England-Highways
Variates	59	200
Timesteps	17520 (+8784)	17520 (+8784)
Granularity	1 h	1 h

We verified our model on NYC-TLC and England-Highways. NYC-TLC refers to the official TLC Trip Record Data of the New York Taxi Management Committee, which uses the traffic flow statistics of 59 observation stations in Manhattan from 2017 to 2018, and takes the traffic flow statistics of 2016 as the historical sequence. England-Highways refers to the highway data set in England, which uses the traffic flow statistics of 200 observation stations from 2013 to 2014, and takes the traffic flow statistics of 2012 as the historical sequence. We introduce the same data pre-processing procedures as in Graph WaveNet [11]. The readings of the sensors are aggregated into 1-hour windows. The datasets are split with 70% for training, 10% for validation and 20% for testing. Detailed dataset statistics are provided in Table 1.

4.3   Experimental Setups

For each dataset, we have introduced look-back window $= 168$ ($L = 168$) and forecasting horizon $T \in \{24, 168\}$. Each time step is 1 h, and the window size of $L = 168$ ensures that the problem belongs to LTSF task.

We train our model using Adam optimizer with an initial learning rate of 0.001. Dropout with $p = 0.3$ is applied to the outputs of the graph convolution layer. The evaluation metrics we choose include Mean Absolute Error (MAE), Root Mean Squared Error (RMSE), and Mean Absolute Percentage Error (MAPE).

4.4   Main Results

The experiment compared the prediction effects of our model and each baseline on 24 and 168 horizons on two datasets. It can be seen that our model has significantly improved compared to other spatial-temporal models, whether they are 24 horizons or 168 horizons. Moreover, an interesting phenomenon is that HA and VAR based on statistical models outperform some depth models on two different datasets, indicating that Transformer-based models are not necessarily effective on LTSF tasks, and simple models may instead achieve better prediction results for LTSF tasks. Our model did not use RNN or TCN methods but instead introduced a simple graph convolutional network(Temporal GCN) to handle temporal relationships. At the same time, we introduced a Historical Attention Mechanism to obtain the historical similarity of long-term time series. Historical Attention Mechanism introduced some ideas similar to Historical Average methods, taking into account the impact of historical periodicity on long-term time series, and achieved significant improvements in both datasets compared to other baselines. This phenomenon can indicate that the architecture of our model has strong adaptability and processing ability for each time stage on LTSF tasks. Table 2 shows our experiment results.

Table 2. Performance comparison of our model and other baseline models, which used look-back window $L = 168$ and forecasting horizon $T \in \{24, 168\}$. Our model achieves the best results in two different settings of two datasets.

Data	Model	24 Horizons			168 Horizons		
		MAE	RMSE	MAPE	MAE	RMSE	MAPE
NYC	HA	35.0452	62.4502	0.3634	35.0452	62.4502	0.3634
	VAR	31.3275	50.8490	0.4163	31.5550	54.6807	0.3839
	LSTM	36.9160	82.5474	0.2651	40.2252	85.7591	0.3259
	GRU	36.3860	81.5329	0.2693	38.6779	84.1623	0.2902
	Informer	33.2689	56.2861	0.4134	37.5730	65.0702	0.4394
	FEDformer	33.0348	56.3305	0.4020	36.9107	63.5396	0.4276
	DCRNN	31.7710	55.2832	0.3044	43.5301	68.6279	0.3877
	Graph WaveNet	22.6950	41.5109	0.2356	27.7610	51.8740	0.3245
	GCN-HAM	**20.0958**	**36.2961**	**0.1916**	**23.8514**	**44.7799**	**0.2458**
England	HA	209.9545	370.1746	0.4340	209.9545	370.1746	0.4340
	VAR	254.6897	384.8239	0.5842	263.0017	409.1418	0.5524
	LSTM	269.9341	448.3828	0.6487	315.2454	513.3620	0.6757
	GRU	259.6071	440.0119	0.6340	282.6938	459.1665	0.6650
	Informer	258.7048	404.2317	0.5951	264.8824	416.1994	0.5886
	FEDformer	237.5420	369.2095	0.5401	268.6748	412.2495	0.5589
	DCRNN	279.4150	439.7152	0.4310	293.4731	462.7639	0.5009
	Graph WaveNet	173.3522	327.4648	0.3921	194.7303	379.4614	0.4361
	GCN-HAM	**144.9969**	**265.6714**	**0.3521**	**178.1745**	**320.5873**	**0.4117**

4.5 Ablation Studies

To verify the effectiveness of our proposed Temporal GCN and Historical Attention Mechanism, we conducted experiments on our model using three different configurations. We chose Graph WaveNet as the baseline for comparison, and Table 3 shows the average scores of MAE, RMSE, and MAPE on 24 and 168 horizons. Regardless of the setting, using Temporal GCN alone can improve the performance of the model, while using Historical Attention Mechanism alone performs average at 24 horizons and improves at 168 horizons. This indicates that for longer time series, historical periodicity has a greater impact. The combination of Temporal GCN and Historical Attention Mechanism can significantly improve the performance of the model.

Table 3. Experimental results for different configurations.

Data	Model	24 Horizons			168 Horizons		
		MAE	RMSE	MAPE	MAE	RMSE	MAPE
NYC	Baseline	22.6950	41.5109	0.2356	27.7610	51.8740	0.3245
	Temporal GCN Only	20.9422	38.0926	0.2056	24.1250	45.2557	0.2507
	Historical Attention Only	22.8747	42.1555	0.2424	26.1639	50.2090	0.2702
	GCN-HAM	**20.0958**	**36.2961**	**0.1916**	**23.8514**	**44.7799**	**0.2458**
England	Baseline	173.3522	327.4648	0.3921	194.7303	379.4614	0.4361
	Temporal GCN Only	152.6054	283.1029	0.3598	191.1585	334.3697	0.4281
	Historical Attention Only	174.0279	332.5160	0.3684	193.7849	366.5838	0.4145
	GCN-HAM	**144.9969**	**265.6714**	**0.3521**	**178.1745**	**320.5873**	**0.4117**

5 Conclusion

In this paper, we propose a novel spatial-temporal graph modeling model for LTSF tasks. Our model captures spatial correlation by modeling space using Spatial GCN. Unlike previous studies, we used a simple Graph Convolutional Network: Temporal GCN to capture temporal correlation, inspired by the periodicity inherent in the long-term time series of LTSF tasks, and validated the effectiveness of Temporal GCN through experiments. In addition, we consider that long-term time series have a long historical periodicity, thereby introducing a Historical Attention Mechanism. By introducing historical sequences, the model integrates the information of current and historical sequences, captures the external dependencies of the time series, and expands the receptive field of the model from local relationships to historical relationships. This also avoids the problem of excessive complexity caused by the excessively long direct input sequence. On the NYC-TLC and England-Highways datasets, our model has achieved significant improvements compared to baseline. Our model can provide a new direction for solving LTSF tasks in the future.

Acknowledgement. This work was supported by the National Natural Science Foundation of China (62272023, 51991391, 51991395).

References

1. Bai, S., Kolter, J.Z., Koltun, V.: An empirical evaluation of generic convolutional and recurrent networks for sequence modeling. arXiv preprint arXiv:1803.01271 (2018)
2. Box, G.E., Jenkins, G.M., Reinsel, G.C., Ljung, G.M.: Time Series Analysis: Forecasting and Control. Wiley, Hoboken (2015)
3. Cho, K., et al.: Learning phrase representations using RNN encoder-decoder for statistical machine translation. arXiv preprint arXiv:1406.1078 (2014)
4. Du, B., et al.: Deep irregular convolutional residual LSTM for urban traffic passenger flows prediction. IEEE Trans. Intell. Transp. Syst. **21**(3), 972–985 (2019)
5. Hamilton, J.D.: Time Series Analysis. Princeton University Press, Princeton (2020)
6. Li, Y., Yu, R., Shahabi, C., Liu, Y.: Diffusion convolutional recurrent neural network: data-driven traffic forecasting. arXiv preprint arXiv:1707.01926 (2017)
7. Ma, X., Zhang, J., Du, B., Ding, C., Sun, L.: Parallel architecture of convolutional bi-directional LSTM neural networks for network-wide metro ridership prediction. IEEE Trans. Intell. Transp. Syst. **20**(6), 2278–2288 (2018)
8. Sundermeyer, M., Schlüter, R., Ney, H.: LSTM neural networks for language modeling. In: Thirteenth Annual Conference of the International Speech Communication Association (2012)
9. Vaswani, A., et al.: Attention is all you need. In: Advances in Neural Information Processing Systems, vol. 30 (2017)
10. Wu, Z., Pan, S., Long, G., Jiang, J., Chang, X., Zhang, C.: Connecting the dots: multivariate time series forecasting with graph neural networks. In: Proceedings of the 26th ACM SIGKDD International Conference on Knowledge Discovery and Data Mining, pp. 753–763 (2020)
11. Wu, Z., Pan, S., Long, G., Jiang, J., Zhang, C.: Graph wavenet for deep spatial-temporal graph modeling. arXiv preprint arXiv:1906.00121 (2019)
12. Ye, J., Sun, L., Du, B., Fu, Y., Tong, X., Xiong, H.: Co-prediction of multiple transportation demands based on deep spatio-temporal neural network. In: Proceedings of the 25th ACM SIGKDD International Conference on Knowledge Discovery and Data Mining, pp. 305–313 (2019)
13. Zhou, H., et al.: Informer: beyond efficient transformer for long sequence time-series forecasting. In: Proceedings of the AAAI Conference on Artificial Intelligence, vol. 35, pp. 11106–11115 (2021)
14. Zhou, T., Ma, Z., Wen, Q., Wang, X., Sun, L., Jin, R.: Fedformer: frequency enhanced decomposed transformer for long-term series forecasting. In: International Conference on Machine Learning, pp. 27268–27286. PMLR (2022)

Multi-hop Reading Comprehension Learning Method Based on Answer Contrastive Learning

Hao You[1,2], Heyan Huang[3,4]($\boxtimes$), Yue Hu[1,2], and Yongxiu Xu[1,2]

[1] Institute of Information Engineering, Chinese Academy of Sciences, Beijing, China
{youhao,huyue,xuyongxiu}@iie.ac.cn
[2] School of Cyber Security, University of Chinese Academy of Sciences,
Beijing, China
[3] School of Computer Science and Technology, Beijing Institute of Technology,
Beijing, China
hhy63@bit.edu.cn
[4] Southeast Academy of Information Technology, Beijing Institute of Technology,
Putian, China

Abstract. Multi-hop reading comprehension generally requires the model to give the answer and complete the prediction of supporting facts. However, previous works mainly focus on the interaction between question and context, and ignore the problem that many entities or short spans in sentences are similar to the true answer, so they do not take advantage of the differentiation information between true and plausible answers. To solve the above problems, we propose a learning method based on answer contrastive learning for multi-hop reading comprehension, which makes full use of answer judgment information to reduce the interference of confusing information to the model. Specifically, similar entity and random span data augmentation methods are proposed firstly from the perspective of answer for contrastive learning. Secondly, we implement multi-task joint learning by combining answer contrastive learning and graph neural network model through a shared encoder, and use several subtasks to mine shared information to assist in answer extraction and supporting fact prediction. Especially, the learning method forces the model to pay more attention to the true answer information through answer contrastive learning, which helps the model distinguish the start and end positions of answers. We validate our proposed learning method on the HotpotQA dataset, and the experimental results show that it performs better than the competitive baselines on several evaluation metrics.

Keywords: Multi-hop Reading Comprehension · Question Answering · Pre-trained Model · Contrastive Learning · Graph Neural Network

1 Introduction

As a hot research direction in natural language processing (NLP), multi-hop reading comprehension (RC) has attracted the attention of many researchers in

Z. Jin et al. (Eds.): KSEM 2023, LNAI 14120, pp. 124–139, 2023.
https://doi.org/10.1007/978-3-031-40292-0_11

recent years. Different from traditional single-hop RC [24], multi-hop RC [32,37] needs to integrate multiple sentences or paragraphs for reasoning, such as comparison, bridging, etc., and this task generally requires evidence to be provided for interpretability. One of the current paradigms for multi-hop RC task is "retriever + reader" [23]. This paradigm first uses a retriever to retrieve relevant context information composed of sentences or paragraphs from multiple candidate paragraphs and then uses a reader to perform reading comprehension based on the retrieved context to reason the answer. In addition to annotated answers, some datasets such as HotpotQA [37] also provide supporting facts or evidence to explain the predicted answer results.

Question: What screenwriter with credits for "Evolution" co-wrote a film starring Nicolas Cage and Téa Leoni?

Paragraph 1 (Title: David Weissman):
David Weissman is a screenwriter and director. His film credits include "The Family Man" (2000), "Evolution" (2001), and "When in Rome" (2010).

Paragraph 2 (Title: The Family Man):
The Family Man is a 2000 American romantic comedy-drama film directed by Brett Ratner, written by David Diamond and David Weissman, and starring Nicolas Cage and Téa Leoni. Cage's production company, Saturn Films, helped produce the film. The film centers on a man who sees what could have been had he made a different decision 13 years prior.

Paragraph 3:...

Answer: David Weissman

Supporting Facts: ["David Weissman",0], ["David Weissman",1], ["The Family Man",0]

Fig. 1. A sample from the HotpotQA dev dataset showing only two relevant paragraphs. The evidence marked in green corresponds to the yellow highlighted part of the paragraph, and "0" represents the first sentence in the paragraph. The red font indicates that spans similar to the true answer may exist in one or more sentences contained in the context, and the traditional model has difficulty distinguishing the start and end positions of the true answer. (Color figure online)

At present, some works [7,23,28] in multi-hop RC are devoted to the application of graph neural network (GNN) in reader model to enhance the ability of reasoning. The current evaluation results of these GNN-based models on the HotpotQA dataset show that they have achieved very good performance in terms of supporting fact metrics, however, they still have low EM and F1 values in answer extraction. One of the reasons that we speculate is the way to predict supporting facts and answers. Specifically, the reader generally uses binary classification to judge whether sentences are supporting facts, while it usually extracts answers by predicting the start and end positions. Although the answers are usually only a few tokens, there are many short spans that are very similar to true answers. As a result, the reader is misinformed about the start and end positions. Figure 1 shows an example of the multi-hop RC task. As can be seen from the figure, only using paragraph 1 (David Weissman) or paragraph 2 (The Family Man) cannot give the answer, while the traditional multi-hop model can use the information provided by the question to jump from paragraph 1 to paragraph 2 by bridging, then conduct subsequent answer reasoning. However, since the semantics of "David Weissman" and "David Diamond" are very close, the traditional model may not be able to distinguish them accurately, resulting in the model potentially predicting the wrong answer "David Diamond".

To solve the above problem, we propose a learning method based on Answer Contrastive Learning for multi-hop RC (ACLRC), whose core modules include data augmentation, answer contrastive learning, and multi-task joint learning. Firstly, we put forward two answer-based data augmentation methods, similar entity and random span, to augment the original dataset in terms of semantic similarity and lexical overlap, respectively. Secondly, answer contrastive learning is proposed to help the model learn richer representation information to distinguish plausible answers from true answers. Thirdly, considering the information aggregation ability of GNN, we combine contrastive learning and GNN through a shared encoder to implement multi-task joint learning. In this way, the model can benefit from mining the shared information of multiple subtasks to improve the extraction of answers and the prediction ability of supporting facts. In particular, the two data augmentation methods we propose are heuristic and do not require additional annotation of existing datasets, which can provide a new solution for contrastive learning of reading comprehension.

Our main contributions are as follows:

- We propose a new learning method for multi-hop RC based on answer contrastive learning. This method can utilize differentiation information of true and plausible answers to enhance the discrimination and inference ability of the model.
- We present two novel answer-based data augmentation methods and use them to implement contrastive learning, which makes the model pay more attention to the information of true answers.
- Multi-task joint learning is realized by combining contrastive learning and GNN where multiple subtasks are used to mine rich shared information.
- Experimental results on the multi-hop RC dataset demonstrate that ACLRC performs better than the baseline models on multiple evaluation metrics of answer extraction and supporting fact prediction.

2   Related Work

2.1   Multi-hop RC

In recent years, the research work on multi-hop RC has been growing increasingly. In this paper, current multi-hop RC work is divided into four categories: multi-hop RC based on evidence chain, multi-hop RC based on attention, multi-hop RC based on question decomposition, and multi-hop RC based on GNN.

Multi-hop RC models based on evidence chain, such as AIR [35] and WAIR [36], firstly use unsupervised retrieval method to retrieve explainable evidence from context, and then use reader based on the pre-trained model to predict answers. Path-net [15] and RoBERTa-Para [3] extract evidence by training the evidence extraction model to provide a more condensed context for subsequent answer prediction.

Multi-hop RC models based on attention, such as EPAr [13] and TAP [2], generally use attention mechanisms, such as bi-attention [25] and self-attention [30] to integrate question and context information to extract answers. QFE [20] and SuQA [12] models focus on the generation of interpretable evidence, the former is inspired by the extractive summarization models, and the latter uses a semi-supervised generative summarization explainer to generate more compact explanations.

More directly, multi-hop RC models based on question decomposition such as DecompRC [19] and ONUS [22] decompose questions into sub-questions, thereby turning multi-hop RC task into one-hop RC task. Especially, from the perspective of interpretable NLP, Xie et al. [34] construct probes through the decomposition of questions to generate explainable evidence so that users know when the answers predicted by the system are trustable.

The main feature of multi-hop RC models based on GNN is the different construction of graphs. For example, MHQA-GRN [26] and Entity-GCN [5] use named entity recognition, coreference resolution, and other methods to construct entity graphs, and use different GNNs to propagate information. HDE graph [29], HGN [7] and ClueReader [8] use the information of different granularity, such as entity, sentence, paragraph, etc., to construct the heterogeneous graph to make the rich information between different types of nodes interact during inference. Gated-RGCN [27] combines graph-based and path-based methods to construct a path-based reasoning graph and uses attention and question-aware gating mechanism to simulate human reasoning process.

Most methods based on GNN have better performance in reading comprehension compared with other methods. Therefore, we take the graph neural network as the basic structure of the ACLRC learning method.

2.2 Contrastive Learning

At present, contrastive learning has achieved excellent results in many fields, such as recommendation [33], question-answer pairs ranking [6], visual representation learning [4], sentence representation learning [9] and so on. In the field of question answering (QA) and reading comprehension, DPR [14] uses the rule method to construct positive and negative samples, and then uses contrastive learning to retrieve passages related to the question. Lee et al. [16] add phrase retrieval to enhance the retrieval performance of the coarse-grained retrieval model. Based on the constructed graph, Liao et al. [17] use structure dropout and representation dropout augmentation strategies to establish contrastive heterogeneous graphs for multi-hop RC reasoning.

To solve the problem of consecutive tokens similar to the true answer in lexicon or semantics, we use contrastive learning to enhance the answer discrimination ability of the model.

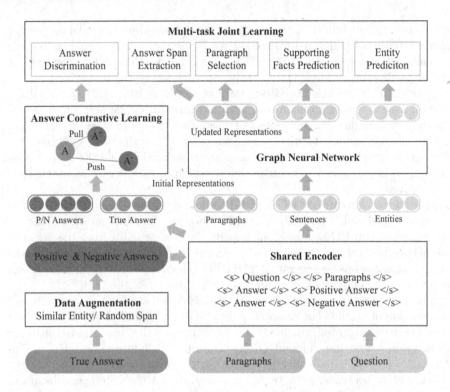

Fig. 2. The framework of the ACLRC learning method. Green, blue, pink, orange, and golden colors represent true answer, generated plausible answers, paragraphs, sentences, and entities, respectively. (Color figure online)

3 Model

The ACLRC learning framework is shown in Fig. 2. ACLRC is mainly composed of five modules: data augmentation, shared encoder, answer contrastive learning, graph neural network, and multi-task joint learning. Specifically, this method uses the pseudo-samples generated by the data augmentation method for contrastive learning, forcing the model to pay more attention to the true answer information. Then, multi-task joint learning is implemented by combining answer contrastive learning and graph neural network through the shared encoder, which makes the learned representation more general and effective by mining shared information. These modules are described in detail sequentially in the following.

3.1 Data Augmentation

Figure 3 shows the similar entity and random span data augmentation strategies proposed in this paper, where the original sentences are part of the paragraph corresponding to the question. The generated data are used for following answer

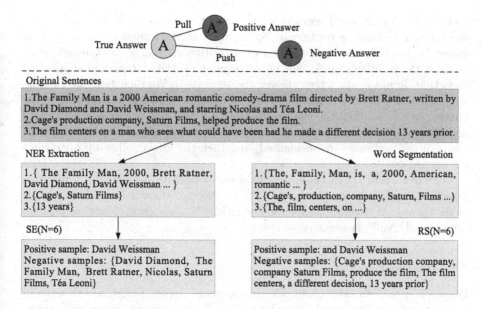

Fig. 3. Similar Entity and Random Span data augmentation methods.

contrastive learning. Since this paper focuses on the data augmentation of extractive answers, samples of "yes" and "no" answer types are excluded first. Next, the above two methods are described in detail.

Similar Entity (SE). Since some entities contained in the context are semantically similar to the true answer, we use semantic similarity calculation to generate positive and negative samples to enhance the semantic differentiation ability of the model in the subsequent contrastive learning. Firstly, all sentences in all candidate paragraphs corresponding to the question are obtained, and all entities in the sentences are extracted by the named entity recognition model fine-tuned on pre-trained model used by DFGN [23]. Then, we use SimCSE [9] to generate true answer representations and entity representations corresponding to the question, which are used to calculate similarity through the cosine similarity method. If the similarity is greater than the threshold β, the entity is considered to be similar to the true answer and is regarded as the positive sample; otherwise, the entity is regarded as the negative sample.

Random Span (RS). In addition to semantic similarity, some of the short spans may have common tokens with the true answer, or even the true answer is a subset of some short spans. To enhance the robustness of the model to judge the start and end positions of answers, we use a rule-based method to generate positive and negative samples composed of consecutive tokens. First, find the sentence that contains the true answer from the candidate paragraphs, and use the NLTK word segmentation method to segment the sentence to get the token set. Then, according to the position of the sentence where the true answer is located, a span composed of n continuous tokens is obtained by n-gram as the positive sample. For negative samples, the sentences in supporting facts that do not contain true answer are segmented. We then generate random start and end positions whose difference of absolute values is n according to the number of tokens, then the span consisting of n continuous tokens is taken as a negative sample. If the number of generated negative samples does not meet the needs, other sentences are segmented, and then the above follow-up operations are carried out.

Through SE or RS method, we can obtain 1 positive sample and N negative samples for each answer. For both of the methods, if there is no positive sample or the number of negative samples is lower than N, we append "None" as positive sample and "Null" as negative samples.

3.2 Shared Encoder

We use a shared encoder to encode the question, paragraphs, true answer, and positive and negative answer samples so that the downstream contrastive training model and the graph neural network model share parameters, which helps the whole model learn richer information.

Paragraph Selection. Before encoding, we need to select paragraphs that are relevant to the question from candidate paragraphs to reduce the interference of irrelevant information. First, we train a RoBERTa model [18] with a binary classifier as a paragraph selector. At most two paragraphs are then selected using a combination of title-question phrase matching, paragraph selector, and paragraph entity-question matching. Then, according to the hyperlink provided by Wikipedia, the second-hop paragraph is selected through the evidence and entities in the first-hop paragraph.

Encoding. After paragraph selection, the relevant paragraphs we obtain are formed into context C, which is connected with the question Q into the RoBERTa encoder, and then fed into a bi-attention layer [25]. We denote encoded question and context as $\mathbf{Q} = [\mathbf{q}_i]_{i=1}^{|Q|}$ and $\mathbf{C} = [\mathbf{c}_j]_{j=1}^{|C|}$, respectively. Here, $\mathbf{q}_i$ is the embedding vector of i-th token in the representation matrix $\mathbf{Q}$, $|Q|$ is the length of question Q, and the definitions of $\mathbf{c}_j$ and $\mathbf{C}$ are similar. Especially, each $\mathbf{q}_i$ and $\mathbf{c}_j \in \mathbb{R}^d$, and d is dimension.

The context representation $\mathbf{C}$ is then fed into a shared BiLSTM [11], and the result is denoted as $\mathbf{M} \in \mathbb{R}^{2d}$. To realize the subsequent subtasks such as paragraph selection, supporting fact prediction, and entity prediction, the hidden state of backward LSTM at the start position and the hidden state of forward LSTM at the end position are concatenated to obtain the representations of paragraphs, sentences, and entities. In particular, we use max-pooling to obtain the question representation, after which the above representations are fed into the graph neural network:

$$\mathbf{p}_i = \mathrm{MLP}_1\left(\left[\mathbf{M}[P^{(i)}_{start}][d:]];[\mathbf{M}[P^{(i)}_{end}][d:]]\right) \in \mathbb{R}^d$$

$$\mathbf{s}_i = \mathrm{MLP}_2\left(\left[\mathbf{M}[S^{(i)}_{start}][d:]];[\mathbf{M}[S^{(i)}_{end}][d:]]\right) \in \mathbb{R}^d$$

$$\mathbf{e}_i = \mathrm{MLP}_3\left(\left[\mathbf{M}[E^{(i)}_{start}][d:]];[\mathbf{M}[E^{(i)}_{end}][d:]]\right) \in \mathbb{R}^d$$

$$\mathbf{q} = \text{max-pooling}(\mathbf{Q}) \in \mathbb{R}^d, \tag{1}$$

where $P^{(i)}_{start}$, $S^{(i)}_{start}$ and $E^{(i)}_{start}$ mean the start positions of i-th paragraph, sentence, and entity. Similarly, $P^{(i)}_{end}$, $S^{(i)}_{end}$, and $E^{(i)}_{end}$ mean end positions. MLP($\cdot$) means multilayer perceptron, and ; means vertical concatenation.

To keep the length of positive and negative samples consistent with the length of the true answer, they are padded with integer 0, and the maximum length is denoted as l. Then we encode the true answer, the positive and negative samples generated by the two data augmentation methods.

Specifically, the true answer is fed into the RoBERTa shared encoder with positive and negative samples generated by SE and RS respectively, and the hidden state in the last layer of the first token is taken as vector representation. We denote encoded true answer as $\mathbf{a}_i$, $N+1$ representations of positive and negative samples obtained by the SE augmentation method as $\mathbf{A}'_i = [\mathbf{a}'_{i,+}, \mathbf{a}'_{i,1}, \ldots, \mathbf{a}'_{i,N}] \in \mathbb{R}^{(N+1)\times d}$, where $\mathbf{a}'_{i,+} \in \mathbb{R}^d$ is the only positive sample and $\mathbf{a}'_{i,N} \in \mathbb{R}^d$ is negative samples. Similarly, $N+1$ span representations of positive and negative samples obtained by the RS method as $\mathbf{A}''_i = [\mathbf{a}''_{i,+}, \mathbf{a}''_{i,1}, \ldots, \mathbf{a}''_{i,N}] \in \mathbb{R}^{(N+1)\times d}$.

3.3 Answer Contrastive Learning

In this paper, the contrastive learning method is used to discriminate true answers from plausible answer samples. Its objective is to maximize the consistency between the true answer and positive sample, and minimize the consistency between true answer and negative samples so that the distance between vectors of the former is smaller than that of the latter, which forces the pre-trained model to pay more attention to the true answer information. In particular, we choose the dot product to calculate the similarity between vectors, so as to make the similar answer vectors closer in the embedding space through training.

Similar to DPR [14], the SE loss function is the negative log likelihood of the positive sample:

$$\mathcal{L}_{se} = -\log \frac{e^{\text{sim}(\mathbf{a}_i, \mathbf{a}'_{i,+})}}{e^{\text{sim}(\mathbf{a}_i, \mathbf{a}'_{i,+})} + \sum_{j=1}^{N} e^{\text{sim}(\mathbf{a}_i, \mathbf{a}'_{i,j})}} \tag{2}$$

Similarly, the RS loss function is formulated as:

$$\mathcal{L}_{rs} = -\log \frac{e^{\text{sim}(\mathbf{a}_i, \mathbf{a}''_{i,+})}}{e^{\text{sim}(\mathbf{a}_i, \mathbf{a}''_{i,+})} + \sum_{j=1}^{N} e^{\text{sim}(\mathbf{a}_i, \mathbf{a}''_{i,j})}}, \tag{3}$$

where sim($\cdot$) is the dot product of vectors.

3.4   Graph Neural Network

Due to the powerful information aggregation and reasoning ability of GNN, we use it to predict other subtasks such as answer extraction and supporting fact prediction. Given that the existing HGN model [7] performs well in graph reasoning, we adopt it as the graph neural network module of ACLRC. Next, we give a brief introduction to the graph reasoning process (readers are advised to read the original HGN paper carefully due to the limited pages).

After the representations are obtained through the shared encoder, GNN is used to transform them into higher-level features. We use p_i, s_i, e_i and q to obtain $H = \{q, P, S, E\}$. After that, Graph Attention Network (GAT) [31] is used for message propagation over the graph, we can get $H' = \{h'_0, h'_1, \ldots, h'_g\}$ and each updated representation P', S', E' and q'. Then, context representation M and graph representation H' are combined for answer span extraction through the gated attention mechanism [7], and the final gated representation is G.

3.5   Multi-task Joint Learning

Once the representations are updated, we use them for different task predictions. Specifically, we feed P', S', E' into different two-layer perceptrons, which are used for determining whether a paragraph contains true supporting facts, judging whether a sentence is a supporting fact, and entity multi-classification prediction task respectively. For the answer extraction task, we feed G into two different two-layer perceptrons respectively for the judgment of the start and end positions of the answer span. In particular, we feed the hidden representation of the first token of G into a two-layer perceptron for answer classification. In the decoding process, the answers are first classified. If the type is "yes" or "no", it is directly used as the answer.

For the above tasks, we calculate their losses through the cross-entropy loss function. Contrastive learning based on two data augmentation methods is used to implement the subtask of answer discrimination, and the loss is used as an auxiliary loss to enhance the ability of the model to discriminate between answer segments and non-answers. Then, we jointly train the contrastive learning model and the graph neural network model to achieve the purpose of multi-task joint learning, and the target loss is shown in the formula below:

$$\mathcal{L}_{final1} = \mathcal{L}_{start} + \mathcal{L}_{end} + \lambda_1\mathcal{L}_{para} + \lambda_2\mathcal{L}_{sent} + \lambda_3\mathcal{L}_{entity} + \lambda_4\mathcal{L}_{type} + \lambda_5\mathcal{L}_{se}, \tag{4}$$

$$\mathcal{L}_{final2} = \mathcal{L}_{start} + \mathcal{L}_{end} + \lambda_1\mathcal{L}_{para} + \lambda_2\mathcal{L}_{sent} + \lambda_3\mathcal{L}_{entity} + \lambda_4\mathcal{L}_{type} + \lambda_6\mathcal{L}_{rs} \tag{5}$$

where λ_i is hyperparameter, $\mathcal{L}_{start}$ and $\mathcal{L}_{end}$ are the start and end loss of answer span, $\mathcal{L}_{para}$ and $\mathcal{L}_{sent}$ are paragraph selection and supporting fact prediction loss respectively, $\mathcal{L}_{entity}$ and $\mathcal{L}_{type}$ are entity prediction and answer type prediction loss respectively.

Table 1. Statistical information of HotpotQA-distractor training and dev set.

Type	Instances	Question Len. (Avg)	Context Len. (Avg)	Answer Len. (Avg)	Paragraph Num. (Avg)	Sentence Num. (Avg)
Train	90447	18	886	2.22	10	41
Dev	7405	16	897	2.46	10	42

4 Experiments and Analyses

In this section, the experimental results of ACLRC are compared with other baseline methods, and the results of ACLRC are further analyzed.

4.1 Dataset

HotpotQA [37] is one of the most popular multi-hop QA datasets including distractor and fullwiki version, and its background corpus is the entire English Wikipedia dump. In this paper, we use the HotpotQA-distractor dataset and its default divided passages and sentences.

Because the test set of HotpotQA-distractor is blind, the statistics for training and dev set are shown in Table 1. The context here refers to all paragraphs corresponding to each question, so the average context length is the average number of words contained in the contexts of all questions. Since the average length of answers is 2.22 and 2.46 in the train and dev set, we set n in n-gram of the RS data augmentation to 3.

4.2 Baselines and Metrics

To demonstrate the validity of our learning method, we compared it with other baselines: Baseline [37], QFE [20], DFGN [23], LongFormer-large [1], QUARK [10], SAE (RoBERTa) [28], HGN [7] and IRC [21].

Based on the metrics adopted in Baseline [37], we use Answer EM, Answer F1, Supporting Facts EM, Supporting Facts F1, Joint EM of answer and supporting facts, and Joint F1 to evaluate the models in many aspects.

4.3 Experiment Settings

For the shared encoder, we use RoBERTa-large pre-trained model. We finetune the whole model on the training set for 5 epochs, with batch size as 8, learning rate as 1e-5, max length of context as 512, max length of query and l as 50, LSTM and GNN dropout rate both as 0.3, λ_1 as 1, λ_2 as 5, λ_3 as 1, λ_4 as 1. Moreover, λ_5, λ_6 and threshold β are all set as 0.5, and the number of negative samples N in SE and RS are both set as 10. We search hyperparameters for learning rate from {1e-5, 2e-5, 3e-5}, dropout rate from {0.1, 0.3, 0.5}, λ_5 and λ_6 from {0.1, 0.5, 1.0, 2.0} and N from {1, 5, 10, 15}. Specially, we conduct experiments in one Nvidia A100 GPU and use FP16 mixed precision training.

Table 2. Experimental results of ACLRC on HotpotQA-distractor dev set. Bold indicates the best value achieved on the current metric. "–" denotes no results are available.

Row	RC Model	HotpotQA-distractor Dev					
		Ans EM	Ans F1	Sup Em	Sup F1	Joint EM	Joint F1
1	Baseline [37]	44.44	58.28	21.95	66.66	11.56	40.86
2	QFE [20]	53.70	68.70	58.80	84.70	35.40	60.60
3	DFGN [23]	55.66	69.34	53.10	82.24	33.68	59.86
4	LongFormer-large [1]	–	81.00	-	85.80	–	71.40
5	SAE(RoBERTa) [28]	67.70	80.75	**63.30**	87.38	**46.81**	72.75
6	QUARK [10]	67.75	81.21	60.72	86.97	44.35	72.76
7	HGN [7]	–	81.00	–	87.93	–	73.01
8	IRC [21]	58.60	72.90	36.60	79.80	–	–
9	ACLRC (SE)	**68.60**	**82.04**	61.92	87.98	45.62	73.81
10	ACLRC (RS)	68.48	81.96	61.47	**88.06**	45.25	**73.84**

4.4   Experimental Results

Table 2 compares the results of ACLRC with those of other baseline models. As can be seen from the table, ACLRC(SE) and ACLRC(RS) learning methods achieve better results on most evaluation metrics. Among them, ACLRC(SE) achieves higher scores than QUARK in Ans EM/F1 of 68.60/82.04 with 0.85/0.83 improvement, and ACLRC(RS) outperforms HGN which has the best score in Sup F1 and Joint F1 with an absolute improvement of 0.13/0.83, which verifies the effectiveness of ACLRC. Especially in terms of the two metrics of the answer, ACLRC is much better than the best baseline model, which is attributed to the fact that answer contrastive learning can effectively help the model determine the start and end positions of the answer. In particular, SE is significantly ahead of RS on three EM metrics, while it is almost the same on three F1 metrics. This may be because the RS method adopts n-gram to obtain spans rather than the complete entities, and the EM metric mainly evaluates the ability of accurate matching of the model, so the trained model is worse than the SE method on EM. In addition, although neither SE nor RS augmentation strategies are designed to supporting facts, both ACLRC(SE) and ACLRC(RS) are marginally better than baseline HGN in supporting facts EM and F1, suggesting that the proposed multi-task joint learning including contrastive learning and GNN has a positive effect on supporting fact prediction.

Considering the better performance of ACLRC(SE), the following experiments are carried out on the basis of ACLRC(SE).

4.5   Ablation Study

Table 3 shows the ablation results of ACLRC(SE) on the HotpotQA-distractor dev set. When the multi-task joint training module is removed, the model degenerates to RoBERTa-Large, so the performance suffers the most. When the GNN

Table 3. Ablation study of ACLRC(SE) model on HotpotQA-distractor dev set.

Model	Ans EM	Ans F1	Sup EM	Sup F1	Joint EM	Joint F1
ACLRC (SE)	**68.60**	**82.04**	**61.92**	**87.98**	**45.62**	**73.81**
w/o Multi-task Joint Learning	65.01	79.20	58.96	87.09	41.34	70.67
w/o Graph Neural Network	66.08	80.20	59.93	87.46	42.09	71.75
w/o Contrastive Learning	67.45	81.11	61.50	87.93	44.46	73.00

module is removed, the performance of ACLRC(SE) also decreases significantly, which indicates the effectiveness of GNN for multi-hop RC. When the answer contrastive learning module is removed, the performance of ACLRC(SE) in the term of answer metric declines more significantly than that on the metric of supporting fact. This is because the data augmentation method is designed for answer, which also indicates that answer contrastive learning does contribute more to the prediction of answers.

Table 4. Different impacts of varying the loss weight λ_5 and the numbers of negative samples N on the performance of ACLRC(SE) on HotpotQA-distractor dev set.

λ_5(SE)	0.1	0.5	1.0	2.0	N(SE)	1	5	10	15
Ans EM	67.90	**68.60**	68.08	68.47	Ans EM	68.04	68.45	**68.60**	67.77
Ans F1	81.55	**82.04**	81.95	81.71	Ans F1	81.63	82.00	**82.04**	81.28
Sup EM	61.92	61.92	**62.04**	60.62	Sup EM	61.28	61.74	**61.92**	61.12
Sup F1	87.82	87.98	**88.00**	87.87	Sup F1	87.83	**88.05**	87.98	**88.05**
Joint EM	45.15	**45.62**	45.36	44.44	Joint EM	44.60	45.27	**45.62**	44.50
Joint F1	73.37	**73.81**	73.72	73.41	Joint F1	73.34	**73.82**	73.81	73.23

4.6 Hyperparameter Analysis

In this section, we analyze the loss weight λ_5 and the number of negative samples N in ACLRC(SE) on HotpotQA-distractor dev sets to explore the influence of changing the hyperparameter on the performance of the model.

The left part of Table 4 shows the impact of λ_5. It is evident that when $\lambda = 0.5$, ACLRC(SE) performs better on most metrics. We speculate that when λ_5 is small, the contrastive loss is small, leading to the model being unable to make full use of the judgment ability between the plausible answers provided by the SE data augmentation method and the true answer. However, when the value is too large, the representation weights learned by the model deviate, which affects the information fusion of graph neural networks used for other subtasks.

The right part of Table 4 shows the impact of N. When $N = 10$, the performance of ACLRC(SE) is better in most metrics, which shows that the appropriate number of negative samples plays an important role in contrastive learning.

But when $N = 1$ or $N = 15$, the performance of ACLRC(SE) degrades. We speculate that when N is small, it is difficult for the model to obtain sufficient judgment information by using a small number of negative samples. However, if N is too large, the negative sample set contains more noise, which weakens the effect of contrastive learning.

1. Both are correct: 43%	2. Correct Answers & Wrong SFs: 41%
ID: 5a877e5d5542993e715abf7d	**ID:** 5ab56e32554299637185c594
Question: The Livesey Hal War Memorial commemorates the fallen of which war, that had over 60 million casualties?	**Question:** Are Random House Tower and 888 7th Avenue both used for real estate?
True Supporting Facts: [["David Weissman", 0], ["David Weissman", 1], ["The Family Man", 0]]	**True Supporting Facts:** [["888 7th Avenue",0], ["Random House Tower",0]]
Predicted Supporting Facts: [["David Weissman",0], ["David Weissman",1], ["The Family Man",0]]	**Predicted Supporting Facts:** [["Random House Tower",0], ["888 7th Avenue",2]]
True Answer: David Weissman	**True Answer:** no
Predicted Answer: David Weissman	**Predicted Answer:** no
3. Wrong Answers & Correct SFs: 4%	**4. Both are wrong: 12%**
ID: 5ae6050f55429929b0807a5e	**ID:** 5a879adb5542996e4f30887f
Question: This singer of A Rather Blustery Day also voiced what hedgehog?	**Question:** What other political position did the person who introduced the DISCLOSE Act hold?
True Supporting Facts: [["A Rather Blustery Day",1], ["Jim Cummings",1]]	**True Supporting Facts:** [["DISCLOSE Act",0], ["Chris Van Hollen",0]]
Predicted Supporting Facts: [["A Rather Blustery Day",1], ["Jim Cummings",1]]	**Predicted Supporting Facts:** [["DISCLOSE Act",0], ["Chris Van Hollen",1]]
True Answer: Sonic	**True Answer:** United States Senator
Predicted Answer: Dr. Robotnik from "Sonic the Hedgehog"	**Predicted Answer:** U.S. Representative for Maryland 's 8 congressional district

Fig. 4. Case analysis of ACLRC(SE) on the HotpotQA-distractor dev set (100 instances are sampled randomly and only 4 of them are shown). Pink indicates the proportion of current type of samples in 100 random samples, blue indicates that the prediction is consistent with the true result, and yellow means that the prediction is wrong. (Color figure online)

4.7 Case Study

Figure 4 shows the sample prediction of ACLRC(SE) on the HotpotQA-distractor dev set. 43% of the first type of samples correctly predict supporting facts and answers, and 41% of the second type of samples correctly predict answers while supporting facts are predicted incorrectly, such as predicting fewer or more supporting fact sentences. Only 4% of the third type of samples predict correct supporting facts and wrong answers. 12% of the fourth type of samples predict wrong both in supporting facts and answers.

Both type 1 and 2 predict answers correctly, but supporting facts are predicted correctly in type 1 and wrong in type 2. This shows that although the correct prediction rate of both answers is as high as 84%, ACLRC(SE) cannot guarantee that the correct supporting facts are provided to explain the correct answer prediction. Although the proportion of type 3 is very low, it still indicates that even if ACLRC(SE) can accurately distinguish the supporting facts in this case, it is difficult to extract the start and end positions of the answers, leading to the inaccuracy of the predicted answers. Overall, only about 16% of the samples have wrong predicted answers, indicating that ACLRC(SE) is still very effective in answer extraction.

5   Conclusion

We propose a learning method based on answer contrastive learning for multi-hop reading comprehension. Our method firstly conducts answer contrastive learning according to positive and negative sample pairs generated by the proposed two data augmentation methods, then combines graph neural network used for other subtasks to realize multi-task joint learning, so as to enhance the reasoning ability of the model on the basis of fusing the answer discrimination information. Experimental results show that the ACLRC performs better than the baseline models on the HotpotQA dataset in terms of answers, supporting facts, and other metrics. In the future, we will study other contrastive learning methods in different aspects to explore whether we can further improve the performance of the multi-hop reading comprehension model.

References

1. Beltagy, I., Peters, M.E., Cohan, A.: Longformer: the long-document transformer. arXiv preprint arXiv:2004.05150 (2020)
2. Bhargav, G.S., et al.: Translucent answer predictions in multi-hop reading comprehension. In: Proceedings of the AAAI Conference on Artificial Intelligence, vol. 34, pp. 7700–7707 (2020)
3. Chen, J., Lin, S.T., Durrett, G.: Multi-hop question answering via reasoning chains. arXiv preprint arXiv:1910.02610 (2019)
4. Chen, T., Kornblith, S., Norouzi, M., Hinton, G.: A simple framework for contrastive learning of visual representations. In: International Conference on Machine Learning, pp. 1597–1607. PMLR (2020)
5. De Cao, N., Aziz, W., Titov, I.: Question answering by reasoning across documents with graph convolutional networks. In: Proceedings of the 2019 Conference of the North American Chapter of the Association for Computational Linguistics: Human Language Technologies, Volume 1 (Long and Short Papers), pp. 2306–2317 (2019)
6. Deng, Y., Zhang, W., Lam, W.: Learning to rank question answer pairs with bilateral contrastive data augmentation. In: Proceedings of the Seventh Workshop on Noisy User-Generated Text (W-NUT 2021), pp. 175–181 (2021)
7. Fang, Y., Sun, S., Gan, Z., Pillai, R., Wang, S., Liu, J.: Hierarchical graph network for multi-hop question answering. In: Proceedings of the 2020 Conference on Empirical Methods in Natural Language Processing (EMNLP), pp. 8823–8838 (2020)
8. Gao, F., Ni, J.C., Gao, P., Zhou, Z.L., Li, Y.Y., Fujita, H.: Heterogeneous graph attention network for multi-hop machine reading comprehension. arXiv preprint arXiv:2107.00841 (2021)

9. Gao, T., Yao, X., Chen, D.: SimCSE: simple contrastive learning of sentence embeddings. In: Proceedings of the 2021 Conference on Empirical Methods in Natural Language Processing, pp. 6894–6910 (2021)

10. Groeneveld, D., Khot, T., Sabharwal, A., et al.: A simple yet strong pipeline for hotpotQA. In: Proceedings of the 2020 Conference on Empirical Methods in Natural Language Processing (EMNLP), pp. 8839–8845 (2020)

11. Hochreiter, S., Schmidhuber, J.: Long short-term memory. Neural Comput. **9**(8), 1735–1780 (1997)

12. Inoue, N., Trivedi, H., Sinha, S., Balasubramanian, N., Inui, K.: Summarize-then-answer: Generating concise explanations for multi-hop reading comprehension. In: Proceedings of the 2021 Conference on Empirical Methods in Natural Language Processing, pp. 6064–6080 (2021)

13. Jiang, Y., Joshi, N., Chen, Y.C., Bansal, M.: Explore, propose, and assemble: an interpretable model for multi-hop reading comprehension. In: Proceedings of the 57th Annual Meeting of the Association for Computational Linguistics, pp. 2714–2725 (2019)

14. Karpukhin, V., et al.: Dense passage retrieval for open-domain question answering. In: Proceedings of the 2020 Conference on Empirical Methods in Natural Language Processing (EMNLP), pp. 6769–6781 (2020)

15. Kundu, S., Khot, T., Sabharwal, A., Clark, P.: Exploiting explicit paths for multi-hop reading comprehension. In: Proceedings of the 57th Annual Meeting of the Association for Computational Linguistics, pp. 2737–2747 (2019)

16. Lee, J., Wettig, A., Chen, D.: Phrase retrieval learns passage retrieval, too. In: Proceedings of the 2021 Conference on Empirical Methods in Natural Language Processing, pp. 3661–3672 (2021)

17. Liao, J., Zhao, X., Li, X., Tang, J., Ge, B.: Contrastive heterogeneous graphs learning for multi-hop machine reading comprehension. World Wide Web **25**(3), 1469–1487 (2022)

18. Liu, Y., et al.: RoBERTa: a robustly optimized BERT pretraining approach. arXiv preprint arXiv:1907.11692 (2019)

19. Min, S., Zhong, V., Zettlemoyer, L., Hajishirzi, H.: Multi-hop reading comprehension through question decomposition and rescoring. In: Proceedings of the 57th Annual Meeting of the Association for Computational Linguistics, pp. 6097–6109 (2019)

20. Nishida, K., et al.: Answering while summarizing: Multi-task learning for multi-hop QA with evidence extraction. In: Proceedings of the 57th Annual Meeting of the Association for Computational Linguistics, pp. 2335–2345 (2019)

21. Nishida, K., Nishida, K., Saito, I., Yoshida, S.: Towards interpretable and reliable reading comprehension: a pipeline model with unanswerability prediction. In: 2021 International Joint Conference on Neural Networks(IJCNN), pp. 1–8. IEEE (2021)

22. Perez, E., Lewis, P., Yih, W.T., Cho, K., Kiela, D.: Unsupervised question decomposition for question answering. In: Proceedings of the 2020 Conference on Empirical Methods in Natural Language Processing (EMNLP), pp. 8864–8880 (2020)

23. Qiu, L., et al.: Dynamically fused graph network for multi-hop reasoning. In: Proceedings of the 57th Annual Meeting of the Association for Computational Linguistics, pp. 6140–6150 (2019)

24. Rajpurkar, P., Zhang, J., Lopyrev, K., Liang, P.: Squad: 100,000+ questions for machine comprehension of text. In: Proceedings of the 2016 Conference on Empirical Methods in Natural Language Processing, pp. 2383–2392 (2016)

25. Seo, M., Kembhavi, A., Farhadi, A., Hajishirzi, H.: Bidirectional attention flow for machine comprehension. In: International Conference on Learning Representations (2017)
26. Song, L., Wang, Z., Yu, M., Zhang, Y., Florian, R., Gildea, D.: Exploring graph-structured passage representation for multi-hop reading comprehension with graph neural networks. arXiv preprint arXiv:1809.02040 (2018)
27. Tang, Z., Shen, Y., Ma, X., Xu, W., Yu, J., Lu, W.: Multi-hop reading comprehension across documents with path-based graph convolutional network. In: Proceedings of the Twenty-Ninth International Conference on International Joint Conferences on Artificial Intelligence, pp. 3905–3911 (2021)
28. Tu, M., Huang, K., Wang, G., Huang, J., He, X., Zhou, B.: Select, answer and explain: Interpretable multi-hop reading comprehension over multiple documents. In: Proceedings of the AAAI Conference on Artificial Intelligence, vol. 34, pp. 9073–9080 (2020)
29. Tu, M., Wang, G., Huang, J., Tang, Y., He, X., Zhou, B.: Multi-hop reading comprehension across multiple documents by reasoning over heterogeneous graphs. In: Proceedings of the 57th Annual Meeting of the Association for Computational Linguistics, pp. 2704–2713 (2019)
30. Vaswani, A., et al.: Attention is all you need. In: Advances in Neural Information Processing Systems, vol. 30 (2017)
31. Veličković, P., Cucurull, G., Casanova, A., Romero, A., Liò, P., Bengio, Y.: Graph attention networks. In: International Conference on Learning Representations (2018)
32. Welbl, J., Stenetorp, P., Riedel, S.: Constructing datasets for multi-hop reading comprehension across documents. Trans. Assoc. Comput. Linguist. **6**, 287–302 (2018)
33. Wu, J., et al.: Self-supervised graph learning for recommendation. In: Proceedings of the 44th International ACM SIGIR Conference on Research and Development in Information Retrieval, pp. 726–735 (2021)
34. Xie, K., Wiegreffe, S., Riedl, M.: Calibrating trust of multi-hop question answering systems with decompositional probes. In: Findings of the Association for Computational Linguistics: EMNLP 2022, pp. 2888–2902 (2022)
35. Yadav, V., Bethard, S., Surdeanu, M.: Unsupervised alignment-based iterative evidence retrieval for multi-hop question answering. In: Proceedings of the 58th Annual Meeting of the Association for Computational Linguistics, pp. 4514–4525 (2020)
36. Yadav, V., Bethard, S., Surdeanu, M.: If you want to go far go together: unsupervised joint candidate evidence retrieval for multi-hop question answering. In: Proceedings of the 2021 Conference of the North American Chapter of the Association for Computational Linguistics: Human Language Technologies, pp. 4571–4581 (2021)
37. Yang, Z., et al.: HotpotQA: a dataset for diverse, explainable multi-hop question answering. In: Proceedings of the 2018 Conference on Empirical Methods in Natural Language Processing, pp. 2369–2380 (2018)

Importance-Based Neuron Selective Distillation for Interference Mitigation in Multilingual Neural Machine Translation

Jiarui Zhang[1,2,4] , Heyan Huang[3(✉)], Yue Hu[1,2], Ping Guo[1,2], and Yuqiang Xie[1,2]

[1] Institute of Information Engineering, Chinese Academy of Sciences, Beijing, China
{zhangjiarui,huyue,guoping,xieyuqiang}@iie.ac.cn
[2] School of Cyber Security, University of Chinese Academy of Sciences, Beijing, China
[3] School of Computer Science and Technology, Beijing Institute of Technology, Beijing, China
hhy63@bit.edu.cn
[4] Southeast Academy of Information Technology, Beijing Institute of Technology, Putian, China

Abstract. Multilingual neural machine translation employs a single model to translate multiple languages, enabling efficient cross-lingual transferability through shared parameters. However, multilingual training suffers from negative language interference, especially interference with high-resource languages. Existing approaches generally use language-specific modules to distinguish heterogeneous characteristics among different languages but suffer from the parameter explosion problem. In this paper, we propose a "divide and conquer" multilingual translation training method based on the importance of neurons that can mitigate negative language interference effectively without adding additional parameters. The key technologies can be summarized as estimation, pruning, distillation, and fine-tuning. Specifically, we estimate the importance of existing pre-trained model neurons, dividing them into the important ones representing general knowledge of each language and the unimportant ones representing individual knowledge of each low-resource language. Then, we prune the pre-trained model, retaining only the important neurons, and train the pruned model supervised by the original complete model via selective distillation to compensate for some performance loss due to unstructured pruning. Finally, we restore the pruned neurons and only fine-tune them. Experimental results on several language pairs demonstrate the effectiveness of the proposed method.

Keywords: Multilingual translation · Importance estimation · Pruning · Selective knowledge distillation · Negative language interference

Z. Jin et al. (Eds.): KSEM 2023, LNAI 14120, pp. 140–150, 2023.
https://doi.org/10.1007/978-3-031-40292-0_12

1   Introduction

In recent years, multilingual neural machine translation (MNMT) [5,7] has attracted considerable interest due to its ability to handle multiple translation directions in a single model. Nevertheless, multilingual training is hampered by the problem of *negative language interference* [4]. The multilingual model performs worse than its bilingual counterpart regarding high-resource translations. That is the precise manifestation of the negative interference caused by the intense competition in multiple training directions between **high-resource languages** (HRLs) and **low-resource languages** (LRLs).

Existing solutions to this issue typically involve incorporating language-specific modules [12,15] to distinguish heterogeneous characteristics among different languages. Although these techniques reduce language interference, there are still some issues: (1). Parameter inflation arises when language-specific modules are introduced, which increases the model's complexity and inefficiency. (2). These methods frequently require onerous and difficult-to-scale manual design.

Another promising direction in the field of MNMT is to expand both the depth and breadth of the MNMT model and construct large-scale corpora to enhance model capacity and incorporate a more diverse range of languages [8,19]. However, it still incurs substantial training and inference costs.

In this paper, we present a divide-and-conquer multilingual training method that manages considerable disagreements during language transfer and maintains a constant model size. Inspired by the analysis works on NMT [1], we argue that some critical neurons in a well-trained MNMT model play an important role among all languages during translation, and other neurons are only helpful for partial languages. To achieve this, we first pre-train a model using only high-resource corpora. This initial training phase allows the model to build a strong foundation by learning high-resource languages' shared knowledge. Next, we prune the model by activation value estimation to remove the less important neurons. Then, the pruned model is taught on all corpora using selective knowledge distillation under the supervision of the original complete model. This method allows the pruned model to learn the teacher model's output distribution. Finally, we restore the model to its original size and fine-tune the re-added neurons with low-resource data. Experimental results on various languages demonstrate the validity of our approach.

Our contributions can be summarized as follows:

- We propose a divide-and-conquer MNMT training method without adding additional parameters that can effectively mitigate language interference, especially the interference suffered by high-resource languages.
- Our method quantifies the importance of pre-trained model neurons and utilises selective knowledge distillation to transfer general knowledge from high-resource to low-resource.
- The experimental results demonstrate that our training method performs equally or surpasses bilingual translation models in high-resource languages, while its translation performance in low-resource languages is far superior to the current multilingual baseline model.

2   Background

We briefly review the background from three aspects, i.e., multilingual translation, knowledge distillation and negative language interference.

Multilingual Translation. In the standard MNMT paradigm, all parameters
are shared across languages, and the model is trained on multiple language pairs
under the encoder-decoder framework simultaneously [7]. Adding a unique language token to the original text indicates the target language. We use the Transformer [14] architecture as the backbone of all our models. The model is optimized by minimizing a cross-entropy loss ($\mathcal{L}_{CE}$) of the ground-truth sequence.

Knowledge Distillation. The most common method for transferring knowledge between models is knowledge distillation [3,6]. Typically, the teacher network is regarded as having the greater capability. By imitating the output distribution of the instructor network on the same data, a smaller student network can
be trained to perform comparably or even better. Assume that we are training a
classifier $p(y|x; \theta)$ with $|\mathcal{V}|$ classes and have access to a previously trained teacher
$q(y|x)$. Knowledge distillation employs the teacher model prediction $q(y|x)$ as a
soft target and minimizes the loss:

$$\mathcal{L}_{KD}(\theta) = -\sum_{k=1}^{|\mathcal{V}|} q(y = k|x) \times \log p(y = k|x; \theta) \qquad (1)$$

Negative Language Interference. Various groups of languages have heterogeneous characteristics, such as dictionaries and grammar, that are distinct.
Previous works have demonstrated that knowledge transfer is not beneficial for
all languages when all parameters are shared [18]. As [2,17] show, HRLs are
conducive to LRLs but may be inhibited by other HRLs and LRLs in turn.

3   Method

The main idea of our method is that disparate neurons exhibit varying significance and fulfill distinct functions. Our method involves four steps, shown in
Fig. 1. In step 1, we pre-train only on HRL pairs to construct a semantic space
containing a large quantity of knowledge. In step 2, we estimate the importance
of different neurons and then prune the model to remove the less critical neurons. In step 3, utilizing the entire data of the high-resource and low-resource
languages, we use selective knowledge distillation to transfer knowledge from
the high to the low. The unpruned model serves as the **teacher**, and the pruned
model serves as the **student**. In step 4, we restore the pruned model to its
original size and only fine-tune the re-added neurons with LRL pairs.

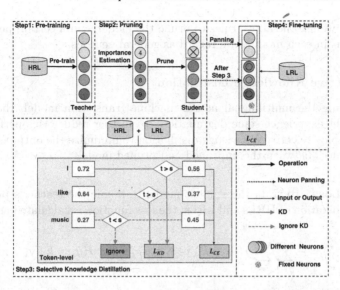

Fig. 1. The whole training process of the proposed method. Our method consists of four steps: (1) *Pre-training* on HRL pairs, (2) *Pruning* for removing unimportant neurons, (3) *Selective Knowledge Distillation* for learning beneficial knowledge from the original model, and (4) *Fine-tuning* with LRL pairs.

3.1   Pruning

The basic idea of pruning in our MNMT model is to determine which neurons are essential to all languages and which are responsible for low-resource languages while maintaining the original performance as much as possible. We can optimize the model for improved translation performance and computational efficiency by identifying these critical neurons. For a neuron i, the average importance $\mathcal{I}$ across language pairs is defined as follow:

$$\mathcal{I}(i) = \frac{1}{M} \sum_{m=1}^{M} \Theta^m(i) \tag{2}$$

where $\Theta(\cdot)$ denotes the importance estimation function and M denotes the number of language pairs. This value correlates positively with the neuron's significance across all languages. For $\Theta(\cdot)$, we employ the magnitude-based pruning scheme [13], in which the absolute value of each neuron's activation value is regarded as its significance. To facilitate the back propagation calculation, we have organized the equations slightly:

$$\Theta^m(i^l) = \frac{1}{T_m} \sum_{t} |h_i^l|. \tag{3}$$

where h_i^l is the activation value of the i-th neuron of l-th layer and T_m is the amount of the training examples of language pair m.

Finally, we use the above rules to prune the model, and a certain percentage ρ of neurons in each module are regard as general neurons.

3.2 Selective Knowledge Distillation

After pruning the multilingual neural machine translation model, the performance might experience some degradation. To further reduce this performance loss, we employ selective knowledge distillation to minimize the output distribution differences between the unpruned and pruned models.

Training Loss. To train the student model to mimic the teacher's prediction on the combination of HRLs and LRLs, the loss function is calculated as follows:

$$\mathcal{L}_{\text{KD}}\left(\theta_T, \theta_T^*\right) = -\sum_{j=1}^{J}\sum_{k=1}^{|\mathcal{V}|} q\left(y_j = k \mid \mathbf{y}_{<j}, \mathbf{x}; \theta_T^*\right) \times \log p\left(y_j = k \mid \mathbf{y}_{<j}, \mathbf{x}; \theta_T\right) \quad (4)$$

where $|\mathcal{V}|$ is the size of target vocabulary, $\mathbf{y}_{<j} = (y_1, \ldots, y_{j-1})$, $q(\cdot|\cdot)$ and $p(\cdot|\cdot)$ are conditional probabilities of the teacher and student models parameterized by θ_T^* and θ_T, respectively.

The student model benefits from the teacher model's knowledge and generalization capabilities, which helps the student model maintain high translation performance despite having fewer parameters.

Knowledge Detection. In some cases, the teacher model performs poorly on some pairs. Hence, it is crucial to discern the segment of the teacher model's supervision that will prove advantageous to the student model, denoted as *knowledge detection*. More specifically, given a batch of training data $\mathcal{B}$, knowledge detection attempts to divide the target tokens in $\mathcal{B}$ into two subsets $\mathcal{B}_+$ and $\mathcal{B}_-$ based on a beneficialness metric $\mathcal{F}$:

$$\mathcal{B}_+ := \{y_j \mid \mathcal{F}\left(y_j, \theta_T^*\right) \geq \mathcal{F}\left(y_j, \theta_T\right)\} \quad (5)$$

$$\mathcal{B}_- := \{y_j \mid \mathcal{F}\left(y_j, \theta_T^*\right) < \mathcal{F}\left(y_j, \theta_T\right)\} \quad (6)$$

In this paper, we adopt token-level cross-entropy as $\mathcal{F}$.

After convergence, the parameters of the student model (θ_T) will be solely responsible for HRLs and will also participate in the translation of LRLs.

3.3 Fine-Tuning

After obtaining the well-trained student model, the original removed parameters (denoted as θ_N) are re-added. These re-added parameters are then fine-tuned with LRL pairs, supervised by the ground truth sequences. The parameters of the student model (denoted as θ_T) remain fixed during this training phase.

This approach combines the knowledge of the student model, which captures the general translation capabilities, with fine-tuning the re-added parameters

Table 1. BLEU scores of English→10 languages translation with bilingual (En → 1), English-to-many (En → X), and many-to-many (X → X) systems. The languages are ordered from high-resource (left) to low-resource (right).

En → X test sets		#Params	Fr	Cs	De	Fi	Lv	Et	Ro	Hi	Tr	Gu	Avg$_{all}$
En → 1	BiNMT [14]	242M	36.3	22.3	40.2	15.2	16.5	15.0	23.0	12.2	13.3	7.9	20.2
En → X	MNMT [7]	**242M**	33.8	20.1	39.4	15.0	18.1	20.1	25.7	12.9	16.3	11.9	21.3
	mBART [9]	611M	33.9	20.8	40.2	14.8	18.2	20.5	26.1	15.4	16.8	12.9	22.0
	HLT-MT [17]	381M	**36.2**	22.2	**41.7**	**16.6**	18.9	21.0	26.3	15.7	17.1	14.6	23.0
	Our method	**242M**	36.0	**22.7**	41.1	16.3	**19.9**	**21.5**	**26.8**	**16.1**	**18.1**	**15.2**	**23.4**
X → X	MNMT [7]	**242M**	33.3	19.8	38.8	14.9	18.3	20.1	26.1	15.1	16.7	12.1	21.5
	mBART [9]	611M	33.4	20.0	39.2	15.1	18.0	**21.2**	25.1	15.7	17.1	14.3	21.9
	HLT-MT [17]	381M	35.7	22.0	**41.3**	**16.1**	19.5	21.0	26.3	15.7	17.6	14.7	23.0
	Our method	**242M**	**35.8**	**22.3**	41.0	**16.1**	**20.1**	21.1	**26.9**	**16.4**	**18.3**	**15.6**	**23.3**

using low-resource languages. The model retains its generalization capabilities while improving its performance on specific low-resource language-related tasks. The fixed parameters (θ_T) ensure that the model maintains its previously learned knowledge, while the re-added parameters (θ_N) are optimized to capture the nuances of the low-resource languages. The loss function is:

$$\mathcal{L}(\theta_T, \theta_N) = -\frac{1}{J} \sum_{j=1}^{J} \sum_{k=1}^{|\mathcal{V}|} (y_j = k) \times \log p\left(y_j = k \mid \mathbf{y}_{<j}, \mathbf{x}; \theta_T, \theta_N\right) \qquad (7)$$

The notations in the above equation are the same as those in the Eq. 4. After convergence, the parameters of the student model (θ_T) and the re-added parameters (θ_N) are combined together for generating HRL and LRL translation.

4 Experiments

4.1 Data Preparation

WMT-10. Following [10,16], we collect parallel data from publicly available WMT datasets in different languages to evaluate the models. The parallel data is between English and other ten languages, including French (Fr), Czech (Cs), German (De), Finnish (Fi), Latvian (Lv), Estonian (Et), Romanian (Ro), Hindi (Hi), Turkish (Tr), and Gujarati (Gu). It contains 32.5 million sentence pairs in the training set. We categorize language pairs greater than 1M as HRLs and the remainder as LRLs. We use the same development and test set as [16].

4.2 Model Details and Baselines

We use the open-source toolkit, *Fairseq-py* [11], as our Transformer system. We adopt the *transformer_big* setting [14] with a 6-layer encoder and decoder. The dimensions of word embeddings, hidden states, and non-linear layers are 1024, 1024, and 4096, respectively.

Table 2. BLEU scores of 10 languages→English translation with bilingual $(1 \rightarrow En)$, many-to-English $(X \rightarrow En)$, and many-to-many $(X \rightarrow X)$ systems. The languages are ordered from high-resource (left) to low-resource (right).

$X \rightarrow En$ test sets		#Params	Fr	Cs	De	Fi	Lv	Et	Ro	Hi	Tr	Gu	Avg_{all}
$1 \rightarrow En$	BiNMT [14]	242M	36.2	28.5	40.2	19.2	17.5	19.7	29.8	14.1	15.1	9.3	23.0
$X \rightarrow En$	MNMT [7]	242M	34.8	28.8	40.1	20.6	20.1	25.7	34.1	21.8	20.6	16.7	26.3
	mBART [9]	611M	35.7	28.9	40.0	22.2	20.6	27.2	37.2	23.3	**25.7**	21.7	28.2
	Our method	242M	**36.1**	**29.9**	**41.8**	**23.1**	**21.9**	**28.3**	**38.7**	**24.9**	25.6	**22.4**	**29.3**
$X \rightarrow X$	MNMT [7]	242M	33.9	28.1	39.0	19.9	19.5	24.5	33.7	22.4	22.0	17.2	26.0
	Our method	242M	**35.9**	**29.5**	**40.4**	**22.1**	**21.2**	**27.8**	**37.2**	**24.1**	**25.7**	**23.6**	**28.8**

All models are optimized with Adam with $\beta_1 = 0.9$, $\beta_2 = 0.98$. The learning rate is set as $5e-4$ with a warm-up step of 4,000. We train the models with the label smoothing cross-entropy with a smoothing ratio of 0.1. In the second step, we prune the last 30% unimportant neurons.

Our method is compared to bilingual and multilingual methods. **BiNMT** [14] is the bilingual Transformer model trained on each language pair separately. **MNMT** [7] is jointly trained on all directions, where the symbol of the target language is prepended to the input sentence. **mBART** [9] is a pre-trained 12-layer encoder-decoder model. **HLT-MT** [17] is trained on various high-resource corpora with the additional selective language-specific modules.

4.3   Main Results

Translation results of the ten languages translated from and to English are presented in Tables 1 and 2, respectively. Our method has the highest average bleu value on all datasets. Furthermore, we get the following conclusions:

First, the traditional multilingual baseline outperforms the single bilingual model on LRLs but not on HRLs like Fr, Cs, and De. In contrast, our approach is comparable to or surpasses the bilingual baseline in terms of high resource translation, such as De → En translation(+1.6 BLEU points). This indicates that our method effectively mitigates the interference of other languages with high-resource languages and improves multilingual translation.

Second, expanding the model reduces negative language interference. mBART employs a 12-layer encoder-decoder structure with parameters for all languages. The structure's robustness is enhanced, thereby reducing the impact of negative language interference. Compared with mBART, our method enables even greater enhancements. The significant parameters are separated for training and subsequent fine-tuning by selective knowledge distillation, thereby minimizing the interference of other low-resource languages.

Lastly, HLT-MT employs language-specific modules that can divide each HRL pair into separate parameter pool. Our method has marginally lower BLEU scores than HLT-MT for some high-resource languages. Nevertheless, our method outperforms HLT-MT on low-resource languages, as HLT-MT continues

Table 3. Ablation study of our proposed approach on the En → X benchmark. "Avg$_{high}$" and "Avg$_{low}$" refer to the average performance over high-resource and low-resource corpora, respectively. "†" denotes that no parameters are fixed.

Id	System	First	Second	Third	Fourth	Avg$_{high}$	Avg$_{low}$	Avg$_{all}$
1	first	lrl	activation	skd	lrl	23.9	18.9	21.4
2		all	activation	skd	lrl	26.0	19.3	22.7
3	second	hrl	random	skd	lrl	21.3	18.2	19.8
4	third	hrl	activation	w/o skd	lrl	25.9	18.9	22.4
5		hrl	activation	kd	lrl	26.8	19.3	23.0
6		hrl	activation	hrl	lrl	27.0	19.1	23.1
7		hrl	activation	lrl	lrl	26.8	19.4	23.1
8	fourth	hrl	activation	skd	all	27.1	19.2	23.2
9		hrl	activation	skd	hrl	**27.2**	18.1	22.7
10	our method	hrl	activation	skd	lrl	**27.2**	**19.5**	**23.4**

to employ the shared parameters method for handling low-resource languages. In addition, our method does not include any extra parameters and is more practical because it does not necessitate specialized model architecture. Only the pruning ratio needs to be modified as a hyperparameter.

4.4 Ablation Study

To gain a deeper understanding of the effects of each phase of our method, we conduct additional studies by removing or substituting certain steps.

The different systems used in the study are numbered from 1 to 10 in the first column of Table 3. The table displays the settings for the first, second, third, and fourth steps of the approach for each system and the average performance across all steps. Lines 1 and 2 show that pre-training just on HRLs can better construct a universal semantic space, boosting model performance and reducing interference from low-resource languages. Row 3 shows that specific neurons encapsulate multilingual knowledge. Lines 4–7 demonstrate the efficacy of selecting knowledge distillation and that fine-tuning the student model with all available data would be more beneficial for transferring knowledge from high to low resource levels. As seen in lines 8 and 9, assigning the neurons removed in stage 2 to low resources in step 4 can improve low-resource machine translation.

Overall, the table provides a comprehensive overview of the impact of different modifications to the proposed approach on translation performance. Our approach ameliorates all translation directions.

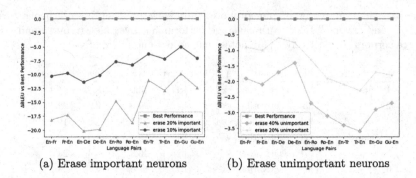

(a) Erase important neurons   (b) Erase unimportant neurons

Fig. 2. ΔBLEU score over best performance when erasing the important or unimportant neurons randomly on many-to-many translation tasks.

4.5 Analysis

Verifying the Function of Important Neurons. To further verify that specific modules or neurons can capture knowledge that is applicable across multiple languages, we conduct the following experiments. We randomly erase 10% or 20% of the important neurons from the best checkpoints of our method on many-to-many translation tasks, meaning that we mask the output values of these neurons to 0 and then use them to generate translations. For comparison, we also perform experiments with erasures of unimportant neurons.

As shown in Fig. 2, when the important neurons are eliminated, the BLEU scores of all language pairs decrease significantly, indicating that the specific neurons selected by our method do capture general knowledge across languages. Unimportant neurons have less effect on high resources because we transfer knowledge from high resources to important neurons knowledge distillation.

5 Conclusion

Current standard models of multilingual neural machine translation do not adequately address the issue of negative language interference. At the same time, recent researchers have focused on pursuing specific knowledge while expanding the model's capacity, necessitating fine-grained manual design. To address this issue, we employ the "divide and conquer" strategy by separating the model's neurons into general and low-resource language-specific components. Based on this, our method consists of several steps: pre-training, model pruning, selective knowledge distillation, and fine-tuning. Experiments on languages of different scales demonstrate that our approach can achieve significant improvements without adding any additional parameters and outperforms the bilingual machine translation model on most language pairs.

6 Limitations and Future Work

Our approach has shown strong performance on English-centric datasets, but has not been able to demonstrate capability on other datasets. In addition, we need further potential theoretical explanations of the real mechanism behind negative language interference.

In future work, we will validate the effectiveness of our approach on additional datasets, further investigate the intrinsic mechanism of the model and identify better ways to address negative interference.

Acknowledgements. This work is supported by the National Natural Science Foundation of China (Grant No. U21B2009). This research is also supported by the Strategic Priority Research Program of Chinese Academy of Science, Grant No. XDC02030400.

References

1. Bau, A., Belinkov, Y., Sajjad, H., Durrani, N., Dalvi, F., Glass, J.R.: Identifying and controlling important neurons in neural machine translation. In: 7th International Conference on Learning Representations. ICLR (2019)
2. Baziotis, C., Artetxe, M., Cross, J., Bhosale, S.: Multilingual machine translation with hyper-adapters. In: Proceedings of the 2022 Conference on Empirical Methods in Natural Language Processing, pp. 1170–1185, December 2022
3. Duh, H.K.B.T.K., Koehn, P.: Regularized training objective for continued training for domain adaptation in neural machine translation. In: ACL 2018, p. 36 (2018)
4. Gong, H., Li, X., Genzel, D.: Adaptive sparse transformer for multilingual translation. arXiv preprint arXiv:2104.07358 (2021)
5. Gu, J., Hassan, H., Devlin, J., Li, V.O.: Universal neural machine translation for extremely low resource languages. arXiv preprint arXiv:1802.05368 (2018)
6. Hinton, G., Vinyals, O., Dean, J.: Distilling the knowledge in a neural network. arXiv preprint arXiv:1503.02531 (2015)
7. Johnson, M., et al.: Google's multilingual neural machine translation system: enabling zero-shot translation
8. Kong, X., Renduchintala, A., Cross, J., Tang, Y., Gu, J., Li, X.: Multilingual neural machine translation with deep encoder and multiple shallow decoders. arXiv preprint arXiv:2206.02079 (2022)
9. Liu, Y., et al.: Multilingual denoising pre-training for neural machine translation. Trans. Assoc. Comput. Linguist. **8**, 726–742 (2020)
10. Ma, S., et al.: XLM-t: scaling up multilingual machine translation with pretrained cross-lingual transformer encoders
11. Ott, M., et al.: FairSeq: a fast, extensible toolkit for sequence modeling. arXiv preprint arXiv:1904.01038 (2019)
12. Philip, J., Berard, A., Gallé, M., Besacier, L.: Monolingual adapters for zero-shot neural machine translation. In: Proceedings of the 2020 Conference on Empirical Methods in Natural Language Processing (EMNLP), pp. 4465–4470 (2020)
13. See, A., Luong, M.T., Manning, C.D.: Compression of neural machine translation models via pruning. In: Proceedings of the 20th SIGNLL Conference on Computational Natural Language Learning, pp. 291–301 (2016)
14. Vaswani, A., et al.: Attention is all you need. In: Advances in Neural Information Processing Systems, vol. 30 (2017)

15. Wang, Y., Zhou, L., Zhang, J., Zhai, F., Xu, J., Zong, C.: A compact and language-sensitive multilingual translation method. In: Proceedings of the 57th Annual Meeting of the Association for Computational Linguistics, pp. 1213–1223 (2019)
16. Wang, Y., Zhai, C., Awadalla, H.H.: Multi-task learning for multilingual neural machine translation. In: Proceedings of the 2020 Conference on Empirical Methods in Natural Language Processing (EMNLP), pp. 1022–1034 (2020)
17. Yang, J., Yin, Y., Ma, S., Zhang, D., Li, Z., Wei, F.: High-resource language-specific training for multilingual neural machine translation. In: Raedt, L.D. (ed.) Proceedings of the Thirty-First International Joint Conference on Artificial Intelligence, IJCAI 2022, Vienna, Austria, 23–29 July 2022, pp. 4461–4467 (2022)
18. Yu, T., Kumar, S., Gupta, A., Levine, S., Hausman, K., Finn, C.: Gradient surgery for multi-task learning. Adv. Neural. Inf. Process. Syst. **33**, 5824–5836 (2020)
19. Zhang, B., Williams, P., Titov, I., Sennrich, R.: Improving massively multilingual neural machine translation and zero-shot translation. In: Proceedings of the 58th Annual Meeting of the Association for Computational Linguistics, pp. 1628–1639 (2020)

Are GPT Embeddings Useful for Ads and Recommendation?

Wenjun Peng[1,2], Derong Xu[1,2], Tong Xu[1,2(✉)], Jianjin Zhang[3],
and Enhong Chen[1,2]

[1] University of Science and Technology of China, Hefei, China
{pengwj,derongxu}@mail.ustc.edu.cn
[2] State Key Laboratory of Cognitive Intelligence, Hefei, China
{tongxu,cheneh}@ustc.edu.cn
[3] Microsoft STC Asia, Beijing, China
jianjin.zhang@microsoft.com

Abstract. Advertisement (ads) and recommendation are important for companies to drive their business objectives and improve user loyalty. A key strategy for these services is semantic modeling, which involves extracting useful knowledge or information from text. Large language models (LLMs) such as GPT-3 and LaMDA have incredible natural language understanding capabilities and their text embeddings have achieved excellent performance in various NLP tasks. Despite their potential, the discussion about whether text embeddings of LLMs can help ads and recommendation services is limited. In order to explore the utilization of GPT embeddings for ads and recommendation, we propose three strategies to integrate LLMs' knowledge into basic PLMs and improve their performance. These strategies consider GPT embedding as a feature (EaaF) to enrich text semantics, as a regularization (EaaR) to guide text token embedding aggregation, and as a pre-training task (EaaP) to replicate the capability of LLMs, respectively. Our experiments demonstrate that, by incorporating GPT embeddings, basic PLMs can improve their performance in both ads and recommendation tasks. Our code is available at https://github.com/Wenjun-Peng/GPT4SM

Keywords: knowledge extraction · semantic modeling · large language model

1 Introduction

Advertisement (ads) and recommendation can effectively increase company revenue and improve user experience. As a crucial technique for these services, semantic modeling aims at extracting helpful knowledge or features from text. To improve the modeling of text semantics, many studies [7,13,16,25,30,32] have adopted basic PLMs [5,6,9,14,15] to learn text representation and have achieved significant progress. For example, [13] demonstrate that BERT can learn text representation effectively to support document ranking tasks. [30] employ PLMs with out-of-domain knowledge to learn user-news semantic representation at

Z. Jin et al. (Eds.): KSEM 2023, LNAI 14120, pp. 151–162, 2023.
https://doi.org/10.1007/978-3-031-40292-0_13

multiple levels for personalized news recommendation. However, limited by the model size and training corpus, basic PLMs can't fully catch text features and are unable to deeply model text semantics.

On the other hand, recent years have witnessed the rapid development of large language models (LLMs). Although LLMs and basic PLMs are both pre-trained on unlabeled text data, LLMs generally contain more parameters, attention layers and are trained with a larger training corpus. Therefore, LLMs such as GPT-3 [3] and LaMDA [18] can certainly model rich semantic features in text and learn the relationships between words, resulting in more powerful capability in text understanding. Nevertheless, due to non-open source policy or limited resources, LLMs are usually unable to be further fine-tuned on downstream tasks or deployed on online platforms. Fortunately, we can obtain LLM embeddings from the embedding service[1] provided by technology corporations like OpenAI to improve basic PLMs performance. But it raises a heavy problem that how to better extract the semantic knowledge from LLMs' embeddings, since the training objectives of these embeddings are not aimed at ads or recommendation tasks, resulting in inconsistencies between the embedding features and the knowledge required for downstream tasks. We believe it is non-trivial to integrate the LLMs' embeddings when fine-tuning a basic PLM.

In this paper, we explore three strategies for utilizing the capabilities of LLMs in semantic modeling: embedding as a feature (EaaF), embedding as a regularization (EaaR), and embedding as a pre-training task (EaaP). These strategies can significantly improve performance on ads and recommendation tasks. 1) The **EaaF** strategy takes the LLMs embedding as global features and concatenates it with each token embedding of basic PLMs to enrich the semantic knowledge of text representation. 2) The **EaaR** strategy is designed to guide the text encoder of basic PLM to learn general knowledge from LLMs by introducing a regularization term, which contains a mean square loss to minimize the difference between the first token embedding of basic PLM and LLM embedding. 3) The **EaaP** strategy aims to enable basic PLMs to replicate the capabilities of LLMs by copying the embeddings of LLMs, and fine-tuning the EaaP model to adapt to downstream tasks. Experiments on two real-world datasets prove that our strategies can effectively improve model performance when compared to methods without these strategies.

2   Related Works

2.1   Text Semantic Modeling

Text semantic modeling techniques have been have been widely used in advertisement and news recommendation services to enhance user experience and achieve business objectives. It aims to extract key information from text and help find best matching text according to the relevance between query and candidate text. Many existing works [2,21,22,24] adopt traditional NLP model to

---

[1] https://api.openai.com/v1/embeddings.

model text semantics. However, such models are usually trained with a specific dataset and lack general knowledge, limiting their ability to mine text semantic information. In recent years, pre-trained language models (PLMs) such as BERT [5] and GPT [14] have demonstrated strong capability in various natural language processing (NLP) tasks. To leverage this advantage, many studies [7,13,16,25,30,32] have adopted PLMs to model text semantics and have achieved significant progress. For examples, [13] employ BERT as text encoder to learn its behavior and performance in text retrieval tasks. They demonstrate that BERT can effectively help text semantic mining and benefit seq2seq matching for passage ranking. [30] employ PLMs with out-of-domain knowledge to learn user-news semantic representation at word-level and news-level to captures multi-grained user-news matching signals for personalized news recommendation. [25] empower news recommendation system with multiple PLMs and improve model performance both online and offline.

However, the basic PLMs contain relatively few training parameters, making it impossible to fully capture the rich semantic knowledge in the text. Furthermore, the corpus used to train them is usually relatively small, which hinders their ability to learn the interaction between words and sentences in natural language understanding.

2.2 Large Language Models

Large Language Models (LLMs) [3,4,17–19] refer to a language model that has been trained on a large corpus and contains hundreds of billions of parameters. Although LLMs share a similar transformer architecture and pre-training objectives with basic PLMs, such huge capacity improvement of LLMs significantly enhances the model ability of semantic mining and natural language understanding capabilities. However, due to the non-open source policy or huge resource consumption, LLMs are usually unable to be further fine-tuned on downstream tasks or deployed on online platforms. Fortunately, many companies like OpenAI, Google and Microsoft deploy LLMs on cloud APIs, which provide a more convenient way for common or business users to use LLMs, without the need of running the model locally. For example, a series of GPT APIs are available to the public, including ada, babbage, curie, davinci, text-ada-001, text-babbage-001, and text-curie-001. These APIs generate text embeddings containing rich general knowledge that can benefit various NLP tasks.

Despite the enormous potential of LLM embeddings, the discussion about their utilization for semantic modeling is limited. Therefore, there is a need to investigate the use of GPT embeddings for ads and recommendation.

3 Methodology

3.1 Overall Framework

We design a framework utilizing **GPT** embedding to help **S**emantic **M**odeling, called **GPT4SM**. The GPT4SM for ads matching, as illustrated in Fig. 1, consists of a basic PLM, a guiding&pooling module, and a relevance prediction

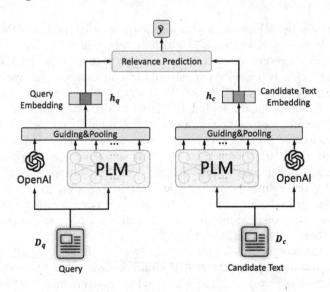

Fig. 1. Framework of our method for ads.

module. Given a query text $D_q = \{w_{q_1}, w_{q_2}, \cdots, w_{q_N}\}$ and a candidate text $D_c = \{w_{c_1}, w_{c_2}, \cdots, w_{c_M}\}$, the basic PLM first encode each tokens in D_q and D_c to obtain their token embeddings, donated as $\mathbf{E}_q = \{\mathbf{e}_{q_1}, \mathbf{e}_{q_2}, \cdots, \mathbf{e}_{q_N} | \mathbf{e}_{q_i} \in \mathbb{R}^{d_1}\}$ and $\mathbf{E}_c = \{\mathbf{e}_{c_1}, \mathbf{e}_{c_2}, \cdots, \mathbf{e}_{c_M} | \mathbf{e}_{c_i} \in \mathbb{R}^{d_1}\}$ respectively. Then, with three proposed strategies, a guiding&pooling module integrates GPT embedding knowledge into the basic PLM and guide token embeddings pooling to obtain the query and candidate text representation, which are donated as $\mathbf{h}_q = pool(\mathbf{E}_q), \mathbf{h}_c = pool(\mathbf{E}_c)$ respectively. The pooling operation can be first token pooling [13], mean pooling [8] or attention pooling [25]. Finally, the query representation $\mathbf{h}_q$ and candidate text representation $\mathbf{h}_c$ will be fed into the relevance prediction module to calculate their matching score $\hat{y}$. The relevance prediction module can be implemented by multi-layer perceptron (MLP) [8,27], inner product [1,11,12] or cosine similarity [2,31].

Unlike ad matching, there is no explicit query text for recommendation. Therefore, following [25], we use user-browsed text as query semantics. As shown in Fig. 2, we first employ the PLM of GPT4SM to encode user-browsed text to get their representation $\mathbf{h}_{i,i=0,1,\cdots,k}$. Then, a text pooling method is used to aggregate browsed text representation to obtain the query representation $\mathbf{h}_q$. The candidate text encoding and relevance prediction are consistent with ads matching. For simplicity, we next explain how our three strategies work for the ads matching task. The recommendation task is similar to ads matching, but it requires an additional step to calculate the weighted summation of browsed text representation.

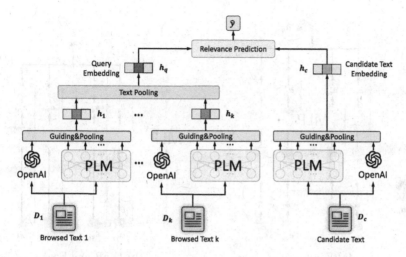

Fig. 2. Framework of our method for recommendation.

3.2 Embedding as a Feature (EaaF)

This strategy regards GPT embeddings as global semantic features to enrich the semantic knowledge for each token embeddings generated by PLMs. As shown in Fig. 3a, to get the query representation, we first concatenate each query token embedding with the GPT embedding. We then employ additive attention to aggregate these concatenated embeddings to get $\mathbf{h_q}$:

$$\mathbf{v}_{q_i} = concat(\mathbf{e}_{q_i}, \mathbf{u}_q), \mathbf{e}_{q_i} \in \mathbf{E}_q, \tag{1}$$

$$\alpha_{q_i} = \frac{\exp\left(\mathbf{w}_p^T \mathbf{v}_{q_i}/\sqrt{d}\right)}{\sum_{j=1}^{N} \exp\left(\mathbf{w}_p^T \mathbf{v}_{q_j}/\sqrt{d}\right)}, \tag{2}$$

$$\mathbf{h}_q = \sum_{q_i} \alpha_{q_i} * \mathbf{v}_{q_i}, \tag{3}$$

where $\mathbf{E}_q$ is set of query token embeddings, $\mathbf{u}_q \in \mathbb{R}^{d_2}$ is GPT embedding of the query, $\mathbf{w}_p \in \mathbb{R}^{d_1+d_2}$ is a learnable parameter vector, $\mathbf{h}_q$ is the query representation. The process of obtaining the candidate text representation $\mathbf{h}_c$ is consistent with the above steps.

The query representation $\mathbf{h}_q$ and the candidate text representation $\mathbf{h}_c$ are fed into the relevance prediction module to calculate their matching score $\hat{y}$. We use the cross entropy loss for model training.

3.3 Embedding as a Regularization (EaaR)

This strategy regards embeddings as regularization terms to guide the basic PLM to learn general knowledge from LLMs. As shown in Fig. 3b, to achieve this goal,

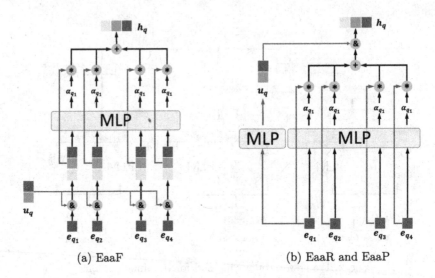

(a) EaaF   (b) EaaR and EaaP

Fig. 3. Strategies of our method. & means concatenate, + means summation

we first apply additive attention to aggregate query token embeddings to get the pooling embedding $\mathbf{p}_q$. And the first token embedding will be transformed to obtain regularization embedding which has the same dimension as the GPT embedding to calculate the mean square loss between them. Finally, the pooling embedding will be concatenated with the regularization embedding to strengthen its semantic knowledge. The process of getting $\mathbf{h}_q$ can be expressed as:

$$\mathbf{c}_q = \mathbf{W}_c^T \mathbf{e}_{\mathbf{qo}}, \tag{4}$$

$$\mathbf{h}_q = concat(\mathbf{c}_q, \mathbf{p}_q), \tag{5}$$

where $\mathbf{W}_c \in \mathbb{R}^{d_1 \times d_2}$ is a learnable parameter matrix, $\mathbf{e}_{\mathbf{qo}} \in \mathbb{R}^{d_1}$ is the first token embedding output from the PLM, $\mathbf{p}_q \in \mathbb{R}^{d_1}$ is the pooling token embedding. The process of obtaining candidate text representation $\mathbf{h}_c$ is consistent with the above steps.

To incorporate the knowledge of LLMs into the training of basic PLMs, we use the mean square loss as a regularization term in the training objective. The final loss can be expressed as:

$$\mathcal{L} = - \sum y \log \hat{y} + w_r * || \frac{\mathbf{c}_q}{||\mathbf{c}_q||_2} - \mathbf{u}_q ||, \tag{6}$$

where y is the groundtruth relevance between query and candidate text, $\hat{y}$ is the predicted relevance, $\mathbf{c}_q \in \mathbb{R}^{d_2}$ is the regularization embedding which learns knowledge from LLMs, $\mathbf{u}_q \in \mathbb{R}^{d_2}$ is the GPT embedding output from LLMs, w_r is the regularization weight.

3.4 Embedding as a Pre-traning Task (EaaP)

Previous studies [10, 20, 28, 29] have proved that attackers can extract the target model encapsulated in the API through model extraction attack, even without knowledge of the model structure and training data. Inspired by this, we propose EaaP which regards embedding as a pre-training task to enable the basic PLM to replicate the capabilities of LLMs. The process of obtaining $\mathbf{h}_q$ and $\mathbf{h}_c$ of EaaP is consistent with EaaR. However, EaaP's training process is divided into two parts. During the first N_{ep} epochs, the model imitates the output of LLMs. We use the transformed first token embedding as replication embeddings to learn the knowledge of GPT embedding. The mean square loss is used to minimize the difference between GPT embeddings and replication embeddings. During the last few epochs, fine-tuning is performed to adapt the model to downstream tasks. We use the cross-entropy loss for click prediction training.

4 Experiments

4.1 Datasets and Baselines

Table 1. Statistics of the MIND and Ads datasets.

Ads		MIND	
# query	935,175	# impression (imp)	2,600,844
# ads	935,175	# news	125,590
# positive interaction	562,154	# clicks	3,972,959
Avg. # words per query	4.17	Avg. # words per news	10.75
Avg. # words per ads	2.51	Avg. # news per imp	39.10

We conducted experiments on two real-world datasets in the fields of ads matching and news recommendation. The first dataset was sampled from Microsoft advertising logs over the past two years and contains 935,175 pairs of (query, ads keywords), each of which was manually labeled for relevance. The second dataset is the MIND [26], collected for personalized news recommendation. It includes user-browsed and clicked news in Microsoft News for six weeks. Their detailed statistics are shown in Table 1.

We compared our methods against multiple baselines, including GPT Emb, GPT Emb+MLP, BERT, BERT+Attention, and BERT+GPT Emb. GPT Emb does not require training, and directly utilizes cosine similarity as its matching score to determine the most similar candidate text for a given query. The GPT embedding comes from the ada2 model of OpenAI[2]. BERT uses its pooling output as text representation, and BERT+Attention uses an attention mechanism to

---

[2] https://openai.com/blog/new-and-improved-embedding-model/.

aggregate token embedding to obtain text representation. Besides, BERT+GPT Emb concatenates BERT's pooling output and GPT embedding as text representation. For all baselines, except GPT Emb, the text representation of the query and candidate text is concatenated and fed into an MLP to calculate their relevance.

Table 2. Performance of methods on Ads and MIND. The best results are in bold, and the second-best results are underlined. Since GPT Emb has no trainable parameters, we do not show its standard deviation. AUC is used as the metric for the Ads dataset to maintain consistency with the industrial evaluation process, while AUC, MRR, and nDCG are used as metrics for the MIND dataset to maintain consistency with the MIND platform.

Methods	Ads	MIND			
	AUC ↑	AUC ↑	MRR ↑	nDCG@5↑	nDCG@10↑
GPT Emb	59.33	64.31	31.10	34.01	39.77
GPT Emb+MLP	70.57 ± 0.51	66.34 ± 0.03	32.25 ± 0.10	34.81 ± 0.10	40.61 ± 0.09
BERT	70.89 ± 0.24	67.88 ± 0.10	33.18 ± 0.09	36.06 ± 0.08	41.77 ± 0.09
BERT+Attention	70.66 ± 2.67	68.25 ± 0.05	33.73 ± 0.05	36.71 ± 0.07	42.38 ± 0.07
BERT+GPT Emb	70.69 ± 0.45	68.36 ± 0.08	33.52 ± 0.04	36.43 ± 0.06	42.18 ± 0.06
GPT4SM (EaaF)	72.89 ± 0.26	68.84 ± 0.15	34.23 ± 0.07	37.29 ± 0.08	42.96 ± 0.07
GPT4SM (EaaR)	**75.37** ± 0.46	68.36 ± 0.27	33.90 ± 0.19	36.88 ± 0.23	42.53 ± 0.22
GPT4SM (EaaP)	74.29 ± 0.15	**69.23** ± 0.25	**34.51** ± 0.15	**37.61** ± 0.17	**43.27** ± 0.18

4.2 Methods Performance

In Fig. 2, it is evident that the integration of GPT embeddings with the BERT-Base backbone improves the performance of multiple methods on both real-world datasets from different fields. This improvement is attributed to the fact that LLMs have more model parameters and general knowledge, which aids in the semantic mining, and their embeddings effectively benefit the training of basic PLMs. To elaborate, EaaR leverages the GPT embedding as a regularization term to guide the text encoder training, resulting in the best performance on the Ads dataset. Specifically, EaaR achieves an AUC of 75.37%, outperforming BERT-Attention, which only achieves an AUC of 70.66%.

We also found that simply concatenating BERT with GPT embeddings does not lead to improved performance, as shown in BERT+GPT Emb. This is because such an approach fails to drive BERT to learn knowledge of the LLMs. When comparing EaaF with EaaR and EaaP in the Ads dataset, we observed that the "learn and fine-tune" approach used in EaaR and EaaP yielded better results than the "directly use embedding as a feature" approach used in EaaF. We believe this is because the GPT embedding provides excellent guidance in this dataset. And EaaR and EaaP combine the imitation of embeddings with

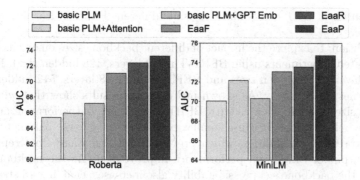

Fig. 4. Performance of baselines and our methods with different backbones.

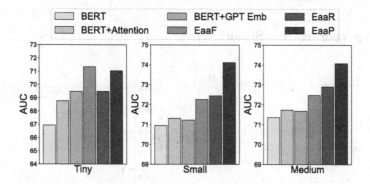

Fig. 5. Performance of baselines and our methods with different backbone size.

the training objectives of downstream tasks, allowing them to acquire knowledge from LLMs' embeddings while adapting to the ads matching. In addition, the performance of EaaR is not significantly improved on the MIND dataset. This is because LLMs are typically trained on general corpora and lack specific transformations for downstream tasks, resulting in embeddings that cannot fully adapt to each task, which can be reflected by the poor performance of GPT Emb+MLP. And EaaR can be viewed as a multi-task learning process, which leads to the model learning noise of GPT embedding when fitting downstream tasks.

4.3 Impact of Backbone

To validate the model-agnostic nature of our strategies, we performed experiments on the Ads dataset to compare the performance of baselines and our methods with different backbones, including Roberta [9] and MiniLM [23]. As shown in Fig. 4, our methods significantly outperform baselines based on all backbones. This demonstrates that our three methods excel in leveraging the rich semantics of GPT embeddings to guide different PLMs in learning general knowledge.

In addition, to explore the impact of different backbone sizes on our methods, we conducted experiments using BERT-Tiny (2 layers, 128 hidden size), BERT-Small (4 layers, 512 hidden size) and BERT-Medium (8 layers, 512 hidden size) as backbones, respectively. As shown in Fig. 5, the results show that when the backbone size is small, such as with BERT-Tiny, EaaF outperforms EaaR and EaaP. We believe this is because smaller backbones have fewer parameters and limited expressive capabilities, which prevent EaaR and EaaP from reproducing the output of LLMs and performance improvement. As the backbone size increases, the backbone's expression ability also increases, enabling all strategies to learn from the LLMs and enhance their semantic mining ability, resulting in performance improvement.

4.4   Hyperparameters Sensitivity

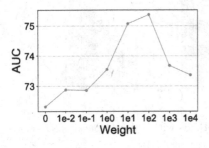 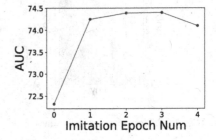

(a) Impact of regularization weight w_r in EaaR

(b) Impact of imitation epoch number N_{ep} in EaaP

Fig. 6. Impact of hyperparameters

In this section, we analyze the impact of hyperparameters on the performance of EaaR and EaaP. The first is the weight w_r of the regularization term in EaaR, which varies from 0 to 1e4. It can be found that when w_r is 0, it fails to learn any GPT embedding knowledge, and the model performs the worst. With the increase of w_r, the model performance gradually improves, with the best performance achieved when w_r is set to 1e2. This is because the GPT embedding and regularization embedding are normalized, thus its mean square loss value is very small, which makes the model ignoring the regularization term. Properly increasing w_r can make the model pay more attention to the task of learning from GPT embeddings. However, as w_r continues to increase, the model's performance begins to decline. This is because the primary objective of the model training shifts towards imitating the LLM rather than learning text semantic relevance (Fig. 6).

The second one is imitation epoch number N_{ep} in EaaP. We observed that the model performs the worst when N_{ep} is set to 0, since it is unable to learn from the GPT embeddings. As N_{ep} increases, the model gradually acquires more GPT embedding knowledge, resulting in improved performance. The best performance is achieved when N_{ep} is set to 2 or 3. However, as N_{ep} continues to increase, the model over-fits to the noise of GPT embeddings, ultimately leading to a decline in performance.

5 Conclusion

In this paper, we introduce three novel strategies, namely EaaF, EaaR, and EaaP, aimed at improving the semantic mining capabilities of basic PLMs by utilizing LLM embeddings. These strategies involve treating GPT embedding as an input feature, a regularization term, and a pre-training task to integrate LLM knowledge into basic PLMs and guiding token embedding aggregation. They facilitate model training and lead to improved performance. Our experimental results, based on two real datasets, demonstrate the effectiveness of our strategies in enhancing the performance of basic PLMs for tasks such as ads matching and news recommendation, regardless of the backbone type and size of the PLMs.

Acknowledgments. This work was supported by the grants from National Natural Science Foundation of China (No. 62222213, 62072423), and the USTC Research Funds of the Double First-Class Initiative (No. YD2150002009).

References

1. Ai, Q., Hill, D.N., Vishwanathan, S., Croft, W.B.: A zero attention model for personalized product search. In: CIKM, pp. 379–388 (2019)
2. Ai, Q., Zhang, Y., Bi, K., Chen, X., Croft, W.B.: Learning a hierarchical embedding model for personalized product search. In: SIGIR, pp. 645–654 (2017)
3. Brown, T., et al.: Language models are few-shot learners. NIPS **33**, 1877–1901 (2020)
4. Chowdhery, A., et al.: Palm: scaling language modeling with pathways. arXiv preprint arXiv:2204.02311 (2022)
5. Devlin, J., Chang, M.W., Lee, K., Toutanova, K.: BERT: pre-training of deep bidirectional transformers for language understanding. In: NAACL, pp. 4171–4186 (2019)
6. Dong, L., et al.: Unified language model pre-training for natural language understanding and generation. NIPS **32** (2019)
7. Jia, Q., Li, J., Zhang, Q., He, X., Zhu, J.: RmBERT: news recommendation via recurrent reasoning memory network over BERT. In: SIGIR, pp. 1773–1777 (2021)
8. Li, D., et al.: VIRT: improving representation-based text matching via virtual interaction. In: EMNLP, pp. 914–925 (2022)
9. Liu, Y., et al.: RoBERTa: a robustly optimized BERT pretraining approach. arXiv preprint arXiv:1907.11692 (2019)
10. Liu, Y., Jia, J., Liu, H., Gong, N.Z.: Stolenencoder: stealing pre-trained encoders in self-supervised learning. In: CCS, pp. 2115–2128 (2022)

11. Okura, S., Tagami, Y., Ono, S., Tajima, A.: Embedding-based news recommendation for millions of users. In: SIGKDD, pp. 1933–1942 (2017)
12. Qi, T., Wu, F., Wu, C., Huang, Y.: Personalized news recommendation with knowledge-aware interactive matching. In: SIGIR, pp. 61–70 (2021)
13. Qiao, Y., Xiong, C., Liu, Z., Liu, Z.: Understanding the behaviors of BERT in ranking. arXiv preprint arXiv:1904.07531 (2019)
14. Radford, A., Narasimhan, K., Salimans, T., Sutskever, I., et al.: Improving language understanding by generative pre-training (2018)
15. Raffel, C., et al.: Exploring the limits of transfer learning with a unified text-to-text transformer. JMLR **21**(1), 5485–5551 (2020)
16. Reimers, N., Gurevych, I.: Sentence-BERT: sentence embeddings using Siamese BERT-networks. arXiv preprint arXiv:1908.10084 (2019)
17. Taylor, R., et al.: Galactica: a large language model for science. arXiv preprint arXiv:2211.09085 (2022)
18. Thoppilan, R., et al.: Lamda: language models for dialog applications. arXiv preprint arXiv:2201.08239 (2022)
19. Touvron, H., et al.: Llama: open and efficient foundation language models. arXiv preprint arXiv:2302.13971 (2023)
20. Wallace, E., Stern, M., Song, D.: Imitation attacks and defenses for black-box machine translation systems. In: EMNLP, pp. 5531–5546 (Nov 2020)
21. Wang, H., Wu, F., Liu, Z., Xie, X.: Fine-grained interest matching for neural news recommendation. In: ACL, pp. 836–845 (2020)
22. Wang, H., Zhang, F., Xie, X., Guo, M.: DKN: deep knowledge-aware network for news recommendation. In: WWW, pp. 1835–1844 (2018)
23. Wang, W., Wei, F., Dong, L., Bao, H., Yang, N., Zhou, M.: Minilm: deep self-attention distillation for task-agnostic compression of pre-trained transformers. NIPS **33**, 5776–5788 (2020)
24. Wu, C., Wu, F., Qi, T., Huang, Y.: User modeling with click preference and reading satisfaction for news recommendation. In: IJCAI, pp. 3023–3029 (2020)
25. Wu, C., Wu, F., Qi, T., Huang, Y.: Empowering news recommendation with pre-trained language models. In: SIGIR, pp. 1652–1656 (2021)
26. Wu, F., et al.: Mind: a large-scale dataset for news recommendation. In: ACL, pp. 3597–3606 (2020)
27. Xi, Y., et al.: Multi-level interaction reranking with user behavior history. In: SIGIR, pp. 1336–1346 (2022)
28. Xu, Q., He, X., Lyu, L., Qu, L., Haffari, G.: Beyond model extraction: Imitation attack for black-box NLP APIs. arXiv e-prints arXiv-2108 (2021)
29. Zanella-Béguelin, S., et al.: Analyzing information leakage of updates to natural language models. In: CCS, pp. 363–375 (2020)
30. Zhang, Q., et al.: UnBERT: user-news matching BERT for news recommendation. In: IJCAI, pp. 3356–3362 (2021)
31. Zhu, Q., Zhou, X., Song, Z., Tan, J., Guo, L.: Dan: deep attention neural network for news recommendation. In: AAAI, vol. 33, pp. 5973–5980 (2019)
32. Zhuang, S., Zuccon, G.: CharacterBERT and self-teaching for improving the robustness of dense retrievers on queries with typos. In: SIGIR, pp. 1444–1454 (2022)

Modal Interaction-Enhanced Prompt Learning by Transformer Decoder for Vision-Language Models

Mingyue Liu[1], Honggang Zhao[1], Longfei Ma[1], Xiang Li[1], Yucheng Ji[1], and Mingyong Li[1,2(✉)]

[1] Chongqing Normal University, Chongqing, China
limingyong@cqnu.edu.cn
[2] National Center for Applied Mathematics in Chongqing, Chongqing, China

Abstract. In the current multimodal retrieval field, CoOp is the preferred approach among many models due to its simplicity and powerful adaptive capability. However, CoOp mainly concentrates on optimizing prompt execution contrast learning and does not consider image-text interactions. In this work, we propose a prompt tuning method for simulating image-text interaction based on CoOp: Decoding context optimization (DeCoOp). Through extensive experiments on 11 image classification datasets, 7 datasets under the few-shot setting and all 11 datasets under the zero-shot setting are ahead of CoOp in our method. Experiments on four target datasets of ImageNet show a model performance improvement of more than 10%, demonstrating that our approach substantially outperforms the baseline model CoOp in terms of point domain generalization and robustness. In addition, ablation experiments performed on three representative datasets confirmed the effectiveness and further improvement of the accuracy of DeCoOp. Finally, experiments are performed on 11 datasets using different visual backbones, and it is not difficult to find that the gap between our approach and hand-crafted prompts is large in all architectures and shows better performance than CoOp.

Keywords: Modal Interaction · CLIP · Prompt Learning · Self-Attention

1 Introduction

Advanced visual language models, and large-scale high-quality datasets, have led to significant improvements in the accuracy of visual understanding tasks, such as classification [12], target detection [7], and semantic segmentation [13]. The development of large-scale self-supervised methods [4] [18] has been also greatly improved. Visualization tasks for large, high-quality datasets are laborious and expensive to collect. Many optimization strategies have been put out as a result of the development of efficient visual language models. Visual-Language pre-training models such as CLIP [17] have been used as a promising alternative to visual representation learning. The main approach is to use two independent

Z. Jin et al. (Eds.): KSEM 2023, LNAI 14120, pp. 163–174, 2023.
https://doi.org/10.1007/978-3-031-40292-0_14

encoders to align the image and the original text so that every modality corresponds to one encoder. For example, CLIP describes the learning goal as contrast loss, which aggregates images and their text descriptions while separating mismatched pairs in the feature space.

Recently, many efforts have been made to enhance the transfer of CLIP models to downstream visual categorization tasks. For example, adding adapters [6,24] to CLIP, can change the language model's output so that it better matches new tasks. As well as CoOp [25], which automates Prompt Engineering by fine-tuning the pre-trained CLIP patterns. Specifically, CoOp changes the hand-crafted prompt of CLIP and turns it into a contextual prompt that can be learned. The change performed much better than manual prompts in terms of domain generalization, achieving good downstream performance and efficiency, and providing powerful evidence of the potential of fast learning in large visual models. The CoOp's work based on zero-shot migration learning shows good performance while leaving the issue of image-text interaction virtually undiscussed.

In this paper, we propose the DeCoOp model to explore the improvement of model performance by image-text interaction optimization prompting. Unlike the previous CLIP and CoOp which simply use contextual text as prompt optimization, our DeCoOp does masking of image features before performing contrast learning with the original joint. Then together with the text features, the text-image interaction is simulated with transformer decoder [21]. Finally, the residuals are used to combine the former contextual prompt vectors. Thus the text part of contrast learning not only is a learnable contextual prompt, but also incorporates visual features. This approach pulls in the distance between the image and the text and enhances the robustness of our model. The results show that our model is more conducive to discovering those invisible classes in the dataset, has a stronger generalization ability, and is better able to capture more generalizable elements that are critical to broad scene identification. Figure 1 shows the experimental results of our model on the fine-grained texture dataset DTD, with improved accuracy compared to zero-shot and CoOp. In summary, our contributions can be summarized as follows:

1. Based on the CoOp context prompt, a novel image-text interaction optimization prompt method is proposed. From the perspective of simulating the interaction between vision and text, we optimize the context prompt and achieved good results on eleven datasets.
2. Compared with CoOp, our model is implemented on four target datasets of ImageNet, and the results prove that our model is more robust and has stronger domain generalization ability.

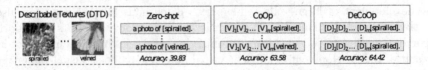

Fig. 1. Prompt engineering vs Decoding Context Optimization (DeCoOp).

2 Methodology

2.1 Text Prompt for Few-Shot Learning

Text Prompt of CLIP A contrast vision-language learning model, the Pre-trained Model (CLIP) shows the potential of learning visual concepts. CLIP is built by two coders, one for image and one for text. During training, CLIP adopts contrast loss to learn the joint embedding space of the two modes. Specifically, for a small batch of image-text pairs, CLIP maximizes the cosine similarity of each image to the matched text while minimizing the cosine similarity to all other unmatched text. And the loss is computed in a similar way for each text.

CLIP finds that the class label is directly used as the text description, many texts are just a label, lacking specific context, and inconsistent with CLIP training data. To solve this problem, CLIP uses the hand-crafted prompt as the input of the text encoder. The text input is converted from a single class label to a text description. For example, the class label: "dog" is converted to "a photo of dog", The effect is better than using the class label directly.

For the CLIP model, let f be the image feature extracted by the image encoder for the image, and $\{w_i\}_{i=1}^{K}$ be a set of weight vectors generated by the text encoder. K indicates the number of classes. Each w_i comes from a prompt that may be in the form of "a photo of a $[CLASS]$ ". Where the class label is replaced by a specific class label, such as "cat", "dog" or "car". The final predicted probability is calculated as:

$$p(y = i \mid x) = \frac{\exp(\cos(w_i, f)/\tau)}{\sum_{j=1}^{K} \exp(\cos(w_j, f)/\tau)}. \tag{1}$$

where τ is a temperature parameter learned through CLIP and $\cos(\cdot, \cdot)$ represents cosine similarity.

Text Prompt of CoOp By employing continuous vectors that have been learned end-to-end from the data, CoOp on context modeling enhances CLIP manually crafted prompts into learnable prompts. The text input is transformed from a one-sentence text description to a set of learnable vectors. Embedding class tokens and finally the vectors whole as text input into the text encoder. According to the implementation approach of the prompt, CoOp divides the optimization context into two categories, namely unified context, and design class-specific context, as follows:

Unified context: All classes share the same context. This means that the contextual statements are learned by modeling, converting them into a vector of a certain length, and then embedding the class label in it. In addition to embedding them at the end of the sequence, the class label can also be placed in the middle of the sequence. The specific forms are shown in Eqs. 2 and 3.

$$t = [V]_1 [V]_2 \cdots [V]_M [CLASS]. \tag{2}$$

$$t = [V]_1 \cdots [V]_{\frac{M}{2}} [CLASS] [V]_{\frac{M}{2}+1} \cdots [V]_M. \tag{3}$$

Each $[V]_m$ $(m\epsilon\{1,\cdots M\})$ is a vector with the same dimension as the word embedding, and M is a hyperparameter specifying the number of context label.

We can obtain the classification weight vector representing the visual concept by forwarding the prompt t to the text encoder $g\left(\cdot\right)$. The predicted probability is calculated as Eqs. 4:

$$p(y=i\mid x)=\frac{\exp(\cos(g(t_i),f)/\tau)}{\sum_{j=1}^{K}\exp(\cos(g\left(t_i\right),f)/\tau)}. \tag{4}$$

The class label in each prompt t_i is replaced by the corresponding word embedding vector of the class label. This increases the flexibility of learning – Prompt can not only fill in the following cells with supplementary descriptions but also use termination signals such as periods to cut sentences in advance.

Design class-specific context: The context vector is independent of each class. For different classes, the context vectors are not equal. As shown in Eq. 5:

$$[V]_1^i[V]_2^i\cdots[V]_M^i\,[CLASS]\neq[V]_1^j[V]_2^j\cdots[V]_M^j\,[CLASS]. \tag{5}$$

where $i\neq j$, and $i,j\epsilon\{1,\cdots,K\}$.

According to the description of CoOp, designing the class-specific context is particularly useful for some fine-grained classification tasks. However, our method chooses the uniform context with the best performance and the class label at the end of the sequence.

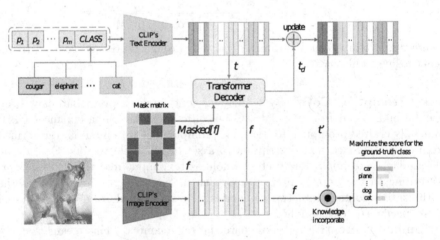

Fig. 2. Overview of Decoding Context Optimization.

2.2 The Proposed Method

In CLIP, text and images are processed in parallel, putting the images and text through the encoder and learning directly by comparative learning, without considering the interaction of text and images. In addition, CoOp focuses primarily on optimizing prompts for contrast learning, but does not consider image-text interactions and the impact on the model when incorporating visual information into the prompts. To address the above issues, our DeCoOp uses the context optimization approach, which is based on modeling contextual words with continuous vectors learned end-to-end from the data. The difference is that we have adopted a visual text interaction perspective inspired by DenseCLIP. We are inserting the Transformer decoder after the image and text encoders. This enables the cross-attention mechanism of the decoder to be employed to simulate the interaction between vision and text. The overview is shown in Fig. 2.

The input of the Transformer Decoder is derived from text features and image features, respectively. Specifically, we choose a masking matrix to mask the visual features f to obtain $\bar{f}$ as in Eq. 6. The matrix is randomly masked with a probability of 0.2 for the features. After the visual features are masked, some visual-spatial information is retained randomly and is consistent with the behavior of the spatial information of f. So $\bar{f}$ can be adopted as the feature map. Combining $\bar{f}$ with f enhances the visual information and balances the deficiency of contextual prompts derived entirely from textual information. The interaction of visual text is next carried out in the form shown in Eq. 7, where $D(\cdot)$ is the transformer decoder whose input is the prompt text, and the visual features after the union. For the context prompts in the textual input part, we choose the M=16 context behind the best-performing class label in CoOp, as shown in Eq. 2. Finally, the text features are updated with the output of the transformer decoder through residual concatenation, as in Eq. 8. Thus, the final text features for comparison learning contain both textual and visual information.

$$\bar{f} = Masked.(f).$$ (6)

$$v_d = D\left(t, [\bar{f}, f]\right).$$ (7)

$$t \leftarrow t + \gamma v_d.$$ (8)

In Eq. 8, $\gamma \epsilon R^c$ is a learnable parameter that controls the residuals scaling, initialized with a very small value (*e.g.*, 10^{-4}), that maximally preserves linguistic priors in the text feature.

3 Experiments

3.1 Few-Shot Learning

Training Settings Datasets We have selected 11 datasets that are the same as CLIP and CoOp to verify the validity of our model. Specifically, benchmarks include ImageNet [3] and Caltech101 [5], which are applied to classify common objects. Oxford Pets [16], Stanford Cars [11], Flowers102 [15], Food101 [1] and

FGVCAircraft [14], are for fine-grained classification. SUN397 [23] is employed for scene recognition. UCF101 [20] is for action recognition. DTD [2] is occupied for texture classification. Finally, EuroSAT [8] is used for satellite image recognition.

Details Referring to CoOp, we apply a single A6000 GPU for all experiments and train our model at shots 1, 2, 4, 8, and 16. We use the same training hyperparameters as CoOp, including a training batch size of 32 and a learning rate of 1×10^{-5}.

Baseline Models Compared our DeCoOp to three baselines: the first baseline is Zero-shot CLIP [17] based on the hand-crafted prompt. The second baseline is Linear probe CLIP [17], an additional linear classifier trained following a few-shot training approach on its visual encoder. The third baseline is CoOp [25] based on continuous prompt learning. To make the comparison fair, we choose the best-performing variant of CoOp. It is shared between different classes, with the class token placed in the context at the end of the continuous prompt. The Zero-shot CLIP uses the shared hand-crafted prompt, our model is built to use the same class token position as the best-performing variant of CoOp.

Performance Comparison and Analysis The main results of the experiment are shown in Fig. 3. From the average accuracy of the 11 datasets shown in the graph, across all different shot training conditions, DeCoOp regularly performed much better than the other three baseline models in seven of them. And in all datasets, persistently significantly outperform the other three baseline models in one-shot tactical situations, showing the proposed method's superior ability to learn fewer shots.

Compared with **zero-shot CLIP**, our method achieves significant performance improvement on 10 datasets and comparable performance with zero-shot CLIP on 1 dataset. Figure 4 illustrates the rank of the 11 datasets' absolute performance improvements in the 16-shot training condition. Our approach enhances effectiveness on fine-grained and task-specific datasets including EuroSAT, Flowers102, and DTD by more than 20% to 45%. As well as a 5.55% improvement on the challenging 1000-category dataset ImageNet. On the two datasets OxfordPets and Food101, despite the slight DeCoOp improvement, the original results of Zero-shot CLIP have been enhanced. DeCoOp's 10%+ performance gain on the remaining five datasets, including datasets related to scene and action recognition: SUN397 and UCF101, is also noteworthy.

Compared with **Linear Probe CLIP**, as shown in Fig. 3, the performance of our model shows obvious advantages. It is significantly better than the linear probe CLIP. And the advantage is more obvious in extremely low data areas (such as one-shot and two-shot training settings). For instance, in the one-shot and two-shot training settings, the absolute improvement in the Oxford-Pets dataset is 60.47% and 47.17%, respectively, and the Food101 dataset is 46.71% and 34.88%, respectively. And that of the Food101 dataset is 46.71% and 34.88%, respectively. This indicates that our approach is much more effective

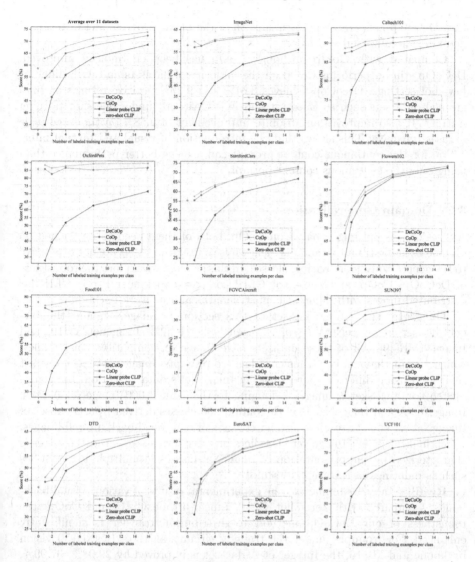

Fig. 3. Main results of few-shot learning on the 11 datasets. DeCoOp display shows the best performance than the previous baseline in 7 datasets and different training lenses. In all 11 datasets, One-shot always represents the best performance than the previous baseline.

for few-shot learning than learning Linear Probe CLIP from scratch. Although the Linear Probe CLIP and CLIP+DeCoOp perform similarly on two specialized tasks (DTD and Eurostat) and several fine-grained datasets (Flowers102 and FGVCAircraft), our DeCoOp continues to indicate better potential on most datasets when the training shots become more numerous, which demonstrates that DeCoOp gains more performance than the linear probe model in terms of domain generalization.

Compared with **CoOp**, although CoOp has been enormously improved, DeCoOp still outperforms CoOp on the majority of datasets and with different few-shot settings. DecoCop achieves 8.61% and 9.26% positive returns on fine-grained data sets such as Eurostat and FGVCAircraft under one-shot training settings. It also improves an absolute improvement of 2.58% on the large-scale dataset ImageNet.This shows that the introduction of visual and textual interaction for the continuous context prompt can achieve better performance than using only the continuous context prompt.

3.2   Domain Generalization

As DeCoOp is optimized based on CoOp, both of them need to be trained on specific data distributions and may learn false correlations that are not conducive to the generalization of invisible classes. In this section, we explore the robustness of DeCoOp, CoOp, and Zero-shot CLIP compared to Linear Probe CLIP for distributed moves with different context lengths and network backbones.

Datasets The source dataset of this section is ImageNet, and the target dataset is ImageNetV2 [19], Imagenet-Sketch [22], Imagenet-A [10] and ImageNet-R [9]. All of these datasets have ImageNet-compatible class names, which permit the seamless transfer of learned prompts. ImageNetV2 is a test set replicated using different sources during ImageNet's data collection. Imagenet-Sketch contains sketch images belonging to the same 1,000 ImageNet classes. ImageNet-A and ImageNet-R both contain 200 classes derived from a subset of ImageNet's 1,000 classes. The former consists of real-world back-filtered images, which makes current ImageNet classifiers produce low results. And the latter is characterized by the presentation of ImageNet classes in multiple image styles such as painting, caricature, and sculpture.

Results Table 1 summarizes the experimental results of various visual backbones. Compared with Zero-shot CLIP, Linear Probe CLIP, and CoOp, the robustness of our DeCoOp method to distribution transfer is significantly enhanced. For example, under the training circumstances of ResNet-50 vision backbone and M=16, the ImageNet-A dataset is improved by 29.08%, 37.99%, and 28.61%, meanwhile the ImageNet-R dataset is enhanced by 15.25%, 36.39%, and 16.29%, respectively. This suggests that the prompt learned through our approach is more generalizable than CoOp. In contrast, the linear probe CLIP yields much worse results on these target datasets, exposing its weakness in domain generalization.

Table 1. Comparison with Zero-shot CLIP on robustness to distribution shift using different vision backbones. M: CoOp's context length.

Method	Source ImageNet	-Target -V2	-Sketch	-A	-R
ResNet-50					
Zero-shot CLIP	58.18	51.34	33.32	21.65	56.00
Linear Probe CLIP	55.87	45.97	19.07	12.74	34.86
CLIP+CoOp(M=4)	63.33	55.40	34.67	23.06	56.60
CLIP+CoOp(M=16)	62.95	55.11	32.74	22.12	54.96
CLIP+DeCoOp(M=4)	63.34	58.97	42.09	43.36	68.29
CLIP+DeCoOp(M=16)	**63.61**	**66.04**	**48.38**	**50.73**	**71.25**
ResNet-101					
Zero-shot CLIP	61.62	54.81	38.71	28.05	64.38
Linear Probe CLIP	59.75	50.05	26.80	19.44	47.19
CLIP+CoOp(M=4)	65.98	58.60	40.40	29.60	64.98
CLIP+CoOp(M=16)	66.60	58.66	39.08	28.89	63.00
CLIP+DeCoOp(M=4)	66.19	61.67	48.27	49.49	74.62
CLIP+DeCoOp(M=16)	**66.63**	**67.13**	**54.55**	**55.95**	**76.94**
ViT-B/32					
Zero-shot CLIP	62.05	54.79	40.82	29.57	65.99
Linear Probe CLIP	59.58	49.73	28.06	19.67	47.20
CLIP+CoOp(M=4)	66.34	58.24	41.48	31.34	65.78
CLIP+CoOp(M=16)	66.85	58.08	40.44	30.62	64.45
CLIP+DeCoOp(M=4)	66.34	62.35	49.07	49.53	75.51
CLIP+DeCoOp(M=16)	**67.05**	**65.78**	**55.18**	**56.40**	**77.74**
ViT-B/16					
Zero-shot CLIP	66.73	60.83	46.15	47.77	73.96
Linear Probe CLIP	65.85	56.26	34.77	35.68	58.43
CLIP+CoOp(M=4)	71.73	64.56	47.89	49.93	75.14
CLIP+CoOp(M=16)	71.92	64.18	46.71	48.41	74.32
CLIP+DeCoOp(M=4)	71.45	67.67	55.67	66.69	82.85
CLIP+DeCoOp(M=16)	**72.09**	**72.03**	**61.55**	**71.68**	**84.79**

Bold value indicates best performance

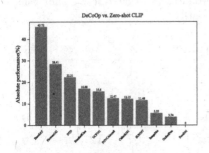
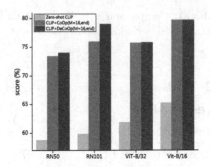

Fig. 4. The absolute performance gain of DeCoOp over the hand-crafted prompt in different datasets.

Fig. 5. Investigation of the various visual backbones of DeCoOp.

Table 2. Ablation experiments on the masking matrix and the transformer decoder.

	Masking matrix	Transformer Decoder	ImageNet	DTD	UCF101
A(CoOp)	✗	✗	61.75	62.17	75.67
B	✗	✔	62.12	63.56	76.79
C(ours)	✔	✔	**63.61**	**64.42**	**77.48**

Bold value indicates best performance

3.3 Ablation Studies

We perform several ablation studies for DeCoOp, choosing whether to use the mask matrix and the transformer decoder for control, and the experiments are compared in terms of accuracy at the 16 shots setting. We selected three datasets, ImageNet, DTD, and UCF101, as representative datasets providing generalizability, fine-grained, and action recognition, for the ablation study, respectively. As shown in Table 2, Group B adds the transformer decoder relative to Group A, while Group C incorporates the mask matrix on top of Group B. The experimental results on the three datasets show that Group C data is ahead of Groups A and B, while Group B in turn shows better performance than Group A. This proves that our introduction of the mask matrix as well as the transformer decoder facilitates the model to learn better features.

3.4 Further Analysis

Vision Backbones Fig. 5 summarizes the results of experiments on 11 datasets applying different visual backbones. The result is obvious: performance is positively related to the backbone, the more advanced the backbone, the better the performance. It is not difficult to find that in all the architectures, the gap between our method and the hand-crafted prompt is large, and the performance is better or more comparable to CoOp.

4   Conclusions

We propose DeCoOp as an optimized CoOp continuous text prompt optimization method. DeCoOp reproduces the "Pretrain-fine-tuning" paradigm by fine-tuning contextual prompts. We use a transformer decoder to interact the text with the image features that are processed by the mask matrix in conjunction with the original features. Finally, the hyperparametric dynamic mixture knowledge is connected to the visual features using residuals. This approach reduces the space between text images and improves the generalization ability of the modal. The experimental results demonstrate further improvements in the effectiveness and accuracy of DeCoOp, confirming the better feature aggregation capability of our designed DeCoOp model. In the future, we will also optimize the hints to further unleash the power of the CLIP backbone.

Acknowledgement. This work was partially supported by the Chongqing Natural Science Foundation of China(Grant No. CSTB2022NSCQ-MSX1417)and the Science and Technology Research Program of Chongqing Municipal Education Commission (Grant No. KJZD-K202200513).

References

1. Bossard, L., Guillaumin, M., Van Gool, L.: Food-101 – Mining Discriminative Components with Random Forests. In: Fleet, D., Pajdla, T., Schiele, B., Tuytelaars, T. (eds.) ECCV 2014. LNCS, vol. 8694, pp. 446–461. Springer, Cham (2014). https://doi.org/10.1007/978-3-319-10599-4_29
2. Cimpoi, M., Maji, S., Kokkinos, I., Mohamed, S., Vedaldi, A.: Describing textures in the wild. In: Proceedings of the IEEE Conference on Computer Vision and Pattern Recognition. pp. 3606–3613 (2014)
3. Deng, J., Dong, W., Socher, R., Li, L.J., Li, K., Fei-Fei, L.: ImageNet: a large-scale hierarchical image database. In: 2009 IEEE Conference on Computer Vision and Pattern Recognition. pp. 248–255. IEEE (2009)
4. Devlin, J., Chang, M.W., Lee, K., Toutanova, K.: Bert: Pre-training of deep bidirectional transformers for language understanding. arXiv preprint arXiv:1810.04805 (2018)
5. Fei-Fei, L., Fergus, R., Perona, P.: Learning generative visual models from few training examples: An incremental bayesian approach tested on 101 object categories. In: 2004 Conference on Computer Vision and Pattern Recognition Workshop. pp. 178–178. IEEE (2004)
6. Gao, P., Geng, S., Zhang, R., Ma, T., Fang, R., Zhang, Y., Li, H., Qiao, Y.: Clip-adapter: Better vision-language models with feature adapters. arXiv preprint arXiv:2110.04544 (2021)
7. Gao, P., Zheng, M., Wang, X., Dai, J., Li, H.: Fast convergence of detr with spatially modulated co-attention. In: Proceedings of the IEEE/CVF International Conference on Computer Vision. pp. 3621–3630 (2021)
8. Helber, P., Bischke, B., Dengel, A., Borth, D.: EuroSAT: a novel dataset and deep learning benchmark for land use and land cover classification. IEEE J. Sel. Topics Appl. Earth Observations Remote Sens. **12**(7), 2217–2226 (2019)

9. Hendrycks, D., et al.: The many faces of robustness: a critical analysis of out-of-distribution generalization supplementary material
10. Hendrycks, D., Zhao, K., Basart, S., Steinhardt, J., Song, D.: Natural adversarial examples. In: Proceedings of the IEEE/CVF Conference on Computer Vision and Pattern Recognition. pp. 15262–15271 (2021)
11. Krause, J., Stark, M., Deng, J., Fei-Fei, L.: 3D object representations for fine-grained categorization. In: Proceedings of the IEEE International Conference on Computer Vision Workshops. pp. 554–561 (2013)
12. Krizhevsky, A., Sutskever, I., Hinton, G.E.: ImageNet classification with deep convolutional neural networks. Commun. ACM **60**(6), 84–90 (2017)
13. Long, J., Shelhamer, E., Darrell, T.: Fully convolutional networks for semantic segmentation. In: Proceedings of the IEEE Conference on Computer Vision and Pattern Recognition. pp. 3431–3440 (2015)
14. Maji, S., Rahtu, E., Kannala, J., Blaschko, M., Vedaldi, A.: Fine-grained visual classification of aircraft. arXiv preprint arXiv:1306.5151 (2013)
15. Nilsback, M.E., Zisserman, A.: Automated flower classification over a large number of classes. In: 2008 Sixth Indian Conference on Computer Vision, Graphics & Image Processing. pp. 722–729. IEEE (2008)
16. Parkhi, O.M., Vedaldi, A., Zisserman, A., Jawahar, C.: Cats and dogs. In: 2012 IEEE Conference on Computer Vision and Pattern Recognition. pp. 3498–3505. IEEE (2012)
17. Radford, A., et al.: Learning transferable visual models from natural language supervision. In: International Conference on Machine Learning. pp. 8748–8763. PMLR (2021)
18. Radford, A., Narasimhan, K., Salimans, T., Sutskever, I., et al.: Improving language understanding by generative pre-training (2018)
19. Recht, B., Roelofs, R., Schmidt, L., Shankar, V.: Do imagenet classifiers generalize to imagenet? In: International Conference on Machine Learning. pp. 5389–5400. PMLR (2019)
20. Soomro, K., Zamir, A.R., Shah, M.: Ucf101: A dataset of 101 human actions classes from videos in the wild. arXiv preprint arXiv:1212.0402 (2012)
21. Vaswani, A.,et al.: Attention is all you need. Adv. Neural Inf. Proces. Syst. **30** (2017)
22. Wang, H., Ge, S., Lipton, Z., Xing, E.P.: Learning robust global representations by penalizing local predictive power. Adv. Neural Inf. Proces. Syst. **32** (2019)
23. Xiao, J., Hays, J., Ehinger, K.A., Oliva, A., Torralba, A.: Sun database: large-scale scene recognition from abbey to zoo. In: 2010 IEEE Computer Society Conference on Computer Vision and Pattern Recognition. pp. 3485–3492. IEEE (2010)
24. Zhang, R., et al.: Tip-adapter: Training-free clip-adapter for better vision-language modeling. arXiv preprint arXiv:2111.03930 (2021)
25. Zhou, K., Yang, J., Loy, C.C., Liu, Z.: Learning to prompt for vision-language models. Int. J. Comput. Vision **130**(9), 2337–2348 (2022)

Unveiling Cybersecurity Threats from Online Chat Groups: A Triple Extraction Approach

Zhen Yang, Cheng Huang[✉], and Jiayong Liu

School of Cyber Science and Engineering, Sichuan University, Chengdu, China
r1ngs@stu.scu.edu.cn, {codesec,ljy}@scu.edu.cn

Abstract. In recent years, instant messaging software has become a popular platform for hackers to exchange knowledge and discuss cybersecurity issues. To trace the source of key hackers and identify potential cybersecurity threats, it is necessary to extract relational triples from hacker dialogues in chat logs. In this paper, we propose a feasible scheme for extracting cybersecurity knowledge triples from an extensive corpus of diverse chat data. We developed a heuristic algorithm based on the BERT next sentence prediction task to separate sequential and asynchronous chat logs into shorter dialogues and disentangle these threads within them, which can improve the accuracy of the subsequent relation extraction process. We also annotated a dialogue relation extraction dataset and developed a relation extraction model tailored for cybersecurity domain. Experimental results demonstrate that our average F1 scores on the thread disentanglement task and the dialogue relation extraction task are 74.9 and 88.4, respectively.

Keywords: Online Chat Group · Cybersecurity Knowledge Triples · Relation Extraction

1 Introduction

Public chat groups and instant messaging platforms have become the primary channels for hackers to exchange attack intelligence, share attack techniques, and announce attack targets. Prior to the release of attack warnings and traceability analysis reports by security vendors or experts, these disclosures were thoroughly discussed in chat groups and other forms of social media [6]. As a result, the collection of Cyber Threat Intelligence (CTI) from chat groups has become increasingly feasible.

Information extraction is a crucial technique for acquiring CTI from unstructured data. It involves extracting cybersecurity knowledge triples *(subject, relation, object)* through Named Entity Recognition (NER) and Relationship Extraction (RE) subtasks, which are prerequisites for building a Cybersecurity Knowledge Graph (CKG). The CKG captures the relationships between different cybersecurity entities and provides a comprehensive view of the entire security landscape. Constructing a CKG of chat groups enables the identification of key hackers in a higher dimension based on their behavior and intentions.

Z. Jin et al. (Eds.): KSEM 2023, LNAI 14120, pp. 175–188, 2023.
https://doi.org/10.1007/978-3-031-40292-0_15

Unlike well-written forum posts or security news, chat logs are informal and often contain irrelevant or distracting content. Chat logs can be considered as a series of asynchronous dialogues covering a wide range of topics. The arguments presented in the dialogues often exhibit cross-sentence relations, making them challenging to analyze. For example, a 9-turn dialogue (shown in Table 1) involving four speakers demonstrates how speaker 1 and speaker 2 may exhibit an apparent attack on a website, while others may have no such intention. In this case, the dialogue contains two cybersecurity knowledge triples: *(S1, targets,* https://www.****.com:7443/) and *(S2, targets,* https://www.****.com:7443/).

Table 1. A dialogue in a chat group. We replace the real domain name with *. S1 to S4: anonymous speakers.

S1: **https://www.****.com:7443/** 你找到后台说不定我可以 (if you can find the backend maybe I can do something)
S2: 我都注册进去了，修改密码那里没用过滤，0.0 (I have already registered in, it didn't filter my request to change a password, 0.0)
S3: 然后呢 (And then what)
S2: cdn 好搞 (cdn is vulnerable)
S4: 黑客，举报了 (Hacker, reported)
S1: 友好的测试一下 (Just penetration testing)
S3: 拿下了嘛 (Is it done?)
S1: 发一次ban一次 (Every request got banned)
S2: 被 BAN，这破网站有封装，有前后端分离，SSH-2.0-OpenSSH_7.4p1 Debian-10+deb9u7 (BANNED, this website uses encapsulation and separation of front-end and backend, SSH-2.0-OpenSSH_7.4p1 Debian-10+deb9u7)

Dialogue-level RE aims to predict the relation type between a pair of two arguments (usually not in a turn) mentioned in a dialogue from a set of predefined relations. This step is typically the last step in extracting cybersecurity knowledge triples from dialogues. DialogRE [15], the first human-annotated dialogue-level RE dataset, has been constructed. The dialogues in this dataset come from transcripts of the TV show *Friends*, a globally preferred show that covers everyday conversations. However, there is a lack of research on the applicability and effectiveness of dialogue-level RE in the cybersecurity domain.

For the purpose of extracting cybersecurity knowledge triples from chat logs, we propose an end-to-end scheme. To begin with, we present a novel algorithm capable of extracting dialogues with the same topic from chat logs. The algorithm employs a two-step approach, where chat logs are first segmented into sessions based on time and turn-structure, and then session-level thread disentanglement is performed. A conversation thread refers to a set of messages exchanged between users as they converse with each other, where the messages are relevant to the discussion at hand. Since multi-participant online chat involves asynchronous and simultaneous conversations, messages tend to be interwoven between the different discussions. The goal of thread disentanglement is to identify these coherent message streams of associated thoughts. We argue that the *schism* problem in thread disentanglement can be better addressed by the Next Sentence Prediction (NSP) training task of BERT, as opposed to other methods such as semantic similarity [1,8]. Next, we extract cybersecurity entities with high recall rates using rule-based and dictionary-based techniques and present a dialogue-level RE dataset for cybersecurity. Finally, we employ dialogue-level RE methods to acquire the cybersecurity knowledge triples.

Our main contributions are as follows.

- We propose a heuristic algorithm based on BERT NSP to enhance the accuracy of subsequent RE processes by effectively separating dialogues with the same topic from asynchronous chat logs.
- We analyze the chat content and develop a cybersecurity ontology specific to chat group scenarios. This ontology serves as the foundation for constructing the first dialogue-level RE dataset for the cybersecurity domain.
- Experimental studies demonstrate the effectiveness and applicability of real-time CTI discovery from chat groups.

2   Related Work

2.1   Thread Disentanglement

Disentangling threads can facilitate subsequent relation extraction by focusing on a single dialogue. Shen et al. [7] introduced the thread disentanglement problem, defining each thread as containing a single topic. Elsner and Charniak [1] presented the first corpus of Internet Relay Chat (IRC) dialogue for thread disentanglement and proposed a graph-theoretic model using discourse structure and utterance content. They found that timestamps and speaker identities were better cues than message content for thread disentanglement tasks.

Subsequent studies have generally followed a two-stage approach. The first stage involves link prediction, which models the *reply-to* relation between two utterances. The second stage is a clustering step, which utilizes the results from link prediction to construct individual conversation threads [16].

Although these methods achieve good performance, there is still an ongoing exploration of heuristic methods. Sinha et al. [8] designed an innovative pipeline based on heuristics, utilizing co-reference resolution and semantic similarity to identify the thread to which a message belongs. Meanwhile, when studying dialogue disentanglement in French chat, Riou et al. [5] found that a simple heuristic can be as effective as complex trainable systems when conversations are lightly entangled. Therefore, corpus characteristics should be taken into account to choose an appropriate approach.

2.2   Dialogue-Level RE

Yao et al. [14] presented DocRED, a large-scale document-level RE dataset based on distant supervision. They adopted CNN, LSTM, and BiLSTM models to experiment on DocRED, and these three models are also used as baselines on DialogRE. However, directly applying the document-level RE method to dialogues will lead to the neglect of the speakers [15].

For dialogue-level RE, the approaches based on graph neural networks are state-of-the-art at present. GDPNet, proposed by Xue et al. [12], is able to find indicative words from dialogues for effective RE. They construct a latent multi-view graph with a Gaussian Graph Generator (GGG) to model various possible relationships among tokens. The graph is then refined through multiple interactions of graph convolution and Dynamic Time Warping Pooling (DTWPool) to select important words for relation prediction. It is worth noting, however, that transformer-based models are still competitive [13].

3   Design and Implementation

The proposed scheme is shown in Fig. 1, which consists of three components: a data collector, a dialogue extractor and a knowledge triple extractor. We aim to convert asynchronous and sequential chat logs into short dialogues on the same topic, extract entities and relational triples at the dialogue level, and build a CKG of chat groups.

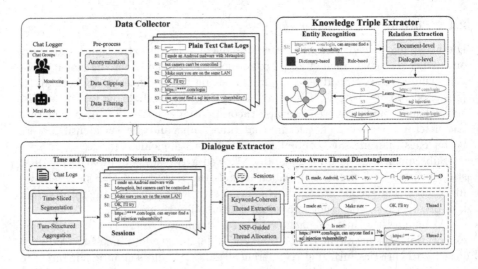

Fig. 1. Overall scheme.

3.1   Data Collector

Our data comes from active QQ chat groups relevant to cybersecurity topics. QQ chat groups typically consist of a group owner, several administrators, and ordinary members. These groups can be discovered by searching for a unique group number or keywords. The group owner usually sets up an entrance verification question to prevent advertising robots and irrelevant people from joining. For example, the question might ask the new member to name an encryption algorithm.

We develop a QQ robot that records the chat logs of more than 100 public chat groups from July 2021 to March 2022 in real time. Specifically, we use Mirai[1], a high-performance and multi-platform framework that provides protocol support for QQ, as a means of monitoring chat content. We search for keywords such as *Cybersecurity* and *Penetration Testing* to find chat groups with cybersecurity topics. Then, we manually fill in the entrance verification information to gain access to the groups. We store each message in our database in real-time, recording seven key pieces of information for each message: the speaker's nickname, the speaker's unique QQ number, the speaker's role (owner, administrator, or member), the content of the message, the timestamp when the message is sent, the group name, and the unique group number.

To ensure the quality and relevance of the data used in subsequent analysis, a data pre-processing step is applied, consisting of three sub-steps: anonymization, data clipping, and data filtering. Anonymization is achieved by assigning each speaker a unique number and replacing their nickname with a generic name, such as *Speaker 1*. Data clipping involves excluding messages that are either less than two characters long or greater than 100 characters long, as well as messages that contain line breaks.

Data filtering is an essential sub-step to eliminate noisy data. To this end, several criteria have been identified to remove messages that lack valuable information. For instance, *QQ red packet* messages, repetitive messages, emojis, and other meaningless content are filtered out. Furthermore, multimedia content such as images, videos, and voice messages which do not contain text information, is also removed. In addition, robot messages are excluded, as they are automatically generated and sent at regular intervals.

Once the pre-processing step is complete, the chat logs are obtained in plain text format.

3.2   Ontology Construction

Speakers in chat groups typically do not discuss comprehensive and conclusive information about cybersecurity attacks, making it difficult to use ontologies designed for information extraction from sources such as forum posts, security bulletins, and APT reports. To address this issue, we conduct an analysis of chat logs and develop the Dialogue Cybersecurity Ontology (DCO) that builds on the relationships and classes defined in the latest Structured Threat Information Expression (STIX) 2.1[2]. By doing so, we are able to ensure that our entities and relationships can be readily converted to STIX format for CTI exchange.

---

[1] https://github.com/mamoe/mirai.
[2] https://oasis-open.github.io/cti-documentation/stix/intro.

Classes in DCO. We define six classes with reference to *STIX Domain Objects* and *Cyber-observable Objects*:

- *Vulnerability*: An entity that refers to weaknesses in software that can be directly exploited by hackers, e.g., CVE-2017-0144, MS17-010.
- *Attack-pattern*: An entity that describes how hackers attempt to compromise targets, e.g., DDOS, Privilege Escalation.
- *Tool*: An entity that refers to legitimate software different from malware and can be used by hackers to perform attacks, e.g., arpspoof, LOIC.
- *Infrastructure*: An entity that refers to physical or virtual resources used as part of an attack or defense, including IPV4 address, domain, and URL.
- *Software*: An entity representing vulnerable software, e.g., Weblogic.
- *Threat-actor*: An entity that refers to a speaker with clear or potential intentions to conduct attacks.

Relations in DCO. We have established a set of fine-grained relations between classes to provide valuable insights into the cybersecurity domain within conversation scenes, as STIX allows user-defined relation types (Table 2). For example, the relation *Attack-pattern targets Software* describes the attack technique that exploits a vulnerability in a particular software.

Table 2. Relationships in DCO.

ID	Subject	Relation Type	Object
1	Threat-actor	uses	Tool
2	Threat-actor	uses	Attack-pattern
3	Threat-actor	targets	Infrastructure
4	Threat-actor	targets	Software
5	Threat-actor	targets	Vulnerability
6	Threat-actor	learns	Attack-pattern
7	Threat-actor	owns	Infrastructure
8	Attack-pattern	uses	Tool
9	Attack-pattern	targets	Software
10	Attack-pattern	targets	Infrastructure

3.3 Dialogue Extractor

The information density in chat logs is relatively low and there are often off-topic discussions [10]. Therefore, to extract relevant information effectively, focusing on short dialogues with the same topic is more practical than analyzing the entire chat log. Previous studies have tried grouping messages in blocks of several minutes or setting a time delay threshold to identify the start of a new dialogue [3]. However, this approach can result in non-cybersecurity-related noise in the dialogues and disrupt the coherence of the dialogue.

To extract dialogues with asynchronous topics, it is essential to understand the linguistic characteristics of chat messages, as thread disentanglement performance may significantly vary depending on corpus characteristics [5]. Our goal is to enhance context and reduce interference information for subsequent entity recognition and relation extraction tasks rather than to accurately restore the complete dialogue between users.

For this purpose, we have developed an efficient heuristic algorithm specifically designed for Chinese users' speaking habits and consists of two main parts: session extraction based on time and turn structure and thread disentanglement within sessions. Our algorithm produces the dialogue scenario in Table 1.

Time and Turn-Structured Session Extraction. We present a two-step approach for extracting sessions from plain text chat logs. In the first step, time-sliced segmentation involves dividing the chat logs into segments based on a threshold value (th_1), which determines the maximum time delay between consecutive messages in a segment.

In the second step, turn-structured aggregation is applied to merge messages from the same speaker within a short period and construct them as a single turn, providing a more coherent representation of the speaker's intent. This approach is motivated by the observation that Chinese users tend to split a complete sentence into multiple parts and send them sequentially, which is a crucial difference from English users.

Session-Aware Thread Disentanglement. We define two states for each conversation thread: active and dead. The fate of a thread depends on its Time-To-Live (TTL), which is defined as the maximum number of times that no new utterance can be contributed to the thread. In essence, the TTL value measures how *active* the conversation is. Upon initializing each thread, we set an initial TTL value, denoted by $iTTL$. When a thread's TTL value reaches 0, it is considered dead, and we treat it as a full dialogue to be processed by subsequent modules.

We start by creating an active thread with the first turn and iterate through each turn chronologically. We then sequentially use the following two methods to assign the new utterance to the appropriate active thread. Whenever an utterance is added to a thread, we update its TTL value to the current number of speakers and decrease the TTL value of other active threads by 1. At the same time, we check whether any threads have reached a TTL value of 0, indicating the end of the conversation.

The first method involves identifying keywords in each turn and using them to determine whether an utterance is coherent with an existing thread. Keywords are words other than Chinese stop words[3] after word segmentation, which hold meaning in an utterance. An utterance is considered coherent with an active

---

[3] https://github.com/goto456/stopwords.

thread if only one thread has overlapping keywords with the utterance. To implement this method, we iterate through all active threads, segment the utterances with jieba[4] and remove stop words to obtain keyword lists. We then calculate the keyword overlaps between the current utterance and all utterances in each thread. If only one thread has overlapping keywords with the current utterance, we add it to that thread. We believe that keyword retrieval is more efficient and accurate than co-reference resolution.

Algorithm 1. NSP-Guided Thread Allocation

Require: Active $THREADS$, current utterance $cUtterance$
Ensure: $maxThread$ with the maximum probability
1: **for** each $thread \in THREADS$ **do**
2:     **for** each $utterance \in thread.utterances$ **do**
3:         $prob = BERTNSPProb(utterance, cUtterance)$
4:         $tProb.append(prob)$
5:     **end for**
6:     $threadProb = avg(tProb)$
7:     **if** $threadProb > maxProb$ **then**
8:         $maxProb = threadProb$
9:         $maxThread = thread$
10:     **end if**
11: **end for**
12: **if** $maxProb > th_2$ **then**
13:     return $maxThread$
14: **else**
15:     return $None$
16: **end if**

If the keyword decision method fails, we utilize BERT NSP to allocate the utterance to an appropriate thread. The NSP task involves assessing whether two sentences are consecutive, which we employ to compute the probability that the current utterance belongs to an active thread (Algorithm 1). Specifically, we leverage a pre-trained BERT model for the NSP task to estimate the probability that the current utterance is a continuation of each utterance in a given thread. We then average these probabilities to represent the probability that the current utterance follows a single thread. If a thread's probability exceeds the threshold th_2, we add the current utterance to the active thread with the highest probability; otherwise, we create a new thread with the current utterance.

To implement the $BERTNSPProb$ function, we use the *bert-base-chinese* model from Hugging Face [11]. We first concatenate the two input sentences s_1 and s_2 with the separator token $[SEP]$ and the classification token $[CLS]$, creating the input for BERT as $[CLS]s_1[SEP]s_2[SEP]$. And then the hidden vector of the last layer corresponding to the $[CLS]$ token is mapped to a 2-dimensional

---

[4] https://github.com/fxsjy/jieba.

space using a linear layer. The probability that s_1 and s_2 are consecutive is obtained by applying the softmax function.

3.4   Knowledge Triple Extractor

The public chat groups are populated by young people who engage in a diverse range of topics, including current news, video games, and casual everyday conversations. As a result, many dialogues do not contain cybersecurity-related content at all. To address this issue, we employ rule-based and dictionary-based methods to identify entities within the dialogues and then discard dialogues that do not contain any relevant entities. We have refrained from using deep learning models trained on well-formed text as they are unsuitable for short and noisy chat messages [8].

Entity Recognizion. The recognition methods of the five entities other than Threat-actor will be explained in detail below.

Tool: We build a dictionary of security tools, comprising both open-source tools on GitHub and non-GitHub tools. We manually add non-GitHub tools, as there are not many of them. Popular English tools such as AWVS, Chinese tools such as 菜刀 (Chopper), and Kali Linux built-in tools such as Ophcrack are included. For GitHub tools, we build the dictionary from the following two sources.

- We crawl websites that introduce GitHub security tools and organize the items.
- We manually compile a list that includes hundreds of well-known and authoritative GitHub experts, including international researchers, security analysts working for security firms, and skilled white hat hackers. We assume that the repositories they follow are security tools.

After de-duplication and manual checking, our dictionary contains 40,309 security tools. We first segment Chinese words and then use the dictionary for lookup to extract security tools in the messages. Since security experts stay active on GitHub, our dictionary can be updated regularly.

Attack-pattern: We construct a dictionary of frequently mentioned attack-patterns among Chinese users. Our approach involves several steps. First, we map the top 10 risks of the Open Web Application Security Project (OWASP) into a set of initial attack-patterns, including injection and Server-Side Request Forgery (SSRF). Next, we pick out dialogues containing these attack-patterns and use them to discover new patterns, thereby expanding the dictionary. We repeat this process until no new patterns are added to the list, resulting in a final set of 44 attack-patterns. We then create regular expressions based on these patterns.

Infrastructure: We summarize three primary purposes for speakers to send URLs or IP addresses in chat groups.

- Knowledge sharing, such as links to Chinese Software Developer Network (CSDN) and GitHub.
- Deliberate attacks, such as the website shown in Table 1.
- Braggings, such as showcasing the infrastructure they use or own, including Command-and-Control (C&C) servers and The Onion Router (TOR) links.

We focus primarily on the second and third cases, where speakers intend to attack or demonstrate infrastructure. We use the msticpy[5] library developed by Microsoft to extract URLs, domains, and IP addresses. To avoid noise in the first case, we remove results for domains ranked in the Alexa top 10,000. We also remove private IP addresses from our analysis.

Vulnerability: We utilize regular expressions to extract CVE IDs with a uniform format. For vulnerabilities in Microsoft software, we compile a dictionary by crawling the monthly security bulletins released by the Microsoft Security Response Center from 1998 to 2017. Notably, we observe that many users habitually abbreviate, such as MS08-067 being abbreviated to 08067. Therefore, we create an abbreviation dictionary for matching after Chinese word segmentation.

Software: Our focus is on vulnerable software or components like log4j and jboss. To build a dictionary that covers all software with CVE IDs, we extract the Common Platform Enumeration (CPE) naming format of vulnerable software from a continuously updated project[6], which contains the detailed descriptions of all CVE IDs. We also check for duplicates of software and tools, as we don't take into account the multi-label problem where software can also be a tool simultaneously.

Relation Extraction. After obtaining the dialogues that contain cybersecurity entities, we use brat [9] to annotate the relations between the entities in each dialogue. For example, in Fig. 2, we recognize *SSH* as a tool, but it has no relation to any other entities, nor does *OpenSSH*. If a dialogue does not contain any relation, we discard it.

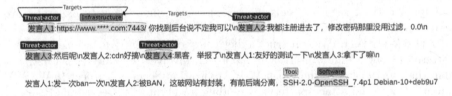

Fig. 2. An example of using brat for relation annotation.

The 10 fine-grained relations we have defined in Table 2 are tailored for RE for cybersecurity. To distinguish the 10 types of relations, we also add some negative

---

[5] https://github.com/microsoft/msticpy.
[6] https://github.com/olbat/nvdcve.

samples of relations corresponding to the OTHER type. Our dataset ultimately consists of 3647 dialogues, on which we perform RE experiments using state-of-the-art dialogue-level and document-level methods.

4 Evaluation

4.1 Experiments for Thread Disentanglement

Dataset. We annotate data on an active multi-party chat group from 22 July 2021 to 11 August 2021. The chat group has over 1300 group members, and our annotation results include 1076 plain text messages and 208 threads.

Methods. We evaluate our method against six other methods, which are described below.

Our method: Our process involves setting three parameters: the initial value of the thread's TTL, denoted as $iTTL$, which we set to 3 to ensure that threads are easy to terminate; the threshold value for time slicing, denoted as th_1, which we set to 5 min based on our analysis of the time interval between adjacent messages; and the threshold for thread allocation, denoted as th_2, which we set to 0.9 based on our experience.

An innovative pipeline [8]: We re-implement the method of Sinha et al. for identifying the thread to which a message belongs using co-reference resolution and semantic similarity. For co-reference resolution, we utilize HanLP, the most effective Chinese tool [2]. To compute semantic similarity, we employ word2vec to convert words into vectors and obtain sentence vectors, which are used to calculate cosine similarity between sentence pairs. We use the same pre-processing settings as in our method, as well as the thread settings, and then set the semantic similarity threshold to 0.1.

All same [1]: The entire transcript is one conversation.

All different [1]: Each utterance is a separate conversation.

Speaker [1]: Each speaker's consecutive utterances are treated as a single conversation.

Blocks of k [1]: Each consecutive group of k utterances is a conversation. We set k to 5, the average number of messages contained in the threads in our dataset.

Pause of k [1]: Each pause of k seconds separates two conversations. We set k to the threshold th_2.

Results. To evaluate the performance of thread disentanglement, the Shen-F score serves as a comprehensive metric that combines both precision and recall [7]. Table 3 presents the performance of different baselines. Our method stands out with a 12.1% improvement over the best baseline, Pause of k. Notably, the method of Sinha et al. underperforms, even ranking lower than trivial systems, which we attribute to discrepancies in the corpus. These results highlight that a straightforward heuristic algorithm can be sufficient for a lightly entangled system [5].

Table 3. Thread disentanglement results compared to each baseline.

Method	Shen-F
All same (Elsner and Charniak 2008)	2.8
All different (Elsner and Charniak 2008)	28.5
Speaker (Elsner and Charniak 2008)	39.6
Blocks of k (Elsner and Charniak 2008)	50.7
Pause of k (Elsner and Charniak 2008)	62.8
An innovative pipeline (Sinha et al. 2020)	47.3
Our method	**74.9**

4.2   Experiments for Relation Extraction

Dataset. We analyze 34 active QQ groups out of more than 100 we have joined. Our dataset covers the period from 22 July 2021 to 27 February 2022 and contains 3,647 dialogues, 9,169 entities, and 7,047 relations, with 90.1% of the subjects in relational triples being speakers. We observe that most of the conversations in the chat groups are relatively short, with an average of 3.6 turns per dialogue.

Methods. We compare document-level and dialogue-level methods for RE using various models, including:

CNN, LSTM, and BiLSTM [14]: We re-implement these three document-level models for our Chinese dataset, using a 300-dimensional Chinese word embedding trained by Li et al. [4].

BERT [15]: Initialized with the pre-trained parameters of Bert-base-chinese, BERT serves as a fine-tuning baseline for document-level RE. The input sequence consists of the dialogue content d and the entity pair (e_1, e_2) in the following format: $[CLS]d[SEP]e_1[SEP]e_2[SEP]$. The final hidden vector corresponding to the token $[CLS]$ is used for classification.

BERTs [15]: A speaker-aware extension to the BERT model, with a modified input sequence of $[CLS]\hat{d}[SEP]\hat{e}_1[SEP]\hat{e}_2[SEP]$. Here, $\hat{d}$ is obtained by replacing every mention of e_i ($i \in 1, 2$) in d with $\hat{e}_i$, which is a newly introduced token $[S_i]$ if e_i is a speaker name, and e_i otherwise.

GDPNet [12]: A graph neural network model that builds on BERTs. It finds indicative words from long sequences by constructing a multi-view latent graph and refining the graph.

Our method: We propose a modification of the BERTs model for input sequences by introducing ground truth argument types. This modification is made possible by capturing entity types during the entity recognition phase. Specifically, if e_i ($i \in \{1, 2\}$) is not speaker name, we replace it and every mention of e_i in d with a newly introduced special token $[T_j]$ ($j \in \{1, 2, 3, 4, 5\}$), representing the argument type.

Table 4. Performance of relation extraction.

Method	Dev(σ)	Test(σ)
CNN (Yao et al. 2019)	56.5(1.2)	57.6(1.4)
LSTM (Yao et al. 2019)	60.4(1.1)	62.1(0.5)
BiLSTM (Yao et al. 2019)	60.0(1.2)	62.2(0.4)
BERT (Yu et al. 2020)	80.5(0.7)	81.4(0.8)
BERTs (Yu et al. 2020)	87.0(0.2)	86.3(0.8)
GDPNet (Xue et al. 2021)	87.0(0.3)	86.3(0.1)
Our method	**90.1(0.7)**	**88.4(0.2)**

Results. The dataset is randomly split into the train, development, and test sets with a ratio of 6:2:2. We use the F1 score for evaluation, which is the harmonic mean of precision and recall. Each experiment is run five times, and we report the mean and standard deviation results of the F1 score in Table 4.

Our model achieves the best results by introducing the ground truth argument type. It is worth noting that the BERTs model also achieves good results, improving the F1 score by 4.9% over BERT. This could be because most of our relational triples involve speakers.

5   Conclusion

In this paper, we have investigated the potential of discovering threat intelligence and extracting cybersecurity knowledge triples from online chat groups. Our proposed NSP-based heuristic algorithm efficiently extracts dialogues with the same topics from a vast number of chat logs. We also developed DCO, a comprehensive dialogue ontology for cybersecurity, which includes six entity classes and ten relation classes.

We extracted entities from dialogues using dictionary-based and rule-based approaches, and annotated a dialogue-level relation extraction dataset. Additionally, we experimented with document-level and dialogue-level relation extraction methods using this dataset. Our experimental results suggest that by introducing ground truth argument types, dialogue-level methods can be more effective in extracting valuable knowledge from chat group conversations.

Acknowledgements. This work was supported in part by National Key Research and Development Program of China (No.2021YFB3100500) and Sichuan Science and Technology Program (No.2023YFG0162).

References

1. Elsner, M., Charniak, E.: You talking to me? a corpus and algorithm for conversation disentanglement. In: Proceedings of ACL-08: HLT. pp. 834–842 (2008)
2. He, H., Choi, J.D.: The stem cell hypothesis: Dilemma behind multi-task learning with transformer encoders. In: Proceedings of the 2021 Conference on Empirical Methods in Natural Language Processing. pp. 5555–5577 (2021)
3. Iqbal, F., Fung, B.C., Debbabi, M., Batool, R., Marrington, A.: Wordnet-based criminal networks mining for cybercrime investigation. IEEE Access **7**, 22740–22755 (2019)
4. Li, S., Zhao, Z., Hu, R., Li, W., Liu, T., Du, X.: Analogical reasoning on chinese morphological and semantic relations. In: Proceedings of the 56th Annual Meeting of the Association for Computational Linguistics (Volume 2: Short Papers). pp. 138–143 (2018)
5. Riou, M., Salim, S., Hernandez, N.: Using discursive information to disentangle french language chat. In: 2nd Workshop on Natural Language Processing for Computer-Mediated Communication (NLP4CMC 2015)/Social Media at GSCL Conference 2015. pp. 23–27 (2015)
6. Sabottke, C., Suciu, O., Dumitras, T.: Vulnerability disclosure in the age of social media: Exploiting twitter for predicting real-world exploits. In: 24th {USENIX} Security Symposium ({USENIX} Security 15). pp. 1041–1056 (2015)
7. Shen, D., Yang, Q., Sun, J.T., Chen, Z.: Thread detection in dynamic text message streams. In: Proceedings of the 29th annual international ACM SIGIR conference on Research and development in information retrieval. pp. 35–42 (2006)
8. Sinha, A., Midhush Manohar, T.K., Subramanian, S., Das, B.: Text segregation on asynchronous group chat. Procedia Comput. Sci. **171**, 1371–1380 (2020)
9. Stenetorp, P., Pyysalo, S., Topić, G., Ohta, T., Ananiadou, S., Tsujii, J.: Brat: a web-based tool for nlp-assisted text annotation. In: Proceedings of the Demonstrations at the 13th Conference of the European Chapter of the Association for Computational Linguistics. pp. 102–107 (2012)
10. Wang, D., Liu, Y.: A pilot study of opinion summarization in conversations. In: Proceedings of the 49th annual meeting of the Association for Computational Linguistics: Human language technologies. pp. 331–339 (2011)
11. Wolf, T., et al.: Transformers: State-of-the-art natural language processing. In: Proceedings of the 2020 Conference on Empirical Methods in Natural Language Processing: System Demonstrations. pp. 38–45 (2020)
12. Xue, F., Sun, A., Zhang, H., Chng, E.S.: GdpNet: refining latent multi-view graph for relation extraction. In: Proceedings of the AAAI Conference on Artificial Intelligence. vol. 35, pp. 14194–14202 (2021)
13. Xue, F., Sun, A., Zhang, H., Ni, J., Chng, E.S.: An embarrassingly simple model for dialogue relation extraction. In: ICASSP 2022–2022 IEEE International Conference on Acoustics, Speech and Signal Processing (ICASSP). pp. 6707–6711. IEEE (2022)
14. Yao, Y., et al.: DocRED: a large-scale document-level relation extraction dataset. arXiv preprint arXiv:1906.06127 (2019)
15. Yu, D., Sun, K., Cardie, C., Yu, D.: Dialogue-based relation extraction. In: Proceedings of the 58th Annual Meeting of the Association for Computational Linguistics. pp. 4927–4940 (2020)
16. Yu, T., Joty, S.: Online conversation disentanglement with pointer networks. In: Proceedings of the 2020 Conference on Empirical Methods in Natural Language Processing (EMNLP). pp. 6321–6330 (2020)

KSRL: Knowledge Selection Based Reinforcement Learning for Knowledge-Grounded Dialogue

Zhanyu Ma[1,2,3], Jian Ye[1,2,3(✉)], and Shuang Cheng[1,2,3]

[1] Institute of Computing Technology, Chinese Academy of Sciences, Beijing, China
{mazhanyu21s,chengshuang22s}@ict.ac.cn
[2] University of Chinese Academy of Sciences, Beijing, China
[3] Beijing Key Laboratory of Mobile Computing and Pervasive Device, Beijing, China
jye@ict.ac.cn

Abstract. In the domain of multi-turn knowledge-grounded dialogues, the sequential coherence among knowledge elements chosen across various conversational turns presents potential cues for knowledge selection. However, this aspect has been largely overlooked in preceding studies. To tackle this issue, the present study introduces an innovative methodology that employs reinforcement learning to enhance knowledge selection in open-domain dialogue systems. By recasting the knowledge selection challenge as a sequential decision-making task and implementing reinforcement learning, the dialogue system is capable of discerning which knowledge to choose based on the conversational context and preceding dialogue turns, thereby generating high-quality responses. The system acquires a reward signal contingent upon the quality of the generated responses and subsequently updates its policy to maximize the expected reward over time. Harnessing the capabilities of reinforcement learning, our proposed method effectively learns to identify the most pertinent knowledge, thereby generating superior-quality responses. The study assesses the proposed approach using multiple open-domain dialogue datasets, demonstrating that it surpasses the performance of prior methodologies.

Keywords: Dialogue · Knowledge-grounded · Reinforcement Learning

1 Introduction

Open-domain dialogue systems have demonstrated potential in generating natural and engaging responses [5,9]. Nonetheless, a significant challenge in developing these systems is the selection of pertinent external knowledge for inclusion in

The research work is supported by National Key R&D Program of China (No.2022YFB3904700), Key Research and Development Program of in Shandong Province (2019JZZY020102), Key Research and Development Program of Jiangsu Province (No.BE2018084), Industrial Internet Innovation and Development Project in 2021 (TC210A02M, TC210804D), Opening Project of Beijing Key Laboratory of Mobile Computing and Pervasive Device.

responses [6]. The appropriate knowledge selection is a multifaceted problem, as it relies on various factors such as context, user persona, and task requirements [3,19].

To enhance knowledge selection, researchers have investigated diverse approaches, including the utilization of external knowledge sources, the integration of domain-specific knowledge, and the incorporation of knowledge-seeking mechanisms within model architectures [4]. However, these methods exhibit limitations concerning their flexibility and adaptability to various dialogue scenarios [17]. For example, methods depending solely on the prior distribution of knowledge may struggle to effectively learn which knowledge to select for specific contexts [15], while approaches involving domain-specific knowledge might not be suitable for open-domain dialogue [16].

To address these limitations, we propose a novel approach that leverages reinforcement learning to improve knowledge selection in open-domain dialogue systems. Reinforcement learning is a machine learning technique that allows an agent to learn by interacting with an environment to achieve a specific goal. In the case of dialogue systems, the goal is to generate high-quality responses that are both informative and engaging. By applying reinforcement learning, we can train the dialogue system to learn which knowledge to select for a given context, based on the feedback received from the environment in the form of rewards or penalties.

Specifically, our approach formulates the knowledge selection problem as a sequential decision-making task, where the dialogue system selects the most appropriate knowledge based on the context and previous dialogue turns. The system receives a reward signal based on the quality of the generated responses, and it updates its policy to maximize the expected reward over time. By leveraging the power of reinforcement learning, our approach can effectively learn to select the most relevant knowledge and generate high-quality responses.

We evaluate our approach on several open-domain dialogue datasets and show that it outperforms prior methods that rely solely on the prior distribution over knowledge. Our method can generate more informative and engaging responses while also being more flexible and adaptable to different dialogue scenarios. We believe that our approach has the potential to significantly improve the performance of open-domain dialogue systems and could also be applied to other natural language processing tasks that require knowledge selection.

Natural language has also been used to improve RL in various ways. The most relevant ones use language abstraction for exploration. [10] rewards the agent for finishing any semantically meaningful low-level such as 'picking up a key' and gradually build up a dataset for learning to correlate the high-level instructions with low-level descriptions. [11,13] use language or visual language models to discover novel states for intrinsic rewards at the semantic level. These works focus on learning a better policy in single agent RL setting by addressing the hard exploration problem.

Natural language has also been used to improve RL in various ways. The most relevant ones use language abstraction for exploration. [10] rewards the agent for finishing any semantically meaningful low-level such as 'picking up a key' and gradually build up a dataset for learning to correlate the high-level instructions with low-level descriptions. [11,13] use language or visual language models to discover novel states for intrinsic rewards at the semantic level. These works focus on learning a better policy in single agent RL setting by addressing the hard exploration problem. Prior works have explored using foundation models for reward specifications in RL. The in-context learning capability of the large foundation models allows user to specify reward function with natural language descriptions. MineDojo [2] collects a large scale multi-modal Minecraft dataset from the internet and trains a CLIP [12] style contrastive video-text model.

2   Model

KSRL aims to augment knowledge selection via an optimized structured representation highlighting vital task-related structures. Our method consists of three key components: the Policy Network (PN), Knowledge Representation Network (KRN), and Knowledge Selection Network (KSN). PN, employing a stochastic policy, generates an action sequence translated into a structured representation by the KRN. KSN uses this representation for classification and provides PN with reward computation, which is entirely dependent on the action sequence.

PN employs the stochastic policy $\pi\left(a_t \mid \mathbf{s_t}; \Theta\right)$, uses a delayed reward for policy learning, and samples an action at each state. After determining all actions, KSN computes $P(y \mid X)$ from the structured representation, which is used as a reward for policy learning. The state, including current input and prior contexts, is defined variably in two representation models. In Information Distilled LSTM (IDLSTM) [18], the action space maps a set of knowledge candidates, with each action indicating structure selection (Fig. 1).

$$\pi\left(a_t \mid \mathbf{s_t}; \Theta\right) = \sigma\left(\mathbf{W} * \mathbf{s_t} + \mathbf{b}\right) \tag{1}$$

We adopt a stochastic policy that uses the sigmoid function to compute the probability of choosing an action at a given state. During training, the action is sampled based on the probability computed by the policy. During testing, the action with the highest probability is selected to obtain superior prediction. The policy is defined as follows:

$$a_t^* = \operatorname{argmax}_a \pi\left(a \mid \mathbf{s_t}; \Theta\right) \tag{2}$$

where $\pi\left(a_t \mid \mathbf{s_t}; \Theta\right)$ represents the probability of choosing the action at, σ denotes the sigmoid function, and $\Theta = W, b$ represents the parameters of PNet.

In summary, the Policy Network implements a stochastic policy that samples actions based on a delayed reward, while the representation models convert these actions into a structured representation. Binary actions represent structure selection in both models, and a stochastic policy is employed during training and testing. Once the Policy Network has sampled all actions, the representation models determine the structured representation of a sentence. This representation is then passed to the KSN to acquire $P(y \mid X)$, where y denotes the class

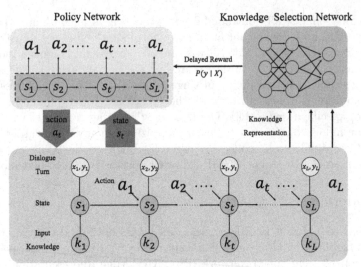

Fig. 1. Framework of KSRL

label. The reward is computed from the predicted distribution $P(y \mid X)$, and a factor accounts for the propensity of structure selection, which will be elucidated later.

This constitutes a typical delayed reward, as it can only be obtained once the final representation is established. The REINFORCE algorithm [18], and policy gradient methods are employed to optimize the parameters of PNet, maximizing the expected reward. The objective function is presented below:

$$J(\Theta) == \sum_{s_1 a_1 \cdots s_L a_L} \prod_t \pi_\Theta (a_t \mid \mathbf{s_t}) R_L \tag{3}$$

Note that this reward is computed over only one sample, say $X = x_1 x_2 \cdots x_L m$. Since the state at step t+1 is fully determined by the state and action at step t, the probability p(s1) and $p(\mathbf{s_{t+1}} \mid \mathbf{s_t}, a_t)$ are equal to 1.

We update the policy network using the gradient of the log-likelihood ratio by applying the likelihood ratio trick. The following gradient is used:

$$\nabla_\Theta J(\Theta) = \sum_{t=1}^{L} R_L \nabla_\Theta \log \pi_\Theta (a_t \mid \mathbf{s_t}) \tag{4}$$

The reward is calculated using the predicted distribution from KSN, and the parameters of PNet are optimized through the REINFORCE algorithm and policy gradient methods to maximize the expected reward. The objective function is determined for a single sample, and the policy network is updated using the gradient of the log-likelihood ratio. We generate the response at turn t, given the current context $\mathbf{x}^t$ and selected knowledge sentence $\mathbf{k}_s^t$.

Their concatenated embedding, $\mathbf{H}^t_{xk_s} = [\mathbf{H}^t_x; \mathbf{H}^t_{k_s}]$, is fed into the decoder p_θ. To amplify the influence of the chosen knowledge during response generation, we employ the Copy mechanism. [7] with Transformer decoder [14].

3 Experimental Evaluation

Our evaluation is centered on the Wizard of Wikipedia dataset [1] to assess the effectiveness of our approach flowing [6]. We compare our results quantitatively and qualitatively with other state-of-the-art models.

Wizard of Wikipedia encompasses a total of 18,430 dialogues for training, 1,948 dialogues for validation, and 1,933 dialogues for testing. The test set is divided into two subsets: *Test Seen*, containing 965 dialogues on topics overlapping with the training set, and *Test Unseen*, consisting of 968 dialogues on topics not previously encountered in the training and validation sets (Table 1).

Table 1. Quantitative results on the Wizard of Wikipedia dataset. The method with [*] does not use the knowledge loss. The scores of E2E Transformer MemNet[†] and Transformer (no knowledge)[†] are from the original paper.

Method	Test Seen				Test Unseen			
	PPL	R-1	R-2	Acc	PPL	R-1	R-2	Acc
Random knowledge selection	–	8.4	1.4	2.7	–	8.0	1.2	2.3
Repeat last utterance	–	14.5	3.1	7	–	14.1	2.9	–
Transformer (no knowledge)[†]	**41.8**	17.8	–	–	87.0	14.0	–	–
E2E Transformer MemNet[†]	63.5	16.9	–	22.5	97.3	14.4	–	12.2
PostKS*	79.1	13.0	1.0	4.8	193.8	13.1	1.0	4.2
E2E BERT	53.5	16.8	4.5	23.7	105.7	13.5	2.2	13.6
PostKS + Knowledge Loss	54.5	18.1	5.3	23.4	144.8	13.5	2.0	9.4
E2E BERT + PostKS	54.6	17.8	5.3	25.5	113.2	13.4	2.3	14.1
E2E BERT + PostKS + Copy	52.2	19.0	6.5	25.5	83.4	15.6	3.9	14.4
Ours	52.1	**19.4**	**6.7**	**26.7**	**81.3**	**16.2**	**4.1**	**18.2**

Evaluation Metrics. To evaluate our system's performance, we followed the evaluation protocol of Wizard of Wikipedia [1,6]. We used unigram F1 (R-1), bigram F2 (R-2), and perplexity (PPL) to assess response generation performance and accuracy to evaluate knowledge selection flowing [6]. Before computing the n-gram metrics, we removed all punctuation and commonly used words such as "a," "an," and "the." A lower perplexity and higher n-gram (R-1, R-2) scores indicated better performance, while a model's prediction was considered accurate if it matched at least one of the correct answers for knowledge accuracy evaluation.

Table 2. Multi-turn human evaluation results on the Wizard of Wikipedia. We report the averages and standard deviations (in parentheses).

Method	Test Seen	Test Unseen
E2E Transformer MemNet	2.33 (1.31)	2.18 (0.91)
Ours	2.38 (0.92)	2.32 (0.99)
Human	4.09 (1.03)	4.25 (0.93)

Baselines. We compared our system's performance with two state-of-the-art knowledge-grounded dialogue models: E2E Transformer MemNet [1] and PostKS [8]. E2E Transformer MemNet utilized a Transformer memory network for knowledge selection and a Transformer decoder for utterance prediction. On the other hand, PostKS used the posterior knowledge distribution as a pseudo-label for knowledge selection. To ensure a fair comparison, we replaced all GRU layers in PostKS with Transformers flowing [6]. We used the official BERT tokenizer to tokenize words and the predefined BERT vocabulary ($\mathcal{V} = 30522$) to convert tokens to indices. All the baselines, except for PostKS, used the same inputs as our model. PostKS did not use knowledge labels as proposed in the original paper.

3.1   Quantitative Results

In Table reftab:results, we compared the effectiveness of different methodologies on the Wizard of Wikipedia dataset flowing [6]. In every metric for knowledge selection (accuracy) and utterance generation (unigram F1, bigram F1), our model outperformed contemporary knowledge-grounded dialogue models. PostKS, which was trained without a knowledge label, exhibited weak knowledge selection accuracy that was only marginally superior to random guessing. However, it outperformed E2E Transformer MemNet with knowledge loss in the WoW Test Seen, indicating that prior and posterior knowledge distribution is effective for knowledge-grounded dialogue, while the addition of a KSRL improved performance even further. BERT improved the accuracy of knowledge selection less than TextQA due to the variability of knowledge selection in conversations. The E2E BERT + PostKS + Copy achieved the greatest results among the baselines, but they were not as impressive as ours, confirming that KSRL modeling was required to improve the accuracy of knowledge selection and, consequently, utterance generation. Moreover, the performance differences between our model and the baselines were greater in Test Unseen, indicating that the KSRL possessed superior generalization capabilities. Adding the copy mechanism to the baseline significantly enhanced the accuracy of utterance generation while having little effect on knowledge selection, demonstrating the effectiveness of the KSRL. Transformer (no knowledge) exhibited the least perplexity on the WoW Test Seen, primarily as a result of its propensity to generate only general and uncomplicated statements. This behavior may be advantageous for perplexity, whereas other knowledge-based models ran the risk of incorrectly predicting knowledge, which was detrimental to perplexity.

3.2   Qualitative Results

Multi-turn Human Evaluation. In addition to the previous evaluation, we performed a human evaluation in a multi-turn setting utilizing the evaluation toolkit from Wizard of Wikipedia [1]. Human participants were paired with one of the models and engaged in a conversation about a specific topic (chosen from 2–3 options) for 3–5 dialogue turns. After the conversation, they rated their dialogue partners on a scale of 1–5, with the score indicating how much they *liked* the conversation. We gathered votes for 110 randomly selected conversations from 11 distinct turkers. Table 2 presents a comparison of the results for different methods in the multi-turn evaluation. Human annotators showed a preference for our results over the baselines, with a more significant gap in Test Unseen.

4   Conclusion

In summary, we propose a novel approach that leverages reinforcement learning to improve knowledge selection in open-domain dialogue systems. By formulating knowledge selection as a sequential decision-making task and applying reinforcement learning, we can train the dialogue system to select the most appropriate knowledge and generate high-quality responses. Our approach has several advantages over other methods, including its flexibility and adaptability to different dialogue scenarios. We hope that our approach will inspire further research in this area and lead to more effective and efficient methods for knowledge selection in natural language processing.

References

1. Dinan, E., Roller, S., Shuster, K., Fan, A., Auli, M., Weston, J.: Wizard of wikipedia: Knowledge-powered conversational agents. In: International Conference on Learning Representations
2. Fan, L., et al.: MineDojo: building open-ended embodied agents with internet-scale knowledge (2022). https://doi.org/10.48550/ARXIV.2206.08853, https://arxiv.org/abs/2206.08853
3. Feng, R., Chen, M.: Multi-sensor data fusion for short-term traffic flow prediction: a novel multi-channel data structure integrated with mixed-pointwise convolution and channel attention mechanism. In: Artificial Neural Networks and Machine Learning-ICANN 2022: 31st International Conference on Artificial Neural Networks, Bristol, UK, September 6–9, 2022, Proceedings; Part IV, pp. 731–742. Springer (2022). https://doi.org/10.1007/978-3-031-15937-4_61
4. Fu, D., Zhang, C., Yu, J., Sun, Q., Zhan, Z.: Improving dialogue generation with commonsense knowledge fusion and selection. In: Knowledge Science, Engineering and Management: 15th International Conference, KSEM 2022, Singapore, August 6–8, 2022, Proceedings, Part I, pp. 93–108. Springer (2022). https://doi.org/10.1007/978-3-031-10983-6_8
5. Holtzman, A., Buys, J., Forbes, M., Choi, Y.: The curious case of neural text degeneration. In: International Conference on Learning Representations (ICLR) (2020)

6. Kim, B., Ahn, J., Kim, G.: Sequential latent knowledge selection for knowledge-grounded dialogue. arXiv preprint arXiv:2002.07510 (2020)

7. Li, Z., Niu, C., Meng, F., Feng, Y., Li, Q., Zhou, J.: Incremental transformer with deliberation decoder for document grounded conversations. In: Proceedings of the 57th Annual Meeting of the Association for Computational Linguistics, pp. 12–21 (2019)

8. Lian, R., Xie, M., Wang, F., Peng, J., Wu, H.: Learning to select knowledge for response generation in dialog systems. In: IJCAI International Joint Conference on Artificial Intelligence, p. 5081 (2019)

9. Ma, Z., Ye, J., Yang, X., Liu, J.: HCLD: a hierarchical framework for zero-shot cross-lingual dialogue system. In: Proceedings of the 29th International Conference on Computational Linguistics, pp. 4492–4498 (2022)

10. Mirchandani, S., Karamcheti, S., Sadigh, D.: ELLA: exploration through learned language abstraction. arXiv preprint arXiv:2103.05825 (2021)

11. Mu, J., et al.: Improving intrinsic exploration with language abstractions (2022). https://doi.org/10.48550/ARXIV.2202.08938, https://arxiv.org/abs/2202.08938

12. Radford, A., et al.: Learning transferable visual models from natural language supervision. arXiv preprint arXiv:2103.00020 (2021)

13. Tam, A.C., et al.: Semantic exploration from language abstractions and pretrained representations (2022). https://doi.org/10.48550/ARXIV.2204.05080, https://arxiv.org/abs/2204.05080

14. Vaswani, A., et al.: Attention is all you need. In: Advances in Neural Information Processing Systems. vol. 30 (2017)

15. Wang, C., Li, Y., Fei, C., Huang, X.: Labeled knowledge-based decision making with assumption-based argumentation. In: Knowledge Science, Engineering and Management: 15th International Conference, KSEM 2022, Singapore, August 6–8, 2022, Proceedings, Part I, pp. 450–465. Springer (2022). https://doi.org/10.1007/978-3-031-10983-6_35

16. Wang, Y., Zhu, X., Zhang, H.: Relation prediction based on source-entity behavior preference modeling via heterogeneous graph pooling. In: Knowledge Science, Engineering and Management: 15th International Conference, KSEM 2022, Singapore, August 6–8, 2022, Proceedings, Part I, pp. 425–436. Springer (2022). https://doi.org/10.1007/978-3-031-10983-6_33

17. Xu, J., Wang, H., Niu, Z.Y., Wu, H., Che, W.: Knowledge graph grounded goal planning for open-domain conversation generation. In: AAAI Conference on Artificial Intelligence (AAAI) (2020)

18. Zhang, T., Huang, M., Zhao, L.: Learning structured representation for text classification via reinforcement learning. In: Proceedings of the AAAI Conference on Artificial Intelligence. vol. 32 (2018)

19. Zou, P., Teng, Y., Niu, T.: Multi-scale feature extraction and fusion for online knowledge distillation. In: Artificial Neural Networks and Machine Learning-ICANN 2022: 31st International Conference on Artificial Neural Networks, Bristol, UK, September 6–9, 2022, Proceedings; Part IV, pp. 126–138. Springer (2022). https://doi.org/10.1007/978-3-031-15937-4_11

Prototype-Augmented Contrastive Learning for Few-Shot Unsupervised Domain Adaptation

Lu Gong, Wen Zhang, Mingkang Li, Jiali Zhang, and Zili Zhang[✉]

College of Computer and Information Science, Southwest University,
Chongqing 400715, China
zhangzl@swu.edu.cn

Abstract. Unsupervised domain adaptation aims to learn a classification model from the source domain with much-supervised information, which is applied to the utterly unsupervised target domain. However, collecting enough labeled source samples is difficult in some scenarios, decreasing the effectiveness of previous approaches substantially. Therefore, a more challenging and applicable problem called few-shot unsupervised domain adaptation is considered in this work, where a classifier trained with only a few source labels needs to show strong generalization on the target domain. The prototype-based self-supervised learning method has presented superior performance improvements in addressing this problem, while the quality of the prototype could be further improved. To mitigate this situation, a novel Prototype-Augmented Contrastive Learning is proposed. A new computation strategy is utilized to rectify the source prototypes, which are then used to improve the target prototypes. To better learn semantic information and align features, both in-domain prototype contrastive learning and cross-domain prototype contrastive learning are performed. Extensive experiments are conducted on three widely used benchmarks: Office, OfficeHome, and DomainNet, achieving accuracy improvement of over 3%, 1%, and 0.5%, respectively, demonstrating the effectiveness of the proposed method.

Keywords: Unsupervised domain adaptation · Self-supervised learning · Few-shot learning · Prototype learning · Contrastive learning

1 Introduction

Domain adaptation (DA) has attracted much attention over the past few years as a subfield of transfer learning. The goal of domain adaptation is to learn a model which can perform well on the target domain by leveraging knowledge from a discrepant while related source domain [13]. In traditional domain adaptation, the source and target domains are usually labeled. But in many real-world scenarios, the target domain may have little or no labeled data available, making traditional domain adaptation methods hard to apply. In the object recognition task, the model trained on clear pictures may face massive unlabeled images taken

Z. Jin et al. (Eds.): KSEM 2023, LNAI 14120, pp. 197–210, 2023.
https://doi.org/10.1007/978-3-031-40292-0_17

in multiple environments (light intensity, morphology change, background clutter, etc.). To deal with this situation, unsupervised domain adaptation (UDA) has received wide attention and made considerable progress due to its wide applications, including image classification, object detection, speech recognition, and machine translation. Several UDA approaches show excellent performance by fully leveraging labeled source samples and unlabeled target samples, such as reducing distribution discrepancy by minimizing distribution distance [6,26], generating domain-invariant features based on adversarial approaches [5,14] and other techniques based on semi-supervised learning [20,21].

From the perspective of time consumption and labeling expense, however, it is hard for us to collect sufficient labeled samples for source domain in some cases. In sentiment analysis, large amounts of textual data need to be labeled to determine their emotional polarity, which costs a lot and requires specialized knowledge. Therefore, obtaining large-scale annotated data is a challenge.

In this work, to deal with source domain annotation costs, we consider the problem called few-shot unsupervised domain adaptation (FS-UDA), where extremely scarce supervised source information is available. The instance-level self-supervised learning (SSL) [10] shows remarkable performance improvements on this issue. However, the instance-based approach involves two drawbacks: (i) the semantic information of the category is not captured during training, and (ii) the performance of domain adaptation degrades severely due to abnormal samples. Recently, the prototype-level SSL is proposed in [31], which learns discriminative features through in-domain prototypical contrastive learning and achieves domain alignment through cross-domain instance-prototype SSL. Although significant performance improvements have brought in [31] compared with instance-level SSL, this approach has a fundamental problem: a large mis-clustering may appear during random clustering, resulting in deviation in prototype calculation. Then, mis-matching occurs during instance-prototype learning, making semantic information learned inconsistent with categories.

To mitigate this situation, a new Prototype-Augmented Contrastive Learning (PAC) method is proposed, which selects the source data with high confidence to enrich semantic information of categories, as shown in Fig. 1. Then the source prototypes are employed as initial centers to cluster the target data to improve the quality of target prototypes. Motivated by [31], in-domain instance-prototype contrastive learning is performed to increase the discriminability of features. A novel cross-domain alignment approach is adopted in our model to reduce domain shift. The main contributions in this work are summarized as follows:

- A new two-stage prototype augmentation method is proposed. Different prototype calculation strategies are utilized in the source domain compared to the prototype obtained by random clustering. Moreover, the source prototype is used to rectify the target prototype.
- A novel cross-domain prototype contrastive learning is proposed. Cross-domain contrastive loss is introduced to our model for better semantic information learning and domain alignment.

– Extensive experiments are performed on three widely used benchmarks, demonstrating that the proposed method achieves comparable performance improvements in image classification.

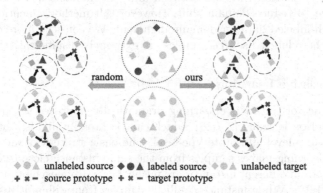

unlabeled source ◆ ● ▲ labeled source ◆ ● ▲ unlabeled target
+ ✗ – source prototype + ✗ – target prototype

Fig. 1. Comparison of our method (right) with random clustering (left) in prototype computation. The cluster obtained by random clustering contains more kinds of samples, making the prototype highly impure. To alleviate this issue, we iteratively append highly confident unlabeled samples to each category to rectify source prototypes, further used to improve target prototypes.

The remainder contents are organized as follows: Sect. 2 introduces the related work on unsupervised domain adaptation using contrastive learning. Section 3 illustrates the proposed method in detail. Then Sect. 4 reports the results of our experiments. Finally, Sect. 5 gives a conclusion to this work.

2 Related Work

Unsupervised domain adaptation is a promising research area in transfer learning. In this section, we concentrate on self-supervised learning for domain adaptation and illustrate its specific applications that are most relevant to our work.

2.1 Unsupervised Domain Adaptation

The traditional UDA is designed to apply knowledge learned from a fully-labeled source domain to a fully-unlabeled target domain [29]. Numerous UDA approaches have been proposed in recent years. Discrepancy-based approaches measure and minimize various distribution distances to align feature distribution [24,26], which mainly lie on some predefined distance. Adversarial-based approaches perform adversarial training to train a domain-invariant encoder, which learns domain-invariant features by minimizing an adversarial loss [16,23,32], and can be viewed as a learnable distance. The emergence of semi-supervised learning presents promising results in UDA. Entropy-based approaches [15,21] perform entropy minimization or maximization to alleviate the gap between domains. In [3], the pseudo-label strategy is used in the target domain to extend the source training set, further improving the model's generalization. Currently, some methods based on optimal transport [4,30] are introduced, which map the data between different domains to the same distribution space to reduce domain shift. However, all methods mentioned above require much-labeled data for domain alignment. We consider more challenging situations where labeled source samples are extremely insufficient.

2.2 Contrastive Learning

The emergence of contrastive learning dramatically improves the performance of representation learning [2,7,11], which can be broadly divided into two categories: instance-level and prototype-level. The basic strategy of instance-based contrastive learning makes samples from the same instance close to each other, and samples from different instances are pushed away from each other in the feature space [1,17]. While instance conflict (samples from different instances but the same category) exists in this approach, making it hard to obtain representations with intra-class consistency and inter-class discrimination [28]. Currently, prototype-based contrastive learning is proposed in [12,22] and shows promising directions in representation learning. Instead of instance-instance matching, prototype-based approaches perform contrastive learning between an instance and its corresponding prototype. This approach can effectively reduce the influence of abnormal samples and seize high-level semantic information of the category, further increasing the quality of representations.

2.3 Contrastive Learning for Unsupervised Domain Adaptation

Recently, the unsupervised domain adaptation based on contrastive learning introduces the contrastive loss into the deep model to learn discriminative features and align cross-domain features [10,28,31]. In [10], the cross-domain instance-level contrastive loss is introduced for domain adaptation. Furthermore, the cross-domain instance-prototype self-supervised loss is proposed in [31] to capture better semantic information. This approach calculates prototypes using random clustering for both domains, which differs from ours. Regarding domain adaptation, [31] performs cross-domain instance-prototype self-supervised learning (SSL) to train domain-invariant features and uses an entropy optimization-based loss calculation strategy, which is also not the same as ours. Hence, a new prototype rectification strategy is proposed to improve the effectiveness of contrastive learning in domain adaptation.

3   Method

We now illustrate the proposed prototype-augmented module and self-supervised learning method, and the main framework is shown in Fig. 2. For source domain, let $D^s = \{(x_i^s, y_i)\}_{i=1}^{N^s}$ denotes limited labeled samples and $D^{su} = \{x_i\}_{i=1}^{N^{su}}$

denotes all the remaining unlabeled samples. For target domain, we use $D^{tu} = \{x_i\}_{i=1}^{N^{tu}}$ to indicate all unlabeled samples. We aim to learn a classifier from D^s, D^{su}, and D^{tu}, then applying it on D^{tu}.

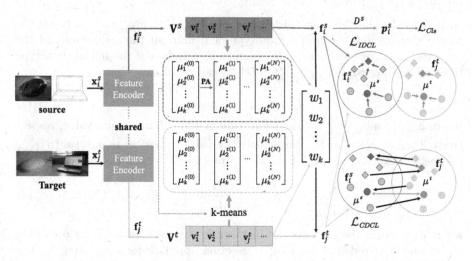

Fig. 2. Illustration of the proposed PAC method for FS-UDA. Different prototype computation strategies are utilized in the source domain to rectify prototypes gradually, which are further acted as initial centers to cluster target data to improve target prototypes. A cosine classifier is introduced and updated by features from memory banks. In-domain and cross-domain prototype contrastive learning are performed in both domains to capture discriminative features and mitigate domain shift.

3.1   Two-Stage Prototype Computation for Source Domain

The effect of prototype-based contrastive learning is greatly affected by the quality of the prototype. PCL [12] is a famous method that obtains prototypes through random clustering and then conducts contrastive learning with samples within the cluster to capture semantic information. [31] introduces it to the UDA setting and extends it to an end-to-end approach. However, the clusters obtained by random clustering will involve many samples from different classes, resulting in poor performance of calculated prototypes.

To better capture the semantic information of the categories and make full use of the unlabeled samples in the source domain, a two-stage prototype computation method is proposed to improve the quality of the prototype. Firstly, we introduce two memory banks $\boldsymbol{V}^s$ and $\boldsymbol{V}^t$ to store the source and target features.

$$\boldsymbol{V}^s = \left[v_1^s, v_2^s, ..., v_{(N_s+N_{su})}^s \right], \boldsymbol{V}^t = \left[v_1^t, v_2^t, ..., v_{N_t}^t \right] \tag{1}$$

v_i is the feature vector corresponding to x_i, initialized with $\mathbf{f}_i$, which is computed by feature extractor $F(\cdot)$, $i.e.$, $\mathbf{f}_i = F(x_i)$ and updated in each batch with a momentum coefficient θ, i.e., $v_i = (1 - \theta)v_i + \theta f_i$. We define $\boldsymbol{C}^s = \{C_j^s\}_{j=1}^k$, which indicates the initial set of labeled samples for each category and is gradually updated by D^{su} in each round. Then we calculate the initial normalized prototype $\{\mu_j^s\}_{j=1}^k$ from $\boldsymbol{C}^s$, specifically, $\mu_j^s = \frac{u_j^s}{\|u_j^s\|}$, where $u_j^s = \frac{1}{|C_j^s|} \sum_{v_j^s \in C_j^s} v_j^s$. Next, we calculate the cosine similarity $p^s = [p_1^s, p_2^s, ..., p_{(N_{su}+N_s)}^s]$ between the source samples and the initial prototype, and find out the maximum and the sub-maximum cosine similarity between each sample and the initial prototype to compute interval. For $x_i \in D^{su} \cup D^s$, d_i can be computed as:

$$d_i = g_{(1)}(p_i) - g_{(2)}(p_i) \tag{2}$$

where $g_{(0)}(\cdot)$ and $g_{(1)}(\cdot)$ return the maximum and sub-maximum value, respectively. Then we calculate the mean similarity $\{m_j\}_{j=1}^k$ and mean interval $\{n_j\}_{j=1}^k$ between labeled samples and the initial prototype.

$$m_j = \frac{1}{|C_j^s|} \sum_{c(i)=u_j^s} g_{(1)}(p_i), n_j = \frac{1}{|C_j^s|} \sum_{c(i)=u_j^s} d_i, j = 1, 2, ..., k. \tag{3}$$

where $c(\cdot)$ return the prototype of instance in current domain. After obtaining the m and n, We define the sample selection approach for each category. Let $E = \{e_j\}_{j=1}^k$ represent the sample selection conditions of the two stages.

$$e_j = \begin{cases} 0, & \text{if } g_{(1)}(p) > m \text{ or } d > n \\ 1, & \text{if } g_{(1)}(p) > m \text{ and } d > n \end{cases} \tag{4}$$

We iteratively add a certain number of high-confident samples to the corresponding category each time. The greater the maximum cosine similarity or prediction interval, the higher the credibility of the pseudo-label is. While some pseudo-label samples may be misclassified, there will be a significant prototype calculation deviation. So different prototype calculation strategies are utilized to reduce the impact of misclassification.

$$u_j^{s(z)} = \begin{cases} \frac{1}{|C_j^{s(z)}|} \sum_{v_i \in C_j^{s(z)}} v_i & , if \ e_j = 0 \\ \sum_{v_i \in C_j^{s(z)}} w_i \cdot v_i & , if \ e_j = 1 \end{cases} \tag{5}$$

where $u_j^{s(z)}$ represents the prototype in round z and w_i indicates the weight and can be computed as:

$$w_i = \frac{exp\left(v_i \cdot u_j^{s(z-1)}/\varepsilon\right)}{\sum_{v \in C_j^{s(z)}} exp\left(v \cdot u_j^{s(z-1)}/\varepsilon\right)} \tag{6}$$

where ε is a scalar coefficient and $u_j^{s(z-1)}$ represents the prototype in previous round. The higher the cosine similarity between the newly added sample and the base prototype, the better effect the prototype rectification is. With the addition of high-confident samples, the calculated prototype is closer to the expected prototype.

3.2   Prototype Computation for Target Domain

Owing to the scarcity of labeled data in the target domain, k-means clustering is performed on D^{tu} to obtain pseudo label. However, the clusters generated based on random clustering may contain multiple semantically unrelated samples, which may cause much deviation between the calculated and expected prototypes. So the number of target clusters is set to be consistent with the number of categories to alleviate this situation. The source prototypes are used as the initial clustering center of the target because both domains share similar semantic information for the same classes [28]. Concretely, we take the source prototype as the initial clustering center of the target in each round. For the j-th class in round z, $u_j^{t(z)}$ can be indicated:

$$u_j^{t(z)} \leftarrow u_j^{s(z)} \tag{7}$$

Then we cluster the target domain through the carefully initialized center and acquire the pseudo-label of the target. The cosine similarity between each sample and its clustering center is calculated. Since the cluster also contains some shots with low similarity, the quality of the target prototype may be affected. So only the unlabeled samples whose similarity values exceed the threshold are selected to recalculate the prototype.

3.3   In-Domain Prototype Contrastive Learning

To obtain a feature encoder with good discriminant ability, in-domain instance-prototype contrastive learning is performed on both domains. Given feature vector f which is encoded by F, i.e., $f = F(\text{x})$ and $\{\mu_j\}_{j=1}^k$, the contrastive loss can be expressed as:

$$\mathcal{L}_{InCL} = \sum_{f \in D^s \cup D^{su} \cup D^{tu}} \log \frac{\sum_{j=1}^{k} \exp\left(\mu_j \cdot f / \varepsilon\right)}{\exp\left(c\left(f\right) \cdot f / \varepsilon\right)} \tag{8}$$

where ε is a coefficient indicating the degree of concentration and μ represents the prototype corresponding to the current domain. As we perform several prototype calculations, the total in-domain prototype contrastive loss is:

$$\mathcal{L}_{IDCL} = \frac{1}{N} \sum_{i=1}^{N} \mathcal{L}_{InCL}^{(i)} \tag{9}$$

3.4   Cross-Domain Prototype Contrastive Learning

Similar to in-domain prototype contrastive learning, we performed cross-domain instance-prototype and prototype-prototype contrastive learning to reduce domain shift and improve the discriminability of cross-domain features. Therefore, the cross-domain prototype contrastive loss is calculated as follows:

$$\mathcal{L}_{CrossCL} = \sum_{f \in D^s \cup D^{su} \cup D^{tu}} \log \frac{\sum_{j=1}^{k} \exp\left(\mu_j^* \cdot f/\tau\right) \cdot \sum_{j=1}^{k} \exp\left(\mu_j^* \cdot c\left(f\right)/\tau\right)}{\exp\left(\left[f + c\left(f\right)\right] \cdot c^*\left(f\right)/\tau\right)} \qquad (10)$$

where $*$ indicates the same operation in the reverse domain. τ is a scale factor set to 0.1 during training. Likewise, the overall cross-domain prototype contrastive loss can be abbreviated as:

$$\mathcal{L}_{CDCL} = \frac{1}{N} \sum_{j=1}^{N} \mathcal{L}_{CrossCL}^{(j)} \qquad (11)$$

3.5   PAC Learning for FS-UDA

To better learn cross-domain category semantic information, inspired by [31], a cosine classifier C composed of weight vectors $W = [w_1, w_2, ..., w_k]$ and a coefficient T is introduced. We classify the input feature f through C, and then the output is processed by softmax to acquire the final result $R\left(x\right) = softmax\left(\frac{1}{T} W^T f\right)$. Since there are also a few labeled samples in the source domain, we directly use the cross-entropy loss to train F and C:

$$\mathcal{L}_{cls} = \mathbb{E}_{(\mathbf{x},y) \in D_s} \mathcal{L}_{CE}\left(R\left(\mathbf{x},y\right)\right) \qquad (12)$$

It is difficult for us to obtain a C with good performance for the target domain due to insufficient labels in the source domain. So from the initial stage, We update the weight of the classifier by using the prototypes calculated from the labeled and the high-confident unlabeled samples from both domains. Additionally, we remove those whose predicted value and interval are under the threshold. Together with in-domain prototype contrastive loss and cross-domain prototype contrastive loss, our final learning objective can be formulated as follows:

$$\mathcal{L}_{PAC} = \mathcal{L}_{Cls} + \eta \cdot \mathcal{L}_{IDCL} + \gamma \cdot \mathcal{L}_{CDCL} \qquad (13)$$

4   Experiments

In this section, we assess the effectiveness of the proposed PAC approach on three commonly used benchmarks. We display the experimental setup, report the results, and analyze the findings in the following subsections.

4.1   Experimental Settings

Datasets. Office [19] contains 31 object categories, each with 4,652 images from three domains: Amazon (A), Webcam (W), and DSLR (D), where experiments are performed with 1-shot and 3-shots labels in each source class. **OfficeHome**

[25] dataset involves 65 object categories, composed of 4,000 shots from four domains: Art (Ar), Clipart (Cl), Product (Pr), and Real-World (Rw), which exists more domain shift than Office and we follow [31] and set 3% and 6% labels in each class during training. **DomainNet** [18] is a larger dataset which has 121 object categories. We follow [20] and choose four domains (Clipart (C), Real (R), Painting (P), Sketch (S)) to train because of noise samples within some domains. We also set 1-shot and 3-shots per class during validation.

Implementation Details. ResNet-50 pre-trained on ImageNet is adopted as our feature encoder for both datasets. To ensure a fair comparison with [31], the last fully-connected layer is replaced with a 512D randomly initialized linear layer. The learning rate ratio between the linear and convolution layers is 1 : 0.1. We utilize SGD with a momentum of 0.9, a weight decay of 0.0005, a learning rate of 0.01, and a batch size of 64. The temperature value ϵ is adaptively calculated according to [12]. The momentum coefficient θ is set to a fixed value of 0.5. The hyper-parameters η and γ belong to $\{0.5, 1\}$.

Table 1. Office: Acc (%) comparison on 1-shot and 3-shots per class

method	Office: Target Acc. on 1-shot | 3-shots						
	A-D	A-W	D-A	D-W	W-A	W-D	Avg
SO	27.5 | 49.2	28.7 | 46.3	40.9 | 55.3	65.2 | 85.5	41.1 | 53.8	62.0 | 86.1	44.2 | 62.7
MME [20]	21.5 | 51.0	12.2 | 54.6	23.1 | 60.2	60.9 | 89.7	14.0 | 52.3	62.4 | 91.4	32.3 | 66.5
CDAN [14]	11.2 | 43.7	6.2 | 50.1	9.1 | 65.1	54.8 | 91.6	10.4 | 57.0	41.6 | 89.8	22.2 | 66.2
SPL [27]	12.0 | 77.1	7.7 | 80.3	7.3 | 74.2	7.2 | 93.5	7.2 | 64.4	10.2 | 91.6	8.6 | 80.1
CAN [9]	25.3 | 48.6	26.4 | 45.3	23.9 | 41.2	69.4 | 78.2	21.2 | 39.3	67.3 | 82.3	38.9 | 55.8
MDDIA [8]	45.0 | 62.9	54.5 | 65.4	55.6 | 67.9	84.4 | 93.3	53.4 | 70.3	79.5 | 93.2	62.1 | 75.5
CDS [10]	33.3 | 57.0	35.2 | 58.6	52.0 | 67.6	59.0 | 86.0	46.5 | 65.7	57.4 | 81.3	47.2 | 69.3
PCS w/o MIM	59.0 | 75.9	58.6 | 76.5	76.2 | 76.4	87.8 | 93.2	68.7 | 74.7	89.8 | 95.0	73.5 | 82.0
DANN+E	32.5 | 57.6	37.2 | 54.1	36.9 | 54.1	70.1 | 87.4	43.0 | 51.4	58.8 | 89.4	46.4 | 65.7
MME+E	37.6 | 69.5	42.5 | 68.3	48.6 | 66.7	73.5 | 89.8	47.2 | 63.2	62.4 | 95.4	52.0 | 74.1
CDAN+E	31.5 | 68.3	26.4 | 71.8	39.1 | 57.3	70.4 | 88.2	37.5 | 61.5	61.9 | 93.8	44.5 | 73.5
CDS+E	40.4 | 61.2	44.7 | 66.7	66.4 | 73.1	71.6 | 90.6	58.6 | 71.8	69.3 | 86.1	58.5 | 74.9
PCS [31]	60.2 | 78.2	69.8 | **82.9**	76.1 | **76.4**	**90.6** | 94.1	71.2 | **76.3**	**91.8** | **96.0**	76.6 | **84.0**
PAC(ours)	**73.3** | **78.3**	**76.9** | 78.9	**76.2** | 75.6	90.1 | **94.6**	**74.3** | 74.8	88.0 | 93.4	**79.8** | 82.6

E: entropy minimization

4.2 Experimental Results

Baselines. To illustrate the effectiveness of PAC in FS-UDA, we compare our method with other UDA approaches: **SO, CDAN** [14], **DANN** [5], **MDDIA** [8], **MME** [20], **CAN** [9], **CDS** [10], and **PCS** [31]. SO is an approach only trained in the labeled source. The target of CDAN, DAAN, and MDDIA is to train a cross-domain classifier for domain adaptation. MME uses a minimax conditional entropy strategy to train the feature encoder and classifier. CAN jointly train the features for both domains through an adversarial network to reduce distribution discrepancy. CDS uses pseudo-labels generated by self-supervised learning to assist conditional classifier training to realize target domain classification. PCS is the one-stage approach based on cross-domain prototype self-supervised learning. We also compare our method with other situations (**CDAN + ENT, DANN + ENT, MME + ENT, CDS + ENT**). We follow the setup suggested by [31], where each category is divided using the same number or proportion of samples.

Table 2. OfficeHome: Acc (%) comparison on 3% and 6% labeled shots per class.

method	Office-Home: Target Acc. (%)											
	A-C	A-P	A-R	C-A	C-P	C-R	P-A	P-C	P-R	R-A	R-C	R-P	Avg
3% labeled source													
SO	24.4	38.3	43.1	26.4	34.7	33.7	27.5	26.5	42.6	41.2	29.0	52.3	35.0
MME [20]	4.5	15.4	25.0	28.7	34.1	37.0	25.6	25.4	44.9	39.3	29.0	52.0	30.1
CDAN [14]	5.0	8.4	11.8	20.6	26.1	27.5	26.6	27.0	40.3	38.7	25.5	44.9	25.2
MDDIA [8]	21.7	37.3	42.8	29.4	43.9	44.2	37.7	29.5	51.0	47.1	29.2	56.4	39.1
CAN [9]	17.1	30.5	33.2	22.5	34.5	36.0	18.5	19.4	41.3	28.7	18.6	43.2	28.6
CDS [10]	33.5	41.1	41.9	45.9	46.0	49.3	44.7	37.8	51.0	51.6	35.7	53.8	44.4
DANN+E	19.5	30.2	38.1	18.1	21.8	24.2	31.6	23.5	48.1	40.7	28.1	50.2	31.2
MME+E	31.2	35.2	40.2	37.3	39.5	37.4	48.7	42.9	60.9	59.3	46.4	58.6	44.8
CDAN+E	20.6	31.4	41.2	20.6	24.9	30.6	33.5	26.5	56.7	46.9	29.5	48.4	34.2
CDS+E	39.2	46.1	47.8	49.9	50.7	54.1	48.0	43.5	59.3	58.6	44.3	59.3	50.1
PCS [31]	42.1	61.5	63.9	52.3	**61.5**	61.4	58.0	47.6	73.9	**66.0**	**52.5**	75.6	59.7
PAC(ours)	**42.2**	**62.0**	**65.5**	**54.6**	61.2	**64.3**	**62.9**	**47.7**	**74.3**	65.2	52.3	**77.0**	**60.8**
6% labeled source													
SO	28.7	45.7	51.2	31.9	39.8	44.1	37.6	30.8	54.6	49.9	36.0	61.8	42.7
MME [20]	27.6	43.2	49.5	41.1	46.6	49.5	43.7	30.5	61.3	54.9	37.3	66.8	46.0
CDAN [14]	26.2	33.7	44.5	34.8	42.9	44.7	42.9	36.0	59.3	54.9	40.1	63.6	43.6
MDDIA [8]	25.1	44.5	51.9	35.6	46.7	50.3	48.3	37.1	64.5	58.2	36.9	68.4	50.3
CAN [9]	20.4	34.7	44.7	29.0	40.4	38.6	33.3	21.1	53.4	36.8	19.1	58.0	35.8
CDS [10]	38.8	51.7	54.8	53.2	53.3	57.0	53.4	44.2	65.2	63.7	45.3	68.6	54.1
DANN+E	22.4	32.9	43.5	23.2	30.9	33.3	33.2	26.9	54.6	46.8	32.7	55.1	36.3
MME+E	37.2	42.4	50.9	46.1	46.6	49.1	53.5	45.6	67.2	63.4	48.1	71.2	51.8
CDAN+E	23.1	35.5	49.2	26.1	39.2	43.8	44.7	33.8	61.7	55.1	34.7	67.9	42.9
CDS+E	42.9	55.5	59.5	55.2	55.1	59.1	54.3	46.9	68.1	65.7	50.6	71.5	57.0
PCS [31]	46.1	65.7	69.2	57.1	**64.7**	66.2	61.4	**47.9**	75.2	67.0	**53.9**	76.6	62.6
PAC(ours)	**47.0**	**66.9**	**71.0**	**60.7**	64.4	**68.9**	**64.3**	46.0	**77.8**	**67.2**	51.0	**77.5**	**63.6**

Table 3. DomainNet: Acc (%) comparison on 1-shot and 3-shots per class

method	DomainNet: Target Acc. on 1-shot/3-shots						
	R-C	R-P	P-C	P-R	C-S	S-P	Avg
SO	18.4|30.2	16.7|25.7	16.2|24.6	28.9|49.8	12.7|24.2	10.5|23.2	19.1|31.7
MME [20]	13.8|22.8	29.2|46.5	16.0|25.1	26.0|50.0	13.4|20.1	14.4|24.9	17.5|29.1
CDAN [14]	16.0|30.0	25.7|40.1	12.6|21.4	19.5|40.8	7.2|17.1	8.0|19.7	14.6|27.3
MDDIA [8]	18.0|41.4	30.6|50.7	15.4|31.4	27.4|52.9	9.3|23.1	10.2|24.1	18.1|37.3
CAN [9]	18.3|28.1	22.1|33.5	13.2|24.7	23.9|46.9	11.1|23.3	12.1|20.1	16.8|28.8
CDS [10]	16.7|35.0	24.4|43.8	14.1|34.1	15.9|36.8	13.4|31.1	19.0|34.5	16.4|36.0
CDS+E	21.7|44.5	30.1|52.2	17.4|40.0	20.5|47.2	18.6|33.0	22.7|40.1	21.5|42.5
PCS [31]	**39.0|45.2**	**51.7|59.1**	26.4|**41.0**	38.8|**66.6**	23.7|**31.9**	23.6|37.4	34.7|**46.9**
PAC(Ours)	38.5|42.3	51.5|56.2	**28.7**|38.2	**43.5**|66.0	**24.5**|31.2	**25.0|38.2**	**35.2**|45.4

Results. We conduct extensive experiments on Office, OfficeHome, and DomainNet, with results reported in Tables 1, 2, and 3. We discover PAC outperforms the previous approaches in two benchmarks with improvements: 2.5% and 1% on Office, 1%, and 1.4% on Office-Home. At the same time, PAC shows remarkable results in some cases (e.g., **13.1%** Acc improvement in amazon-to-webcam on Office with 1-shot and over **4.9%** improvement in product-to-art on OfficeHome with 3% labeled shots) without using the entropy minimization (ENT) in the source domain. In the DomainNet, although with larger domain shift and more categories, PAC improves transfer accuracies between multiple domains in the 1-shot per class situations. Due to pool qualities of labeled shots in some categories, the prototypes are effected, decreasing the accuracies. Overall, PAC presents substantial performance improvements in the label-scarce scenario.

Table 4. Office: performance contribution of each part

method	Office: Target Acc. on 1-shot/3-shots						
	A-D	A-W	D-A	D-W	W-A	W-D	Avg
$\mathcal{L}_{Cls}$	53.2|60.8	49.0|59.6	61.1|64.3	79.3|89.6	58.7|60.7	78.9|89.3	63.4|70.7
$+\mathcal{L}_{IDCL}$	65.4|66.7	60.2|68.5	65.3|68.9	87.3|90.1	67.0|68.1	82.1|90.2	73.8|78.5
$+\mathcal{L}_{CDCL}$	73.3|78.3	76.9|78.9	76.2|75.6	90.1|94.6	74.3|74.8	88.0|93.4	**79.8**|82.6

Table 5. OfficeHome: performance contribution of each part

method	OfficeHome: Target Acc. (%)											
	A-C	A-P	A-R	C-A	C-P	C-R	P-A	P-C	P-R	R-A	R-C	R-P	Avg
3% labeled source												
$\mathcal{L}_{Cls}$	27.9	43.4	51.4	40.0	46.0	46.3	41.4	29.3	59.1	48.8	29.4	59.4	43.5
$+\mathcal{L}_{IDCL}$	35.6	55.1	58.9	51.1	56.4	55.0	55.4	38.8	67.6	56.3	42.3	70.5	53.6
$+\mathcal{L}_{CDCL}$	42.2	62.0	65.5	54.6	61.2	64.3	62.9	47.7	74.3	65.2	52.3	77.0	**60.8**
6% labeled source												
$\mathcal{L}_{Cls}$	31.0	45.2	54.5	43.3	51.5	50.8	46.6	32.1	63.9	54.0	34.5	63.0	47.5
$+\mathcal{L}_{IDCL}$	39.3	60.4	63.9	52.2	57.3	61.2	54.9	40.9	71.9	60.1	43.8	70.6	56.4
$+\mathcal{L}_{CDCL}$	47.0	66.9	71.0	60.7	64.4	68.9	64.3	46.0	77.8	67.2	51.0	77.5	**63.6**

4.3   Ablation Study

We conduct experiments on Office and OfficeHome datasets to evaluate the contributions of each part in PAC. We gradually combine the loss terms: (i) classification loss ($\mathcal{L}_{Cls}$), (ii) in-domain prototype contrastive loss ($\mathcal{L}_{IDCL}$), and (iii) cross-domain prototype contrastive loss ($\mathcal{L}_{CDCL}$) to the model, and the classification accuracies are shown in Tables 4 and 5. The proposed method achieves remarkable effects between multiple cases when all parts are included. The classification accuracy is minimum when only involving $\mathcal{L}_{Cls}$, which indicates that the encoder can't learn high-level semantic information of each category for both domains due to the lack of labeled samples. As adding $\mathcal{L}_{IDCL}$, the classification result has a noticeable improvement, indicating that in-domain prototype contrastive learning effectively captures discriminative features in the single domain. Further improvement is achieved when $\mathcal{L}_{CDCL}$ is introduced, confirming that cross-domain prototype contrastive learning reduces the gap between domains to a certain extent. Meanwhile, we can see that PAC outperforms the previous approaches in most cases. Especially in 1-shot or 3% shots per class, PAC achieves comparable performance.

5   Conclusion

In this work, a Prototype-Augmented Contrastive Learning (PAC) method was proposed for Few-shot Unsupervised Domain Adaptation, where only a few source samples are labeled. A two-stage prototype computation approach was utilized to rectify the source prototypes, which are then employed as the initial clustering center to cluster the target domain to improve the target prototypes. Furthermore, in-domain and cross-domain prototype contrastive learning were performed to train a discriminative feature extractor and reduce domain shift. Our extensive experiments demonstrated the effectiveness of PAC in the Few-shot Unsupervised Domain Adaptation setting.

References

1. Chen, T., Kornblith, S., Norouzi, M., Hinton, G.: A simple framework for contrastive learning of visual representations. In: International Conference on Machine Learning, pp. 1597–1607 (2020)
2. Chen, X., Fan, H., Girshick, R., He, K.: Improved baselines with momentum contrastive learning. arXiv preprint arXiv:2003.04297 (2020)
3. Cicek, S., Soatto, S.: Unsupervised domain adaptation via regularized conditional alignment. In: Proceedings of the IEEE/CVF International Conference on Computer Vision, pp. 1416–1425 (2019)
4. Damodaran, B.B., Kellenberger, B., Flamary, R., Tuia, D., Courty, N.: DeepJDOT: deep joint distribution optimal transport for unsupervised domain adaptation. In: Proceedings of the European Conference on Computer Vision, pp. 447–463 (2018)
5. Ganin, Y., et al.: Domain-adversarial training of neural networks. J. Mach. Learn. Res. **17**(1), 1–35 (2016)
6. Gretton, A., Borgwardt, K.M., Rasch, M.J., Schölkopf, B., Smola, A.: A kernel two-sample test. J. Mach. Learn. Res. **13**(1), 723–773 (2012)
7. He, K., Fan, H., Wu, Y., Xie, S., Girshick, R.: Momentum contrast for unsupervised visual representation learning. In: Proceedings of the IEEE/CVF Conference on Computer Vision and Pattern Recognition, pp. 9729–9738 (2020)
8. Jiang, X., Lao, Q., Matwin, S., Havaei, M.: Implicit class-conditioned domain alignment for unsupervised domain adaptation. In: International Conference on Machine Learning, pp. 4816–4827 (2020)
9. Kang, G., Jiang, L., Yang, Y., Hauptmann, A.G.: Contrastive adaptation network for unsupervised domain adaptation. In: Proceedings of the IEEE/CVF Conference on Computer Vision and Pattern Recognition, pp. 4893–4902 (2019)
10. Kim, D., Saito, K., Oh, T.H., Plummer, B.A., Sclaroff, S., Saenko, K.: Cross-domain self-supervised learning for domain adaptation with few source labels. arXiv preprint arXiv:2003.08264 (2020)
11. Le-Khac, P.H., Healy, G., Smeaton, A.F.: Contrastive representation learning: a framework and review. IEEE Access **8**, 193907–193934 (2020)
12. Li, J., Zhou, P., Xiong, C., Hoi, S.C.: Prototypical contrastive learning of unsupervised representations. arXiv preprint arXiv:2005.04966 (2020)
13. Long, M., Cao, Y., Wang, J., Jordan, M.: Learning transferable features with deep adaptation networks. In: International Conference on Machine Learning, pp. 97–105 (2015)
14. Long, M., Cao, Z., Wang, J., Jordan, M.I.: Conditional adversarial domain adaptation. arXiv e-prints, pp. arXiv-1705 (2017)
15. Long, M., Zhu, H., Wang, J., Jordan, M.I.: Unsupervised domain adaptation with residual transfer networks. arXiv e-prints, pp. arXiv-1602 (2016)
16. Long, M., Zhu, H., Wang, J., Jordan, M.I.: Deep transfer learning with joint adaptation networks. In: International Conference on Machine Learning, pp. 2208–2217 (2017)
17. Oord, A.V.D., Li, Y., Vinyals, O.: Representation learning with contrastive predictive coding. arXiv preprint arXiv:1807.03748 (2018)
18. Peng, X., Bai, Q., Xia, X., Huang, Z., Saenko, K., Wang, B.: Moment matching for multi-source domain adaptation. In: Proceedings of the IEEE/CVF International Conference on Computer Vision, pp. 1406–1415 (2019)

19. Saenko, K., Kulis, B., Fritz, M., Darrell, T.: Adapting visual category models to new domains. In: Daniilidis, K., Maragos, P., Paragios, N. (eds.) ECCV 2010. LNCS, vol. 6314, pp. 213–226. Springer, Heidelberg (2010). https://doi.org/10.1007/978-3-642-15561-1_16

20. Saito, K., Kim, D., Sclaroff, S., Darrell, T., Saenko, K.: Semi-supervised domain adaptation via minimax entropy. In: Proceedings of the IEEE/CVF International Conference on Computer Vision, pp. 8050–8058 (2019)

21. Saito, K., Watanabe, K., Ushiku, Y., Harada, T.: Maximum classifier discrepancy for unsupervised domain adaptation. In: Proceedings of the IEEE Conference on Computer Vision and Pattern Recognition, pp. 3723–3732 (2018)

22. Tanwisuth, K., et al.: A prototype-oriented framework for unsupervised domain adaptation. Adv. Neural Inf. Process. Syst. **34**, 17194–17208 (2021)

23. Tzeng, E., Hoffman, J., Saenko, K., Darrell, T.: Adversarial discriminative domain adaptation. In: Proceedings of the IEEE Conference on Computer Vision and Pattern Recognition, pp. 7167–7176 (2017)

24. Tzeng, E., Hoffman, J., Zhang, N., Saenko, K., Darrell, T.: Deep domain confusion: Maximizing for domain invariance. arXiv preprint arXiv:1412.3474 (2014)

25. Venkateswara, H., Eusebio, J., Chakraborty, S., Panchanathan, S.: Deep hashing network for unsupervised domain adaptation. In: Proceedings of the IEEE Conference on Computer Vision and Pattern Recognition, pp. 5018–5027 (2017)

26. Wang, J., Chen, Y., Hao, S., Feng, W., Shen, Z.: Balanced distribution adaptation for transfer learning. In: 2017 IEEE International Conference on Data Mining, pp. 1129–1134 (2017)

27. Wang, Q., Breckon, T.: Unsupervised domain adaptation via structured prediction based selective pseudo-labeling. In: Proceedings of the AAAI Conference on Artificial Intelligence. vol. 34, pp. 6243–6250 (2020)

28. Wang, R., Wu, Z., Weng, Z., Chen, J., Qi, G.J., Jiang, Y.G.: Cross-domain contrastive learning for unsupervised domain adaptation. arXiv preprint arXiv:2106.05528 (2021)

29. Wilson, G., Cook, D.J.: A survey of unsupervised deep domain adaptation. ACM Trans. Intell. Syst. Technol. **11**(5), 1–46 (2020)

30. Xu, R., Liu, P., Wang, L., Chen, C., Wang, J.: Reliable weighted optimal transport for unsupervised domain adaptation. In: Proceedings of the IEEE/CVF Conference on Computer Vision and Pattern Recognition, pp. 4394–4403 (2020)

31. Yue, X., et al.: Prototypical cross-domain self-supervised learning for few-shot unsupervised domain adaptation. In: Proceedings of the IEEE/CVF Conference on Computer Vision and Pattern Recognition, pp. 13834–13844 (2021)

32. Zhang, W., Ouyang, W., Li, W., Xu, D.: Collaborative and adversarial network for unsupervised domain adaptation. In: Proceedings of the IEEE Conference on Computer Vision and Pattern Recognition, pp. 3801–3809 (2018)

Style Augmentation and Domain-Aware Parametric Contrastive Learning for Domain Generalization

Mingkang Li, Jiali Zhang, Wen Zhang, Lu Gong, and Zili Zhang[✉]

College of Computer and Information Science, Southwest University,
Chongqing 400715, China
zhangzl@swu.edu.cn

Abstract. The distribution shift between training data and test data degrades the performance of deep neural networks (DNNs), and domain generalization (DG) alleviates this problem by extracting domain-invariant features explicitly or implicitly. With limited source domains for training, existing approaches often generate samples of new domains. However, most of these approaches confront the issue of losing class-discriminative information. To this end, we propose a novel domain generalization framework containing style augmentation and Domain-aware Parametric Contrastive Learning (DPCL). Specifically, features are first decomposed into high-frequency and low-frequency components, which contain shape and style information, respectively. Since the shape cues contain class information, the high-frequency components remain unchanged. Then Exact Feature Distribution Mixing (EFDMix) is used for diversifying the low-frequency components, which fully uses each order statistic of the features. Finally, both components are re-merged to generate new features. Additionally, DPCL is proposed, based on supervised contrastive learning, to enhance domain invariance by ignoring negative samples from different domains and introducing a set of parameterized class-learnable centers. The effectiveness of the proposed style augmentation method and DPCL is confirmed by experiments. On the PACS dataset, our method improves the state-of-art average accuracy by 1.74% using ResNet-50 backbone and even achieves excellent performance in the single-source DG task.

Keywords: Domain Generalization · Deep Learning · Data Augmentation · Contrastive Learning · Object Recognition

1 Introduction

Deep neural networks (DNNs) have achieved remarkable performance, assuming the testing dataset follows the same distribution as the training dataset. Unfortunately, this assumption rarely holds in practice. For example, in clinical practice, we may only have data from several patient populations (source domains) during training. However, we have to make predictions for data from

© The Author(s), under exclusive license to Springer Nature Switzerland AG 2023
Z. Jin et al. (Eds.): KSEM 2023, LNAI 14120, pp. 211–224, 2023.
https://doi.org/10.1007/978-3-031-40292-0_18

another patient population (unseen target domain) during testing. As another example, we need to make predictions on sketch images when only photograph and cartoon image datasets are available during training. In these cases, the "distribution gap" between the training and testing datasets will lead to the poor performance of the model. Due to the frequent occurrence of this problem in practice, domain generalization (DG) has aroused much concern.

Given a training set consisting of single or multiple source domains, the goal of DG is to train a model that generalizes well on unseen domains. Previous works tackled this problem via domain alignment [19,22,24], meta-learning [1,2,27], and data augmentation [14,15,20,34]. With the assumption that the "distribution gap" between source and target domains could be narrowed through extensive data augmentation, approaches based on data augmentation expose models to various source domains to learn generalizable representation. Zhang *et al.* [34] proposed EFDMix that matches high-order feature statistics to generate more diverse feature augmentations for DG. However, this method fails to preserve the class semantics in the high-frequency components of features, resulting in the distortion of class semantics during stylization. Additionally, most data augmentation methods do not consider the consistency of augmented samples. Jeon *et al.* [14] utilized supervised contrastive learning to achieve feature-level consistency, but the positives are not pulled strongly enough toward the anchor in this method, undermining the consistency.

In this paper, a novel domain generalization framework is proposed to mitigate the above shortcomings. The framework contains style augmentation and Domain-aware Parametric Contrastive Learning (DPCL). Motivated by the assumption that a domain can be characterized by the styles of its images [21,23], we augment the styles of images to enhance the generalization ability of DNNs. Specifically, features of the images are decomposed into high-frequency and low-frequency components, which comprise shape and style information [33], respectively. Since the shape cues preserve the high-level semantic information of the object and maintain consistency across different domains [29], we keep the high-frequency components unchanged. Then Exact Feature Distribution Mixing (EFDMix) [34] is utilized for diversifying the low-frequency components, which can take full advantage of each order statistic. Finally, the diversified low-frequency and original high-frequency components are re-merged to obtain new features. By incorporating them into the training process, the model can learn more, and its robustness can be improved.

Besides, DPCL is proposed to align the source domains and reduce the distance between the augmented and original features, achieving consistency at the feature level. Specifically, DPCL is a loss function improved over the Supervised Contrastive learning (SupCon) [16]. First, inspired by a recent long-tail learning method [8], a set of parameterized class-learnable centers are introduced into the SupCon loss, which can increase the intensity of pushing samples close to those samples that belong to the same class. Moreover, the SupCon loss is inconsistent with the objective of domain generalization since it keeps negative samples from different domains away from the anchor, which widens the "distribution gap" between the source domains. To this end, negative samples from different domains are ignored in DPCL to maintain domain invariance. Experimental results show the effectiveness of the proposed style augmentation method and DPCL loss.

To sum up, our main contributions are shown as follows:

- Firstly, a novel domain generalization framework is proposed, and various features are generated by the proposed style augmentation method. Generated features are used to improve the generalization capability of DNNs.
- Secondly, a novel Domain-aware Parametric Contrastive Learning loss is introduced to enhance domain invariance. This is achieved by introducing a set of parameterized class-learnable centers and contrasting features based on the domain and class labels.
- The effectiveness of the proposed style augmentation method and DPCL is demonstrated through ablation studies. Furthermore, experimental results show that the proposed method outperforms previous methods, achieving leading performance on widely-used benchmarks: PACS and Office-Home. Even in the single-source domain generalization task, the proposed method has a significant improvement over the baseline.

In the rest of the paper, Sect. 2 introduces the related work, and Sect. 3 describes our method in detail. In Sect. 4, the results of applying our method to various benchmarks are presented. Finally, Sect. 5 presents the conclusions of the study.

2   Related Work

Domain generalization (DG) is a hot spot currently in transfer learning. In this section, we mainly concentrate on reviewing two aspects most relevant to our work. One is data augmentation, and the other is contrastive learning.

2.1   Data Augmentation

Data augmentation has recently emerged as a promising approach due to its simplicity. Recent works [9,13] demonstrated that style information is preserved in the early layers of CNN. Based on such observation, researchers tend to perform feature statistics perturbation to get style-augmented training samples for DG. To this end, Mixstyle [38] linearly interpolated feature statistics (i.e. mean and variance) between instances. Meanwhile, Zhang et al. [34] matched high-order feature statistics to generate more diverse augmented features for DG. However, these methods distort the class semantic information in the high-frequency components of the features. Jeon et al. [14] sampled domain style vectors from the manipulated distribution of batch-wise feature statistics. Nevertheless, this method ignores higher-order statistics of features, leading to the loss of class-discriminative information. Our proposed style augmentation method maximally preserves the original semantics in terms of both feature statistics and semantic information in frequency.

2.2 Contrastive Learning

Recent works [4,19,22,24] reduced the distribution distance among multiple domains to learn domain invariant features. For instance, Li *et al.* [19] used adversarial learning and the maximum mean discrepancy criteria to carry out domain alignment, while Liu *et al.* [22] proposed to reduce both the conditional and label shifts. Unlike these methods, we use contrastive learning to carry out domain alignment.

Contrastive learning aims to learn a representation by contrasting similar (positive) and dissimilar (negative) samples in a latent space. To avoid the influence of trivial solutions on the model, SimCLR [5] added a projection head to avert model collapse. MoCo [11] improved the stability and accuracy of learning by introducing a momentum update strategy. Besides, Khosla *et al.* [16] proposed supervised contrastive learning to maximize the similarity between samples from the same class and minimize the similarity between samples from different classes. Our method is proposed based on this [16]. For domain generalization, Kim *et al.* [17] facilitated the application of metric learning using only positive pairs without negative pairs, while Yao *et al.* [32] proposed a novel proxy-based contrastive learning technique for domain generalization. Different from these, our method is motivated by [8] to introduce a set of parameterized class-learnable centers to ensure domain invariance.

3 Method

3.1 Problem Definition

When K source domains $D = \{D_1, D_2, ..., D_k\}$ with different distributions are available to train, domain generalization aims to learn a model which generalizes well to unseen domain D_t. Each source domain D_i contains a number of images $X^i = \{x_1^i, x_2^i, ..., x_{n_i}^i\}$, and the corresponding class label set for these images is $Y^i = \{y_1^i, y_2^i, ..., y_{n_i}^i\}$, where n_i denotes the amount of images in the i-th source domain. Note that both source domains and target domains share the same label space.

3.2 Overall Framework of the Model

The overall framework of our method is shown in Fig. 1 (a). The proposed DG framework contains a feature extractor g, a single fully-connected layer h, and the DPCL module. Among these, g consists of multiple convolutional layers and the proposed style augmentation module. The output feature of the l-th convolutional layer is denoted by z_l. Besides, h provides a set of parameterized class-learnable centers $\mathbf{C}$ to the DPCL module during training and acts as a classifier during inference. The DPCL loss is computed by the DPCL module that follows the framework of MoCo [6,11].

During training, the feature of the input image is extracted by the convolutional layers and diversified by the style augmentation module. Thus, we can

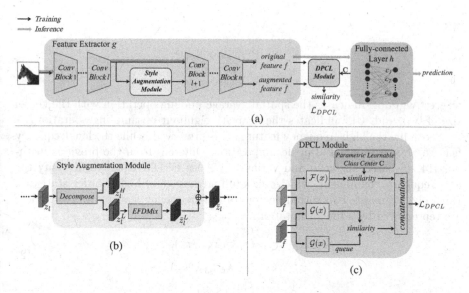

Fig. 1. Overall flowchart. (a) Our network with a number of convolutional blocks, the proposed style augmentation module and DPCL module. (b) The detailed structure of the style augmentation module. (c) The detailed structure of the DPCL module.

obtain the original feature f and the augmented feature $\bar{f}$. Then, these two features are fed into the DPCL module to produce the similarities. The DPCL loss, constituted by these similarities with $\mathbf{C}$, is utilized for training the whole model. The style augmentation and DPCL module are explained in detail in Sect. 3.3 and Sect. 3.4, respectively.

During the inference, the style augmentation module from the forward path is detached. Meanwhile, the single fully-connected layer h receives the original feature and makes a prediction.

3.3 Style Augmentation

Intuitively, the more samples from different domains a model sees, the better the generalization ability of the model is [28]. Therefore, we can synthesize new domains to enrich the source domains. Under the assumption that a domain can be represented by the styles of its images, the low-frequency component of the feature, which contains style information [33], can be diversified during training. Meanwhile, the high-frequency component of the feature, which contains shape information [33], remains unchanged since it is necessary to preserve the original semantics (*e.g.* shape) of the feature. The specific process is shown in Fig. 1 (b) and explained as follows.

First, inspired by a photo-realistic style transfer model [33], the feature z_l is decomposed into high-frequency and low-frequency components, *i.e.*, z_l^H and

z_l^L:

$$z_l^L = \text{UP}(\text{AvgPool}(z_l)),$$
$$z_l^H = z_l - z_l^L, \tag{1}$$

where "AvgPool" indicates the spatial average pooling operation with the kernel size of two, and "UP" indicates the nearest neighbour upsampling operation.

Secondly, the high-frequency feature z_l^H is preserved, while the low-frequency feature z_l^L is diversified after decomposition. Different from the previous methods [14,20] based on mean and variance, we use EFDMix [34] to diversify the low-frequency component, which takes full advantage of higher-order statistics. Precisely, we match two sorted vectors of low-frequency features whose indices are represented by a line of notation:

$$z_l^L : \tau = (\tau_1 \ \tau_2 \ \tau_3 \dots \tau_n),$$
$$z'^L_l : k = (k_1 \ k_2 \ k_3 \dots k_n), \tag{2}$$

where z'^L_l is the low-frequency feature of another image in the mini-batch, and $\{z_{l\tau_i}^L\}$ and $\{z'^L_{lk_i}\}$ are sorted values of z_l^L and z'^L_l in ascending order. In other words, $z_{l\tau_1}^L = \min(z_l^L)$, $z_{l\tau_n}^L = \max(z_l^L)$, and $z_{l\tau_i}^L \leq z_{l\tau_j}^L$ if $i < j$. $z'^L_{lk_i}$ is similarly defined. To synthesize more diverse styles, we interpolate these two sorted vectors by EFDMix and obtain a new low-frequency component $\bar{z}_l^L$:

$$\text{EFDMix}(z_l^L, z'^L_l) : \bar{z}_{l\tau_i}^L = z_{l\tau_i}^L + (1-\lambda)z'^L_{lk_i} - (1-\lambda)\langle z_{l\tau_i}^L \rangle, \tag{3}$$

where $\langle \cdot \rangle$ represents the stop-gradient operation [7]. The instance-wise mixing weight λ is adopted and λ is sampled from the Beta-distribution: $\lambda \sim Beta(\alpha, \alpha)$, where $\alpha \in (0, \infty)$ is a hyper-parameter. The value of α is set to 0.1.

At last, the synthesized low-frequency feature $\bar{z}_l^L$ is combined with the original high-frequency feature z_l^H and we obtain the augmented feature $\bar{z}_l$, which is formulated as

$$\bar{z}_l = z_l^H + \bar{z}_l^L. \tag{4}$$

Note that the proposed style augmentation module can be embedded after any layer of the feature extractor g. The optimal position l of the style augmentation module is analyzed via ablation studies.

3.4   Domain-Aware Parametric Contrastive Learning

Supervised Contrastive Learning (SupCon) [16] can be utilized in DG, and there are two main reasons for this. On the one hand, compared with the cross-entropy loss, SupCon loss has proved more robust in deep learning [16]. On the other hand, the augmented embeddings should be adjacent to the original counterpart. Therefore, the distance between the original features (anchors) and their style-augmented features can be minimized based on the dot product similarity in the SupCon loss. For better classification efficiency, the SupCon loss is presented in the framework of MoCo [6,11] that contains a *queue*. The SupCon loss is formulated as

$$\mathcal{L}_{SupCon} = -\sum_{f_i \in I} \frac{1}{|P(i)|} \sum_{f_+ \in P(i)} \log \frac{\exp(T(f_i) \cdot f_+ / \tau)}{\sum_{f_k \in A(i)} \exp(T(f_i) \cdot f_k / \tau)}, \quad (5)$$

where f represents an output feature from the feature extractor, $I \equiv \{f_1...f_{2B}\}$ indicates the output features in the mini-batch and their style-augmented features, $A(i) \equiv I \setminus \{f_i\} \cup queue$ contains the features from I but the anchor and the features from the *queue*, $P(i)$ denotes all positives to the anchor. Besides, the softmax function with temperature τ scaling is utilized on the similarity matrix of the anchor.

However, there exist two significant shortcomings in the SupCon loss: (i) the positives are not pulled strongly enough toward the anchor in the SupCon loss, undermining the consistency, and (ii) DG aims to shorten the domain gap while the negatives from different domains are pulled away from the anchor in the SupCon loss, leading to the increasing domain gap. Therefore, we improve the SupCon loss and propose the Domain-aware Parametric Contrastive Learning (DPCL) loss, which is more suitable for the DG task.

Specifically, inspired by a recent long-tail learning method [8], a series of parametric class-wise learnable centers $\mathbf{C} = \{c_1, c_2, ..., c_n\}$ are first introduced into the SupCon loss to overcome the first drawback. In this way, positives can be pushed closer to their corresponding centers. Therefore, we ensure the augmented features are closer to their original feature and achieve feature-level consistency. Besides, to overcome the second drawback, the negative samples in different domains from the anchor are ignored in the DPCL loss. The DPCL loss is defined as

$$\mathcal{L}_{DPCL} = -\sum_{f_i \in I} \frac{1}{|P(i)| + 1} \sum_{f_+ \in P(i) \cup \{c_y\}} \omega(f_+) \log \frac{\exp(T(f_i) \cdot f_+ / \tau)}{\sum_{f_k \in A'(i) \cup \mathbf{C}} \exp(T(f_i) \cdot f_k / \tau)}, \quad (6)$$

where

$$\omega(f_+) = \begin{cases} \gamma, & f_+ \in P(i) \\ 1.0, & f_+ \in \{c_y\}, \end{cases}$$

and

$$T(f_i) \cdot f_a = \begin{cases} \mathcal{G}(f_i) \cdot f_a, & f_a \in A'(i) \\ \mathcal{F}(f_i) \cdot f_a, & f_a \in \mathbf{C}. \end{cases}$$

In Eq. (6), $P(i)$ is the same with SupCon in Eq. (5), while $A'(i) \equiv A(i) \setminus \{f_l \mid y_l \neq y_i, d_l \neq d_i\}$, where y_i and d_i are the label and domain of f_i, respectively. The transform $\mathcal{G}(\cdot)$ denotes a two-layer MLP and $\mathcal{F}(\cdot)$ denotes the identity mapping, *i.e.*, $\mathcal{F}(x) = x$. γ is one hyper-parameter in $(0,1)$. $f_a \in \{f_+, f_k\}$ denotes the positive or negative. Moreover, following Cui *et al.* [8], the momentum encoder in MoCo [6,11] is removed to make the model more robust as shown in Fig. 1 (c). Therefore, both key and query share the same encoder, *i.e.*, the feature extractor g.

4 Experiments

4.1 Experiment Details

Datasets. Our method is evaluated on two DG benchmarks: (1) PACS [18] is an object recognition dataset consisting of four domains, *i.e.*, Photo (1,670 images), Art Painting (2,048 images), Cartoon (2,344 images) and Sketch (3,929 images). There are 9,991 images in PACS and each with a resolution of 227* 227. The dataset consists of 7 categories: 'dog', 'elephant', 'giraffe', 'guitar', 'horse', 'house', and 'person'. (2) Office-Home [10] is an object recognition dataset comprising four different domains, *i.e.*, Artistic, Clip, Product, and Real world. Each domain contains images of 65 common object categories found in the office and home. The total number of images is 15,500.

Evaluation. Domain generalization is often evaluated using a common protocol called "leave-one-domain-out" [18], which involves selecting one domain as the target domain and using the remaining domains as source domains. The model is trained on the source domains and then tested on the target domain. It is worth noting that the samples from the target domain are unavailable during training. This process is repeated for each domain to ensure that each domain is used as the target domain exactly once, and the accuracy is averaged over all domains.

Implementation Details. To make a fair comparison with previous research, we utilize ResNet-18 and ResNet-50 [12] pre-trained on ImageNet. Stochastic gradient descent (SGD) optimization is used to train our network. We set an initial learning rate of 0.004. A single mini-batch consists of 64 images for each source domain.

Moreover, the temperature parameter τ of $\mathcal{L}_{DPCL}$ is set to 0.15 following MoCo [6,11]. For better classification efficiency, the size of the *queue* in MoCo is set to 2048. Following [8], γ of $\mathcal{L}_{DPCL}$ is set to 0.5. Our model is developed upon the popular implementation of Zhou *et al.* [37].

4.2 Comparison with State-of-the-art Methods

Results on PACS. Table 1 presents a comparison of our method with previous DG methods on the PACS dataset [18]. The baseline model is trained only with cross-entropy loss. Compared with the state-of-the-art method, our method has an average accuracy improvement of 0.61% with ResNet-18. Moreover, when using the ResNet-50 as the backbone, our method sets a new record with an average accuracy of 89.70%, which is an improvement of 1.74% over the best competitor.

The experimental results demonstrate significant performance improvements when the photo and cartoon domains are selected as target domains, likely due to our method's ability to generate richer styles. Since the shape cues are preserved, our method maintains high performance in the art and sketch domain. Our style augmentation module requires no additional network parameters, making our model more memory-efficient than other methods.

Table 1. Quantitative leave-one-domain-out results on PACS. Entries are separated based on the backbones.

Accuracy(%)						
	Method	Art	Cartoon	Photo	Sketch	Avg.
ResNet-18	Baseline [18]	77.63	76.77	95.85	69.50	79.94
	MetaReg [1]	83.70	77.20	95.50	70.30	81.70
	Jigen [3]	79.42	75.25	96.03	71.35	80.51
	DDAIG [35]	84.20	78.10	95.30	74.70	83.10
	L2A-OT [36]	83.30	78.20	96.20	73.60	82.80
	EISNet [30]	81.89	76.44	95.93	74.33	82.15
	SagNet [23]	83.58	77.66	95.47	76.30	83.25
	MixStyle [38]	84.10	78.80	96.10	75.90	83.70
	DSON [25]	84.67	77.65	95.87	**82.23**	85.11
	FACT [31]	**85.37**	78.38	95.15	79.15	84.51
	DSU [20]	83.60	79.60	95.80	77.60	84.10
	EFDMix [34]	83.90	79.40	96.80	75.00	83.90
	FSDCL [14]	85.30	81.31	95.63	81.19	85.86
	Ours	85.18	**82.73**	**96.88**	81.07	**86.47**
ResNet-50	Baseline [18]	84.94	76.98	97.64	76.75	84.08
	MetaReg [1]	87.20	79.20	97.60	70.30	83.60
	EISNet [30]	86.64	81.53	97.11	79.07	85.84
	DSON [25]	87.04	80.62	95.99	82.90	86.64
	FACT [31]	89.63	81.77	96.75	84.46	88.15
	EFDMix [34]	90.60	82.50	98.10	76.40	86.90
	FSDCL [14]	88.48	83.83	96.59	**82.93**	87.96
	Ours	**91.31**	**86.28**	**98.65**	82.54	**89.70**

Results on Office-Home. Table 2 shows the results of our method on the Office-Home benchmark [10], where our approach achieve a leading performance using ResNet-18, with an average accuracy of 66.84%. Notably, our method improves the performance of all target domains, indicating its effectiveness in diverse settings. Overall, the comparison results confirm the effectiveness of our proposed style augmentation and contrastive loss for enhancing domain generalization performance.

4.3 Single-Source Domain Generalization

In the single-source DG task, the model is only trained on a single source domain while tested on the remaining domain on the PACS dataset. Each row in Table 3 represents the source domain, and each column represents the target domain. We utilize the same hyper-parameter settings as described in the previous section.

Table 2. Quantitative leave-one-domain-out results on Office-Home.

	Method	Art	Clipart	Product	Real	Avg.
Accuracy(%)						
ResNet-18	Baseline [18]	57.88	52.72	73.57	74.80	64.72
	MMD-AAE [19]	56.50	47.30	72.10	74.80	62.70
	CrossGrad [26]	58.40	49.40	73.90	75.80	64.40
	Jigen [3]	53.04	47.51	71.47	72.79	61.20
	SagNet [23]	60.20	45.38	70.42	73.38	62.34
	DDAIG [35]	59.20	52.30	74.60	76.00	65.50
	MixStyle [38]	58.70	53.40	74.20	75.90	65.50
	L2A-OT [36]	**60.60**	50.10	74.80	**77.00**	65.60
	FACT [31]	60.34	54.85	74.48	76.55	66.56
	FSDCL [14]	60.24	53.54	74.36	76.66	66.20
	Ours	59.19	**57.63**	**75.01**	75.52	**66.84**

Table 3. Results of single-source domain generalization on PACS. Each row and column indicates the source and target domain, respectively. We report the accuracy with the absolute gain from the baseline in brackets. Positive and negative gains are colored green and red, respectively.

	Accuracy(%) (Absolute gain from baseline)			
	Art	Cartoon	Photo	Sketch
Art	99.46 (+0.00)	73.04 (+16.81)	97.13 (+0.54)	67.18 (+23.19)
Cartoon	73.34 (+12.68)	99.51 (+0.06)	89.16 (+4.73)	75.97 (+13.57)
Photo	65.19 (+7.62)	32.00 (+12.59)	99.79 (−0.09)	58.38 (+32.27)
Sketch	41.11 (+11.57)	66.42 (+22.18)	43.47 (+11.07)	99.44 (+0.00)

Our results show improvements in most domain generalization scenarios, except for the diagonal elements where the source and target domains are the same. The most significant performance gains are observed in the "Art-to-Sketch", "Cartoon-to-Sketch", "Photo-to-Sketch", and "Sketch-to-Cartoon" settings. Notably, when the sketch serves as the source domain, there is a noticeable increase in performance, indicating the style diversification ability of our method even with only simple shape cues available for training.

4.4   Analysis

In this section, we evaluate our method and conduct a series of ablation studies using ResNet-18 as the backbone on the PACS benchmark. Our first objective is to inspect the effect of each component of our method. Next, the optimal position of the style augmentation module will be analyzed. Note that all hyperparameters will remain constant throughout the ablation studies.

Table 4. Ablation study on each component. † denotes that augmented features are aggregated for cross-entropy loss.

Style Augmentation	$\mathcal{L}_{DPCL}$ with only I_1	$\mathcal{L}_{DPCL}$ with only I_2	Accuracy(%)				
			P	A	C	S	Avg.
			95.85	77.63	76.77	69.50	79.94
$\checkmark^{\dagger}$			96.59	83.84	77.39	80.97	84.70
$\checkmark$	$\checkmark$		96.42	84.23	82.38	80.30	85.83
$\checkmark$		$\checkmark$	95.69	81.58	81.27	78.67	84.30
$\checkmark$	$\checkmark$	$\checkmark$	**96.88**	**85.18**	**82.73**	**81.07**	**86.47**

Ablation Study on Components. We conducted an ablation study to investigate the effects of incorporating style augmentation and domain-aware parametric contrastive learning (DPCL) loss. Note that the DPCL loss contains two improvements based on the SupCon, *i.e.*, introducing a set of parameterized class-learnable centers and ignoring negative samples from different domains. We denote these two improvements as I_1 and I_2 and conduct an ablation study to inspect their contribution.

Table 4 demonstrates that each component enhances the model's generalization ability compared to the baseline. Specifically, the contribution of style augmentation is observable in terms of average accuracy, and the overall performance is improved by around 4.76%. In addition, it is observed that both of the two improvements to SupCon play a positive role in DG task.

Table 5. Ablation study on the location of style augmentation module.

Layer	Accuracy(%)				
	P	A	C	S	Avg.
Conv	94.37	81.93	80.23	78.54	83.77
ResBlock$_1$	94.91	81.54	82.08	78.67	84.30
ResBlock$_2$	**96.88**	**85.18**	**82.73**	**81.07**	**86.47**
ResBlock$_3$	94.73	81.49	81.74	77.39	83.84
ResBlock$_4$	94.31	78.61	80.16	70.54	80.91

Location of the Style Augmentation Module. We explore the optimal location for the proposed style augmentation module. The ResNet architecture is re-grouped into five layers, `Conv` and `ResBlock` `1-4`. Among these, `Conv` represents the first convolutional layer before residual blocks.

Table 5 shows that the optimal position for the style augmentation module is following the second residual block in the neural network. The results indicate that features following the second residual block capture both detailed structural information and higher-level class information.

5   Conclusion

In this paper, a novel framework involving style augmentation and Domain-aware Parametric Contrastive Learning is proposed to mitigate the distribution shift. In detail, low-frequency features are diversified by EFDMix while high-frequency features are preserved. In this way, important class semantic information can be preserved, and feature statistics can be fully utilized to augment samples. Additionally, the supervised contrastive learning loss is improved by ignoring negative samples from different domains and incorporating a set of parameterized class-learnable centers. The improved loss is called DPCL loss, which can align the domains further and ensure the consistency of augmented samples. The effectiveness of the proposed augmentation method and loss function is demonstrated through comparisons and experimental analyses on two widely-used benchmarks.

References

1. Balaji, Y., Sankaranarayanan, S., Chellappa, R.: MetaReg: towards domain generalization using meta-regularization. In: Proceedings of the 32nd International Conference on Neural Information Processing Systems, pp. 1006–1016 (2018)
2. Bui, M.H., Tran, T., Tran, A., Phung, D.: Exploiting domain-specific features to enhance domain generalization. Adv. Neural Inf. Process. Syst. **34**, 21189–21201 (2021)
3. Carlucci, F.M., D'Innocente, A., Bucci, S., Caputo, B., Tommasi, T.: Domain generalization by solving jigsaw puzzles. In: Proceedings of the IEEE/CVF Conference on Computer Vision and Pattern Recognition, pp. 2229–2238 (2019)
4. Chen, S., Wang, L., Hong, Z., Yang, X.: Domain generalization by joint-product distribution alignment. Pattern Recogn. **134**, 109086 (2023)
5. Chen, T., Kornblith, S., Norouzi, M., Hinton, G.: A simple framework for contrastive learning of visual representations. In: International Conference on Machine Learning, pp. 1597–1607 (2020)
6. Chen, X., Fan, H., Girshick, R., He, K.: Improved baselines with momentum contrastive learning. arXiv preprint arXiv:2003.04297 (2020)
7. Chen, X., He, K.: Exploring simple Siamese representation learning. In: Proceedings of the IEEE/CVF Conference on Computer Vision and Pattern Recognition, pp. 15750–15758 (2021)
8. Cui, J., Zhong, Z., Liu, S., Yu, B., Jia, J.: Parametric contrastive learning. In: Proceedings of the IEEE/CVF International Conference on Computer Vision, pp. 715–724 (2021)

9. Dumoulin, V., Shlens, J., Kudlur, M.: A learned representation for artistic style. arXiv preprint arXiv:1610.07629 (2016)
10. Finn, C., Abbeel, P., Levine, S.: Model-agnostic meta-learning for fast adaptation of deep networks. In: International Conference on Machine Learning, pp. 1126–1135 (2017)
11. He, K., Fan, H., Wu, Y., Xie, S., Girshick, R.: Momentum contrast for unsupervised visual representation learning. In: Proceedings of the IEEE/CVF Conference on Computer Vision and Pattern Recognition, pp. 9729–9738 (2020)
12. He, K., Zhang, X., Ren, S., Sun, J.: Deep residual learning for image recognition. In: Proceedings of the IEEE Conference on Computer Vision and Pattern Recognition, pp. 770–778 (2016)
13. Huang, X., Belongie, S.: Arbitrary style transfer in real-time with adaptive instance normalization. In: Proceedings of the IEEE International Conference on Computer Vision, pp. 1501–1510 (2017)
14. Jeon, S., Hong, K., Lee, P., Lee, J., Byun, H.: Feature stylization and domain-aware contrastive learning for domain generalization. In: Proceedings of the 29th ACM International Conference on Multimedia, pp. 22–31 (2021)
15. Kang, J., Lee, S., Kim, N., Kwak, S.: Style Neophile: constantly seeking novel styles for domain generalization. In: Proceedings of the IEEE/CVF Conference on Computer Vision and Pattern Recognition, pp. 7130–7140 (2022)
16. Khosla, P., et al.: Supervised contrastive learning. Adv. Neural Inf. Process. Syst. **33**, 18661–18673 (2020)
17. Kim, D., Yoo, Y., Park, S., Kim, J., Lee, J.: SelfReg: self-supervised contrastive regularization for domain generalization. In: Proceedings of the IEEE/CVF International Conference on Computer Vision, pp. 9619–9628 (2021)
18. Li, D., Yang, Y., Song, Y.Z., Hospedales, T.M.: Deeper, broader and artier domain generalization. In: Proceedings of the IEEE International Conference on Computer Vision, pp. 5542–5550 (2017)
19. Li, H., Pan, S.J., Wang, S., Kot, A.C.: Domain generalization with adversarial feature learning. In: Proceedings of the IEEE Conference on Computer Vision and Pattern Recognition, pp. 5400–5409 (2018)
20. Li, X., Dai, Y., Ge, Y., Liu, J., Shan, Y., Duan, L.Y.: Uncertainty modeling for out-of-distribution generalization. arXiv preprint arXiv:2202.03958 (2022)
21. Li, Y., Wang, N., Liu, J., Hou, X.: Demystifying neural style transfer. arXiv preprint arXiv:1701.01036 (2017)
22. Liu, X., et al.: Domain generalization under conditional and label shifts via variational bayesian inference. arXiv preprint arXiv:2107.10931 (2021)
23. Nam, H., Lee, H., Park, J., Yoon, W., Yoo, D.: Reducing domain gap via style-agnostic networks. arXiv preprint arXiv:1910.11645 (2019)
24. Nie, Z., Lin, Y., Yan, M., Cao, Y., Ning, S.: An adversarial training method for improving model robustness in unsupervised domain adaptation. In: Qiu, H., Zhang, C., Fei, Z., Qiu, M., Kung, S.-Y. (eds.) KSEM 2021. LNCS (LNAI), vol. 12817, pp. 3–13. Springer, Cham (2021). https://doi.org/10.1007/978-3-030-82153-1_1
25. Seo, S., Suh, Y., Kim, D., Kim, G., Han, J., Han, B.: Learning to optimize domain specific normalization for domain generalization. In: Vedaldi, A., Bischof, H., Brox, T., Frahm, J.-M. (eds.) ECCV 2020. LNCS, vol. 12367, pp. 68–83. Springer, Cham (2020). https://doi.org/10.1007/978-3-030-58542-6_5
26. Shankar, S., Piratla, V., Chakrabarti, S., Chaudhuri, S., Jyothi, P., Sarawagi, S.: Generalizing across domains via cross-gradient training. arXiv preprint arXiv:1804.10745 (2018)

27. Shu, Y., Cao, Z., Wang, C., Wang, J., Long, M.: Open domain generalization with domain-augmented meta-learning. In: Proceedings of the IEEE/CVF Conference on Computer Vision and Pattern Recognition, pp. 9624–9633 (2021)

28. Tobin, J., Fong, R., Ray, A., Schneider, J., Zaremba, W., Abbeel, P.: Domain randomization for transferring deep neural networks from simulation to the real world. In: 2017 IEEE/RSJ International Conference on Intelligent Robots and Systems (IROS), pp. 23–30 (2017)

29. Wang, J., Du, R., Chang, D., Liang, K., Ma, Z.: Domain generalization via frequency-domain-based feature disentanglement and interaction. In: Proceedings of the 30th ACM International Conference on Multimedia, pp. 4821–4829 (2022)

30. Wang, S., Yu, L., Li, C., Fu, C.-W., Heng, P.-A.: Learning from extrinsic and intrinsic supervisions for domain generalization. In: Vedaldi, A., Bischof, H., Brox, T., Frahm, J.-M. (eds.) ECCV 2020. LNCS, vol. 12354, pp. 159–176. Springer, Cham (2020). https://doi.org/10.1007/978-3-030-58545-7_10

31. Xu, Q., Zhang, R., Zhang, Y., Wang, Y., Tian, Q.: A fourier-based framework for domain generalization. In: Proceedings of the IEEE/CVF Conference on Computer Vision and Pattern Recognition, pp. 14383–14392 (2021)

32. Yao, X., et al.: PCL: proxy-based contrastive learning for domain generalization. In: Proceedings of the IEEE/CVF Conference on Computer Vision and Pattern Recognition, pp. 7097–7107 (2022)

33. Yoo, J., Uh, Y., Chun, S., Kang, B., Ha, J.W.: Photorealistic style transfer via wavelet transforms. In: Proceedings of the IEEE/CVF International Conference on Computer Vision, pp. 9036–9045 (2019)

34. Zhang, Y., Li, M., Li, R., Jia, K., Zhang, L.: Exact feature distribution matching for arbitrary style transfer and domain generalization. In: Proceedings of the IEEE/CVF Conference on Computer Vision and Pattern Recognition, pp. 8035–8045 (2022)

35. Zhou, K., Yang, Y., Hospedales, T., Xiang, T.: Deep domain-adversarial image generation for domain generalisation. In: 34th AAAI Conference on Artificial Intelligence, pp. 13025–13032 (2020)

36. Zhou, K., Yang, Y., Hospedales, T., Xiang, T.: Learning to generate novel domains for domain generalization. In: Vedaldi, A., Bischof, H., Brox, T., Frahm, J.-M. (eds.) ECCV 2020. LNCS, vol. 12361, pp. 561–578. Springer, Cham (2020). https://doi.org/10.1007/978-3-030-58517-4_33

37. Zhou, K., Yang, Y., Qiao, Y., Xiang, T.: Domain adaptive ensemble learning. IEEE Trans. Image Process. 30, 8008–8018 (2021)

38. Zhou, K., Yang, Y., Qiao, Y., Xiang, T.: Domain generalization with mixstyle. arXiv preprint arXiv:2104.02008 (2021)

Recent Progress on Text Summarisation Based on BERT and GPT

Binxia Yang[1], Xudong Luo[1]([✉]), Kaili Sun[1], and Michael Y. Luo[2]

[1] Guangxi Key Lab of Multi-Source Information Mining & Security,
School of Computer Science and Engineering Guangxi Normal University,
Guilin, China
binxiay@stu.gxnu.edu.cn, luoxd@mailbox.gxnu.edu.cn
[2] Emmanuel College, Cambridge University, Cambridge, UK
myl41@cam.ac.uk

Abstract. Text summarisation is one of the essential topics in natural language processing. Pre-trained language models, especially BERT and GPT, are the most advanced methods for various natural language processing tasks; thus, many researchers have tried to use BERT and GPT for text summarisation. To facilitate further research on this topic, this paper surveys its state-of-the-art. Specifically, we summarise the topic's main research issues and BERT- and GPT-based solutions, compare these methods (especially their pros and cons), explore their applications, and discuss the challenges to future research.

Keywords: Natural language processing · Pre-trained language model · BERT · GPT · Text summarisation

1 Introduction

Automated information extraction is an efficient technique for consumers, academics and decision-makers to comprehend critical information in text data rapidly. Thus, Text Summarisation (TS) is becoming increasingly important as one of the essential Natural Language Processing (NLP) tasks [13]. TS has been applied in many domains, including news article summaries, email summaries and medical information summaries [7].

On the other hand, Pre-trained Language Models (PLMs) can learn universal language representations through unsupervised training on vast amounts of text and the probability distribution of each word or word occurrence. Their labels are their contexts, allowing for training with almost complete large-scale corpora. Through training, a PLM can achieve outstanding results in numerous downstream tasks.

Among various PLMs [32], the most popular are the BERT family and the GPT family.

- At the end of 2018, Devlin *et al.* [9] presented PLM BERT (Bidirectional Encoder Representations from Transformers), which utilises a Masked Language Model (MLM) and Next Sentence Prediction (NSP) for deep bidirectional joint training. The difference between BERT's pre-training and downstream task-specific training lies in the top output layer. Consequently, BERT achieves remarkable performance on 11 fundamental tasks of NLP. Since then, researchers have proposed many improved versions of BERT. For example, RoBERTa [19] employs a larger dataset for training, changes static masks to dynamic masks, and eliminates the NSP task.
- In 2018, Radford *et al.* [28] developed the GPT (Generative Pretrained Transformer) model. Its pre-training consists of two stages as follows. (1) *Unsupervised pre-training*: learning a high-capacity language model on a large text corpus. (2) *Supervised fine-tuning*: adapting the model to discriminative tasks with labelled data. In 2019, Radford *et al.* [29] developed GPT-2. It still employs the unidirectional transformer model of GPT, but its training data has significantly improved in quantity, quality, and breadth. The network parameters have also increased to answer questions, summarise, and translate text without domain-specific training. In 2020, Brown *et al.* [3] further developed GPT-3, with 175 billion parameters. In 2022, OpenAI realised ChatGPT (GPT-3.5). Finally, in March 2023, they released GPT-4.

Since BERT and GPT are the most advanced methods for various NLP tasks, many researchers use them for TS [26]. We survey this topic in this paper to help researchers quickly grasp the state-of-the-art TS models based on BERT and GPT. Specifically, we summarise their main research issues and the methods to address them, compare them (especially their pros and cons), discuss their applications in legal, news, and healthcare domains, and identify future challenges.

Our survey in this paper is distinct from those on PLM and TS. For example, in 2021, El-Kassas *et al.* [12] summarised and reviewed various TS models but little about PLM-based TS ones. In contrast, our entire survey is about PLM-based TS. In 2022, Sun *et al.* [32] surveyed PLMs but not PLM-based TS models. Moreover, theirs only covers papers published before their survey; we include many others published since. Finally, in 2022, Syed *et al.* [33] surveyed abstractive TS using PLMs. However, they primarily analysed PLMs to identify issues and challenges in fine-tuning PLMs for TS. Instead, ours highlights various types of TS and how to use BERT and GPT to solve these TS problems rather than how to fine-tune PLMs for better performance of TS. Moreover, unlike ours, theirs focuses on something other than BERT- and GPT-based TS. Additionally, ours covers some later TS models.

The rest of this paper is organised as follows. Section 2 reviews BERT-based TS models. Section 3 examines GPT-based TS models. Section 4 briefly discusses BERT&GPT-based TS models. Section 5 explores the applications of BERT-based and GPT-based TS models. Section 6 identifies future research directions. Finally, Sect. 7 concludes this paper.

2   BERT-Based Model

This section will discuss how researchers use BERT according to the desired type of TS. Table 1 compares these models.

2.1   Single Document Summarisation

(1) **Short Text Summarisation**: In 2022, Ma *et al.* [23] fine-tuned BERT and applied it to automatically generate titles for a specific input abstract based on a sample collection of published literature. The model comprises an encoder module, a decoder module, and a training module. The encoder and decoder are connected by a multi-stage function, giving the TS model a multi-task learning architecture. Their experiments show that their model outperforms other baseline models, achieving a BLEU (BiLingual Evaluation Understudy)[1] of 67.6 and a ROUGE-L (Recall-Oriented Understudy for Gisting Evaluation)[2] score of 84.6.

(2) **Long Text Summarisation**: Although BERT has been used for document coding in some TS models, it often generates redundant or uninformative phrases in the extracted summaries. Besides, since BERT is pre-trained on sentence pairs rather than complete documents, capturing long-range dependencies in the entire document can be challenging. To address these issues, in 2019, Xu *et al.* [36] presented DiscoBert, a discourse-aware BERT-based TS model. The model uses discourse units as the minimal selection basis to reduce summarisation redundancy. To capture the long-range dependencies between discourse units, they constructed a structured discourse graph and encoded it using a convolutional graph network. Their experiments show that DiscoBert outperforms BERT-based baseline models, with ROUGE-1, ROUGE-2, and ROUGE-L (ROUGE-1, -2, and -L) scores better by 1.30, 1.29, and 1.82, respectively.

Although NLP has adopted the practice of fine-tuning large PLMs for downstream tasks, current transformer-based architectures have limitations when the target task requires reasoning on long documents. To address this issue, in 2021, Grail *et al.* [15] proposed globalising BERT-based Transformer architectures for long TS by adding propagation layers that spread information between multiple transformer windows. Their model outperforms other adaptations of BERT and previously proposed models for an extractive TS task. The authors achieved ROUGE-1, -2, and -L scores of 42.93, 19.81, and 39.20, respectively.

(3) **Variable-length Text Summarisation**: In 2020, Su *et al.* [31] proposed a TS model capable of both fluent and variable-length TS. The model first divides the input text into segments using BERT and a Bi-directional Long and Short-Term Memory (BiLSTM) based on the Transformer. The most important sentences from each segment are then extracted using the BERT-based TS

---

[1] BLEU measures precision: how many words in the machine-generated summaries are also in the human reference summaries.

[2] ROUGE measures recall: how many words in the human reference summaries are also in the machine-generated summaries.

Table 1. Comparison of various BERT-based methods for TS

Ref	Citation	Issue addressed	Method	Pro	Con	Data source
Ma et al. [23] (2022)	13	generate the titles for the input abstract of a given paper	give BERT a multi-task learning architecture	can be fine-tuned even with small dataset	weak presentation of the model	Geological journals in China
Xu et al. [36] (2019)	207	capture long-range dependencies in documents	improve BERT using discourse units as a minimum basis for selection	can generate accurate and informative summaries with low redundancy	compromised grammaticality and consistency of the output	New York Times and CNN/Daily-Mail
Grail et al. [15] (2021)	27	limitations of current transformer-based long TS	use layered components between the layers of BERT	build informative representations for extractive TS	the model's performance influenceable by sentence position	CNN/Daily Mail
Su et al. [31] (2020)	27	generate variable length summaries	segmentation of input text with BERT and bidirectional LSTM	consider simultaneously fluency and variable length of the generated summaries	the short text that was cut may contain insufficient information	ChWiki_181k and Wiki_300
Ramina et al. [30] (2020)	12	topic-level TS of large amounts of information	use BERT as encoder and Transformer as decoder	can summarise according to user keywords	cannot understand the context accurately	CNN DailyMail
Ma et al. [24] (2021)	27	long text dependencies and using latent topic mapping for TS	joint learning of topic modelling and BERT TS	use the pretrained external knowledge and topic mining to capture accurate contexts	unsuitable for long documents with multiple themes	CNN/Daily mail and XSum datasets
Lamsiyah et al. [18] (2021)	7	summarise multiple documents	fine-tune BERT using multi-task learning	improve the model's performance	less effective than multi-task fine-tuning	GLUE benchmark datasets and UC'2002-2004 datasets
Ghadimi et al. [14] (2022)	5	longer multi-document summaries	use BERT to encode sentences in a context-aware way	eliminating longer sequences also reduces computation time	require a large amount of computational power	DUC 2002, DUC 2004, Multi-News and CNN DailyMail
Kano et al. [16] (2021)	5	impact of automatic speech recognition errors on speech abstraction	replace the input embeddings of BERT with the sum of embedding vectors weighted	can mitigate the effects of identification errors	may not have sufficient information in the generated summary	How2 dataset and TED-based dataset
Zhao et al. [39] (2020)	5	make BERTl better for Chinese short TS	integrate a keyword based clause division with BERT's	significantly improve the abstractive TS quality	cannot improve the extractive TS quality	LCSTS dataset
Farahani et al. [13] (2021)	8	an abstract approach to TS in Persian	use ParsBERT and mT5	close to real TS on meaning and wording	lack of baseline comparison	pn-summary dataset
Wang et al. [34] (2019)	44	TS through a strategy gradient of reinforcement learning	integrate BERT word embedding with reinforcement learning	take the advantage of the rich semantic features of BERT embedding	cannot use BERT for abstract summarisation tasks	CNN/Daily Mail and DUC 2002

model (BERTSUM). They co-train the segmentation and TS modules until convergence. On the ChWiki_181k database, they experimentally demonstrate that their model can effectively capture the relationships between sentences. However, on the LCSTS dataset, a human subjective evaluation reveals its maximum accuracy is 70.0% (not very high).

(4) **Topic-level/aware Text Summarisation**: A topic-level summary is a collective one consisting of information about a topic, which could be a concept, an idea, or a term the user wants. In 2020, Ramina et al. [30] proposed a topic-level TS model. First, it searches for relevant information about a keyword on Wikipedia and Hinduism according to a user's input. Then, a topic-level summary is generated using BERT based on the relevant information. Their model's ROUGE-1, -2, and -L scores are 41.72, 19.39, and 38.76, respectively.

With great encoding capabilities, pre-trained word embedding and sequence-to-sequence models can extract meaningful information from a social network. However, they must effectively capture long text dependencies and exploit potential topic mappings. To address the issue, in 2021, Ma et al. [24] presented a TS model named T-BERTSum. It can infer topics and produce summaries from social texts. Via a neural topic model, the encoded potential topic representations are compared to the embedded representations of BERT's as a guide for topic generation. Transformers are used to learn long-term dependencies as part of an end-to-end exploration of topic inference and TS. On top of the extraction model, LSTM is stacked to capture serial temporal information. Then, gate networks are built on the abstract model to filter valid information. A two-stage extraction-abstraction model is also used to share information. Their experiments show that their model outperforms state-of-the-art ones on the CNN/Daily Mail and XSum datasets in ROUGE by nearly 3.

2.2 Multi-Document Summarisation

(1) **Using BERT to Get Sentence Embeddings**: Text representation is essential for TS models. Most of these representations, however, need to consider the order and semantic relationships between words in a sentence; otherwise, the representation cannot convey the whole meaning of the sentence. To address the issue, in 2021, Lamsiyah et al. [18] proposed a transfer learning method based on BERT sentence embedding. It is an unsupervised method for multi-document TS. Moreover, they used single and multi-task fine-tuning methods on a supervised intermediate task on the GLUE benchmark dataset to fine-tune BERT to improve sentence representation learning. On a standard DUC 2002-2004 dataset, their experiments show that fine-tuned BERT with multi-task learning can considerably improve TS performance.

(2) **Using BERT to Remove Redundant Information**: In 2022, Ghadimi and Beigy [14] proposed an abstractive multi-document TS model named HMSumm. First, the model preserves the critical parts of the input documents for abstractive TS and removes redundant information (a global problem in multi-document) using BERT-based similarity to compute the redundancy. Then, the obtained extractive summary is input into PLMs BART and T5 to

generate two abstractive summaries. Finally, they used the diversity of sentences in each summary to choose one of them as the final one. On the datasets of DUC 2002, DUC 2004, Multi-News, and CNN/Daily Mail, their experiments show that HMSumm outperforms the state-of-the-art baselines, with an average score of 43.4 and 16.6 for ROUGE-1 and ROUGE-2.

2.3   Speech Summarisation

Speech summarisation can be achieved by using a Transformer for Automatic Speech Recognition (ASR) and BERT for TS. However, ASR errors may directly affect the quality of the output summaries in the cascade method. To address this issue, in 2021, Kano et al. [16] proposed a speech TS model robust to ASR errors. First, they used the sum of the posterior value weights of the subword embedding vectors provided by the ASR system as input to a BERT-based TS system. They then introduced a more general scheme that uses an attention-based fusion module added to a pre-trained BERT module. On the How2 and newly assembled TED-based datasets, their experiments show that their model can improve TS performance, with the attention-based fusion module being particularly effective (improving ROUGE-1 by 2 points on the How2 corpus).

2.4   Non-English Text Summarisation

(1) **Chinese Short Text Summarisation**: Although BERT is one of the most advanced PLMs, its potential has yet to be released entirely in Chinese short TS. To address the issue, in 2020, Zhao et al. [39] proposed a BERT-based TS model with keyword templates. They used the templates to extract keywords, guiding BERT in TS. They also integrated a keyword-based sentence division method with the original BERT one. On the LCSTS dataset, their experiments show that their model can generate higher-quality summaries than a baseline model, with improvements of 3.8, 3.0, and 2.5 on ROUGE-1, -2, and -L scores.

(2) **Persian Text Summarisation**: In 2021, Farahani et al. [13] proposed two Persian TS models and established a dataset named pn-summary for Persian TS. Their PLM is an encoder-decoder version of the ParsBERT model (a family member of BERT trained on the Persian dataset). These models are fine-tuned on the pn-summary dataset. Their experiments show their model's ROUGE-1, -2, and -L scores are 44.01, 25.07, and 37.76, respectively. Since their model is the first of its kind, it may serve as a baseline for future work.

2.5   Hybrid Method

In 2019, Wang et al. [34] proposed a BERT-based TS model. First, they converted human-summarised summaries into labels. Then, they used BERT word embeddings as text representations and separately pre-trained an extractive TS model and an abstractive TS model. Finally, they used reinforcement learning to connect the two models to form a final TS model. On the CNN/Daily Mail dataset, their experiments show that its ROUGE-1, -2, and -L scores are better than a baseline model by 1.07, 2.46, and 0.95, respectively.

Table 2. Comparison of various GPT-based methods for TS

Ref.	Citation	Issue addressed	Method	Pro	Con	Dataset
Liu et al. [20] (2021)	3	Chinese legal judgment report TS	use GPT-2 for text compression and integration	effective generation of summaries	rougher on long text extraction	Law Research Cup Judicial Summarising Dataset
Deepika et al. [7] (2021)	1	the summarisation of the medical document	pre-process the minimum number of documents in the dataset	produce better results in terms of performance	not high enough accuracy	the COVID-19 Open Research Dataset
Chintagunta et al. [6] (2021)	42	medical dialogue summarisation	GPT-3 based medically-aware data tagger	generate high quality training data	consider no other medical priori factors	a random subset of dialogues from their chat Telemedicine
Prodan et al. [27] (2022)	1	reliable static methods of creating hints for various types of conversation TS	design templates for pre-training GPT-3	save memory space and time	high calculation cost	SAMSum Corpus, DialogSum, and MediaSum
Liu et al. [21] (2021)	0	optimise Chinese text automatic summary model	use the Adabound method to optimise GPT-2 for TS	significant improved in terms of ROUGE	single evaluation indicator	online data on catastrophic incidents and emergencies
Zhu et al. [42] (2022)	1	apply PLMs to Chinese TS	extend the GPT-2 based Chinese TS model to downstream tasks	obtain relevant, informative and coherent summaries	experiments not conducted on larger Chinese dataset	LCSTS datasets
Alexandr et al. [1] (2021)	11	Russian news summarisation	fine-tune ruGPT3 on Russian news corpus	reduce the randomness of model output	easy to change named entities in an original text	Gazeta dataset
Dhivyaa et al. [10] (2022)	2	summarise online news in Tamil	extract relevant features using a phonetic GPT-2 based model	reduce repetitions in the generated summaries	lack of baseline comparison	Daliythandi, Dinamani, Hindu Tamil, and One India Tamil

3 GPT-Based Model

Most studies of PLM-based TS models use BERT, but a few use GPT. This section will review how researchers use GPT for TS. Table 2 compares these models.

3.1 Long Document Summarisation

In legal practice, it is unavoidable for ordinary people and professionals to check the judgement documents of previous similar cases (typically very lengthy). To reduce their efforts for such things, in 2021, Liu et al. [20] proposed a model of summarising a legal case judgement document. First, they extracted five critical components of a case judgement document. Thus, the long TS problem becomes

Table 3. Comparison of various BERT&GPT-based methods for TS

Ref	Citation	Issue addressed	Method	Pro	Con	Dataset
Kieuvong-ngam et al. [17] (2020)	53	TS of the COVID-19 medical dataset	use BERT to get document embedding and use GPT-2 to summarise	can infer more precise summaries from keywords	mostly limited by computation power	the COVID-19 Open Research Dataset (CORD-19)
Lucky et al. [22] (2022)	1	single document abstract TS in Indonesian	use BERTSum to get the embedding of the document, then feed it into the GPT	more embeddings can improve the performance of the model	unstable fine tuning at the same hyperparameters	IndoSum dataset
Yoon et al. [37] (2022)	3	abstractive summarisation of Korean legal judgement report	combine BERT and GPT as the encoder and the decoder	better performance, higher quality summaries	its performance deteriorates as the length of the input sentence increases	the precedents released on the Korean Court Comprehensive Legal Information website

five short TS ones. They then fine-tuned the five models of GPT-2 for TS of each component. Next, they used five models to summarise each. Finally, they put together all the summaries of the five parts to obtain a complete summary of the entire case judgement document. Their experiments show the model's effectiveness. Its average F1-score on the five datasets reaches above 57.

3.2 Multi-Document Summarisation

In 2021, Deepika et al. [7] used BERT, TextRank, and GPT-2 to preprocess and model several documents in the COVID-19 dataset. They found GPT-2 is the best among these models, with a precision of 96.7 in ROUGE-1.

3.3 Dialogue Summarisation

It is exciting to use PLMs for dialogue TS. However, it is hard to learn an effective model for medical conversation TS due to the difficulty of obtaining labelled data. To address the issue, in 2021, Chintagunta et al. [6] proposed a GPT-3 based algorithm for creating a synthetic training dataset that explicitly captures relevant medical information. Using low-shot learning and ensemble methods, they scaled 210 human-labelled examples, comparable to those using 6,400 human-labelled examples. Their experiments show that their model produces high-quality training data mergeable with human-labelled data, resulting in substantially more accurate and compelling summaries than those trained on human data alone, reaching ROUGE-L of 53.39.

Another way to overcome the lack of labelled data is to create cue templates for a small amount of training. However, a static method of creating prompts may cause unreliable results for different dialogue classes. To address the issue, in 2022, Prodan et al. [27] improved the training of a small number of shots by focusing on the structural properties of dialogues. In addition, they used GPT-3 experimentally and found improved results regarding ROUGE scores and human evaluations on three large-scale datasets.

3.4 Non-English Text Summarisation

(1) **Chinese Text Summarisation**: Natural disasters and emergencies happen often. The enormous volume of Internet disasters, incident data, and emergency case-handling procedures can offer technical references and support decision-making when social catastrophes arise. To collect incident case summaries automatically, in 2021, Liu *et al.* [21] developed a Chinese TS model. The model's primary network structure is GPT-2. The Adabound technique optimises the model, so it converges to a global minimum after training and is not perturbed by extreme learning rates. In addition, it fixes the Adam optimisation algorithm's issue, where the model reaches a local minimum due to high learning rates. Adabound's hyperparameters have also been optimised using the Jaya method to perform well. Their experiments show that their model significantly improves the ROUGE score by 1.75, compared to the original model.

In 2022, Zhu *et al.* [42] also proposed a GPT-2 based model for a Chinese TS model. It uses GPT-2 to acquire relevant, contentful, and coherent summarisation. On the LCSTS datasets, their experiments show that their model outperforms the state-of-the-art BERTSUM-based TS model by 25.22 on ROUGE-1.

(2) **Russian News Summarisation**: There are many English TS models but few Russian ones. To address the issue, in 2021, Alexandr *et al.* [1] proposed a ruGPT3-based TS model for Russian news. They employed hyper-parameter tuning to make the model's output less random and more tied to the original text. By a set of metrics, their method outperforms state-of-the-art models without requiring additional structure or loss function changes. However, despite their ability to produce good summaries, their model has shortcomings, such as changing named entities in the original text (such as surnames, places, and dates), ignoring the facts stated in the document, and repeating information.

(3) **Tamil News Summarisation**: In 2022, Dhivyaa *et al.* [10] developed a GPT-2 based TS model for online news in Tamil. It extracts sentence position, hot code, number of entities, term frequency, and inverse document frequency to summarise online news. Furthermore, they presented an attention-based LSTM-NMT decoding model for Tamil-English translation to evaluate the model's performance. Moreover, they compared three pre-trained models: the fine-tuned GPT-2, the Text-to-Text Conversion Translator (T-5), and BERT. Their evaluation data are from multiple online sources. The enhanced transliteration model is assessed using a bilingual evaluation method, whereas the GPT-2 based TS model is evaluated using the ROUGE score. Their experiments show that the fine-tuned GPT-2 model outperforms BERT and T5 on ROUGE-1, -2, and -L scores by 1.54/8.18, 0.68/8.38, and 1.17/6.23, respectively.

4   BERT and GPT-Based Text Summarisation

This section will brief BERT&GPT-based TS models (not commonly found in the literature). Table 3 compares them.

4.1   English Text Summarisation

Since the sudden outbreak of COVID-19, it has been challenging for researchers to keep abreast of the rapidly growing literature about the virus. To address the issue, in 2020, Kieuvongngam *et al.* [17] proposed a BERT & GPT-2 based TS model. Specifically, they used BERT to convert each sentence in a document into 768-dimensional vectors. Then, they clustered these vectors with K-medoid to extract abstracts paired with keywords and input them into GPT-2 for training it to generate summary results. Finally, their experiments show that their model can infer a summary with greater precision from keywords.

Table 4. Comparison of BERT-Based and GPT-based TS applications

Ref	Citation	Issue addressed	Method	Pro	Con	Dataset
Batra et al. [2] (2021)	4	summary of COVID-19 news articles	use BERT for extractive TS	can generate short, concise summaries	use single model	COVID-19 Public Media Dataset
Moradi et al. [25] (2020)	47	summarisation of biomedical literature	use BERT to capture a sentence context and a clustering algorithm to identify its relevant sentences	much better performance and effective context capture in biomedical TS	over-fitting and lack of generalisability	English Wikipedia and BooksCorpus
Cai et al. [5] (2022)	9	provide reliable draft summaries	pre-train BERT on a biomedical corpus	significantly improve other TS models	the results may have duplicate content	COVID-19 Open Dataset
Xie et al. [35] (2022)	10	extractive TS of biomedical literature	enhance BERT, RoBERTa, BioBERT, and PubMedBERT with medical evidence knowledge	outperform strong baselines	unclear whether it is applicable to TS in other domains	CORD-19, PubMed, S2ORC
Du et al. [11] (2020)	25	extractive summarisation of biomedical literature	use a BERT-like PLM pre-trained on a biomedical corpus as an encoder, and further fine-tune the PLM	outperform the state-of-the-art models	multiple overlapping words exist and are affected by sentence length	PubMed dataset
Cai et al. [4] (2021)	10	summarise a chest radiology report	pre-train BERT on a radiology corpus	outperform other neural network based TS models	small size and high memory consumption	Open-I 2 and MIMIC-CXR 3

4.2   Non-English Text Summarisation

In Indonesian, most studies on TS focus on multi-document variations; hence, similar methods may not work optimally in single-document variations. To address this issue, in 2022, Lucky and Suhartono [22] proposed a BERT&GPT-based model for Indonesian TS. First, the model uses BERTSum as an encoder to get a document's embeddings and then inputs them into GPT to obtain the abstractive summary of the paper. On the IndoSum dataset, their experiments show that their model improves the ROUGE score and BERTS score of TS. Moreover, more embeddings led to higher model performance, achieving an average of over 60 on the ROUGE score.

Language barriers and expertise limit artificial intelligence applications in the Korean legal field. To address the issue, in 2022, Yoon et al. [37] proposed a BERT&GPT-based model for summarising Korean legal judgment documents. They used PLMs BERT2BERT (BERT integrated with the Seq2Seq model) and BART in the encoder-decoder architecture. BERT2BERT is pre-trained with BERT on both the encoder and decoder. BART integrates BERT and GPT as the encoder and the decoder. BERT can predict noisy tokens via a bidirectional encoder, and GPT can predict the next token. They also publicly release the dataset they collected and used for training, testing, and validating their model. Their experiments show that their model outperforms BERT2BERT regarding ROUGE-1, -2, and -L scores by 3.2, 6.2, and 5.6, respectively.

5 Application

This section will brief BERT- and GPT-based TS in legal, news, and healthcare domains. Table 4 compares them, excluding ones already in previous sections.

5.1 Legal Domain

The studies in the legal domain are the work of Liu et al. [20] in Sect. 3 and that of Yoon et al. [37] in Sect. 4.

5.2 News Text Summarisation

(1) **COVID-19 News**: In 2021, the accelerating growth of news articles related to COVID-19 made it difficult for the general public to keep up with all the latest information during the pandemic. However, if news articles could be summarised, the public could get the gist of the entire article without having to read it in full. To address the issue, Batra et al. [2] compared PLMs BERT, GPT-2, XLNet, BART, and T5 for TS on the COVID-19 public media dataset. The first three models were used for extractive summarisation, while the last two were for abstractive summarisation. Their experiments show that BERT outperformed the other models in ROUGE-2 and ROUGE-L scores (i.e., 36.4 and 35.4, respectively, and on average 9.3 and 10.3 more than the others). Thus, their web application "CoVShorts" uses BERT to summarise COVID-19 news articles. Besides, as part of validating the TS task, they also visually analysed the dataset to identify the most commonly used words in COVID-19 news articles.

(2) **Non-English News**: This kind has two in Sect. 3: a GPT-3 based TS model of Russian News [1] and a GPT-2 based TS model of Tamil news [10].

5.3 Healthcare Domain

(1) **Biomedical Literature Summarisation**: Biomedical TS is critical for comprehending the vast and expanding biomedical literature but must be done

in a meaningful context. To tackle this challenge, in 2020, Moradi *et al.* [25] proposed a TS model that leverages contextual embeddings produced by BERT. They combine various versions of BERT with clustering techniques to extract the most pertinent and informative sentences from an input document. Their experiments show that their model outperforms a set of domain-specific and domain-independent methods, and using BERT-large's ROUGE-1 and -2 are up to .75.04 and 33.12, respectively. Their work provides a starting point for investigating deep contextualised PLMs for biomedical TS.

Many researchers work hard to diagnose, treat, and vaccinate against COVID-19. However, in addition to publishing their latest research advances through scientific papers, researchers also write abstracts for papers manually, increasing their writing burdens significantly. To address this issue, in 2022, Cai *et al.* [5] proposed a language-rich SciBERT-based TS model called COVID-Sum, which automatically provides researchers with reliable draft abstracts. The model first extracts salient sentences from the source papers to construct word co-occurrence graphs. Subsequently, it encodes the sentence and word co-occurrence graphs using a SciBERT-based sequence encoder and a graph-attention network-based encoder. Finally, it fuses the above two encodings to summarise each scientific paper. On the publicly available COVID-19 open research dataset, their experiments show that their model outperforms other TS models, achieving ROUGE-1, -2, and -L scores of 44.56, 18.89, and 36.53, respectively.

Existing PLM-based TS models typically fine-tune PLMs directly on target corpora without considering that fine-grained domain knowledge can help generate coherent summaries by identifying the required context. To address this issue, in 2022, Xie *et al.* [35] proposed KeBioSum, a framework for knowledge infusion training. To fine-tune a PLM for extractive TS, they used adapter fusion techniques to inject domain knowledge into the PLM. Their experiments show that including KeBioSum knowledge adapters improves the existing PLMs (BERT, RoBERTa, BioBERT, and PubMedBERT) for the extractive TS task on three biomedical literature datasets, and their model outperforms the strong baselines with ROUGE-1, -2, and -L scores improved by 1, 1.5, and 3, respectively.

Deep neural networks can significantly improve extractive TS. However, required is domain-aware external knowledge if these methods are used for biomedical extractive summarisation, and their methods omit document structure features. To address these issues, in 2020, Du *et al.* [11] proposed a BioBERT-based TS model called BioBERTSum. BioBERT is a member of the BERT family, trained on a large-scale biomedical corpus as an encoder and further fine-tuned for extractive TS. Primarily, they embed sentence position information into the model to learn positional sentence information. On the PubMed dataset, they experimentally demonstrate that their model outperforms state-of-the-art models, achieving ROUGE-1, -2, and -L scores of 37.45, 17.59, and 29.58, respectively.

In addition, this kind of work also includes a TS model of COVID-19 literature [17] in Sect. 4.1.

Table 5. Summary of various PLMs for various TS tasks

		BERT family											GPT				BERT & GPT
		BERT	DiscoBert	BERTSum	T-BERTSum	ParsBERT	BERT2BERT	SciBERT	RoBERTa	BioBERT	PubMedBERT	ChestXRayBERT	GPT	GPT-2	GPT-3	ruGPT-3	
TS tasks	short TS	✓	×	×	×	×	×	×	×	×	×	×	×	×	×	×	×
	long TS	✓	✓	×	×	×	×	×	×	×	×	×	×	✓	×	×	×
	variable-length TS	×	×	✓	×	×	×	×	×	×	×	×	×	×	×	×	×
	topic-level/aware TS	✓	×	×	✓	×	×	×	×	×	×	×	×	×	×	×	×
	multi-document TS	✓	×	×	×	×	×	×	×	×	×	×	×	✓	×	×	×
	speech TS	✓	×	×	×	×	×	×	×	×	×	×	×	×	×	×	×
	dialogue TS	×	×	×	×	×	×	×	×	×	×	×	×	×	✓	×	×
	non-English TS	✓	×	✓	×	✓	×	×	×	×	×	×	✓	✓	×	✓	✓
	legal domain TS	✓	×	×	×	×	✓	×	×	×	×	×	✓	✓	×	×	×
	news domain TS	✓	×	×	×	×	×	×	×	×	×	×	×	✓	✓	×	×
	healthcare domain TS	✓	×	×	×	×	×	✓	✓	✓	✓	✓	×	×	✓	×	✓

(2) **Medical Report Summarisation**: By summarising as much of the salient information in the result section of a radiology report as possible, its impressions section can facilitate more effective communication between radiologists and referring physicians. However, due to domain-specific terminology in radiology, existing TS models cannot be directly applied to radiology reports. To address this issue, in 2021, Cai *et al.* [4] developed a PLM, ChestXRayBERT, for chest radiology. Specifically, they first collected radiology-related scientific papers and pre-trained ChestXRayBERT on them. They then proposed a TS model integrating ChestXRayBERT with a Transformer decoder. Finally, they fine-tuned the model on chest X-ray reports. On the public OPEN-I and MIMIC-CXR datasets, their experiments show that this model outperforms other neural network-based TS models with ROUGE-1, -2, and -L scores of 41.3, 28.6, and 41.5, respectively.

(3) **Medical Dialogue Summarisation**: We find only one of this kind, *i.e.*, the work of Chintagunta *et al.* [6]. We have already discussed it in Sect. 3.

6 Challenges

Through the analysis of the literature on PLM-based TS, we believe the following are the main challenges in the future: (1) To fine-tune or develop various PLMs for TS in individual application domains. Several researchers, such as Cai *et al.* [4], Zhong *et al.* [40], and Zhou *et al.* [41], have directed efforts in this direction, but it is far from enough. (2) To apply PLMs for TS in more application domains, we use Google Scholar to search for the applications of BERT- and GPT-based TS models and find that they are applied in three domains (legal, news, and healthcare). However, TS models not based on PLMs have been applied in many more domains [8]. As such, it is certainly worth applying PLM-based TS to these domains and investigating whether or not PLM-based models can improve upon non-PLM-based ones. (3) To use more PLMs, especially the most advanced ones and non-English ones, for TS. For example, there are many Chinese PLMs [32], and few TS models are based on these Chinese PLMs. It is also worth studying which of the existing PLMs is best for which application domain or task. (4) To develop automated survey technology of scientific literature based on PLM-based TS models and the remarkable ChatGPT. Using TS for a single paper may make little sense; however, it is far more significant to automatically survey the literature on a certain topic. This differs from multi-document TS because a survey has to summarise multiple papers, sort and analyse them, and identify their further research issues. Although this direction is very significant, little work has been done. In 2022, Yu [38] attempted to address the issue but made limited contributions (highlighting that current TS evaluation metrics are insufficient in measuring TS accuracy).

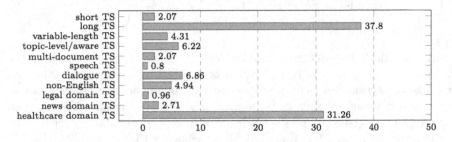

Fig. 1. The citation percentage of papers on various TS tasks

7   Conclusion

BERT and GPT families are the two most powerful PLM families for various NLP tasks, particularly various TS tasks (see Table 5 for the summary of various PLMs for various TS tasks and see Fig. 1 for the citation percentage of papers on various TS task). This paper surveys the state-of-the-art on the topic to aid future research. We observe that researchers use BERT family and GPT primarily for TS of short, long, and variable-length single documents, multi-documents, speech, and dialogue. Most of these methods are for English, while a few are for other languages, including Chinese, Korean, Tamil, Russian, Arabic, Persian, and Indonesian. Moreover, these methods are mainly applied in legal, news, and healthcare domains. In the legal domain, we find two methods for summarising legal judgement documents. In the news domain, we find five methods for summarising COVID-19 news, financial news, and general news. In the healthcare domain, there are several methods for summarising biomedical literature, one for medical reports, and one for medical conversations.

For each of these methods, we discuss their motivations (*i.e.*, what issues their authors aimed to solve) and how BERT and GPT have been used to address these issues. Furthermore, we compare these methods, including their pros and cons, so that future researchers can accordingly choose the most suitable approaches for their projects or develop their own methods. Finally, we identify four future research directions. Among them, we believe the automatic scientific literature survey is the most significant.

References

1. Alexandr, N., Irina, O., Tatyana, K., Inessa, K., Arina, P.: Fine-tuning GPT-3 for Russian text summarization. In: Silhavy, R., Silhavy, P., Prokopova, Z. (eds.) CoMeSySo 2021. LNNS, vol. 231, pp. 748–757. Springer, Cham (2021). https://doi.org/10.1007/978-3-030-90321-3_61
2. Batra, H., et al.: CoVShorts: news summarization application based on deep NLP transformers for SARS-CoV-2. In: 2021 9th International Conference on Reliability, Infocom Technologies and Optimization (Trends and Future Directions), pp. 1–6 (2021)
3. Brown, T., Mann, B., et al.: Language models are few-shot learners. In: Advances in Neural Information Processing Systems, vol. 33, pp. 1877–1901 (2020)
4. Cai, X., Liu, S., Han, J., Yang, L., Liu, Z., Liu, T.: ChestXRayBERT: a pre-trained language model for chest radiology report summarization. IEEE Transactions on Multimedia (2021)
5. Cai, X., et al.: COVIDSum: a linguistically enriched SciBERT-based summarization model for COVID-19 scientific papers. J. Biomed. Inform. **127**, 103999 (2022)
6. Chintagunta, B., Katariya, N., Amatriain, X., Kannan, A.: Medically aware GPT-3 as a data generator for medical dialogue summarization. In: Proceedings of the 6th Machine Learning for Healthcare Conference, pp. 354–372 (2021)
7. Deepika, S., Shridevi, S., et al.: Extractive text summarization for COVID-19 medical records. In: 2021 Innovations in Power and Advanced Computing Technologies (i-PACT), pp. 1–5 (2021)
8. Dehru, V., Tiwari, P.K., Aggarwal, G., Joshi, B., Kartik, P.: Text summarization techniques and applications. IOP Conf. Ser. Mater. Sci. Eng. **1099**, 012042 (2021). IOP Publishing (2021)
9. Devlin, J., Chang, M.W., Lee, K., Toutanova, K.: BERT: pre-training of deep bidirectional transformers for language understanding. In: Proceedings of the 1st 2019 Conference of the North American Chapter of the Association for Computational Linguistics: Human Language Technologies, pp. 4171–4186 (2019)
10. Dhivyaa, C., Nithya, K., Janani, T., Kumar, K.S., Prashanth, N.: Transliteration based generative pre-trained transformer 2 model for Tamil text summarization. In: 2022 International Conference on Computer Communication and Informatics, pp. 1–6 (2022)
11. Du, Y., Li, Q., Wang, L., He, Y.: Biomedical-domain pre-trained language model for extractive summarization. Knowl.-Based Syst. **199**, 105964 (2020)
12. El-Kassas, W.S., Salama, C.R., Rafea, A.A., Mohamed, H.K.: Automatic text summarization: a comprehensive survey. Expert Syst. Appl. **165**, 113679 (2021)
13. Farahani, M., Gharachorloo, M., Manthouri, M.: Leveraging ParsBERT and pre-trained mT5 for Persian abstractive text summarization. In: 2021 26th International Computer Conference, Computer Society of Iran, pp. 1–6 (2021)

14. Ghadimi, A., Beigy, H.: Hybrid multi-document summarization using pre-trained language models. Expert Syst. Appl. **192**, 116292 (2022)
15. Grail, Q., Perez, J., Gaussier, E.: Globalizing BERT-based transformer architectures for long document summarization. In: Proceedings of the 16th Conference of the European Chapter of the Association for Computational Linguistics: Main volume, pp. 1792–1810 (2021)
16. Kano, T., Ogawa, A., Delcroix, M., Watanabe, S.: Attention-based multi-hypothesis fusion for speech summarization. In: 2021 IEEE Automatic Speech Recognition and Understanding Workshop, pp. 487–494 (2021)
17. Kieuvongngam, V., Tan, B., Niu, Y.: Automatic text summarization of COVID-19 medical research articles using BERT and GPT-2 (2020). arXiv preprint arXiv:2006.01997
18. Lamsiyah, S., Mahdaouy, A.E., Ouatik, S.E.A., Espinasse, B.: Unsupervised extractive multi-document summarization method based on transfer learning from BERT multi-task fine-tuning. J. Inf. Sci. **49**(1), 0165551521990616 (2021)
19. Li, L.H., Yatskar, M., Yin, D., Hsieh, C.J., Chang, K.W.: VisualBERT: a simple and performant baseline for vision and language (2019). arXiv preprint arXiv:1908.03557
20. Liu, J., Wu, J., Luo, X.: Chinese judicial summarising based on short sentence extraction and GPT-2. In: Qiu, H., Zhang, C., Fei, Z., Qiu, M., Kung, S.-Y. (eds.) KSEM 2021. LNCS (LNAI), vol. 12816, pp. 376–393. Springer, Cham (2021). https://doi.org/10.1007/978-3-030-82147-0_31
21. Liu, M., Wang, Z., Wang, L.: Automatic Chinese text summarization for emergency domain. J. Phys: Conf. Ser. **1754**(1), 012213 (2021)
22. Lucky, H., Suhartono, D.: Investigation of pre-trained bidirectional encoder representations from transformers checkpoints for Indonesian abstractive text summarization. J. Inf. Commun. Technol. **21**(1), 71–94 (2022)
23. Ma, K., Tian, M., Tan, Y., Xie, X., Qiu, Q.: What is this article about? Generative summarization with the BERT model in the geosciences domain. Earth Sci. Inf. **15**(1), 21–36 (2022)
24. Ma, T., Pan, Q., Rong, H., Qian, Y., Tian, Y., Al-Nabhan, N.: T-BERTSum: Topic-aware text summarization based on BERT. IEEE Trans. Comput. Soc. Syst. **9**(3), 879–890 (2021)
25. Moradi, M., Dorffner, G., Samwald, M.: Deep contextualized embeddings for quantifying the informative content in biomedical text summarization. Comput. Methods Programs Biomed. **184**, 105117 (2020)
26. Patel, P.M.: Financial news summarisation using transformer neural network (2022). https://doi.org/10.21203/rs.3.rs-2132871/v1
27. Prodan, G., Pelican, E.: Prompt scoring system for dialogue summarization using GPT-3. TechRxiv Preprint (2022)
28. Radford, A., Narasimhan, K., Salimans, T., Sutskever, I., et al.: Improving language understanding by generative pre-training, openAI (2018)
29. Radford, A., Wu, J., Child, R., Luan, D., Amodei, D., Sutskever, I.: Language models are unsupervised multitask learners. OpenAI Blog **1**(8), 9 (2019)
30. Ramina, M., Darnay, N., Ludbe, C., Dhruv, A.: Topic level summary generation using BERT induced abstractive summarization model. In: Proceedings of 4th International Conference on Intelligent Computing and Control Systems, pp. 747–752 (2020)
31. Su, M.H., Wu, C.H., Cheng, H.T.: A two-stage transformer-based approach for variable-length abstractive summarization. IEEE/ACM Trans. Audio Speech Lang. Process. **28**, 2061–2072 (2020)

32. Sun, K., Luo, X., Luo, M.Y.: A survey of pretrained language models. In: Memmi, G., Yang, B., Kong, L., Zhang, T., Qiu, M. (eds.) Knowledge Science, Engineering and Management. KSEM 2022. Lecture Notes in Computer Science, vol. 13369, pp. 442–456. Springer, Cham (2022). https://doi.org/10.1007/978-3-031-10986-7_36

33. Syed, A.A., Gaol, F.L., Boediman, A., Matsuo, T., Budiharto, W.: A survey of abstractive text summarization utilising pretrained language models. In: Nguyen, N.T., Tran, T.K., Tukayev, U., Hong, TP., Trawinski, B., Szczerbicki, E. (eds.) Intelligent Information and Database Systems. ACIIDS 2022. Lecture Notes in Computer Science, vol. 13757, pp. 532–544. Springer, Cham (2022). https://doi.org/10.1007/978-3-031-21743-2_42

34. Wang, Q., Liu, P., Zhu, Z., Yin, H., Zhang, Q., Zhang, L.: A text abstraction summary model based on BERT word embedding and reinforcement learning. Appl. Sci. **9**(21), 4701 (2019)

35. Xie, Q., Bishop, J.A., Tiwari, P., Ananiadou, S.: Pre-trained language models with domain knowledge for biomedical extractive summarization. Knowl.-Based Syst. **252**, 109460 (2022)

36. Xu, J., Gan, Z., Cheng, Y., Liu, J.: Discourse-aware neural extractive text summarization (2019). arXiv preprint arXiv:1910.14142

37. Yoon, J., Junaid, M., Ali, S., Lee, J.: Abstractive summarization of Korean legal cases using pre-trained language models. In: Proceedings of the 16th International Conference on Ubiquitous Information Management and Communication, pp. 1–7 (2022)

38. Yu, B.: Evaluating pre-trained language models on multi-document summarization for literature reviews. In: Proceedings of the 3rd Workshop on Scholarly Document Processing, pp. 188–192 (2022)

39. Zhao, S., You, F., Liu, Z.Y.: Leveraging pre-trained language model for summary generation on short text. IEEE Access **8**, 228798–228803 (2020)

40. Zhong, M., Liu, Y., Xu, Y., Zhu, C., Zeng, M.: DialogLM: pre-trained model for long dialogue understanding and summarization. In: Proceedings of the AAAI Conference on Artificial Intelligence, vol. 36, pp. 11765–11773 (2022)

41. Zhou, Y., Portet, F., Ringeval, F.: Effectiveness of French language models on abstractive dialogue summarization task. In: Proceedings of the 13th Language Resources and Evaluation Conference, pp. 3571–3581 (2022)

42. Zhu, Q., Li, L., Bai, L., Hu, F.: Chinese text summarization based on fine-tuned GPT2. In: 3rd International Conference on Electronics and Communication; Network and Computer Technology. vol. 12167, pp. 304–309 (2022)

Ensemble Strategy Based on Deep Reinforcement Learning for Portfolio Optimization

Xiao Su, Yalan Zhou[✉], Shanshan He, and Xiangxia Li

School of Information Science, Guangdong University of Finance and Economic,
Guangzhou 510320, China
zhouylan@163.com

Abstract. Although deep reinforcement learning for portfolio optimization has attracted the attention of more and more researchers, existing research focuses on the improvement of a single algorithm. According to No Free Lunch Theorem (NFL), single algorithms are always limited, especially in complex financial environment. In this paper, an ensemble strategy that combines the advantages of three deep reinforcement learning algorithms is proposed to select appropriate agents at different stages. The ensemble strategy is composed of Deep Deterministic Policy Gradient (DDPG), Soft Actor-Critic (SAC) and Twin Delayed Deep Deterministic Policy Gradient (TD3). Compared with other model and algorithms, our model on experimental datasets shows better performance.

Keywords: Portfolio optimization · Investment portfolio · Deep reinforcement learning · Ensemble strategy · Quantitative trading

1   Introduction

Appropriate investment strategies can enable investors to obtain more income, but it is well known that the investment is accompanied by risks. Portfolio optimization is to search the optimal investment portfolio with the aim of achieving investment goals such as maximal profits or minimal risks. In the face of complex financial environment, the reliability and effectiveness of investment transactions based on human judgment are relatively low [1]. At present, the use of computer technology to realize automated transactions has become the focus of research by major financial institutions and researchers. Due to the perception and decision-making ability of Deep Reinforcement Learning (DRL), the use of DRL to optimize investment portfolios has gradually become one of the research focus [2,3]. In recent years, more and more researchers have tried to optimize the portfolio problem by improving various single DRL algorithms, and have achieved good results [4,5], but a single algorithm model always has certain limitations. For example, many researchers have chosen the classic DQN algorithm and its variants [6], but DQN is still not suitable for dealing with a large number of assets [7]. The theoretical properties of the PPO algorithm are

Z. Jin et al. (Eds.): KSEM 2023, LNAI 14120, pp. 242–249, 2023.
https://doi.org/10.1007/978-3-031-40292-0_20

attractive, but PPO is too conservative and tends to give almost equal weight to the assets it invests in [8]. The DDPG algorithm is an excellent model for stock portfolio trading because of its stability, but it may not be able to find the optimal portfolio [1].

According to No Free Lunch Theorem (NFL), there is no single machine learning algorithm can perform the best in all situations. Since different algorithms have different advantages and are suitable for different market environments. In this paper, in order to adapt to the changing market environment and make the model more robust, an ensemble strategy is proposed for portfolio optimization by combining the advantages of the algorithms. The proposed ensemble strategy combines Deep Deterministic Policy Gradient (DDPG), Soft Actor-Critic (SAC) and Twin Delayed Deep Deterministic Policy Gradient (TD3). Train the three agents simultaneously, and finally select the optimal agent based on the Sharpe ratio. Experiments are carried on the US market datasets and the Chinese market datasets. The experimental results show the proposed ensemble strategy model outperforms other integrated strategy model, the single algorithm models and the baselines.

2 Problem Description

Investment portfolio refers to any combination of financial assets such as funds, stocks, and cash. As one of the important components, stocks have attracted the attention of many people because of their high returns and quick payback. The portfolios in this paper are mainly applicable to the stock market. In the stock market, the stock trading process of portfolio optimization is a stochastic optimization process. And the Markov decision process (MDP) is an architectural model for how decisions are made in a state that is partially random and partially controllable by the decision maker. The process of stock trading can be modeled as a MDP (as shown in Fig. 1). MDP means that the decision maker observes the environment periodically or continuously, and then selects an action a from a limited action set A to make a decision in turn according to the observed state s_t, thereby generating the next random state s_{t+1}. In addition, MDP also contains reward R and discount coefficient γ.

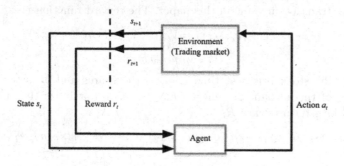

Fig. 1. Markov decision process for the portfolio

2.1   State Space

Eight parts of information composed to represent the state space of the portfolio trading environment: $S_t = [b_t, p_t, m_t, MACD_t, BOLL_t, RSI_t, CCI_t, SMA_t]$. The specific meaning is as follows:

$b_t \in R^+$: the balance of the account at time t. $p_t \in R^+$: the stock price at time t. $m_t \in Z^+$: the current shares corresponding to each stock. $MACD_t \in R$: Moving Average Convergence/Divergence (MACD) is used to research and judge the market. $BOLL_t \in R^+$: Bolinger Bands (BOLL) is used to determine the fluctuation range and future trend of the stock price. $RSI_t \in R^+$: Relative Strength Index (RSI) is convenient for predicting the direction of the stock market. $CCI_t \in R$: Commodity Channel Index (CCI) is used to measure whether the stock price has exceeded the normal distribution range. $SMA_t \in R^+$: Simple Moving Average (SMA) can simply and directly reflect changes in stock prices.

Among them, R^+ represents positive real numbers, Z^+ represents non-negative integers.

2.2   Action Space

The action space A is defined as $\{-k, ..., -1, 0, 1, ..., k\}$, where k denotes the number of shares we can trade. In addition, $k \leq m_{max}$, where m_{max} is the maximum quantity that can be purchased under balance b. In short, as shown in Eq. 1, the sign of the value indicates the action of buying and selling and the absolute value indicates the share of the trade. This kind of action is applicable in each stock. For each stock x, the action $a[x]$ can be represented as:

$$a[x] = \begin{cases} k, k \in (0, m_{\max}] : buy \ k \ x \ stocks, \\ 0 : hold, \\ -k, k \in [-m_{\max}, 0) : sell \ k \ x \ stocks. \end{cases} \tag{1}$$

2.3   Reward Function

The reward function $r(s_t, a_t, s_{t+1})$ is defined as the change in portfolio value when a new state s_{t+1} is reached by taking an action a_t at state s_t. For the robustness of the model, transaction cost (TC) is also considered, which is assumed to be 0.001 of the transaction value in this paper. The reward function is

$$r(s_t, a_t, s_{t+1}) = V_{t+1} - V_t - TC_t \tag{2}$$

$$V_t = p_t m_t + b_t \tag{3}$$

where p_t is the stock prices at time t, m_t is the shares and b_t is the remaining balance of the account at time t. Our goal is to maximize the cumulative discounted long-term reward R_t:

$$R_t = r(s_t, a_t, s_{t+1}) + \gamma r(s_{t+1}, a_t, s_{t+2}) + ... + \gamma^{T-1} r(s_T, a_T, s_{T+1})$$

$$= \sum_{i=t}^{t+T} \gamma^{i-t} r(s_i, a_i, s_{i+1}) \tag{4}$$

where γ is a discount coefficient in the range of 0 to 1.

3   The Ensemble Strategy

3.1   Selection of the Base Trading Agent

Value function-based and policy gradient-based methods have been widely used
to deal with large portfolio problems. The methods based on the combination of
value function and policy gradient, combines the advantages of value function-
based and policy gradient-based methods. Therefore, the following three models
(the SAC, DDPG, and TD3) are adopted as our basic trading agents. Each model
has its own advantages in different markets. These three models are chosen as
the basic trading agents because of their different strengths and their superior
performance in the initial single-algorithm model tests. SAC [9] adopts a random strategy to adapt to the unpredictable stock market. At the same time,
the maximum entropy is used to increase randomness and exploration, creating
more possibilities for transactions, and more conducive to finding the best decisions. DDPG [10] can handle high-dimensional action space, has high algorithm
efficiency and strong anti-risk ability, can adapt to changes in the stock market.
The TD3 algorithm [11] reduces the overestimation of the value function, avoids
suboptimal strategies, and is conducive to finding the best strategy.

3.2   Ensemble Strategy

This ensemble strategy is based on the Sharpe ratio to automatically select the
best agent for trading among SAC, DDPG, and TD3, so that the appropriate
agent can be selected at different stages. The framework of the proposed ensemble
strategy is showed in Fig. 2. The whole process is as follows:

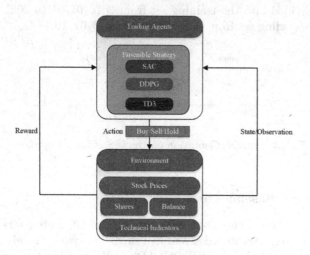

Fig. 2. The Framework of the Proposed Ensemble Strategy

Step1: window scrolling training. Train according to the training interval, set the retraining window period to 3 months (63 trading days), and retrain the three agents at the same time.

Step 2: validation and selection. After training, verify the three agents through validation rolling window of 63 trading days, and choose the best agent with the highest Sharpe Ratio (SR). The equation for SR is as follows:

$$SR = \frac{E(R_p - R_f)}{\sigma_p} \tag{5}$$

where R_p is the expected rate of return on the portfolio, R_f is the risk-free rate, and σ_p is the standard deviation of the excess return on the portfolio.

Step 3: trade by the selected agent. The agent selected in the previous step will be used for the next quarter of the transaction.

Repeat the above step 1~step 3 until the trading time interval ends.

The higher the Sharpe ratio, the higher the increase in return per unit of risk. Therefore, the most suitable agent can be selected to a certain extent.

4   Experiments

4.1   Experimental Environment and Datasets

In this paper, the experimental environment and models are built based on the OpenAI Gym, the FinRL library and stablebaselines3. And γ is set to 0.99.

Two datasets are selected: 30 Dow Jones stocks from the US market and 50 stocks from SSE 50 Index of the Chinese stock market. The data set of 30 Dow Jones stocks of the US market is downloaded from Yahoo Finance. The data set of 50 stocks from SSE 50 Index of the Chinese stock market is obtained from Tushare. The segmentation of the entire datasets is shown in Fig. 3. The data samples are divided into the training set from 2010/01/01 to 2021/10/01, and the validation/trading set from 2021/10/01 to 2023/01/19.

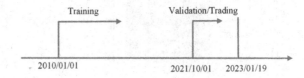

Fig. 3. Data segmentation on the U.S./Chinese markets

4.2   Evaluation Baselines and Indicators

The models used for comparison include another integrated strategy model (ASTE [12]), DJIA, SSE 50 Index and five single-algorithm models. Five single-algorithm models include SAC, DDPG, TD3, A2C, and PPO algorithms.

The following six indicators are used to evaluate the performance of models. **Cumulative Return**: it is the ratio of the final return of the portfolio to the initial value. It reflects the final benefit obtained at the end of the investment period. **Annualized Return**: it is the rate of return on investment for one year, usually converted from the rate of return on investment over the holding time. **Annualized Volatility**: a measure of the risk of investment volatility. It is the annualized standard deviation of returns. **Sharpe Ratio**: it is a measure of both risk and return. The larger the Sharpe ratio, the higher the return per unit risk of the asset. **Max Drawdown**: it is the maximum decline of the product in a selected time frame. **Sortino Ratio**: it is used to measure the relative performance of a portfolio and is more oriented towards loss analysis.

4.3   Performance Comparisons

The comparison results between the US market and the Chinese market are shown in Table 1 and Table 2, respectively. It can be seen from Table 1, in the US market, our ensemble strategy model has the highest annualized rate of return, cumulative rate of return and Sharpe ratio. And compared with DJIA, our annualized volatility and the absolute value of the maximum drawdown are smaller, which means that our model has a stronger ability to resist risks. In addition, the indicators of PPO model and A2C model are better than DJIA, indicating that they are suitable for the US market. Among them, the annualized volatility and the absolute value of maximum drawdown of the PPO agent are the smallest, and the stability is good. The A2C model is similar to the PPO model.

Table 1. Performance evaluation on 30 U.S. stocks

(2022/01/03-2023/01/03)	Ensemble(ours)	ASTE	SAC	PPO	A2C	DDPG	TD3	DJIA
Annual Return	−0.9%	−17.9%	−18.5%	−1.6%	−6.9%	−18.0%	−13.0%	−9.4%
Cumulative Return	−0.9%	−17.9%	−18.5%	−1.6%	−6.9%	−18.0%	−13.0%	−9.4%
Annual volatility	18.0%	19.7%	17.0%	**1.8%**	4.5%	17.1%	14.6%	19.9%
Sharpe Ratio	**0.04**	−0.91	−1.12	−0.90	−1.58	−1.09	−0.89	−0.40
Max Drawdown	−14.1%	−29.6%	−23.0%	**−2.4%**	−7.7%	−22.0%	−16.6%	−21.9%
Sortino Ratio	**0.06**	−1.21	−1.49	−1.25	−2.04	−1.45	−1.20	−0.56

Table 2. Performance evaluation on 50 Chinese stocks

(2022/01/06-2023/01/18)	Ensemble(ours)	ASTE	SAC	PPO	A2C	DDPG	TD3	SSE50
Annual Return	**16.6%**	−27.0%	−22.6%	−0.0%	−3.4%	−10.8%	−10.0%	−28.3%
Cumulative Return	**16.6%**	−27.0%	−22.6%	−0.0%	−3.4%	−10.8%	−10.0%	−28.3%
Annual volatility	25.4%	20.7%	16.5%	**0.0%**	2.0%	28.7%	28.8%	40.0%
Sharpe Ratio	**0.73**	−1.42	−1.48	−0.96	−1.67	−0.26	−0.22	−0.75
Max Drawdown	−19.5%	−29.0%	−25.8%	**−0.0%**	−3.9%	−34.8%	−34.7%	−36.8%
Sortino Ratio	**1.10**	−1.80	−1.90	−1.17	−2.12	−0.35	−0.31	−1.04

It can be seen from Table 2 that our model is much higher than other models and baselines in terms of annualized rate of return, cumulative rate of return and Sharpe ratio. All of the three indicators are positive and perform very well. Combined with Table 1, it can be seen that the PPO model is very good at dealing with the bear market, with good stability and anti-risk ability, followed by the A2C model. But the earning power of the two models is weak. Furthermore, all models outperform SSE50. In Table 1 and Table 2, our model shows strong profitability and strong anti-risk ability. And it performs well on both U.S. and Chinese markets, and also shows good robustness and adaptability.

In order to better display the development trend of accumulated income, the cumulative income curve is shown in Fig. 4 and Fig. 5. From Fig. 4 and Fig. 5, it can be seen that the income of our model has always been better than another integrated strategy model, SAC model, DDPG model, TD3 model and baselines. It shows an overall upward trend, and can still be adjusted quickly after market shocks, and even surpass the stable PPO model in the end. These models perform better in the Chinese market than in the U.S. market. In addition, from the comparison of the annualized volatility and the maximum drawdown, the risk of the Chinese market is greater. The Chinese market, where the market changes greatly, may be a good training environment for deep reinforcement learning models.

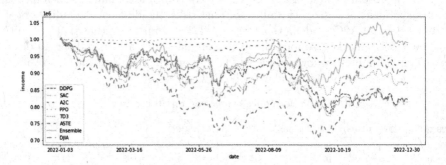

Fig. 4. Trends of value of assets of models for 2022/01/03-2023/01/03 on U.S. market

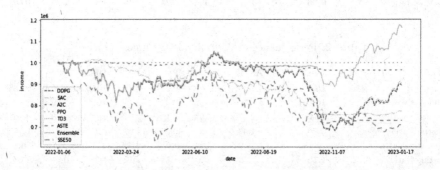

Fig. 5. Trends of value of assets of models for 2022/01/06-2023/01/18 on Chinese market

5   Conclusion

In this paper, an ensemble strategy combining the advantages of the three algorithms (SAC, DDPG, and TD3), is proposed for portfolio optimization. The ensemble strategy can adapt to the changing market environments. The results show that our ensemble strategy model outperforms another integrated strategy model, the single-algorithm models and the baselines. And the cumulative return grows rapidly in both the US market and the Chinese market, surpassing all control models in the later period. In addition, in the bearish market, it can also have good robustness and anti-risk ability. In all, experiments have showed that the ensemble strategy combines the advantages of each algorithm well, and achieves the effect of surpassing its constituent algorithms.

Acknowledgements. This work was supported by the Natural Science Foundation of Guangdong Province (2021A1515012298), the Project of Philosophy and Social Science Planning of Guangdong (GD21YGL16).

References

1. Zhang, Y., Zhao, P., Wu, Q., et al.: Cost-sensitive portfolio selection via deep reinforcement learning. IEEE Trans. Knowl. Data Eng. **34**(1), 236–248 (2022)
2. Tianxin, L., Xiaoping, Y., Liang, W., et al.: Research and development of financial trading system based on reinforcement learning. J. Softw. **30**(03), 845–864 (2019)
3. Bing, Y., Ting, L., Jian, X., et al.: Deep reinforcement learning based on transformer and U-Net framework for stock trading. Knowl.-Based Syst. **262**, 1–10 (2023)
4. Tianxiang, C., Shusheng, D., Huan, J., et al.: Portfolio constructions in cryptocurrency market: A CVaR-based deep reinforcement learning approach. Econ. Model. **119**, 1–9 (2023)
5. Giulio, M., Raffaele, M.: Shrinkage estimation with reinforcement learning of large variance matrices for portfolio selection. Intell. Syst. Appl. **17**, 1–11 (2023)
6. Jie, X., Yukun, Z., Chunxiao, X.: Research on financial trading algorithms based on deep reinforcement learning. Comput. Eng. Appl. **58**(07), 276–285 (2022)
7. Hyungjun, P., Kyu, S.M., Gu, C.D.: An intelligent financial portfolio trading strategy using deep Q-learning. Expert Syst. Appl. **158**, 1–16 (2020)
8. Mohamed, A.A., Xu, Z., Lee, C.-G.: What is the value of the cross-sectional approach to deep reinforcement learning? Quantitative Finan. **22**(6), 1091–1111 (2022)
9. Tuomas, H., Aurick, Z., Pieter, A., et al.: Soft actor-critic: off-policy maximum entropy deep reinforcement learning with a stochastic actor. In: Proceedings of the 35th International Conference on Machine Learning, pp. 1861–1870. PMLR (2018)
10. Lillicrap Timothy, P., Hunt Jonathan, J., Alexander, P., et al.: Continuous control with deep reinforcement learning. In: International Conference on Learning Representations (2016)
11. Scott, F., van Herke, H., David, M.: Addressing function approximation error in actor-critic methods. In: Proceedings of the 35th International Conference on Machine Learning, pp. 1587–1596. PMLR (2018)
12. Yang, H., Liu, X.-Y., Zhong, S., et al.: Deep reinforcement learning for automated stock trading: an ensemble strategy. In: Proceedings of the First ACM International Conference on AI in Finance, pp. 1–8. Association for Computing Machinery, New York (2020)

A Legal Multi-Choice Question Answering Model Based on BERT and Attention

Guibin Chen, Xudong Luo$^{(\boxtimes)}$, and Junlin Zhu

Guangxi Key Lab of Multi-Source Information Mining and Security School
of Computer Science and Engineering, Guangxi Normal University, Guilin, China
gbchen@stu.gxnu.edu.cn, luoxd@mailbox.gxnu.edu.cn

Abstract. Legal question answering is one of the critical topics in the
field of legal intelligence, and the judicial examination is a multi-choice
question-answering task. However, previous scoring-based methods for
the multi-choice task suffer from the classification bias problem and can
not fully exploit the relationship between reference books, questions,
and multi-choice answers. To address the issues, in this paper, we propose a BERT and attention based model for the judicial examination
task. Specifically, we first use the BM25 algorithm to retrieve articles
in the reference law books to provide certain information to answer a
given question. Second, we input a question, its multi-choice answers,
and the retrieved relevant articles to BERT for encoding. Third, we input
the encoded information to the module of information fuse and match
through attention mechanism to find deep relationships in articles, questions, and multi-choice answers. Finally, we concatenate the output of
the attention mechanism and input it to a binary classifier to determine
whether an answer option to the question is correct. We have done extensive experiments to show that our model significantly outperforms the
baselines in accuracy. We also experimentally demonstrate the effectiveness of some components of our model. Moreover, we applied our method
in the Challenge of AI in Law 2022 (CAIL 2022) and won the third prize
in the judicial examination task in this competition.

Keywords: Question answering · Legal intelligence · Attention
mechanism · Binary classification · Pre-trained language model

1 Introduction

Legal intelligence refers to applying Artificial Intelligence (AI) and other
advanced technologies to address legal domain problems [2,4,22]. It involves
using machine learning algorithms, natural language processing, and other forms
of AI to automate and improve various legal processes such as contract management, legal research, document analysis, and decision-making. As a result, legal
intelligence can help legal practitioners improve their work's accuracy, speed,
and efficiency, reduce costs, and increase access to justice. Legal intelligence is

Z. Jin et al. (Eds.): KSEM 2023, LNAI 14120, pp. 250–266, 2023.
https://doi.org/10.1007/978-3-031-40292-0_21

a rapidly growing field, and its potential for transforming the legal industry is becoming increasingly apparent.

Legal Question Answering (LQA) is a critical one in the field of legal intelligence. An effective LQA system can provide appropriate legal consulting services for ordinary people and help legal professionals work more efficiently. The Judicial Examination is a Legal Multi-Choice QA (LMCQA) task, which is one of China's most challenging examination programs today in the legal domain. Its source of questions contains the primary laws and legal codes currently in force, which is the threshold for legal practitioners to practice law. It requires reading some articles associated with a question and then answering it from multiple answers. Their typical method selected answers are sequence matching and then scoring the output sequence with the highest rating as the final correct answer.

However, the existing methods [17,18] for judicial examination suffer from the classification bias problem and cannot fully use the relationship in reference books, questions, and multi-choice answers. To address the issues, we propose a judicial examination model based on BERT [1] and Attention machinism [14]. Specifically, firstly, we concatenate the question with answer options and regard them as the query sequence, then use the BM25 algorithm [12] to retrieve articles in the reference law books to provide certain information to answer a given question. Secondly, we concatenate sequences in the form of $\langle articles, question, answer \rangle$. If an answer option is correct in this triple, we set this triple's label to 1; otherwise, we set it to 0. Next, we input this triple into the BERT pre-trained language model for independent encoding. Matching to the articles helps answer the question, but it also introduces some noise, so we focus on the relationship between the question and the answer options. Inspired by Zhu et al. [26], we use the information fuse module and the information match module through the attention mechanism to capture the deep relationships in articles, the question and its multi-choice answers. Finally, we concatenate the output of the attention mechanism and input it to a binary classifier to determine whether an answer option to the question is correct. If the classifier's output positive score is bigger than the negative score, the current answer option is correct for this sequence and its label is 1; otherwise, 0. We can integrate all the option labels of the question to get the final answer to the questions.

Our main contributions of this paper are as follows. (1) We propose a hybrid model of BERT and Attention for the judicial examination task. (2) We use binary classification to overcome the bias problem of scoring-based classification. (3) We exploit the relationship between reference books, questions, and multi-choice answers to increase the accuracy of answers to a given question. (4) We do extensive experiments to show the effectiveness of our model. Our method also won the third prize in the judicial examination task in the competition of Challenge of AI in Law 2022 (CAIL 2022).[1]

The rest of this paper is structured as follows. Section 2 details our model. Section 3 evaluates our model experimentally. Section 4 compare our work with related work. Finally, Sect. 5 concludes the paper with future work.

---

[1] http://cail.cipsc.org.cn/task_summit.html?raceID=0&cail_tag=2022.

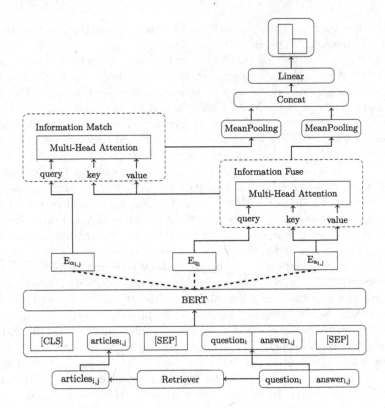

Fig. 1. Overall architecture of our model

2 Model Structure

This section will present the details of our model. Our model aims to select all the correct answers from the answer set of a given question. Figure 1 shows its main structure consisting of four main modules: the article retriever (Sect. 2.2), the information fuser (Sect. 2.4), the information matcher (Sect. 2.5), and the answer choose (Sect. 2.6).

2.1 Dataset of Articles, Questions, and Answer Options

In the JEC-QA dataset of judicial examination [23], there are a set of questions:

$$Q = \{q_1, \cdots, q_n\}, \tag{1}$$

where n is the number of questions. For a set of questions Q, the corresponding answer option set is:

$$A = \{(a_{1,1}, \cdots, a_{1,4}), \cdots, (a_{n,1}, \cdots, a_{n,4})\}, \tag{2}$$

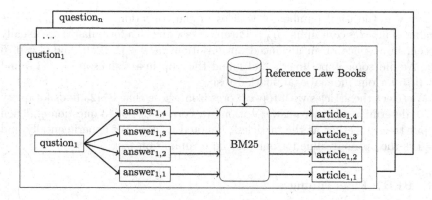

Fig. 2. Retriever module

where $a_{i,j}$ denotes the j-th answer option for i-th question and $i \in \{1, \cdots, n\}$ and $j \in \{1, 2, 3, 4\}$. Besides, the dataset also has some reference law books containing articles that would help answer questions. Suppose a question q_i and a corresponding answer option $a_{i,j}$ have m relate article(s) $\alpha_{i,j,1} \cdots, \alpha_{i,j,m}$. Then, the set of all the articles relevant to the question set Q is:

$$\mathcal{A} = \{(\alpha_{1,1}, \cdots, \alpha_{1,4}), \cdots, (\alpha_{n,1}, \cdots, \alpha_{n,4})\}, \tag{3}$$

where $\alpha_{i,j} = (\alpha_{i,j,1}, \cdots, \alpha_{i,j,m})$.

2.2 Article Retriever

For a given question q_i and its answer option $a_{i,j}$, the retrieval module (Fig. 2) uses the BM25 algorithm [12] to retrieve relevant articles in reference law books to determine whether or not an answer option is correct to the question.

Formally, let a pair of a question q_i and an answer option $a_{i,j}$ be denoted as:

$$\varrho_{i,j} = (q_i, a_{i,j}). \tag{4}$$

Then, given a query $\varrho_{i,j}$ containing keywords $\varrho_{i,j,1}, \cdots, \varrho_{i,j,\eta}$ (obtained by the Chinese Jieba segmentation tool), the BM25 score of an article $\alpha_{i,j,\iota}$ is:

$$\text{score}(\alpha_{i,j,\iota}, \varrho_{i,j}) = \sum_{\tau=1}^{\eta} \text{IDF}(\varrho_{i,j,\tau}) \frac{f(\varrho_{i,j,\tau}, \alpha_{i,j,\iota})(\kappa + 1)}{f(\varrho_{i,j,\tau}, \alpha_{i,j,\iota}) + \kappa \left(1 - \beta + \beta \frac{|\alpha_{i,j,\iota}|}{\tilde{l}_{\alpha_{i,j,\iota}}}\right)}, \tag{5}$$

where $f(\varrho_{i,j,\tau}, \alpha_{i,j,\iota})$ is $\varrho_{i,j,\tau}$'s term frequency in article $\alpha_{i,j,\iota}$; $|\alpha_{i,j,\iota}|$ is the length of $\alpha_{i,j,\iota}$ in words; $\tilde{l}_{\alpha_{i,j,\iota}}$ is the average article length in the text collection from which articles are drawn; κ and β are tuning parameters that control the impact of term frequency and document length on the score; and $\text{IDF}(\varrho_{i,j,\tau})$ is the IDF (Inverse Document Frequency) weight of the query term $\varrho_{i,j,\tau}$, defined as follows:

$$\text{IDF}(\varrho_{i,j,\tau}) = \ln \left(\frac{N - n(\varrho_{i,j,\tau}) + 0.5}{n(\varrho_{i,j,\tau}) + 0.5} + 1 \right), \tag{6}$$

where N is the total number of articles in the collection, and $n(\varrho_{i,j,\tau})$ is the number of articles containing $\varrho_{i,j,\tau}$. Parameters κ and β in formula (5) are usually chosen, in absence of an advanced optimisation, as $\kappa \in [1.2, 2.0]$ and $\beta = 0.75$ [13]. We did some experiments and found their optimal values are $\kappa = 1.5$ and $\beta = 0.75$ for our judicial examination task.

We select the articles with top-k scores from those that BM25 finds for query $\varrho_{i,j}$ to determine whether answer option $a_{i,j}$ correct or not to question q_i. Then we put them together as the "articles", denoted as $\alpha'_{i,j}$. We experimentally find $k = 1$ is the optimal value for our judicial examination task.

2.3 BERT Fine-Tuning

Now we discuss how to fine-turn BERT for obtaining the input tokens' embeddings with rich semantic information. Specifically, for a given question q_i, an answer option $a_{i,j}$ to this question q_i, and its corresponding articles $\alpha'_{i,j}$ (i.e., $\langle \alpha'_{i,j}, q_i, a_{i,j} \rangle$), its label is set to 1 if answer option $a_{i,j}$ is correct to question q_i; otherwise, 0. Then, we use a PLM such as BERT or DeBERTa [3] to get its embedding with rich semantic information, i.e.,

$$\left(E_{\alpha'_{i,j}}, E_{q_i}, E_{a_{i,j}} \right) = \text{BERT} \left(\langle \alpha'_{i,j}, q_i, a_{i,j} \rangle \right), \tag{7}$$

where

$$E_{\alpha'_{i,j}} = \left[e_{\alpha'_{i,j},1}, \ldots, e_{\alpha'_{i,j},n_{\alpha'_{i,j}}} \right], \tag{8}$$

$$E_{q_i} = \left[e_{q_{i,1}}, \ldots, e_{q_{i,n_{q_i}}} \right], \tag{9}$$

$$E_{a_{i,j}} = \left[e_{a_{i,j},1}, \ldots, e_{a_{i,j},n_{a_{i,j}}} \right], \tag{10}$$

where $e_{\alpha'_{i,j},m}$, $e_{q_i,m}$, and $e_{a_{i,j},m}$ are the m-th token embeddings of articles $\alpha'_{i,j}$, question q_i and answer option $a_{i,j}$, respectively; and $n_{\alpha'_{i,j}}$, n_{q_i}, and $n_{a_{i,j}}$ is the token numbers of articles $\alpha'_{i,j}$, question q_i and $a_{i,j}$, respectively. So , embedding $E_{\alpha'_{i,j}}$ is a real number matrix of $n_{\alpha'_{i,j}} \times 768$, embedding E_{q_i} is a real number matrix of $n_{q_i} \times 768$ and embedding $E_{a_{i,j}}$ is a real number matrix of $n_{a_{i,j}} \times 768$.

2.4 Information Fusion

Since BM25 is a character-matching method, it cannot find articles that semantically match question q_i and answer option $a_{i,j}$, making a certain amount of noise in the article retrieving. Therefore, we should consider the relationship between question q_i and its answer option $a_{i,j}$ to obtain deeper information.

Thus, we use the multi-head attention mechanism [14] to capture the relation. First, we calculate the attention representation of E_{q_i} and $E_{a_{i,j}}$ as follows:

$$\text{MHA}(q_i, a_{i,j}) = \text{Concat} \left(\text{head}_{qa,1}, \ldots, \text{head}_{qa,h} \right) W_{qa,O}, \tag{11}$$

where h denotes the number of heads, $W_{qa,O} \in \mathbb{R}^{hd_v \times 786}$ is the parameter matrix (here d_v is the dimensions of vector *Value* in the attention mechanism), and

$$\text{head}_{qa,m} = \text{softmax} \left(\frac{E_{q_i} W_{q_i,m} (E_{a_{i,j}} W_{K_a,m})^T}{\sqrt{d_k}} \right) E_{a_{i,j}} W_{V_a,m}, \qquad (12)$$

where $W_{q_i,m} \in \mathbb{R}^{768 \times d_q}$, $W_{K_a,m} \in \mathbb{R}^{768 \times d_k}$, and $W_{V_a,m} \in \mathbb{R}^{768 \times d_v}$ are parameter matrices (here d_q, d_k, and d_v denote the dimensions of vectors *Query*, *Key*, and *Value* in the attention mechanism, respectively).

2.5   Information Match

Now we match articles embeddings $E_{\alpha' i,j}$ with the information fusion output to help to answer question q_i. Specifically, similar to information fusion module, we calculate the attention representation of $\text{MHA}(q_i, a_{i,j})$ and $E_{\alpha' i,j}$ as follows:

$$\text{MHA}(\alpha'_{i,j}, q_i a_{i,j}) = \text{Concat}(\text{head}_{\alpha' qa,1}, \ldots, \text{head}_{\alpha' qa,h}) W_{\alpha' qa,O}, \qquad (13)$$

where h denotes the number of heads, $W_{\alpha' qa,O} \in \mathbb{R}^{hd_v \times 786}$ is the parameter matrix , and

$$\text{head}_{\alpha' qa,m} = \text{softmax} \left(\frac{E_{\alpha'_{i,j}} W_{\alpha'_{i,j},m} \left(\text{MHA}(q_i, a_{i,j}) W_{K_{qa},m} \right)^T}{\sqrt{d_k}} \right)$$
$$\times \text{MHA}(q_i, a_{i,j}) W_{V_{qa},m}, \qquad (14)$$

where $W_{\alpha'_{i,j},m} \in \mathbb{R}^{768 \times d_q}$, $W_{K_{qa},m} \in \mathbb{R}^{768 \times d_k}$, and $W_{V_{qa},m} \in \mathbb{R}^{768 \times d_v}$ are parameter matrices.

2.6   Answer Choose

Now we apply mean pooling to information fusion module output $\text{MHA}(q_i, a_{i,j})$ (see formula (11)) and information match module output $\text{MHA}(\alpha'_{i,j}, q_i a_{i,j})$ (see formula (13)) to get semantic features $\widetilde{\text{MHA}}(q_i, a_{i,j})$ and $\widetilde{\text{MHA}}(\alpha'_{i,j}, q_i a_{i,j})$, i.e.,

$$\widetilde{\text{MHA}}(q_i, a_{i,j}) = \text{MeanPooling}(\text{MHA}(q_i, a_{i,j})), \qquad (15)$$

$$\widetilde{\text{MHA}}(\alpha'_{i,j}, q_i a_{i,j}) = \text{MeanPooling}(\text{MHA}(\alpha'_{i,j}, q_i a_{i,j})). \qquad (16)$$

$\widetilde{\text{MHA}}(q_i, a_{i,j})$ and $\widetilde{\text{MHA}}(\alpha'_{i,j}, q_i a_{i,j})$ are two 768-dimension vectors.

Then, we concatenate $\widetilde{\text{MHA}}(q_i, a_{i,j})$ and $\widetilde{\text{MHA}}(\alpha'_{i,j}, q_i a_{i,j})$ to get the final representation output as follows:

$$O_{i,j} = \text{Concat} \left(\widetilde{\text{MHA}}(q_i, a_{i,j}), \widetilde{\text{MHA}}(\alpha'_{i,j}, q_i a_{i,j}) \right), \qquad (17)$$

where $O_{i,j} \in \mathbb{R}^{1 \times 1536}$.

Table 1. An example of knowledge-driven question

Which of the following cases need to apply for trademark changes?
✓ A. Change of name of the registrant
✗ B. Change of trademark logo
✓ C. Change of registered address
✗ D. Different categories of goods want to use the same trademark.

Table 2. An example of case-analysis question

The defendant, Sun, had a psychotic episode during the court hearing, making it impossible to continue the case for a longer period. Which of the following was the correct approach by the court?
✗ A. The verdict declared Sun not criminally responsible
✓ B. Adjudication of stay of trial
✗ C. Adjudication of adjournment
✗ D. Adjudication of termination

Finally, we use a fully-connected layer to binary-classify the fussed information and a softmax layer for normalisation to obtain its positive-class score $s_{i,j}$ and its negative-class score $(1 - s_{i,j})$. Formally, we have:

$$s_{i,j} = \text{softmax}(O_{i,j}W_{s_{i,j}} + b_{i,j}), \tag{18}$$

where $W_{s_{i,j}} \in \mathbb{R}^{1536 \times 2}$ is the weight matrix for classifier and $b_{i,j}$ is the bias term.

When the positive score is bigger than the negative score, the answer to the current output sequence is judged to be positive, and the label is set to 1; otherwise, 0. The final answer to each question is derived by integrating the labels of all answer options. For example, suppose the labels of question q_i's four answer options $a_{i,1}$, $a_{i,2}$, $a_{i,3}$, and $a_{i,4}$ are 1, 0, 1, and 0, respectively. Then, question q_i corresponding answer is AC.

2.7   Model Training

Our model is trained end-to-end by minimising the loss of all $\langle \alpha'_{i,j}, q_i, a_{i,j} \rangle$ [21], i.e.,

$$\mathcal{L} = - \sum_{i \in \{1, \cdots, n\}, j \in \{1, \cdots, 4\}} (y_{i,j} \log s_{i,j} + (1 - y_{i,j}) \log(1 - s_{i,j})), \tag{19}$$

where $y_{i,j}$ is the label of class. In the training set, if answer option $a_{i,j}$ is correct to question q_i, $y_{i,j} = 1$; otherwise, $y_{i,j} = 0$.

3   Experiments

This section will experimentally evaluate our model.

3.1   Dataset

We use JEC-QA, one of the largest QA datasets in legal domain [23]. In the dataset, each data entry a 4-choice question (one question and four answer options, and at least one of them is correct) from real Chinese judicial exams

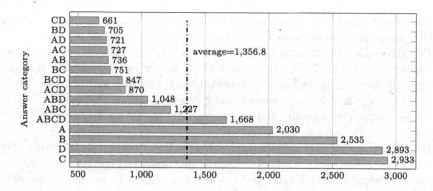

Fig. 3. Answer distribution over category

Table 3. Dataset statistics of JEC-QA

	Knowledge-drive	Case-analysis	Full
Single-Q	3,548	6,843	10,391
Multi-Q	3,907	6,054	9,961
All	7,455	12,897	20,352

from 2009 to 2017, and has two types: Knowledge-Driven (KD) (see Table 1 for an example) and Case-Analysis (CA) (see Table 2 for an example). The former is on memorising concepts. The latter is on problem-specific understanding, and answering the questions of this kind requires strong reasoning skills.

Figure 3 shows the distribution of each answer category. Among them, the numbers of categories A, B, C, D, and $ABCD$ exceed the average value of $1,356.8$. We removed the repeated data entries in the JEC-QA dataset and get a new version of JEC-QA with a total of $20,352$ data entries. Table 3 shows the statistics of the new version of the dataset. We randomly selected $12,210$ data entries as the training set, $4,071$ ones as the validation set, and $4,071$ ones as the test set at a ratio of 6:2:2.

3.2 Baselines

We re-implemented the following baselines on the JEC-QA dataset for comparison with our model:

1. **DeBERTa**: It uses a disentangled attention mechanism with an enhanced mask decoder. Compared with RoBERTa Large [9], DeBERTa, even trained on half of the training data, consistently performs better on various NLP tasks. It also uses a virtual adversarial training method to improve its generalisation performance effectively. We use its V2 version in our experiments.
2. **Lawformer**: It is trained on the legal corpus containing tens of millions of legal documents, including both criminal and civil cases. To keep in line with the original paper, we link questions and answer options together as input to

Lawformer, and then it determines which ones among the four answer options to a given question are correct as a text classification task.

3. **DCMN+** [20]: It extracts the relation in the triple of passage, question, and answer bidirectionally. Then, it fuses them into word embeddings through a gating mechanism and uses passage sentence selection and option interaction to mimic how humans solve reading comprehension. The model predicts answer options by a bi-directional matching module. We refer to the officially published code[2] and re-implement it.

4. **DUMA**: It uses a dual multi-headed collaborative attention model to directly model the relationship triple of passages, questions, and answers in multiple-choice reading comprehension tasks, which can work with popular large-scale PLMs while simply and efficiently improving model performance. We refer to the officially published code[3] and re-implement it.

Besides, we retrieve top-1 article for each answer option (see Sect. 2.1) and solve it as a reading comprehension task. Since the output of baseline models is only suitable for the single-answer questions, we formalise it as a text classification task to fit it to the multi-answer questions of JEC-QA.

3.3 Settings

For a fair comparison, all the models (except for Lawformer) use the Chinese version of DeBERTa-v2-Base (with 97 million parameters) as the encoder. We implemented all models based on Hugging Face[4] and fine-tuned them on a single GPU (A100). The total training rounds for all the models are 25 epochs, and the optimizer uses the AdamW function [10]. The early stop mechanism we used is: before 25 epochs, if the accuracy of the models on the validation set cannot be increased for 4 epochs, the model training will stop. Finally, we set the batch size as 32 and the learning rate as 2×10^{-5}.

3.4 Benchmark Experiment

We use accuracy as an evaluation metric: the model's answer to a multi-choice question is accurate if the answer options of the question that the model determines as correct are exactly the same as the standard.

Figure 4 shows that our model outperforms all the baselines overall. Specifically, Fig. 5 shows that the baselines perform worse for multi-choice questions. The baselines are better only for single-answer questions and category $ABCD$ because the number of single-answer questions and category $ABCD$ in the JEC-QA dataset is larger than the number of multiple-answer questions. The imbalance of answer categories causes the scoring-based methods used in the baselines to learn this bias during fine-tuning, so they tend to select single-answer

---

[2] https://github.com/Qzsl123/dcmn.
[3] https://github.com/pfZhu/duma_code.
[4] https://github.com/huggingface/transformers.

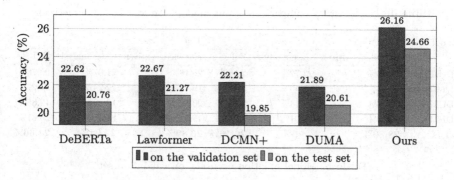

Fig. 4. The model accuracy comparison on the validation set and the test set

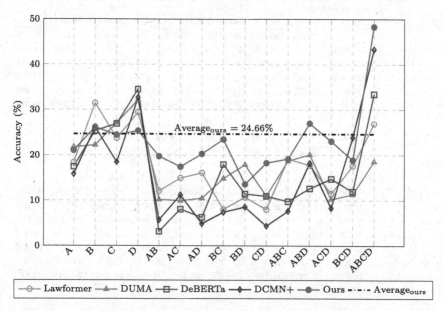

Fig. 5. The accuracy of per categories on test set

questions and category $ABCD$ with a higher probability of occurrence during inference.

We also found that the baseline methods and our model in single-answer questions and category $ABCD$ have higher accuracy than multiple-answer questions. However, the gap in our method is smaller than the scoring-based methods used in the baselines. The binary classification method used in our model can maintain a certain balance between categories with a higher probability of occurrence and those with a lower probability of occurrence. It improves the accuracy of the fewer categories while maintaining a certain accuracy of the more numerous categories, thus mitigating the bias due to the unbalanced number of categories and improving the final accuracy.

Table 4. The accuracy comparison of our model with four baseline methods

model	Validation			Test		
	Knowledge-driven	Case-analysis	Full	Knowledge-driven	Case-analysis	Full
DeBERTa	20.70%	23.72%	22.62%	20.18%	21.07%	20.76%
Lawformer	21.24%	23.49%	22.67%	19.48%	22.24%	21.27%
DCMN+	22.33%	22.14%	22.21%	20.88 %	19.29%	19.85%
DUMA	19.76%	23.01%	21.89%	19.34%	21.30%	20.61%
Ours	**28.89%**	**24.6%**	**26.16%**	**26.89%**	**23.04%**	**24.66%**

Table 5. Model ablation accuracy on validation set

model	Validation								
	Knowledge-driven			Case-analysis			Full		
	Single-Q	Multi-Q	All-KD	Single-Q	Multi-Q	All-CA	Single-Q	Multi-Q	All
Score	25.92%	16.23%	20.70%	**30.21%**	16.02%	23.72%	**28.80%**	16.10%	22.62%
Score+Fuse	27.38%	18.49%	22.60%	27.86%	18.89%	23.76%	27.70%	18.73%	23.34%
Score+Fuse+Match	27.09%	17.36%	21.85%	29.14%	16.95%	23.56%	28.47%	17.11%	22.94%
Bi	24.16%	24.53%	24.36%	22.96%	20.49%	21.83%	23.35%	22.11%	22.75%
Bi+Fuse	**27.96%**	26.42%	27.13%	24.96%	23.78%	24.41%	25.93%	24.84%	25.40%
Our full model	26.94%	**30.57%**	**28.89%**	25.66%	**23.36%**	**24.60%**	26.08%	**26.25%**	**26.16%**

Table 6. Model ablation accuracy on test set

model	Test								
	Knowledge-driven			Case-analysis			Full		
	Single-Q	Multi-Q	All-KD	Single-Q	Multi-Q	All-CA	Single-Q	Multi-Q	All
Score	26.36%	14.84%	20.18%	**26.97%**	14.19%	21.07%	**26.78%**	14.44%	20.76%
Score+Fuse	25.15%	17.58%	21.09%	26.62%	20.26%	**23.68%**	26.15%	19.22%	22.77%
Score+Fuse+Match	25.0%	16.80%	20.60%	26.76%	18.29%	22.85%	26.20%	17.72%	22.06%
Bi	22.74%	25.39%	24.16%	22.04%	18.46%	20.39%	22.26%	21.14%	21.71%
Bi+Fuse	24.40%	26.56%	25.56%	23.17%	23.08%	22.97%	23.56%	24.36%	23.95%
Our full model	**26.51%**	**27.21%**	**26.89%**	23.45%	**23.46%**	23.46%	24.42%	**24.91%**	**24.66%**

Table 4 shows that there are also some differences in the performances of all
the models over knowledge-driven and case-analysis questions. The baselines for
the case-analysis questions outperform those for the knowledge-driven questions
(except for DCMN+), so scoring-based methods may be more appropriate for
case-analysis questions. In contrast, our model performs better on knowledge-
driven questions than case-analysis questions, meaning that our model is more
suitable for knowledge-driven questions. However, our model outperforms the
baselines for both knowledge-driven and case-analysis questions, indicating that
our model can do the judicial examination task better than the baseline methods.

3.5 Ablation Experiment

We also conducted a series of ablation experiments to validate the specific
components of the model. Specifically, we experimented separately using only
scoring-based classification (Score), adding the fuse module to scoring-based

Table 7. Different numbers of article(s) performance on validation set

No. of article(s)	Validation								
	Knowledge-Driven			Case-Analysis			Full		
	Single-Q	Multi-Q	All-KD	Single-Q	Multi-Q	All-CA	Single-Q	Multi-Q	All
Top-1	26.94%	**30.57%**	**28.89%**	**25.66%**	23.36%	**24.60**	**26.08%**	**26.25%**	**26.16%**
Top-2	**27.38%**	27.04%	27.20%	22.67%	22.85%	22.75%	24.21%	24.53%	24.37%
Top-3	24.30%	25.53%	24.97%	23.95%	**23.44%**	23.72%	24.07%	24.28%	24.17%

Table 8. Different numbers of article(s) performance on test set

No. of article(s)	Test								
	Knowledge-Driven			Case-Analysis			Full		
	Single-Q	Multi-Q	All-KD	Single-Q	Multi-Q	All-CA	Single-Q	Multi-Q	All
Top-1	**26.51%**	**27.21%**	**26.89%**	**23.45%**	**23.46%**	**23.46**	24.42%	24.91%	24.66%
Top-2	22.74%	26.17%	24.58%	22.89%	21.0%	22.02%	22.84%	23.0%	22.92%
Top-3	20.48%	24.87%	22.84%	23.24%	21.16%	22.28%	22.36%	22.60%	22.48%

classification (Score+Fuse), and continuing the match module after adding the fuse module (Score+Fuse+Match). Moreover, we experimented with a binary classification method only (Bi) and added the fuse module to the binary classification method (Bi+Fuse). Finally, to ensure a fair comparison, we used the same hyper-parameters as described in Sect. 3.3.

Tables 5 and 6 show our experiment results:

1. Similar to the results in Sect. 3.4, the scoring-based method achieves better results on single-answer and case-analysis questions. In contrast, the binary classification-based method performs better on knowledge-driven questions than on case-analysis questions.
2. Using the binary classification method effectively improves the model's performance when other structures are identical.
3. With the addition of the fuse module, the scoring-based and binary classification methods have effectively improved the model's performance. In the overall performance of the test set, the scoring-based method improved by approximately 2.01%, and the binary classification-based method improved by about 2.24%.
4. After adding the match module on top of the fuse module, the scoring-based method shows some performance degradation. However, it achieves the best performance in our full model, with a 0.71% improvement in the test set compared to the combined binary classification and fuse module (Bi+Fuse).

In conclusion, each component in our approach is necessary, and all the components work together, achieving the best model performance.

3.6 Experiments of Article Number

We have done some experiments to explore whether the number of articles affects the model's performance.

Tables 7 and 8 display the model's performance with different numbers of articles. The model performs best when we use only the top-1 article because the word matching-based BM25 algorithm cannot semantically retrieve articles relevant to the question and its answer options. Furthermore, the excessive use of the BM25 algorithm to retrieve resulting articles introduces a lot of noise into the data, which affects the model's performance. Therefore, the model that uses only the top-1 article performs better than those using top-2 or top-3.

3.7 Benchmark with ChatGPT

We benchmark our model with ChatGPT. ChatGPT is based on the GPT-3.5 model, which was released in November 2022 and can understand and generate natural language or code. The latest version of ChatGPT currently iterates to GPT-4. However, since GPT-4 does not currently provide an API interface and limits the number of conversations a user can have, we use "GPT-3.5 Turbo", which is optimised for chat and traditional tasks and is the most capable and cost-effective model in the GPT-3.5 family.

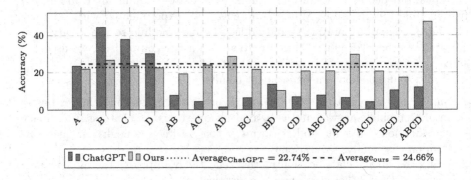

Fig. 6. The accuracy of ChatGPT (GPT 3.5) and Ours in each category

In our experiments, we used the API interface to enter all questions into ChatGPT in the format: "Please give the correct answers to the following question directly: Question A. Option 1, B. Option 2, C. Option 3, D. Option 4." Since there is no fixed format for the answers it generates, we selected half of the data (2,036 items) from the test set, entered it into ChatGPT, and manually integrated the generated answers to compare them with the correct ones. We obtained the answers generated by ChatGPT from our repository.[5]

Figure 6 shows the experimental results that indicate ChatGPT has an accuracy of 22.74%, while our method has an accuracy of 24.66%. Specifically, our method's accuracy is 1.92% higher than ChatGPT. ChatGPT performs better than our model on single-answer questions but worse than our model on multi-answer questions. Overall, our model outperforms ChatGPT.

---

[5] https://github.com/gbchen99/chatGPT_result.

4 Relate Work

This section will compare our work with related work to show how our work advances the state of the art in the field.

4.1 Multi-Choice Question Answering

There are some studies on Multi-Choice Question Answering (MCQA). Li et al. [7] propose a neural-symbolic approach that uses an adaptive logic graph network to enhance neural and symbolic reasoning mutually and iteratively to improve the model's logical reasoning over text. Wang and Pan [16] connect a hierarchical attentive reader with a multi-hop reasoner to solve the problem of information extraction and complex reasoning in multi-hop reading comprehension. Xu et al. [19] employ external entity descriptions, further enhancing the model's capabilities. Jin et al. [5] and Xu et al. [19] have shown that coarse-tuning and out-of-domain datasets and multi-task learning stages using a larger in-domain dataset can help the model generalise better with limited data. Zhang et al. [20] and Zhu et al. [26] have also demonstrated that attention mechanisms can use the relationships between the given context, question, and answer options to improve the model's performance.

However, although our work in this paper is also on MCQA, it differs from the above studies in the following way. Their datasets are articles or passages that correspond to the questions and have only one correct answer to a question, so they can directly construct the relationship in $\langle context, question, answers \rangle$ and straightforwardly use the highest scoring option as the answer to the question. Instead, in the judicial examination dataset, no passages or articles correspond to each question, and each question may have one or more correct answer options. Therefore, the above method cannot be applied directly to our task.

4.2 Legal Question Answering

There are LQA models for similar case retrieval [11], but ours is different from them. In 2019, Liu, Luo, and Yang [8] presented a QA model of this kind. Their method use the semantics and structure similarity between a new case and existing cases, not using any machine learning method. In 2022, Zhu, Luo, and Wu [24] also presented such a QA model, but they employ a PLM to propose a BERT-based two-stage ranking method. In 2023, Zhu et al. [25] presented a CNN-based QA model for similar case retrieval. The prototype system has been deployed on the WeChat platform and can answer the user's queries like ChatGPT. They use real-cases related COVID-19 to train the CNN model. However, unlike these model, ours in paper is not for similar case retrieval, but judge whether answer option is correct to a given legal question according to law.

There are also some LQA models for legal knowledge retrieval, but our work is different from them. In 2021, Kourtin et al. [6] presented a QA model to answer legal questions in a natural language according to a structured knowledge base built on an ontology. The ontology is based on legal domain concepts and relationships. In 2022, Wang et al. [15] presented a legal knowledge QA model. Specifically, they first use BERT to obtain the vector representation of a question. Then they use the Milvus vector search engine to match the question-answer pair in the knowledge base and return the answer which question is the most similar to the question the user asks. This sort of QA models aim to find the answer to an a given question, while in our model, the answers to a question already exist but it is unknown whether they are correct and so ours needs to judge them.

For LMCQA, in 2021, Wu et al. [17] propose a BERT-based alignment and gated graph attention networks to utilize all question-answer pairs' global information. and in 2021, Xiao et al. [18] released Lawformer, the first legal pre-training language model for the long legal text that can handle thousands of token documents. Lawformer can also be applicable to LMCQA, as we did in Sect. 3.4. However, our LMCQA models differs from theirs. The above two models use a scoring-based method for the judicial examination task, which suffers from classification bias problems. Rather, our model alleviates the issue by doing bi-classification for each answer option.

5   Conclusion

Legal question-answering is an essential part of legal intelligence. This paper proposes a legal multi-choice question-answering model based on BERT and attention-based. The model first retrieves relevant articles using the BM25 algorithm and then utilises the fuse module and match module through the attention mechanism to obtain a deep relationship among law articles, questions, and answer options. Next, the model concatenates the output representations of the attention mechanism and inputs them through a binary classifier to determine whether an answer option to the question is correct. Finally, it integrates all option labels to finalise the answers to the question. We have done extensive experiments to show that our model outperforms the baseline. And also, our model won the third prize in the judicial examination task of the Challenge of AI in Law 2022 (CAIL 2022). However, there is still considerable noise in the information retrieved by the BM25 algorithm, and the model accuracy performance could be even better. Therefore, enhancing the articles' retrieval accuracy and model performance remains an open problem that needs to be addressed.

Acknowledgements. This work was partially supported by a Research Fund of Guangxi Key Lab of Multi-source Information Mining Security (22-A-01-02) and a Graduate Student Innovation Project of School of Computer Science and Engineering, Guangxi Normal University (JXXYYJSCXXM-2021-001).

References

1. Devlin, J., Chang, M., Lee, K., Toutanova, K.: BERT:pre-training of deep bidirectional transformers for language understanding. In: Proceedings of the 2019 Conference of the North American Chapter of the Association for Computational Linguistics: Human Language Technologies, vol. 1, pp. 4171–4186 (2019)

2. Governatori, G., Bench-Capon, T., Verheij, B., Araszkiewicz, M., Francesconi, E., Grabmair, M.: Thirty years of artificial intelligence and law: the first decade. Artif. Intell. Law **30**(4), 481–519 (2022)
3. He, P., Liu, X., Gao, J., Chen, W.: DeBERTa: decoding-enhanced BERT with disentangled attention. In: Proceedings of the 9th International Conference on Learning Representations (2021)
4. Huang, Q., Luo, X.: State-of-the-art and development trend of artificial intelligence combined with law. Computer Sci. **45**(12), 1–11 (2018)
5. Jin, D., Gao, S., Kao, J.Y., Chung, T., Hakkani-Tur, D.: MMM: Multi-stage multi-task learning for multi-choice reading comprehension. In: Proceedings of the AAAI Conference on Artificial Intelligence, vol. 34, pp. 8010–8017 (2020)
6. Kourtin, I., Mbarki, S., Mouloudi, A.: A legal question answering ontology-based system. In: Bekavac, B., Kocijan, K., Silberztein, M., Šojat, K. (eds.) NooJ 2020. CCIS, vol. 1389, pp. 218–229. Springer, Cham (2021). https://doi.org/10.1007/978-3-030-70629-6_19
7. Li, X., Cheng, G., Chen, Z., Sun, Y., Qu, Y.: AdaLoGN: adaptive logic graph network for reasoning-based machine reading comprehension. In: Proceedings of the 60th Annual Meeting of the Association for Computational Linguistics, vol. 1, pp. 7147–7161 (2022)
8. Liu, Y., Luo, X., Yang, X.: Semantics and structure based recommendation of similar legal cases. In: 2019 IEEE 14th International Conference on Intelligent Systems and Knowledge Engineering (ISKE), pp. 388–395 (2019)
9. Liu, Y., et al.: RoBERTa: a robustly optimized BERT pretraining approach. arXiv preprint arXiv:1907.11692 (2019)
10. Loshchilov, I., Hutter, F.: Fixing weight decay regularization in Adam. In: Proceedings of the 7th International Conference on Learning Representations, pp. 1–8 (2019)
11. Martinez-Gil, J.: A survey on legal question-answering systems. Comput. Sci. Rev. **48**, 100552 (2023)
12. Robertson, S., Zaragoza, H., et al.: The probabilistic relevance framework: BM25 and beyond. Found. Trends® Inf. Retriev. **3**(4), 333–389 (2009)
13. Schütze, H., Manning, C.D., Raghavan, P.: Introduction to information retrieval. Cambridge University Press (2008)
14. Vaswani, A., et al.: Attention is all you need. In: Advances in Neural Information Processing Systems 30 (2017)
15. Wang, C., Luo, X.: A legal question answering system based on BERT. In: Proceedings of the 2021 5th International Conference on Computer Science and Artificial Intelligence, pp. 278–283 (2022)
16. Wang, W., Pan, S.: Deep inductive logic reasoning for multi-hop reading comprehension. In: Proceedings of the 60th Annual Meeting of the Association for Computational Linguistics, vol. 1, pp. 4999–5009 (2022)
17. Wu, J., Luo, X.: Alignment-based graph network for judicial examination task. In: Qiu, H., Zhang, C., Fei, Z., Qiu, M., Kung, S.-Y. (eds.) KSEM 2021. LNCS (LNAI), vol. 12817, pp. 386–400. Springer, Cham (2021). https://doi.org/10.1007/978-3-030-82153-1_32
18. Xiao, C., Hu, X., Liu, Z., Tu, C., Sun, M.: Lawformer: a pre-trained language model for Chinese legal long documents. AI Open **2**, 79–84 (2021)
19. Xu, Y., Zhu, C., Xu, R., Liu, Y., Zeng, M., Huang, X.: Fusing context into knowledge graph for commonsense question answering. In: Findings of the Association for Computational Linguistics: ACL-IJCNLP 2021, pp. 1201–1207 (2021)

20. Zhang, S., Zhao, H., Wu, Y., Zhang, Z., Zhou, X., Zhou, X.: DCMN+: dual co-matching network for multi-choice reading comprehension. In: Proceedings of the AAAI Conference on Artificial Intelligence, vol. 34, pp. 9563–9570 (2020)

21. Zhang, Z., Sabuncu, M.: Generalized cross entropy loss for training deep neural networks with noisy labels. In: Advances in Neural Information Processing Systems, vol. 31 (2018)

22. Zhong, H., Xiao, C., Tu, C., Zhang, T., Liu, Z., Sun, M.: How does NLP benefit legal system: a summary of legal artificial intelligence. In: Proceedings of the 58th Annual Meeting of the Association for Computational Linguistics, pp. 5218–5230 (2020)

23. Zhong, H., Xiao, C., Tu, C., Zhang, T., Liu, Z., Sun, M.: JEC-QA: a legal-domain question answering dataset. In: Proceedings of the AAAI Conference on Artificial Intelligence, vol. 34, pp. 9701–9708 (2020)

24. Zhu, J., Luo, X., Wu, J.: A BERT-based two-stage ranking method for legal case retrieval. In: Memmi, G., Yang, B., Kong, L., Zhang, T., Qiu, M. (eds.) Knowledge Science, Engineering and Management. KSEM 2022. Lecture Notes in Computer Science, vol. 13369, pp. 534–546. Springer, Cham (2022). https://doi.org/10.1007/978-3-031-10986-7_43

25. Zhu, J., Wu, J., Luo, X., Liu, J.: Semantic matching based legal information retrieval system for COVID-19 pandemic. Artificial Intelligence and Law, pp. 1–30 (2023)

26. Zhu, P., Zhang, Z., Zhao, H., Li, X.: DUMA: reading comprehension with transposition thinking. IEEE/ACM Trans. Audio Speech Lang. Process. **30**, 269–279 (2021)

Offline Reinforcement Learning with Diffusion-Based Behavior Cloning Term

Han Wang, Youfang Lin, Sheng Han, and Kai Lv[✉]

Beijing Key Laboratory of Traffic Data Analysis and Mining, School of Computer and Information Technology, Beijing Jiaotong University, Beijing 100044, China
lvkai@bjtu.edu.cn

Abstract. To address the distributional shift problem in offline reinforcement learning, policy constraint methods aim to minimize the divergence between the current policy and the behavior policy. One type of policy constraint method is the regularization constraint method, which adds regularization terms to online reinforcement learning algorithms. However, some of these regularization terms may be too restrictive and limited by the expressive power of the generative model. To relax the strict distribution matching constraint, this paper proposes TD3+diffusion-based BC algorithm, which contains a behavior cloning term incorporating the diffusion model as a regularization constraint term. The diffusion model has a strong expressive power and can achieve support set matching, which means it can learn actions with a high probability in a given state and avoid actions outside of the distribution. Our algorithm matches or surpasses state-of-the-art algorithms on most tasks in the D4RL benchmark, as shown by the experimental results.

Keywords: Offline reinforcement learning · Policy constraint · Diffusion model · Behavior cloning

1 Introduction

Reinforcement learning has proven successful in many real-life tasks [16,24,28]. However, due to its huge interaction costs, some recent studies focus on offline reinforcement learning settings, which require agents to learn policy from a fixed dataset without interacting with the environment. Compared to standard reinforcement learning, it improves sample efficiency and avoids expensive or unsafe real-world interaction costs.

The main problem in offline reinforcement learning is distributional shift, which refers to a certain gap between the behavior policy used to collect the offline dataset and the learned policy. To address this issue, a series of algorithms have been proposed. Among them, model-free algorithms can be roughly divided into three categories: constraining learned policy as close to behavior policy as possible; giving lower Q-values to out-of-distribution actions [14]; completely avoiding accessing actions outside of the dataset [12]. Our method belongs to the first category.

Z. Jin et al. (Eds.): KSEM 2023, LNAI 14120, pp. 267–278, 2023.
https://doi.org/10.1007/978-3-031-40292-0_22

Regularization methods are a widely used and effective type of policy constraint. Currently, most of them use stochastic policies and regularization terms such as KL divergence, Maximum Mean Discrepancy, Fisher divergence, and Wasserstein distance to measure the distance between the learned policy and behavior policy [11,13,26]. However, this approach has some limitations. The behavior policy and the distance estimate may be inaccurate, and strictly limiting the two distributions to be similar may prevent learning a better policy beyond the behavior policy. The TD3+BC [4] method uses a deterministic policy and adds a behavior cloning term to the TD3 [5] algorithm, which is simple and works well. However, its requirements are also strict. Trying to achieve the goal of making the neural network learn all the actions in the dataset precisely is challenging, especially when some actions are difficult to access or have low reward values. In such cases, learning this part of the data may not be useful.

In this paper, we propose TD3+diffusion-based BC, a method that incorporates the diffusion model into the regularization policy constraint algorithm and pre-trains the diffusion model as a behavior policy. It restricts the actions to those generated by the generative model, which implicitly implements the support constraint and avoids strict distribution constraint [13]. In addition, we use pre-trained behavior policy samplings as a warm-start at the beginning of the policy evaluation step, so that the Q-values are not overestimated at the start.

The contributions of this paper can be summarized as follows:

1. We pre-train a diffusion model and use a diffusion-based behavior cloning term to enforce the support constraint;
2. Our method, TD3+diffusion-based BC, achieves comparable or superior performance to state-of-the-art methods on most datasets for the D4RL locomotion task.

2   Related Works

Generative Models in Offline RL. In recent years, generative models have been widely used in computer vision [15,20], reinforcement learning, and other fields. One of the most common ways to use generative models in offline reinforcement learning is to use them to implement data augmentation [17,21,23] and the use of augmented datasets improves the performance of various algorithms. In model-based reinforcement learning methods, a Gaussian model is often used to fit the dynamics model of the environment [10,27]. In planning-based approaches, Diffuser [9] uses a diffusion model for the first time in offline reinforcement learning, using it to generate trajectories. Generative models are also commonly used for policy modeling. Offline datasets may be derived from human demonstrations, sub-optimal policies or a mixture of policies, making it difficult to estimate the behavior policy. Most previous algorithms use the Gaussian model or conditional VAE modeling policy, but they may not fit the distribution of data well due to the limited expressive power of the model. Recent algorithms use diffusion model modeling policy. Diffusion model [8,22] is highly expressive and can capture multi-modal information of the data well.

Policy Constraint Methods. Policy constraint methods bring current policy closer to the behavior policy, which can be classified into two categories: parameterization constraint and regularization constraint. The former directly uses generative models to estimate behavior policy while incorporating reinforcement learning techniques for training [1, 6, 7, 25, 29]. BCQ [6] trains a conditional VAE model and a perturbation model combined as the final policy; Diffusion-QL [25] trains a conditional diffusion model while adding Q-value guidance to the loss function as the final policy; BPPO [29] pre-trains a Gaussian model as a behavior policy, after which monotonically promotes the policy in a similar way to PPO; SfBC [1] decouples the policy model into a pre-trained diffusion model and an action evaluation model, and performs weighted sampling with Q-value as the weight from action candidate set generated by diffusion model. The latter solves optimization problems with constraint by using the Lagrange multiplier to put constraint into the optimization goal or transforms the optimization goal into the form of weighted maximum likelihood estimation [4, 11, 13, 18, 19, 26]. BEAR [13] pre-trains a conditional VAE model with sampling-based MMD constraint for policy support matching; BRAC [26] also pre-trains the conditional VAE model, adds a penalty term to the value function or policy and calculates the distance between two distributions using four measures including Kernel MMD, KL-Divergence, f-divergence, and Wasserstein Distance. TD3+BC [4] adds a behavior cloning term as a constraint. AWR [19] and AWAC [18] methods use the advantage function as the behavior cloning weight to make policy prefers actions with higher reward.

3 Preliminaries

3.1 Offline Reinforcement Learning

Reinforcement learning problems are often modelled by Markov Decision Process, which is usually defined as a six-tuple $(S, A, r, \rho, P, \gamma)$, consisting of the state space S, the action space A, the reward function $r(s, a)$, the initial state distribution ρ, the transition dynamics $P(s' \mid s, a)$ and the discount factor γ. The goal of reinforcement learning is to find an optimal policy that maximizes the expected discounted return: $\mathbb{E}_{s_0 \sim \rho, a_t \sim \pi_\theta(\cdot|s_t), s_{t+1} \sim P(\cdot|s_t, a_t)} \left[\sum_{t=0}^{T} \gamma^t r(s_t, a_t) \right]$. The state-action value function is usually defined as:
$Q^\pi(s_t, a_t) = \mathbb{E}_{s_0 \sim \rho, a_i \sim \pi_\theta(\cdot|s_i), s_{i+1} \sim P(\cdot|s_i, a_i)} \left[\sum_{i=t}^{T} \gamma^i r(s_i, a_i) \right]$.

In offline reinforcement learning, you can only get offline datasets $D = (s_i, a_i, r_i, s_i')_{i=1}^{N}$, and there is no interaction with environment. Some offline reinforcement learning algorithms use the Actor-Critic framework to iterate between policy evaluation and policy improvement to improve policy:

$$
\begin{cases}
\phi^{k+1} \leftarrow \underset{\phi}{\arg\min}\, \mathbb{E}_{(s, a, r, s') \sim D} \left[\left(\left(r(s, a) + \gamma \mathbb{E}_{a' \sim \pi_{\theta'}^k(a'|s')} \left[Q_{\phi'}^k(s', a') \right] \right) \right. \right. \\
\qquad\qquad\qquad\qquad\qquad\qquad \left. \left. -\, Q_\phi(s, a) \right)^2 \right] \; (policy\ evaluation) \qquad , \; (1) \\
\theta^{k+1} \leftarrow \underset{\theta}{\arg\max}\, \mathbb{E}_{s \sim D, a \sim \pi_\theta^k(a|s)} \left[Q_{\phi'}^{k+1}(s, a) \right] \; (policy\ improvement)
\end{cases}
$$

where $Q_\phi(s, a)$ is the parameterized Q function, $\pi_\theta(s)$ is the parameterized policy network, and $Q_{\phi'}(s, a)$ and $\pi_{\theta'}(s)$ are the target networks. As the policy improvement step maximizes the Q-value, it may make the policy select OOD actions, and the Q-values of these actions will be incorrectly overestimated.

3.2 Diffusion Model

DDPM (Denoising Diffusion Probabilistic Model) [8] is a type of diffusion model that has both forward and reverse diffusion processes. The forward diffusion process adds Gaussian noise to the sample $x_0 \sim q(x_0)$ in T steps as shown in Eq. 2 until the data becomes random noise:

$$q(x_t \mid x_{t-1}) = \mathcal{N}\left(x_t; \sqrt{1 - \beta_t} x_{t-1}, \beta_t I\right), \tag{2}$$

where β_t is the variance used in each step and is fixed using the variance schedule. By defining $\alpha_t = 1 - \beta_t$, $\bar{\alpha}_t = \prod_{i=1}^{t} \alpha_i$ and using the reparameterization technique, we can obtain $x_t = \sqrt{\bar{\alpha}_t} x_0 + \sqrt{1 - \bar{\alpha}_t} \epsilon$. The reverse diffusion process learns to remove noise from data points and generate new samples. We use a neural network to parameterize the reverse process as:

$$p_\theta(x_{t-1} \mid x_t) = \mathcal{N}(x_{t-1}; \mu_\theta(x_t, t), \Sigma_\theta(x_t, t)). \tag{3}$$

After a series of derivations, the optimization objective is transformed into Eq. 4:

$$\mathcal{L}(\theta) = \mathbb{E}_{t \sim \mathcal{U}(1,T), \epsilon \sim \mathcal{N}(0,I), x_0} \left[\left\| \epsilon - \epsilon_\theta \left(\sqrt{\bar{\alpha}_t} x_0 + \sqrt{1 - \bar{\alpha}_t} \epsilon, t \right) \right\|^2 \right], \tag{4}$$

where ϵ_θ represents the predicted noise.

4 Method

4.1 The Design of Behavior Cloning Term

As the simplest imitation learning method, behavior cloning minimizes the difference between the learned policy and behavior policy through supervised learning. The goal of behavior cloning is to make the action distribution of the current policy in state s as close as possible to that of the offline dataset in the same state, and performing maximum likelihood estimation is equivalent to minimizing KL divergence:

$$\operatorname*{argmax}_{\theta} \mathbb{E}_{s \sim D, a \sim \pi_\beta} [\log \pi_\theta(a \mid s)] \iff \operatorname*{argmin}_{\theta} KL(\pi_\beta(a \mid s) \| \pi_\theta(a \mid s)). \tag{5}$$

Behavior cloning is effective when the offline dataset contains high-quality data. When reward information is available, we can choose to imitate only a portion of the relatively high-value state-action pairs [2]. However, the performance of the policy trained only by the behavior cloning method cannot surpass that of the behavior policy. Some offline reinforcement learning methods combine behavior cloning to improve policy, among which the design of behavior cloning terms is crucial.

For each state s, assuming that the action output of the policy $\pi_\theta(s)$ follows a Gaussian distribution $\mathcal{N} \sim \left(\mu_\theta(s), \sigma_\theta^2(s)\right)$. When the variance is a constant independent of the parameters, the log-likelihood function is converted into Eq. 6:

$$\underset{\theta}{\text{argmin}} \sum_{(s,a)\in D} \frac{(a - \mu_\theta(s))^2}{2\sigma_\theta^2(s)} + \frac{1}{2} \log\left(2\pi\sigma_\theta^2(s)\right) \Rightarrow \underset{\theta}{\text{argmin}} \sum_{(s,a)\in D} (a - \mu_\theta(s))^2.$$
(6)

The TD3+BC algorithm adds the same behavior cloning term as Eq. 6 on the basis of the TD3 algorithm to maximize the Q-value while minimizing the mean squared error:

$$\underset{\theta}{\text{argmax}} \, \mathbb{E}_{(s,a)\sim D} \left[\lambda Q(s, \pi_\theta(s)) - (\pi_\theta(s) - a)^2 \right],$$
(7)

where $\lambda = \frac{\alpha}{\frac{1}{N}\sum_{(s_i,a_i)} |Q(s_i,a_i)|}$. As a relatively simple algorithm with a competitive effect, the TD3+BC algorithm is often regarded as a benchmark method for algorithm comparison in the field of offline reinforcement learning. However, the policy directly fits each state-action pair in the offline dataset, which may be too restrictive. There may be a portion of actions under a state s in the offline dataset that can only be accessed with low probability, and learning this portion of actions to bring the current policy close to the behavior policy may degrade policy performance, which is inconsistent with the concept of policy support constraint.

Support constraint has been proposed and used in previous works [7,13] as an effective method to solve the problem of distributional shift. The support constraint can be interpreted as only selecting actions with an action density greater than a certain threshold ε for the currently trained policy π_θ under a certain state s, i.e.

$$\forall a, \pi_\beta(a \mid s) < \varepsilon \rightarrow \pi_\theta(a \mid s) = 0.$$
(8)

We will therefore design a behavior cloning term so that it satisfies the concept of support constraint.

4.2   Practical Implementation

Diffusion-Based Behavior Policy. We train a generative model by supervised learning to fit the data distribution and this model serves as an estimated behavior policy. To satisfy the support constraint, we only allow the trained policy to take actions from the output space of this model.

The choice of generative model is critical and a good model needs to correctly cover the space of state-actions pairs while avoiding learning out-of-distribution actions. Currently, there are some algorithms that explicitly model behavior policy to solve problems in offline reinforcement learning. Some methods choose the Gaussian model [29] or conditional VAE [6,7] as the behavior policy, but their effects may be limited by the expressive ability of the model itself. Recently, diffusion models have demonstrated great capabilities in image generation. Their successful use in offline reinforcement learning [1,25] has also demonstrated the advantages over other models.

Therefore, we pre-train the diffusion model as a behavior policy to implement the behavior cloning term. We train a conditional diffusion model based on the simplified training objective in DDPM paper [8]:

$$\mathcal{L}_d\left(\hat{\beta}\right) = \mathbb{E}_{t\sim\mathcal{U}(1,T),\epsilon\sim\mathcal{N}(0,I),(s,a)\sim D}\left[\left\|\epsilon - \epsilon_{\hat{\beta}}\left(\sqrt{\bar{\alpha}_t}a + \sqrt{1-\bar{\alpha}_t}\epsilon, s, t\right)\right\|^2\right], \quad (9)$$

where T is the number of diffusion model timesteps and t is taken from a uniform distribution between 1 and T. The training objective is to make the noise predicted by the neural network identical to the real noise. The process of sampling an action from the diffusion model is as follows: first sample a noise as the initial action $a_T \sim \mathcal{N}(0,I)$, and then go through the reverse diffusion process, for $t = T, ..., 1$:

$$a_{t-1} = \frac{1}{\sqrt{\alpha_t}}\left(a_t - \frac{1-\alpha_t}{\sqrt{1-\bar{\alpha}_t}}\epsilon_{\hat{\beta}}\left(a_t, s, t\right)\right) + \sigma_t z, z \sim \mathcal{N}(0,I). \quad (10)$$

Policy Evaluation. For a given state s, we replace the actions in the offline dataset with the actions generated by the diffusion model. The diffusion model defines a support set of state-action pairs and selects an arbitrary high-probability action from the in-support dataset at a given state, as shown in Eq. 11. Here $\pi_{\hat{\beta}}$ refers to the above conditional diffusion model:

$$\underset{\theta}{\mathrm{argmax}}\,\mathbb{E}_{(s,a)\sim D}\left[\frac{Q\left(s,\pi_\theta\left(s\right)\right)}{\frac{1}{N}\sum_{(s_i,a_i)}|Q\left(s_i,a_i\right)|} - \alpha\left(\pi_\theta\left(s\right) - \pi_{\hat{\beta}}\left(s\right)\right)^2\right]. \quad (11)$$

Policy Improvement. We use the action generated by the diffusion model as a warm-start for Q-value update as shown in Eq. 12:

$$\underset{\phi}{\mathrm{argmin}}\,\mathbb{E}_{(s,a,r,s')\sim D}\left[\left(\left(r\left(s,a\right) + \gamma\mathbb{E}_{a'\sim\pi_{\hat{\beta}}(a'|s')}\left[Q_{\phi'}\left(s',a'\right)\right]\right) - Q_\phi\left(s,a\right)\right)^2\right], \quad (12)$$

which ensures that the action taken in the next state is within the support set and the Q-values are not overestimated. And the policy evaluation after step t is the same as in Eq. 1. The algorithm flow is summarized in Algorithm 1.

Algorithm 1. TD3 + diffusion-based BC

// *Pre-training the diffusion model as behavior policy*
Initialize diffusion model $\epsilon_{\hat{\beta}}$
for $t = 1$ to T_1 **do**
    Sample mini-batch (s, a) from dataset D
    Update diffusion model by minimizing Equation 9
end for
// *Training Q-value function and policy*
Initialize policy network π_θ, critic networks Q_{ϕ_1}, Q_{ϕ_2} and target networks $\pi_{\theta'}$, $Q_{\phi_1'}$,
$Q_{\phi_2'}$, $\theta' \leftarrow \theta, \phi_1' \leftarrow \phi_1, \phi_2' \leftarrow \phi_2$
for $t = 1$ to T_2 **do**
    Sample mini-batch (s, a, r, s') from dataset D
    if $t < \frac{1}{10}T_2$ **then**
        Update Q_{ϕ_1} and Q_{ϕ_2} by minimizing Equation 12
    else
        Update Q_{ϕ_1} and Q_{ϕ_2} by performing policy evaluation step in Equation 1
    end if
    if $t\%d$ **then**
        Sample M $a \sim \pi_{\hat{\beta}}(a \mid s)$ by Equation 10
        Update policy by minimizing Equation 11
        Update target networks $\theta' \leftarrow \tau\theta' + (1 - \tau)\theta$, $\phi_i' \leftarrow \tau\phi_i' + (1 - \tau)\phi_i$ for $i = 1, 2$
    end if
end for

---

5   Experiments

5.1   Performance on D4RL Benchmark

Datasets. We conduct experiments on three Gym-Mujoco tasks (Halfcheetah, Hopper, Walker2d) in the D4RL benchmark [3], each containing three quality datasets:

- **medium:** dataset collected from a policy that uses the online SAC algorithm and achieves $1/3$ performance on the expert dataset by early stopping.
- **medium-replay:** dataset consisting of the replay buffer of a policy trained up to medium performance using online SAC.
- **medium-expert:** dataset containing half medium dataset and half expert dataset.

Baselines. We compare TD3+diffusion-based BC proposed in this paper with a number of model-free offline reinforcement learning algorithms, including (1) BC, %BC [2], which are classic behavior cloning methods; (2) CQL [14], which learns conservative Q function by minimizing the Q-values of OOD actions; (3) IQL [12], which uses in-sample actions exclusively; (4) TD3+BC [4], which adds a behavior cloning term as a policy constraint term; and (5) Diffusion-QL [25], which trains a diffusion model as the policy to achieve parameterization constraint. We obtain results of Diffusion-QL algorithm on the "-v2" datasets from Diffusion-QL paper [25] and the results of other algorithms on the same datasets from IQL paper [12].

Table 1 presents the experimental results compared with different benchmark algorithms. Each environment is trained for 1M gradient steps. The results indicate that our algorithm matches or exceeds benchmark algorithms in most environments. Additionally, results using a warm-start step outperform the algorithm without this step in a portion of the environments. In contrast to parameterization constraint method Diffusion-QL, our algorithm takes advantage of the diffusion model's ability to capture data distributions by pre-training, while designing a behavior cloning term as a regularization term to avoid direct policy modeling. Our approach uses less time for training and is convenient for subsequent migration or online fine-tuning.

Table 1. Normalized scores for all methods on Gym-Mujoco task. Our method shows the mean and standard deviation under 5 random seeds. Scores within the top 5% of each task are highlighted in bold. "w-s" is short for warm-start.

Dataset(v2)	BC	%10BC	CQL	IQL	TD3+BC	Diffusion-QL	Ours (w/o w-s)	Ours (w/ w-s)
halfcheetah-m	42.6	42.5	44.0	47.4	48.3	51.5	**58.6±0.5**	**58.7±0.1**
hopper-m	52.9	56.9	58.5	66.3	59.3	**96.6**	95.6±5.6	**98.6±4.8**
walker2d-m	75.3	75.0	72.5	78.3	**83.7**	87.3	86.1±1.1	83.7±2.4
halfcheetah-m-r	36.6	40.6	45.5	44.2	44.6	48.3	55±1.1	55.9±1.4
hopper-m-r	18.1	75.9	95.0	94.7	60.9	**102.0**	101.9±0.2	97.1±8.5
walker2d-m-r	26.0	62.5	77.2	73.9	81.8	**98.0**	90.4±1.6	96.8±2.5
halfcheetah-m-e	55.2	**92.9**	91.6	86.7	90.7	**97.2**	92.4±0.5	88.2±0.4
hopper-m-e	52.5	110.9	105.4	91.5	98.0	112.3	110.2±3.1	**111.4±0.1**
walker2d-m-e	107.5	109.0	108.8	109.6	110.1	**111.2**	108.6±0.8	108.6±0.4

5.2   Ablation Study

Diffusion vs. VAE We compare the training results with the VAE and diffusion models. The parameter settings are the same except for a different choice of the generative model, and the results are shown in Fig. 1. It can be seen that the results using the diffusion model in "hopper" environments are significantly better than those of the VAE model, which demonstrates that the choice of generative model is crucial and that the generative model needs to accurately determine the support set of state-action pairs to avoid accessing out-of-distribution actions.

Effect of Hyperparameter α α is an important parameter for weighing reinforcement learning and behavior cloning. Here we further adjust the parameter by choosing from four values $\{0.05, 0.1, 0.5, 1.0\}$. The optimal choice of parameter α for each environment is shown in Table 2.

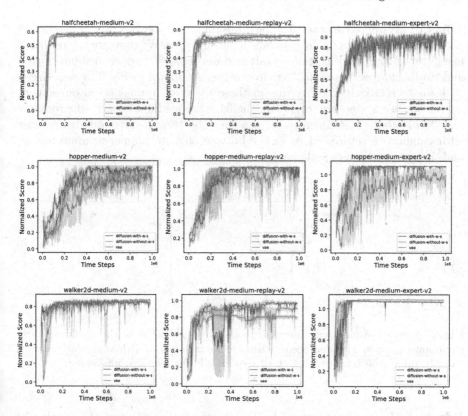

Fig. 1. Ablation studies with different generative models. We show the results in all Gym-Mujoco environments under 5 random seeds.

Table 2. Selection of hyperparameter α in all Gym-Mujoco environments.

Dataset(v2)	α
halfcheetah-medium	0.05
hopper-medium	0.1
walker2d-medium	1
halfcheetah-medium-replay	0.05
hopper-medium-replay	0.1
walker2d-medium-replay	0.1
halfcheetah-medium-expert	1
hopper-medium-expert	0.5
walker2d-medium-expert	1

Effect of Hyperparameter T. The diffusion model step size T is an important parameter that affects model generation performance. We compare the results of using steps $\{15, 25, 50\}$ in "halfcheetah-medium-replay", "hopper-medium-replay" and "walker2d-medium-replay" environments. As shown in Fig. 2, a step size of 25 leads to relatively good results in these three environments. In our experiments, we use a step size of 100 in "halfcheetah-medium-expert" environment and 25 in other environments. We use the %bc trick to filter out trajectories with cumulative return values in the bottom 50% in "hopper-medium-replay" and "hopper-medium-expert" environments.

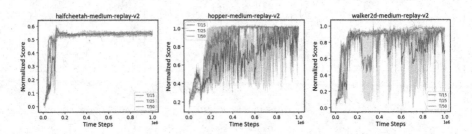

Fig. 2. Ablation studies with diffusion model steps T. We show the results in three environments under 3 random seeds, where we use trajectories with a cumulative return value in the top 50% for training at all step sizes in "hopper-medium-replay".

Effect of Hyperparameter M. We investigate the effect of the number of samples M. We conduct experiments with different numbers of sampling actions $\{1, 2, 3, 5\}$ in "hopper" environments and present the results in Fig. 3. Since we obtain similar results for all the hyperparameters tested, we choose a sampling size of 3 in all environments.

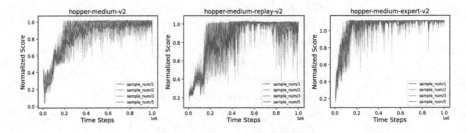

Fig. 3. Ablation studies with the number of samples M. We show the results in three environments under 3 random seeds.

6   Conclusion

In this paper, we propose the TD3+diffusion-based BC algorithm, which combines the benefits of reinforcement learning and behavior cloning. First, we use the conditional diffusion model, which has a powerful ability to generate data, to learn the distribution of the offline dataset collected by hybrid policies. Then, we design a behavior cloning term with the diffusion model as a regularization constraint, which implicitly achieves support set matching, avoids selecting actions that are out of distribution, and relaxes the strict requirement of fitting each state-action pair. We evaluate our algorithm on the D4RL benchmark and show that it matches or surpasses state-of-the-art algorithms in most tasks.

In the future, we consider further improving the policy by combining the method of uncertainty estimation. Multiple diffusion models are pre-trained as behavior policies to compensate for the inaccuracy of single model estimation.

Acknowledgements. This work was supported by the National Natural Science Foundation of China under Grant 62206013.

References

1. Chen, H., Lu, C., Ying, C., Su, H., Zhu, J.: Offline reinforcement learning via high-fidelity generative behavior modeling. ArXiv abs/2209.14548 (2022)
2. Emmons, S., Eysenbach, B., Kostrikov, I., Levine, S.: Rvs: what is essential for offline RL via supervised learning? In: International Conference on Learning Representations (2022)
3. Fu, J., Kumar, A., Nachum, O., Tucker, G., Levine, S.: D4rl: datasets for deep data-driven reinforcement learning. arXiv preprint arXiv:2004.07219 (2020)
4. Fujimoto, S., Gu, S.S.: A minimalist approach to offline reinforcement learning. Adv. Neural. Inf. Process. Syst. **34**, 20132–20145 (2021)
5. Fujimoto, S., Hoof, H., Meger, D.: Addressing function approximation error in actor-critic methods. In: International Conference on Machine Learning, pp. 1587–1596. PMLR (2018)
6. Fujimoto, S., Meger, D., Precup, D.: Off-policy deep reinforcement learning without exploration. In: International Conference on Machine Learning, pp. 2052–2062. PMLR (2019)
7. Ghasemipour, S.K.S., Schuurmans, D., Gu, S.S.: Emaq: expected-max q-learning operator for simple yet effective offline and online RL. In: International Conference on Machine Learning, pp. 3682–3691. PMLR (2021)
8. Ho, J., Jain, A., Abbeel, P.: Denoising diffusion probabilistic models. Adv. Neural. Inf. Process. Syst. **33**, 6840–6851 (2020)
9. Janner, M., Du, Y., Tenenbaum, J., Levine, S.: Planning with diffusion for flexible behavior synthesis. In: International Conference on Machine Learning (2022)
10. Kidambi, R., Rajeswaran, A., Netrapalli, P., Joachims, T.: Morel: model-based offline reinforcement learning. Adv. Neural. Inf. Process. Syst. **33**, 21810–21823 (2020)
11. Kostrikov, I., Fergus, R., Tompson, J., Nachum, O.: Offline reinforcement learning with fisher divergence critic regularization. In: International Conference on Machine Learning, pp. 5774–5783. PMLR (2021)

12. Kostrikov, I., Nair, A., Levine, S.: Offline reinforcement learning with implicit q-learning. In: International Conference on Learning Representations (2022)
13. Kumar, A., Fu, J., Soh, M., Tucker, G., Levine, S.: Stabilizing off-policy q-learning via bootstrapping error reduction. Advances in Neural Information Processing Systems 32 (2019)
14. Kumar, A., Zhou, A., Tucker, G., Levine, S.: Conservative q-learning for offline reinforcement learning. Adv. Neural. Inf. Process. Syst. **33**, 1179–1191 (2020)
15. Lv, K., Sheng, H., Xiong, Z., Li, W., Zheng, L.: Pose-based view synthesis for vehicles: a perspective aware method. IEEE Trans. Image Process. **29**, 5163–5174 (2020)
16. Lv, K., Sheng, H., Xiong, Z., Li, W., Zheng, L.: Improving driver gaze prediction with reinforced attention. IEEE Trans. Multim. **23**, 4198–4207 (2021)
17. Lyu, J., Li, X., Lu, Z.: Double check your state before trusting it: Confidence-aware bidirectional offline model-based imagination. In: Advances in Neural Information Processing Systems (2022)
18. Nair, A., Dalal, M., Gupta, A., Levine, S.: Accelerating online reinforcement learning with offline datasets. ArXiv abs/2006.09359 (2020)
19. Peng, X.B., Kumar, A., Zhang, G., Levine, S.: Advantage-weighted regression: Simple and scalable off-policy reinforcement learning. ArXiv abs/1910.00177 (2019)
20. Sheng, H., Lv, K., Liu, Y., Ke, W., Lyu, W., Xiong, Z., Li, W.: Combining pose invariant and discriminative features for vehicle reidentification. IEEE Internet Things J. **8**(5), 3189–3200 (2021)
21. Sinha, S., Mandlekar, A., Garg, A.: S4rl: surprisingly simple self-supervision for offline reinforcement learning in robotics. In: Conference on Robot Learning, pp. 907–917. PMLR (2022)
22. Song, Y., Sohl-Dickstein, J., Kingma, D.P., Kumar, A., Ermon, S., Poole, B.: Score-based generative modeling through stochastic differential equations. In: International Conference on Learning Representations (2021)
23. Wang, J., Li, W., Jiang, H., Zhu, G., Li, S., Zhang, C.: Offline reinforcement learning with reverse model-based imagination. Adv. Neural. Inf. Process. Syst. **34**, 29420–29432 (2021)
24. Wang, S., Wu, Z., Hu, X., Lin, Y., Lv, K.: Skill-based hierarchical reinforcement learning for target visual navigation. IEEE Trans. Multimed., 1–13 (2023). https://doi.org/10.1109/TMM.2023.3243618
25. Wang, Z., Hunt, J.J., Zhou, M.: Diffusion policies as an expressive policy class for offline reinforcement learning. arXiv preprint arXiv:2208.06193 (2022)
26. Wu, Y., Tucker, G., Nachum, O.: Behavior regularized offline reinforcement learning. arXiv preprint arXiv:1911.11361 (2019)
27. Yu, T., Thomas, G., Yu, L., Ermon, S., Zou, J.Y., Levine, S., Finn, C., Ma, T.: MOPO: model-based offline policy optimization. Adv. Neural. Inf. Process. Syst. **33**, 14129–14142 (2020)
28. Zhang, H., Lin, Y., Han, S., Lv, K.: Lexicographic actor-critic deep reinforcement learning for urban autonomous driving. IEEE Trans. Veh. Technol. **72**(4), 4308–4319 (2023)
29. Zhuang, Z., Lei, K., Liu, J., Wang, D., Guo, Y.: Behavior proximal policy optimization. arXiv preprint arXiv:2302.11312 (2023)

Evolutionary Verbalizer Search for Prompt-Based Few Shot Text Classification

Tongtao Ling, Lei Chen$^{(\boxtimes)}$ [ID], Yutao Lai, and Hai-Lin Liu [ID]

Guangdong University of Technology, Guangzhou, China
{chenlei3,hlliu}@gdut.edu.cn

Abstract. Recent advances for few-shot text classification aim to wrap textual inputs with task-specific prompts to cloze questions. By processing them with a masked language model to predict the masked tokens and using a verbalizer that constructs the mapping between predicted words and target labels. This approach of using pre-trained language models is called prompt-based tuning, which could remarkably outperform conventional fine-tuning approach in the low-data scenario. As the core of prompt-based tuning, the verbalizer is usually handcrafted with human efforts or suboptimally searched by gradient descent. In this paper, we focus on automatically constructing the optimal verbalizer and propose a novel evolutionary verbalizer search (EVS) algorithm, to improve prompt-based tuning with the high-performance verbalizer. Specifically, inspired by evolutionary algorithm (EA), we utilize it to automatically evolve various verbalizers during the evolutionary procedure and select the best one after several iterations. Extensive few-shot experiments on five text classification datasets show the effectiveness of our method.

Keywords: Few-shot text classification · Prompt-based tuning · Evolutionary algorithm

1 Introduction

In recent years, pre-trained language models (PLMs) [3] have achieved great success in NLP tasks such as natural language understanding and natural language generation. The conventional method of utilizing PLMs for downstream tasks is fine-tuning, where we add a classifier to the top of PLMs and further train on sufficient labeled data [8]. Fine-tuning achieves satisfactory results on supervised downstream tasks. However, since the additional classifier requires sufficient training instances for fitting, it can not replicate the same success in low-resource scenarios (zero and few-shot tasks). In addition, training the additional classifier is usually difficult due to the gap between pre-trained tasks (e.g., masked language modeling) and downstream tasks (e.g., text classification). To this end, prompt-tuning, a novel paradigm of NLP has risen to be a powerful way for low-resource works to narrow the gap between pre-trained stage and downstream tasks stage [18].

© The Author(s), under exclusive license to Springer Nature Switzerland AG 2023
Z. Jin et al. (Eds.): KSEM 2023, LNAI 14120, pp. 279–290, 2023.
https://doi.org/10.1007/978-3-031-40292-0_23

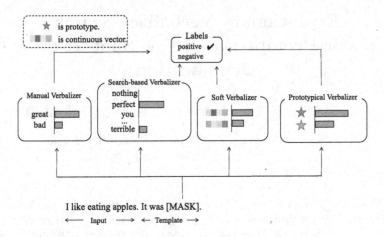

Fig. 1. Illustration of current verbalizer construction methods.

The core of prompt-tuning is to re-formalize a classification task to a cloze-style task. For example, in a sentiment classification task, given an original input sentence "I like eating apples", we add a task-specific prompt (also called template) "It is [MASK]" after the sentence, then the PLMs will predict the token [MASK] token and the token is further mapped to the target label by a **verbalizer** (e.g., "great" to "positive"). Verbalizer can be seen as a mapping function from label word (label word means the set of predicted words corresponding labels) space to label space. It is the connection between [MASK] token outputs and final predicted results [6]. Since the verbalizer can directly determine the effectiveness of the classification result, how to construct the verbalizer is a critical issue in prompt-tuning [12].

Recently, the construction of verbalizer is mainly divided into the following categories: manual verbalizer, search-based verbalizer, soft verbalizer, and prototypical verbalizer. We show an illustration of them in Fig. 1. The most commonly used verbalizer is the manual verbalizer, which can be divided into two categories: One2One and One2Many. One2One verbalizer means that each label only has one label word, which requires human effort and domain knowledge to select the best label word. But One2One limits the coverage of label words because it cannot summarize the semantic information of the label using one label word. Therefore, to enrich the semantic information of label words for a specific label, [9] proposes to select some related words from a large knowledge base to construct the One2Many verbalizer, which has multiple label words for each label. These approaches can greatly improve the semantics of labels, but related words of the different label may overlap, which expect human efforts to filter some overlapped words and select the remaining suitable words to construct a task-specific verbalizer. To solve these issues, search-based verbalizer aims to find suitable label words with various algorithms [17] and soft verbalizer treats label words as trainable tokens which are optimized in the training process [7].

However, when the amount of annotated data is not sufficient, the search-based is not necessarily better than the manual verbalizer. To this end, the prototypical verbalizer aims to obtain a semantic representation of labels and project the hidden vectors of [MASK] to the embedding space and learn prototypes with few data for each label to serve as a verbalizer. Despite these efforts, the challenge of obtaining the high-performance verbalizer under low-resource scenario for prompt-tuning still exists, and previous works pointed out that the current gradient-based verbalizer search is usually suboptimal [12].

It is challenging to automatically find the optimal verbalizer for prompt-tuning. Inspired by the Evolutionary Algorithm (EA) [1], we propose a novel search-based verbalizer approach for this purpose. Evolutionary algorithms are a kind of metaheuristic method inspired by natural population evolution. Compared to the traditional gradient-based search, EA can conduct a more robust and global search by leveraging the internal parallelism of the search population. To search for optimal label words as verbalizer, in this paper, we introduce a novel Evolutionary Verbalizer Search (EVS) algorithm to find the optimal One2Many verbalizer for text classification on a tiny set of labeled data. EVS does not require updating any model parameters because it relies on a small development set for validation rather than training. To verify the effectiveness of the proposed EVC, extensive experimental studies are conducted on benchmark datasets, and the experimental results are compared with various verbalizes. Our experiments show that EVS can achieve substantial improvements over the baseline of manual verbalizer and other search-based verbalizers, and it also outperformed the other state-of-the-art verbalizers.

In summary, the main contributions of this paper are as follows:

- We design a novel evolutionary verbalizer search algorithm that can automatically find the high-performance verbalizer on a small development set.
- For the few-shot scenario, we conduct experiments with other state-of-the-art verbalizers, and our proposed methods outperform other existing search-based verbalizers in the same few-shot setting and achieve similar performance with manual verbalizers.
- We carefully investigate the effects of hyperparameters in the proposed method. And we also find that our searched verbalizers are semantically related to the corresponding class.

2   Related Work

In this section, the related work to this study is introduced briefly.

2.1   Verbalizer Construction

In this paper, we investigate the search-based method for verbalizer construction in prompt-tuning. As a crucial component of prompt-tuning, verbalizer aims to transform model outputs to target labels and has a strong influence on the

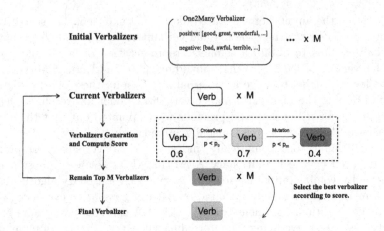

Fig. 2. Illustrative procedure of EVS algorithm. The core of EVS is borrowed from evolutionary algorithm.

performance of prompt-tuning [6]. Most previous works focused on manual verbalizers, which require manual elaboration and enough human prior knowledge. To avoid the drawbacks of manual verbalizers, some studies propose to construct an automatic verbalizer by using search-based methods [17], which are expected to find suitable label words during the training process. In addition to using discrete words to construct verbalizers, soft verbalizers have been proposed by [7], which treat labels as trainable tokens and optimize in the training process. Some other works design prototypical verbalizers [2,19], which learn prototype vectors as verbalizers by contrastive learning.

2.2   Evolutionary Algorithm

Due to the properties of gradient-free and highly parallelism, Evolutionary Algorithm (EA) [1] has been applied to extensive applications. For instance, automated machine learning (AutoML), a typical combination of deep learning techniques and evolutionary algorithms, has demonstrated promising results in the areas of parameter optimization and neural architecture search (NAS) [5]. More than that, EAs have been applied to NLP tasks successfully. [15] use classical NLP methods incorporated with Genetic Programming (GP) to predict the next words with an input word. Furthermore, the complementary relationship between large language models and evolutionary computing is discussed in [10]. However, this field is still worth exploring like how to leverage the benefits of EA for NLP tasks effectively.

3   Evolutionary Verbalizer Search

In this section, the core idea of the proposed Evolutionary Verbalizer Search (EVS) is introduced first, and then the verbalizer generation strategies are given in detail.

3.1   Encoding and Decoding

To conduct an evolutionary verbalizer search, proper encoding and decoding methods are first needed. Formally, denote $\mathcal{M}$, $\mathcal{T}$ as a masked language model (MLM) and a task-specific template function, respectively. We first sample a tiny labeled data as development set D_{dev} and each instance x in D_{dev} is wrapped by $\mathcal{T}$ with a [MASK] token, the prompt input can be formulated as:

$$x_t = \mathcal{T}(x) \tag{1}$$

Then, we input x_t into $\mathcal{M}$ to compute the hidden vectors of [MASK] token $h_{[mask]} \in \mathbb{R}^V$, which represents the probability distribution of the whole vocabulary. It can be calculated as:

$$h_{[mask]} = \mathcal{M}(x_t) \tag{2}$$

where V is the vocabulary size. In EVS, we input the whole D_{dev} to $\mathcal{M}$ and compute each label average representation $h^i_{[mask]} \in \mathbb{R}^V$, $i \in \{label_1, ..., label_N\}$, N is the number of labels. So we can get the initialized matrix $h_{init} \in \mathbb{R}^{N \times V}$. After that, let N_c be the number of candidates for each label, which means that we need to select label words from candidates. Then, for each $label_i$, $i \in N$, we sort the elements of $h^i_{[mask]}$ and select top N_c candidates to acquire $h^i_c \in \mathbb{R}^{N_c}$. The encoding matrix can be computed as follows:

$$h_{encode} = \begin{bmatrix} h^1_c \\ \vdots \\ h^N_c \end{bmatrix}, h_{encode} \in \mathbb{R}^{N \times N_c} \tag{3}$$

After that, we use a square matrix $X^* \in \mathbb{R}^{N_c \times N_c}$ to multiply h_{encode} as decoding:

$$h_{decode} = h_{encode} \cdot X^*, h_{decode} \in \mathbb{R}^{N \times N_c} \tag{4}$$

Finally, let N_l be the number of label words for each label, which represents the number of label words we expect to choose. And we also sort the elements of h^i_c and memorize the index of vocabulary, then we select top N_l elements to acquire $\hat{h}^i_c \in \mathbb{R}^{N_l}$ and change it into corresponding words by indexes. The decoding verbalizer is defined as:

$$h^* = \begin{bmatrix} \hat{h}^1_c \\ \vdots \\ \hat{h}^N_c \end{bmatrix} = \begin{bmatrix} w_{11} & \cdots & w_{1N_l} \\ \vdots & \ddots & \vdots \\ w_{N1} & \cdots & w_{NN_l} \end{bmatrix}, h^* \in \mathbb{R}^{N \times N_l} \tag{5}$$

where w means the label word.

Algorithm 1: Evolutionary Procedure

---

1 **Input:** S^0; D_{dev}; f; M; N_{iter}; P_m; P_c;
2 **Output:** The best optimized individual: X^* ;
3 Initialize population $S^0 = \{X_1, ..., X_M\}$; $n = 0$;
4 **while** $n < N_{iter}$ **do**
5   compute score of $X_i \in S^n$ using f and remain top M individuals;
6   Initialize a new empty population $S_{new} = \{\}$; $m = 0$;
7   **while** $m < M$ **do**
8   select two individuals X_i, X_j from S^n ;
9   **if** *random(0,1)* $< P_c$ **then**
10              $X_{i,j}^C = $ Crossover(X_i, X_j);
11   **if** *random(0,1)* $< P_m$ **then**
12                  $X_{i,j}^M = $ Mutation($X_{i,j}^C$) and add $X_{i,j}^M$ in S_{new};
13   **else**
14   add $X_{i,j}^C$ in S_{new};
15   **end**
16   **end**
17          $m = m + 1$;
18   **end**
19      $S^{n+1} = S^n + S_{new}$;
20      $n = n + 1$;
21 **end**
22 from $S^N = \{X_*^1, ..., X_*^N\}$, select the best individual X^*;
23 **return** X^*;

3.2 Population Evaluation

We formalize $X_k \in \mathbb{R}^{N_c \times N_c}, k \in \{1, M\}$, as an individual in population, M is the population size. To conduct the environmental selection, all members of the search population are evaluated. Our aim is to obtain the best X^* during the evolutionary procedure. The procedure is described in **Algorithm 1**.

In the initialization of the evolutionary procedure, S^0 is an initialized population and f is the fitness function to compute the score of each individual X_k and rank by the score to decide which individual will be reserved or eliminated at each iteration. Specifically, we use X_k to get verbalizer by Eq. 4 and Eq. 5 and subsequently evaluate on the validation set to compute accuracy as fitness score. N_{iter} is the maximum number of iterations. P_m and P_c are mutation probability and crossover probability, respectively.

The core of the evolutionary process is to reproduce the current generation of individuals and use the fitness function to select elite individuals iteratively. For each iteration, we firstly compute scores of $X_k \in S^n$ by using f and remain top M individuals. Then, we create a new empty set to store the generation of individuals. In the process of generation, we use the Roulette Wheel Selection algorithm [1] to select two individuals from S^n and generate new individuals by crossover and mutation with probability. The new generation will be added in S^n and continue to iterate until the population has doubled in size.

After several steps of evolutionary search, we will collect the optimal individual X^* from the final population and use Eq. 4 and Eq. 5 to obtain the final verbalizer. We show an illustration in Fig. 2.

3.3 Verbalizer Generation Strategies

In the evolutionary verbalizer search, new verbalizers are generated in each generation, and the following verbalizer generation strategies are designed.

Crossover Operator. The Crossover operator is the process by which two individuals exchange some of their genes with each other in some way based on the crossover probability. The crossover operation plays a key role in EA and is the main method for generating new individuals. In the process of biological evolution, the probability of crossover is higher. In EVS, P_c is set to 0.8. We randomly swap the elements of two rows of the matrix X_k to obtain a new individual.

Mutation Operator. A mutation operator is the replacement of some gene values in an individual with other gene values based on the probability of mutation, resulting in a new individual. P_m is set to 0.1. We randomly initialize a matrix X_m with the same shape as X_k and these two matrices are multiplied together to obtain a new individual.

4 Experiments

The optimal result of EVS is **EvoVerb**. We conducted our experiments on five text classification datasets under few-shot settings to demonstrate the effectiveness of **EvoVerb**. In this section, we first describe the dataset and experimental settings. Then, we analyze and discuss the experimental results.

4.1 Experimental Settings

Dataset. We conduct our experiment on five text classification benchmark datasets, including three topic classification datasets (AG's News [20], DBPedia [11], and Yahoo [20]) and two sentiment classification datasets (IMDB [14] and Amazon [16]). For Amazon, we randomly select 10000 instances from the original test set to construct a new test set. The statistics of each dataset are shown in Table 1.

Template. Due to the rich prior knowledge of human-picked templates, manual templates are better than auto-generated templates in few-shot settings. Following the previous works [9], we use the same four manual templates for each dataset. We test all baselines and our method by using four manual templates, and report both the average results (with standard error) of the four templates and the results of the best template.

Evaluation. We use accuracy as micro-F1 for our experiments. We repeat 5 times with 5 different random seeds.

Table 1. The statistics of each dataset.

Dataset	Type	#Class	#Training Size	#Test Size
AG's News	Topic	4	120000	7600
DBPedia	Topic	14	560000	70000
Yahoo	Topic	10	1400000	60000
Amazon	Sentiment	2	3600000	10000
IMDB	Sentiment	2	25000	25000

4.2 Baselines

To verify the effectiveness of our method, we compare our method under few-shot setting with various approaches: fine-tuning, prompt-tuning with various state-of-the-art verbalizers. Fine-tuning, which uses the last layer's hidden state of [CLS] to a classification layer to make predictions. For prompt-tuning, we compare with: (1) **One2OneVerb**, using the class name as the only one label word for each class; (2) **One2ManyVerb**, using multiple label words for each class; (3) **KnowVerb** [9], which selects related words from the large knowledge base to construct One2ManyVerb; (4) **AutoVerb** [17], searching label words from vocabulary automatically, which maximizes the likelihood of the training data; (5) **SoftVerb** [7], which treats the label words as trainable tokens and optimizes it with cross-entropy loss in the training processing; (6) **ProtoVerb** [2] learns prototype vectors as verbalizers by contrastive learning. The prototypes summarize training instances and can include rich label-level semantics.

4.3 Implementation Details

All our experiments are based on Transformers[1] and OpenPrompt [4] framework. We employ RoBERTa-large [13] as our pre-trained language model backbone and use AdamW optimizer with learning rate 3e-5 to optimize it. For few-shot setting, we conduct 1,4,8,16-shot experiments. For a *k-shot* experiment, we sample k instances of each class from the original training set to form the few-shot training set and sample another k instances per class to form the validation set. The max sequence length is set to 256, and we train the model for 5 epochs with the batch size set to 8 and choose the best checkpoint in validation set for each experiment. In EVS, the validation set is also used as the development set to search verbalizers. The size of population is set to 30 and the maximum iteration is set to 5. N_c and N_l are set to 1000 and 100 respectively. We run all experiments using PyTorch 1.7.0 on a single Nvidia RTX 3090 GPU. Our code is available at https://github.com/rickltt/evs.

---

[1] https://github.com/huggingface/transformers.

Table 2. Micro-F1 and standard deviation on five text classification datasets. **Bold**: best results in brackets and the best results among all methods for the same k-shot experiment.

K	Verbalizer	AG's News	DBPedia	Yahoo	Amazon	IMDB
1 shot	Fine-tuning	29.5 ± 5.4 (35.3)	26.6 ± 1.6 (31.3)	13.1 ± 3.3 (16.6)	45.5 ± 4.2 (50.4)	51.4 ± 2.4 (54.6)
	One2OneVerb	71.9 ± 7.2 (81.4)	87.0 ± 1.0 (88.4)	49.3 ± 1.2 (51.4)	89.1 ± 3.1 (92.1)	86.0 ± 3.3 (89.7)
	One2ManyVerb	74.3 ± 7.6 (**82.8**)	89.8 ± 2.5 (92.3)	50.9 ± 1.8 (52.6)	88.7 ± 3.0 (91.6)	88.4 ± 6.4 (**93.0**)
	KnowVerb	**75.7** ± 3.6 (78.4)	**90.3** ± 3.7 (**93.6**)	**61.4** ± 3.6 (**63.5**)	**89.4** ± 4.2 (**92.8**)	**91.4** ± 2.4 (92.7)
	AutoVerb	55.9 ± 2.8 (60.4)	77.1 ± 1.7 (79.5)	22.9 ± 4.2 (26.8)	65.7 ± 9.3 (73.2)	72.4 ± 7.1 (79.9)
	SoftVerb	65.1 ± 3.2 (68.8)	62.9 ± 1.7 (65.7)	32.5 ± 5.1 (37.2)	71.7 ± 2.5 (74.2)	79.1 ± 3.4 (82.2)
	ProtoVerb	64.3 ± 5.1 (72.4)	74.9 ± 4.0 (79.4)	48.3 ± 3.6 (51.4)	69.6 ± 4.7 (73.6)	79.3 ± 3.0 (83.5)
	EvoVerb (ours)	69.4 ± 3.4 (73.1)	72.8 ± 1.4 (74.1)	44.4 ± 3.2 (47.7)	73.4 ± 1.1 (73.9)	72.7 ± 1.5 (73.6)
4 shot	Fine-tuning	46.9 ± 3.2 (48.5)	91.6 ± 1.2 (92.3)	43.1 ± 8.2 (51.6)	53.5 ± 3.3 (56.4)	56.4 ± 1.4 (57.3)
	One2OneVerb	77.9 ± 1.9 (79.4)	94.2 ± 1.0 (95.8)	**62.8** ± 1.2 (64.7)	90.4 ± 1.8 (92.5)	87.4 ± 7.2 (91.9)
	One2ManyVerb	78.5 ± 4.2 (83.5)	94.3 ± 1.2 (96.0)	62.5 ± 2.6 (**65.5**)	93.1 ± 2.5 (93.6)	91.2 ± 1.1 (**93.5**)
	KnowVerb	80.4 ± 5.6 (**84.8**)	93.8 ± 2.5 (95.3)	61.9 ± 4.8 (64.6)	93.2 ± 1.2 (**94.1**)	91.8 ± 0.6 (92.2)
	AutoVerb	73.1 ± 1.8 (74.8)	92.4 ± 1.3 (94.0)	57.7 ± 3.3 (60.0)	87.8 ± 3.1 (91.2)	90.0 ± 3.7 (93.4)
	SoftVerb	76.9 ± 4.7 (81.5)	93.8 ± 1.6 (96.5)	48.4 ± 3.9 (54.7)	92.4 ± 2.5 (93.7)	87.1 ± 3.3 (90.6)
	ProtoVerb	79.6 ± 1.6 (82.3)	**95.5** ± 0.7 (96.2)	60.5 ± 3.9 (64.6)	90.2 ± 1.5 (92.0)	91.5 ± 2.5 (92.2)
	EvoVerb (ours)	**80.7** ± 1.7 (82.1)	94.6 ± 2.8 (**96.7**)	57.2 ± 4.1 (60.9)	**93.4** ± 1.4 (93.6)	**92.5** ± 1.7 (93.3)
8 shot	Fine-tuning	73.5 ± 4.4 (78.9)	92.5 ± 0.5 (93.2)	48.1 ± 2.5 (53.6)	83.8 ± 2.3 (86.7)	77.3 ± 3.7 (81.4)
	One2OneVerb	82.4 ± 2.0 (84.7)	95.9 ± 1.2 (97.2)	64.5 ± 0.3 (64.9)	90.5 ± 2.7 (92.2)	91.3 ± 1.4 (93.6)
	One2ManyVerb	84.3 ± 1.9 (86.9)	97.3 ± 0.7 (98.0)	64.4 ± 0.8 (65.5)	93.6 ± 0.6 (94.3)	91.1 ± 3.6 (93.2)
	KnowVerb	83.3 ± 5.6 (86.8)	89.8 ± 2.5 (92.3)	66.9 ± 1.8 (68.6)	93.7 ± 0.5 (94.2)	92.1 ± 1.3 (92.7)
	AutoVerb	80.0 ± 4.7 (85.2)	95.7 ± 2.0 (97.8)	60.5 ± 1.6 (62.5)	88.5 ± 8.4 (94.1)	91.6 ± 2.5 (92.9)
	SoftVerb	81.4 ± 1.9 (82.8)	96.5 ± 0.3 (97.0)	51.5 ± 6.5 (58.0)	91.0 ± 3.1 (93.0)	91.6 ± 0.7 (92.3)
	ProtoVerb	85.4 ± 1.9 (87.9)	97.4 ± 0.6 (**98.2**)	66.7 ± 1.2 (68.0)	92.4 ± 1.8 (94.4)	89.1 ± 5.0 (92.6)
	EvoVerb (ours)	**86.5** ± 1.5 (**88.1**)	**97.8** ± 0.3 (98.1)	**69.4** ± 0.7 (**69.9**)	**94.0** ± 1.1 (**94.5**)	**92.7** ± 1.6 (**93.7**)
16 shot	Fine-tuning	84.1 ± 3.5 (87.1)	95.6 ± 1.2 (96.3)	57.1 ± 2.7 (60.5)	85.3 ± 2.1 (88.6)	76.4 ± 1.4 (77.3)
	One2OneVerb	85.5 ± 1.6 (88.3)	97.5 ± 0.4 (98.2)	66.5 ± 1.7 (69.2)	**93.1** ± 0.7 (94.0)	92.1 ± 1.0 (92.8)
	One2ManyVerb	86.9 ± 0.8 (87.7)	97.3 ± 0.6 (98.0)	65.9 ± 3.1 (69.1)	90.6 ± 3.3 (94.4)	92.3 ± 5.2 (**93.9**)
	KnowVerb	85.2 ± 4.6 (86.8)	97.8 ± 1.5 (97.8)	68.1 ± 0.9 (68.6)	91.7 ± 2.4 (93.6)	91.4 ± 1.4 (92.7)
	AutoVerb	86.6 ± 2.7 (88.0)	96.2 ± 2.0 (97.7)	64.4 ± 1.8 (67.5)	92.9 ± 1.7 (93.9)	91.5 ± 2.4 (93.1)
	SoftVerb	85.6 ± 0.9 (86.6)	97.8 ± 0.1 (98.0)	62.8 ± 1.8 (64.5)	91.0 ± 3.1 (94.2)	90.4 ± 4.4 (93.7)
	ProtoVerb	85.7 ± 1.6 (87.3)	97.3 ± 0.7 (98.2)	69.0 ± 1.1 (70.2)	92.5 ± 1.7 (**94.5**)	89.7 ± 1.6 (92.6)
	EvoVerb (ours)	**87.2** ± 0.6 (**88.6**)	**98.0** ± 0.4 (**98.3**)	**70.3** ± 0.7 (**70.7**)	93.4 ± 2.3 (93.7)	**93.2** ± 1.4 (93.5)

4.4 Results

In this part, we analyze the results of few-shot experiments with different verbalizers and provide insights of EvoVerb.

From Table 2, we find out that all prompt-based methods outperform fine-tuning methods under five datasets. The gap is decreasing as the shot increases. Compared to other baseline verbalizers, One2ManyVerb performs slightly better than One2OneVerb and KnowVerb wins over One2ManyVerb by a slight margin. The result proves that one-many mapping can considerably enhance the probability of making correct predictions and one-one mapping lacks enough information for predictions. KnowVerb introduces an external knowledge base to enrich the coverage of label words, so it can yield better performance. Although free of manual design, AutoVerb, SoftVerb and ProtoVerb have poor performance under data scarcity. As the training data increase sufficiently, they get

Table 3. The result of label words for each label on AG's News dataset obtained using EVS. Select top 5 label words for each label.

Label	$K = 1$	$K = 16$
World	headlines, news, report, foreign, country	governance, politics, world, government, national
Sports	score, match, playoff, replay, repeat	racing, sprinter, netball, sporting, athletics
Business	chemical, cbs, systemic, committee, auditor	company, bank, corruption, billboard, taxpayer
Tech	device, security, digital, phone, energy	facebook, technical, computer, internet, nanotechnology

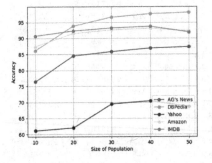

Fig. 3. Ablation results on the size of population.

Fig. 4. Ablation results on the number of EVS iterations.

even exceeding scores. The reason is obvious, that these methods require enough data to optimize during the training process.

When comparing EvoVerb with the other optimize-based verbalizers, we find EvoVerb outperforms other baseline methods on 8 and 16 shot and achieves similar performance on 4-shot. But it is quite unsatisfactory on 1-shot. We attribute the reason why our methods do not perform as well as other verbalizers in 1-shot and 4-shot scenarios to too few training and development samples, which result in inadequate initialization for evolutionary verbalizer search. When in 8-shot and 16-shot settings, our method achieves better performance in prompt-tuning, which indicates that more instances can result in a better representation of the initialization labels and promote EVS to search high performance verbalizer.

4.5   Analysis

In this subsection, we discuss several factors that affect EVS.

The Size of Development Set. In EVS, the development set plays an important role in the initialization of each label representation and is also critical to the final high-performance verbalizer from EVS. To investigate the best searched verbalizer with different size of development set, we present k-shot experiments for 1 and 16 on AG's News dataset. From Table 3, we see that: (1) Even if there is only one example per class, the searched verbalizer is meaningful. (2) With more examples, EVS can find more appropriate label words. Most similar label words are closely related to the corresponding label topics.

Population Size. The population size is also a critical hyperparameter for EVS. As shown in Fig. 3, the overall performance on all datasets improves first and then declines with population growth, which indicates that large population sizes do not optimize the results of the evolutionary algorithm.

The Number of EVS Iterations. Another critical hyperparameter is the number of iterations for the evolutionary verbalizer search. We conduct experiments from 1 to 10 iterations on five datasets and the results are shown in Fig. 4. It can be seen that some datasets such as Yahoo and IMDB achieve the best results in iteration 5, but other datasets achieve the best results in iteration 6. EVS requires enough iterations to find the high-performance verbalizers. In order to balance time cost and performance, the default iteration is set to 5 in EVS.

5   Conclusion

In this paper, we propose a novel approach for automatic verbalizer construction in prompt-based tuning. To obtain a high-performance and meaningful verbalizer, we optimize models by utilizing evolutionary algorithm. We compare it to other current verbalizers and the experimental results demonstrate that EvoVerb outperforms various baselines and verifies its effectiveness. For future work, we will focus on extending EvoVerb for effective strategies of evolutionary algorithm.

Acknowledgements. This work was supported in part by the National Natural Science Foundation of China (62006044, 62172110), in part by the Natural Science Foundation of Guangdong Province (2022A1515010130), and in part by the Programme of Science and Technology of Guangdong Province (2021A0505110004).

References

1. Blickle, T., Thiele, L.: A comparison of selection schemes used in evolutionary algorithms. Evol. Comput. 4(4), 361–394 (1996)
2. Cui, G., Hu, S., Ding, N., Huang, L., Liu, Z.: Prototypical verbalizer for prompt-based few-shot tuning. In: Proceedings of the 60th Annual Meeting of the Association for Computational Linguistics (ACL), pp. 7014–7024 (2022)
3. Devlin, J., Chang, M.W., Lee, K., Toutanova, K.: BERT: Pre-training of deep bidirectional transformers for language understanding. In: Proceedings of the 2019 Conference of the North American Chapter of the Association for Computational Linguistics: Human Language Technologies (NAACL-HLT), pp. 4171–4186 (2019)
4. Ding, N., et al.: OpenPrompt: an open-source framework for prompt-learning. In: Proceedings of the 60th Annual Meeting of the Association for Computational Linguistics: System Demonstrations (ACL), pp. 105–113 (2022)
5. Elsken, T., Metzen, J.H., Hutter, F.: Neural architecture search: a survey. J. Mach. Learn. Res. 20(1), 1997–2017 (2019)
6. Gao, T., Fisch, A., Chen, D.: Making pre-trained language models better few-shot learners. In: Proceedings of the 59th Annual Meeting of the Association for Computational Linguistics and the 11th International Joint Conference on Natural Language Processing (ACL-IJCNLP), pp. 3816–3830 (2021)

7. Hambardzumyan, K., Khachatrian, H., May, J.: WARP: word-level Adversarial ReProgramming. In: Proceedings of the 59th Annual Meeting of the Association for Computational Linguistics and the 11th International Joint Conference on Natural Language Processing (ACL-IJCNLP), pp. 4921–4933 (2021)

8. Howard, J., Ruder, S.: Universal language model fine-tuning for text classification. In: Proceedings of the 56th Annual Meeting of the Association for Computational Linguistics (ACL), pp. 328–339 (2018)

9. Hu, S., et al.: Knowledgeable prompt-tuning: incorporating knowledge into prompt verbalizer for text classification. In: Proceedings of the 60th Annual Meeting of the Association for Computational Linguistics (ACL), pp. 2225–2240 (2022)

10. Lehman, J., Gordon, J., Jain, S., Ndousse, K., Yeh, C., Stanley, K.O.: Evolution through large models. arXiv preprint arXiv:2206.08896 (2022)

11. Lehmann, J., et al.: Dbpedia-a large-scale, multilingual knowledge base extracted from Wikipedia. Semantic web **6**(2), 167–195 (2015)

12. Liu, P., Yuan, W., Fu, J., Jiang, Z., Hayashi, H., Neubig, G.: Pre-train, prompt, and predict: a systematic survey of prompting methods in natural language processing. arXiv preprint arXiv:2107.13586 (2021)

13. Liu, Y., et al.: Roberta: a robustly optimized bert pretraining approach. arXiv preprint arXiv:1907.11692 (2019)

14. Maas, A., Daly, R.E., Pham, P.T., Huang, D., Ng, A.Y., Potts, C.: Learning word vectors for sentiment analysis. In: Proceedings of the 49th Annual Meeting of the Association for Computational Linguistics: Human Language Technologies, pp. 142–150 (2011)

15. Manzoni, L., Jakobovic, D., Mariot, L., Picek, S., Castelli, M.: Towards an evolutionary-based approach for natural language processing. In: Proceedings of the 2020 Genetic and Evolutionary Computation Conference, pp. 985–993 (2020)

16. McAuley, J., Leskovec, J.: Hidden factors and hidden topics: understanding rating dimensions with review text. In: Proceedings of the 7th ACM Conference on Recommender Systems, pp. 165–172 (2013)

17. Schick, T., Schmid, H., Schütze, H.: Automatically identifying words that can serve as labels for few-shot text classification. In: Proceedings of the 28th International Conference on Computational Linguistics, pp. 5569–5578 (2020)

18. Schick, T., Schütze, H.: Exploiting cloze-questions for few-shot text classification and natural language inference. In: Proceedings of the 16th Conference of the European Chapter of the Association for Computational Linguistics (EACL), pp. 255–269 (2021)

19. Wei, Y., Mo, T., Jiang, Y., Li, W., Zhao, W.: Eliciting knowledge from pretrained language models for prototypical prompt verbalizer. In: Artificial Neural Networks and Machine Learning - ICANN 2022, pp. 222–233 (2022)

20. Zhang, X., Zhao, J., LeCun, Y.: Character-level convolutional networks for text classification. Advances in neural information processing systems 28 (2015)

Graph Contrastive Learning Method with Sample Disparity Constraint and Feature Structure Graph for Node Classification

Gangbin Chen[1], Junwei Cheng[1], Wanying Liang[1], Chaobo He[1,2(✉)], and Yong Tang[1,2]

[1] School of Computer Science, South China Normal University, Guangzhou 510631, China
{gbchan,jung,sylvialaung,hechaobo,ytang}@m.scnu.edu.cn
[2] Pazhou Lab, Guangzhou 510330, Guangdong, China

Abstract. Most of the existing graph contrastive learning methods for node classification focus on exploiting topological information of the attributed networks, with little attention to the attribute information of the networks. Furthermore, in most graph contrastive learning methods, both positive and negative sample representations are generated by the same encoder, which makes them somewhat coupled and not conducive to distinguishing between them. But to our knowledge, most of these methods ignore the coupling between positive and negative sample representations, which may negatively affect the performance of the methods. To address these two issues, we propose a new method called DCFSG, in which we generate a feature structure graph from the attribute matrix, and then learn the node representations jointly from the topological structure graph and the feature structure graph. In addition, we impose a disparity constraint on the positive and negative samples and add corresponding loss to the objective function, which can help to lower the coupling between positive and negative samples and improves the performance of our method. The experimental results on real networks validate the effectiveness of our method.

Keywords: Graph contrastive learning · Node classification · Attributed networks · Feature structure graph · Disparity constraint

1 Introduction

Attributed networks have been widely used to represent relationships between objects in the real world, and they consist of nodes that are enriched with attribute information. For example, in the citation network, each node represents a document with its own attributes (e.g., keywords), and the edges represent the citation relationships between documents. The analysis of attributed networks can capture the attributes of objects to help people better understand real-world relationships, which is clearly meaningful and challenging.

Z. Jin et al. (Eds.): KSEM 2023, LNAI 14120, pp. 291–303, 2023.
https://doi.org/10.1007/978-3-031-40292-0_24

Graph node classification is one of the most popular topics in the analyses of attributed networks. It aims to partition nodes of the network into different categories, which can help us understand the relationships between different nodes and infer the category of the nodes. In general, there are several broad categories of methods for graph node classification, such as Graph Neural Networks-based (GNNs) methods [1,11,15,19], Graph Autoencoder-based (GAE) methods [6,8,9], Graph Contrastive Learning-based (GCL) methods [2,4,16] and so on. Among these, GCL has received much attention because of several advantages for classification tasks. One is that GCL does not require label information and relies heavily on the graph structure itself, so it can be applied to the datasets without label information, improving the applicability and scalability of the method. Moreover, GCL can learn features by purely comparing similarity between different nodes with a small number of positive and negative samples, which can enhance the robustness of the classification method.

Recently, numerous researchers have put forward novel methods to effectively tackle node classification task within the realm of GCL. Velikovi et al. [14] proposed a classical GCL framework (i.e., DGI), whose main idea is to maximize the mutual information between the node embedding and the global summary vector of the whole graph. Yu et al. [20] proposed the SimGCL method, which discards the graph enhancement mechanism and instead adds uniform noise to the embedding space to create a contrast view. And their experiments showed that graph augmentation operations play only a minor role in the recommendation domain, which used to be considered necessary. Jing et al. [5] proposed HDMI method, which combines extrinsic and intrinsic mutual information for learning node embeddings of attributed networks and attributed multiplex networks. They also introduced a new method, called High-order Deep Informax, to optimize the high-order mutual information, which can better capture the structure and interactions in complex networks to learn more optimal representations for classification. All of the aforementioned methods have played a pivotal role in driving the development of GCL for the task of node classification.

Though the above methods have proven successful in the field of classification based on GCL, they may still have two issues that can be addressed. The first one is that most GCL methods for classification tasks focus on exploiting topological information of the attributed network to extract representations of graph nodes, but fail to fully utilize the attribute information of the graph. This means that the node representations we learn do not accurately reflect the nodes well in the attributed networks. The second one is that there is a slight coupling between the positive and negative sample representations because both positive and negative sample representations are generated by the same graph encoder. And most GCL methods do not take into account whether there are couplings between the positive and negative samples. Therefore, if we do not make full use of the attribute information in the attributed networks and ensure the disparities of the positive and negative samples, then the graph encoder performance obtained by the GCL methods may be suboptimal, which is not conducive to our subsequent node classification task.

Addressing the aforementioned two issues is crucial for improving the quality of graph node embeddings and enhancing the performance of graph node classification method. In this paper, we propose a novel method called DCFSG, which is based on general framework of GCL and it can solve both issues mentioned above. For the issue of not making full use of the attribute information in the attributed networks, we propose to use the K-Nearest Neighbor (KNN) graph generated by the node attributes as the feature structure graph. Then we learn the embedding of graph nodes based on the feature structure graph and the topological structure graph. In this way, we can better integrate node attribute information with graph topological information, which helps us to learn high-quality node representations and improves the performance of node classification method. For another issue, we use the Hilbert-Schmidt Independence Criterion (HSIC) [12] as a constraint to measure the disparity of the node embeddings of positive and negative samples. And it can enhance the disparity between these two types of embeddings, which help us to obtain a optimal graph encoder for classification. Our main contributions are summarized as follows:

- We propose a novel method DCFSG for learning node representations to tackle node classification task. Our method makes full use of the graph attribute information and constrains the positive and negative samples, which can improve the performance of the method on node classification task.
- We propose to learn the representations of nodes simultaneously from the topological structure graph and feature structure graph, in which we generate the KNN graph as the feature structure graph. Also, we propose to use HSIC as a constraint to enhance the diparity of positive and negative samples. More specifically, we add the corresponding loss to our objective function to improve the performance of our classification method.
- We conduct sufficient experiments on a series of benchmark datasets and the results demonstrate that DCFSG is superior over most methods or on par performance with existing methods.

2 Preliminaries

2.1 Attributed Networks

Attributed networks are a type of network where each node contains a set of attributes, and each edge represents a relationship between nodes. The attributed networks can be represented by $G(\mathbf{A}, \mathbf{X})$, where $\mathbf{A} \in \mathbb{R}^{N \times N}$ indicates the adjacency matrix and N indicates the number of nodes. $\mathbf{X} \in \mathbb{R}^{N \times M}$ indicates the attribute matrix and M indicates the dimension of attributes.

2.2 Graph Contrastive Learning

GCL is a self-supervised learning method for learning the representations of the nodes of graphs. And it use the concept of mutual information, which can be used to measure the correlation between two random variables, and the mutual information of a and b can be expressed as $I(a,b)$. GCL also uses global summary vectors as a way to efficiently compute mutual information. By maximizing the mutual information between node embeddings h and global summary vectors S, GCL can improve the distinguishability of nodes in the embedding space, which contributes to achieving good performance on various graph data tasks.

In summary, most GCL methods first generate a negative network $\tilde{G}$ by a corruption function $\mathcal{C}$. Secondly they generate the positive samples $\{h_1,\ldots,h_N\}$ for positive network as well as the negative samples $\{\tilde{h}_1,\ldots,\tilde{h}_N\}$ for the negative network by the same graph encoder $\mathcal{E}$ (e.g., GCN [7]). Then it use a readout function $\mathcal{R}$ to get the summary vector $S = \mathcal{R}(\{h_1,\ldots,h_N\})$ of the positive network G. Lastly, with S as input, it use the discriminator $\mathcal{D}$ to distinguish the positive node embeddings $\{h_1,\ldots,h_N\}$ from those negative node embeddings$\{\tilde{h}_1,\ldots,\tilde{h}_N\}$.

In most GCL methods, the maximization of $I(h_n, S)$ can be expressed as the maximization of the objective function $\mathcal{L}$, defined as follows:

$$\mathcal{L} = \sup\mathbb{E}[\log\mathcal{D}(h_n;S)] + \mathbb{E}[\log(1 - \mathcal{D}(\tilde{h}_n;S))] \tag{1}$$

where the discriminator $\mathcal{D}$ is used to differentiate the real node embedding h_n from the negative node embedding $\tilde{h}_n$ and the expectation is denoted by $\mathbb{E}$.

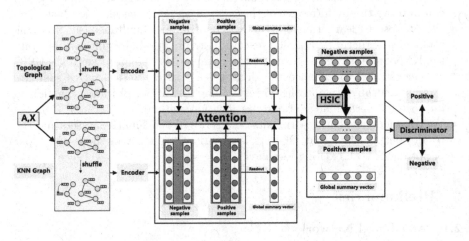

Fig. 1. The framework of DCFSG.

3   The Proposed Method

In this section, we introduce three main modules of our method DCFSG, which is shown in Fig. 1. In the first module, we construct the KNN graph as our feature structure graph, which is based on the node attributes by using the cosine similarity method. In the second module, we firstly use the topological and feature structure graphs to generate the corresponding positive and negative samples. Based on positive samples from both types of graphs, then we can obtain the global summary vectors for each graph. Lastly, we use an attention mechanism to adaptively fuse node embeddings of the same type, such as positive samples embeddings, negative samples embeddings, and global summary vectors. In the last module, we use HSIC to impose constraints on the representations of both positive and negative samples, which ensure the disparity between positive and negative sample representations. Finally, we add the corresponding loss to the objective function, which is beneficial for us to improve the performance of the method.

3.1   Feature Structure Graph Construction

To make full use of the attribute information of the nodes in the attributed networks, we construct KNN graph $G_f = (\mathbf{A}_f, \mathbf{X})$ based on the attribute matrix $\mathbf{X}$, and $\mathbf{A}_f$ is the adjacency matrix of KNN graph. More specifically, we first calculate the similarity matrix $\mathbf{Y} \in \mathbb{R}^{N \times N}$ among N nodes by the cosine similarity method. And we present this method here, in which $\mathbf{y}_i$ and $\mathbf{y}_j$ are feature vectors of node i and j. Then we use the cosine value of the angle between two vectors to measure the similarity, the calculation formula is as follows:

$$\mathbf{Y}_{ij} = \frac{y_i \cdot y_j}{|y_i||y_j|} \tag{2}$$

After calculating the similarity matrix $\mathbf{Y}$, then we can select the top K similar node pairs for each node to establish edges, and subsequently obtain the adjacency matrix $\mathbf{A}_f$. Usually, the value of K here is chosen by us.

3.2   Node Embeddings Generation

Now we have the topological structure graph $G = (\mathbf{A}, \mathbf{X})$ and the feature structure graph $G_f = (\mathbf{A}_f, \mathbf{X})$. Taking these two graphs as positive samples, we can use the corruption function $\mathcal{C}$ to construct negative samples for these two graphs, i.e., $(\tilde{\mathbf{A}}, \tilde{\mathbf{X}}) = \mathcal{C}(\mathbf{A}, \mathbf{X})$ and $(\tilde{\mathbf{A}}_f, \tilde{\mathbf{X}}) = \mathcal{C}(\mathbf{A}_f, \mathbf{X})$.

In this paper, we employ the corruption function based on random node permutation and specifically randomize the rows of the attribute matrix $\mathbf{X}$.

We use the graph encoder $\mathcal{E}$ to encode the graph nodes. Specifically, we use a single layer GCN as $\mathcal{E}$:

$$\mathbf{H} = ReLU(\hat{\mathbf{D}}^{-\frac{1}{2}}\hat{\mathbf{A}}\hat{\mathbf{D}}^{-\frac{1}{2}}\mathbf{X}\Theta) \tag{3}$$

where $\hat{\mathbf{A}} = \mathbf{A} + \mathbf{I}_N$ denotes the adjacency matrix with inserted self-loops and $\hat{\mathbf{D}}$ denotes its degree matrix. $\mathbf{H} \in \mathbb{R}^{N \times d}$ denotes the node embedding matrix, where d denotes the dimension of the node embeddings. Also, Θ is a learnable linear transformation that is applied to every node and ReLU denotes the nonlinear function.

Similarly we can obtain $\tilde{\mathbf{H}}$, $\mathbf{H}_f$ and $\tilde{\mathbf{H}}_f$ via Eq. 3. In general, we now have four node embedding matrices. $\tilde{\mathbf{H}}$ denotes the node embedding matrix obtained from the topological structure graph. Also, $\mathbf{H}_f$ and $\tilde{\mathbf{H}}_f$ represent the node embedding matrices generated by the feature structure graph. Notably, $\mathbf{H}$ and $\mathbf{H}_f$ denote positive sample embedding matrices while $\tilde{\mathbf{H}}$ and $\tilde{\mathbf{H}}_f$ denote negative sample embedding matrices.

Finally, we obtain the global summary vectors S and S_f by using average pooling as $\mathcal{R}$:

$$S = \mathcal{R}(\mathbf{H}) = \frac{1}{N} \sum_{n=1}^{N} h_n \tag{4}$$

where $h_n \in \mathbb{R}^{1 \times d}$ is the n-th rows of $\mathbf{H}$. S and $S_f \in \mathbb{R}^{1 \times d}$ represent the global summary vectors of topological structure graph and feature structure graph, respectively. Now we have two categories of positive sample node embeddings (i.e., h and h_f) from topological and feature structure graphs, respectively, as well as two classes of global summary vectors (i.e., S and S_f). In addition, we have $\tilde{h}$ and $\tilde{h}_f$ as negative sample node embeddings from above two mentioned graphs.

Considering that the node information should be learned from the topological and feature structure graphs, we use the attention mechanism to learn their corresponding importance as follows:

$$(\alpha_t, \alpha_f) = att(\mathbf{H}, \mathbf{H}_f) \tag{5}$$

where α_t and $\alpha_f \in \mathbb{R}^{N \times 1}$ denote the attention values of positive samples $\mathbf{H}$ and $\mathbf{H}_f$. Similarly, we can get the (β_t, β_f) and (γ_t, γ_f) through $att(\tilde{\mathbf{H}}, \tilde{\mathbf{H}}_f)$ and $att(S, S_f)$. β_t and β_f here denote the attention values of negative samples. γ_t and γ_f denote the attention values of different global summary vectors.

Specifically, we focus on node i, whose embedding in $\mathbf{H}$ is represented by $h^i \in \mathbb{R}^{1 \times d}$. Firstly we transform the embedding through a nonlinear transformation, and then use one shared vector $q \in \mathbb{R}^{d' \times 1}$ to calculate the attention value, where d' is the dimension of the output layer of the first linear layer in the attention mechanism. The specific calculation of the attention value ω_t^i is as follows:

$$\omega_t^i = q_\omega \cdot tanh(\mathbf{W}_\omega \cdot (h^i)^T + b_\omega) \tag{6}$$

Similarly, we can get the attention values ω_f^i for node i in embedding matrix $\mathbf{H}_f$ as follows:

$$\omega_f^i = q_\omega \cdot tanh(\mathbf{W}_\omega \cdot (h_f^i)^T + b_\omega) \tag{7}$$

Moreover, by replacing $(h^i)^T$ in Eq. (6) with $(\tilde{h}^i)^T$ and $(s^i)^T$ respectively, we can obtain the corresponding attention values ψ_t^i and ϕ_t^i. Also, by replacing $(h_f^i)^T$ in Eq. (7) with $(\tilde{h}_f^i)^T$ and $(s_f^i)^T$ separately, we can obtain the attention values ψ_f^i and ϕ_f^i. Here $\mathbf{W} \in \mathbb{R}^{d' \times d}$ is the weight matrix and $b \in \mathbb{R}^{d' \times 1}$ denotes the bias vector. Then we can normalize the attention values ω_t^i and ω_f^i with softmax function to calculate the final weights, as follows:

$$\alpha_t^i = softmax(\omega_t^i) = \frac{exp(\omega_t^i)}{exp(\omega_t^i) + exp(\omega_f^i)} \tag{8}$$

$$\alpha_f^i = softmax(\omega_f^i) = \frac{exp(\omega_f^i)}{exp(\omega_t^i) + exp(\omega_f^i)} \qquad (9)$$

Similarly, we can calculate β_t^i and β_f^i from ψ_t^i and ψ_f^i. Also, we can obtain γ_t and γ_f from ϕ_t^i and ϕ_f^i. Finally, we have the learned weights $\alpha_t = [\alpha_t^i]$, $\alpha_f = [\alpha_f^i] \in \mathbb{R}^{N \times 1}$. Similarly we can get β_t, β_f, γ_t and γ_f. Then we can combine these embeddings with the attention values to obtain the final embeddings, as follows:

$$\mathbf{H}^* = \alpha_t \cdot \mathbf{H} + \alpha_f \cdot \mathbf{H}_f \qquad (10)$$

$$\tilde{\mathbf{H}}^* = \beta_t \cdot \tilde{\mathbf{H}} + \beta_f \cdot \tilde{\mathbf{H}}_f \qquad (11)$$

$$S^* = \gamma_t \cdot S + \gamma_f \cdot S_f \qquad (12)$$

3.3   Disparity Constraint and Optimisation of Objective Functions

After we have the final node embeddings as described above (i.e., $\mathbf{H}^*, \tilde{\mathbf{H}}^*, S^*$), we can use the discriminator $\mathcal{D}$ [14] to score global summary vector S^* and positive samples $\mathbf{H}^*$, as well as global summary vector and negative samples $\tilde{\mathbf{H}}^*$, as follows:

$$\mathcal{D}(h_n^*, S^*) = \sigma(h_n^{*T} \mathbf{M}_E S^*)$$
$$\mathcal{D}(\tilde{h}_n^*, S^*) = \sigma((\tilde{h}_n^*)^T \mathbf{M}_E S^*) \qquad (13)$$

where $\mathbf{M}_E \in \mathbb{R}^{d \times d}$ is parameter matrix and σ is the sigmoid activation function. $h_n^* \in \mathbf{H}^*$ and $\tilde{h}_n^* \in \tilde{\mathbf{H}}^*$ represent positive and negative sample node embeddings, respectively. Although h_n^* and $\tilde{h}_n^*$ are node embeddings learned from different graph structures, they are generated by the same graph encoder $\mathcal{E}$. The two types of node embeddings are likely to have a certain degree of coupling. Therefore, if we want to learn a good discriminator, then we need to ensure that the positive and negative samples input to the discriminator have some disparities. In this paper, we use HSIC to enhance the disparity of these two embeddings. Formally, we define the disparity constraint $\mathcal{L}_h$ as follows:

$$\mathcal{L}_h = HSIC(\mathbf{H}^*, \tilde{\mathbf{H}}^*) = (n-1)^{-2} tr(\mathbf{R}\mathbf{K_T}\mathbf{R}\mathbf{K_{CT}}) \qquad (14)$$

where $\mathbf{K}_T$ and $\mathbf{K}_{CT}$ are matrices defined as $k_{T,ij} = k_T(\mathbf{h}^i, \mathbf{h}^j)$ and $k_{CT,ij} = k_{CT}(\tilde{\mathbf{h}}^i, \tilde{\mathbf{h}}^j)$, respectively. $\mathbf{R} = \mathbf{I} - \frac{1}{n}ee^T$, where e is an all-one column vector and $\mathbf{I}$ is an identity matrix.

Ultimately, imposing the loss corresponding to the disparity constraint on our objective function based on Eq. (1), we can obtain the final objective function as follows:

$$\mathcal{L}_E = \mathbb{E}[log\mathcal{D}(h_n^*, S^*)] + \mathbb{E}[log(1 - \mathcal{D}(\tilde{h}_n^*, S^*))] \qquad (15)$$

$$\mathcal{L} = \mathcal{L}_E + \lambda_h \mathcal{L}_h \qquad (16)$$

where λ_h is tunable coefficient. Our method is based on the basic GCL framework, which maximizes the mutual information of the final node embeddings

h_i^* and S^*. Also, it imposes disparity constraint on the positive and negative samples. Finally, we can update parameters involved in $\mathcal{E}$, $\mathcal{D}$ and $\mathcal{R}$ by applying gradient descent to maximize Eq. (16). We list the whole process of our proposed method in Algorithm 1.

Algorithm 1. Framework of DCFSG.

Input: Original Graph $G = (\mathbf{A}, \mathbf{X})$, Maximum epoch value T_{max};
Output: Node embeddings $\mathbf{H}$, Classification results;
1: ▶ **Generate a KNN graph:**
2:    $G = (\mathbf{A}_f, \mathbf{X})$ via Eq. (2) ;
3: **while** epoch $< T_{max}$ or our method has not yet converged **do**
4:    ▶ **Generate representations**
5:       Use encoder $\mathcal{E}$ to generate $\mathbf{H}$, $\tilde{\mathbf{H}}$, $\mathbf{H}_f$ and $\tilde{\mathbf{H}}_f$ via Eq. (3);
6:       Use Readout function $\mathcal{R}$ to generate S and S_f via Eq. (4);
7:    ▶ **Using the attention mechanism**
8:       Calculate the values of $\alpha_t, \alpha_f, \beta_t, \beta_f, \gamma_t$ and γ_f via Eq. (5),
          Eq. (6), Eq. (7), Eq. (8) and Eq. (9);
9:       Obtain $\mathbf{H}^*$, $\tilde{\mathbf{H}}^*$ and S^* via Eq. (10), Eq. (11) and Eq. (12);
10:   ▶ **Calculate the loss** λ
11:      Calculate the HSIC via Eq. (14);
12:      Use the discriminator $\mathcal{D}$ to score via Eq. (13);
13:      Calculate the loss via Eq. (15) and Eq. (16);
14:      Update parameters of the attention mechanism and HSIC;
15:      Update parameters involved in $\mathcal{E}$, $\mathcal{D}$ and $\mathcal{R}$;
16: **end while**
17: **return** Node embeddings $\mathbf{H}$, Classification results through inputting $\mathbf{H}$ into the MLP.

---

4   Experiments

4.1   Experimental Setup

(1) Datasets. We conduct experiments on three real-world datasets, i.e., Cora, Citeseer and Pubmed[1], which are summarized in Table 1.

(2) Baselines. We compare the metrics (i.e., Accuracy (ACC) and macro F1-score (F1)) of our method with other methods. These methods are: DeepWalk [10], Planetoid [18], GCN [7], GraphSAGE [3], GAT [13], GIN [17] ,DGI [14]. And we report the ACC and F1 of all these methods after several runs of training. Lastly we summary the results in Table 2.

(3) Parameter Settings. For our method, we use the learned representations to tackle node classification task through an MLP. Also, we use the Adam optimizer and set the learning rate to 0.001. For the Cora, Citeseer and Pubmed datasets, we set the dimension of the hidden layer in the encoder $\mathcal{E}$ to 896, 512 and 512, respectively. And the dimension of the hidden layer in the attention mechanism is 16. Also, the value of K is fixed as 7, which is used to generate the KNN graph as the feature structure graph. Lastly, for Cora, Citeseer and Pubmed datasets, we set the dimension of the output layers of the MLP to 7, 6 and 3, respectively.

---

[1] https://github.com/GDM-SCNU/Datasets.

Table 1. Summary of the datasets used in our experiments.

Dataset	Nodes	Edges	Attributes	Classes
Cora	2708	5429	1433	7
Citeseer	3327	4732	3703	6
Pubmed	19717	44338	500	3

Table 2. Classification results on three datasets. (Bold: best)

Dataset	Cora		Citeseer		Pubmed	
Metric	ACC	F1	ACC	F1	ACC	F1
Planetoid	0.771	0.766	0.646	0.616	0.753	0.749
DeepWalk	0.689	0.683	0.454	0.437	0.748	0.729
GCN	0.816	0.809	0.708	0.679	0.773	0.679
GraphSAGE	0.791	0.788	0.708	0.679	0.760	0.758
GAT	0.792	0.782	0.722	0.689	0.780	0.769
GIN	0.748	0.751	0.637	0.601	0.774	0.770
DGI	**0.823**	**0.810**	0.718	0.675	0.771	0.773
DCFSG	0.820	**0.810**	**0.724**	**0.693**	**0.812**	**0.810**

4.2 Classification Performance Analysis

The node classification results are reported in Table 2, from which we have the following observations:

(1) Our proposed DCFSG achieves better results than most methods on the three real datasets. For the Cora, Citeseer and Pubmed datasets, DCFSG's ACC improved by a maximum of 13.1%, 27% and 6.4% as well as the F1 of DCFSG improved by a maximum of 12.1%, 25.3% and 13.1%. Furthermore, our proposed method achieves the best performance on both the Citeseer and Pubmed datasets when compared to other methods. And the ACC on the Cora dataset is only 0.3% lower than DGI.

(2) Overall, we achieve the greatest performance advantage on the larger dataset, Pubmed. On the smaller dataset Cora, our proposed method also performs well compared to other methods, but does not reach the most optimal. This shows that our model performs well in learning node embeddings and classifying nodes on large graphs, but does not perform well on small graphs. Probably because when the graph is small, the number of positive and negative samples is small, which is not conducive to learning a good encoder for the graph.

(3) On the other hand, the classification performance of the DCFSG outperforms most of the supervised and unsupervised learning methods, which indicates that our method can extract graph information better than other methods and can learn better node representations.

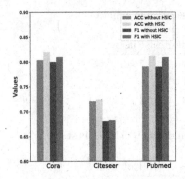

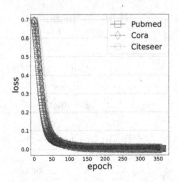

Fig. 2. Ablation study.   **Fig. 3.** Convergence experiment.

4.3 Hyperparameter Analysis

Hyperparameter Analysis of λ_h. The analysis of hyperparameter λ_h is divided into two parts, namely ablation study analysis and sensitivity experimental analysis, based on whether λ_h in Eq. (16) is zero or λ_h is greater than zero.

(I) When $\lambda_h=0$, this experiment represents the ablation study analysis. We compare DCFSG with its one variant on all benchmark datasets. From the result in Fig. 2, we can have the following observations:

- The experimental results show that our method with HSIC performs better than that without HSIC on the three datasets. The method with HSIC has significantly better ACC than the method without HSIC on the three datasets, and for F1, the performance of the method with HSIC is significantly better on Pubmed and Cora, while the difference with and without HSIC is not significant on the Citeseer dataset.
- The experimental results demonstrate that our use of HSIC to enhance the disparity between positive and negative samples is effective, which indicates that our use of HSIC can improve the ability of our method to learn graph node embeddings and improve the accuracy of classification.

(II) When $\lambda_h > 0$, this experiment represents the sensitivity analysis and the result is shown in Fig. 4. We analyze the effect of hyperparameter λ_h on classification performance and the result shows that the performance of our method changes very little as the value of λ_h increases. In general, experiments on the performance of our method under different hyperparameters λ_h show that our method is not sensitive to hyperparameter λ_h. In a way, it means that our method is more stable, and our insensitivity to this hyperparameter λ_h reduces the complexity of parameter tuning and speeds up the training of our method.

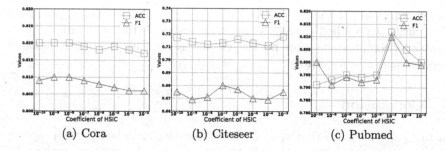

Fig. 4. λ_h-sensitivity analysis on three datasets.

K-Sensitivity Analysis. We analyze the impact of the value of K on the classification performance, where K is used to determine the construction of the KNN graph. From the result shown in Fig. 5, we can have the following observations:

(1) In Cora dataset, ACC and F1 tend to decrease overall as the value of K increases. But for Citeseer dataset, ACC and F1 exhibit minimal variation. As the value of K increases, we find that there is significant variation in both ACC and F1 in Pubmed dataset.

(2) Within a certain range of the value of K changes, this hyperparameter K has a relatively small effect on changes in the model performance. This means that even if the value of this hyperparameter K changes, the performance of our method may not change significantly.

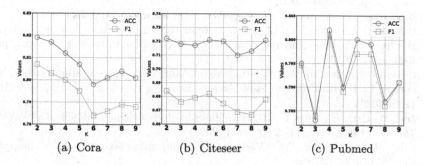

Fig. 5. Results of K-sensitivity analysis on three datasets.

4.4 Convergence Analysis

We verify the convergence of our method using Cora, Citeseer and Pubmed datasets, respectively. The experimental results shown in Fig. 3 demonstrate that our method converges quickly, with the losses calculated on the three datasets starting to converge at around 50 epochs and stabilising at around 200 epochs. This indicates that our method has a good generalisation ability to a certain extent, which enables us to facilitate hyperparameter tuning and experimentation. Since the method converges quickly, it allows us to verify various hyperparameter combinations more rapidly, ultimately reducing the time required for hyperparameter optimization.

5   Conclusion

In this paper, we find that most GCL methods focus on using graph topological information to extract the representations of nodes, without making full use of the node attribute information. Moreover, most existing methods do not explicitly consider the impact of the disparity of positive and negative samples within a graph on method performance. Therefore, we propose a novel method, called DCFSG, which exploits both graph topological and attribute information to jointly learn node representations, and enhances the disparities between the positive and negative node embeddings by adding the disparity constraint. The extensive experimental data demonstrates the effectiveness of our method.

Acknowledgement. This work was supported in part by the National Natural Science Foundation of China under Grant 62077045, and Grant U1811263.

References

1. Abu-El-Haija, S., Kapoor, A., Perozzi, B., Lee, J.: N-GCN: multi-scale graph convolution for semi-supervised node classification. In: Uncertainty in Artificial Intelligence, pp. 841–851 (2020)
2. Brzozowski, U., Siemaszko, K.: Representation learning on graphs (2021)
3. Hamilton, W.L., Ying, Z., Leskovec, J.: Inductive representation learning on large graphs. In: Annual Conference on Neural Information Processing Systems, pp. 1024–1034 (2017)
4. Hassani, K., Ahmadi, A.H.K.: Contrastive multi-view representation learning on graphs. In: ICML. Proceedings of Machine Learning Research, vol. 119, pp. 4116–4126 (2020)
5. Jing, B., Park, C., Tong, H.: HDMI: high-order deep multiplex infomax. In: WWW: The Web Conference, pp. 2414–2424 (2021)
6. Kipf, T.N., Welling, M.: Variational graph auto-encoders. arXiv preprint abs/1611.07308 (2016)
7. Kipf, T.N., Welling, M.: Semi-supervised classification with graph convolutional networks. In: ICLR (2017)
8. Niknam, G., Molaei, S., Zare, H., Clifton, D., Pan, S.: Graph representation learning based on deep generative gaussian mixture models. Neurocomputing **523**, 157–169 (2023)
9. Pan, S., Hu, R., Long, G., Jiang, J., Yao, L., Zhang, C.: Adversarially regularized graph autoencoder for graph embedding. In: IJCAI, pp. 2609–2615 (2018)
10. Perozzi, B., Al-Rfou, R., Skiena, S.: DeepWalk: online learning of social representations. In: ACM, pp. 701–710 (2014)
11. Rong, Y., Huang, W., Xu, T., Huang, J.: DropEdge: towards deep graph convolutional networks on node classification. In: ICLR (2020)

12. Song, L., Smola, A.J., Gretton, A., Borgwardt, K.M., Bedo, J.: Supervised feature selection via dependence estimation. In: ICML, vol. 227, pp. 823–830. ACM (2007)
13. Velickovic, P., Cucurull, G., Casanova, A., Romero, A., Liò, P., Bengio, Y.: Graph attention networks. In: ICLR (2018)
14. Velickovic, P., Fedus, W., Hamilton, W.L., Liò, P., Bengio, Y., Hjelm, R.D.: Deep graph infomax. In: ICLR (2019)
15. Wang, X., Zhu, M., Bo, D., Cui, P., Shi, C., Pei, J.: AM-GCN: adaptive multi-channel graph convolutional networks. In: SIGKDD, pp. 1243–1253 (2020)
16. Wang, Z., Yan, S., Zhang, X., da Vitoria Lobo, N.: Self-supervised visual feature learning and classification framework: based on contrastive learning. In: ICARCV, pp. 719–725. IEEE (2020)
17. Xu, K., Hu, W., Leskovec, J., Jegelka, S.: How powerful are graph neural networks? In: ICLR (2019)
18. Yang, Z., Cohen, W.W., Salakhutdinov, R.: Revisiting semi-supervised learning with graph embeddings. In: Balcan, M., Weinberger, K.Q. (eds.) ICML, vol. 48, pp. 40–48 (2016)
19. Yao, L., Mao, C., Luo, Y.: Graph convolutional networks for text classification. In: AAAI, pp. 7370–7377 (2019)
20. Yu, J., Yin, H., Xia, X., Chen, T., Cui, L., Nguyen, Q.V.H.: Are graph augmentations necessary?: Simple graph contrastive learning for recommendation. In: SIGIR, pp. 1294–1303 (2022)

Learning Category Discriminability for Active Domain Adaptation

Jiali Zhang, Mingkang Li, Wen Zhang, Lu Gong, and Zili Zhang[✉]

College of Computer and Information Science, Southwest University,
Chongqing 400715, China
zhangzl@swu.edu.cn

Abstract. Active Domain Adaptation (ADA) attempts to improve the adaptation performance on a target domain by annotating informative target data with a limited budget. Previous ADA methods have significantly advanced by incorporating domain representativeness and predictive uncertainty. However, they only focus on domain-level alignment and ignore the category discriminability of two domains, which may cause classwise mismatching. These mismatched data are overlooked by the above query strategy. To solve this, a Learning Category Discriminability approach is proposed for active domain adaptation. Specifically, it achieves semantic-level alignment and selects the informative target data consistent with the domain adaptation based on task-specific classifiers. To overcome the class imbalance from the small queried data, progressive augmentation of the queried set with confident pseudo labels is designed in our work. In addition, discriminability and diversity learning for unlabeled target samples are performed to improve the reliability of pseudo labels, which makes the classification boundaries more applicable to the target domain. Extensive experiments on two benchmarks, Office-31 and Office-Home, demonstrate the superiority of the proposed method.

Keywords: Active learning · Domain adaptation · Active domain adaptation · Classifier discrepancy · Learning category discriminability

1 Introduction

In recent years, the success of deep neural networks (DNNs) in various tasks has been evident to all. However, their excellent performance relies on massive high-quality annotations, which is time-consuming and expensive for practical applications. Aware of this problem, Unsupervised Domain Adaptation (UDA) has gained wide attention since it can transfer knowledge from labeled to unlabeled domains, mainly reducing the formidable cost of data annotation [11,32]. UDA has shown excellent generalization performance by minimizing distribution distance [7,30], or adversarial approaches [14,28]. However, there is still tremendous potential to catch up with the supervised counterpart, especially when the distribution gap is enormous. The non-negligible performance gap is the biggest

Z. Jin et al. (Eds.): KSEM 2023, LNAI 14120, pp. 304–317, 2023.
https://doi.org/10.1007/978-3-031-40292-0_25

obstacle to applying UDA in practice. In real-world scenarios, annotating a few target data is achievable. Shown as [12], the information from the target domain is more valuable than that of the source domain. Labeling a few target samples can significantly improve the model adaptation. Therefore, a new paradigm called Active Domain Adaptation (ADA) draws attention due to its promising performance, which labels the most informative target instances to assist domain adaptation [20,27].

The active domain adaptation task faces two significant challenges: (i) selecting target samples that can benefit the model most within a limited annotation budget; (ii) how to utilize these chosen samples effectively. Traditional active learning methods aim to select samples based on predictive uncertainty [8,29] or maximal disagreement assessed by committee [3]. Nevertheless, they are less effective for active domain adaptation because they overlook the distribution shift. Aware of this, recent ADA methods incorporate sample uncertainty and domain representativeness as query criteria [5,27]. However, they only consider the generation of domain-invariant features, e.g., using domain discriminator [27], but ignore the category discriminability of target features. Some samples are mismatched to the source domain and failed to be detected by the query strategy. In addition, given a few labeled target data, it is critical to address the class imbalance issue, which is ignored in previous ADA methods [5,20]. They treat the labeled target data and source as one dataset in the training process. However, due to the influence of a large amount of source data, the impact of a small amount of labeled target data is weakened.

To address the above issues, a novel Learning Category Discriminability (LCD) method is proposed for active domain adaptation. It performs domain-level and semantic-level alignment built on an improved collaborative alignment framework [23,31], and annotates valuable target data that are consistent with the domain adaptation. Maximizing the target prediction discrepancy makes the decision boundaries closer to different source classes. Training the generator to minimize the target prediction discrepancy, target samples are matched with source data classwise. Thus, ambiguous target data are exposed between the two classifiers in this adversarial manner. Inspired by this, a two-stage selection strategy is designed to choose informative target data. The target samples with significant prediction discrepancy are queried as a candidate set. Then consistent uncertainty based on two classifiers is further designed to estimate the uncertainty of candidates. A progressive adding confident pseudo-labels approach is adopted to mitigate the class imbalance of labeled target data. Motivated by [2], category discriminability and diversity learning of the target domain are used to adjust the decision boundaries, making them pass through the low-density region of the target domain. To sum up, our contributions are as follows:

- A novel two-stage query strategy is proposed based on task-specific classifiers, selecting informative target samples consistent with domain adaptation. It is lightweight compared to the discriminator-based approaches.
- A progressive adding confident pseudo-labels approach is proposed to augment the labeled target data. Category discrimination and diversity learning are introduced to increase the reliability of pseudo labels.

– Extensive experimental results demonstrate that the proposed method out-performs others in various ADA scenarios.

The remainder of the paper is organized as follows. Related work is introduced in Sect. 2. In Sect. 3, the proposed approach is illustrated in detail. The performance of the proposed method is fully demonstrated in Sect. 4. Finally, Sect. 5 summarizes the work and puts forward the outlook.

2   Related Work

Active domain adaptation is a combination of active learning and domain adaptation. The subsection below introduces the development state and existing problems of active learning, domain adaptation and active domain adaptation.

2.1   Active Learning (AL)

Active learning (AL) attempts to maximize model performance with limited labeled data [22], and the core idea of AL is to actively inquire which samples should be annotated by query strategy [1,4]. Pool-based active learning methods have been successfully applied to various tasks. It mainly queries samples by uncertainty, representativeness, and committee. Uncertainty-based method annotates samples the model is most uncertain about evaluated via entropy or margin [8,29]. Representativeness-based strategy chooses data representing target distribution in the feature space by clustering [24]. Query by committee uses multiple classifiers voting to select the disagreement samples [25]. In addition, the loss-based method [33] is proposed to assess the impact of samples on the model. However, these query strategies are designed for a single domain, which may be less effective under the domain shift.

2.2   Domain Adaptation (DA)

A typical effort in domain adaptation is Unsupervised Domain Adaptation(UDA), which works well on an utterly label-free target domain by transferring knowledge learned from the source domain. Early UDA methods narrow the gap between domains by minimizing the margin distribution distance [7,13] or adversarial learning [19,28,31]. However, compared with supervised training methods, the accuracy of unsupervised domain adaptation is still far worse. Although obtaining all the target label information is expensive, labeling a small number of target samples is achievable. With this consideration, Semi-Supervised Domain Adaptation (SSDA) [16] and Few-Shot Domain Adaptation (FSDA) [18] have been proposed. However, they label the target samples by randomly selecting or predefined rules, which may select the instances that already match the source domain well. On the contrary, active domain adaptation methods select the most valuable target samples through query strategies, which have more significant potential than random criteria.

2.3   Active Domain Adaptation (ADA)

\Active Domain Adaptation (ADA) aims to improve the model adaptation by labeling the most informative target samples through query strategy. Unlike traditional active learning, active domain adaptation methods incorporate uncertainty and representativeness as selection criteria to alleviate the domain shift. AADA [27] and TQS [5] use a domain discriminator as representativeness cues to assist active selection. S3VAAD [21] combines three scores via a submodular to determine the selected set and trains with improved VADA [26]. However, the feature distribution learning based on domain discriminator only considers domain-level alignment, ignoring semantic-level alignment. This results in many target samples being incorrectly matched into the source category. As a result, this part of the data is ignored during the selection process based on query strategy, leading to the selected data are not necessarily advantageous for classifiers.

Based on the issues mentioned above, the category discriminative features of target samples have been taken into account in some domain adaptation methods [23,31]. They construct two different classifiers as a discriminator to train with a generator in an adversarial manner. Class-recognizable features of target samples are extracted in this way. Motivated by these efforts, a new query strategy is proposed based on task-specific classifiers, labeling the target samples that are most useful for the model consistent with domain adaptation. Besides, the training of labeled source, labeled target, and unlabeled target is improved in our work, further enhancing adaptation performance under the ADA setting.

3   Method

3.1   Overall Framework

Problem Formulation. In ADA, we access a source domain $D_s = (x_s^i, y_s^i)_{i=1}^{n_s}$ with n_s samples, where y_s^i is the corresponding label of x_s^i, and an unlabeled target domain $D_t = (x_t^i)_{i=1}^{n_t}$ with n_t unlabeled instances. Both domains have the same label space but draw from two different margin distributions. During the training process, a small number of target samples are labeled by query selection. Therefore, the entire target domain consists of labeled and unlabeled pools. Such query selections are repeated until the labeling budget is exhausted.

Method Overview. We exploit the prediction discrepancy to label informative target samples and enhance adaptation performance. The framework of our proposed method is illustrated in Fig. 1. The model has a generator (G) and two task-specific classifiers (C_1 and C_2). θ is defined as the parameter of the whole frame, composed of a parameter θ_G of the feature extractor and two parameters θ_{C_1}, θ_{C_2} of the classifiers. Two task-specific classifiers are constructed as a discriminator and trained adversarially with a generator to extract discriminative target features. The training process is divided into three steps, further explained in Sect. 3.2. Then a novel and easy-to-implement query strategy is proposed based on task-specific classifiers, described in Sect. 3.3. A progressive amplifying of the queried set with confident pseudo labels is proposed, mitigating the imbalance issue of small labeled target data, described in Sect. 3.4. Our Learning Category Discriminability(LCD) approach for active domain adaptation is illustrated in Algorithm 1.

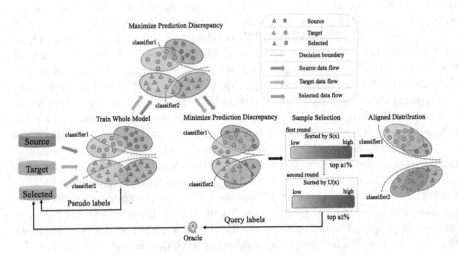

Fig. 1. Outline of the LCD. For training process, two different classifiers are constructed as a discriminator train with a feature generator in the form of adversarial. It achieves both domain and semantic alignment. For selection process, 1% of target samples are quired to annotate in each selection round. We first select a set of $\alpha_1\%$ candidates with big difference between two classifiers. Then we label $\alpha_2\%$ instances from candidates with biggest consistent uncertainty.

3.2 Learning Discriminative Features via Co-training Two Classifiers

The distribution gap between the source and target domains is the biggest obstacle to transferring the model. [23] is a famous method that first utilized task-specific classifiers as a discriminator and achieved semantic-level alignment. Building upon this, [31] further reduces the discrepancy between the feature distributions for better transfer performance. But the model tends to give higher predictions to the classes with higher frequencies, which leads to low diversity of predictions. Thus, an improved collaborative alignment framework is performed blew.

Step 1. Ensure that the model correctly classifies source samples. Thus, the model is trained with cross-entropy loss

$$\min_{\theta_g,\theta_{C1},\theta_{C2}} \mathcal{L}_s(x_s,y_s) = \frac{1}{2n_s}\sum_{i=1}^{n_s}\sum_{j=1}^{2}\mathcal{L}_{ce}(C_j(G(x_s),y_s). \tag{1}$$

Due to the domain shift, although the model can correctly classify the source samples, it does not guarantee that the model can be well applied to the target domain. The decision boundaries may pass through the high-density area of the target domain, resulting in extensive data being misjudged by classifiers. A classic approach is strengthening the target prediction discriminability by minimizing entropy [6,15]. However, entropy-based methods only focus on individual samples and ignore the structural information of the data. This results in instances that actually belong to minority classes being pushed into majority classes. Considering this, a batch nuclear-norm maximization [2] approach is adopted to improve the prediction discriminability of target samples while avoiding low diversity. The objective function reads

$$\mathcal{L}_{BNM}(x_t) = -\frac{1}{B}\sum_{j=1}^{2}||C_j(G(x_t))||_*, \tag{2}$$

where $C_j(G(x_t))$ represents a batch target prediction matrix. $||C_j(G(x_t))||_*$ means the kernel-norm of the prediction matrix. Class discriminability and diversity of unlabeled samples can be improved by maximizing the batch kernel-norm, as deduced in [2].

Thus, to improve the adaptation performance, the model is trained simultaneously using cross-entropy loss and batch kernel norm to maximize loss,

$$\min_{\theta_g,\theta_{C1},\theta_{C2}} \mathcal{L}_{da} = \mathcal{L}_s(x_s,y_s) + \lambda\mathcal{L}_{BNM}(x_t), \tag{3}$$

where λ is a trade-off parameter to balance the two losses.

Step 2. Two distinct classifiers are trained as a discriminator under a fixed generator. To learn tighter decision boundaries, maximizing the target output discrepancy is performed in this step. Therefore, target samples that are far from the source distribution can be detected by the classifiers. The predictions of the source data should be guaranteed to be accurate when maximizing the prediction discrepancy. So the objective should satisfy

$$\min_{\theta_{C_1},\theta_{C_2}} \mathcal{L}_{da} - \mathcal{L}_d,$$
$$\mathcal{L}_d = \frac{1}{n_t}\sum_{i=1}^{n_t} D(C_1(G(x_{ti})), C_2(G(x_{ti}))), \tag{4}$$

where $D(\cdot,\cdot)$ is used to estimate the target prediction divergence between two classifiers, e.g., L1 norm or Wasserstein distance.

Step 3. To extract the discriminative target feature, the generator is trained by minimizing the target prediction discrepancy for fixed classifiers. Narrowing the distance between feature distributions is proposed to achieve domain-level alignment. The optimization objectives on both domain and semantic levels are as follows,

$$\min_{\theta_g} \mathcal{L}_d + \mathcal{L}_{dom}(F_s, F_t) + \lambda\mathcal{L}_{BNM}(x_t). \tag{5}$$

Algorithm 1. Learning Category Discriminability for Active Domain Adaptation

---

Input: Labeled source data S, unlabeled target data T_u and labeled target set T_l, maximum epoch E, iterations per epoch I, selection ratios α_1, α_2

Output: Optimal parameters $\theta_G, \theta_{C_1}, \theta_{C_2}$

1: **for** $e = 0$ to E **do**
2:     **if** need active querying **then**
3:         Select $\alpha_1\%$ samples from T_u as a candidate set Q_1 as described in Eq. (6)
4:         Select $\alpha_2\%$ samples from Q_1 as query set Q with label from oracle as described in Eq. (8)
5:         $T_l = T_l \bigcup Q, T_u = T_u \backslash Q$
6:     **end if**
7:     Initialize $M = T_l$
8:     **for** $iter = 0$ to I **do**
9:         **if** $T_l = \emptyset$ **then**
10:            Sample batches $(x_s, y_s) \sim S, x_t \sim T_u$
11:            Step 1: Update the model with Eq. (3)
12:        **else**
13:            Sample batches $(x_s, y_s) \sim S, (x_m, y_m) \sim M, x_t \sim T_u$
14:            Step 1: Update the model with Eq. (9)
15:            $p_n = (C_1(G(x_t))) + (C_2(G(x_t))), y_n = argmax\ p_n$
16:            **if** $p_n[y_n] > t$ **then**
17:                $M \leftarrow M \bigcup \{(x_n, y_n)\}$
18:            **end if**
19:        **end if**
20:        Step 2: Update the model with Eq. (4)
21:        Step 3: Update the model with Eq. (5)
22:     **end for**
23: **end for**

3.3   Active Query with Task-Specific Classifiers

The transfer performance on an utterly unlabeled target domain can significantly decrease when the domain gap is enormous. So a few informative target data are queried to be labeled, improving the transfer performance. Based on the above training, a novel query strategy is proposed. Local semantic consistency is implemented to match source samples classwise. Consequently, the target samples with contradictory predictions are detected, indicating they are far from the source distribution and challenging to recognize. To this end, two distinct classifiers are employed as a discriminator to query a candidate set. Our acquisition objective is

$$S(x_t) = D(C_1(G(x_t)), C_2(G(x_t))), \tag{6}$$

where $D(\cdot, \cdot)$ denotes the discrepancy between target predictions of each unlabeled instance. The straightforward L1 distance between predictions $C_1(G(x_t))$ and $C_2(G(x_t))$ is applied in [23]. Nevertheless, the L1-norm ignores the constraint of the relevant information between classes. [10] utilizes cosine similarity to calculate the ambiguous score of target samples. However, cosine similarity only focuses on differences in direction, overlooking the magnitude of specific values. On the contrary, an improved measurement method is exploited to measure the target prediction discrepancy, which is inspired by sliced Wasserstein distance (SWD). It can leverage intrinsic geometric properties to calculate the distribution distance. Refer to [9], we first sample M samples from a unit sphere $\mathbb{S} = \{\theta \in \mathbb{R}^{|Y|s} \mid ||\theta|| = 1\}$. M is fixed at 256 in this paper. For one target sample x_{ti}, we project its classifier predictions to 1-D space by $\{\theta_m\}_{m=1}^{M}$. Then, the prediction discrepancy between two classifiers is calculated as

$$D = \frac{1}{M} \sum_{m=1}^{M} |S^i((V_t^m|_{i=1}^{n_t})_1) - S^i((V_t^m|_{i=1}^{n_t})_2)|, \tag{7}$$

$$(V_{ti}^m)_j = \langle C_j(G(x_{ti})), \theta_m \rangle = \theta_m^{\top} C_j(G(x_{ti})), \; j = 1,2$$

where S represents a sorting function from small to large. S^i is the value of the i-th element after sorting.

Consistent Uncertainty. Some instances are close to one decision boundary but far from another, indicating they are not the most challenging samples to identify. But they still are selected by the above query criterion. To further annotate the most significant target samples for the model adaptation, consistent uncertainty of two classifiers is proposed to evaluate the pieces in the candidate set. At the same time, constant uncertainty avoids variance and unreliable results relying on a single classifier. Unlike most entropy-based methods, we use the margin of the highest and the second-highest probability in the predicted distribution $p = C(G(x_t))$. The consistent uncertainty based on the two distinct classifiers can be formulated as

$$U(x_t) = \sum_{m=1}^{2} \frac{(1 - (p^* - p'))}{2}, \tag{8}$$

where $p^* = \max p$ and $p' = \max_{p \setminus p^*} p$ are the highest probability and the second-highest probability, respectively. A smaller margin means higher uncertainty. The consistent uncertainty only assigns a high score to the most ambiguous samples evaluated by two classifiers, reducing the uncertainty estimation bias under the domain shift.

3.4 Training with a Progressively Augmented Labeled Target Set

The small queried data may lead to class imbalance when the active selection focuses on partial categories. Previous active domain adaptation methods join the queried set to the source data. However, compared to the large source, the influence of the small queried group is weakened. To handle the issue, a gradually adding confident pseudo labels method is designed to supplement the small labeled target data. A temporal set M is initialized with current T_l at the beginning of an epoch. In each iteration, high-confidence samples are selected from a target mini-batch and added to M for supervised training. The objective in Eq. 3 becomes

$$\min_{\theta_g,\theta_{C1},\theta_{C2}} \mathcal{L}_{ada} = \mathcal{L}_{da} + \frac{1}{2n_m} \sum_{i=1}^{n_m} \sum_{j=1}^{2} \mathcal{L}_{ce}(C_j(G(x_m)), y). \qquad (9)$$

The latter two training processes are consistent with unsupervised domain adaptation. The model trained solely on the source domain is unreliable on the target domain under domain shift, so we consider gradually increasing the pseudo-labeled samples after active selection. Reliable pseudo labels are selected after the model learns more target information. Meanwhile, the category discriminability and diversity learning in the target domain further improve the predictive credibility.

4   Experiments

We evaluate the performance of the proposed method on two popular image classification datasets and compare with various methods, including Source-only, Random (randomly label some target data), BvSB [8], Entropy [29], CoreSet [24], Active Adversarial Domain Adaptation (AADA) [27], Active Deep Model Adaptation (ADMA) [27], Discrepancy-Based Active Learning for Domain Adaptation (DBAL) [17], S3VAADA: Submodular Subset Selection for Virtual Adversarial Active Domain Adaptation (S3VAAD) [21], Active Domain Adaptation via Clustering Uncertainty-weighted Embeddings (CLUE) [20], Transferable Query Selection for Active Domain Adaptation (TQS) [5].

4.1   Datasets and Implementations

We conduct our proposed algorithm on two benchmark datasets.

Office-31 is a standard benchmark including 31 classes of 4110 images. It contains three distinct domains: Amazon (A, images downloaded from online merchants), DSLR (D, high-resolution images captured by digital SLR cameras), and Webcam (W, low-resolution images recorded by web cameras).

Office-Home is a larger dataset with an enormous domain distribution discrepancy, which is more challenging than Office-31. It includes 15,588 images collected from four different domains with 65 categories: Artistic (Ar), Clipart (Cl), Product (Pr), and Real-World (Rw). We carry out 8 active domain adaptation tasks in this dataset.

Implementation Details. All experiments are implemented by PyTorch, which adopts the ResNet-50 pre-trained model on ImageNet as backbone networks, containing a feature extractor and substituting three fully connected layers as classifiers. In the experiments, we utilize mini-batch SGD with momentum 0.9 and a learning rate annealing strategy as [31]. Besides, we introduce one hyperparameter to balance the source domain supervised loss and the target domain loss, setting $\lambda = 0.1$ for all the experiments without tuning.

Table 1. Accuracy (%) on Office-31 with 5% target samples as the labeling budget.

Method	A→D	A→W	D→A	D→W	W→A	W→D	Avg
Source only	81.5	75.0	63.1	95.5	65.7	99.4	80.0
Random	87.1	84.1	75.5	98.1	75.8	99.6	86.7
BvSB	89.8	87.9	78.2	99.0	78.6	100.0	88.9
Entropy	91.0	89.2	76.1	99.7	77.7	100.0	88.9
CoreSet	82.5	81.1	70.3	96.5	72.4	99.6	83.7
AADA	89.2	87.3	78.2	99.5	78.7	100.0	88.8
ADMA	90.0	88.3	79.2	**100.0**	79.1	**100.0**	89.4
DBAL	88.2	88.9	75.2	99.4	77.0	100.0	88.1
CLUE	92.0	87.3	79.0	99.2	79.6	99.8	89.5
S3VAAD	93.0	93.7	75.9	99.4	78.2	100.0	90.0
TQS	92.8	92.2	80.6	100.0	80.4	100.0	91.1
LCD	**96.7**	**95.7**	**82.2**	99.1	**81.3**	99.8	**92.4**

4.2   Main Results

The average results of different methods with 5% annotating budget on Office-31 and Office-Home are reported in Table 1 and Table 2, respectively. Our method performs better than the baseline. Especially in challenging task D→A and W→A scenarios, our method achieves more than 81% accuracy only using 5% annotations. In the Ar→Cl and Pr→Cl tasks of the Office-Home dataset, our approach also shows excellent adaptation performance, which emphasizes the benefit of learning category discriminability.

Table 2. Accuracy (%) on Office-Home with 5% target samples as the labeling budget.

Method	Ar→Cl	Ar→Pr	Cl→Ar	Cl→Pr	Cl→Rw	Pr→Ar	Pr→Cl	Rw→Cl	Avg
Source only	42.1	66.3	50.7	59.0	62.6	51.9	37.9	42.6	51.6
Random	52.5	74.3	56.3	69.7	68.9	57.7	50.9	54.6	60.6
BvSB	56.3	78.6	58.1	74.0	70.9	59.5	52.6	56.4	63.3
Entropy	58.0	78.4	60.5	73.0	72.6	60.4	54.2	58.0	64.3
CoreSet	51.8	72.6	58.3	68.5	70.1	58.8	48.8	52.7	60.2
AADA	56.6	78.1	58.5	73.7	71.0	60.1	53.1	57.0	63.5
ADMA	57.2	79.0	58.2	74.0	71.1	60.2	52.2	57.5	63.6
S3VAAD	57.3	73.9	60.3	76.5	71.1	57.6	56.0	**63.1**	64.4
TQS	58.6	**81.1**	61.1	76.1	73.3	61.2	54.7	58.9	65.6
DBAL	**58.7**	77.3	61.7	73.8	73.3	62.6	54.5	59.9	65.2
LCD	58.5	79.9	**68.0**	**80.4**	**76.6**	**64.2**	**59.2**	62.0	**68.5**

4.3   Analysis

Varying Labeling Budget. This experiment shows that the LCD consistently outperforms other active domain adaptation approaches with various annotation budgets. Given 10% annotation budget in Office-31, the comparison results are shown in Table 3.

Table 3. Accuracy (%) on Office-31 with 10% target samples as the labeling budget.

Method	A→D	A→W	D→A	D→W	W→A	W→D	Avg
AADA	94.0	93.4	84.4	**100.0**	84.6	100.0	92.7
ADMA	93.5	93.1	83.2	99.7	84.2	100.0	92.3
CLUE	93.5	93.1	83.2	99.7	84.2	100.0	92.3
S3VAAD	98.0	95.6	81.0	99.4	81.6	100.0	92.6
TQS	96.4	96.4	**86.4**	100.0	**87.1**	100.0	94.4
LCD	**98.3**	**98.9**	85.5	99.9	84.9	100.0	**94.6**

Ablation Study. To validate each component of LCD, the experimental results with diverse settings are presented in Table 4. The improvement of the second row over the first row shows that the proposed query strategy is effective. The accuracy is increased by 0.5% when $\mathcal{L}_{BNM}$ is included, which verifies that learning target category discriminability and diversity is critical for active domain adaptation. The accuracy is boosted by 0.9% in the last row, proving the excellent performance of augmenting the queried set with pseudo labels.

Table 4. Ablation study on Office-31 with 5% budget. Ac-Sel: select informative target data; $\mathcal{L}_{BNM}$: batch nuclear-norm maximization loss; Pl-Aug: augment queried set with pseudo-labeled confident target data.

Ac-Sel	$\mathcal{L}_{BNM}$	Pl-Aug	O31
			88.4
✓			91.0
✓	✓		91.5
✓	✓	✓	92.4

Analysis of Selection Ratios. To analyze the affection of the selection ratio, we report the accuracy on Office-31($D \rightarrow A$) with varying α_1, shown as Fig. 2. It is worth noting that when α_1 is 1% or 100%, the model performance decreases. We leave it as future work to explore their more effective combinations.

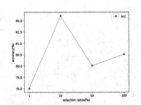

Fig. 2. Selection ratios analysis

5 Conclusion

This paper proposes a Learning Category Discriminability(LCD) approach for active domain adaptation, built on an improved collaborative alignment framework based on task-specific classifiers. Our method utilizes target prediction discrepancy and consistent uncertainty to select informative instances consistent with domain adaptation. Then, gradually augmenting queried data with confident pseudo labels is advocated to mitigate the issue of small queried data and obtain more target information. In addition, the reliability of pseudo labels is improved by learning target category discriminability and diversity. Extensive experiments demonstrate the efficacy of LCD in various active domain adaptation scenarios.

References

1. Bachman, P., Sordoni, A., Trischler, A.: Learning algorithms for active learning. In: International Conference on Machine Learning, pp. 301–310 (2017)
2. Cui, S., Wang, S., Zhuo, J., Li, L., Huang, Q., Tian, Q.: Towards discriminability and diversity: batch nuclear-norm maximization under label insufficient situations. In: Proceedings of the IEEE/CVF Conference on Computer Vision and Pattern Recognition, pp. 3941–3950 (2020)
3. Dagan, I., Engelson, S.P.: Committee-based sampling for training probabilistic classifiers. In: Machine Learning Proceedings 1995, pp. 150–157. Elsevier (1995)
4. Dasgupta, S.: Two faces of active learning. Theoret. Comput. Sci. **412**(19), 1767–1781 (2011)
5. Fu, B., Cao, Z., Wang, J., Long, M.: Transferable query selection for active domain adaptation. In: Proceedings of the IEEE/CVF Conference on Computer Vision and Pattern Recognition, pp. 7272–7281 (2021)
6. Grandvalet, Y., Bengio, Y.: Semi-supervised learning by entropy minimization. In: Proceedings of the 17th International Conference on Neural Information Processing Systems, pp. 529–536 (2004)
7. Gretton, A., Borgwardt, K., Rasch, M.J., Scholkopf, B., Smola, A.J.: A kernel method for the two-sample problem. arXiv preprint arXiv:0805.2368 (2008)
8. Joshi, A.J., Porikli, F., Papanikolopoulos, N.: Multi-class active learning for image classification. In: 2009 IEEE Conference on Computer Vision and Pattern Recognition, pp. 2372–2379. IEEE (2009)
9. Lee, C.Y., Batra, T., Baig, M.H., Ulbricht, D.: Sliced Wasserstein discrepancy for unsupervised domain adaptation. In: Proceedings of the IEEE/CVF Conference on Computer Vision and Pattern Recognition, pp. 10285–10295 (2019)
10. Li, S., Gong, K., Xie, B., Liu, C.H., Cao, W., Tian, S.: Critical classes and samples discovering for partial domain adaptation. IEEE Trans. Cybern. 1–14 (2022)
11. Li, S., et al.: Transferable semantic augmentation for domain adaptation. In: Proceedings of the IEEE/CVF Conference on Computer Vision and Pattern Recognition, pp. 11516–11525 (2021)
12. Long, M., Cao, Y., Cao, Z., Wang, J., Jordan, M.I.: Transferable representation learning with deep adaptation networks. IEEE Trans. Pattern Anal. Mach. Intell. **41**(12), 3071–3085 (2018)

13. Long, M., Cao, Y., Wang, J., Jordan, M.: Learning transferable features with deep adaptation networks. In: International Conference on Machine Learning, pp. 97–105 (2015)
14. Long, M., Cao, Z., Wang, J., Jordan, M.I.: Conditional adversarial domain adaptation. arXiv e-prints, arXiv-1705 (2017)
15. Long, M., Zhu, H., Wang, J., Jordan, M.I.: Unsupervised domain adaptation with residual transfer networks. arXiv e-prints, arXiv-1602 (2016)
16. Luo, Z., Zou, Y., Hoffman, J., Fei-Fei, L.: Label efficient learning of transferable representations across domains and tasks. arXiv e-prints, arXiv-1712 (2017)
17. de Mathelin, A., Deheeger, F., Mougeot, M., Vayatis, N.: Discrepancy-based active learning for domain adaptation. arXiv preprint arXiv:2103.03757 (2021)
18. Motiian, S., Jones, Q., Iranmanesh, S.M., Doretto, G.: Few-shot adversarial domain adaptation. arXiv e-prints, arXiv-1711 (2017)
19. Nie, Z., Lin, Y., Yan, M., Cao, Y., Ning, S.: An adversarial training method for improving model robustness in unsupervised domain adaptation. In: Knowledge Science, Engineering and Management (KSEM), pp. 3–13 (2021)
20. Prabhu, V., Chandrasekaran, A., Saenko, K., Hoffman, J.: Active domain adaptation via clustering uncertainty-weighted embeddings. In: Proceedings of the IEEE/CVF International Conference on Computer Vision (ICCV), pp. 8505–8514 (October 2021)
21. Rangwani, H., Jain, A., Aithal, S.K., Babu, R.V.: S3Vaada: submodular subset selection for virtual adversarial active domain adaptation. In: Proceedings of the IEEE/CVF International Conference on Computer Vision (ICCV), pp. 7516–7525, October 2021
22. Ren, P., et al.: A survey of deep active learning. ACM Comput. Surv. **54**(9), 1–40 (2021)
23. Saito, K., Watanabe, K., Ushiku, Y., Harada, T.: Maximum classifier discrepancy for unsupervised domain adaptation. In: Proceedings of the IEEE Conference on Computer Vision and Pattern Recognition, pp. 3723–3732 (2018)
24. Sener, O., Savarese, S.: Active learning for convolutional neural networks: a core-set approach. arXiv preprint arXiv:1708.00489 (2017)
25. Seung, H.S., Opper, M., Sompolinsky, H.: Query by committee. In: Proceedings of the Fifth Annual Workshop on Computational Learning Theory, pp. 287–294 (1992)
26. Shu, R., Bui, H.H., Narui, H., Ermon, S.: A dirt-t approach to unsupervised domain adaptation. arXiv preprint arXiv:1802.08735 (2018)
27. Su, J.C., Tsai, Y.H., Sohn, K., Liu, B., Maji, S., Chandraker, M.: Active adversarial domain adaptation. In: Proceedings of the IEEE/CVF Winter Conference on Applications of Computer Vision, pp. 739–748 (2020)
28. Tzeng, E., Hoffman, J., Saenko, K., Darrell, T.: Adversarial discriminative domain adaptation. In: Proceedings of the IEEE Conference on Computer Vision and Pattern Recognition, pp. 7167–7176 (2017)
29. Wang, D., Shang, Y.: A new active labeling method for deep learning. In: 2014 International Joint Conference on Neural Networks (IJCNN), pp. 112–119. IEEE (2014)
30. Wang, J., Chen, Y., Hao, S., Feng, W., Shen, Z.: Balanced distribution adaptation for transfer learning. In: 2017 IEEE International Conference on Data Mining (ICDM), pp. 1129–1134. IEEE (2017)
31. Xie, B., Li, S., Lv, F., Liu, C.H., Wang, G., Wu, D.: A collaborative alignment framework of transferable knowledge extraction for unsupervised domain adaptation. IEEE Trans. Knowl. Data Eng. (2022)

32. Xu, R., Li, G., Yang, J., Lin, L.: Larger norm more transferable: an adaptive feature norm approach for unsupervised domain adaptation. In: Proceedings of the IEEE/CVF International Conference on Computer Vision, pp. 1426–1435 (2019)
33. Yoo, D., Kweon, I.S.: Learning loss for active learning. In: Proceedings of the IEEE/CVF Conference on Computer Vision and Pattern Recognition, pp. 93–102 (2019)

Multi-level Contrastive Learning
for Commonsense Question Answering

Quntian Fang[1], Zhen Huang[1], Ziwen Zhang[1], Minghao Hu[2(✉)], Biao Hu[1], Ankun Wang[1], and Dongsheng Li[1]

[1] National Key Laboratory of Parallel and Distributed Processing, National University of Defense Technology, Changsha, China
{fangquntian,huangzhen,ziwen,hubiao,wak,dsli}@nudt.edu.cn
[2] Information Research Center of Military Science, Beijing, China
huminghao16@gmail.com

Abstract. Recent studies have shown that the integration of external knowledge greatly improves the performance of commonsense question answering. However, the problems of semantic representation discrepancy between questions and external knowledge as well as weak discrimination between choices have not been well ameliorated. To address the above problems, we propose Multi-Level Contrastive Learning named MLCL for commonsense question answering, which includes instance-level and class-level contrastive learning modules. The instance-level contrastive module aims to align questions with knowledge of correct choice in semantic space, and class-level contrastive module focuses on how to make it easier to distinguish between correct and wrong choices. The model achieves state-of-the-art result in CommonsenseQA dataset and outperforms competitive approaches in OpenBookQA. In addition, adequate experiments verify the effectiveness of contrastive learning in multi-choice commonsense question answering.

Keywords: Contrastive learning · Commonsense question answering · External knowledge

1 Introduction

Commonsense question answering is an important and challenging task, which requires reasoning over questions, knowledge and answers. In multi-choice commonsense question answering domain, there are two major research directions, the knowledge graphs (KGs) methods and context methods. For KGs methods, there have been several approaches coupling language models with various forms of KGs, including relational paths [8], graph relation network [4], joint graph reasoning [27] and simple MLP graph neural network [23]. Nevertheless, though KGs can capture structured and topological knowledge, the context method DEKCOR [26] points out that KGs methods lack context information. Meanwhile, DEKCOR introduces definitions of concepts from Wiktionary for

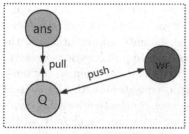 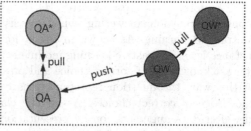

instance-level contrastive learning   **class-level contrastive learning**

Fig. 1. Intuitive demonstration of proposed MLCL. **Q** and **ans/wr** stand for question, knowledge of correct/wrong choices, while **QA/QW** stand for the input sequences containing correct/wrong choices. * stands for the corresponding data augmentation.

each choice to achieve remarkable result in the CommonsenseQA [21] research benchmark. Based on DEKCOR, KEAR [25] reaches human parity on CommonsenseQA by introducing more adequate context knowledge. The knowledge of each choice includes KG triplets, Wiktionary definitions of concept and extra retrieval training data.

Though context methods indicate great potentiality, context knowledge usually comes from a variety of sources. And the context methods leverage attention mechanism of transformer [22] to construct the connection between questions and context. However, the discrepancy of their representations in semantic space still exists. In the KEAR method, the knowledge graph triplets extracted are formatted as (s, r, t) and Wiktionary definitions generally are redundant and declarative sentences. Various knowledge suggests the correct answer, but there are reasoning gaps between the retrieved knowledge and original questions. This problem results in inconsistent semantic representations after PLM encoding (see Fig. 3).

Moreover, in multi-choice commonsense question answering, existing context methods only score the concatenation of question and context knowledge of each choice. They do not care about the association of different choices when scoring, which results in weak discrimination between choices. For example, consider a multi-choice commonsense question "*Some people prefer releasing energy through work while others prefer to release it through what? (A) motion (B) stretch (C) exercise (D) movement (E) muscles*". Since that "*exercise*" and "*movement*" are similar in interpretation, the human parity model KEAR [25] predicts '(D) *movement*' as answer, while the answer choice is '(C) *exercise*'. Context methods do not take into account knowledge of different choices at the same time, whereas human commonly compare the context knowledge of different choices in a comprehensive way [13] to derive the answer. To compare different choices, generative method [16] utilizes prompt patterns to generate contrastive explanation for binary classification commonsense reasoning, which is limited and complicated for multi-choice questions. In contrast, contrastive learning methods have been proved to be effective in improving representations [5] and distinguishing between classes [7] without the problems of generative methods.

Therefore, we propose Multi-Level Contrastive Learning (MLCL) for commonsense question answering, which consists of instance-level and class-level contrastive learning. As shown in Fig. 1, for the semantic representations, the instance-level contrastive learning module is proposed to pull questions closer to context knowledge of correct choice and push questions away from wrong ones. In this way, the question representations can be consistent with the context knowledge of correct choices. As for the class-level contrastive learning module, after data augmentation by presentation concatenation, we classify all the representation sequences based on whether containing the knowledge of correct choice. Then supervised contrastive learning is performed in terms of labels to pull the same class representations closer and push the different class representations away. Due to the existence of weak discrimination between choices, hard negative cases better promote the effects of contrastive learning [7]. As thus, correct and wrong choices can be more easily distinguished through class-level contrastive learning. Finally, the contrastive loss of two modules are obtained and combined in a certain proportion.

To evaluate the effectiveness of our proposed method, we conduct a series of experiments on CommonsenseQA and OpenBookQA. The experimental results show that MLCL outperforms other methods and also works on existing problems improvements.

2   Related Work

Commonsense Question Answering. Commonsense Question Answering has been a hot research in QA domain recent years. Generally, it requires real-world knowledge to understand and reason. Therefore, many previous works are devoted to how to leverage knowledge so as to answer commonsense questions. The works [3,15,17,28] have studied that pre-trained language models(PLMs) can be latent knowledge bases, while it is not enough in some cases. In order to provide explicit and interpretable knowledge, two main research direction including knowledge graph and context emerges. The knowledge graphs methods [4,8,23,27] apply graph neural network to commonsense reasoning based on some commonsense knowledge graphs like ConceptNet [20] and ATOMIC [18], which achieve remarkable results on many commonsense datasets.

In addition to knowledge graphs, context method DEKCOR [26] uses the Wiktionary definitions of the question concepts and answer concepts as external knowledge. KEAR [25] borrows REINA [24] method, which retrieves relevant questions and answers from the training data as external knowledge for commonsense question answering.

Contrastive Learning. Contrastive learning has been widely used in self-supervised learning for Computer Vision and Natural Language Processing. Supervised contrastive learning [7] extends the self-supervised batch contrastive approach to the fully-supervised setting.

In multi-choice commonsense question answering domain, there are a few contrastive thought methods proposed, such as elBERto [29] which introduces five additional self-supervised tasks and prompting template method [16] which designs the prompt patterns for generating contrastive explanation. In contrast, our proposed method fully utilize label information to mine the relationship between questions and knowledge of choices. On the other hand, we do not resort to patterns and generation, which is more universal and concise.

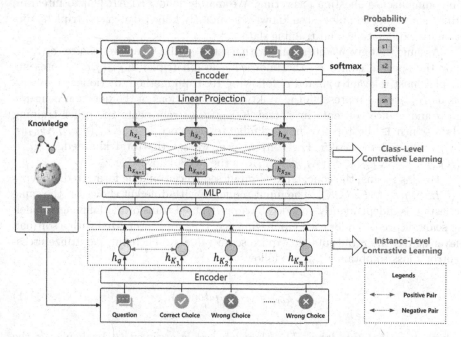

Fig. 2. Overview of our MLCL method. The bottom half part is instance-level contrastive learning and the above part is class-level contrastive learning. Green parts stand for the representations containing knowledge of correct choice and red parts stand for the representations containing knowledge of wrong choices. (Color figure online)

3   Methods

Problem Formulation. We focus on the task of multi-choice commonsense question answering. Formally, given a natural language commonsense question q and a set of candidate answer choices $c_1, ... c_n$, the task is to select the correct choice from the set of candidate answer choices. Whether KGs methods introduce structured knowledge graphs or context methods introduce context information to assist in answering, knowledge integration is essential for our research problem.

3.1 Knowledge Integration

In some cases, the commonsense questions do not contain any mention and context about answers. Moreover, most of the choices are tokens or phrases that do not provide sufficient semantic information. Therefore, knowledge integration, which provides a panoramic view of each concept is vital for contrastive learning in commonsense question answering. We mainly follow KEAR [25] to integrate three sources of commonsense knowledge, namely knowledge graph triplets, dictionary explanations and training data.

Assume that given a question q with a set of candidate answer choices $c_1, ...c_n$. For the specific choice c_i, the knowledge graph triplet $K_{KG}(q, c_i)$ represents triplet most relevant to q and c_i following KCR [9] method, dictionary explanations $K_{dict}(q, c_i)$ represents the Wiktionary definitions of the question concepts in q and choice concepts in c_i and $K_{train}(q, c_i)$ represents the other training data which is the top five most similar to sequence $[q; c_i; K_{KG}(q, c_i); K_{dict}(q, c_i)]$ evaluated by BM25. For convenience, we set the total knowledge $K_i = [K_{KG}(q, c_i); K_{dict}(q, c_i); K_{train}(q, c_i)]$ as the extra knowledge.

By this means, the concatenated input sequence could be formatted as: $X_i = [\langle CLS \rangle, q, c_i, \langle SEP \rangle, K_i]$. The input sequence with different choice for the same question is independently encoded by a pre-trained transformer language model. A scalar is predicted for each input sequence, then it is normalized with a softmax layer across the n outputs to acquire score value s_i. Thereout, we utilize cross-entropy loss to obtain $\mathcal{L}_{score}$ as follows:

$$\mathcal{L}_{score} = -\sum_{i=1}^{n} p_i log(s_i), \tag{1}$$

where p_i is the class label. The class label p_i is assigned to 1 when c_i is the answer to q otherwise it is assigned to 0.

3.2 Multi-level Contrastive Learning

In this section, we introduce our proposed method **Multi-Level Contrastive Learning (MLCL)** for multi-choice commonsense question answering including instance-level and class-level contrastive learning modules.

Instance-Level Contrastive Learning. Due to the various sources of contextual knowledge, there are significant discrepancies in semantic representations between questions and knowledge. To enable the model to learn more consistent representations between question and knowledge of choices, we design an instance-level contrastive learning module that allows questions and the knowledge of choices to be compared and contrasted with each other.

In contrastive learning, it's necessary to construct positive and negative cases. For a multi-choice commonsense question, we consider the knowledge of correct choice as positive case, and the knowledge of the remaining choices as negative cases.

In details, the knowledge of correct choice is denoted by K_p. q matching with K_p forms a positive pair (q, K_p), while q matching with others forms negative pairs. As the bottom half of Fig. 2 illustrates, we leverage one single pre-trained language model to acquire representations of questions h_q and representations of the knowledge $\{h_{K_1}, \cdots, h_{K_p}, \cdots, h_{K_n}\}$. Hence, the objective InfoNCE Loss [14] can be obtained as follows:

$$\mathcal{L}_{ins} = -\log \frac{e^{sim(h_q, h_{K_p})/\tau_{ins}}}{\sum_{i=1}^{n} e^{sim(h_q, h_{K_i})/\tau_{ins}}}, \tag{2}$$

where τ_{ins} is the configurable temperature hyperparameter, and following function [1] we select the cosine similarity as the $sim(\cdot)$ in this way:

$$sim(h_q, h_{K_p}) = \frac{f_q(h_q)^\top f_k(h_{K_p})}{\|f_q(h_q)\| \|f_k(h_{K_p})\|}, \tag{3}$$

where $f_q(\cdot)$ and $f_k(\cdot)$ are two diverse linear projection to project the representations into a lower dimension, which are applied to enhance their semantic capability.

Class-Level Contrastive Learning. The knowledge integration does not solve the weak discrimination between choices. Therefore, we introduce á class-level contrastive learning method, which divides the input sequences into two classes, the correct class and the wrong class. On the basis of this, supervised contrastive learning [7] method can be devised. The representations of the same class are closer to each other otherwise away from each other.

Specifically, for the original input sequence X_i that is encoded as h_{X_i} by the same PLM as the instance-level contrastive learning module, we perform data augmentation by concatenating h_q and h_{K_i} mentioned in instance-level contrastive learning. The augmented representation is denoted by $h_{X_{i+n}} = [h_q; h_{K_i}]$. Therefore, the representations of original n input sequences are augmented to get the corresponding n representations. Finally, all the representation sequences are formatted as $\{h_{X_1}, h_{X_2}, \cdots, h_{X_n}, h_{X_{n+1}}, \cdots, h_{X_{2n}}\}$. Based on the above description, we define the objective $\mathcal{L}_{class}$ as follows:

$$\mathcal{L}_{class} = -\sum_{i=1}^{2n} \frac{1}{2n_{p_i} - 1} \sum_{j=1, j \neq i}^{2n} l_{p_i = p_j} \left\{ \log \frac{e^{sim(h_{X_i}, h_{X_j})/\tau_{class}}}{\sum_{k=1, k \neq i}^{2n} e^{sim(h_{X_i}, h_{X_k})/\tau_{class}}} \right\}, \tag{4}$$

where τ_{class} is the configurable temperature hyperparameter, p_i is the class label described earlier, n_{p_i} is the number of original samples whose labels are p_i, $l_{p_i = p_j} \in \{0, 1\} = 1$ if $p_i = p_j$; otherwise $l_{p_i = p_j} \in \{0, 1\} = 0$, and $sim(\cdot)$ is similar to Eq. 3, while the concatenated representations are fed into a two-layer MLP which is different from the simple linear projection.

3.3 Training Objective

The final training objective contains three parts which is shown in Fig. 2. We can formulate the overall objective function as follows:

$$\mathcal{L}_{total} = \mathcal{L}_{score} + \alpha\mathcal{L}_{ins} + \beta\mathcal{L}_{class}, \qquad (5)$$

where α, β are weighting hyperparameters.

4 Experiments

4.1 Datasets and Baselines

In this paper, we evaluate our model on two benchmark datasets of multi-choice commonsense question answering: CommonsenseQA (CSQA) [21] and Open-BookQA (OBQA) [12].

CommonsenseQA. This is a popular 5-way multi-choice question answering dataset containing 12102 questions. The test set of CommonsenseQA is not publicly available, and model predictions can only be evaluated once every two weeks on the official leaderboard. Therefore, our main experiments follows the data split [8], which takes 1241 examples from official 9741 training examples as in-house (IH) test set and the rest 8500 examples as in-house training set, official 1221 dev examples as in-house dev set.

OpenBookQA. This is a 4-way multiple choice question answering dataset which consists of 5,957 elementary-level science questions. Since KEAR does not experiment on OpenBookQA dataset, we follow the preprocess steps of KEAR to process it. When processing, we replace the extra training data knowledge with the top 5 science facts retrieved by BM25 [11].

Baselines. We apply our method on two datasets and compare with other baseline models to test the contribution of contrastive learning modules. Specifically, for CommonsenseQA dataset, we pay more attention to KEAR [25] and DEK-COR [26] which both introduce similar context knowledge, and for OpenBookQA dataset, to be compared under the same conditions, we focus on single models without answer facts.

4.2 Implementation Details

Our method mainly follows the hyperparameters setting in KEAR, which includes max sequence length 512 and optimizer AdamW [10] with learning rate from $\{4e-6, 6e-6, 9e-6\}$ in DeBERTaV3-large PLM. The weight decay is in $\{0, 0.01, 0.1\}$ for 10 epoch on two datasets. For the linear projections' dimensions in Eq 3, we search over $d \times \{\frac{d}{2}, \frac{d}{4}, \frac{d}{8}\}$, and the two-layer MLP's dimensions are searched over $2d \times \{d, \frac{d}{2}, \frac{d}{4}\} \times \{\frac{d}{2}, \frac{d}{4}, \frac{d}{8}\}$ where d is the hidden size in PLM. The temperature hyperparameters τ_{ins} and τ_{class} are searched over in $\{0.1, 0.3, 0.5, 0.7, 1\}$. Finally, we search over α and β in $\{0.025, 0.05, 0.075, 0.1\}$. Due to the lack of GPU resources, we use the 4 times gradient accumulation with a batch size of 1 on 2 T V100 GPUs to follow batch size of 4 in KEAR.

Table 1. Performance comparison under data split [8] on CommonsenseQA.

Methods	IHdev-Acc	IHtest-Acc
RGCN [19]	72.7	68.4
KagNet [8]	73.5	69.0
MHGRN [4]	74.5	71.1
QAGNN [27]	76.5	73.4
GSC [23]	79.1	74.9
ChatGPT* [2]	–	74.0
DEKCOR [26]	83.5	81.4
KEAR [25]	90.3	87.7
MLCL (Ours)	**91.1**	**89.3**

Table 2. Performance of competitive models on the OpenBookQA test leaderboard.

Methods	Accuracy
BERT-Large	59.4
BERT + Careful Selection	72.0
DeBERTa + QAGNN	79.0
KF + SIR	80.0
ALBERT + KB	81.0
ALBERT + PG-Full	81.8
ChatGPT*	73.0
DEKCOR	82.4
KEAR	84.0
MLCL (Ours)	**85.2**

4.3 Main Results

To make a fair comparison, for CommonsenseQA, we reproduce DEKCOR and KEAR experiments under data split [8], which is more intuitive to see the effectiveness of our proposed method. We adopt the **Acc** evaluation metrics for performance comparison. We also compared the performance based on the current popular large language model ChatGPT. The method [2] only conducts experiment on random 100 samples, so the results are marked with * for reference only. The results may better illustrate that more effort is still needed in commonsense question answering.

CommonsenseQA Results. As shown in Table 1, it can be seen that our proposed method in single model achieves the state-of-the-art result. The results above line are based on graph reasoning, and under the line are based on extra context, which shows that the methods based on context knowledge have greater

Table 3. Ablations of different kind of contrastive loss. **Ins**, **Class** and **Class**^{M} indicate instance-level, class-level and multi class-level contrastive learning respectively.

Model	CSQA IHtest	OBQA test
MLCL	**89.3**	**85.2**
-Ins	88.7	84.8
cre -Class	88.1	84.2
-Class +Class^M	89.0	84.8

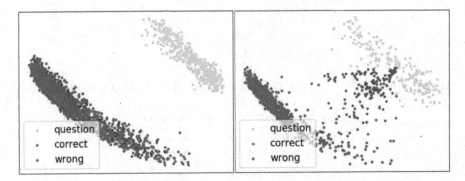

Fig. 3. Representations comparison on CSQA IHdev set. The left is the learned representations by KEAR, the right is by MLCL. Question and correct/wrong points represent question and knowledge of correct/wrong choices representations

potentiality. Compared with KEAR, on the IHdev set, there is 0.8% performance gain and on the IH-test set, there is 1.6% performance gain.

OpenBookQA Results. For the OpenBookQA results, as shown in Table 2, we did not employ the answer facts provided in OpenBookQA and we just use BM25 to retrieve the top-5 related facts as the extra input. For KEAR, we have implemented it on OpenBookQA. Compared with the single models without the answer facts on OpenBookQA test set, we outperform them.

4.4   Ablation Study

To illustrate the efficacy of our proposed two kinds of contrastive loss, we conduct an ablation study on CommonsenseQA and OpenBookQA test set. Table 3 demonstrates the performance of removing different contrastive loss. When the instance-level module is removed, it can be seen that 0.6% performance drop on the CSQA and 0.4% performance drop on the OBQA, which illustrates that the instance-level module contributes in the task.

For the class-level module, we additionally design a method called multi class-level contrastive learning (Class^M) which treats each choice as a single class instead of binary classification. From our experiments, it can be seen that

Table 4. Discrimination comparison on CSQA IHtest set. Ratio means the ratio of bad granularity wrong cases to all the wrong cases.

Model	Acc	Wrong cases	Bad granularity wrong cases	Ratio
KEAR	87.7	153	45	29.4
MLCL	**89.3**	**133**	**34**	**25.6**

both methods contribute, but binary classification based on whether the choice is correct performs better. The specific reason may be that the method [6] shows that binary classification results perform better than scoring each choice separately when the difference between the choices is large. The contrastive learning enhances the difference, which leads to better results for binary classification.

4.5   Effects of Problems Improvement

To better analyze the effects of our proposed method on problems improving, we conduct a series of comparative experiments on the CommonsenseQA. We mainly focus on whether the weak discrimination is ameliorated and how the representations improve compared to KEAR.

Representations Improvement. To better illustrate the consistency of semantic representations, we random select 500 samples from CSQA IHdev set and demonstrate their representations by PCA method. As shown in Fig. 3, from the left part KEAR method it can be seen that questions and knowledge are far apart, which suggests that they are inconsistent in semantic space, while in the right part MLCL method, questions are closer with knowledge especially correct knowledge. Through the comparison of the two parts, it can be seen the representations improvement of our proposed method.

Discrimination Improvement. In CommonsenseQA [21], it defines that the correct answer has finer granularity compared to one of the distractors as **bad granularity**. The bad granularity cases make weak discrimination more likely, which makes context methods more prone to error. As shown in Table 4, we conduct discrimination comparison experiments on CSQA IHtest set. It is obvious that our method MLCL has performance gain. For KEAR method, 45 of the 153 wrong cases with ratio 29.4 are due to bad granularity, while MLCL method only has 34 of the 133 wrong cases with ratio 25.6. Therefore, our proposed method has a superior improvement on weak discrimination.

4.6   Generality Analysis

In order to better illustrate robustness and generalization of our method on commonsense question answering, we conduct experiments to test the effect of our proposed method with different knowledge. The knowledge can be divided into two categories, including implicit knowledge PLMs and explicit knowledge

Table 5. Performance comparison on various PLMs. DV3-l stands for DeBERTaV3-large, RB-l stands for RoBERTa-large, AB-2 stands for Albert-base-v2 and E-l stands for ELECTRA-large.

Model	CSQA IHdev				OBQA Dev			
	DV3-l	RB-l	AB-2	E-l	DV3-l	RB-l	AB-2	E-l
KEAR [25]	90.3	79.5	71.8	84.6	82.2	72.0	66.2	78.6
MLCL(Ours)	**91.1**	**80.0**	**72.8**	**85.5**	**83.2**	**72.6**	**66.8**	**79.2**

Table 6. Performance comparison with different explicit knowledge on CSQA IHdev set.

Model	Triplets	Wiktionary	Training Data	None
KEAR	86.7	85.1	87.1	84.6
MLCL	**87.9**	**87.6**	**88.5**	**85.2**

K. KEAR only has relevant experimental results on the CSQA dev set, so in order to comparison, we mainly analyze on the dev set.

Implicit Knowledge. As shown in Table 5, we conduct experiments on CSQA IHdev set and OBQA dev set with different PLMs which performs well on most of commonsense question answering datasets. It is obvious that our method MLCL has performance gain on all PLMs. On the two datasets, there are maximum of 1% and at least 0.5% performance gains. In general, our proposed method MLCL performs better on different PLMs, which illustrates the generalization of MLCL.

Explicit Knowledge. We also probe the influence of MLCL on the extra explicit knowledge introduced. As shown in Table 6, we design the experiments with different explicit knowledge on CSQA IHdev set. The results show that there are performance gains on each type of knowledge, especially in Wiktionary knowledge 2.5% improvement. Few performance gains despite without extra knowledge, which indicates that the extra knowledge provides sufficient semantic information for contrastive learning to help performance gain. The robustness is demonstrated by experiments performance gain with different explicit knowledge.

4.7   Case Study

In this section, we analyze two examples from CSQA IHdev and OBQA dev set to illustrate how MLCL reasons more accurately than KEAR. As shown in Table 7, for the first question in CSQA, KEAR selects the wrong choice "satisfaction" probably due to the misleading triplet ["helping", "Causes", "satisfaction"], while the MLCL magnifies the differences in other knowledge between choices. Through this way, MLCL successfully selects the correct choice. The latter question in

Table 7. Case study for the effect of contrastive learning. We list two questions from the CSQA IHdev and OBQA dev set). The correct answers that MLCL selects are in **bold**, and KEAR model selects the wrong choices which are marked with an underline. Misleading means the knowledge that may cause KEAR to select the wrong choice.

CommonsenseQA:	
Question	She was always helping at the senior center, it brought her what?
Choices	A) satisfaction, B) heart, C) feel better, D) pay, **E) happiness**
Misleading Triplet	["helping", "Causes", "satisfaction"]
OpenBookQA:	
Question	Why can an Owl retain its body temperature during the winter?
Choices	A) It's neither,
	B) It's both,
	C) It's cold blooded,
	D) It's warm blooded,
Misleading Retrieval	June is during the winter in the southern hemisphere

OBQA should have been easy to answer correctly, while for the choice C, the misleading retrieval knowledge may cause KEAR to select wrong, since June is usually considered to be hot. MLCL pays more attention to contrast between "cold" and "warm". Therefore, in many cases, the performance of MLCL could be better.

5   Conclusion

In this paper, we propose MLCL, a multi-level contrastive learning framework for commonsense question answering including instance-level and class-level contrastive learning modules, which can effectively alleviate the problems found in context methods. Instance-level contrastive learning module makes the questions representations more consistent with knowledge representations, and class-level contrastive learning module makes it easier to distinguish between correct and wrong choices to improve the model performance. We also conducted a series of experiments on CommonsenseQA and OpenBookQA to demonstrate its effectiveness. For future work, we will apply the technique to other multi-choice tasks to improve language model performance with contrastive learning.

Acknowledgments. This work was supported by the National Natural Science Foundation of China (No. 62006243). We thank the reviewers for their helpful comments and suggestions.

References

1. Barkan, O., Caciularu, A., Dagan, I.: Within-between lexical relation classification. In: Proceedings of the 2020 Conference on Empirical Methods in Natural Language Processing (EMNLP), pp. 3521–3527 (2020)
2. Bian, N., Han, X., Sun, L., Lin, H., Lu, Y., He, B.: ChatGPT is a knowledgeable but inexperienced solver: an investigation of commonsense problem in large language models. arXiv preprint arXiv:2303.16421 (2023)
3. Bosselut, A., Rashkin, H., Sap, M., Malaviya, C., Celikyilmaz, A., Choi, Y.: Comet: commonsense transformers for automatic knowledge graph construction. In: Proceedings of the 57th Annual Meeting of the Association for Computational Linguistics, pp. 4762–4779 (2019)
4. Feng, Y., Chen, X., Lin, B.Y., Wang, P., Yan, J., Ren, X.: Scalable multi-hop relational reasoning for knowledge-aware question answering. In: Proceedings of the 2020 Conference on Empirical Methods in Natural Language Processing (EMNLP), pp. 1295–1309 (2020)
5. Gao, T., Yao, X., Chen, D.: SimCSE: simple contrastive learning of sentence embeddings. In: Proceedings of the 2021 Conference on Empirical Methods in Natural Language Processing, pp. 6894–6910 (2021)
6. Ghosal, D., Majumder, N., Mihalcea, R., Poria, S.: Two is better than many? Binary classification as an effective approach to multi-choice question answering. arXiv preprint arXiv:2210.16495 (2022)
7. Khosla, P., et al.: Supervised contrastive learning. Adv. Neural. Inf. Process. Syst. **33**, 18661–18673 (2020)
8. Lin, B.Y., Chen, X., Chen, J., Ren, X.: KagNet: knowledge-aware graph networks for commonsense reasoning. In: Proceedings of the 2019 Conference on Empirical Methods in Natural Language Processing and the 9th International Joint Conference on Natural Language Processing (EMNLP-IJCNLP), pp. 2829–2839 (2019)
9. Lin, J.: Knowledge chosen by relations (2020). https://github.com/jessionlin/csqa/blob/master/Model_details.md
10. Loshchilov, I., Hutter, F.: Decoupled weight decay regularization. In: International Conference on Learning Representations (2018)
11. Manning, C.D.: Introduction to Information Retrieval. Syngress Publishing (2008)
12. Mihaylov, T., Clark, P., Khot, T., Sabharwal, A.: Can a suit of armor conduct electricity? A new dataset for open book question answering. In: Proceedings of the 2018 Conference on Empirical Methods in Natural Language Processing, pp. 2381–2391 (2018)
13. Miller, T.: Contrastive explanation: a structural-model approach. Knowl. Eng. Rev. **36** (2021)
14. Oord, A.v.d., Li, Y., Vinyals, O.: Representation learning with contrastive predictive coding. arXiv preprint arXiv:1807.03748 (2018)
15. Pan, X., et al.: Improving question answering with external knowledge. In: Proceedings of the 2nd Workshop on Machine Reading for Question Answering, pp. 27–37 (2019)
16. Paranjape, B., Michael, J., Ghazvininejad, M., Hajishirzi, H., Zettlemoyer, L.: Prompting contrastive explanations for commonsense reasoning tasks. In: Findings of the Association for Computational Linguistics: ACL-IJCNLP 2021, pp. 4179–4192 (2021)

17. Petroni, F., et al.: Language models as knowledge bases? In: Proceedings of the 2019 Conference on Empirical Methods in Natural Language Processing and the 9th International Joint Conference on Natural Language Processing (EMNLP-IJCNLP), pp. 2463–2473 (2019)
18. Sap, M., et al.: Atomic: an atlas of machine commonsense for if-then reasoning. In: Proceedings of the AAAI Conference on Artificial Intelligence, vol. 33, pp. 3027–3035 (2019)
19. Schlichtkrull, M., Kipf, T.N., Bloem, P., van den Berg, R., Titov, I., Welling, M.: Modeling relational data with graph convolutional networks. In: Gangemi, A., et al. (eds.) ESWC 2018. LNCS, vol. 10843, pp. 593–607. Springer, Cham (2018). https://doi.org/10.1007/978-3-319-93417-4_38
20. Speer, R., Chin, J., Havasi, C.: Conceptnet 5.5: an open multilingual graph of general knowledge. In: Thirty-First AAAI Conference on Artificial Intelligence (2017)
21. Talmor, A., Herzig, J., Lourie, N., Berant, J.: CommonSenseQA: a question answering challenge targeting commonsense knowledge. In: Proceedings of the 2019 Conference of the North American Chapter of the Association for Computational Linguistics: Human Language Technologies, Volume 1 (Long and Short Papers), pp. 4149–4158 (2019)
22. Vaswani, A., et al.: Attention is all you need. In: Advances in Neural Information Processing Systems, vol. 30 (2017)
23. Wang, K., Zhang, Y., Yang, D., Song, L., Qin, T.: GNN is a counter? Revisiting GNN for question answering. In: International Conference on Learning Representations
24. Wang, S., et al.: Training data is more valuable than you think: a simple and effective method by retrieving from training data. In: Proceedings of the 60th Annual Meeting of the Association for Computational Linguistics (Volume 1: Long Papers), pp. 3170–3179 (2022)
25. Xu, Y., et al.: Human parity on commonsenseQA: augmenting self-attention with external attention. arXiv preprint arXiv:2112.03254 (2021)
26. Xu, Y., Zhu, C., Xu, R., Liu, Y., Zeng, M., Huang, X.: Fusing context into knowledge graph for commonsense question answering. In: Association for Computational Linguistics (ACL) (2021)
27. Yasunaga, M., Ren, H., Bosselut, A., Liang, P., Leskovec, J.: QA-GNN: reasoning with language models and knowledge graphs for question answering. In: Proceedings of the 2021 Conference of the North American Chapter of the Association for Computational Linguistics: Human Language Technologies, pp. 535–546 (2021)
28. Ye, Z.X., Chen, Q., Wang, W., Ling, Z.H.: Align, mask and select: a simple method for incorporating commonsense knowledge into language representation models. arXiv preprint arXiv:1908.06725 (2019)
29. Zhan, X., Li, Y., Dong, X., Liang, X., Hu, Z., Carin, L.: elBERTo: self-supervised commonsense learning for question answering. Knowl.-Based Syst. **258**, 109964 (2022)

Efficient Hash Coding for Image Retrieval Based on Improved Center Generation and Contrastive Pre-training Knowledge Model

Ye Liu[1,2,3,5], Yan Pan[1,5], and Jian Yin[4,5(✉)]

[1] School of Computer Science and Engineering, Sun Yat-sen University,
Guangzhou, China
liuye7@mail2.sysu.edu.cn, {panyan5,issjyin}@mail.sysu.edu.cn
[2] Artificial Intelligence Department, Lizhi Inc., Beijing, China
[3] Big Data Department, Lizhi Inc., Guangzhou, China
[4] School of Artificial Intelligence, Sun Yat-sen University, Zhuhai, China
[5] Guangdong Key Laboratory of Big Data Analysis and Processing,
Guangzhou, China

Abstract. In image retrieval tasks, effective hash coding methods can achieve better similarity preservation, so as to gain efficient retrieval results. Existing methods are usually divided into constructing global center constraints and utilizing local feature constraints. These methods mainly use the category labels of images as numbers, and do not fully exploit the value of classification labels as textual knowledge information. In this paper, we propose a novel and efficient hash coding framework. In the proposed method, the generation method of hash centers is improved, so that each image can correspond to multiple hash centers. In this way, the loss function for local similarity constraint is proposed, and the joint loss function for deep model is designed. Furthermore, based on the text-image pre-trained large model, we extract the text of the category label from the image as knowledge information, which is used to construct better hash codes for the image retrieval query, so as to improve the image retrieval evaluation effect. Extensive experiments on several large-scale datasets verify that the proposed method achieves better results than the state-of-the-art hash coding methods.

Keywords: Hash coding · Image retrieval · Center generation · Contrastive pre-training · Knowledge model

1 Introduction

Image representation can be used for classification, object detection, image segmentation, face recognition and other real world application scenarios. Since the breakthrough of deep neural networks architecture, deep learning methods become the cornerstone of image classification. In the supervised task of image classification, deep networks can predict class label and generate image

Z. Jin et al. (Eds.): KSEM 2023, LNAI 14120, pp. 332–342, 2023.
https://doi.org/10.1007/978-3-031-40292-0_27

representation simultaneously. Typically, deep neural networks pre-trained from large-scale image datasets are used to generate image representation as sample features for different kinds of downstream tasks.

For the image retrieval task, it is usually necessary to convert the images into the form of feature representations, and measure the distance between the image features. When given images are used to query as input, based on the image feature representation and distance measurement, the image retrieval framework can retrieve from the image database set similar to the image query set in content and form as output. The output image representations based on the deep neural network model are generally high-dimensional real number features, which take up more space in storage. Meanwhile, high-dimensional real number features also cost higher computing resources when calculating distance metric. In order to solve the problem of storage and computing efficiency in image retrieval, image hash coding frameworks and algorithms are widely studied and used [17].

Similarity maintenance is the key to achieve good results in deep hash coding. A two-stage hash coding algorithm is proposed in CNNH [23], it is one of the original deep hashing algorithms. By using the improved Network-in-Network deep network and adding a new triplet loss function, the end-to-end NINH [12] method is proposed and achieves better results than CNNH. Very recently, CSQ [24] proposes to generate global hash centers and use them as key tags in the supervised training process of deep hashing. However, CSQ constructs hash centers as supervised features from a global perspective, and does not make good use of local similarity features of images and image classification labels.

In recent years, the research of pre-training large model in natural language processing has made continuous progress. CLIP [19] is a model that is pre-trained with very large dataset of text and image pairs. After pre-training, text can be used for zero-shot transfer of the model to downstream image tasks. In most deep hashing algorithms, the category labels of images are usually expressed by 0 and 1, which obviously ignores the knowledge information of the natural language text that describes the category labels. With the text-image pre-training model, it is feasible to extract text knowledge from images in zero-shot mode. Through text knowledge extraction, image and text information can be combined and fully used in the scene of image retrieval.

In this paper, by improving the generation of global centers in CSQ, combining local similarity features with global constraints, and extracting text knowledge from images by pre-training model based on CLIP, the novel hash coding framework for image retrieval tasks is proposed. Figure 1 shows our proposed framework based on improved center generation and contrastive pre-training knowledge model.

2 Related Work

2.1 Deep Hash Coding for Image Retrieval

Hashing methods used for image retrieval tasks usually include traditional hashing and deep hashing [14]. The traditional hashing methods (LSH [6], ITQ [8],

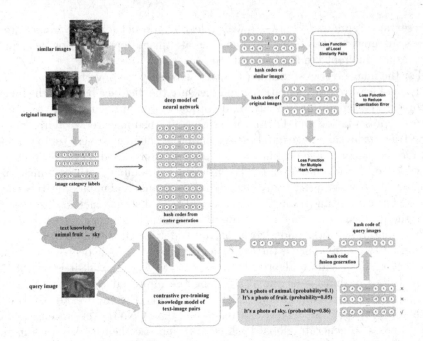

Fig. 1. Overview of the efficient hash coding architecture of improved center generation and contrastive pre-training knowledge model.

SDH [22], etc.) mainly use the hand-crafted image features, and obtain the hash codes through optimization algorithms. Since deep neural networks can learn the features of images at a deep level, and improve the training effect by using the related label information of images, supervised deep hashing method is the current mainstream. The initially proposed deep hashing algorithms (CNNH [23], MBH [16]) include a two-stage framework for learning. Firstly, the similarity matrix is constructed by image labels and the hash codes corresponding to the image for training are generated. Then the deep hashing model can be obtained by deep network training. In recent deep hashing work (DHN [25], HashNet [3], DCH [2], NINH [12]), the end-to-end models are realized by directly constructing the relationship with similarity or dissimilarity of local image features into the form of deep neural network loss function. Considering that adding global constraints can improve the retrieval accuracy of hash coding, CSQ [24] proposed a method to quickly construct a single hash center for each image and train deep neural network to fit the Hamming codes of hash center to the corresponding image.

2.2   Pre-training Model for Knowledge Feature Extraction

Image classification is to distinguish different types of images according to the semantic information of images. It is an important basic task in computer vision and the basis of other high-level visual tasks such as image retrieval, object detection, image segmentation, object tracking, face recognition, behavior analysis, etc. Image feature extraction through pre-training model of deep convolutional neural network is the mainstream paradigm at present. Pre-trained AlexNet [11] deep model is usually used for simple image feature extraction scenarios. In recent years, with the progress of residual network research, ResNet [9] has become the most important backbone of deep pre-trained models.

With the development of pre-training large models for natural language (BERT [5], GPT [20], T5 [21]), the text-image pre-training model CLIP [19] in multi-modal scenarios has been proposed immediately. By pre-training on large-scale real-world datasets, CLIP is applied to a variety of downstream tasks. In image retrieval task, CLIP can be used to extract textual knowledge from images.

3   The Proposed Framework and Method

In the task of hash coding for image retrieval, the mapping function Φ is defined, which is used to convert the high-dimensional image feature vector into a low-dimensional encoding form. The input of function Φ is the image dataset, define Q as the input image dataset, then the formal representation of Q is $Q = \{Q_x\}_{x=1,2,...,N} \in \mathcal{Q}$, where $\mathcal{Q}$ denotes the vector space of image features. Then the output of the mapping function Φ can be defined as $H = \{H_x\}_{x=1,2,...,N}$, where H_x denotes the output encoding of q bits. Similarity preservation is the key measure of hash coding quality. For the image feature pairs that are similar in the input Q of the original image space, the hash encoding pairs output by the mapping function Φ in the H space should also be similar.

3.1   Hash Coding Framework for Image Retrieval

Large-scale image datasets contain multiple category labels, more information can be used in the deep hashing framework to improve the effectiveness of hash coding by extracting and using the appropriate classification label knowledge information. The hash coding framework for image retrieval proposed in this paper consists of several components:

- Based on the existing method that each image corresponds to a single hash center Hamming coding, extended hash center generation procedure of multiple hash centers is improved for adapting multi-label images.
- The learning loss function is redesigned by gaining insight into the relationship of global hash centers and local similarity image features, which concludes the joint loss of multiple hash centers, local similarity pairs and reducing quantization error.
- A pre-trained deep model is used as the backbone network for fine-tuning to extract proper image feature information and generate the hash codes. Then another pre-trained deep model with text and image pairs is adopted for extracting text knowledge information from images in zero-shot mode.

3.2   Improved Hash Center Generation Procedure

For image data with multiple category labels, the knowledge information of class labels can be used to improve the effect of hash coding. In recent multi-label image hashing works, the deep models are used for training several times by segmenting the image or covering different parts of the image. Inspired by the end-to-end training procedure, we simplify and extend the construction method of multi-label image hash centers, so that the hash centers of each image are directly integrated into the deep network model training process, without the need for multiple training separately. The hash center generation process is based on the improvement of the research [24]. The difference is that each image can only correspond to one fused hash center in the original work, while our improved method enables each image to correspond to multiple hash centers.

3.3   Loss Function Designed for Deep Model

We design the loss function of efficient hash coding with deep model for image retrieval tasks, and the proposed joint loss function consists of three components.

Loss Function for Multiple Hash Centers
Through the improved hash center generation procedure, each image can generate one or more hash centers corresponding to different image category labels. To formally represent, the hash center codes of image dataset can be denoted as $C = \{C_{i,j}\}_{i=1,2,...,N \ and \ j=1,2,...,NUM(i)}$ and $NUM(i)$ represents the number of labels of the corresponding image category, then $C_{i,j}$ denotes the q bits binary hash codes. Similarly, for the hash encoding of the image dataset, we denote $\hat{H} = \{\hat{H}_i\}_{i=1,2,...,N}$, where $\hat{H}_i$ represents the real number encoding of q bits obtained from H_i by a simple transformation refer to the previous definition. Furthermore, we introduce the variable k to represent the k-th position corresponding to the encodings, so that we can use $H_{i,k}$, $\hat{H}_{i,k}$ and $C_{i,j,k}$ more concisely in the following formula representation.

With the above definition, the loss function of multiple hash center L_{mhc} is defined as below:

$$L_{mhc} = \frac{1}{q} \sum_{i=1}^{N} \sum_{j=1}^{NUM(i)} \sum_{k=1}^{q} \frac{C_{i,CLS(i,j),k} \log \hat{H}_{i,k} + (1 - C_{i,CLS(i,j),k}) \log (1 - \hat{H}_{i,k})}{NUM(i)}$$

(1)

where formula $NUM(i)$ is used to represent the number of category labels corresponding to image i, and the function $CLS(i,j)$ is denoted to show the position of the j-th class label of image i among all the class labels.

Loss Function of Local Similarity Pairs
In image retrieval tasks, local similarity can be used to improve the effect of hash coding, so similar image pairs can be constructed by category labels, and similarity preservation can be achieved by loss function constraints.

With the smooth loss proposed in [7], the loss function of local similarity pairs can be denoted as below:

$$L_{lps} = \begin{cases} \frac{1}{qN} \sum_{i=1}^{N} \sum_{k=1}^{q} 0.5(H_{i,k} - H'_{i,k})^2 & if \ |H_{i,k} - H'_{i,k}| < 1 \\ \frac{1}{qN} \sum_{i=1}^{N} \sum_{k=1}^{q} |H_{i,k} - H'_{i,k}| - 0.5 & otherwise \end{cases} \quad (2)$$

where H'_i is denoted as the encoding of similar image in each training mini-batch for H_i locally.

Loss Function to Reduce Quantization Error

In the process of hash coding model training, the output codes obtained directly from the deep model are real numbers, and the actual form of Hamming code needs to be generated eventually. So it is necessary to construct a quantization loss function to reduce the influence of quantization error.

So we define the following loss function to reduce the quantization error of image hash codes:

$$L_{rqe} = \frac{1}{q} \sum_{i=1}^{N} \sum_{j=1}^{q} (\|H_{i,j}\|_1 - 1)^2 \quad (3)$$

Joint Loss Function for Training Deep Model

In summary, we obtain the joint loss function for deep model training procedure, which is expressed as follows.

$$L = \lambda_1 L_{mhc} + \lambda_2 L_{lps} + \lambda_3 L_{rqe} \quad (4)$$

3.4   Contrastive Pre-training Knowledge Model

The pre-training knowledge model CLIP [19] used in the proposed hash coding framework is a contrastive learning based multi-modal deep model that trains a transferable vision model by using text as a supervised signal. The training data of the model is text-image pairs, an image and its corresponding text description, and the matching relationship between text-image pairs can be learned by contrastive learning model.

For image retrieval tasks, the hash coding process of each query image is divided into several stages. Firstly, the hash codes of the intermediate stage is obtained by the fine-tuned image deep model with the joint loss function. Secondly, the text knowledge information of the image category labels is used as the basis to construct multiple texts for describing the image, the contrastive pre-training model is used to obtain the probability of matching multiple texts to the query image in a zero-shot manner, and the text knowledge with high probability is filtered by a threshold. Furthermore, the text knowledge information with high probability is obtained, which corresponds to the image category label text in reverse, so as to obtain the hash codes of category centers with the hash center generation process. Finally, the hash codes of category centers and the hash codes in the intermediate stage of the query image are synthesized by embedding method to generate the final hash codes of the query image.

4 Experiments

4.1 Datasets and Baselines

In the following comparative experiments, we select three classical datasets for image tasks, and the datasets are divided into training, query and database for image retrieval evaluation.

- **MS-COCO** [13] is a well-known large-scale dataset for image segmentation and recognition, containing 80 different image categories. In the experiment, 10,000 images are randomly selected as the training set, and 5,000 images are chosen for test queries. Furthermore, 117,218 images are used as the database for image retrieval with hash codes.
- **NUS-WIDE** [4] is a labeled image data collection that contains images from websites with several tags. In the experiment, we used 81 categories as multi-label data, and randomly sampled 10,000 images as training set and 5,000 images for query, then selected 168,692 images as database retrieval set in the remaining part.
- **MIRFLICKR** [10] is an image set of 25,000 images selected from the Flickr dataset, which contains a total of 38 classification categories. Similarly, 4,000 images are used as the training set and 1,000 images were selected as the query dataset. Then the remaining 20,000 images were chosen to construct the search database.

Hash coding frameworks usually include traditional hashing methods and state-of-the-art deep hashing methods. We selected eight benchmark methods of traditional hashing and deep hashing as the evaluation reference in the comparative experiments, including KSH [15], ITQ [8], SDH [22], CNNH [23], NINH [12], DHN [25], HashNet [3] and CSQ [24].

4.2 Evaluation Metric and Implementation Details

As the experimental evaluation criterion, we selected the mean average precision (mAP [1]) metric commonly used for hash coding methods. Specifically, mAP evaluation is defined by the following formula:

$$mAP = \frac{1}{N_q} \sum_{i=1}^{N_q} AP_i \tag{5}$$

where AP_i represents the average precision of the i-th image.

The comparison experiments in this paper are carried out based on the Pytorch framework [18]. The training and testing procedures of hash coding are implemented on the GeForce RTX series GPUs cluster. In terms of the cornerstone model selection of deep neural network, ResNet is selected as the backbone network for training based on its extensibility and validity, which is used in the contrastive experiment of the deep hashing methods. For the hyper-parameter settings in the experiment, the size of each mini-batch is set to 64, and we train the proposed deep hash coding model with 30 epochs each time.

4.3 Experimental Results and Analysis

On MS-COCO dataset, we compare the proposed method with eight benchmark hash encoding methods, and the experimental results are shown in Table 1. The comparative experimental results show that the proposed method achieves the best result in mAP measure compared with the baseline method, and it can improve by 6.84%/2.53%/3.76% compared with the best benchmark experimental result on 16/32/64 bits hash codes.

Table 1. mAP of Hamming ranking w.r.t different number of bits on MS-COCO.

Method	MS-COCO (mAP)		
	16 bits	32 bits	64 bits
KSH	0.5232	0.5356	0.5362
ITQ	0.5671	0.5632	0.5125
SDH	0.5549	0.5641	0.5812
CNNH	0.6001	0.6183	0.6221
NINH	0.6447	0.6521	0.6477
DHN	0.7208	0.7322	0.7452
HashNet	0.7456	0.7729	0.7879
CSQ	0.7612	0.8521	0.8653
Ours	**0.8133**	**0.8737**	**0.8978**

On NUS-WIDE dataset, the proposed method achieves the best results on the compared baseline algorithms. According to the analysis of the experimental results, the proposed hash coding framework achieves 1.49%/4.78%/5.92% improvement in mAP measurement results on 16/32/64 bits respectively (Table 2).

Table 2. mAP of Hamming ranking w.r.t different number of bits on NUS-WIDE.

Method	NUS-WIDE (mAP)		
	16 bits	32 bits	64 bits
KSH	0.3562	0.3326	0.3363
ITQ	0.4597	0.4049	0.3462
SDH	0.4753	0.5541	0.5811
CNNH	0.5687	0.5822	0.5987
NINH	0.5972	0.6153	0.6383
DHN	0.6372	0.6629	0.6713
HashNet	0.6625	0.6982	0.7161
CSQ	0.7251	0.7451	0.7478
Ours	**0.7359**	**0.7807**	**0.7921**

On MIRFLICKR dataset, the proposed method achieves better results, so due to the length of the paper, Table 3 only shows the comparison results with the best baseline algorithm. As can be seen from the experimental results, the proposed method gain an increase of 5.76%/10.70%/13.57% with 16/32/64 bits hash codes compared to the best contrast method.

Table 3. mAP of Hamming ranking w.r.t different number of bits on MIRFLICKR.

Method	MIRFLICKR (mAP)		
	16 bits	32 bits	64 bits
CSQ	0.6852	0.6935	0.6943
Ours	**0.7247**	**0.7677**	**0.7885**

5   Conclusion

In this paper, we propose a novel efficient hash coding framework for image retrieval, and implement the improved hash center generation procedure. At the same time, we design a loss function for deep model training. In addition, the contrastive pre-training knowledge model is introduced from the perspective of image knowledge extraction. The effectiveness of the method is verified by comparative experiments on multiple datasets. In future work, we consider trying to add the vision transformer architecture to the training and extraction of the knowledge model to further improve the effect.

Acknowledgements. This work is supported by the National Natural Science Foundation of China (61772567, U1811262, U1911203, U2001211, U22B2060), Guangdong Basic and Applied Basic Research Foundation (2019B1515130001, 2021A1515012172, 2023A1515011400), Key-Area Research and Development Program of Guangdong Province (2020B0101100001).

References

1. Baeza-Yates, R., Ribeiro-Neto, B., et al.: Modern Information Retrieval, vol. 463. ACM Press, New York (1999)
2. Cao, Y., Long, M., Liu, B., Wang, J.: Deep Cauchy hashing for hamming space retrieval. In: Proceedings of the IEEE Conference on Computer Vision and Pattern Recognition, pp. 1229–1237 (2018)
3. Cao, Z., Long, M., Wang, J., Yu, P.S.: Hashnet: deep learning to hash by continuation. In: Proceedings of the IEEE International Conference on Computer Vision, pp. 5608–5617 (2017)
4. Chua, T.S., Tang, J., Hong, R., Li, H., Luo, Z., Zheng, Y.: Nus-wide: a real-world web image database from national university of Singapore. In: Proceedings of the ACM International Conference on Image and Video Retrieval, pp. 1–9 (2009)

5. Devlin, J., Chang, M.W., Lee, K., Toutanova, K.: BERT: pre-training of deep bidirectional transformers for language understanding. arXiv preprint arXiv:1810.04805 (2018)
6. Gionis, A., Indyk, P., Motwani, R., et al.: Similarity search in high dimensions via hashing. In: VLDB, vol. 99, pp. 518–529 (1999)
7. Girshick, R.: Fast R-CNN. In: Proceedings of the IEEE International Conference on Computer Vision, pp. 1440–1448 (2015)
8. Gong, Y., Lazebnik, S., Gordo, A., Perronnin, F.: Iterative quantization: a procrustean approach to learning binary codes for large-scale image retrieval. IEEE Trans. Pattern Anal. Mach. Intell. **35**(12), 2916–2929 (2012)
9. He, K., Zhang, X., Ren, S., Sun, J.: Deep residual learning for image recognition. In: Proceedings of the IEEE Conference on Computer Vision and Pattern Recognition, pp. 770–778 (2016)
10. Huiskes, M.J., Lew, M.S.: The MIR Flickr retrieval evaluation. In: Proceedings of the 1st ACM International Conference on Multimedia Information Retrieval, pp. 39–43 (2008)
11. Krizhevsky, A., Sutskever, I., Hinton, G.E.: ImageNet classification with deep convolutional neural networks. Commun. ACM **60**(6), 84–90 (2017)
12. Lai, H., Pan, Y., Liu, Y., Yan, S.: Simultaneous feature learning and hash coding with deep neural networks. In: Proceedings of the IEEE Conference on Computer Vision and Pattern Recognition, pp. 3270–3278 (2015)
13. Lin, T.-Y., et al.: Microsoft COCO: common objects in context. In: Fleet, D., Pajdla, T., Schiele, B., Tuytelaars, T. (eds.) ECCV 2014. LNCS, vol. 8693, pp. 740–755. Springer, Cham (2014). https://doi.org/10.1007/978-3-319-10602-1_48
14. Liu, H., Wang, R., Shan, S., Chen, X.: Deep supervised hashing for fast image retrieval. In: Proceedings of the IEEE Conference on Computer Vision and Pattern Recognition, pp. 2064–2072 (2016)
15. Liu, W., Wang, J., Ji, R., Jiang, Y.G., Chang, S.F.: Supervised hashing with kernels. In: 2012 IEEE Conference on Computer Vision and Pattern Recognition, pp. 2074–2081. IEEE (2012)
16. Liu, Y., Pan, Y., Lai, H., Liu, C., Yin, J.: Margin-based two-stage supervised hashing for image retrieval. Neurocomputing **214**, 894–901 (2016)
17. Luo, X., et al.: A survey on deep hashing methods. ACM Trans. Knowl. Discov. Data **17**(1), 1–50 (2023)
18. Paszke, A., et al.: PyTorch: an imperative style, high-performance deep learning library. In: Advances in Neural Information Processing Systems, vol. 32 (2019)
19. Radford, A., et al.: Learning transferable visual models from natural language supervision. In: International Conference on Machine Learning, pp. 8748–8763. PMLR (2021)
20. Radford, A., Narasimhan, K., Salimans, T., Sutskever, I., et al.: Improving language understanding by generative pre-training (2018)
21. Raffel, C., et al.: Exploring the limits of transfer learning with a unified text-to-text transformer. J. Mach. Learn. Res. **21**(1), 5485–5551 (2020)
22. Shen, F., Shen, C., Liu, W., Tao Shen, H.: Supervised discrete hashing. In: Proceedings of the IEEE Conference on Computer Vision and Pattern Recognition, pp. 37–45 (2015)
23. Xia, R., Pan, Y., Lai, H., Liu, C., Yan, S.: Supervised hashing for image retrieval via image representation learning. In: Twenty-Eighth AAAI Conference on Artificial Intelligence (2014)

24. Yuan, L., et al.: Central similarity quantization for efficient image and video retrieval. In: Proceedings of the IEEE/CVF Conference on Computer Vision and Pattern Recognition, pp. 3083–3092 (2020)
25. Zhu, H., Long, M., Wang, J., Cao, Y.: Deep hashing network for efficient similarity retrieval. In: Proceedings of the AAAI Conference on Artificial Intelligence, vol. 30 (2016)

Univariate Time Series Forecasting via Interactive Learning

Yu Li, Haonan Li, Peng Wang[✉], Xu Cui, and Zhenguo Zhang

Department of Computer Science and Technology, Yanbian University,
977 Gongyuan Road, Yanji 133002, China
{2021050054,2022050081,pwang,xcui,zgzhang}@ybu.edu.cn

Abstract. For time series forecasting tasks, it is necessary to capture the temporal dependencies from observed variables. Although many deep learning models have gained good performance, they still lack an effective modeling of temporal dependencies. Additionally, statistical features of time series often change over time, resulting in distribution shift issues. This is also one of the main challenges for time series forecasting. In this paper, we propose a module called Interactive Temporal-spatial Attention (ITSA), which combines interactive convolution and attention mechanism to effectively model the dependence between time and suppress the distribution shift problem. First, the time series is normalized and decomposed into trend and seasonal components. We then use an interactive learning strategy to extract the temporal dependencies of observed values at different data resolutions. Next, a normalized temporal-spatial attention mechanism is employed to capture the temporal-spatial features of the time series to prevent information loss. Finally, the true distribution is obtained by inverting the normalized data to achieve the purpose of suppressing the distribution shift. We employ a hierarchical way to stack the proposed ITSA, namely HITSA, to complete the forecasting task. The experimental results show that the model has good predictive performance in datasets of electricity and MOOC, and is significantly superior to other baseline methods, which indicates that the proposed ITSA can extract representative features from time series.

Keywords: Time Series Forcasting · Interactive Convolution · Temporal-Spatial Attention

1 Introduction

Time series forecasting (TSF) constitutes a crucial research field, encompassing diverse domains such as healthcare [1], energy management, traffic flow [15], financial investment [2], education [7], etc. In dealing with time series forecasting tasks, different methodologies are available, with the statistics-based and deep learning-based approaches representing the two most prevalent techniques.

During the decades, there are lots of methods for TSF task. Statistical learning based methods are first considered to solve the task. Autoregressive moving

Z. Jin et al. (Eds.): KSEM 2023, LNAI 14120, pp. 343–355, 2023.
https://doi.org/10.1007/978-3-031-40292-0_28

average model (ARMA) and its variants ARIMA, Seasonal ARIMA (SARIMA). ARMA assumes that the data is static, which is not suitable for reality. Although ARIMA changes this limitation, the data has no seasonality. SARIMA comprehensively considers the problem of data stationary and seasonal. With the wide application of deep learning models in TSF tasks and the good results achieved, the research focus has shifted to deep learning based methods.

Deep learning-based methods have become prevalent in time series forecasting (TSF) and can be categorized into three types: Recurrent Neural Network (RNN)-based [3], Transformer-based [11], and Convolutional Neural Network (CNN)-based [8]. RNN-based methods, such as FC-LSTM [14] etc. have emerged as a preferred choice in TSF due to their ability to retain past information in an internal memory state within the RNN structure. However, enabling parallel computation in RNN-based models remains a challenging issue. Attention mechanisms have recently emerged as a key driver of enhanced performance in long-term dependency learning [11], and attention-based approaches such as Informer [15] and Autoformer [13] have been proposed for TSF with favorable outcomes. Convolution-based methods, including Temporal Convolutional Network (TCN), have shown remarkable performance in capturing locally invariant relationships across temporal and spatial dimensions through 1D convolution operations. Nonetheless, discerning temporal connections between observations remains constrained in these approaches due to the lack of information on the temporal dimension of the series.

Although the aforementioned methodologies offer promising solutions for time series forecasting (TSF), a few challenges still exist. For instance, the statistical properties of time series data, such as the mean and variance, may change over time. Additionally, capturing temporal dependencies between observations and identifying critical features can be difficult, especially in multilayer models dealing with long-term time series data. To address these issues, we propose an effective data processing and feature extraction mechanism that leverages interactive learning to extract features from diverse resolution data. Our proposed framework first normalizes the time series to eliminate variations in statistical characteristics. It is then divided into two parts representing the trend term and the residual term, which are input to our model unit for interactive convolution operation. Furthermore, we have incorporated an attention module following the interaction operation to facilitate better understanding of the relationships between observations. Finally We have proposed the architectures named Hierarchical structures to undertake TSF tasks. To evaluate our approach, we have conducted experiments on two diverse time series datasets (ETT and education) and achieved robust performance in terms of forecasting accuracy.

2   Related Works

In this section, we first enumerate various time series forecasting methods and their limitations, and then explore the attention mechanism and its related limitations.

2.1 Time Series Forecasting Methods

The RNN-based TSF method can model complex internal rules without prior parameter calculation or excessive constraints on the time series properties [6]. This approach is more advanced than traditional methods and considers the intricate nature of the time series data [10]. However, constructing such a network can be complex due to the need for data preprocessing and fine-tuning multiple hyperparameters.

Google introduced the Transformer model in 2017 [11], which effectively replaces RNN models due to its use of self-attention mechanism in sequence modeling tasks. Transformers are better at predicting long time series than RNN models, as it propagates information over a short distance without requiring complex cyclic structures. Transformer-based TSF methods such as [5] combine high-performance multi-span forecasting with interpretable insights into spatiotemporal dynamics, leveraging interpretable self-attention layers to learn long-term dependencies. Proven to be effective in predicting long sequences, but these models have significant overhead, and ongoing research is aimed at addressing this issue.

2.2 Attention-Based Blocks

The attention mechanism is prevalent in deep learning models due to its ability to capture the relationships between features and sequences. One example of such a mechanism is the Squeeze and Excitation (SE) module [4], which compresses the feature map obtained from convolution to obtain global features at the channel level. The SE module performs text processing on these global features and learns the relationship between channels, generating weights for different channels. The final feature is obtained by multiplying with the original feature map. Essentially, the SE module executes attention or gating operations in the channel dimension, enabling models to concentrate more on channel features with important information while suppressing unimportant ones. Another point is that the SE module is generic, so it can be embedded in existing network architectures. However, experimental outcomes did not show a significantly improvement after the addition of the SE module.

The BAM module (Bottleneck Attention Module) [9] improves time series forecasting accuracy by directing the model's attention towards the most important parts of the time series, while also enhancing the model's generalization ability by identifying the key features of the time series that it should focus on. However, the BAM module's automatic selection and adjustment of the data parts that the model focuses on results in reduced interpretability, making it difficult for users to understand why the model generates specific forecasting.

The Convolution Block Attention Module (CBAM) [12] comprises two attention mechanism modules, namely the channel attention module and the spatial attention module. The former processes feature maps of different channels and instructs the model to pay closer attention to them, while the latter processes feature regions of the feature map and highlights which regions should receive greater emphasis. However, receptive field that CBAM can utilize is limited.

3   Methodology

Given a time series T and a look-back window of fixed length L, at timestamp t, time series forecasting is to predict $\hat{T}(t+1:t+\tau) = T_{(t+1)}, \cdots, T_{(t+\tau)}$ based on the past L steps. Here, τ is the length of the forecast horizon, $X_t \in R^d$ is the value at time step t, and d is the number of dimension. For simplicity, in the following, we will omit the subscripts, and use T and $\hat{T}$ represent the historical data and the forecasting, respectively.

3.1   Time Series Decomposilion

Wu et al. [13] propose seasonal trend decomposition of time series data, and confirm the validity of the idea through experiments. Therefore, we borrow the idea and divide the original time series into two parts, trend term T_{tre} and residual term T_{res}. We use a sliding average kernel to extract trend and seasonal components from the normalized time series.

For time series T, its statistical characteristics change unpredictably with increasing time steps, leading to the issue of distribution shift. Normalizing the time series at the outset effectively mitigates distribution differences, but reverse normalization is needed to restore output to the correct distribution. After normalizing the time series, a moving average kernel is applied to extract trend components T_{tre} and seasonal components T_{res} by eliminating random noise and aiding in decomposition of the time series. Calculation of the moving average occurs from beginning to end, with each data point averaged by the same kernel. Feature extraction through the moving average kernel facilitates better extraction of time-dependent relationships among observed values.

3.2   Interactive Temporal-Spatial Attention (ITSA) Block

ITSA is a module that integrates convolution and normalized temporal-spatial attention mechanisms by a interactive way, and its organizational structure is illustrated in Fig. 1. ITSA involves two layers of interactive convolution and normalized temporal-spatial attention mechanisms on processed input data. The primary objective is to achieve information interaction and capture of time-dependent relationships within the data.

Interactive Learning. The pre-processing of time series involves decomposing the data which benefits the model in capturing the temporal properties, However, it often results in information loss. To compensate for drawback, we employs a novel interactive learning strategy that learns affine transformation parameters for each subsequence, which is an information exchange way to ensure information integrity. The interaction convolution calculation process in ITSA begins by normalizing T to suppress statistical characteristic changes with increasing time steps. Then, T is decomposed into T_{tre} and T_{res} representing the trend and seasonal components respectively to highlight the temporal characteristics.

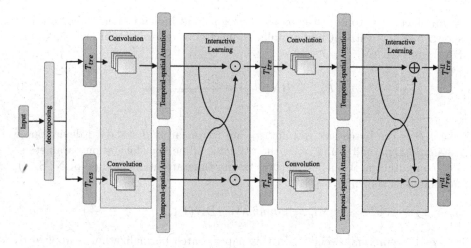

Fig. 1. The architecture of our ITSA block.

The two parts, T_{tre} and T_{res}, are handled through 1D convolution and NTSA modules with different structures. These modules project T_{tre} and T_{res} into hidden states. After normalization with spatiotemporal attention mechanism, information interaction is performed between them. This process can be viewed as scale transformation on T_{tre} and T_{res}, where the scaling factor is learned. *LeakyReLU* is utilized after the first convolutional layer due to its temporal nature and potential for reducing gradient vanishing, while *Tanh* is applied after the second convolutional layer to keep positive and negative features within the range of $[-1, 1]$.

Afterwards, T_{tre} and T_{res} are projected into two additional hidden states via 1D convolution and NTSA modules. Information interaction occurs between these updated features. Then, two operations, addition and subtraction, are employed to retain the feature information left. Two updated sub-features, T_{tre} and T_{res}, are output by the interactive learning module. Extracted features contain both isomorphic and heteromorphic information due to the independence of the convolutional kernels, augmenting feature attributes. See Eq. 1 and Eq. 2 for the detailed calculation process.

$$T_{tre}^l = T_{tre} \odot conv(T_{res}), \quad T_{res}^l = T_{res} \odot conv(T_{tre}) \tag{1}$$

$$T_{tre}^{ll} = T_{tre}^l \pm conv(T_{res}^l), \quad T_{res}^{ll} = T_{res}^l \pm conv(T_{tre}^l) \tag{2}$$

Normalized Temporal-Spatial Attention (NTSA). NTSA is primarily designed to address the weight issues in attention mechanisms during computation, as well as capture the temporal dependency among observation values. It integrates CBAM and redesigns the attention sub-module. In this paper, we aim to enhances attention by utilizing the importance of weights represented by the scaling factor of Batch Normalization. The temporal attention sub-module uses scaling factor w_γ to adjust channel variations and indicate their importance as shown in Eq. 3, without adding fully connected or convolutional layers like SE, BAM, and CBAM.

$$B_{out} = BN(B_{in}) = \frac{B_{in} - \mu_\beta}{\sqrt{\sigma_\beta^2 + \varepsilon}} + \beta \qquad (3)$$

where B is the batch size, μ_β and σ_β are the mean and standard deviation of the mini-batch, and γ and β are the trainable affine transformation parameters. The computation of output features in the time attention module of NTSA is calculated as shown in Eq. 4.

$$M_c = sigmoid(W_\gamma(BN(F1)) \qquad (4)$$

where W_γ represents weights. In this paper, batch normalization is applied to the spatial dimension, which is referred to as spatial normalization. The output features of the spatial attention module in NTSA are shown in Eq. 5.

$$M_s = sigmoid(W_\lambda(BN_s(F2)) \qquad (5)$$

where W_λ represents weight. The sum of these two sub-modules represents the proportionality factors. In NTSA, the Loss function is shown in Eq. 6:

$$Loss = \sum_{(x,y)} L(f(x, W), y) + p\sum g(\gamma) + p\sum g(\lambda) \qquad (6)$$

To suppress insignificant weights, a regularization term $g(.)$ is added to the loss function. L1 regularization with $g(s) = \|s\|$ is a common approach. The coefficient p balances weights $g(\gamma)$ and $g(\lambda)$, and its value can adjust model performance. Regularization of scale factors γ and λ is applied in the loss function $\sum_{(x,y)} L(f(x, W), y)$, where γ maps each channel's output to a new scale. combined with sparse regularization, unimportant channels and their corresponding scale factors are set to 0. Then, we remove smaller scale factors and corresponding channels to reduce parameter count and computational complexity.

3.3   Hierarchical Stacking of ITSA

In this section, we build our overall model (HITSA) in a Hierarchical way, which use a stack of multiple ITSA modules. Figure 2 shows the structure.

In HITSA, normalized and de-normalized operation are used before data input and output respectively. After that, effective feature learning of different time resolutions is allowed through step-by-step decomposition of time series and information interaction processing. Generally, information from previous levels will accumulate, and deeper features will contain additional and finer temporal information. In this way, the short-term and long-term dependencies can be captured. The *Concat&Realign* representation rearranges the output into a new

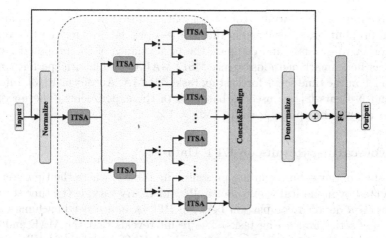

Fig. 2. The architecture of our hierarchical HITSA.

sequence, then it is added to the original time series for forecasting. Finally, a fully connected layer is employed to complete the forecasting.

For HITSA, input time series $T(k = 1)$ or feature vector $\hat{T}^{(k-1)} = \hat{t}_1^{(k-1)}, \cdots, \hat{t}_\tau^{(k-1)}$ (for $k > 1$). Figure 1 shows that the ITSA module captures temporal dependencies in time series and feature vectors at different resolutions. Deeper features contain finer time information from shallower levels. This allows short-term and long-term dependencies to be captured in the TSF task. After traversing each HITSA branch, data is merged and concatenated into a new sequential representation. A de-normalization operation is performed to conform to the true distribution. The enhanced sequential representation is decoded into $\hat{T}^k = \hat{t}_1^k, \cdots, \hat{t}_\tau^k$ (for $k > 1$) using fully connected layers. HITSA does not need to downsample the original sequence for feature extraction, as it does not benefit forecasting. Thus, m (number of stacked layers) can be much smaller than the backward view window size $log_2 M$.

4   Experiments

4.1   Experimental Setup

In order to verify the effectiveness of our proposed model, we conduct relevant experiments on the ETT dataset in the power field and the MOOC dataset in the education field. ETT dataset consists of 2 years of electricity data from two counties in China, including hourly subsets ETTh1, ETTh2 and quarter-hourly subset ETTm1. Each data point includes a 'oil temperature' value and 6 power load features. The training, validation, and test sets contain data for 12 months, 4 months, and 4 months, respectively. MOOC dataset used in our study is sourced from the Open University (OU) that analyzed 15 terms of courses from 7 modules in 2013 and 2014 at the Open University. Interaction clickstream data from forums, course content, and resources are used to analyze student dropout rates, resulting in three time-series datasets for the 15 modules.

In order to evaluate and compare the performance of the proposed method and other benchmark methods, we use MSE, MAE to evaluate the performance of the model on the time series forecasting task. ARIMA, Autoformer [13], Informer [15], and N-Beats [8] are used as baselines in the experiments. The maximum number of training epochs is set to 150.

4.2   Forecasting Results on ETT Dataset

The results of our experiment are presented in Table 1, where the time steps are represented by numerical values such as 24 and 48. By varying the time steps, we can obtain a detailed comparison between HITSA and other benchmark models in time series forecasting tasks. The result reveals that the MAE and MSE increase with the increase in time step, for both HITSA and the baseline model. Nevertheless, on the three sub-datasets of the ETT dataset, the MAE and MSE for HITSA only increase by a maximum of 0.24 and 0.283, respectively, which is lower than those of other baseline models. The findings indicate that HITSA exhibits similar performance for long-term time series forecasting as well as for short-term time series forecasting, Hierarchical structure effectively addressing the issue of a significant decline in the evaluation index with longer sequences. When compared to the baseline model, HITSA outperforms at each time step. Compared to ARIMA, HITSA accounts for seasonal factors in time series and utilizes attention mechanisms to better capture temporal dependencies unique to time series data. Although N-beats also incorporates unique properties of time series data and employs residual network architecture for learning trend and seasonal models, it underperforms compared to our model and other baseline models. The unique attention module and hierarchical stacking structure of modules in our proposed model enable us to extract deeper features from the data, including shallow features that are otherwise difficult to extract. This approach enables us to more fully exploit relevant information in the data for improved performance. As a result, our proposed model, HITSA, achieves 22% higher performance than sub-optimal N-beats. This validates the effectiveness of our proposed model's attention module and hierarchical stacking structure.

4.3   Dropout Rates Forecasting for MOOC Dataset

Table 2 presents the performance of our HITSA model on the MOOC dataset. Our results show that compared with the baseline models Informer and Autoformer, HITSA achieves the lowest MAE of 15.76 and MAPE of 9.79 for Social Science courses, and 16.13 and 10.11 for STEM courses, respectively, which achieve the best results. Furthermore, while Autoformer may yield suboptimal outcomes, it has demonstrated comparative advantages over Informer in the extraction and forecast of long-term sequential information in the domain of education, owing to its focused attention on data seasonality modeling and self-attention mechanisms at the subsequence level. HITSA's deep hierarchical

Table 1. Univariate time-series forecasting results on the ETT dataset

sub-dataset	Model	Evaluation	24	48	168	336	720
ETTh1	ARIMA	MSE	0.108	0.175	0.369	0.468	0.659
		MAE	0.284	0.424	0.504	0.593	0.766
	Autoformer	MSE	0.115	0.168	1.224	1.549	2.735
		MAE	0.275	0.33	0.763	1.82	3.253
	Informer	MSE	0.098	0.158	0.183	0.222	0.269
		MAE	0.247	0.319	0.346	0.387	0.435
	N-Beats	MSE	0.042	0.065	0.106	0.127	0.269
		MAE	0.156	0.2	0.255	0.284	0.422
	HITSA	MSE	**0.029**	**0.045**	**0.079**	**0.091**	**0.169**
		MAE	**0.13**	**0.163**	**0.22**	**0.239**	**0.329**
ETTh2	ARIMA	MSE	3.554	3.190	2.8	2.753	2.878
		MAE	0.445	0.474	0.595	0.738	1.044
	Autoformer	MSE	0.199	0.304	2.145	2.096	3.355
		MAE	0.381	0.462	1.068	2.534	4.664
	Informer	MSE	0.093	0.155	0.232	0.263	0.277
		MAE	0.24	0.314	0.389	0.417	0.431
	N-Beats	MSE	0.078	0.123	0.244	0.27	0.281
		MAE	0.21	0.271	0.393	0.481	0.532
	HITSA	MSE	**0.064**	**0.076**	**0.113**	**0.173**	**0.243**
		MAE	**0.182**	**0.199**	**0.258**	**0.341**	**0.399**
ETTm1	ARIMA	MSE	0.09	0.179	0.272	0.462	0.639
		MAE	0.206	0.306	0.399	0.558	0.697
	Autoformer	MSE	0.12	0.133	0.194	0.452	1.747
		MAE	0.29	0.305	0.396	0.574	1.874
	Informer	MSE	0.03	0.069	0.194	0.401	0.512
		MAE	0.137	0.203	0.372	0.554	0.644
	N-Beats	MSE	0.031	0.056	0.095	0.157	0.207
		MAE	0.117	0.168	0.234	0.311	0.37
	HITSA	MSE	**0.017**	**0.044**	**0.07**	**0.115**	**0.175**
		MAE	**0.079**	**0.14**	**0.191**	**0.25**	**0.319**

structure allows it to capture both long and short-term temporal dependencies in the MOOC dataset, thus enabling it to better predict dropout rates. Additionally, HITSA's unique normalization and de-normalization operations enable it to preserve data information, which is crucial for accurate forecasting of dropout rates. HITSA decomposes the data into trend and seasonal factors, which makes it well-suited for forecasting in the education domain. These findings highlight

Table 2. The course types are the predicted result of Social Science and STEM

Dataset	course type	Evaluation	Baselines		Ours
			Informer	Autoformer	HITSA
AAA2013J	SocicalScience	MAE	18.87	18.18	**15.76**
		MAPE	18.63	18.91	**14.28**
AAA2014J		MAE	22.81	24.7	**16.84**
		MAPE	14.31	17.12	**10.86**
BBB2013J		MAE	21.42	17.86	**15.8**
		MAPE	13.09	11.45	**9.79**
EEE2013J	STEM	MAE	19.77	18.62	**16.76**
		MAPE	19.23	19.77	**15.22**
EEE2014J		MAE	23.11	25.16	**17.14**
		MAPE	14.72	17.66	**11.02**
FFF2013J		MAE	21.83	18.12	**16.13**
		MAPE	13.72	12.35	**10.11**

the potential of HITSA as a powerful tool for dropout rate forecasting in the field of education.

4.4 The Effect of Hyperparameters

Next, We analyze the influence of K (model stacking size) and L (module stacking depth) on three datasets, using MAE as the evaluation metric. To better observe the differences between the experimental data, we examine how module stacking depth and model stacking size affect MOOC dropout rate forecasting. We keep K fixed at 1 and L fixed at 3.

Figure 3 demonstrates that MAE decreases as L increases, but excessive data loss resulting from the data flow process causes forecasting accuracy to decline when L surpasses 3. Increasing L leads to greater interaction information between modules and more detailed time information from shallower layers, but a large value of L also causes partial data loss through data decomposition, which affects forecasting performance. Figure 4 confirms that fixing L at 3 and increasing K reduces MAE, reaching an optimal result at $K = 2$. However, further increases in K lead to insufficient information for effective MOOC dropout rate forecasting. Therefore, stacking multiple HITSAs can increase model depth and reduce overfitting while learning complex time series patterns. However, when the number of HITSA models exceeds 2, MAE increases due to unstable forecasting results. In conclusion, the optimal configuration for time series forecasting is achieved when K is 2 and L is 3.

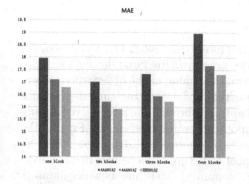
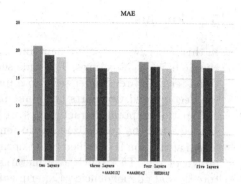

Fig. 3. Effect of the number of HITSA stacks on MAE

Fig. 4. Effect of the number of ITSA stacking layers on MAE

4.5 Ablation Study

To validate proposed modules for TSF tasks, we conduct experiments on MOOC datasets and test multiple variants of the modules on two types of course datasets. After fixing the number of layers of ITSA, we do experiments with four variants. Variant 1 remove NTSA and use a linear structure during stacking, variant 2 remove NTSA and use a hierarchical structure, variant 3 stack a hierarchical structure but removed residual connections, and variant 4 use CBAM instead of NTSA. As shown in Table 3. ITSA stacked in a hierarchical structure showed significantly better performance than in a linear structure. Removing residual connections led to a 10% decrease in model performance. Despite the use of *ReLU* and regularization techniques, a deep network is required to capture large-range time dependencies, and residual connections effectively avoid issues such as gradient vanishing and exploding that may occur during the stacking of large models. In the third variant experiments, the fully connected layer is crucial for high forecasting accuracy, as it extract and fuse relevant temporal information based on supervision. Results in Table 3 show that NTSA outperform CBAM by 12%, which states weight reduction of less significant features can lead to more efficient weight computation. These findings suggest the superior performance of our constructed NTSA in TSF tasks.

Table 3. Component selection experiment of ITSA on AAA2013J, AAA2014J, EEE2013J dataset

NTSA	Hierarchical	Linear	Residual	CBAM	MAE		
					AAA2013J	AAA2014J	EEE2013J
		✓	✓		19.32	22.21	20.21
	✓		✓		18.91	21.42	19.11
✓	✓				17.69	17.13	18.43
	✓		✓	✓	18.02	19.85	19.22
✓	✓		✓		**15.76**	**16.12**	**16.01**

5   Conclusion

In this paper, we propose a new time series forecasting block ITSA and design a Hierarchical architectures. The time series are normalized and decomposed into trend term and remainder term to improve the timing of the observation. Then, the decomposed two parts are input into the model, and the time dependence and spatio-temporal characteristics are captured through the interactive learning strategy and the normalized spatio-temporal attention mechanism. Finally, the true distribution is obtained by de-normalized to suppress distribution shift. The design of the ITSA block as a hierarchical structure is more beneficial to capture the data dependencies. Experiments on multiple real-time sequence datasets show that the proposed model is effective for TSF tasks.

Acknowledgment. This work is supported by the National Natural Science Foundation of China [grant numbers 62162062], the Science and Technology Project of Jilin Provincial Education Department [JJKH20220538KJ, JJKH20230622KJ].

References

1. Bahadori, M.T., Lipton, Z.C.: Temporal-clustering invariance in irregular healthcare time series. arXiv preprint arXiv:1904.12206 (2019)
2. D'Urso, P., De Giovanni, L., Massari, R.: Trimmed fuzzy clustering of financial time series based on dynamic time warping. Ann. Oper. Res. **299**(1), 1379–1395 (2021)
3. Graves, A., Graves, A.: Long short-term memory. Supervised sequence labelling with recurrent neural networks, pp. 37–45 (2012)
4. Hu, J., Shen, L., Sun, G.: Squeeze-and-excitation networks. In: Proceedings of the IEEE Conference on Computer Vision and Pattern Recognition, pp. 7132–7141 (2018)
5. Lim, B., Arık, S.Ö., Loeff, N., Pfister, T.: Temporal fusion transformers for interpretable multi-horizon time series forecasting. Int. J. Forecast. **37**(4), 1748–1764 (2021)
6. Lipton, Z.C., Berkowitz, J., Elkan, C.: A critical review of recurrent neural networks for sequence learning. arXiv preprint arXiv:1506.00019 (2015)
7. Liu, H., Wang, Z., Benachour, P., Tubman, P.: A time series classification method for behaviour-based dropout prediction. In: 2018 IEEE 18th International Conference on Advanced Learning Technologies (ICALT), pp. 191–195. IEEE (2018)
8. Oreshkin, B.N., Carpov, D., Chapados, N., Bengio, Y.: N-beats: neural basis expansion analysis for interpretable time series forecasting. In: International Conference on Learning Representations (2019)
9. Park, J., Woo, S., Lee, J.Y., Kweon, I.S.: Bam: Bottleneck attention module. arXiv preprint arXiv:1807.06514 (2018)
10. Salehinejad, H., Sankar, S., Barfett, J., Colak, E., Valaee, S.: Recent advances in recurrent neural networks. arXiv preprint arXiv:1801.01078 (2017)
11. Vaswani, A., et al.: Attention is all you need. In: Advances in Neural Information Processing Systems, vol. 30 (2017)

12. Woo, S., Park, J., Lee, J.-Y., Kweon, I.S.: CBAM: convolutional block attention module. In: Ferrari, V., Hebert, M., Sminchisescu, C., Weiss, Y. (eds.) ECCV 2018. LNCS, vol. 11211, pp. 3–19. Springer, Cham (2018). https://doi.org/10.1007/978-3-030-01234-2_1
13. Wu, H., Xu, J., Wang, J., Long, M.: Autoformer: decomposition transformers with auto-correlation for long-term series forecasting. Adv. Neural. Inf. Process. Syst. **34**, 22419–22430 (2021)
14. Xiong, B., Lou, L., Meng, X., Wang, X., Ma, H., Wang, Z.: Short-term wind power forecasting based on attention mechanism and deep learning. Electric Power Syst. Res. **206**, 107776 (2022)
15. Zhou, H., et al.: Informer: beyond efficient transformer for long sequence time-series forecasting. In: Proceedings of the AAAI Conference on Artificial Intelligence, pp. 11106–11115 (2021)

Task Inference for Offline Meta Reinforcement Learning via Latent Shared Knowledge

Ying Zhou, Shan Cong, and Chao Yu$^{(\boxtimes)}$

Sun Yat-sen University, Guangzhou, Guangdong 510006, China
yuchao3@mail.sysu.edu.cn

Abstract. Offline Reinforcement Learning (RL) has emerged as a promising approach for learning from existing data without requiring online interactions. However, traditional offline RL algorithms often suffer from poor generalization and overfitting due to limited task diversity in the training data. In this paper, we propose a novel framework called Meta-Task (MeTask) for offline RL that leverages meta-learning techniques to learn a task representation from a diverse set of offline training tasks. Specifically, we introduce a task-shared meta-learning objective that extracts meta-knowledge from the context data of each task and uses it to learn a more generalizable task representation. Additionally, we design a task-infer module that restores the learned meta-knowledge and task-specific information between different tasks to achieve efficient transfer of knowledge. Experiments on a variety of benchmark tasks demonstrate that MeTask achieves state-of-the-art performance compared to traditional offline RL algorithms. These results suggest that leveraging task diversity and meta-learning techniques can significantly improve the efficiency of offline RL methods.

Keywords: Meta learning · Offline reinforcement learning · Knowledge transfer

1 Introduction

Reinforcement Learning (RL) algorithms have achieved remarkable successes in diverse fields such as gaming [15], robot control [6], healthcare [16] and autonomous driving [7]. However, conducting exploration in real environments in certain domains may result in high interaction costs. Instead of exploring and learning online, offline RL [8] learns from a static batch of data that are collected prior to the learning phase. This setting is particularly relevant in scenarios where data collection is expensive or risky, such as in robotics or healthcare applications, where trial-and-error exploration may be unsafe or time-consuming. Despite its practical appeal, offline RL poses unique challenges, including the risk of overfitting to the dataset and the potential loss of exploration-induced diversity. Besides, offline RL methods require a distinct policy to be trained for each

© The Author(s), under exclusive license to Springer Nature Switzerland AG 2023
Z. Jin et al. (Eds.): KSEM 2023, LNAI 14120, pp. 356–365, 2023.
https://doi.org/10.1007/978-3-031-40292-0_29

target task. In a multi-task scenario, such as a robotic arm picking up items from different coordinates or making advertising bid decisions across multiple channels, generating a policy for each task would necessitate millions of policy iterations. This differs from the way of human learning when they can learn new tasks quickly based on past experiences. To address the challenges posed by real-world multi-task scenarios, recent studies have introduced meta-learning approaches to offline RL, which aim to improve the learning efficiency in target tasks by leveraging the knowledge gained from multiple related tasks [3,10,17].

Meta-RL [13] has gained increasing attention in recent years due to its ability to *learn how to learn* in RL settings by learning a set of meta-parameters during the meta-training phase that can be utilized to adapt to new tasks quickly during the meta-testing phase. A number of methods, commonly referred to as *context-based* or *task inference-based* meta-learning methods [5], have been proposed by training a task inference model that aims to leverage limited data to identify the distribution of tasks. Additionally, these kinds of methods can help identify similarities and differences between tasks, which can be used to improve the efficiency of algorithms [1]. In an offline setting, several studies [9,10,17] have introduced context-based meta-RL methods to address the challenges of high data collection costs in RL by leveraging discriminative information from a set of related tasks to differentiate the objectives of different tasks. However, the task-specific features normally account for a small proportion of the whole feature space. For example, when controlling a robotic arm to lift various objects, we prefer the algorithm to learn generic skills such as how to *grasp, pick up* and *turn the wrist* rather than to *identify the target object* for each task. This is because an agent with generic skills only requires a few attempts to detect the target object, while an agent that only recognizes the objects needs to master the skills through extensive learning before it can complete the task. Besides, insufficient or overly similar information in the sampled context can lead to overfitting or poor generalization in methods for extracting discriminative features [1]. With this regard, we contend that in a multi-task setting where tasks are relatively similar or task sampling is limited, it is important to extract common knowledge representations between tasks rather than solely focusing on discriminative identification information. By identifying and leveraging commonalities between tasks, the efficiency and generalization performance of the existing meta-RL algorithms could be further improved, even in the face of limited data.

In this paper, we propose a novel learning objective, which aims to learn a shared task representation capturing the commonalities between tasks for more efficient inter-task knowledge transfer. **Our contributions are summarized as follows:**

- We propose a novel framework MeTask for improving the generalization ability of meta-knowledge using a completely offline dataset, which aims to learn general features by transferring common knowledge between tasks.
- We introduce an objective of task inference that learns representations of shared skills and patterns of tasks to achieve rapid adaptation to new tasks.

– We investigate the impact of using tasks with different levels of similarity during training on the effectiveness of our approach. Experiments show that the proposed method is more effective than different baselines.

2   Method

2.1   Problem Formulation

The task in RL can be modelled as a fully observable Markov Decision Process (MDP), which can be defined as a tuple $M = (S, A, \mathcal{P}, \mathcal{R}, \gamma)$, where S and A represent the state space and action space of the agent, respectively, $\mathcal{P}$ is the transfer dynamics of the environment, $\mathcal{R}$ is the reward function, and $\gamma \in (0, 1)$ is the discount factor for the reward. In this paper, the meta-RL tasks share the same action and state space but have different transfer dynamics or reward functions. In the offline setting, each task follows the distribution $\mathcal{M}_i \sim p(\mathcal{T})$, which consists of an offline trajectory $\mathcal{T}_i = \{(s_{i,j}, a_{i,j}, r_{i,j}, s'_{i,j})\}_{j=1}^k$ collected by an arbitrary behaviour strategy. The meta-learning process typically involves an inner loop and an outer loop. The inner loop learns the initialisation parameter from the training tasks, while the outer loop evaluates and updates this parameter using the testing tasks. This interdependence is a characteristic of meta-learning, enabling efficient adaptation to new tasks with limited data. Specifically, in the inner loop, a considerable amount of data is sampled from a diverse set of training tasks to learn the meta-parameter ω_{old}^*. Then, the performance of ω_{old}^* is evaluated using the training set $\mathcal{D}_{\mathcal{T}}^{tr}$ while updating the parameters of RL model. In this paper, we base on the Soft Actor-Critic (SAC) algorithm [4] with the update parameters denoted as θ^* and ψ^*:

$$\omega_{old}^* = \arg\max_{\omega} \log p\left(\mathcal{D}_{\mathcal{T}}^{tr} | \omega\right), \tag{1}$$

$$\theta_i^*, \psi_i^* = \arg\min_{\theta, \psi} \mathcal{L}^{task}\left(\theta, \psi, \omega_{old}^*, \mathcal{D}_i^{tr}\right), \tag{2}$$

where $\mathcal{L}^{task}\left(\theta, \psi, \omega_{old}^*, \mathcal{D}_i^{tr}\right)$ denotes the loss of the strategy on training task i. The meta-parameter ω_{old}^* is updated based on the testing tasks with the updated parameters θ_i^*, ψ_i^* to obtain the final meta-parameter ω^*:

$$\omega^* = \arg\min_{\omega_{old}^*} \sum_{i=1}^{M} \mathcal{L}^{meta}\left(\theta_i^*, \psi_i^*, \omega_{old}^*, \mathcal{D}_i^{ts}\right), \tag{3}$$

where $\mathcal{L}^{meta}\left(\theta_i^*, \psi_i^*, \omega_{old}^*, \mathcal{D}_i^{ts}\right)$ denotes the loss of testing tasks and M denotes the number of tasks. Under the offline setting, the meta-parameter is the embedding features z_i of contextual information $c_i = \{(s_i, a_i, r_i, s'_i)\}_{i=1}^k$ from the task i collected by the exploration strategy. The ultimate goal of meta-learning is to learn to obtain an optimal learning process $\omega^* = \mu_{\theta, \psi}(\mathcal{D}_{\mathcal{T}}^{tr}, \omega)$ which can adapt to a new task $\mathcal{T}$ from the same distribution using a small dataset $\mathcal{D}_{\mathcal{T}}^{ts}$:

$$\min_{\theta, \psi} \mathbb{E}_{\mathcal{T} \sim p(\mathcal{T})}[\mathcal{L}(\mathcal{D}_{\mathcal{T}}^{ts}, \omega^*)] \quad s.t. \quad \omega^* = \mu_{\theta, \psi}(\mathcal{D}_{\mathcal{T}}^{tr}, \omega), \tag{4}$$

where $\mathcal{D}_{\mathcal{T}}^{tr}$ and $\mathcal{D}_{\mathcal{T}}^{ts}$ denote the training and testing tasks from $p(\mathcal{T})$, respectively, and $\mathcal{L}(\mathcal{D}_{\mathcal{T}}^{ts}, \omega^*)$ denotes the loss of the strategy on the testing tasks.

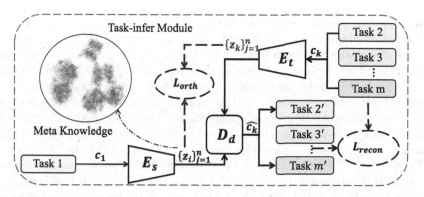

Fig. 1. The task-infer module of MeTask. The encoder E_s extracts the meta knowledge while the encoder E_t extracts the other features of the tasks. The tasks are reconstructed by a decoder D_d.

2.2 MeTask: Learning Meta-knowledge from Tasks

In the offline environment, previous research has addressed the meta-learning problem by using historical trajectory $\tau_{1:t} = \{(s_j, a_j, r_j, s'_j)\}_{j=1}^t$ to infer task-specific information z (e.g., the target object in robotic arm control tasks), which serves as a supplement to the state information for optimizing strategy $\pi(a|z, s_t)$ [10,17]. However, most of the meta-tasks used in these studies share similar environmental settings (e.g., physical laws of the motion of a robot arm) but only differ in goals (e.g., target objects), and thus focusing on extracting task-specific features (i.e., the shape and mass of objects) but neglecting the large amount of shared knowledge (i.e., the skills of how to manipulate the robot arm) among the tasks can cause inefficiency of learning and also poor generalization.

To address the above problem, we propose the MeTask framework in Fig. 1 to learn generalizable representations of tasks, while transferring common knowledge across tasks to assist the learning of shared knowledge. Specifically, MeTask consists of a task-infer module and a policy learning module, which are trained in two phases. First, the task-infer module is trained to encode the shared knowledge across tasks. Concretely, the shared information and the task-specific information of tasks are separately encoded using two encoders E_s, E_t. Subsequently, the tasks are reconstructed by a decoder D_d via the shared information from the current task with different task-specific information to ensure the integrity of the shared knowledge. Then, in the policy learning phase, the pre-trained encoder E_s is used to extract the latent features of the tasks. Subsequently, all features are aggregated by an aggregator E_g using weighted summation, and fine-tuned according to the adaptation of RL. When updating the Q-function $Q_\psi(s, a)$ and the policy $\pi_\phi(a|s)$, we extend the state $\mathcal{S}$ by the latent representation $\mathcal{Z}$ as a dimension of the state $\tilde{\mathcal{S}} \triangleq \mathcal{S} \times \mathcal{Z}$, parameterized with ψ, ϕ.

Learning Shared Knowledge. An ideal task representation can learn the general skills from a series of similar tasks. In other words, we can transfer this common feature between tasks without changing the characteristics of each task. Inspired by the domain generalization research [2], we separate the tasks into a shared knowledge component that contains common knowledge and a target information component that captures task-specific information for each task. The reconstruction process using common knowledge with different task-specific features ensures that the common knowledge retains a minimum of task-dependent information. Concretely, given that M tasks follow the distribution $p(\mathcal{T})$, we sample a batch context c_1 of current task $\mathcal{T}_1$ and another context c_k sampled from other k tasks $\mathcal{T}_k \in \mathcal{T} \setminus \{\mathcal{T}_1\}$. The task-infer model consists of $\hat{c}_k = D(E_s(c_1) + E_t(c_k))$ and $z = E_s(c_1)$, where $\hat{c}_k$ is the reconstruction of inputs c_1 and c_k, while z is the shared knowledge. The goal of training is to minimize the following loss with respect to parameters $\Theta = \{\theta_s, \theta_t, \theta_d\}$:

$$\mathcal{L} = \alpha \mathcal{L}_{orth} + \beta \mathcal{L}_{recon}, \tag{5}$$

where α, β are weights that control the interaction of the loss terms. Let $\mathbf{Z}_1$ and $\mathbf{Z}_k$ be matrices of the features of c_1 and c_k respectively. We introduce the soft subspace orthogonality loss used in DSN [2] to encourage the shared encoder and the target encoder to learn different representations on the latent space $\mathcal{Z}$:

$$\mathcal{L}_{orth} = \|\mathbf{Z}_1^\top \mathbf{Z}_k\|_F^2, \tag{6}$$

where $\| \cdot \|_F^2$ is the squared Frobenius norm. Merely making two batches of tuples extract inconsistent features cannot achieve the goal of extracting common knowledge. Therefore, $\hat{c}_k$ is reconstructed with the task-specific features z_k extracted by $E_t(c_k)$ and the shared knowledge z_1 extracted by $E_s(c_1)$ to ensure the common knowledge z_1 be transferable between tasks. The scale-invariant mean squared error term [2] is used for the reconstruction loss $\mathcal{L}_{recon}$:

$$\mathcal{L}_{recon} = \sum_{i=0}^{M} \mathcal{L}_{si\_mse}(\mathbf{c}_k, \hat{\mathbf{c}}_k), \tag{7}$$

$$\mathcal{L}_{si\_mse}(\mathbf{c}, \hat{\mathbf{c}}) = \frac{1}{y}\|\mathbf{c} - \hat{\mathbf{c}}\|_2^2 - \frac{1}{y^2}([\mathbf{c} - \hat{\mathbf{c}}] \cdot \mathbf{1}_y)^2, \tag{8}$$

where $\| \cdot \|_2^2$ is the squared L_2-norm, y is the number of pixels in input $\mathbf{c}$, M is the number of tasks, and $\mathbf{1}_y$ is the vector of ones of length y.

Algorithm Summary. In this paper, the DQN algorithm [12] is used in an discrete environment, while the SAC algorithm [4] is used in a continuous environment. Under the offline setting, the SAC algorithm provides the benefits of high sample efficiency. During meta-training, we fine-tune the ensemble encoder E_g by combining the losses of the actor and critic in SAC as follows:

$$\mathcal{L}_{critic} = \mathbb{E}_{\substack{\mathbf{z}^* \sim E_g(\mathbf{z}) \\ \pi \sim \Pi}} \left[Q_\theta(s, \cdot, \mathbf{z}^*) - (r + V(s', \mathbf{z}^*)) \right]^2, \tag{9}$$

Algorithm 1. Meta Training

Require: Pre-collected datasets $\{\mathcal{T}_i\}_{i=1}^N \sim p(\mathcal{T})$, learning rate $\alpha_1, \alpha_2.\alpha_3$;
Initialize replay buffer c_i and c_k;
Initialize models parameters $\theta_s, \theta_t, \theta_d, \theta_g, Q_\psi, \pi_\phi$;
Train the meta-knowledge extractor:
1: **while** not done **do**
2:     **for** each $\mathcal{T}_i$ **do**
3:         Sample a batch of transition tuples c_i from task i and the same amount of c_k
            from all other tasks.
4:         $\mathbf{z}_i = E_s(c_i), \mathbf{z}_k = E_t(c_k), \hat{c}_k = D_d(\mathbf{z}_i, \mathbf{z}_k)$
5:         $\mathcal{L}_{orth} = \|\mathbf{Z}_i^\top \mathbf{Z}_k\|_F^2$
6:         $\mathcal{L}_{recon} = \sum_{i=0}^M \mathcal{L}_{si\_mse}(\mathbf{c}_k, \hat{\mathbf{c}}_k)$
7:     **end for**
8:     $\mathcal{L}_i = \mathbb{E}_{\substack{\mathbf{z}_i \sim E_s(\mathbf{z}|c_i) \\ \mathbf{z}_k \sim E_t(\mathbf{z}|c_k)}} (\beta\mathcal{L}_{orth} + \gamma\mathcal{L}_{recon})$
9:     Update $\theta_s, \theta_t, \theta_d$ to minimize loss
10: **end while**
11: **return** θ_s^*
Train the offline policy:
1: **for** step in training steps **do**
2:     **for** each $\mathcal{T}_i$ **do**
3:         Sample context c_i and RL batch b_i from task i
4:         $\mathbf{z}^* = E_g(E_s(c_i))$
5:         $\mathcal{L}_{actor}^i = \mathcal{L}_{actor}(b_i, \mathbf{z}^*)$
6:         $\mathcal{L}_{critic}^i = \mathcal{L}_{critic}(b_i, \mathbf{z}^*)$
7:     **end for**
8:     Update θ_d, ϕ, ψ with offline RL algorithms
9: **end for**

$$\mathcal{L}_{actor} = \mathbb{E}_{\substack{\mathbf{z}^* \sim E_g(\mathbf{z}) \\ \pi \sim \Pi}} \left[D_{KL} \left(\pi_\theta(\cdot|s, \mathbf{z}^*) \middle\| \frac{\exp(Q_\theta(s, \cdot, \mathbf{z}^*))}{\mathcal{Z}_\theta(s)} \right) \right], \tag{10}$$

where $\mathbf{z}$ is the shared knowledge of $\mathcal{T}_i$ learn by E_s, and $\mathbf{z}^*$ is the latent representation gathered by E_g trained with the policy to learn critical part of $\mathbf{z}$ [17]. During meta-testing, a limited number of trajectories c_i are collected using an arbitrary policy and extract their meta-knowledge $\mathbf{z}^* = E_g(E_s(c_i))$, which is added to the state for policy updating. The meta-training process is shown in Algorithm 1 while the meta-testing process is shown in Algorithm 2.

3 Experiments

3.1 Experimental Settings

We compare MeTask with the offline version of PEARL [14], and offline context-based meta-learning methods including FOCAL [10] and CORRO [17]. The environments of the experiments consist of a discrete 2D navigation environment named Point-Robot as well as three continuous environments in MuJoCo. To

Algorithm 2. Meta Testing

Require: Trained models E_s, E_g, Q_ψ, π_ϕ

1: **for** each $\mathcal{T}_i$ **do**
2:     Sample a batch of transition tuples c_i
3:     $\mathbf{z}^* = E_g(E_s(c_i))$
4:     **while** not done **do**
5:         Roll out π_ϕ for evaluation
6:     **end while**
7: **end for**

---

generate different tasks, following [9,10,17], we set different *reward functions* for the tasks in Half-Cheetah-Vel and Ant-Dir environments, while different *dynamic transfer* for tasks in the Hopper-Param environment. Each environment is comprised of 20 training tasks and 20 testing tasks, and unless specified otherwise, the tasks in the training set and testing set are randomly sampled from the same dataset, which means that the distribution of the two data sets is uniform [9,10,17]. The configurations and hyperparameters used in the dataset collection are the same as the settings in CORRO [17], and the architectures of both the encoders and the decoder in MeTask take a four-layer MLP structure, where the size of hidden layers is 64. Several important hyperparameters of MeTask are shown in Table 1. All experimental results are over 5 random seeds.

Table 1. Configurations and hyperparameters in MeTask.

Configurations	Point-Robot	Ant-Dir	Half-Cheetah-Vel	Hopper-Param
Weights (α, β)	(1,1)	(1,1)	(1,1)	(1,1)
Learning rate	3e-4	3e-4	3e-4	3e-4
Context size	200	200	200	200
RL batch size	256	256	256	256
RL network width	64	256	256	256
RL network depth	3	3	3	3
Training steps	2e5	2e5	2e5	2e5

3.2   Results and Analysis

The experimental results in the four environments are illustrated in Fig. 2. In Ant-Dir, MeTask surpasses all other benchmark methods. In Half-Cheetah-Vel and Point-Robot, MeTask outperforms the FOCAL and PEARL methods and demonstrates comparable effectiveness to the CORRO algorithm. In Hopper-Param, all the methods have similar performance but MeTask outperforms other compared algorithms slightly in terms of final converged performance.

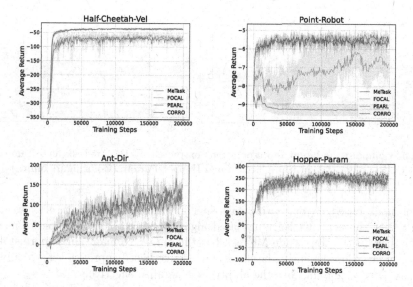

Fig. 2. The performance of MeTask against the baselines in four different environments with the average performance of all test tasks, while shadow area represents the standard deviation from 5 random seeds.

Latent Space Visualization. A transferable meta-knowledge extractor should have the ability to extract common knowledge representations from context across different tasks. To gain a more intuitive illustration of the distribution of the learned meta-knowledge of the tasks, we visualize the task representations by projecting the embedding vectors into a 2D space via t-SNE [11] as shown in Fig. 3. Specifically, we visualize the feature of a batch of context data sampled from a testing task extracted by MeTask and CORRO. The points in the figure with different colours indicate the features extracted from different tasks. The results show that the distribution of latent vectors extracted by the MeTask method for each task are similar, which is consistent with the idea of extracting common features between tasks. By contrast, the features extracted by CORRO methods are mostly separated from each other. This result provides a clear evidence of the effectiveness of MeTask in capturing a common underlying structure across different tasks.

Generalizability and Stability. Compared to the task-specific information, the features that are embedded in the common knowledge among tasks are more robust, especially for relatively similar tasks or with limited task sampling. To validate that, we design an experiment in which the training tasks and the testing tasks are sampled unevenly to achieve a certain difference in the task distribution in Point-Robot. Specifically, the goal positions of 40 tasks are equally distributed on a semicircle, among which 20 tasks in the middle of the semicircle are chosen as the training tasks and the remaining tasks on either side are chosen as the testing tasks. With this setup, we investigate whether MeTask is superior

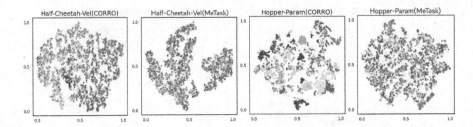

Fig. 3. Compare the latent representations extracted by the MeTask algorithm and the CORRO algorithm in Half Cheetah and Hopper Param. (Color figure online)

to methods based on extracting task-specific information. Figure 4 shows the result that the contrast learning-based algorithms exhibit poorer performance and larger fluctuation, while MeTask has the ability to maintain a more stable performance. Consequently, the shared knowledge-based approach is more robust to task distribution and has the ability to generalize effectively.

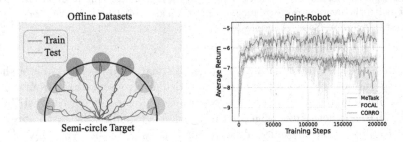

Fig. 4. Specific setting and result in Point Robot. The training tasks and the testing tasks are sampled unevenly. Test returns of MeTask, FOCAL and CORRO methods.

4   Conclusion

In this paper, we propose a novel offline meta-RL method named MeTask which focuses on extracting the common knowledge among tasks instead of the task-specific information to achieve rapid adaptation to new tasks. In the process of learning the task-infer module, a novel learning objective is introduced to learn shared skills and patterns of tasks, even when the training and testing tasks are unevenly distributed. The integrity of the common knowledge is achieved by transferring learning common representations across tasks and reconstructing tasks with their specific information. The experiments demonstrate that MeTask outperforms prior methods in diverse environments and task distributions. MeTask can be combined with any online exploration methods by collecting small amount of task information to further facilitate the adaptation to new tasks. We leave this issue for our future work.

Acknowledgements. We acknowledge support from the National Natural Science Foundation of China (No. 62076259), Fundamental and Applicational Research Funds of Guangdong province (No. 2023A1515012946), and Fundamental Research Funds for the Central Universities-Sun Yat-sen University.

References

1. Beck, J., Vuorio, R., Liu, E.Z., et al.: A survey of meta-reinforcement learning. arXiv preprint arXiv:2301.08028 (2023)
2. Bousmalis, K., Trigeorgis, G., Silberman, N., et al.: Domain separation networks. In: NeurIPS, vol. 29 (2016)
3. Dorfman, R., Shenfeld, I., Tamar, A.: Offline meta reinforcement learning-identifiability challenges and effective data collection strategies. In: NeurIPS, vol. 34, pp. 4607–4618 (2021)
4. Haarnoja, T., Zhou, A., Abbeel, P., et al.: Soft actor-critic: off-policy maximum entropy deep reinforcement learning with a stochastic actor. In: ICML, pp. 1861–1870. PMLR (2018)
5. Humplik, J., Galashov, A., Hasenclever, L., et al.: Meta reinforcement learning as task inference. arXiv preprint arXiv:1905.06424 (2019)
6. Johannink, T., Bahl, S., Nair, A., et al.: Residual reinforcement learning for robot control. In: ICRA, pp. 6023–6029. IEEE (2019)
7. Kiran, B.R., Sobh, I., Talpaert, V., et al.: Deep reinforcement learning for autonomous driving: a survey. IEEE Trans. Intell. Transp. Syst. **23**(6), 4909–4926 (2021)
8. Levine, S., Kumar, A., Tucker, G., et al.: Offline reinforcement learning: tutorial, review, and perspectives on open problems. arXiv preprint arXiv:2005.01643 (2020)
9. Li, L., Huang, Y., Chen, M., et al.: Provably improved context-based offline meta-RL with attention and contrastive learning. arXiv preprint arXiv:2102.10774 (2021)
10. Li, L., Yang, R., Luo, D.: Focal: efficient fully-offline meta-reinforcement learning via distance metric learning and behavior regularization. arXiv preprint arXiv:2010.01112 (2020)
11. Van der Maaten, L., Hinton, G.: Visualizing data using t-SNE. J. Mach. Learn. Res. **9**(11) (2008)
12. Mnih, V., Kavukcuoglu, K., Silver, D., et al.: Human-level control through deep reinforcement learning. Nature **518**(7540), 529–533 (2015)
13. Nagabandi, A., Clavera, I., Liu, S., et al.: Learning to adapt in dynamic, real-world environments through meta-reinforcement learning. arXiv preprint arXiv:1803.11347 (2018)
14. Rakelly, K., Zhou, A., Finn, C., et al.: Efficient off-policy meta-reinforcement learning via probabilistic context variables. In: ICML, pp. 5331–5340. PMLR (2019)
15. Ye, D., Liu, Z., Sun, M., et al.: Mastering complex control in MOBA games with deep reinforcement learning. In: AAAI, vol. 34, pp. 6672–6679 (2020)
16. Yu, C., Liu, J., Nemati, S., Yin, G.: Reinforcement learning in healthcare: a survey. ACM Comput. Surv. (CSUR) **55**(1), 1–36 (2021)
17. Yuan, H., Lu, Z.: Robust task representations for offline meta-reinforcement learning via contrastive learning. In: ICML, pp. 25747–25759. PMLR (2022)

A Quantitative Spectra Analysis Framework Combining Mixup and Band Attention for Predicting Soluble Solid Content of Blueberries

Zhaokui Li[1(✉)], Jinen Zhang[1], Wei Li[2], Fei Li[1], Ke Bi[1], and Hongli Li[1]

[1] School of Computer Science, Shenyang Aerospace University, Shenyang, China
lzk@sau.edu.cn, {zhangjinen,bike,lihongli}@stu.sau.edu.cn,
alinafeili@mail.dlut.edu.cn
[2] School of Information and Electronics, Beijing Institute of Technology, Beijing, China
liwei08@ieee.org

Abstract. Hyperspectral imaging can rapid and non-destructive monitor physical characteristics and intrinsic chemical information of food. In recent years, many studies have applied hyperspectral imaging to evaluate the internal quality of fruits. However, due to the influence of environmental factors, there are abnormal samples in the collected data. Furthermore, the model faces challenges such as limited data availability and insufficient diversity in the dataset. In this study, we collected a total of 1010 hyperspectral images of blueberries and measured their soluble solid content (SSC). To reduce the influence of abnormal samples and increase the diversity of samples, we propose a deep learning framework combining mixup and band attention to predict blueberry SSC. The mixup module performs data augmentation on both spectra and SSC values, enhancing sample diversity and improving the generalization performance of the model. The band attention module captures cross-band information and learns band weights, enabling the model to focus on the bands relevant to SSC. Furthermore, we find that bands with higher weights are consistent with SSC-sensitive bands in existing knowledge, which improves the interpretability of the model.

Keywords: Hyperspectral imaging · Data augmentation · Attention mechanism · Soluble solid content · Non-destructive detection

1 Introduction

Blueberries are a popular fruit with high anti-oxidant capacity and potential anti-cancer effects [3]. The soluble solid content (SSC) is an important indicator of the internal quality of blueberries. The traditional method for measuring SSC is both time-consuming and destructive. Therefore, a rapid, accurate, and non-destructive measurement method would be very useful.

Z. Jin et al. (Eds.): KSEM 2023, LNAI 14120, pp. 366–373, 2023.
https://doi.org/10.1007/978-3-031-40292-0_30

Hyperspectral images (HSIs) can provide rich information concerning the chemical and physical properties of fruits [6], making them a promising non-destructive method for quality assessment in recent years. However, variations in light, temperature, and chemical composition during data collection can introduce noise and errors, making the collected data less reliable. Additionally, data collection is both time-consuming and expensive, resulting in a small sample size, which can lead to model overfitting and negatively affect model robustness and accuracy. To mitigate this issue, spectra data are preprocessed to remove noise. But choosing the appropriate preprocessing methods requires constant trial and error [8]. For problems with limited data, data augmentation techniques can be employed. However, this approach only augments the spectra, not the target variable (e.g., SSC), leading to limited diversity in the samples.

To solve these problems, we introduce a mixup [7] method to augment spectra and SSC values simultaneously, which improves the sample diversity, mitigates the impact of noise on the model, and improves the generalization performance of the model. We refer to Inception-ResNet [4] to design a feature extractor to extract features of different scales in the spectra, and improve the adaptability of the network by using multiple sets of filters. Moreover, a band attention module is designed to capture local cross-band information while learning band weights, ensuring the model focuses on SSC-related bands. We selected the top 10 bands with large weights and analyzed them in combination with the blueberry spectra characteristics. The interpretability of the model is improved.

The main contributions of this paper are as follows. (1) We propose a quantitative spectra analysis framework that uses multiple sets of filters to extract features, which improves the adaptability of the network to local spectra features at different scales. (2) A mixup method is introduced to augment spectra features and SSC values simultaneously, which expands the distribution of the training set and improves the generalization performance of the model. (3) We design a band attention module to capture local cross-band information, and combined it with the spectra characteristics of blueberries for analysis, improving the interpretability of the model.

2 Materials and Methods

2.1 Data Preparation and Acquisition

Blueberries sourced from Dandong, Liaoning and Yuxi, Yunnan in China. 5 batches of samples (13–24 mm in diameter) with sample sizes of 180, 210, 170, 220 and 230 were acquired on October 15, October 21, October 28, November 4, 2022 and February 17, 2023. We use a destructive manner for SSC measurements. Each sample SSC value is the average of three measurements. The overall range of SSC ($^\circ$Brix) in [7.7, 19.8], mean is 13.6 and standard deviation is 1.8.

We use a push-broom hyperspectral camera (GaiaSky-mini2, Dualix Spectral Imaging Technology Co., Ltd.) to collect HSIs. The spectra range is 393.7–1001.4 nm (176 bands), and the spectra resolution is 3.5 nm ± 0.5 nm. The acquisition system also includes four 50W halogen lamps, a conveyor belt, and a computer. Before the acquisition of HSIs, the halogen lamp needs to be adjusted to the appropriate position and preheated for 30 min to ensure uniform and stable light in the line scan area. The conveyor belt's movement speed was set to 2.0 cm/s, and the camera height was set at 29 cm. Different batches had exposure times of 2.5 ms, 6.2 ms, 4.7 ms, 5.2 ms, and 5.4 ms, respectively. To avoid the interference of external light, data acquisition is carried out in a dark room.

Before image acquisition, we used a white Teflon plate to obtain a white reference image. An opaque lens cap is used to cover the camera lens to obtain a dark reference image. The reflectance correction is formulated as follows.

$$R_c = \frac{I_{original} - I_{dark}}{I_{white} - I_{dark}} \times R_{white} \tag{1}$$

where $I_{original}$ is the original hyperspectral image, R_c is the corrected hyperspectral image, I_{white} is the white reference image, I_{dark} is the dark reference image, R_{white} is the reflectance of the white plate (approximately 100%).

2.2   Spectra Extraction

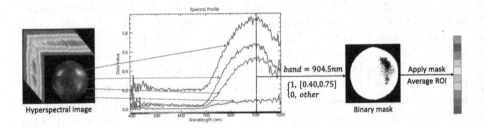

Fig. 1. Flowchart of spectra extraction. (Color figure online)

Firstly, blueberries are spheroidal bodies. The surface curvature variation of spherical fruits leads to uneven light intensity distribution. Figure 1 illustrates the hyperspectral image, wherein multiple areas are highlighted. The area with a higher reflectance is indicated by the blue line. The brown line points to the edge region, which has a lower reflectance. The green line points to the background region. The red line points to the spectra curve in the normal region, where the spectra are what we need to extract.

Secondly, we acquired a grayscale image at 904.5 nm due to the distinctive differences in spectra reflectance between the target region and other areas (highlight, edge, or background). We obtain a binary mask by setting all pixels with reflectance between 0.40 and 0.75 to 1, and all other pixels to 0. The Region of Interest (ROI) of the sample is obtained by multiplying the binary mask with the original image to remove other regions. The average spectra of each band within ROI are calculated as the spectra data of a single sample.

3   Proposed Network

Figure 2 shows our proposed framework combining mixup and band attention (MBA). After spectra extraction, a dataset $D = \{(x_1, y_1), \ldots, (x_N, y_N)\}$ is obtained, where x_i is a feature vector, $x_i \in \mathbb{R}^{1 \times b}$, b is the number of bands, N is the number of samples, and y_i is the SSC measurement value.

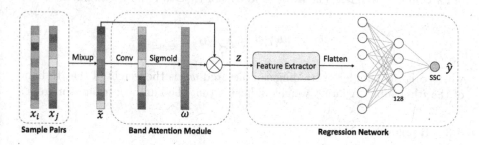

Fig. 2. Framework of proposed MBA.

3.1   Mixup Module

We introduce mixup [7] to enhance sample diversity and reduce the impact of noisy samples. The samples are always changing during the training process, which expands the distribution of the training set and improves the generalization performance of the model. In a set of training data, we randomly select two samples $(x_i, y_i), (x_j, y_j)$, x_i, x_j are spectra feature vectors and y_i, y_j are SSC values, and perform the following operations.

$$\tilde{x} = \lambda x_i + (1 - \lambda) x_j \tag{2}$$

$$\tilde{y} = \lambda y_i + (1 - \lambda) y_j \tag{3}$$

where $\lambda \sim Beta(\alpha, \alpha)$, $\lambda \in [0, 1]$, for $\alpha \in (0, \infty)$. The mixup hyperparameter α controls the strength of interpolation between a feature-target pairs [7]. A larger value of α leads to a higher probability of λ taking a value around 0.5. During training, we randomly shuffle the data of each batch and mixup it with the original batch data. In particular, mixup is not used during the testing phase.

3.2   Band Attention Module

To make the model pay more attention to the bands related to the target variable [1], we design a band attention module to learn the band weights. The input of this module is the spectra vector $\tilde{x}$, and the output is the weighted spectra vector z. The band attention module performs 1D convolution (kernel size is 1×3, stride is 1, and padding is 1) and then uses the Sigmoid function to learn the non-negative band weight tensor, $\omega \in \mathbb{R}^{1 \times b}$. To establish a connection between the initial inputs and its weights, the following is performed.

$$z = \tilde{x} \otimes \omega \qquad (4)$$

where $\otimes$ represents the band-wise production between $\tilde{x}$ and ω. After the training is completed, we can determine the feature bands by averaging the band weights of all training samples. The average weight of the jth band is computed as

$$\bar{w}_j = \frac{1}{S} \sum_{i=1}^{S} w_{ij} \qquad (5)$$

where S is the number of training samples and w_{ij} is the weight of the jth band of the ith sample. A larger weight indicates that the band contributes more.

3.3   Regression Network

The regression network consists of a feature extractor and three fully connected layers. The design of the feature extractor refers to the structure of Inception-ResNet-A [4], which can extract information at different scales. In addition, the residual connection can retain the original input feature map information.

Firstly, in Fig. 3, the blue block denotes BasicConv operations, with detailed operations shown in the upper right corner. A batch normalization layer is used directly after the input layer. Then, through the BasicConv operation, the feature map $M1$ is obtained. $M1$ is fed into three different filter banks and residual connections. Different filter bank combinations can extract features of different scales and improve network adaptability. We concatenate three sets of feature maps with identical sizes along the channel dimension to produce the feature map $M2$. Then, $M4$ is obtained by adding the corresponding positions of $M1$ and $M3$ through the residual connection.

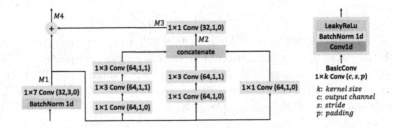

Fig. 3. Feature extractor structure.

Secondly, the feature map $M4$ is flattened and passed through a 3-layer fully connected network to predict SSC. Batch normalization, LeakyRelu, and dropout (with a drop probability of 0.2) are applied to the hidden layer. We use the mean squared error (MSE) as the loss function, which is expressed as

$$\mathcal{L}_{reg} = \frac{1}{S} \sum_{i=1}^{S} (\tilde{y}_i - \hat{y}_i)^2 \tag{6}$$

where S is the number of training samples, $\tilde{y}_i$ is the true SSC value of the ith sample after mixup, and $\hat{y}_i$ is the corresponding predicted SSC value. The model optimizes this loss function.

4   Results and Discussion

4.1   Spectra Profiles

Based on the learned band weights, we average the band weights of all training samples, take the top 10 bands with large weights and mark in Fig. 4 with red dashed lines. The spectra have the same trend. There is an absorption region within the range of 900–980 nm, corresponding to the third overtones (910 nm) of C-H functional groups related to sugar and the second overtones (960 nm) of O-H functional groups related to moisture [2].

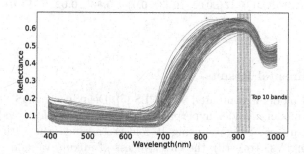

Fig. 4. Spectra curves (randomly selected 100 samples) and top 10 bands. (Color figure online)

From a physical and chemical perspective, a good quantitative spectra analysis model is also important for feature bands. As shown in Fig. 4, we selected the top 10 bands with large weights (marked in red), which are: 919.3 nm, 915.6 nm, 923.0 nm, 911.9 nm, 908.2 nm, 926.7 nm, 904.5 nm, 900.8 nm, 930.4 nm, 897.2 nm. Among them, the bands associated with SSC near 910.0 nm are selected. This improves the interpretability of the model. In addition, these bands are concentrated in the near infrared region, indicating that the spectra in the near infrared region are more helpful for predicting SSC.

4.2   Dataset Partitioning and Experimental Setting

We randomly split each batch of blueberry data into 80% training set and 20% test set. The performance of the model is evaluated based on coefficient of determination (R^2), MSE, and mean absolute error (MAE). The input data are scaled using MaxAbsScaler, and the SSC values are processed using normalization. We use Stochastic Gradient Descent optimizer, and the momentum is set to 0.9. The batch size is set to 64, epoch is set to 5000. The learning rate is set to 0.001, the first 100 epochs are using warm-up methods, then the learning rate is changed using cosine decay. In the last epoch, the learning rate dropped to 1e-9. In addition, Convolutional layers initialized with He method, fully connected layer initialized with Glorot method.

Table 1. Results of different models for SSC (mean ± standard deviation).

Model	α	Train R^2	Train MSE	Train MAE	Test R^2	Test MSE	Test MAE
PLS		0.89 ± 0.01	0.39 ± 0.02	0.49 ± 0.02	0.84 ± 0.02	0.55 ± 0.07	0.56 ± 0.03
CNN		0.97 ± 0.01	0.09 ± 0.02	0.25 ± 0.03	0.83 ± 0.02	0.61 ± 0.05	0.60 ± 0.02
CNN+M	0.2	0.95 ± 0.01	0.15 ± 0.02	0.31 ± 0.03	0.85 ± 0.02	0.55 ± 0.05	0.57 ± 0.03
DS		0.96 ± 0.01	0.14 ± 0.04	0.29 ± 0.04	0.83 ± 0.02	0.62 ± 0.06	0.60 ± 0.03
DS+M	0.2	0.92 ± 0.02	0.23 ± 0.05	0.37 ± 0.04	0.84 ± 0.02	0.57 ± 0.07	0.58 ± 0.04
MBA	0.2	0.95 ± 0.01	0.13 ± 0.02	0.29 ± 0.02	$\mathbf{0.85\pm0.01}$	0.53 ± 0.05	0.56 ± 0.04
	1.2	0.92 ± 0.01	0.16 ± 0.02	0.32 ± 0.02	$\mathbf{0.85\pm0.01}$	0.52 ± 0.04	0.54 ± 0.02
	1.8	0.91 ± 0.01	0.17 ± 0.02	0.33 ± 0.02	$\mathbf{0.86\pm0.02}$	0.51 ± 0.05	0.54 ± 0.02

4.3   Experimental Results

The proposed model is compared with PLS [5], DeepSpectra(DS) [8], and CNN [6]. The PLS model includes hyperparameter latent variables (LVs). Determine the optimal number of LVs by using 10-fold cross-validation, with a maximum value of 30 for LVs. To verify the effectiveness of mixup, we add mixup to the CNN and DS models for experiments (+M in Table 1 indicates adding mixup).

The average predictive performance (10 random weight initializations) of SSC is listed in Table 1. The results show that adding mixup improves the performance on the test set. Note that the performance on the training set decreases after mixup is added. This is because the samples are constantly changing during the training process, which increases the diversity of samples and has a regularizing effect. Compared with other models, our model performs better. To verify the effectiveness of each module of the proposed MBA method, we conduct an ablation study. In the experimental setting of ablation study, we successively add mixup module ($\alpha = 0.2$), and band attention module to the regression network. Table 2 shows ablation study results indicating each module in the paper is essential for improving blueberry SSC prediction performance.

5   Conclusion

This study proposes an end-to-end quantitative spectra analysis framework. We use multiple sets of parallel filters for feature extraction, which improves the

Table 2. Results of ablation experiments ($\alpha = 0.2$).

Regression Network	Mixup Module	Band Attention Module	Test R^2
√			0.830 ± 0.024
√	√		0.848 ± 0.020
√	√	√	0.852 ± 0.014

adaptability of the network. In addition, the band attention module is used to learn the band weights, so that the model pays more attention to the bands related to SSC. By computing the top 10 weighted bands, we found that the frequency bands sensitive to SSC exist within these more heavily weighted bands, which improves interpretability of our model. Aiming at the problem of insufficient data diversity, mixup method is used for data augmentation to increase the diversity of samples and expand the distribution of the training set. The experimental results show our method has better performance than other methods.

Acknowledgements. This work was supported in part by the National Natural Science Foundation of China (62171295), and the Applied Basic Research Project of Liaoning Province (2023JH2/101300204).

References

1. Cai, Y., Liu, X., Cai, Z.: BS-Nets: an end-to-end framework for band selection of hyperspectral image. IEEE Trans. Geosci. Remote Sens. **58**(3), 1969–1984 (2020)
2. Guthrie, J.A., Walsh, K.B., Reid, D.J., Liebenberg, C.J.: Assessment of internal quality attributes of mandarin fruit. 1. NIR calibration model development. Crop Pasture Sci. **56**, 405–416 (2005)
3. Li, S., et al.: Optical non-destructive techniques for small berry fruits: a review. Artif. Intell. Agric. **2**, 85–98 (2019)
4. Szegedy, C., Ioffe, S., Vanhoucke, V., Alemi, A.A.: Inception-v4, inception-ResNet and the impact of residual connections on learning. In: Proceedings of the Thirty-First AAAI Conference on Artificial Intelligence, pp. 4278–4284. AAAI 2017, AAAI Press (2017)
5. Wold, S., Sjöström, M., Eriksson, L.: PLS-regression: a basic tool of chemometrics. Chemometr. Intell. Lab. Syst. **58**(2), 109–130 (2001). pLS Methods
6. Zhang, C., Wu, W., Zhou, L., Cheng, H., Ye, X., He, Y.: Developing deep learning based regression approaches for determination of chemical compositions in dry black goji berries (lycium ruthenicum murr.) using near-infrared hyperspectral imaging. Food Chem. **319**, 126536 (2020)
7. Zhang, H., Cisse, M., Dauphin, Y.N., Lopez-Paz, D.: mixup: Beyond empirical risk minimization (2018)
8. Zhang, X., Lin, T., Xu, J., Luo, X., Ying, Y.: DeepSpectra: an end-to-end deep learning approach for quantitative spectral analysis. Anal. Chim. Acta **1058**, 48–57 (2019)

Contextualized Hybrid Prompt-Tuning for Generation-Based Event Extraction

Yuzhen Zhong, Tong Xu[✉], and Pengfei Luo

School of Data Science, State Key Laboratory of Cognitive Intelligence,
University of Science and Technology of China, Hefei, China
{alivezyz,pfluo}@mail.ustc.edu.cn, tongxu@ustc.edu.cn

Abstract. Recent years have witnessed the wide attention of event extraction task, which highly benefits various downstream applications. Traditionally, prior arts attempt to model this task in the perspective of sequence generation problem with discrete prompts. However, these methods typically construct templates for each event type without considering unique instance characteristics, which may lead to the suboptimal performance and unwanted noise. To address this issue, in this paper, we propose a novel solution for event extraction based on structure generation with contextualized hybrid prompt tuning, called CHPT-EE, in terms of both discrete and continuous prompts. Specifically, CHPT-EE unifies the encoding of event mentions from various event types via a structured event extraction language. Along this line, CHPT-EE could effectively exploit the complementary advantages of different prompts to mitigate the issues encountered by prior methods. Afterwards, for each context, we employ a semantically similar strategy to retrieve answered prompts as discrete prompt *DISC-P*, and obtain context-aware continuous prompt *CONT-P* by aggregating specific event type information and contextual semantic information. Experiments on ACE 2005 and CASIE show that CHPT-EE achieved competitive performance compared with state-of-the-art methods.

Keywords: Event Extraction · Hybrid Prompt-Tuning · Structure Generation · Prefix Tuning · In-Context Learning

1 Introduction

Event Extraction (EE) [1] is a critical task of Information Extraction, requiring the detection and classification of event triggers and their corresponding arguments according to a pre-defined event schema. For example, as shown in Fig. 1, the given context contains a *Data breach* event that is triggered by "*dumping*". By explicitly extracting the event structure in the text, EE can facilitate numerous downstream tasks, such as building knowledge graphs [2,11] and event evolutionary graphs [14], knowledge base population [9] and reading comprehension [28].

© The Author(s), under exclusive license to Springer Nature Switzerland AG 2023
Z. Jin et al. (Eds.): KSEM 2023, LNAI 14120, pp. 374–386, 2023.
https://doi.org/10.1007/978-3-031-40292-0_31

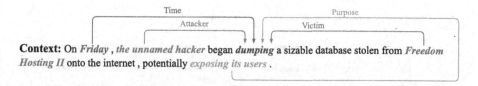

Fig. 1. An example sampled from the CASIE dataset with its event annotation.

Generally, recent approaches for Event Extraction can be divided into two categories. One is formulating this task as a sequence labeling classification problem in a pipeline framework [30], i.e., labels are treated as specific symbols, and the extraction of event triggers and event arguments are tackled in isolation. The other is the end-to-end generation-based method by guiding the model to summarize event information following a pre-defined pattern with manually designed prompts [7] or leveraging sequence-to-structure generation paradigm that applies special decoding strategies [17].

Despite some progress achieved along this line, current methods still suffer from several potential limitations. First, an insufficiency noted in the design and selection of manually designed prompts is the limited scope of event type information, with a lack of focus on the contextual information within the same sentence. Due to the non-specificity of prompt selection with regard to the context itself, it is necessary to enumerate all types during inference and training. Consequently, each context is typically assigned prompts that are suboptimal, which may introduce noise. Second, there exists a semantic gap between structured language and pre-trained language models. Similarly to the illustration in Fig. 2, structured languages usually indicate their hierarchical information by using special symbols, which is different from natural language. Without effective instruction on harnessing their analogical capabilities, models may struggle to generate complex, high-level structural information.

To overcome the aforementioned limitations, we introduce a structure generation based event extraction method with contextualized hybrid prompt-tuning (**CHPT-EE**). Figure 3 illustrates the overall framework of CHPT-EE. Specifically, by designing a structured event extraction language to unify the encoding of event mentions from various event types, there's no need to enumerate all event types during inference and training, thereby enabling our approach that can generalize to continually evolving event ontologies (**Contribution 1**). Furthermore, to leverage the complementary advantages of different prompts, we employ discrete prompt *DISC-P* and continuous prompt *CONT-P* to attain hybrid prompt-tuning. Concretely, for each context, we retrieve semantically analogous examples as *DISC-P* from constructed demonstration repositories via Prompts Retrieval Module, to assist the model in capturing the regularities of structured language. Moreover, we propose a trainable continuous prefix *CONT-P*, which aggregates specific event type information and unique contextual information to ensure the adaptability and specificity of the prompt to the context, thus alleviating the issue of suboptimality (**Contribution 2**).

Structured Event Extraction Language	Example

< Event_Start >
    Event < Mention_Start > *trigger mention*
< Arg_Start >
    Arg < Mention_Start > *argument mention*
< Arg_Start >
    Arg < Mention_Start > *argument mention*
<Arg_Start >
 	
    ....
< Event_End >
	< Event_Start >
	    Data breach < Mention_Start > *dumping*
	< Arg_Start >
	    Attacker < Mention_Start > *the unnamed hacker*
	< Arg_Start >
	    Victim < Mention_Start > *Freedom Hosting II*
	< Arg_Start >
	    Purpose < Mention_Start > *exposing its users*
	< Arg_Start >
	    Time < Mention_Start > *Friday*
	< Event_End >

Fig. 2. "Structured Event Extraction Language" is on the left side of the table. The right side of the table describes a structure language example of "On Friday, the unnamed hacker began dumping a sizable database stolen from Freedom Hosting II onto the internet, potentially exposing its users."

We conduct experiments on two event extraction benchmarks, ACE 2005 and CASIE, with fully-supervised setting and few-shot setting respectively. Experiment results demonstrate that our model achieves competitive results with previous methods (template generation-based and classification-based methods) on both ACE 2005 and CASIE. The ablation studies also prove our hypothesis that leveraging the complementary advantages of prompts in different forms can enhance the stability and superiority of the model performance.

2   Related Work

Traditional event extraction studies [8] rely on manually-crafted features to extract events. In the past decade, lines of work appeared that formulated Event Extraction as token-level classification in a pipeline-style framework [25,29] or followed the joint architecture [12,15,19], with emphasis on detecting both event triggers and arguments and identifying types. Furthermore, there has been a recent trend to view event extraction as a machine reading comprehension task [6,10,27] to investigate the semantics of events.

Recently, generation-based approaches have been proposed. TANL [20] casts structured prediction tasks as translation tasks by designing augmented natural languages. Text2Event [17] design a sequence-to-structure network for unified event extraction, generating with a constrained decoding algorithm during inference. DEGREE [7] utilizes template-generation-based approaches with manually designed discrete prompts. UIE [18] proposes a unified text-to-structure generation framework, that adaptively generates target extractions via a schema-based prompt mechanism. Compared to the aforementioned methods, the hybrid prompt tuning that we adopt is able to make better utilization of event semantics and context information, leverage the complementary advantages of diverse prompts to alleviate the issue of sub-optimality with hand-crafted prompts and stabilize performance on downstream tasks.

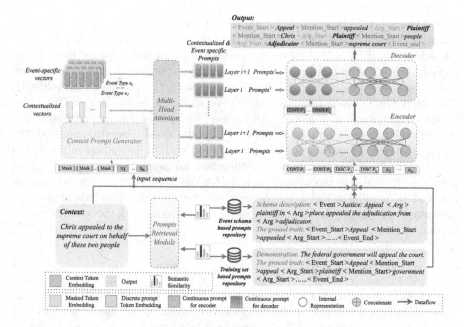

Fig. 3. The overall framework of CHPT-EE.

3 Methodology

3.1 Structure Generation for Event Extraction

Event Extraction can be formulated as a conditional generation task of mapping unstructured text to specific structures, using an encoder-decoder style architecture. Thus we choose T5 [21], a large pre-trained encoder-decoder language model, as our base model. Along this line, CHPT-EE initially concatenates the raw text sequence C with the discrete prompt $DISC\text{-}P$ as input sequence X. Subsequently, X is encoded by the bidirectional encoder, and the decoder predicts the output sequence Y in an auto-regressive manner, where Y is a structured sequence directed by structured event extraction language.

Motivated by the Unified Structure Generation (UIE) method [18], to encode event mentions from various event types into a uniform representation, we design a structured event extraction language based on the characteristics of EE. Concretely, within each structured language expression, it contains three types of semantic units shown in the left part of Fig. 2.

(1) **Event** signifies the presence of a particular trigger mention in the source text that denotes the occurrence of this event type.
(2) **Arg** indicates the existence of argument mention, which is associated with the upper-level Event in Arg way.
(3) **Mention** refers to the textual span of the corresponding trigger or argument in the source text.

Additionally, "⠆" represents the mapping from mention to the corresponding Event or Arg, and the four structure indicators $\langle Event\text{-}Start\rangle$, $\langle Event\text{-}End\rangle$, $\langle Arg\text{-}Start\rangle$ and $\langle Mention\text{-}Start\rangle$ are used to organize the extracted event information into a hierarchical structure. To facilitate the use of this language, we add six new tokens: $\langle Event\rangle$, $\langle Arg\rangle$, $\langle Event\text{-}Start\rangle$, $\langle Event\text{-}End\rangle$, $\langle Arg\text{-}Start\rangle$, $\langle Mention\text{-}Start\rangle$, aside from the special tokens in the vocabulary of T5.

The right part of Fig. 2 illustrates an example of our structured event extraction language. Compared with the template-based generation method, the structure-based generation method presents extracted information in a uniform format, circumventing the need to enumerate all possible event types during inference. If there are multiple arguments for the same role, results can be represented in parallel without the concern of overlapping. Therefore, it has the advantage of reducing the complexity of decoding and sharing the semantic information of labels.

3.2 Hybrid Prompt-Tuning

This section describes the construction of discrete prompt $DISC\text{-}P$ and continuous prompt $CONT\text{-}P$ in detail. The framework of our model with hybrid prompt-tuning is shown in Fig. 3. Compared to methods that employ only one type of prompt, the hybrid prompts can leverage complementary advantages of different prompts to incorporate more comprehensive contextual information into LM.

3.2.1 Discrete Prompts Design

Inspired by in-context learning, we optionally augment the input with multiple answered prompts. Following a semantically similar strategy [3], we retrieve $DISC\text{-}P$ from Event-schema-based and Training-set-based prompts repository via Prompts Retrieval Module.

Event-Schema-Based Prompts Repository. For each event type e_i, there is a pair $\langle d_i, sg_i\rangle$ stored in the repository, where d_i is a manually constructed event description and sg_i is the corresponding ground truth encoding by structured event extraction language. We obtain the event description d_i by rewriting a concise natural language sequence based on work [7]. Specifically, the rewriting process involves replacing the event element placeholders with semantic units from the structured event extraction language. For instance, considering a $Life\text{:}Be\text{-}Born$ event, d_i is "$\langle Event\rangle$ Be-Born $\langle Arg\rangle$ person was born in $\langle Arg\rangle$ place".

Training-Set-Based Prompts Repository. To comprehensively authenticate the effectiveness of our method and ensure experimental soundness, we employ different construction methods based on different experimental settings. In the fully-supervised setting, we initiate the repository with the full training set, consisting of raw texts and corresponding annotations which are encoded by structured event extraction language. In the few-shot setting, by setting a budget, we sample 5% of the examples per event type, including the non-event type.

Semantic-Based Prompts Retrieval Module. In order to measure the semantic similarity between the current context and answered prompts, We employ SBERT [22] as Prompts Retrieval Module, which is a modification of the pre-trained BERT [5] network that uses siamese and triplet network structures to derive semantically meaningful sentence embeddings. This module efficiently identifies text with the highest similarity score while also ensuring a high degree of accuracy is maintained. We feed the context and all the prompts in two repositories to the Prompts Retrieval Module as illustrated in Fig. 3, retrieving the most similar prompts from each repository separately to form $DISC\text{-}P$. We concatenate $DISC\text{-}P$ and the context as the input sequence X^d as follows:

$$X^d = [DISC\text{-}P; X], \tag{1}$$

where [;] denotes the concatenation operation.

3.2.2 Contextually Induced Continuous Prompts

Unlike P-tuning [16] and Prefix-tuning [13], whose prefix is related to the task only, our method is expected to provide additional context information. Thus, we propose a context-aware continuous prompt $CONT\text{-}P$ by aggregating specific event type information and contextual semantic information to optimize the instruction as continuous word embeddings, which is virtually prepended for the encoder and decoder input as shown in Fig. 3.

$$X^{'} = [CONT\text{-}P_{encoder}; X^d], \quad Y^{'} = [CONT\text{-}P_{decoder}; Y]. \tag{2}$$

Event-Specific Prefix. Based on Prefix-tuning [13], except for the LM parameter ϕ, we initialize a trainable embedding tensor $P_\theta \in \mathcal{R}^{|e| \times l \times dim(h_i)}$ (parametrized by θ) for both encoder and decoder to store the Event-specific prefix parameters. Here, $|e|$ denotes the number of event types defined in the event schema, l represents the length of the prefix $CONT\text{-}P$, and $h_i = [h_i^{(1)}; ...; h_i^{(n)}]$ is a concatenation of all activation layers at time step i, and $h_i^{(j)}$ is the activation of the j-th Transformer layer at time step i. To be more specific, for each event type e_i, there exists a corresponding transformer activation sequence $Ep_{e_i} \in \mathcal{R}^{l \times dim(h_i)}$.

Context Prompt Generation. With the intention of obtaining contextualized information when constructing trainable prefixes, we choose to elicit related knowledge from PLMs. To utilize the excellent mask-filling ability of BERT

[5], we employ it as the context prompt generator, to derive the contextualized prompt vectors. Specifically, the input is reconstructed by concatenating a sequence of special tokens $[Mask]$ to the context:

$$\tilde{X} = [Mask]_1, ..., [Mask]_l \oplus C. \tag{3}$$

By feeding $\tilde{X}$ as the input of the prompt generator, we are able to acquire the last hidden state of tokens that can be used as prompt vectors $p_c^1, ..., p_c^l$:

$$p_c^1, ..., p_c^l, ... = Generator(\tilde{X}). \tag{4}$$

This approach enables a more profound capture of the interdependence between prompts and context.

Integrating Prompt by Attention. In order to obtain the final $CONT\text{-}P$, we dynamically integrate the context prompt vectors and Event-specific prefix by multi-head attention [4,24]. For the $CONT\text{-}P_c = \{cont\text{-}p_c^1, ..., cont\text{-}p_c^l\}$ specified by context C,

$$cont\text{-}p_c^k = \text{MultiHeadAttention}(p_c^k, [Ep_{e_1}^k, Ep_{e_2}^k, ..., Ep_{e_\epsilon}^k]), \tag{5}$$

where $k = 1, ..., l$, $Ep_{e_i}^k = P_\theta[e_i, k, :]$.

3.3 Training

In order to separately learn the LM parameters ϕ and $CONT\text{-}P$ parameters θ based on specific training objectives, the training process is divided into two stages. In the first stage, to capture the fundamental text-to-structure mapping ability and generate valid structures defined by structured event extraction language, we train the model to learn the parameters ϕ without $CONT\text{-}P$, performing gradient updates with the following log-likelihood objective:

$$\max_\phi \log P_\phi(\mathbf{y} \mid \mathbf{x}) = \max_\phi \sum_{y_i} \log P_\phi(y_i \mid \mathbf{x}, y_{<i}). \tag{6}$$

In the second stage, the LM parameters ϕ are fixed and $CONT\text{-}P$ parameters θ are the only trainable parameters, whose effects will be propagated upward to all transformer activation layers and rightward to subsequent tokens. The training objective and the computation of the decoder transformer activation vector h_i are as follows:

$$\max_\theta \log P_\theta(\mathbf{y} \mid \mathbf{x}; \phi) = \max_\theta \sum_{y_i} \log P_\theta(y_i \mid h_{<i}; \phi), \tag{7}$$

$$h_i = \begin{cases} cont\text{-}p_c^i, & \text{if } i < l, \\ \text{LM}_\phi(y_i; h_{<i} \mid \mathbf{x}), & \text{otherwise.} \end{cases} \tag{8}$$

4   Experiments

4.1   Experimental Settings

Datasets. We evaluate our method on the most widely used ACE 2005 English corpus [26] and the newly constructed CASIE [23] dataset in the domain of cybersecurity. ACE 2005 contains 599 English documents from various domains, crawled between 2003 and 2005, which are annotated with 33 event types and 22 argument roles. Following the previous work [15,25], we process the datasets through two distinct approaches and obtain two datasets, **ACE05-EN** and **ACE05-EN$^+$**. In addition, for **CASIE**, defining 5 event types along with their semantic roles and 20 event-relevant argument types, our pre-processing method is aligned with the prior study [18].

Metrics. We consider the same evaluation metrics as prior works [17,25], using span-based offset Micro-F1 as the primary metric to evaluate the model. (1) **Tri-C** (trigger classification): an event trigger is correct if its offsets and event type matches a reference trigger. (2) **Arg-C** (argument classification): an event argument is correct if its offsets, role type, and event type match a reference argument mention. Since CHPT-EE generates only string-level extraction results, we reconstruct the offset of predicted trigger/argument mentions by finding the matched utterance in the input sequence one by one.

Baselines. We conduct a comparative analysis of CHPT-EE against a range of representative and competitive baselines, encompassing both classification-based and generation-based methods: (1) DyGIE++ [25], a BERT-based model which captures both within-sentence and cross-sentence context. (2) OneIE [15], an end-to-end IE system that employs global feature and beam search to extract globally optimal event structures, which is the state-of-the-art. (3) BERT_QA [6], which formulates the EE task as a question-answering (QA) task. (4) Text2Event [17], a sequence-to-structure generation method for unified event extraction. (5) UIE [18], a unified text-to-structure generation framework with structural schema instructor. (6) DEGREE [7], a template generation-based approach with manually designed discrete prompts.

Data Split for Low-Resource Setting. In order to verify the performance of the CHPT-EE under the low-resource situation, we follow UIE [18], which conducted experiments on six different partitions of the original ACE05-EN$^+$ training sets (1/5/10 shot, 1/5/10% ratio), separately. For each event type in the low-shot experiment, we sample 1/5/10 instances and leverage the original development set and test set for evaluation. For low-ratio experiments, we sample 1/5/10% of training instances. To avoid the influence of random sampling, we conduct each experiment 10 times with diverse samples and calculate the average of their performance.

382   Y. Zhong et al.

Table 1. Results for Supervised event extraction on ACE05-E, ACE05-E$^+$ and CASIE. The Highest scores are in **bold** and the second-best scores are underlined. "Cls" and "Gen" represent classification-based models and generation-based models, respectively.

Model	Type	ACE05-E		ACE05-E$^+$		CASIE	
		Tri-C	Arg-C	Tri-C	Arg-C	Tri-C	Arg-C
DyGIE++ [25]	Cls	69.7	48.8	–	–	–	–
OneIE [15]	Cls	**74.7**	<u>56.8</u>	72.8	54.8	–	–
BERT_QA [6]	Cls	72.4	53.3	–	–	–	–
Text2Event [17]	Gen	71.9	53.8	71.8	54.4	67.5	59.4
UIE [18]	Gen	–	–	<u>73.3</u>	54.7	<u>69.3</u>	<u>61.3</u>
DEGREE [7]	Gen	73.3	55.8	70.9	**56.3**	–	–
CHPT-EE	Gen	<u>74.2</u>	**57.1**	**73.9**	<u>55.5</u>	**71.4**	**62.0**

Table 2. Results for low-resource event extraction on ACE05-E$^+$.

	Model	1-Shot	5-Shot	10-Shot	1%	5%	10%
ACE05-E$^+$ Event Trigger	CHPT-EE w/o *DISC-P*	32.2	49.3	55.9	44.6	53.8	60.5
	CHPT-EE w/o *CONT-P*	34.5	51.7	54.5	49.1	52.6	62.0
	CHPT-EE	**36.7**	**53.5**	**57.2**	**51.2**	**57.6**	**63.1**
ACE05-E$^+$ Event Argument	CHPT-EE w/o *DISC-P*	10.6	26.2	29.5	16.5	25.0	34.0
	CHPT-EE w/o *CONT-P*	14.9	25.0	31.9	17.3	29.7	35.7
	CHPT-EE	**18.6**	**29.4**	**36.1**	**26.0**	**34.4**	**37.2**

4.2   Results in Fully-Supervised Event Extraction

Table 1 assesses the CHPT-EE performance in supervised settings, showing the trigger classification F1-scores and the argument classification F1-scores. We compare our model with all baseline methods on three datasets. It is worth noting that CHPT-EE exhibits notable competitiveness with regard to trigger extraction and argument extraction tasks. Regarding the Tri-C evaluation, CHPT-EE achieves the highest F1 scores on ACE05-EN$^+$ and CASIE. In particular, with respect to CASIE, CHPT-EE demonstrates a remarkable improvement of 2.1% in F1 scores over the SOTA. In the ACE05-EN dataset, our method outperforms all the baselines except for OneIE, the state-of-the-art classification-based method. Moreover, in terms of the Arg-C, our method consistently delivers superior performance across all three datasets, exhibiting significantly greater robustness than alternative approaches when confronted with varied dataset characteristics. This result proves the stability and superiority of our model.

4.3 Results in Low-Resource Event Extraction

To establish the necessity of our hybrid prompts when adapting CHPT-EE under a low-resource situation, we empirically investigate the impact of *DISC-P* and *CONT-P* on six different partitions of the original ACE05-EN$^+$ training sets. As Table 2 shows, all types of prompts are essential, as removing any one of *DISC-P* and *CONT-P* results in performance degradation. And we observe that *DISC-P* seems to be more beneficial under the extremely low data situation, which demonstrates that contextual answered-prompt can unleash the excellent analogical capability of large pre-trained models. Additionally, it is important to highlight that the substantial volume of non-event type data in ACE05-EN+ may cause issues with imbalanced class sampling during data splitting by ratio, leading to a decrease in model performance. Nonetheless, according to the results, the performance of our method in the 1% setting is on par with that of the 5-shot setting under similar data amounts, which validates the ability of our model to mitigate bias issues caused by imbalanced types in both trigger and argument extraction tasks.

Table 3. Results of various ablation studies.

Model	ACE05-EN		ACE05-EN$^+$		CASIE	
	Tri-C	Arg-C	Tri-C	Arg-C	Tri-C	Arg-C
CHPT-EE	**74.2**	**57.1**	**73.9**	**55.5**	**71.4**	**62.0**
- w/o *All prompts*	71.1	52.4	70.9	51.0	69.3	59.4
- only *DISC-$P_{context}$*	73.3	55.2	72.5	54.6	69.8	60.2
- only *CONT-$P_{context}$*	72.9	53.9	73.0	53.4	70.2	61.2
- only *DISC-P_{random}*	71.5	51.8	70.4	51.0	69.7	58.2
- only *CONT-P_{event}*	72.2	53.4	71.6	52.4	69.4	60.7

4.4 Ablation Study

We conduct comprehensive ablation studies to evaluate the effectiveness of individual components of our approach. The results on ACE05-E, ACE05-E$^+$ and CASIE are presented in Table 3. With respect to discrete prompt *DISC-P*, to demonstrate the impact of different construction methods on performance, we conduct two sets of experiments. We denote the prompts obtained by the semantic-based prompts retrieval module as *DISC-$P_{context}$*, and the prompts randomly retrieved from two repositories as *DISC-P_{random}*. As Table 3 shows, utilizing discrete prompts selected by incorporating contextual information enhances performance, especially for argument extraction tasks. Incorporating prompts that are not relevant to the context may introduce noise for training, consequently leading to performance decay. Regarding continuous prompt

$CONT$-P, we additionally devised dual settings with different constructing rules, naming the prompts that only utilize Event-specific prefix as $CONT$-P_{event}, and the prompts that dynamically aggregate context and event type information as $CONT$-$P_{context}$. Compared with $CONT$-P_{event}, $CONT$-$P_{context}$ respectively exhibits a improvement of 0.7%, 1.4% and 0.8% for Tri-C and 0.5%, 1.0% and 0.5% for Arg-C F1 score across three distinct datasets. It indicates that triggers are more sensitive to context-aware prefixes compared to arguments. Moreover, CHPT-EE employs hybrid prompts consisting of both $DISC$-$P_{context}$ and $CONT$-$P_{context}$. We observe that contextualized hybrid prompt-tuning provides a boost of performance consistently with various datasets and tasks, which confirms our method's ability to leverage the complementary strengths of different prompts.

5   Conclusion and Future Work

In this paper, we cast the task of event extraction as a structure generation problem and designed hybrid prompts for each context by utilizing specific contextual semantic information. Experimental results show that our method achieves competitive performance in both fully-supervised and few-shot settings, which demonstrates its effectiveness. In the future, we plan to 1) explore more efficient structured event extraction languages, and 2) consider alternative methods for aggregating event type information and contextual information.

Acknowledgments. This work was supported by the grants from National Natural Science Foundation of China (No. 62222213, 62072423), and the USTC Research Funds of the Double First-Class Initiative (No. YD2150002009).

References

1. Ahn, D.: The stages of event extraction. In: Proceedings of the Workshop on Annotating and Reasoning about Time and Events, pp. 1–8 (2006)
2. Bosselut, A., Rashkin, H., Sap, M., Malaviya, C., Celikyilmaz, A., Choi, Y.: COMET: commonsense transformers for automatic knowledge graph construction. In: ACL (1), pp. 4762–4779. Association for Computational Linguistics (2019)
3. Chen, L., et al.: Entity summarization via exploiting description complementarity and salience. IEEE Trans. Neural Netw. Learn. Syst. (2022)
4. Chen, L., et al.: Multi-modal Siamese network for entity alignment. In: Proceedings of KDD (2022)
5. Devlin, J., Chang, M., Lee, K., Toutanova, K.: BERT: pre-training of deep bidirectional transformers for language understanding. In: NAACL-HLT (1), pp. 4171–4186. Association for Computational Linguistics (2019)
6. Du, X., Cardie, C.: Event extraction by answering (almost) natural questions. In: EMNLP (1), pp. 671–683. Association for Computational Linguistics (2020)
7. Hsu, I.H., et al.: Degree: a data-efficient generation-based event extraction model. In: Proceedings of the 2022 Conference of the North American Chapter of the Association for Computational Linguistics: Human Language Technologies, pp. 1890–1908 (2022)

8. Ji, H., Grishman, R.: Refining event extraction through cross-document inference. In: Proceedings of ACL-08: Hlt, pp. 254–262 (2008)
9. Ji, H., Grishman, R.: Knowledge base population: successful approaches and challenges. In: Proceedings of the 49th Annual Meeting of the Association for Computational Linguistics: Human Language Technologies, pp. 1148–1158 (2011)
10. Li, F., et al.: Event extraction as multi-turn question answering. In: Findings of the Association for Computational Linguistics: EMNLP 2020, pp. 829–838 (2020)
11. Li, L., et al.: Real-world data medical knowledge graph: construction and applications. Artif. Intell. Med. **103**, 101817 (2020)
12. Li, Q., Ji, H., Huang, L.: Joint event extraction via structured prediction with global features. In: Proceedings of the 51st Annual Meeting of the Association for Computational Linguistics (Volume 1: Long Papers), pp. 73–82 (2013)
13. Li, X.L., Liang, P.: Prefix-tuning: optimizing continuous prompts for generation. In: ACL/IJCNLP (1), pp. 4582–4597. Association for Computational Linguistics (2021)
14. Li, Z., Ding, X., Liu, T.: Constructing narrative event evolutionary graph for script event prediction. In: IJCAI, pp. 4201–4207. ijcai.org (2018)
15. Lin, Y., Ji, H., Huang, F., Wu, L.: A joint neural model for information extraction with global features. In: Proceedings of the 58th Annual Meeting of the Association for Computational Linguistics, pp. 7999–8009 (2020)
16. Liu, X., Ji, K., Fu, Y., Du, Z., Yang, Z., Tang, J.: P-tuning v2: prompt tuning can be comparable to fine-tuning universally across scales and tasks. arXiv preprint arXiv:2110.07602 (2021)
17. Lu, Y., et al.: Text2event: controllable sequence-to-structure generation for end-to-end event extraction. In: ACL/IJCNLP (1), pp. 2795–2806. Association for Computational Linguistics (2021)
18. Lu, Y., et al.: Unified structure generation for universal information extraction. In: ACL (1), pp. 5755–5772. Association for Computational Linguistics (2022)
19. Nguyen, T.H., Cho, K., Grishman, R.: Joint event extraction via recurrent neural networks. In: Proceedings of the 2016 Conference of the North American chapter of the Association for Computational Linguistics: Human Language Technologies, pp. 300–309 (2016)
20. Paolini, G., et al.: Structured prediction as translation between augmented natural languages. In: ICLR. OpenReview.net (2021)
21. Raffel, C., et al.: Exploring the limits of transfer learning with a unified text-to-text transformer. J. Mach. Learn. Res. **21**(1), 5485–5551 (2020)
22. Reimers, N., Gurevych, I.: Sentence-BERT: sentence embeddings using Siamese BERT-networks. In: EMNLP/IJCNLP (1), pp. 3980–3990. Association for Computational Linguistics (2019)
23. Satyapanich, T., Ferraro, F., Finin, T.: Casie: extracting cybersecurity event information from text. In: Proceedings of the AAAI Conference on Artificial Intelligence, vol. 34, pp. 8749–8757 (2020)
24. Vaswani, A., et al.: Attention is all you need. In: Advances in Neural Information Processing Systems, vol. 30 (2017)
25. Wadden, D., Wennberg, U., Luan, Y., Hajishirzi, H.: Entity, relation, and event extraction with contextualized span representations. In: EMNLP/IJCNLP (1), pp. 5783–5788. Association for Computational Linguistics (2019)
26. Walker, C., Strassel, S., Medero, J., Maeda, K.: ACE 2005 multilingual training corpus. Linguistic Data Consortium, Philadelphia **57**, 45 (2006)

27. Wang, S., Yu, M., Chang, S., Sun, L., Huang, L.: Query and extract: refining event extraction as type-oriented binary decoding. In: ACL (Findings), pp. 169–182. Association for Computational Linguistics (2022)
28. Wang, W., Yang, N., Wei, F., Chang, B., Zhou, M.: Gated self-matching networks for reading comprehension and question answering. In: Proceedings of the 55th Annual Meeting of the Association for Computational Linguistics (Volume 1: Long Papers), pp. 189–198 (2017)
29. Yang, S., Feng, D., Qiao, L., Kan, Z., Li, D.: Exploring pre-trained language models for event extraction and generation. In: Proceedings of the 57th Annual Meeting of the Association for Computational Linguistics, pp. 5284–5294 (2019)
30. Zhang, T., Ji, H., Sil, A.: Joint entity and event extraction with generative adversarial imitation learning. Data Intell. 1(2), 99–120 (2019)

udPINNs: An Enhanced PDE Solving Algorithm Incorporating Domain of Dependence Knowledge

Nanxi Chen[1,2], Jiyan Qiu[1,2], Pengcheng Shi[1,2], Wu Yuan[1,2(✉)], and Jian Zhang[1,2]

[1] Computer Network Information Center, Chinese Academy of Sciences, Beijing, China
yuanwu@sccas.cn
[2] University of Chinese Academy of Sciences, Beijing, China

Abstract. Physics-Informed Neural Networks (PINNs) have demonstrated their effectiveness in solving partial differential equations (PDEs) by integrating PDE knowledge into the neural network training process. However, prior methods were restricted to incorporating only PDE knowledge, and could not utilize broader knowledge from computational mathematics, such as the domain of dependence of PDEs. To tackle this limitation, we introduce a distributed PINNs algorithm called udPINNs (unidirectional Physics-Informed Neural Networks), which is founded on a domain decomposition approach and capable of incorporating domain of dependence knowledge into the training process. This enhancement accelerates training speed and elevates solution accuracy. We validate udPINNs on common equations, including heat transfer and incompressible flow, and demonstrate that it surpasses existing XPINNs methods in terms of error reduction and computational efficiency.

Keywords: Distributed deep learning · Differential equations · Knowledge-driven learning · Physics-Informed Neural Networks

1 Introduction

Differential equations are widely used to describe various physical phenomena and are the most important part of knowledge in physical modeling. Therefore, in solving the most fundamental task in this field - the solution of physical equations, researchers are constantly exploring how to incorporate the knowledge of these partial differential equations into the deep learning process. This has led to the development of the Physics-Informed Neural Networks (PINNs) algorithm [1]. PINNs employ networks to fit the solution functions of differential equations and explicitly add partial differential equation losses to the loss function by leveraging the automatic differentiation mechanism of neural networks, thus satisfying physical constraints.

Supported by "Research and Development of CAE Cloud Service Platform for Complex Equipment" (2020YFB1709500).

However, possessing accurate physical equations does not imply that we have fully grasped the underlying physical mechanisms. For instance, in fluid simulation, the Navier-Stokes equations (fundamental equations in fluid mechanics) were established in the early 18th century and have been consistently employed since then. Nevertheless, this does not indicate that the field of computational fluid dynamics has reached its full potential. To genuinely apply these equations to real-world problems, researchers still need to investigate the properties of the equations, discretization methods, and numerical solution strategies.

In this article, we focus on incorporating the domain of dependence property of PDEs into the training of PINNs. For a specific PDE with a known analytical form, we can typically employ mathematical techniques to analyze its properties. PDEs can be classified into elliptic, parabolic, and hyperbolic types. In this paper, we provide a brief overview of their respective characteristics as follows:

Elliptic Equations. The solutions of elliptic equations are influenced by boundary conditions throughout the entire domain.

Hyperbolic/Parabolic Equations. The solutions of these equations are affected by boundary conditions in some regions but not throughout the entire domain.

If the aforementioned concepts seem abstract, let's consider an example: the process of heat gradually reaching equilibrium in a metal block, which involves a heat equation with hyperbolic characteristics in the time direction. This means that the physical field state at a given moment depends only on the historical physical field states. In other words, the current temperature distribution can be affected only by the historical temperature distribution and not by the future temperature distribution.

Our work primarily focuses on incorporating the properties of partial differential equations, derived from mathematical analysis, into the PINNs solving process. We have built upon existing domain decomposition-based distributed deep learning algorithms to implement directional control of information propagation and a specialized communication buffer for stabilizing the training process. Moreover, we have not limited ourselves to the properties of partial differential equations derived from mathematical analysis. In the experimental section on incompressible flow cases, we demonstrate how we control the direction of information propagation based on the known information distribution.

In this paper, we first introduce the background and motivation in Sect. 1. Section 2 reviews related works, focusing on the optimization of PINNs algorithms. In Sect. 3, we present our proposed methodology, udPINNs. Section 4 details the experiments and results for four different cases: ordinary differential equations, single wave equations, heat equations, and incompressible flow equations. Finally, Sect. 5 concludes the paper and discusses future work.

2   Related Works

After the introduction of PINNs (Physics-Informed Neural Networks) by Raissi M [1], this method has become an effective means for solving PDEs by encoding

PDEs into the neural network loss function to handle both forward and inverse problems. For non-stationary problems, PINNs utilize the automatic differentiation mechanism of neural networks to calculate the physical quantity derivatives and train the network based on the control equations and boundary conditions to define the neural network loss function [2–4]. Recent optimizations of the PINNs algorithm for single models include: 1. Difference method: Research has shown that, compared to traditional automatic differentiation mechanisms, using the difference method to calculate derivatives can achieve the same accuracy with fewer sampling points [5,6]. 2. Loss function: The main difficulty in training PINNs lies in setting the weights of the various loss items. Many researchers have proposed innovative methods for determining the weights of PINNs loss items during training [7–10], effectively accelerating the convergence speed of the network during training.

Traditional neural network models can be parallelized through methods such as data parallelism or model parallelism to speed up training. However, data parallelism often has significant communication overhead, and for the problems PINNs handle, i.e., solving partial differential equations, allowing a subnetwork to iterate over the entire solution domain can result in an overly large task for a single network. Therefore, researchers have drawn inspiration from domain decomposition in traditional numerical methods and proposed a series of model parallelism and domain decomposition strategies for PINNs, which greatly improve efficiency compared to training a single large model. These include:

DPINNs [11] assigns network models to individual solution subdomains and constrains the physical quantities and partial differential equation derivatives to be the same at the boundaries. Jagtap et al. [12] first introduced the domain decomposition idea for handling conservation equations in PINNs and named it Conservative Physics-Informed Neural Networks (CPINNs). The same author extended the algorithm to more general cases, capable of handling non-conservative equations, with XPINNs [13]. Building on this work, paper [14] mathematically analyzes the advantages of XPINNs over traditional PINNs, while paper [15] discusses the system design strategies of cPINN and XPINNs in the software framework. Parareal PINNs [16] decomposes longer time domains into multiple short-time subdomains to accelerate the solution of long-time integration PDEs, but it cannot be applied to all types of PDEs. hp-VPINNs [17] proposes a variational PINNs method that combines the advantages of variational methods and neural networks. DDM [18] uses the Schwarz method for overlapping domain decomposition and iteratively trains subnets to improve computational efficiency. Coarse-space accelerated DDM [19] extends the DDM method to improve convergence. To alleviate the spectral bias problem, paper [20] proposes an overlapping domain decomposition algorithm.

3   Proposed Methodology

In this section, we introduce our proposed algorithm and discuss the main improvements compared to the XPINNs algorithm, as illustrated in Fig. 1. Our

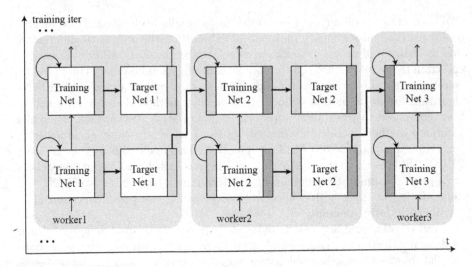

Fig. 1. Structure of our methods (udPINNs): Mainly two improvements - (1) Unidirectional information propagation mechanism based on the dependency relationship of the partial differential equation solution domain, and (2) Caching optimal communication area sampling within a certain time window based on the value of the loss function.

algorithm is based on the prior knowledge of partial differential equations, utilizing the dependency of the solution domain to determine the weight coefficients of the boundary loss. The improvements involved in our algorithm can be divided into two parts:

Unidirectional Information Propagation Mechanism. Setting the weight coefficients of boundary loss in a non-symmetric manner according to the dependency of the solution domain of differential equations,

Caching Mechanism for Communication Area. We have a buffer to store the optimal network in a certain historical window to provide boundary value information for other networks, stabilizing the training process and reducing communication overhead.

Next, we will first review the shortcomings of existing methods and then separately discuss our improvements.

3.1 Shortcomings of Existing Methods

We first use time-dependent partial differential equations (PDEs) as an example to explain our algorithm. Time-dependent PDEs exhibit dependency along the time axis, which is the most common scenario where dependency occurs in the solution domain. For a time-dependent PDE problem, assuming the time interval involved is within $t \in [0,T]$, the original PINNs algorithm usually iterates training within the entire solution domain. To improve training efficiency and reduce computational complexity based on the basic PINNs algorithm, two methods have been adopted in the past:

Sequential Training of Time-Advancing Models. A simple method is to divide the time domain into N subdomains, and then use PINNs models to solve the solution domains. After the training in the interval is completed, the values of the solution function fitted by the network at the time are used as the initial value conditions of the solution domain and N models are trained in sequence. The final result is obtained by concatenating the solutions of each model in their respective regions. The disadvantage of this method is that it requires sequential training of N models, lacking parallelism.

Domain Decomposition. XPINNs type algorithms provide a second model training mechanism aimed at improving parallelism. For instance, in XPINNs, as depicted in the image on the right side of Fig. 2, we still divide the time domain into N subdomains and assign N models to train in each subdomain separately. The main difference from the previous model training is that this process is parallel. During the training process, in addition to the data loss and PDE loss within each model, the equation residuals and value continuity at the model boundaries are also constrained. This achieves the purpose of parallel training and reduces the expressiveness required for individual models. Moreover, XPINNs have stronger parallelism when deployed on multi-node computing clusters with sufficient computing power, and usually achieve better performance.

However, XPINNs algorithm also has some drawbacks. Since XPINNs treat all types of equations as elliptic equations without fully utilizing the equation's characteristics, this may lead to reduced efficiency and insufficient solution accuracy when dealing with other types of equations. In addition, the interdependence between the submodels may slow down the training process. Although XPINNs have advantages in improving parallelism and handling complex geometric problems, their limitations should be considered in practical applications, especially when solving non-elliptic equations or problems with strong dependencies. For these issues, attempts can be made to improve the XPINNs algorithm to better utilize the characteristics of the equations.

3.2   Unidirectional Information Propagation Mechanism

In our algorithm, we address dependency by setting asymmetric loss weight coefficients. For strong dependencies, such as those resulting from equation properties (e.g., Experiments 1, 2, and 3 in the experimental section), we choose to define the interface loss unidirectionally. For certain reconstruction problems (e.g., flow field reconstruction experiments in the experimental section), we set asymmetric loss weight coefficients to construct asymmetric loss terms. Specifically, for the situation shown on the left side of Fig. 2, the area processed by network 2 depends on the area processed by network 1 in the temporal dimension. The loss defined using XPINNs for each network is as follows:

$$J(\widetilde{\Theta}_q) = \mathrm{DataLoss} + \mathrm{PdeLoss} + \mathrm{InterfaceLoss} \tag{1}$$

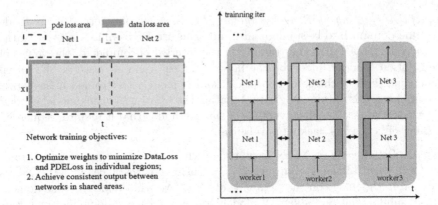

Fig. 2. The left figure shows an example of a decomposed area, using two networks for parallel training to compute the solution within the computation area. The right figure shows the process flow of the benchmark XPINNs algorithm, for comparison with the our method in Fig. 1.

$$\text{DataLoss} = \frac{1}{N_{uq}} \sum_{i=1}^{N_{uq}} \left(u^{(i)} - u_{\widetilde{\Theta}_q}(x_{uq}^{(i)}) \right)^2, \tag{2}$$

$$\text{PdeLoss} = \frac{1}{N_{Fq}} \sum_{i=1}^{N_{Fq}} \left(F_{\widetilde{\Theta}_q}(x_{Fq}^{(i)}) \right)^2. \tag{3}$$

$$\text{InterfaceLoss} = \frac{1}{N_{Iq}} \sum_{i=1}^{N_{Iq}} \left(u_{\widetilde{\Theta}_q}(x_{Iq}^{(i)}) - u_{\widetilde{\Theta}_{q+}}(x_{Iq}^{(i)}) \right)^2 \tag{4}$$

Here, q represents the q-th network, q+ represents the neighboring network, u is the function for network output, and F denotes the residual. We can simply control the unidirectional information transfer by removing the interface loss of Network 1, based on the dependency relationship in time, the udPINNs loss function for two networks id defined as:

$$J(\widetilde{\Theta}_1) = \text{DataLoss}_1 + \text{PdeLoss}_1 \tag{5}$$

$$J(\widetilde{\Theta}_2) = \text{DataLoss}_2 + \text{PdeLoss}_2 + \text{InterfaceLoss}_{12} \tag{6}$$

We can view this process from another perspective: for the common region in Fig. 2, two networks are involved in the iteration. For time-dependent partial differential equations, the solution typically relies on historical information, so the network 1, which is closer to the historical information, is more accurate in training the interface region. In this case, allowing these two networks to learn from each other, as in XPINNs, is not a good strategy. We control the direction of information propagation by controlling the loss weights of the interface region, which helps the networks with worse fitting conditions to unidirectionally learn from the networks with better fitting conditions.

3.3 Caching Mechanism for Communication Area

In the right parts of Fig. 2, Net2 requires the capability to explore the function space in order to accomplish tasks, necessitating continuous adaptation during the training process. However, Net2 also depends on Net1 and Net3 to provide accurate and stable boundary information, aiming for the smoothest possible training process. Each model needs to self-adapt while having accurate and stable neighboring models, resembling the conflict between policy network sampling and evaluation in deep reinforcement learning.

To stabilize the training process and reduce communication overhead, we introduce a buffer mechanism into the algorithm, storing the communication area sampling results of the optimal network within historical windows. Throughout the training process, we use the loss function values obtained from training to evaluate the overall state of the network. When a lower loss value is achieved within a specific training window, the process locally saves the communication area sampling results that may need to be sent to other networks. In this scenario, by setting the hyperparameter for the frequency of information exchange (how often communication occurs between networks during each iteration), each process only requires a few iterations involving network communication, significantly reducing communication overhead. For specific details, please refer to the pseudocode provided in Algorithm 1.

4   Experiments and Results

4.1   Ordinary Differential Equation

In this study, we investigate the following first-order ordinary differential equation:

$$\frac{dy}{dt} = -\sin(\pi t) \tag{7}$$

$$y(0) = 1 \tag{8}$$

The unique analytical solution to the equation is:

$$y(t) = \cos(\pi t) \tag{9}$$

By comparing the numerical computations with the analytical solution, we validate the accuracy of our experimental results.

Algorithm 1. Communication and Computation Behavior of Each Worker, Described in an MPI-like Syntax

---

1: $rank \leftarrow$ GETRANK()
2: $size \leftarrow$ GETSIZE()
3: $CommBlockInfo \leftarrow$ GETCOMMBLOCKINFO($rank$)
4: $SendCommBlock \leftarrow None$
5: $RecvCommBlock \leftarrow None$
6:
7: **for** $i \leftarrow 1$ **to** $total\_iter\_num$ **do**
8:     **if** $method == udPINNs$ **then**
9:         **if** i mod $infoExchangeFreq == 0$ **then**
10:             SEND($SendCommBlock, dst = neighbor(rank)$)
11:             $RecvCommBlock \leftarrow$ RECV($src = neighbor(rank)$)
12:             BARRIER()
13:             $loss\_window\_best \leftarrow \infty$
14:             $SendCommBlock \leftarrow None$
15:         **end if**
16:     **end if**
17:     **if** $method == XPINNs$ **then**
18:         SEND($SendCommBlock, dst = neighbor(rank)$)
19:         $RecvCommBlock \leftarrow$ RECV($src = neighbor(rank)$)
20:         BARRIER()
21:     **end if**
22:     $Net, loss\_current \leftarrow$ TRAIN($Net, RecvCommBlock$)
23:     **if** $method == udPINNs$ **then**
24:         **if** $loss\_current < loss\_window\_best$ **then**
25:             $loss\_window\_best \leftarrow loss\_current$
26:             $SendCommBlock \leftarrow$ EVAL($Net, CommBlockInfo$)
27:         **end if**
28:     **end if**
29: **end for**

Before training, we sample 128 points within the interval $[0, 6]$ as training points and calculate the PDE loss at these points. Note that this is different from traditional data-driven deep learning methods, as we do not actually know the labels of these training points. We simply constrain the network to satisfy the PDE relationship at these points. During training, the only known label data is $y(0) = 1$.

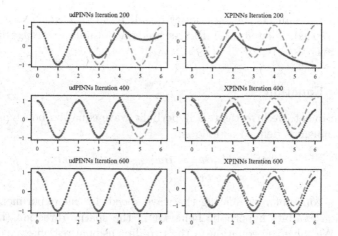

Fig. 3. Dashed line represents the target solution function, and blue dots indicate the predictions of the three parallel working networks. We can see networks corresponding to earlier time intervals tend to train faster. Moreover, our method (udPINNs) can propagate information to the right more quickly, resulting in faster training. (Color figure online)

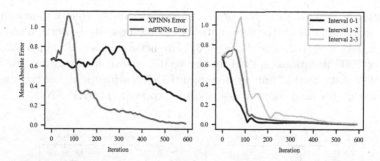

Fig. 4. The left figure shows the change of the mean absolute error during iterations for the two methods, where our method (udPINNs) converges faster than XPINNs. The right figure presents the error change of the three networks in their respective intervals as the iterations progress.

The network training employs the Adam optimizer, with the activation function set to tanh and the network architecture as fully Connected Network [1, 32, 32, 32, 1]. The learning rate is 0.001, and the number of iterations is 600, with all residual and data points being fed each time. The workload is divided among three workers, with each worker training a network to infer the function within the intervals [0, 2], [2, 4], and [4, 6], respectively. A hard propagation direction control is adopted, with an information exchange cycle of 10 iterations.

By analyzing Figs. 3 and 4, we find that udPINNs demonstrates a significant acceleration in training performance for this example. Figure 3 reveals that the udPINNs method is capable of rapidly propagating information to the right.

Figure 4 further confirms the superiority of udPINNs over XPINNs in terms of convergence speed. Therefore, udPINNs holds a notable advantage in solving such problems.

4.2   Wave Equation

In this experiment, we investigate a hyperbolic wave equation benchmark problem. The problem is defined as follows:

$$\frac{\partial u}{\partial t} + a\frac{\partial u}{\partial x} = 0 \tag{10}$$

where a is a constant representing the wave speed. In this experiment, $a = 3$. The equation exhibits hyperbolic behavior in the spatial direction (i.e., the x direction). We solve the equation in the two-dimensional region $t \times x \in [0,1] \times [0,3]$. The initial condition is $u(t = 0, x) = 0$, corresponding to a stationary initial state. The boundary condition $Bound(t)$ is given as a multi-gaussian function as Fig. 5. And the solution of this equation is:

$$u(t, x) = Bound(t - \frac{x}{3}) \tag{11}$$

Due to the equation's hyperbolic characteristics in the spatial dimension, we allocate load intervals for the three networks along the spatial direction according to $x \in [0, 1.1]$, $x \in [1, 2.1]$, and $x \in [2, 3]$. The network scale is $[2,64,64,32,32,1]$, and after 2000 iterations, we obtain the results shown in Figs. 5 and 6. These results demonstrate that our algorithm, udPINNs, achieves higher training efficiency and better final convergence accuracy compared to XPINNs.

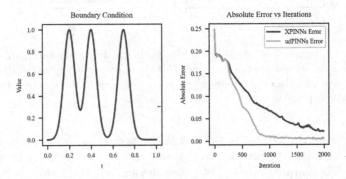

Fig. 5. The left plot shows the boundary condition definition, and the right plot displays the decreasing trend of average absolute error with increasing iterations during training.

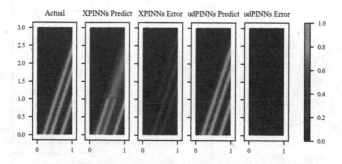

Fig. 6. The figure presents a comparison of the prediction results of XPINNs and udPINNs at the 2000th iteration.

4.3   Heat Equation

The first two experiments demonstrated the powerful capability of our method in handling partial differential equations with dependency properties. In this experiment, we selected a special case to analyze the limitations of our method. The key point is that the strength of the dependency in the physical process corresponding to the partial differential equation will affect the performance of our training. Taking time-dependent partial differential equations as an example, when the solution domain of the partial differential equation in earlier time intervals has a weak impact on the solution domain in later time intervals, our algorithm can accelerate convergence in the initial stage. However, as the number of training rounds increases, the performance of our algorithm and the benchmark XPINNs tend to be close.

We studied the heat transfer problem defined as follows:

$$\frac{\partial u}{\partial t} = a\frac{\partial^2 u}{\partial x^2},\tag{12}$$

where $a = 0.02$. The initial and boundary conditions are illustrated in the left graph of Fig. 7, defined by sine functions, with the known initial thermal field value at $t = 0$, and the constant thermal values at $x = 0$ and $x = 1$. We divided the solution domain along the time direction and distributed the solution domains corresponding to $t \in [0, 1.1]$, $t \in [1, 2.1]$, and $t \in [2, 3]$ across three networks for parallel training. By comparing with the results of numerical simulation programs, we obtained the curve of test error changing with time in the left graph of Fig. 7 and the training results in Fig. 8. At the final iteration round (2000 epochs), both algorithms achieved good solution results. The main difference is that the error convergence of udPINNs was faster in the initial stage of training.

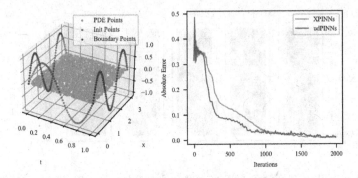

Fig. 7. The left figure shows the physical loss points and data loss points defined by the problem, while the right figure shows the error convergence curves for the comparison of the two methods.

Our hyperparameter settings, such as learning rate, are basically the same as those in the single-wave equation solution example. However, in this case, udPINNs did not have a significant final error advantage. This is mainly because the physical process we are solving is not sensitive to the initial values. As shown in Fig. 8, the field value at $t = 3$ has been very weakly influenced by the initial value at $t = 0$, and mainly depends on the influence of the boundary conditions at $x = 0$ and $x = 1$. This is quite different from the long-term dependence of the single-wave equation. However, it is noteworthy that even with this weaker dependence, we can still accelerate the training process using the udPINNs algorithm. This is very helpful for applications requiring higher real-time performance.

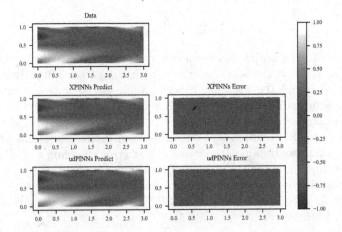

Fig. 8. The final convergence results of two methods at 1000th iteration.

4.4   Incompressible Flow Equations

The governing equations for incompressible flow are as follows:

$$u\frac{\partial u}{\partial x} + v\frac{\partial u}{\partial y} + \frac{\partial p}{\partial x} - \mu\left(\frac{\partial^2 u}{\partial x^2} + \frac{\partial^2 u}{\partial y^2}\right) = 0, \tag{13}$$

$$u\frac{\partial v}{\partial x} + v\frac{\partial v}{\partial y} + \frac{\partial p}{\partial y} - \mu\left(\frac{\partial^2 v}{\partial x^2} + \frac{\partial^2 v}{\partial y^2}\right) = 0, \tag{14}$$

$$\frac{\partial u}{\partial x} + \frac{\partial v}{\partial y} = 0. \tag{15}$$

In this experiment, we address the problem of reconstructing the flow field based on specific observation points. As shown in the left part of Fig. 9, there is a pipe with a semi-circular arc obstacle at the bottom. According to the boundary conditions in fluid mechanics, the velocity at the pipe and the semi-circular arc obstacle is set to zero. We place 10 observation points at both the inlet and outlet, which can be used to measure pressure and velocity information. Now, our goal is to restore the original steady-state flow field based on these observation points.

Mathematically, the incompressible flow equations for elliptic equations have no direct dependence. However, when we divide the entire flow field into three regions: region 1: $[0,1] \times [0,1]$, region 2: $[1,2] \times [0,1]$, and region 3: $[2,3] \times [0,1]$, we find that the data points reflecting the flow field characteristics are located in regions 1 and 3 on both sides. Therefore, for our proposed udPINNs method, we set the weights according to the soft setting method proposed in the methodology section, making the network responsible for the intermediate region learning information from the networks of the two side regions to be dominant.

$$J(\widetilde{\Theta}_1) = \text{DataLoss}_1 + \text{PdeLoss}_1 + 0.1 \cdot \text{InterfaceLoss}_{12} \tag{16}$$

$$J(\widetilde{\Theta}_2) = \text{DataLoss}_2 + \text{PdeLoss}_2 + \text{InterfaceLoss}_{12} + \text{InterfaceLoss}_{23} \tag{17}$$

$$J(\widetilde{\Theta}_3) = \text{DataLoss}_3 + \text{PdeLoss}_3 + 0.1 \cdot \text{InterfaceLoss}_{23} \tag{18}$$

The benchmark flow field data for measuring the error is obtained through numerical simulation. Before network training, we simulate a flow field using a numerical simulation program and extract the values at the observation point locations to obtain 20 data points. Our goal is to restore the original flow field based on these sparse observation points. During training, the scale of each sub-network is $[2, 64, 64, 64, 3]$, and 10,000 iterations are performed. As shown in the error curves in the middle and right parts of Fig. 10, we obtain the error curves of pressure and velocity amplitudes corresponding to the changes in the number of iterations. The results show that the performance of udPINNs is better than that of XPINNs.

From the above results, it can be seen that for some equations without direct solution domain dependence, if the known observation data is unevenly distributed in each region, we can set weights according to the available information in each region to control the direction of information propagation, thus accelerating training and obtaining better convergence results. This makes our method generalizable to some empirical prior knowledge.

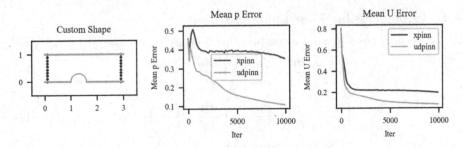

Fig. 9. Problem setup (left figure) and convergence curves of the two methods for pressure p and velocity U (middle and right figures).

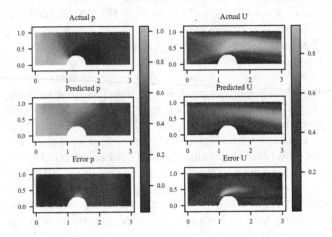

Fig. 10. Flow field obtained by udPINNs at the 10,000th.

5   Conclusion

In this paper, we propose a novel distributed Physics-Informed Neural Networks algorithm (udPINNs), addressing the limitations of traditional PINNs methods in handling partial differential equations (PDEs) by incorporating domain-specific knowledge, such as dependency properties. Our method is the first to introduce dependency properties of PDEs into the PINNs training process, effectively accelerating training speed and enhancing solution accuracy. Experimental results demonstrate that udPINNs outperform existing XPINNs methods in common equations, such as heat transfer and incompressible flow, with lower error rates and computational efficiency. However, our method has limitations, as its performance depends on the equation type. For instance, in Experiment 3's heat conduction problem, due to weak physical dependency, our method's final convergence performance is on par with XPINNs. Nevertheless, the udPINNs algorithm shows significant advantages in handling equations with strong dependencies and provides new research directions for the future development of PINNs methods.

References

1. Raissi, M., Perdikaris, P., Karniadakis, G.E.: Physics-informed neural networks: a deep learning framework for solving forward and inverse problems involving nonlinear partial differential equations. J. Comput. Phys. **378**, 686–707 (2019)
2. Lagaris, I.E., Likas, A., Fotiadis, D.I.: Artificial neural networks for solving ordinary and partial differential equations. IEEE Trans. Neural Netw. **9**(5), 987–1000 (1998)
3. Psichogios, D.C., Ungar, L.H.: A hybrid neural network-first principles approach to process modeling. AIChE J. **38**(10), 1499–1511 (1992)
4. Lagaris, I.E., Likas, A.C., Papageorgiou, D.G.: Neural-network methods for boundary value problems with irregular boundaries. IEEE Trans. Neural Netw. **11**(5), 1041–1049 (2000)
5. Xiang, Z., Peng, W., Zhou, W., Yao, W.: Hybrid finite difference with the physics-informed neural network for solving PDE in complex geometries. arXiv preprint arXiv:2202.07926 (2022)
6. Chiu, P.H., Wong, J.C., Ooi, C., et al.: CAN-PINN: a fast physics-informed neural network based on coupled-automatic-numerical differentiation method. Comput. Methods Appl. Mech. Eng. **395**, 114909 (2022)
7. Wang, S., Teng, Y., Perdikaris, P.: Understanding and mitigating gradient pathologies in physics-informed neural networks. SIAM J. Sci. Comput. **43**(5), A3055–A3081 (2021)
8. Liu, D., Wang, Y.: A Dual-Dimer method for training physics-constrained neural networks with minimax architecture. Neural Netw. **136**, 112–125 (2021)
9. McClenny, L., Braga-Neto, U.: Self-adaptive physics-informed neural networks using a soft attention mechanism. arXiv preprint arXiv:2009.04544 (2020)
10. Xiang, Z., Peng, W., Liu, X., Yao, W.: Self-adaptive loss balanced Physics-informed neural networks. Neurocomputing **496**, 11–34 (2022)
11. Dwivedi, V., Parashar, N., Srinivasan, B.: Distributed physics informed neural network for data-efficient solution to partial differential equations. arXiv preprint arXiv:1907.08967 (2019)
12. Jagtap, A.D., Kharazmi, E., Karniadakis, G.E.: Conservative physics-informed neural networks on discrete domains for conservation laws: applications to forward and inverse problems. Comput. Methods Appl. Mech. Eng. **365**, 113028 (2020)
13. Jagtap, A.D., Karniadakis, G.E.: Extended physics-informed neural networks (XPINNs): a generalized space-time domain decomposition based deep learning framework for nonlinear partial differential equations. In: AAAI Spring Symposium: MLPS (2021)
14. Hu, Z., Jagtap, A. D., Karniadakis, G.E., et al.: When do extended physics-informed neural networks (XPINNs) improve generalization? arXiv preprint arXiv:2109.09444 (2021)
15. Shukla, K., Jagtap, A.D., Karniadakis, G.E.: Parallel physics-informed neural networks via domain decomposition. J. Comput. Phys. **447**, 110683 (2021)
16. Meng, X., et al.: PPINN: parareal physics-informed neural network for time-dependent PDEs. Comput. Methods Appl. Mech. Eng. **370**, 113250 (2020)
17. Kharazmi, E., Zhang, Z., Karniadakis, G.E.: hp-VPINNs: variational physics-informed neural networks with domain decomposition. Comput. Methods Appl. Mech. Eng. **374**, 113547 (2021)
18. Li, W., Xiang, X., Xu, Y.: Deep domain decomposition method: elliptic problems. Mathematical and Scientific Machine Learning. PMLR (2020)

19. Mercier, V., Gratton, S., Boudier, P.: A coarse space acceleration of deep-DDM. arXiv preprint arXiv:2112.03732 (2021)
20. Moseley, B., Markham, A., Nissen-Meyer, T.: Finite basis physics-informed neural networks (FBPINNs): a scalable domain decomposition approach for solving differential equations. arXiv preprint arXiv:2107.07871 (2021)

Joint Community and Structural Hole Spanner Detection via Graph Contrastive Learning

Jingyuan Zhang[1,2], Wenjun Wang[1,2], Tianpeng Li[1,2], Minglai Shao[3(✉)], Jiye Liu[1,2], and Yueheng Sun[1,2]

[1] College of Intelligence and Computing, Tianjin University, Tianjin, China
{zjylyy,wjwang,ltpnimeia,3015216020,yhs}@tju.edu.cn
[2] Georgia Tech Shenzhen Institute, Tianjin University, Tianjin, China
[3] School of New Media and Communication, Tianjin University, Tianjin, China
shaoml@tju.edu.cn

Abstract. Structural hole spanners are nodes in a network that connect different communities, which are located on key information paths and control information flow between different communities, and therefore have an important status from the perspective of network analysis. Due to its definition, the detection of structural hole spanners relies on the partitioning of subgraph or community structures in network, but most existing methods for detecting structural hole spanner rely on known community labels or complex global search, which are difficult to apply to large-scale real-world networks without labels. To address the aforementioned challenges, inspired by success of graph contrastive learning, we propose a self-supervised method for jointly detecting community and structural hole spanner, i.e., a Augmentation-Free contrastive learning framework for jointly detecting Community and structural hole spanner, named **AF-Comm**. Experimental results on multiple real-world networks demonstrate the superiority of our algorithm on both community detection and structural hole spanner detection tasks.

Keywords: complex networks · graph contrastive learning · community detection · structural hole spanner · modularity

1 Introduction

According to the well-known structural hole theory proposed by sociologist Burt [3] in the competitive field, the lack of connections between different communities in a network is called a structural hole (SH), users who fill the "holes" between different user groups or disconnect them gain positional advantages in the network because they control key information pathways, as shown in Fig. 1. These types of users are known as SH spanners. Structural hole spanner detection can play an important role in tasks such as studying social structure [4], information diffusion [33], and link prediction [18]. As the definition of SH spanner, the identification of such nodes is highly dependent on subgraph or community structures in network.

Z. Jin et al. (Eds.): KSEM 2023, LNAI 14120, pp. 403–417, 2023.
https://doi.org/10.1007/978-3-031-40292-0_33

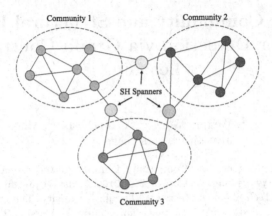

Fig. 1. SH spanners in a simple network with three communities

Community detection is fundamental task in network analysis, identifying clusters or groups of nodes in a network that are connected to each other but relatively disconnected from nodes outside the cluster. This technique is useful for understanding how people form groups and how these groups interact, with practical applications including,identifying protein functions in bioinformatics networks [31] and predicting information diffusion processes in social networks [17].

Many methods have been proposed for detecting SH spanner [16,18,22,25], yet most existing studies rely on known community labels or complex global search, which are difficult to apply to large-scale real-world networks without labels. In recent years, Graph Neural Networks (GNN) [10,13,28] have shown significant performance in various representation learning tasks on attributed graph, and Deep Graph Clustering (DGC) has also received increasing attention in recent years. In general GNN-based community detection frameworks, two-stage approaches are commonly used, where representation learning and clustering are isolated steps. For example, using GAE [14] to learn node embeddings, and then applying clustering methods like K-means. Recently, some one-stage frameworks based on autoencoder [9] have been proposed. However, these methods directly use clustering loss related to edges to learn node representations, but lack effective methods to capture high-order relationships between nodes and communities. Furthermore, studies on these two tasks have been conducted separately, ignoreing the inseparable relationship between SH spanner and community.

To address the aforementioned challenges, we propose a Augmentation-Free contrastive learning framework for jointly detecting Community and SH spanner named AF-Comm. Specifically, we select positive samples from k-NN search when it is either 1) a neighboring node of the target node in the adjacency matrix (local perspective), or 2) belonging to the same cluster as the target node (global perspective). We could capture local structural and global semantic information by maximizing the mutual information between the target node and selected true positives. Furthermore, by adopting BYOL [8] as the backbone of AF-Comm, the model training does not require negative samples. To further capture information about communities, we adapt a trainable clustering layer using soft K-means assignment in our graph neural network, allowing for optimizing node representations and community detection in a unified manner. We finally design a new SH spanner score function depending on community labels which simulates simple information diffusion, effectively identifying SH spanners after obtaining community detection results. Our contributions are summarized as follows:

- We propose a graph contrastive learning model for jointly detecting community and SH spanner named AF-Comm without using graph augmentation techniques or selecting negative samples.
- We add a trainable clustering layer to our model and jointly optimize modularity objective and graph contrastive objective to help learn node representations relevant to communities in a unified manner.
- We design a new SH spanner score function depending on community labels which simulates simple information diffusion to detect SH spanners.
- We conduct extensive experiments on four real-world datasets and demonstrate the superiority of AF-Comm on detecting community and SH spanner.

The rest of this paper is organized as follows. Section 2 briefly reviews related work on community detection, SH spanner detection, and graph contrastive learning. Section 3 introduces the definition of the issue studied and essential notations in this paper. Section 4 describes the proposed algorithm model. Section 5 reports and discusses extensive experiment results. Section 6 concludes the paper.

2   Related Work

2.1   Structural Hole Spanner Detection

To better understand the problem of detecting top-k SH spanners, the algorithms can be divided into two categories based on their approach. The first category is based on information flow [11, 16, 18, 33]. HAM [11] applies harmonic functions to jointly detect communities and SH spanners based on the topological properties between communities and SH spanners. ESH [16] introduces an entropy-based method from the factor diffusion process, attempting to evaluate possibilities through the entropy of the factor distribution process to distinguish SH spanners. The second category mainly detect SH spanners based on the centrality of network structures [22, 25, 35]. Among them, the AP_BICC [22] algorithm combines the inverse closeness centrality of nodes and edges to obtain a more comprehensive centrality evaluation. The recently proposed FSBCDM [35] algorithm uses a method based on marginal utility decay and community forest model to discover SH spanners. These algorithms often rely on complex global search or known community labels, which are inefficient and difficult to apply to real-world networks.

2.2   Community Detection

Methods community detection methods can be divided into two categories: traditional heuristic methods and deep learning-based methods, i.e., Deep Graph

Clustering (DGC). Traditional methods such as spectral methods [1] and methods based on modularity [7] face difficulties in meeting the needs of large-scale networks. More recently, DGC methods have gained more attention, these methods can be divided into two categories: (1) two-stage methods that perform clustering after learning node representations, and (2) one-stage methods that jointly perform clustering and representation learning. Unsupervised graph representation learning methods are usually two-stage methods. For example, GAE [14] and VGAE [14] use a graph autoencoder and a variational variant to learn node embeddings. After learning node embeddings, K-means is used to obtain clustering assignments. DEAGC [30] is a one-stage method that learns graph clustering assignments by combining DEC's clustering loss [32] with the graph attention autoencoder's graph reconstruction loss. Although one-stage methods can obtain node representations relevant to communities, it is difficult to distinguish the cluster of boundary nodes between communities without considering the influence of SH spanner.

2.3   Graph Contrastive Learning

In recent years, due to the great success of self-supervised methods for images, contrastive methods are increasingly being used for graphs. DGI [29] is a pioneering work inspired by Deep InfoMax [12], which learns node representations by maximizing the mutual information between node and graph-level summaries. Inspired by SimCLR [5], GRACE [37] first creates two augmented views of the graph by randomly perturbing nodes/edges and their features. Despite the success of contrastive methods on graphs, they have been criticized for the "sampling bias" problem [2] caused by negative sampling. BGRL [27] addresses the "sampling bias" problem by using two independent encoders without using negative samples to encode the two augmented versions of the graph. AFGRL [15] extends BGRL by conducting k-nearest neighbor (k-NN) searches in the representation space to select positive samples in another view for nodes in the original view, which address the "semantic drift" [26] issue that may arise from graph augmentation.

3   Preliminary

In this section, we introduce notations and definitions, and provide the formulation for the problem. Table 1 gives the frequently-used notations in this paper.

Definition 1. (Attributed Graph) An attributed graph is defined as $G = (A, X, V)$ with a set of n nodes $V = \{v_1, v_2, \ldots, v_n\}$. $A \in \mathbb{R}^{n \times n}$ denotes the binary adjacency matrix which describe the observed graph structure, where $A_{ij} = 1$ if there is a link between v_i and v_j otherwise $A_{ij} = 0$. $X \in \mathbb{R}^{n \times d}$ denotes the attribute matrix where $x_i \in \mathbb{R}^d$ indicates the attribute vector of v_i.

Problem 1. (Community Detection) Given an attributed graph $G = (A, X, V)$ and the number of communities K, learn a cluster assignment matrix $R \in \mathbb{R}_{\geq 0}^{n \times K}$, $r_{ik} \in R$ indicates the probability of node v_i belonging to cluster k.

Problem 2. (Top-k Structural Hole Spanner Detection) Given an attributed graph $G = (A, X, V)$, use the defined SH spanner score to measure the impact of node and find a vertice subset $V_{SHS} \in V$ containing k SH spanners with the top-k largest score values.

Table 1. Table of notations.

Notation	Definition
A_{ij}	adjacency matrix value between node v_i and node v_j
v_i	the i-th node in Graph G
$H \in \mathbb{R}^{n \times d'}$	node embedding matrix
h_i	embedding of node v_i
μ_k	cluster center of community k
$R \in \mathbb{R}_{\geq 0}^{n \times k}$	entire cluster assignment matrix
r_{ik}	the probability to which node v_i is assigned to cluster k
D	degree matrix
d_i	degree of node v_i
$\mathcal{E}$	encoder

4 Method

In this section, we will provide a detailed description of AF-Comm. For clarity, the AF-Comm framework is illustrated in Fig. 2.

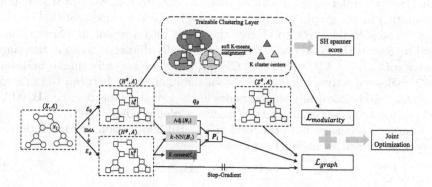

Fig. 2. The overall architecture of AF-Comm. Given an attributed graph, $\mathcal{E}_\theta$ and $\mathcal{E}_\phi$ generate node embeddings H^θ and H^ϕ both of which are used to obtain k-NNs for node v_i, i.e., $\mathbf{B}_i$. Then AF-Comm combines local and global positives, i.e., $\mathbf{N}_i$ and $\mathbf{C}_i$, to obtain real positives, i.e., $\mathbf{P}_i$. A predictor q_θ projects H^θ to Z^θ, which is used to compute the graph loss along with H^ϕ. Meantime, AF-Comm manipulates H^θ with a trainable clustering layer, which is optimized together with the graph loss via modularity loss.

4.1 Augmentation-Free Contrastive Layer

To assign nodes into different communities, we should encode the attributes of each node first. Based on the model structure of BYOL [8], for each node $v_i \in V$ in the graph G, we use the node representations learned by two encoders, i.e., online encoder $\mathcal{E}_\theta(\cdot)$ and target encoder $\mathcal{E}_\phi(\cdot)$, to identify positive samples. Specifically, given the adjacency matrix A and the feature matrix X as inputs, the two encoders respectively compute the online and target representations of each node, i.e., $H^\theta = \mathcal{E}_\theta(X, A)$ and $H^\phi = \mathcal{E}_\phi(X, A)$ whose i-th rows, h_i^θ and h_i^ϕ, are representations for node $v_i \in V$. Then, for a given query node $v_i \in V$, we calculate the cosine similarity between it and all other nodes in the graph, as follows:

$$\mathrm{sim}\,(v_i, v_j) = \frac{h_i^\theta \cdot h_j^\phi}{\left\|h_i^\theta\right\| \left\|h_j^\phi\right\|}, \forall v_j \in V, \tag{1}$$

where the similarity is computed between the online and the target representations. Given the similarity information, we search for k-nearest-neighbors for each node v_i and use the set $\mathbf{B}_i$ to represent them, which can serve as the positive samples candidates for node v_i.

According to the smoothness assumption [36], the neighboring nodes $\mathbf{N}_i$ of node v_i are more likely to have the same label as query node v_i. To further capture the structural information in the graph, we utilize the local structural information among nodes given by the adjacency matrix A and compute the intersection between the nearest neighbors and the neighboring nodes, i.e., $\mathbf{B}_i \cap \mathbf{N}_i$. We refer to the set of these intersection nodes as the *local positive* of node v_i.

From a global perspective, clustering techniques can be used to discover semantically similar entities without shared edges to capture global semantic information in the graph. Specifically, we apply the K-means algorithm on the target representations H^ϕ to cluster the nodes into a set of M clusters, and $c\,(v_i)$ represents the cluster of v_i. Then, we consider the set of nodes in the same cluster with v_i, i.e., $\mathbf{C}_i = \left\{v_j \mid v_j \in C_{c(v_i)}\right\}$, as its semantically similar nodes in the global perspective. Finally, we obtain the intersection between the nearest neighbors and semantically similar nodes in the global perspective, i.e., $\mathbf{B}_i \cap \mathbf{C}_i$, and represent this set of intersecting nodes as *global positive* of v_i.

In order to consider both the local and global information, we define the set of *real positives* for node v_i as follows:

$$\mathbf{P}_i = (\mathbf{B}_i \cap \mathbf{N}_i) \cup (\mathbf{B}_i \cap \mathbf{C}_i). \tag{2}$$

Our contrastive objective function aims to minimize the cosine distance between the query node v_i and its real positives $\mathbf{P}_i$:

$$\mathcal{L}_{graph} = -\frac{1}{N} \sum_{i=1}^{N} \sum_{v_j \in \mathbf{P}_i} \frac{z_i^\theta h_j^{\phi\mathsf{T}}}{\left\|z_i^\theta\right\| \left\|h_j^\phi\right\|}, \tag{3}$$

where $z_i^\theta = q_\theta\left(h_i^\theta\right) \in \mathbb{R}^D$ is the prediction of online embedding $h_i^\theta \in \mathbb{R}^D$, and $q_\theta(\cdot)$ is the predictor network.

4.2 Trainable Clustering Layer and Modularity Objective

In the problem of community detection, the clustering assignment of nodes corresponds to assigning nodes to their respective communities. In this clustering layer, we implement a differentiable K-means clustering, which can a soft assignment of nodes to clusters and cluster centers in the embedding space during training. Considering that the target encoder is stop-gradient, we add the trainable clustering layer in the online encoder. Specifically, we use soft assignment to assign each node to a cluster center based on the distance using the norm $\| \cdot \|$ as negative cosine similarity, and δ is an inverse temperature hyperparameter which defines how hard to employ the clustering process. We optimize the cluster centers using an iterative process similar to the typical K-means update, alternating between:

$$\mu_k = \frac{\sum_i r_{ik} h_i}{\sum_i r_{ik}}, \forall k = 1,\ldots,K,\tag{4}$$

$$r_{ik} = \frac{\exp\left(-\delta \left\|h_i^\theta - \mu_k\right\|\right)}{\sum_{z=1}^{K} \exp\left(-\delta \left\|h_i^\theta - \mu_z\right\|\right)}, \forall k = 1,\ldots,K,\tag{5}$$

where h_i^θ is the representation of node v_i, μ_k is the cluster center of cluster k, $R = \{r_{ik}\}$ is the assignment matrix of soft K-means, where r_{ik} is the degree to which node v_i is assigned to cluster k satisfying $\sum_k r_{ik} = 1$.

Having obtained the cluster assignments R and cluster centers μ in a differentiable manner, we use a modularity [7] measure to interpret the clustering as a soft solution to an optimization problem. Modularity is a classical objective in community detection optimization which estimates the quality of a partition of the network in communities. The general expression of modularity is:

$$Q = \frac{1}{2m} \sum_{ij} \sum_{k=1}^{K} \left(A_{ij} - \frac{d_i d_j}{2m}\right) \hat{r}_{ik}\hat{r}_{jk},\tag{6}$$

where m is the number of edges of the network, and $\hat{r}_{ik}$ is 1 if node v_i is assigned to community k and 0 if not. This measures the number of edges within communities compared to the expected number if edges were placed randomly.

We apply the modularity objective into our clustering layer as:

$$\mathcal{L}_{\text{modularity}} = \frac{1}{2m} \text{Tr} \left[R^T \left(A_{ij} - \frac{d_i d_j}{2m}\right) R\right],\tag{7}$$

which is the expected value of a partition sampled according to assignment R.

4.3 Joint Optimization

The above loss terms capture signals on the graph and the community structure, we jointly optimize the graph representation learning and clustering layer, and define our total objective function as:

$$\mathcal{L} = \mathcal{L}_{\text{graph}} + \mathcal{L}_{\text{modularity}},\tag{8}$$

where $\mathcal{L}_{\text{graph}}$ is the Augmentation-Free graph contrastive loss, $\mathcal{L}_{\text{modularity}}$ is the modularity loss. Via the above loss terms, we can learn node attributes information from the Augmentation-Free contrastive layer, and the modularity pay more attention to edge-related knowledge of communities.

Additionally, the online parameters θ are updated through (8), the target parameters ϕ are updated as an exponential moving average of the online parameters θ, using a decay rate τ, i.e.,

$$\phi \leftarrow \tau\phi + (1 - \tau)\theta. \tag{9}$$

4.4 Structural Hole Spanner Score Function

During the optimization process mentioned above, we can obtain the community detection results directly from the previous optimization results, and the label of node v_i can be estimated as:

$$c_i = \arg\max_k r_{ik}, \tag{10}$$

which is the most probable assignment from the final soft K-means assignment distribution R.

Having obtained an approximate community detection assignment, we compute the score which approximate the process of message diffusion from node of SH spanners for all nodes as follows:

$$score(v_i) = \frac{|N_i^2|}{d_i^2} \times mask_i, \tag{11}$$

where $N_i^2 = \{v : c(v) \neq c_i | v \in (v_k \cup v_j), v_k \in N_i, v_j \in N_k\}$, d_i^2 denotes the number of nodes within 2-hops neighbors of node v_i. According to the definition of SH spanner, we multiply the computed score by a $mask_i$ that is to 1 if node v_i connects multiple communities and 0 if not. Finally, we sort the SH spanner scores, according users need, select top-k SH spanners from nodes.

5 Experiments

To evaluate the effectiveness of AF-Comm, we conducted extensive experiments on real-world networks and compared it with various baseline methods. We first study the performance of AF-Comm on community detection, then investigate the effectiveness on SH spanner detection.

5.1 Datasets

We conduct extensive community detection and SH spanners detection experiments on four wildly used datasets, including Cora [20], Citeseer [6], Pubmed [23], Amazon-Photo [24], i.e. *Photo*. The statistics of the datasets are summarized in Table 2.

Table 2. Basic statistics of the three datasets.

Dataset	#Nodes	#Edges	#Features	#Communities
Cora [20]	2,708	5,429	1,433	7
Citeseer [6]	3,327	4,732	3,703	6
Pubmed [23]	19,717	44,378	500	3
Photo [24]	7,650	119,081	745	8

5.2 Implementation Details

We use a 2-layer GCN model as the encoders, i.e., $\mathcal{E}_\theta(\cdot)$ and $\mathcal{E}_\phi(\cdot)$, which follows the propagation rule:

$$H = \mathcal{E}(X, A) = \sigma\left(\hat{D}^{-\frac{1}{2}}\hat{A}\hat{D}^{-\frac{1}{2}}\left(\sigma\left(\hat{D}^{-\frac{1}{2}}\hat{A}\hat{D}^{-\frac{1}{2}}XW^{(1)}\right)W^{(2)}\right)\right) \quad (12)$$

where $\hat{A} = A + I_n$ is the adjacency matrix with self-loops and $\hat{D} = \sum_i \hat{A}_i$ is the degree matrix, σ is a nonlinear activation function such as PReLU, $W^{(1)}$ and $W^{(2)}$ represent the trainable weight matrixs of the GCN, respectively. We perform grid search on several hyperparameters, such as learning rate η, weight decay τ, node embedding dimension size D. For other hyperparameters like Clustering coefficient δ is set to 30.

5.3 Community Detection

5.3.1 Baselines.

We compare AF-Comm with the following methods on community detection: K-means is a classic clustering method applied to the raw input features. DGI [29] learns node embeddings by maximizing their MI with the graph. GRACE [37], BGRL [27], GCA [38] and AFGRL [15], which are the current state-of-the-art self-supervised methods for learning representations of nodes in a graph. CommDGI [34] is a community-oriented method which utilize mutual information mechanism to capture neighborhood as well as community information in graphs. For methods that produce only node embeddings, we apply K-means to the node embeddings to obtain cluster memberships.

5.3.2 Metrics.

In our experiments on community detection, we focused on the community detection task of attributed graphs and evaluate the performance of all the compared methods using three clustering metrics: ACC (Accuracy), NMI (Normalized Mutual Information), and F1 score. The three metrics all range from 0 to 1 (higher values are better).

Table 3. Performance on SH spanner detection. Best results are in bold, and second best results are underlined.

Method	Cora			Citeseer			Pubmed			Photo		
	ACC	NMI	F1	ACC	NMI	F1	ACC	NMI	F1	ACC	NMI	F1
K-means	0.347	0.221	0.348	0.436	0.206	0.439	0.415	0.230	0.481	0.413	0.324	0.445
DGI [29]	0.665	0.550	0.687	0.629	0.418	0.628	0.651	0.263	0.655	0.738	0.636	0.717
GRACE [37]	0.694	0.533	0.678	0.586	0.391	0.595	0.647	0.257	0.650	0.734	0.647	0.714
GCA [38]	0.631	0.488	0.630	0.604	0.402	0.603	**0.699**	**0.358**	**0.697**	0.692	0.644	0.702
BGRL [27]	0.685	0.523	0.677	0.595	0.393	0.598	0.615	0.296	0.613	0.769	0.668	0.742
AFGRL [15]	0.717	0.534	0.682	0.660	0.403	0.618	0.635	0.301	0.633	0.784	0.702	0.747
CommDGI [34]	0.701	0.552	0.687	0.641	0.408	0.598	0.622	0.291	0.631	0.775	0.674	0.733
AF-Comm	**0.747**	**0.576**	**0.699**	**0.673**	**0.425**	**0.623**	0.668	0.316	0.664	**0.787**	**0.739**	**0.792**

5.3.3 Experiment Result.
In the community detection task, we compare the performance of eight different community detection methods. Table 3 shows the performance of AF-Comm and seven other baseline methods, evaluated by NMI, ACC, and F1-score on community detection results. According to the results, AF-Comm outperforms all other methods in terms of NMI, ACC, and F1-score on the Cora, Citeseer, and Photo, while achieving the second best performance on the Pubmed, which indicates the effectiveness of AF-Comm on the community detection task.

5.4 Structural Hole Spanner Detection

5.4.1 Baselines.
We compare AF-Comm with the following methods on SH spanner detection: PageRank [21] returns the nodes with the top-k page rank scores as the SH spanners. HAM [11] jointly detect community and SH spanners via a harmonic function. AP_BICC [22] efficiently calculate the proposed approximate inverse closeness centrality for each node in the articulation point set to select top-k SH spanners. ESH [16] proposes an entropy-based method from a factor diffusion process, and applied distributed parallel computing for efficient calculation. FSBCDM [35] identifies SH spanner based on community forest model and diminishing marginal utility which jointly detect community and SH spanner.

5.4.2 Metrics.
In this paper, we use the *structural hole influence index* $(SHII)$ [11], which is based on simulating information diffusion processes in a given network, to evaluate the performance of structure hole spanners.

Let s be the given seed, C_p is the community to which the given seed belongs, I_v represents whether a node v is affected by a specific information diffusion model. The formula for $SHII$ is as follows:

$$SHII(s) = \frac{\sum_{C_i \in C \setminus C_p} \sum_{v \in C_i} I_v}{\sum_{C_i \in C} \sum_{v \in C_i} I_v} \tag{13}$$

where C is the set of all the communities. Generally, higher $SHII$ means better performance. In this paper, we use the Linear Threshold (LT) model and the Independent Cascade (IC) model to find the set of influenced nodes.

Table 4. Performance on community detection(average SHII of top-100 SHS). Best results are in bold, and second best results are underlined.

Method	Cora		Citeseer		Pubmed		Photo	
	LT	IC	LT	IC	LT	IC	LT	IC
PageRank [21]	0.485	0.342	0.374	0.315	0.431	0.333	0.544	0.280
HAM [11]	0.397	0.275	0.313	0.282	0.425	0.320	0.491	0.308
AP_BICC [22]	0.512	0.383	0.446	0.373	0.485	0.419	0.519	0.315
ESH [16]	0.571	0.427	0.554	0.489	0.444	0.349	0.508	0.364
FSBCDM [35]	0.594	0.523	0.527	0.462	0.457	0.378	0.615	0.416
AF-Comm	**0.656**	**0.597**	**0.648**	**0.625**	**0.534**	**0.494**	**0.709**	**0.575**

5.4.3 Experiment Result.

From Table 4, we can see that our algorithm outperforms other baseline methods in all datasets for the SH spanner detection task. It can be observed that, based on the excellent community detection results, setting an appropriate SH spanner score can achieve good detection results.

5.5 Ablation Study

We conduct ablation experiments for each component of the framework, and evaluated the contribution of different components to the community detection task based on the NMI results on three datasets. As we can see in Table 5, the addition of local structures and global semantics to positive sample selection has a relatively small improvement on community detection performance, while the modularity objective designed based on the trainable clustering layer has a more significant improvement on performance.

Table 5. The NMI results of ablation experiment on three datasets.

Framework	Cora	Citeseer	Photo
Only k-NN search	0.514	0.390	0.698
+ Local	0.526	0.400	0.695
+ Global	0.534	0.403	0.702
+ Modularity	0.576	0.425	0.739

5.6 Case Study

To demonstrate the effectiveness of our algorithm in identifying SH spanners more clearly, we conducted a case study on the Political Blogs dataset. The dataset records the mutual relationships between political blogs in the United States in 2005, with 1490 nodes and two node labels, i.e. Democratic and Republican (0 and 1), respectively. As the node labels are binary, we selected the top-20 SH spanners.

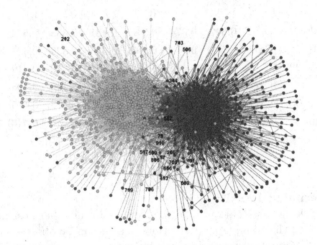

Fig. 3. Visualization of the identified SH spanners in Political Blogs, where the red nodes represent SH spanners discovered by AF-Comm (Color figure online)

The Fig. 3 shows the detected SH spanners in red, and it can be observed that the majority of these nodes are located at the intersection of two communities, in key positions that bridge communication between the two communities.

6 Conclusion

In this paper, we propose a self-supervised learning framework for joint detecting community and structural hole spanner, which does not require augmentation techniques or negative samples to learn graph representations. AF-Comm preserves the semantic of the original graph by selecting nodes that share local structural information and global semantics with the graph as positive samples from an alternative view of the graph. For community detection, the model learns node embeddings by assigning soft labels through soft K-means clustering to capture community-related information, while obtaining top-k SH spanner in network simultaneously. A comparison of the experimental results with various baselines validate AF-Comm's community and SH spanner detection performance.

Furthermore, the detection of SH spanner can be regarded as a part of anomaly detection problem, i.e., structural anomalies [19]. In future work, we could consider incorporating relevant work on anomaly detection to improve the performance of SH spanner detection or feed the learned SH spanners back into the encoder during training to optimize the community assignment.

Acknowledgments. This work is supported by the Shenzhen Sustainable Development Project under Grant (KCXFZ20201221173013036) and NSFC program (No. 62272338).

References

1. Barnard, S.T., Simon, H.D.: Fast multilevel implementation of recursive spectral bisection for partitioning unstructured problems. Concurr. Practi. Exp. **6**(2), 101–117 (1994)
2. Bielak, P., Kajdanowicz, T., Chawla, N.V.: Graph Barlow twins: a self-supervised representation learning framework for graphs. Knowl.-Based Syst. **256**, 109631 (2022)
3. Burt, R.S.: Structural Holes: The Social Structure of Competition. Harvard University Press (1995)
4. Burt, R.S., Kilduff, M., Tasselli, S.: Social network analysis: foundations and frontiers on advantage. Annu. Rev. Psychol. **64**, 527–547 (2013)
5. Chen, T., Kornblith, S., Norouzi, M., Hinton, G.: A simple framework for contrastive learning of visual representations. In: International Conference on Machine Learning, pp. 1597–1607. PMLR (2020)
6. Giles, C.L., Bollacker, K.D., Lawrence, S.: Citeseer: an automatic citation indexing system. In: Proceedings of the Third ACM Conference on Digital Libraries, pp. 89–98 (1998)
7. Girvan, M., Newman, M.E.: Community structure in social and biological networks. Proc. Natl. Acad. Sci. **99**(12), 7821–7826 (2002)
8. Grill, J.B., et al.: Bootstrap your own latent-a new approach to self-supervised learning. Adv. Neural. Inf. Process. Syst. **33**, 21271–21284 (2020)
9. Guo, X., Gao, L., Liu, X., Yin, J.: Improved deep embedded clustering with local structure preservation. In: IJCAI, pp. 1753–1759 (2017)
10. Hamilton, W., Ying, Z., Leskovec, J.: Inductive representation learning on large graphs. In: Advances in Neural Information Processing Systems, vol. 30 (2017)
11. He, L., Lu, C.T., Ma, J., Cao, J., Shen, L., Yu, P.S.: Joint community and structural hole spanner detection via harmonic modularity. In: Proceedings of the 22nd ACM SIGKDD International Conference on Knowledge Discovery and Data Mining, pp. 875–884 (2016)
12. Hjelm, R.D., et al.: Learning deep representations by mutual information estimation and maximization. arXiv preprint arXiv:1808.06670 (2018)
13. Kipf, T.N., Welling, M.: Semi-supervised classification with graph convolutional networks. arXiv preprint arXiv:1609.02907 (2016)
14. Kipf, T.N., Welling, M.: Variational graph auto-encoders. arXiv preprint arXiv:1611.07308 (2016)
15. Lee, N., Lee, J., Park, C.: Augmentation-free self-supervised learning on graphs. In: Proceedings of the AAAI Conference on Artificial Intelligence, vol. 36, pp. 7372–7380 (2022)

16. Li, F., Zou, Z., Li, J., Li, Y., Chen, Y.: Distributed parallel structural hole detection on big graphs. In: Li, G., Yang, J., Gama, J., Natwichai, J., Tong, Y. (eds.) DASFAA 2019. LNCS, vol. 11446, pp. 519–535. Springer, Cham (2019). https://doi.org/10.1007/978-3-030-18576-3_31

17. Lin, S., Hu, Q., Wang, G., Yu, P.S.: Understanding community effects on information diffusion. In: Cao, T., Lim, E.-P., Zhou, Z.-H., Ho, T.-B., Cheung, D., Motoda, H. (eds.) PAKDD 2015. LNCS (LNAI), vol. 9077, pp. 82–95. Springer, Cham (2015). https://doi.org/10.1007/978-3-319-18038-0_7

18. Lou, T., Tang, J.: Mining structural hole spanners through information diffusion in social networks. In: Proceedings of the 22nd international conference on World Wide Web, pp. 825–836 (2013)

19. Ma, X., et al.: A comprehensive survey on graph anomaly detection with deep learning. IEEE Trans. Knowl. Data Eng. (2021)

20. McCallum, A.K., Nigam, K., Rennie, J., Seymore, K.: Automating the construction of internet portals with machine learning. Inf. Retrieval 3, 127–163 (2000)

21. Page, L., Brin, S., Motwani, R., Winograd, T.: The pagerank citation ranking: bringing order to the web. Technical report, Stanford InfoLab (1999)

22. Rezvani, M., Liang, W., Xu, W., Liu, C.: Identifying top-k structural hole spanners in large-scale social networks. In: Proceedings of the 24th ACM International on Conference on Information and Knowledge Management, pp. 263–272 (2015)

23. Sen, P., Namata, G., Bilgic, M., Getoor, L., Galligher, B., Eliassi-Rad, T.: Collective classification in network data. AI Mag. 29(3), 93–93 (2008)

24. Shchur, O., Mumme, M., Bojchevski, A., Günnemann, S.: Pitfalls of graph neural network evaluation. arXiv preprint arXiv:1811.05868 (2018)

25. Song, C., Hsu, W., Lee, M.L.: Mining brokers in dynamic social networks. In: Proceedings of the 24th ACM International on Conference on Information and Knowledge Management, pp. 523–532 (2015)

26. Sun, M., Xing, J., Wang, H., Chen, B., Zhou, J.: MOCL: data-driven molecular fingerprint via knowledge-aware contrastive learning from molecular graph. In: Proceedings of the 27th ACM SIGKDD Conference on Knowledge Discovery and Data Mining, pp. 3585–3594 (2021)

27. Thakoor, S., Tallec, C., Azar, M.G., Munos, R., Veličković, P., Valko, M.: Bootstrapped representation learning on graphs. In: ICLR 2021 Workshop on Geometrical and Topological Representation Learning (2021)

28. Veličković, P., Cucurull, G., Casanova, A., Romeró, A., Lio, P., Bengio, Y.: Graph attention networks. arXiv preprint arXiv:1710.10903 (2017)

29. Velickovic, P., Fedus, W., Hamilton, W.L., Liò, P., Bengio, Y., Hjelm, R.D.: Deep graph infomax. ICLR (Poster) 2(3), 4 (2019)

30. Wang, C., Pan, S., Hu, R., Long, G., Jiang, J., Zhang, C.: Attributed graph clustering: a deep attentional embedding approach. arXiv preprint arXiv:1906.06532 (2019)

31. Winterbach, W., Mieghem, P.V., Reinders, M., Wang, H., Ridder, D.d.: Topology of molecular interaction networks. BMC Syst. Biol. 7, 1–15 (2013)

32. Xie, J., Girshick, R., Farhadi, A.: Unsupervised deep embedding for clustering analysis. In: International Conference on Machine Learning, pp. 478–487. PMLR (2016)

33. Xu, W., Li, T., Liang, W., Yu, J.X., Yang, N., Gao, S.: Identifying structural hole spanners to maximally block information propagation. Inf. Sci. 505, 100–126 (2019)

34. Zhang, T., Xiong, Y., Zhang, J., Zhang, Y., Jiao, Y., Zhu, Y.: CommdGI: community detection oriented deep graph infomax. In: Proceedings of the 29th ACM International Conference on Information and Knowledge Management, pp. 1843–1852 (2020)

35. Zhang, Y., et al.: Finding structural hole spanners based on community forest model and diminishing marginal utility in large scale social networks. Knowl.-Based Syst. **199**, 105916 (2020)

36. Zhu, X., Lafferty, J., Ghahramani, Z.: Combining active learning and semi-supervised learning using gaussian fields and harmonic functions. In: ICML 2003 Workshop on the Continuum from labeled to Unlabeled Data in Machine Learning and Data Mining, vol. 3 (2003)

37. Zhu, Y., Xu, Y., Yu, F., Liu, Q., Wu, S., Wang, L.: Deep graph contrastive representation learning. arXiv preprint arXiv:2006.04131 (2020)

38. Zhu, Y., Xu, Y., Yu, F., Liu, Q., Wu, S., Wang, L.: Graph contrastive learning with adaptive augmentation. In: Proceedings of the Web Conference 2021, pp. 2069–2080 (2021)

A Reinforcement Learning-Based Approach for Continuous Knowledge Graph Construction

Jiao Luo[1], Yitao Zhang[1], Ying Wang[1], Wolfgang Mayer[2], Ningpei Ding[1], Xiaoxia Li[1], Yuan Quan[1], Debo Cheng[2], Hong-Yu Zhang[1(✉)], and Zaiwen Feng[1(✉)]

[1] College of Informatics, Huazhong Agricultural University, Wuhan 430070, China
{zhy630,Zaiwen.Feng}@mail.hzau.edu.cn
[2] Industrial AI Research Centre, University of South Australia,
Mawson Lakes 5095, SA, Australia

Abstract. Currently, the knowledge graph construction from the text mainly relies on document-level relation extraction models. However, these models have lower accuracy due to the limitations in capturing relations across sentences and documents. To address this problem, this paper proposes a novel approach to continuously construct a knowledge graph based on a reinforcement learning framework, which leverages a question generation model, question answering model, and sentence-level relation extraction model to mine cross-document domain knowledge for effective knowledge updating. Three joint rewards are designed to optimize the question generation model, making it generate high-quality questions that facilitate the knowledge graph construction. Automatic evaluation combined with manual evaluation is conducted based on the SQuAD dataset, to assess the quality of the questions and generated knowledge graph respectively. The experiments and analyses demonstrate the effectiveness of our approach in improving the quality of the knowledge graph construction.

Keywords: Knowledge graph construction · Reinforcement learning · Question generation · Question answering · Knowledge updating

1 Introduction

Automatic knowledge graph construction from large amounts of unstructured text data such as scientific literature in various fields has attracted increasing attention in natural language processing research [1]. Knowledge graphs provide a powerful representation for organizing and integrating information [2], enabling efficient knowledge management and facilitating various downstream applications such as question answering and information retrieval.

J. Luo, Y. Zhang and Y. Wang—The authors contributed equally to this work.

Z. Jin et al. (Eds.): KSEM 2023, LNAI 14120, pp. 418–429, 2023.
https://doi.org/10.1007/978-3-031-40292-0_34

However, existing approaches for knowledge extraction from unstructured data largely rely on document-level relation extraction models, which have limitations in capturing relations across sentences and documents, and suffer from low recall and precision rates [3]. To address these challenges, this paper proposes a method for continuously constructing a knowledge graph by actively asking questions [4] to extract knowledge from text. The goal is to create a self-learning system that can improve the quality of knowledge graph and question generation ability over time. Our approach leverages sentence-level relation extraction and cross-document knowledge mining strategies. Our model adopts a reinforcement learning framework, where three rewards are designed to encourage the generation of useful questions that facilitate the expansion of the knowledge graph.

The specific approach involves generating questions based on the content of the text and searching for answers in multiple text. This process condenses and refines knowledge contained in the text into a set of question-answer pairs. Then, the sentence-level relation extraction model is used to extract triples from the question-answer pairs for knowledge graph construction. Finally, The outcomes of whether the question-answering model can generate answers and whether the triples extracted from the question-answer pairs can be utilized for knowledge graph updating will serve as rewards for continuously adjusting the question generation model, guiding it towards generating answerable questions that can unearth new knowledge. In summary, our contributions are:

- A Reinforcement learning-based framework is proposed for continuously constructing knowledge graphs from unstructured text based on a dataset composed of Wikipedia articles (SQuAD).
- Three joint reinforcement learning-based rewards including *Relevance*, *Validity*, and *Updateability* for question generation and question answering are designed to facilitate cross-text knowledge mining and knowledge graph updating.
- Automatic and Human evaluation of the quality of the generated knowledge graph is conducted, with a specific focus on the accuracy of extracted relation triples. The experimental results indicate that the model with rewards significantly improves the number of correct triples.

2 Related Work

The related work of this paper focuses on the research field of generating knowledge graphs from text, which has received a lot of attention in various communities. In recent years, the success of transformer-based language models [5], such as BERT [6,7] and GPT [8,9], in the NLP community has led to attempts to utilize these advanced language models for downstream tasks of knowledge graph construction. Some methods [10,11] propose querying pre-trained models to extract learned facts and common sense knowledge. In addition, there are also methods [12] propose that entities and relations extraction from research publications by employing natural language processing and machine learning techniques and integrated into a large-scale knowledge graph.

Furthermore, some unsupervised methods, such as [13], utilize Semantic Web technology to semantically annotate triples in text, which aims to link and navigate triples to linked data clouds. Other works, such as Grapher [14], propose automated methods for text-to-knowledge-graph construction. Specifically, Grapher predicts entity-entity relationships using pre-trained language model T5 to predict entities in the text combined with position information.

Although these methods have their advantages and limitations, our method focuses on solving the problem of constructing automatically learning knowledge representations based on advanced language models.

3   Methodology

3.1   Overview

The framework of our proposed approach is illustrated in Fig. 1, which consists of three main components. From left to right, there is a Question Generation (QG) module based on reinforcement learning, an intelligent Question Answering (QA) module, and a Knowledge Graph Updating (KGU) module. To be more specific. Firstly, given the input text d_s, the reward-based QG module actively proposes a question q related to d_s through continuous learning. Secondly, the QA module retrieves candidate text d_c from the literature base based on the generated question q, and then generates the answer a to the question by leveraging information from both the original text d_s and the candidate text d_c. Thirdly, the obtained $q.a$ pairs are utilized by the KGU module, which extracts triples from the $q.a$ pairs to construct the knowledge graph G. Finally, the feedback from each module is used as a reward to constantly optimize the QG model, enabling the framework to be iteratively updated to achieve the goal of continuous knowledge graph construction. Each of the modules is described in detail in the following individual sections.

This objective is formalized as the maximization of conditional probability $P(q, a \mid d_s, d_c)$, *i.e.*, maximizing the probability of obtaining $q.a$ pair that can update the knowledge graph.

$$\bar{q}, \bar{a} = \arg\max_{q,a} P(q, a \mid d_s, d_c) \tag{1}$$

$$\bar{G} = Fus(Ext(\bar{q}, \bar{a}), G) \tag{2}$$

where G is original knowledge graph, $\bar{G}$ represents the updated knowledge graph. The function $Ext()$ indicates the knowledge extraction process for $q.a$ pairs, which outputs *(entity, relation, entity)* triples. The function $Fus()$ represents the knowledge fusion process, which outputs the updated knowledge graph $\bar{G}$.

3.2   Reward-Based Question Generation

Generate natural language questions from a given text using a reward-based approach that is capable of updating the knowledge graph. A formal definition

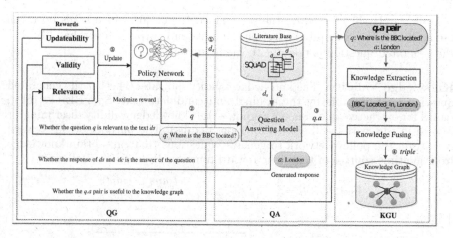

Fig. 1. The Framework of Knowledge Graph Continuous Construction Method Based on Reinforcement Learning.

of QG is as follows: Given an input text d_s, the goal of QG is to generate a natural question $\bar{q}$ related to the information in the input text d_s. The task is formulated as a conditional sequence generation, and the model is optimized to maximize the conditional log-likelihood $P(q \mid d_s)$ as in Eq. (3).

$$\bar{q} = \arg\max_q P(q \mid d_s) = \arg\max_q \sum_{t=1}^{|q|} log P(q_t \mid d_s, q_{<t}) \qquad (3)$$

where q_t represents a word in the generated question, $|q|$ represents the length of the generated question, and q represents the final question generated based on the input text.

The QG module consists of a basic Seq2Seq model and three reward mechanisms (see Eq. 4). The model is continuously adjusted based on feedback through three types of rewards, such as question relevance, knowledge validity, and knowledge updateability reward, to generate effective questions. The QG model is optimized by maximizing the above three rewards. The total loss function is set as follows:

$$L = L_{base} + \gamma_{rel} L_{rel} + \gamma_{val} L_{val} + \gamma_{upd} L_{upd} \qquad (4)$$

where the L_{base} is the loss of the basic QG model, which is described in [15], the three parameters $L_{rel}, L_{val}, L_{upd}$ represent the reward-based loss functions of question relevance, knowledge validity, and knowledge updateability, respectively. The hyper-parameters $\gamma_{rel}, \gamma_{val}, \gamma_{upd}$ specify the trade-off between different kinds of rewards.

Question Relevance. We use a classifier-based discriminator in [15] to judge whether the generated question is relevant to the input text. The discriminator is a binary classifier based on the pre-trained BERT [6], which takes both the input text and the generated question as inputs and outputs the probability that the generated question is relevant to the input text.

Knowledge Validity. The knowledge validity indicates whether the generated question is answerable by the original and candidate text. SpanBERT [16], a model for extractive question answering, as our knowledge validity discriminator is used in this part (see Sect. 3.3 for more details). The purpose of this reward is to train the policy network to generate questions that can obtain knowledge from multiple sources of text. The reward function R_{val} is set as follows:

$$R_{val}(d_{s/c}, q) = \begin{cases} 0, & if\ ans\ is\ empty \\ -log(1 - \phi + \epsilon), & others \end{cases} \tag{5}$$

$$\phi = \max_{1 \le i \le j \le |q|, j-i \le l} \sqrt{P^s_{val}(i|d_{s/c}, q) . P^e_{val}(j|d_{s/c}, q)} \tag{6}$$

where ϵ is a positive factor close to zero to avoid calculating log 0. $P^s_{val}(i)/P^e_{val}(i)$ is the probability that the i-th token is in the start/end span of the answer. l represents the maximum allowed length of the answer.

The total knowledge validity reward function R^T_{val} is a linear combination of reward based on d_s and reward based on d_c.

$$R^T_{val}(d_s, d_c, q) = \alpha R_{val}(d_s, q) + \beta R_{val}(d_c, q) \tag{7}$$

where the hyper-parameters α, β indicates the trade-off between the original text d_s and the candidate text d_c. To optimize the knowledge validity reward in reinforcement learning training, the loss function L_{val} is set as follows:

$$L_{val} = -(R^T_{val}(d_s, d_c, \bar{q}) - \alpha_{val}) \frac{1}{|q|} \sum_{t=1}^{|q|} logP_{QG}(\bar{q}_t \mid d_s, \bar{q}_{<t})) \tag{8}$$

where $\bar{q}_t$ is the t-th token in the predicted question $\bar{q}$, which is sampled from the vocabulary distribution $P_{QG}(q_t \mid q_{<t})$ specified by the RNN decoder of the question generator. α_{val} is a pre-defined negative answer score, which is used as the baseline reward to stabilize the training process.

Knowledge Updateability. The knowledge updateability indicates whether the acquired $q.a$ pair can update the existing knowledge graph. The reward function R_{upd} is set as follows:

$$R_{upd}(q.a, G) = -log(1 - P_{upd}(q.a, G) + \epsilon) \tag{9}$$

where $P_{upd}(q.a, G)$ is the predicted binary result of knowledge fusion(see 3.4 for more details on discriminator). Similar to the knowledge validity reward, the loss function L_{upd} is set as follows:

$$L_{upd} = -(R_{upd}(\bar{q}.\bar{a}, G) - \alpha_{upd}) \frac{1}{|q|} \sum_{t=1}^{|q|} logP_{QG}(\bar{q}_t \mid d_s, \bar{q}_{<t})) \tag{10}$$

where $\bar{a}$ is predicted answer of the predicted question $\bar{q}$ generated by the QA model.

3.3 Question Answering

QA model extracts the correct answer $\bar{a}$ to the generated question $\bar{q}$ from the original text d_s and the candidate text d_c. In this work, an extractive model SpanBERT is adopted to predict a span of the given text as a possible answer to the question. It outputs the probability of the start token $P_{val}^s(i)$ and the end token $P_{val}^e(j)$ in the text, and the subsequence with the highest start and end probabilities is usually chosen as the answer to the question. The SpanBERT model is fine-tuned on the SQuAD v2.0 dataset to enhance its semantic understanding and enable it to output an empty answer when the question cannot be answered based on the given text. Our assumption is that there is only one subsequence that represents the correct answer. Thus, the probability of extracting the answer can be defined by maximizing the probability of all candidate tokens in both the original text and the candidate text, which can be formally defined as follows:

$$\bar{a} = \arg\max_a P(a \mid d_{s/c}, q), \ P(a \mid d_{s/c}, q) = \max_{1 \le i \le j \le |q|} P_{val}^s(i) P_{val}^e(j) \qquad (11)$$

where i and j represent the start and end tokens of the answer in the text, respectively.

3.4 Knowledge Graph Updating

Updating the original knowledge graph G based on the acquired $\bar{q}.\bar{a}$ pair involves entities and relations extraction, as well as checking whether these entities and relations already exist in the knowledge graph. This process can be expressed as a formula (2). The process of KGU mainly consists of knowledge extraction $Ext()$ and knowledge fusion $Fus()$.

Knowledge Extraction. In this part, the generated questions and corresponding answers are taken as input into a sentence-level joint entity relation extraction model SpERT [17], which extracts (*entity, relation, entity*) triples from $\bar{q}.\bar{a}$ pair. These triples consist of a subject, a relation, and an object, which represent the key information contained in the $\bar{q}.\bar{a}$ pair.

Knowledge Fusion. In this part, the (*entity, relation, entity*) triples extracted from the $\bar{q}.\bar{a}$ pair are linked to update original knowledge graph, and then obtain the updated knowledge graph. The linking approach we adopted takes into account both the string similarity of entities and relations, as well as the consistency of entity types. If the entity in a triple has the same entity type and name as an existing entity in the knowledge graph, the entity is considered to

424 J. Luo et al.

already exist in the knowledge graph. Otherwise, the knowledge graph needs to be updated with this new entity. When both the head and tail entities in a triple exist in the knowledge graph, it is necessary to determine whether the relation between these two entities exists in the knowledge graph.

4 Experiments and Results

The basic QG model is a Seq2Seq model with attention, copy, and coverage mechanisms, which is described by [15]. Briefly, the encoder is a 1-layer bi-directional Gate Recurrent Unit (GRU) and the decoder is a 1-layer GRU with a hidden-unit size of 512 [18]. In reinforcement learning training, the baseline reward R_{rel}, R_{val} and R_{upd} are all set to log(2), the hyper-parameters γ_{rel}, γ_{val} and γ_{upd} are all set to 1, α and β are set to 0 and 1 respectively, which follow the best practice in [15] and our experiment. Our model was trained using two Tesla V100 GPUs with 32 cores in Sugon's cloud server.

4.1 Dataset

The SQuAD v1.1 dataset [13], which consists of over 100K questions and corresponding answers extracted by crowd workers from 536 Wikipedia articles, is used for conducting experiments. For training the reward-based QG model, we extract (sentence, question, passage) triples from SQuAD v1.1, where the sentence represents the source text and the paragraph is the candidate text. To ensure that the $q.a$ pairs focus on the entities and relations in the knowledge graph, we filter the SQuAD v1.1 dataset by performing joint entity relation extraction on the gold standard $q.a$ pairs, and select about 7,000 sets of (sentence, question, passage) triples for further fine-tuning the QG model, denoted as SQuAD-7k. The joint entity relation extraction model SpERT is trained on the CoNLL04 dataset, which includes four entity types (Location, Organization, People, Other) and five relation types (Work-For, Kill, Organization-Based-In, Live-In, and Located-In).

4.2 Automatic Evaluation

To compare the impact of different rewards on knowledge graph construction, we train the QG model for 50 epochs using SQuAD v1.1 and SQuAD-7k respectively. We conduct an automatic evaluation using five metrics to assess different reward optimization objectives: a) BLEU1 and 4 [19], b) ROUGE [20], c) METEOR [21], and d) Number of triples updated. The results of the automatic evaluation are shown in Table 1 and Table 2 respectively, the first four metrics reflect the similarity between generated and ground-truth questions, while the number of triples updated is the number of non-repeated triples obtained. The performance of our method under different reward schemes will be evaluated. B1 represents the baseline model, while Sx (where $x \in \{1, 2, 3\}$) denotes the models derived from the baseline by adding relevance, validity, and updateability rewards respectively. Ey (where $y \in \{1, 2, 3, 4\}$) represents the QG model optimized with multiple rewards.

Table 1. The performance of each model trained on *SQuAD v1.1.*

Model	Rewards			Metrics				
	R	V	U	BLEU1	BLEU4	ROUGE	METEOR	Triples
B1				29.56	6.52	28.98	12.24	524
S1	✓			29.30	**6.77**	28.32	**12.73**	**601**
S2		✓		**29.57**	6.56	**29.07**	12.66	490
S3			✓	29.51	6.45	28.91	12.14	474

Performance Comparison. In Table 1, we note that after adding a certain reward, the scores of the first four metrics in the reward-based models are higher than or comparable to the baseline model. However, the number of updated triples by the models with validity or updateability reward is lower than the performance of the baseline, it's probably because the SpERT model used in our study can only extract a limited number of relations from the *q.a* pairs, where the SQuAD v1.1 dataset contains diverse questions.

Table 2. The performance of each model trained on *SQuAD-7K.*

Model	Rewards			Metrics				
	R	V	U	BLEU1	BLEU4	ROUGE	METEOR	Triples
B1				28.08	5.11	27.32	**11.95**	681
S1	✓			26.71	5.06	26.81	11.80	719
S2		✓		27.89	4.97	27.03	11.74	660
S3			✓	26.80	4.98	27.10	11.93	**948**
E1	✓	✓		**28.39**	**5.18**	**27.36**	11.94	824
E2	✓		✓	25.92	4.68	26.58	11.73	865
E3		✓	✓	28.06	5.05	27.29	11.91	799
E4	✓	✓	✓	27.23	4.84	27.03	11.83	794

After fine-tuning the model using the SQuAD-7K dataset, we have the following findings:

(1) The evaluation results of the models in Table 2 are generally higher than those of the models in Table 1 in terms of the number of triples updated. This confirms our previous analysis that the types of questions generated by the model after fine-tuning will concentrate on the relation type set R we provided. However, the overall scores of the first four metrics decreased. This is probably because the rewards focus on different aspects of question quality, not just similarity to the gold question. *i.e.*, the validity reward we designed to cause a bias towards generating questions that deviated from the gold questions in the dataset.

(2) Table 2 shows that adding rewards leads to more triples than the baseline. Compared to adding a single reward alone, training with multiple rewards together can lead to both improved and decreased performance, such as E1 and E3. This shows that different rewards do not exist in isolation, rather, they are interrelated and exhibit a certain level of correlation. When the correlation among rewards is consistent, they reinforce each other, whereas they weaken each other when the correlation is inconsistent.

(3) As can be observed from Tables 1 and 2, the highest number of triples extracted from the test set of approximately 10,000 is only 948, the probable reason for this is the data bias in the training set, which results in generated questions that are often irrelevant to the current knowledge graph.

4.3   Human Evaluation

A common method for evaluating the quality of knowledge graphs is to compare the newly constructed knowledge graph with the existing standard knowledge graph [22]. However, the data we used to construct the knowledge graph comes from the SQuAD v1.1 test set. Since our method encourages the model to generate diverse questions that are useful for KGU, the questions generated by the model may not be the same as the gold questions in the dataset. To the best of our knowledge, there is no knowledge graph construction method based on this unstructured data by this asking question. Without appropriate ground truth, manual judgment is needed to determine the accuracy of the extracted triples.

Table 3. The facts-based accuracy of the knowledge graph constructed by each model.

Annotator	Accuracy of Triples based on facts (%)							
	B1	S1	S2	S3	E1	E2	E3	E4
A	43.90	51.16	46.51	47.37	57.14	55.77	56.25	54.17
B	60.97	69.76	62.79	66.67	67.35	67.31	64.58	64.58
C	60.97	69.76	60.46	61.41	69.39	65.38	72.92	64.58
Majority	51.22	62.79	51.16	54.38	65.31	65.38	66.67	62.50
Defective	28.57	33.33	27.27	54.37	40.62	26.38	34.38	26.67

Performance Comparison. Table 5 shows the Fleiss' kappa score for each model, with the range mainly between 0.4 and 0.6, indicating a moderate level of agreement. After manually evaluating the quality of the triples, we made the following observations:

The main focus of our Human evaluation is the correctness of the content described by the triples. We recruited three human annotators to evaluate the triples extracted from each model. We use A, B, and C to identify the three annotators. Specifically, we randomly sampled 6% triples from each model's triples

Table 4. The $q.a$ pairs-based accuracy of the knowledge graph constructed by each model.

Annotator	Accuracy of Triples based on $q.a$ pairs (%)							
	B1	S1	S2	S3	E1	E2	E3	E4
A	63.41	65.11	53.49	57.89	77.55	67.31	70.83	66.67
B	75.61	83.72	74.41	77.19	91.84	78.85	83.33	85.42
C	80.49	81.39	81.39	77.19	89.79	80.77	83.83	81.25
Majority	70.73	74.41	69.76	70.17	89.75	78.85	87.50	77.08
Defective	27.59	18.75	20.00	50.00	27.27	17.07	30.59	32.43

Table 5. The Fleiss' kappa score for each model.

Type	Fleiss' kappa score							
	B1	S1	S2	S3	E1	E2	E3	E4
fact-based	0.549	0.404	0.477	0.421	0.527	0.507	0.366	0.458
$q.a$-based	0.542	0.411	0.548	0.427	0.520	0.546	0.424	0.430

for evaluation. Each annotator was provided with the original text, the triple, and the types of entities and relations involved in the triple, and was asked to evaluate each triple based on our rules, where 0 indicates inaccuracy, 1 indicates accuracy with minor issues in entities, and 2 indicates complete accuracy. We use the majority-agreed label as the ground truth of the triple, "Majority" refers to the accuracy rate, which is the proportion of labels that are greater than zero, "Defective" denotes the proportion of defective triples, which is calculated as the number of labels marked as 1 divided by the total number of labels marked as greater than 0. The evaluation results are presented in Table 3.

In addition, we also conduct a manual evaluation to determine whether the knowledge described by the triples in the knowledge graph is consistent with the knowledge contained in the $q.a$ pairs. Provided the triple, corresponding $q.a$ pair, and the type of entities to annotators. Annotators used the same evaluation rules to estimate the accuracy of each triple based on the knowledge contained in the corresponding $q.a$ pair. The evaluation results are presented in Table 4.

The performance evaluation of the model can be influenced by the subjective bias of human annotators, which may affect the reliability and accuracy of the annotations. Therefore, assessing the inter-rater agreement among the annotators is essential to ensure the quality of the data. In this study, we calculate the Fleiss' kappa score for each model as a measure of inter-rater agreement among the annotators.

(1) As present in Table 3, the accuracy for triples in each model is approximately 60%. We find that those models with rewards generally achieved higher accuracy than the baseline model, which is consistent with the automatic evaluation that the reward-based fine-tuning mechanisms can indeed provide some improvement over the baseline.

(2) Comparing Tables 3 and 4, we find that the accuracy of the triples extracted based on $q.a$ pairs are significantly higher than the accuracy of the fact-based triples. This finding suggests that $q.a$ pairs themselves contain erroneous knowledge. It is related to the performance of the QG and QA models.

(3) As can be observed from Table 3 and Table 4, the percentage of defective triples is consistently around 30% in almost all the models. To our knowledge, there is currently no research on relation extraction from $q.a$ pairs using a joint entity-relation extraction model, which makes it difficult for the relation extraction model to better understand the semantics of $q.a$ pairs. For example, in our experiments, SpERT identified *"News Network? CNN"* in the $q.a$ pair *"What was the name of the U.S.-based News Network? CNN"* as an entity, but *"CNN"* is the correct entity.

5   Conclusion and Future Work

This paper propose a novel solution for automatically constructing knowledge graphs based on unstructured data. Our approach involves extracting knowledge from the literature by actively asking questions and intelligently obtaining answers, and then updating the knowledge graph using a relation extraction model. In this process, we introduce reinforcement learning mechanisms and design three rewards to guide the question generation. The results demonstrate the effectiveness of validity and Updateability reward designed in improving the quality of the KGU, which has great potential for applications.

In future work, the incorporation of prior knowledge contained within the updated knowledge graph is planned to guide the generation of questions toward meeting the requirements of KGU. In the knowledge fusion stage, incorporation of entity resolution and entity disambiguation will be considered to clean and remove redundant data from triples, thereby improving the quality of the generated knowledge graph.

References

1. Ye, H., Zhang, N., Chen, H., Chen, H.: Generative knowledge graph construction: a review. CoRR (2022). https://doi.org/10.48550/arXiv.2210.12714
2. Ji, S., Pan, S., Cambria, E., Marttinen, P., Philip, S.Y.: A survey on knowledge graphs: representation, acquisition, and applications. IEEE Trans. Neural Netw. Learn. Syst. **33**(2), 494–514 (2021)
3. Xu, B., Wang, Q., Lyu, Y., Zhu, Y., Mao, Z.: Entity structure within and throughout: modeling mention dependencies for document-level relation extraction. In: Proceedings of the AAAI Conference on Artificial Intelligence, vol. 35, pp. 14149–14157 (2021)
4. Krishna, R., Lee, D., Fei-Fei, L., Bernstein, M.S.: Socially situated artificial intelligence enables learning from human interaction. Proc. Natl. Acad. Sci. **119**(39), e2115730119 (2022)

5. Vaswani, A., et al.: Attention is all you need. In: Proceedings of the 31st International Conference on Neural Information Processing Systems, pp. 6000–6010 (2017)
6. Devlin, J., Chang, M.W., Lee, K., Toutanova, K.: BERT: pre-training of deep bidirectional transformers for language understanding. arXiv preprint arXiv:1810.04805 (2018)
7. Liu, Y., et al.: RoBERTa: a robustly optimized BERT pretraining approach. arXiv preprint arXiv:1907.11692 (2019)
8. Radford, A., Narasimhan, K., Salimans, T., Sutskever, I., et al.: Improving language understanding by generative pre-training (2018)
9. Radford, A., Wu, J., Child, R., Luan, D., Amodei, D., Sutskever, I.: Language models are unsupervised multitask learners (2019)
10. Roberts, A., Raffel, C., Shazeer, N.M.: How much knowledge can you pack into the parameters of a language model? In: Conference on Empirical Methods in Natural Language Processing (2020)
11. Shin, T., Razeghi, Y., Logan IV, R.L., Wallace, E., Singh, S.: Autoprompt: eliciting knowledge from language models with automatically generated prompts. arXiv preprint arXiv:2010.15980 (2020)
12. Dessì, D., Osborne, F., Reforgiato Recupero, D., Buscaldi, D., Motta, E., Sack, H.: AI-KG: an automatically generated knowledge graph of artificial intelligence. In: Pan, J.Z., et al. (eds.) ISWC 2020. LNCS, vol. 12507, pp. 127–143. Springer, Cham (2020). https://doi.org/10.1007/978-3-030-62466-8_9
13. Rincon-Yanez, D., Senatore, S.: FAIR knowledge graph construction from text, an approach applied to fictional novels. In: Proceedings of the 1st International Workshop on Knowledge Graph Generation From Text and the 1st International Workshop on Modular Knowledge co-located with 19th Extended Semantic Conference (ESWC 2022), pp. 94–108. CEUR-WS, Hersonissos, Greece (2022)
14. Melnyk, I., Dognin, P., Das, P.: Knowledge graph generation from text. In: Proceedings of the 2022 Conference on Empirical Methods in Natural Language Processing (Findings of EMNLP) (2022)
15. Xie, Y., Pan, L., Wang, D., Kan, M.Y., Feng, Y.: Exploring question-specific rewards for generating deep questions. In: The 28th International Conference on Computational Linguistics (COLING 2020) (2020)
16. Joshi, M., Chen, D., Liu, Y., Weld, D.S., Zettlemoyer, L., Levy, O.: SpanBERT: improving pre-training by representing and predicting spans. arXiv preprint arXiv:1907.10529 (2019)
17. Span-based joint entity and relation extraction with transformer pre-training. In: 24th European Conference on Artificial Intelligence (2020)
18. Li, M., Zhu, Y., Shen, Y., Angelova, M.: Clustering-enhanced stock price prediction using deep learning. World Wide Web 26(1), 207–232 (2023)
19. Papineni, K., Roukos, S., Ward, T., Zhu, W.J.: Bleu: a method for automatic evaluation of machine translation. In: Proceedings of the 40th Annual Meeting of the Association for Computational Linguistics, pp. 311–318 (2002)
20. Lin, C.Y.: Rouge: a package for automatic evaluation of summaries. In: Text Summarization Branches Out, pp. 74–81 (2004)
21. Banerjee, S., Lavie, A.: Meteor: an automatic metric for MT evaluation with improved correlation with human judgments. In: Proceedings of the ACL Workshop on Intrinsic and Extrinsic Evaluation Measures for Machine Translation and/or Summarization, pp. 65–72 (2005)
22. Islam, M.S.: Knowurenvironment: an automated knowledge graph for climate change and environmental issues. In: AAAI 2022 Fall Symposium: The Role of AI in Responding to Climate Challenges (2022)

A Multifactorial Evolutionary Algorithm Based on Model Knowledge Transfer

Xuan Lu, Lei Chen$^{(\boxtimes)}$, and Hai-Lin Liu

School of Mathematics and Applied Mathematics, Guangdong University
of Technology, Guangzhou 510520, China
{chenlei3,hlliu}@gdut.edu.cn

Abstract. Evolutionary multitasking optimization is a newly proposed paradigm that leverages the implicit parallelism of population-based search and transfers genetic information among tasks to solve multifactorial optimization (MFO) problems simultaneously. However, simply migrating implicit genetics is incapable of fully exploring the potential of transfer learning to sum up crucial information and avoid local optima traps. Moreover, the negative transfer will hinder the search for the appropriate solution, leading to a performance collapse of the optimization algorithm. To address those issues, a multifactorial evolutionary algorithm based on model knowledge transfer (MT-MFEA) is proposed for MFO problems in this paper. In MT-MFEA, a clustering model is built based on density-based spatial clustering of applications with noise (DBSCAN) algorithm, which is beneficial to better capturing the position information of the search population for each task. Furthermore, explicit transfer learning is conducted among tasks by selecting higher-quality information from clustering models to enhance searchability and avoid negative transfer. The MT-MFEA is evaluated on various benchmark problems, involving optimization tasks with varying levels of intersecting global optima and similarities. The experimental analysis of the performances and comparisons with four state-of-the-art algorithms demonstrate the efficacy and efficiency of MT-MFEA.

Keywords: Multitasking optimization · knowledge transfer · evolutionary algorithm · clustering model

1 Introduction

A type of optimization problem, namely Multifactorial Optimization (MFO) problem, was introduced in [1]. In MFO, a single- or multi-objective optimization problem is embodied in component tasks, and every task owns a distinct search landscape. For instance, imagine a scenario where the handling of two

This work was supported in part by the National Natural Science Foundation of China (62006044, 62172110), in part by the Natural Science Foundation of Guangdong Province (2022A1515010130), and in part by the Programme of Science and Technology of Guangdong Province (2021A0505110004).

Z. Jin et al. (Eds.): KSEM 2023, LNAI 14120, pp. 430–441, 2023.
https://doi.org/10.1007/978-3-031-40292-0_35

separate tasks is required simultaneously, such as job-shop scheduling and route design. This can be viewed as an MFO problem. Consequently, the evolutionary multitasking paradigm of MFO was introduced to address MFO problems, which involve multiple component optimization tasks to be handled simultaneously. The distinguishing characteristic of this paradigm lies in its comprehensive approach toward all tasks, leveraging the implicit parallelism of population-based search rather than merely searching for feasible trade-off solutions, making MFO problems inherently more complex than typical optimization tasks. Specifically, the process of searching for reliable solutions is time-consuming as it involves performing simulations. This makes it arduous for general algorithms to solve MFO problems. To obtain reliable solutions for MFO problems, a multifactorial evolutionary algorithm (MFEA) was recently introduced in [1]. In order to optimize the effectiveness of population-based search and capitalize on knowledge gained from solving analogous tasks using parallelism, MFEA simultaneously solves MFO problems by transferring genetic information among tasks, using assortative mating and vertical cultural transmission as approaches for genetic communication.

MFEA has consistently demonstrated an impressive ability to accelerate convergence [2], while also increasing the ability to achieve optimal global search results. This has made it an object of intense research focus, and numerous experts have proposed innovative approaches to optimizing it. For example, MTES is an example of an evolutionary multitask algorithm that builds on the multitasking gradient algorithm (MTGD) [3]. By combining the effectiveness of the evolutionary single-task strategy (ES) with the fast convergence rate of MTGD to achieve accelerated convergence, the resulting gradient-free MTES approach offers a powerful optimization tool that can efficiently address complex optimization problems with multiple objectives. Ding et al. proposed a generalized MFEA (G-MFEA) in [4], which incorporates the valuable decision variable translation and practical shuffling strategies. A group-based MFEA (GMFEA) was presented in [5], which groups tasks to improve information exchange among the same group. To address the issue of tasks of varying dimensions, a linearized domain adaptation strategy (LDA-MFEA) was proposed in [6] and is designed to transform the search space from a simple task to a complex task. In [7], a two-level transfer learning method (TLTLA) was presented for evolutionary multitasking. The proposed TLTLA employed the upper and lower level to leverage inter-task transfer learning and enable the transfer of decision variables for across-dimension optimization tasks, respectively. The TMO-MFEA in [8] is notable for its ability to distinguish between diversity-related variables (DVs) and convergence-related variables (CVs), allowing the proposed TMP-MFEA to achieve impressive search performance by grouping decision variables in a way that is informed by related approaches outlined in [9].

Although MFEA has shown excellent performance in many MFO problems, there is still a lot of room for improvement with respect to convergence speed and search accuracy. To improve the original MFEA algorithm, this paper suggests an MFEA based on model knowledge transfer that consists of three new strategies:

the clustering model building strategy, the model knowledge transfer strategy, and the local optimum escaping strategy.

. The significant contributions of the MT-MFEA can be elaborated as follows.

1. A clustering model building strategy is introduced to address MFO problems by applying the density-based spatial clustering with noise (DBSCAN) algorithm [10] to construct Gaussian distribution models, leading to the advantages of extracting crucial information and accelerating the speed of convergence. Thereinto, the DBSCAN algorithm is feasible to arrange nearby points into groups based on density and to identify external points in low-density areas. Consequently, the search speed is significantly improved, and the solutions produced are more reliable.

2. In MT-MFEA, the clustering models that belong to the current tasks and the most similar tasks are used to produce feasible solutions. This approach to transfer learning allows for circumventing repetitive work and avoiding the predicament of the search process. To solve optimization tasks more efficiently, particularly those with discrepancies in the global optima, this paper employs a mean shifting method that helps reduce negative transfer and search for high-quality solutions.

3. To avoid being trapped in local optima during the search process, a strategy is presented to escape local optima. This strategy involves changing the mean of clustering models and changing the arrangement of the offspring genotype, resulting in significantly improved search capabilities.

2   Proposed Algorithm MT-MFEA

In this section, we will delve into the related strategies of MT-MFEA, including the clustering model building strategy, the model knowledge transfer strategy, and the local optimal escaping strategy. Then, the main structure of the proposed TL-MFEA is presented. Afterward, we present the experimental results and accompanying charts for further analysis and research.

2.1   Clustering Model Building Strategy

As the iteration continues, the population of an optimization task tends to concentrate on specific regions due to the selection of highly promising offspring and the elimination of less valuable ones. Empirical observations have shown that these regions with concentrated individuals are more likely to harbor global optima. Inspired by this phenomenon, we propose the strategy of constructing clustering models to enhance the performance of the original multifactorial evolutionary algorithm. Each individual's position can be graphically depicted as a point in a $D_{multitask}$-dimensional space, where $D_{multitask}$ represents the highest dimension of all tasks' search space. In each iteration, MT-MFEA employs the DBSCAN algorithm to group the points, resulting in the classification of closely located points into the same category. By analyzing the distribution information of individuals in each category, Gaussian distribution models are constructed, from which descendants are subsequently produced.

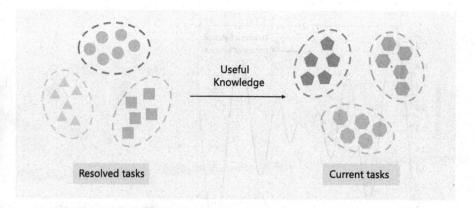

Fig. 1. Illustration of the transfer learning process between similar tasks.

2.2 Model Knowledge Transfer Strategy

In the search process, the significance of transfer learning cannot be overstated. As shown in Fig. 1, the useful knowledge gained from successfully completing tasks is essential to effectively managing future tasks that are similar or related. Adopting the method of transfer learning would allow us to streamline our efforts, avoid unnecessary duplication, and identify viable solutions more effectively. The idea of incorporating transfer learning can be beneficial in our proposed model knowledge transfer strategy. The core concept of the knowledge transfer strategy of the model is to utilize the clustering models obtained from the building strategy of the clustering model to transfer knowledge between tasks. Specifically, for each task, the algorithm first identifies the most similar task based on the distance metric between the task clustering model and the clustering models of other tasks. Then, it transfers knowledge between the two tasks by selecting a random individual from a similar task and generating a new offspring based on the selected individual's genotype and the current task's Gaussian model. This process is repeated several times with each task, and the resulting offspring are evaluated and potentially added to the population. The proposed model knowledge transfer strategy helps to steer clear of local optima and leverage insights gained from related tasks. In addition, it minimizes the computational expenditure associated with solving multiple tasks by recycling information.

It is worth mentioning that not all optimization tasks have the same global optimum, as shown in Fig. 2. This can result in negative transfer in the transfer learning process, leading to poor performance during the search process. To address this issue, if the Gaussian models do not belong to the current task, the mean of the Gaussian distribution needs to be adjusted based on the estimated global optimum, and the modified Gaussian models will assist in searching for feasible solutions for the current task. Furthermore, the skill of identifying the location of the temporary global optima of each task involves calculating the mean position of the best ΔN individuals.

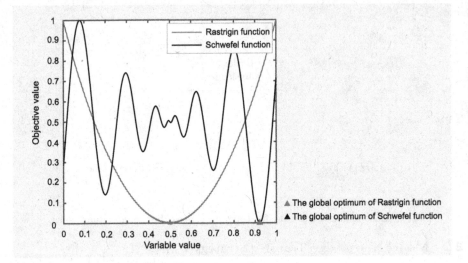

Fig. 2. The example illustrates the difference between two algorithms' global optimums.

2.3 Local Optimum Escaping Strategy

The local optimum escaping strategy aims to enhance the diversity of the population by applying a particular amount of displacement to Gaussian models, thus preventing the population from being trapped in local optima. The amount of movement in each Gaussian model is determined by calculating the factorial cost difference between the current generation and the previous generation. If the factorial cost has not decreased much, the movement amount is increased; otherwise, the movement amount is decreased to ensure that the population will not be allowed to move too far away from the promising solutions. Specifically, the mean of the Gaussian distribution model is shifted randomly within a certain range, and the standard deviation is adjusted by a certain factor to ensure that the Gaussian distribution model enables exploration of a wider range of the search space. The amount of movement is determined by a dynamic adjustment mechanism, and the adjustment factor is inversely proportional to the improvement in factorial cost. The local optimum escaping strategy is applied periodically to ensure the population's diversity and prevent the population from being trapped in a local optimum. The experimental outcomes indicate that the suggested local optimum escaping strategy significantly enhances the search performance of the proposed MT-MFEA.

In each different task, when the factorial costs obtained from every ΔT generation differs by less than a number ΔS, it indicates that the search process has entered a local optimum region, and the location of clustering models needs to be shifted with a specific probability p to overcome this situation. Consider an MFO problem set in a $D_{multitask}$ unified space, where $D_{multitask}$ is the maximum number in $D_k, k = 1, 2, ..., K$, and D_k represents the search space dimension of

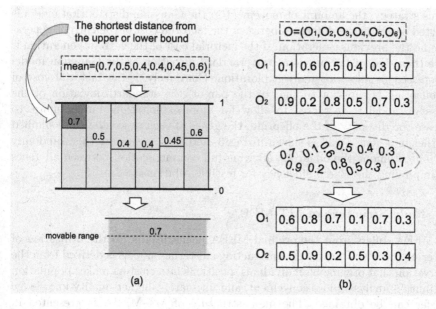

Fig. 3. The details about local optimum escaping strategy. (a) Illustration of how to obtain the amount of movement of the mean of the Gaussian distribution. (b) The example illustrates how to shuffle the genes of offspring individuals.

the kth task, we denote the center location of the original clustering model as $O = (o_1, o_2, ..., o_{D_{multitask}})$, and the formula that calculates the amount of shifting is as follows:

$$F = \begin{cases} \dfrac{1}{10\sqrt{\frac{f_{previous}-f_{current}}{f_{previous}}+3}} & , f_{previous} \neq 0 \\[2ex] \dfrac{1}{3} & , f_{previous} = 0 \end{cases} \tag{1}$$

$$r = F\vartheta max\left\{max\left\{|o_j - 1|\right\}, max\left\{|o_j - 0|\right\}\right\} \tag{2}$$

where $\vartheta \sim U[-1, 1]$, and r denotes the distance of movement of $o_d, d = 1, 2, ..., D_{multitask}$. $f_{previous}$ and $f_{current}$ represent the factorial cost of the previous and current iteration, respectively, and the factorial cost δ_k^i of individual p_i in optimization task T_k is given by $\delta_k^i = \lambda\eta_k^i + f_k^i$, where λ represents a large penalizing multiplier, η_k^i represents the violation of the constraint and f_k^i represents the objective value. Especially, to prevent division by zero, if $f_{previous}$ is zero, the value of F is $\frac{1}{3}$. In this formula, the purpose of calculating the max $|o_j - 1|$ and the max $|o_j - 0|$ is to prevent the relocated offspring from exiting the search area and to manage the shifting amount efficiently. Figure 3 illustrates the main idea of how to obtain the amount of movement of the Gaussian distribution model.

To enhance the diversity of the offspring and prevent them from being trapped in the local optimum, the local optimum escaping strategy is adopted.

In this strategy, the amount of movement in the Gaussian distribution model is adjusted based on the difference between the factorial cost of the current generation and the previous generation. If the factorial cost of the current generation is worse than that of the previous, the standard deviation of the Gaussian model is increased to allow for more exploration. Conversely, if the factorial cost of the offspring is superior to that of the parent, the standard deviation of the Gaussian model is decreased to allow for more exploitation. Furthermore, to increase the diversity of the offspring, the genes of each descendant are shuffled together in a gene pool, as shown in Fig. 3, and these genes are then randomly distributed among the offspring, allowing full communication between all genes and improving the search efficiency for feasible solutions.

2.4   Main Structure of MT-MFEA

MT-MFEA differs from the original MFEA primarily due to the utilization of clustering models. The idea of constructing clustering models is derived from the observation that organizing individuals' positions into clusters makes population distribution analysis more convenient, and ultimately, higher-quality knowledge transfer can be obtained. The main structure of MT-MFEA is presented in Algorithm 1.

Algorithm 1. Structure of MT-MFEA

Input:
  P_k: the individuals associated with kth task;
  g: the number of iteration;
  K: the number of tasks.
Output: The elite population P' for every task.

1: population $P_k, k = 1, 2, ..., K \xrightarrow{map\ to}$ a unified searching space Y;
2: Assign a given skill factor to individuals. The skill factor $\tau_i = mod(i, K) + 1$ in ith tasks;
3: **while** the termination condition is not met **do**
4:     Clustering model building strategy $\rightarrow$ cluster model $\mathbf{M} = \{M_1, M_2, ..., M_K\}$;
5:     **for** $i = 1 : K$ **do**
6:         **if** $rand < rmp$ **then**
7:             Two random parents p_a and $p_b \leftarrow Select(P)$;
8:             Crossover p_a and $p_b \rightarrow$ two offspring;
9:         **else**
10:             Generated two elite individuals P' by model knowledge transfer strategy and local optimum escaping strategy.
11:         **end if**
12:     **end for**
13: **end while**

In each generation, MT-MFEA clusters the positions of individuals and generates clustering models for each task by using the DBSCAN algorithm. During the offspring generation process, the parents of the same task undergo a mutation only if a random number is inferior to the random mating probability (RMP). Otherwise, the clustering models belonging to the current task and the most analogous task are employed to produce offspring for the current task. To ensure offspring quality, all clustering models produce five temporary descendants for the current task. From these, the two best final descendants are selected based on their factorial cost. To circumvent being trapped in local optima, the local optimum escaping strategy has been implemented. After assigning a skill factor to each offspring through vertical cultural transmission, feasible solutions are meticulously selected from the population of parents and current offspring based on their factorial cost. Thereinto, the skill factor τ_i of individual p_i represents the optimization task T_k that p_i performs best. The resulting top-performing elites have then been deemed the parents of the upcoming generation.

3   Experimental Studies

In this section, the presented MT-MFEA is compared with four advanced algorithms: MTES [3], EMaTOMKT [11], MFEA [1], and SOO, where the SOO algorithm is two tasks that search for feasible independently. To verify the effectiveness of these algorithms, an MFO problem [12] is used in this paper. The result of the experiment shows that the proposed MT-MFEA has better performance than other algorithms.

3.1   Test Problems

This paper presents the searchability of the proposed MT-MFEA by employing the test suit [12] provided in Table 1. This test suite comprises nine problems, each consisting of two single-objective optimization tasks. For a more complete description, the benchmark problems are classified into nine test instances to evaluate the proposed algorithm under diverse conditions. These instances are classified by observing their intersection degree, comprising complete intersection (CI), partial intersection (PI), and no intersection (NI).

3.2   Experimental Settings

By drawing on the research of predecessors and taking note of their pertinent experiences of predecessors on this topic, the parameters in this paper are established as follows

- Population Size: The population size N for each task is set to 100.
- Termination Condition: All algorithms' maximum generation is 1000.
- Hybrid Variation Parameter: SBX [13] and polynomial mutation are employed as the operator of crossover and mutation, respectively. Among them, η_n is set to 2 in SBX and the variation parameter of the polynomial η_m is set to 5.
- Number of Runs: All algorithms are run 30 times independently in every test suit.

Table 1. Properties of the single-objective multitask benchmark

Problem	Task NO	Properties	D	Decision space	Landscape
CI+HS	T1	Griwank	50	$[-100, 100]$	multimodal, nonseparable
	T2	Rastrigin	50	$[-50, 50]$	multimodal, nonseparable
CI+MS	T1	Ackley	50	$[-50, 50]$	multimodal, nonseparable
	T2	Rastrigin	50	$[-50, 50]$	multimodal, nonseparable
CI+LS	T1	Ackley	50	$[-50, 50]$	multimodal, nonseparable
	T2	Schwefel	50	$[-500, 500]$	multimodal, separable
PI+HS	T1	Rastrigin	50	$[-500, 500]$	multimodal, nonseparable
	T2	Sphere	50	$[-50, 50]$	unimodal, separable
PI+MS	T1	Ackley	50	$[-50, 50]$	multimodal, nonseparable
	T2	Rosenbrock	50	$[-50, 50]$	multimodal, nonseparable
PI+LS	T1	Ackley	50	$[-50, 50]$	multimodal, nonseparable
	T2	Weierstrass	25	$[-0.5, 0.5]$	multimodal, nonseparable
NI+HS	T1	Rosenbrock	50	$[-50, 50]$	multimodal, nonseparable
	T2	Rastrigin	50	$[-50, 50]$	multimodal, nonseparable
NI+MS	T1	Griwank	50	$[-100, 100$	multimodal, nonseparable
	T2	Weierstrass	50	$[-0.5, 0.5]$	multimodal, nonseparable
NI+LS	T1	Rastrigin	50	$[-50, 50]$	multimodal, nonseparable
	T2	Schwefel	50	$[-500, 500]$	multimodal, separable

- Private Parameter: The probability rmp in Algorithm 1 is set to 0.3.
- Generation Apart: The ΔT in the local optimum escaping strategy is set to 10 generations.
- Criterion number: In the local optimum escaping strategy, the criterion ΔS for whether the search process is trapped into the local optimum is set according to the order of magnitude of its factorial cost. For example, the factorial cost of the current tasks was determined to be 21.2, with a magnitude of 2. To compute ΔS, we calculated 10 to the power of 2 minus 3, which results in a value of 0.1.
- Estimated global optima: the ΔN in local optimum escaping strategy is 40.

3.3   Experimental Results and Analysis

To evaluate the searchability of the proposed MT-MFEA, Table 2 displays the average function values of MT-MFEA and four other algorithms for comparison. The results of MTES are sourced from [3], while the experimental results of the remaining algorithms are obtained by running them on MATLAB2020b. The test suite runs each algorithm 30 times, and the mean function values of the best-performing algorithms are highlighted in bold for ease of interpretation. MT-MFEA demonstrates superior performance, outperforming other algorithms

Table 2. The experiment result of the five algorithms

Problem	Task	MT-MFEA	MTES	EMaTOMKT	MFEA	SOO
CI+HS	T1	**0.00E+00**	1.20E−03(−)	1.05E−02(−)	3.56E−01(−)	1.70E−01(−)
	T2	**0.00E+00**	3.08E+01(−)	7.12E+01(−)	1.88E+02(−)	3.32E+02(−)
CI+MS	T1	**8.88E−16**	3.27E−01(−)	7.82E−01(−)	4.73E+00(−)	3.43E+00(−)
	T2	**0.00E+00**	4.08E+01(−)	8.14E+01(−)	2.20E+02(−)	3.08E+02(−)
CI+LS	T1	**7.70E−14**	2.00E+01(−)	2.01E+01(−)	2.02E+01(−)	2.11E+01(−)
	T2	**6.36E−04**	9.49E+03(−)	3.29E+03(−)	3.84E+03(−)	2.93E+03(+)
PI+HS	T1	**0.00E+00**	3.06E+01(−)	1.29E+02(−)	5.77E+02(−)	3.06E+02(−)
	T2	8.81E−05	**0.00E+00(+)**	8.72E−08(−)	8.69E+00(−)	1.82E+00(−)
PI+MS	T1	**5.17E−05**	5.76E−02(−)	3.99E−01(−)	3.84E+00(−)	3.33E+00(−)
	T2	**5.51E−07**	5.04E+01(−)	1.42E+02(−)	7.28E+02(−)	1.06E+03(−)
PI+LS	T1	**8.88E−16**	2.81E+00(−)	1.11E−05(−)	2.01E+01(−)	3.34E+00(−)
	T2	**−1.99E−18**	6.63E+00(−)	9.90E+00(−)	2.12E+01(−)	1.24E+01(−)
NI+HS	T1	**2.96E−04**	4.25E+01(−)	2.95E+02(−)	8.07E+02(−)	9.32E+02(−)
	T2	**0.00E+00**	3.07E+01(−)	8.19E+01(−)	2.68E+02(−)	3.22E+02(−)
NI+MS	T1	**0.00E+00**	9.76E−02(−)	8.68E−03(−)	4.23E−01(−)	1.59E−01(−)
	T2	**−3.98E−18**	5.78E+00(−)	1.64E+01(−)	2.68E+01(−)	3.76E+01(−)
NI+LS	T1	**0.00E+00**	4.85E+03(−)	1.32E+02(−)	6.12E+02(−)	3.35E+02(−)
	T2	**9.83E+02**	1.33E+04(−)	3.13E+03(+)	3.63E+03(−)	3.03E+03(−)
Summary(−/=/+)		—	(17/0/1)	(18/0/0)	(18/0/0)	(18/0/0)

in 17 out of 18 tasks. The last row of Table 2 further indicates that the number of '−' is significantly more than the number of '+', confirming the advanced nature of MT-MFEA compared to the other listed algorithms. The corresponding observations and analyses are as follows.

1. Test instances 1 and 2 are the easier problems in the test suite, and according to Table 2, MT-MFEA outperforms other algorithms in these test instances. While MFEA and SOO exhibit comparable results, MTES and EMATOMKT demonstrate superior performance over MFEA and SOO. These findings suggest that genetic communication between tasks is crucial in population evolution and that employing a model knowledge transfer strategy improves the transferability of knowledge. However, random genetic transfer in MFEA may lead to negative transfer and poor search performance. To mitigate this, while externally exploiting genetic information, MT-MFEA and EMATOMKT filter the most beneficial information by offsetting the mean of cluster models and choosing highly similar tasks using the maximum mean discrepancy, respectively. Additionally, the cluster model strategy accelerates convergence and significantly improves search efficiency.
2. The superiority of the proposed MT-MFEA over other algorithms becomes clearly evident in test instances 3 and 4, where the global optima are located in disparate positions. These outcomes accentuate the impact of discrepancies in global optimal positions on transfer efficiency and demonstrate the effectiveness of the approach in eliminating disparities and enhancing search

performance. The high reliability of MT-MFEA stems from the measure of compensating the location of clustering models, which mitigates negative transfer and obtains higher-quality information for transfer. MTES outperforms in test instance 4 because of its exceptional method of accelerating convergence. This method employs an enhanced version of the standard gradient descent updates, incorporating a multi-task interaction term to significantly expedite convergence and enhance searchability.

3. The proposed MT-MFEA achieves better performance in problem test instances that overlap partially with medium and low similarity. Despite the greater complexity of these optimization problems, the clustering model strategy is employed to accelerate convergence remarkably. Furthermore, the local optimum escaping strategy significantly improves population diversity, increasing the likelihood of finding global optima. Furthermore, the MTES and EMATOMKT algorithms demonstrate better searchability compared to MFEA and SOO, highlighting the superiority of their distinct population evolution measures in uncovering the most optimal solutions.

4. MT-MFEA outperforms other paradigms in the most challenging problem test instances (sets 7, 8, and 9) due to its superior strategies, including building clustering models, utilizing transfer learning, and implementing measures to escape local optima.

In summary, MT-MFEA exhibits superior performance compared to other comparison approaches owing to its unique strategies. The clustering model-building strategy summarizes the population distribution to steer the search process and distinguishes itself from the traditional transfer of genetic information among tasks. Furthermore, the model knowledge transfer strategy allows transfer learning, improves efficiency, and improves the acquisition of high-quality solutions. The local optimum escaping strategy improves population diversity and elevates the probability of finding the global optimum.

4   Conclusion

This paper presents a pioneering evolutionary algorithm, called MT-MFEA for solving single-objective multitask optimization problems using clustering models, model knowledge transfer, and the method of escaping the local optimum. The clustering model strategy clusters the population and builds models using the DBSCAN algorithm, which accelerates the speed of convergence significantly. The model knowledge transfer strategy involves transferring information about the population's distribution to eliminate hindrances in tackling similar tasks and bolster the quality of solutions significantly. Additionally, a local optimum escaping strategy generates diverse genetic knowledge for more feasible solutions. The comparative study of MT-MFEA against other algorithms solidly demonstrates its superior efficacy. Nevertheless, it is necessary to elevate transfer learning approaches and explore their potential more deeply and comprehensively. More potent forms of transfer learning must be developed and integrated into optimized problems to deliver more comprehensive knowledge sharing among tasks.

References

1. Gupta, A., Ong, Y.-S., Feng, L.: Multifactorial evolution: toward evolutionary multitasking (2015)
2. Ong, Y.-S., Gupta, A.: Evolutionary multitasking: a computer science view of cognitive multitasking (2016)
3. Bai, L., Lin, W., Gupta, A., Ong, Y.-S.: From multitask gradient descent to gradient-free evolutionary multitasking: a proof of faster convergence (2021)
4. Ding, J., Yang, C., Jin, Y., Chai, T.: Generalized multitasking for evolutionary optimization of expensive problems (2017)
5. Tang, J., Chen, Y., Deng, Z., Xiang, Y., Joy, C.P.: A group-based approach to improve multifactorial evolutionary algorithm. In: IJCAI (2018)
6. Bali, K.K., Gupta, A., Feng, L., Ong, Y.S., Siew, T.P.: Linearized domain adaptation in evolutionary multitasking. In: 2017 IEEE Congress on Evolutionary Computation (CEC) (2017)
7. Ma, X., Chen, Q., Yu, Y., Sun, Y., Ma, L., Zhu, Z.: A two-level transfer learning algorithm for evolutionary multitasking (2020)
8. Liaw, R.-T., Ting, C.-K.: Evolutionary many-tasking based on biocoenosis through symbiosis: a framework and benchmark problems. In: 2017 IEEE Congress on Evolutionary Computation (CEC) (2017)
9. Zhang, X., Tian, Y., Cheng, R., Jin, Y.: A decision variable clustering-based evolutionary algorithm for large-scale many-objective optimization (2016)
10. Ester, M., Kriegel, H.-P., Sander, J., Xu, X., et al.: A density-based algorithm for discovering clusters in large spatial databases with noise. In: KDD (1996)
11. Liang, Z., Xu, X., Liu, L., Tu, Y., Zhu, Z.: Evolutionary many-task optimization based on multisource knowledge transfer (2021)
12. Da, B., et al.: Evolutionary multitasking for single-objective continuous optimization: benchmark problems, performance metric, and baseline results (2017)
13. Deb, K., Agrawal, R.B., et al.: Simulated binary crossover for continuous search space (1995)

Knowledge Leadership, AI Technology Adoption and Big Data Application Ability

Siqi Zhu[1], Ping He[1], Jianming Zhou[1(✉)], and Peng Zhang[2]

[1] School of Business Administration, Guangdong University of Finance and Economics, Luntou Road. 21, Guangzhou 510320, People's Republic of China
jmzhou@gdufe.edu.cn
[2] Department of Science and Technology, Guangdong Mechanical and Electrical Polytechnic, Chanchushi East Road. 2, Guangzhou 510515, People's Republic of China

Abstract. This paper examined the relationship between knowledge leadership and R&D team's big data application ability with testing the mediating role of artificial intelligence (AI) technology adoption, and took 113 R&D teams as study samples from 42 Guangzhou enterprises. The structural equation modeling (SEM) test results found that (1) supervisor's knowledge leadership can help R&D team adopting AI technology, improve big data application ability including big data decision-making ability and big data control ability directly; (2) AI technology adoption can improve R&D team's big data application ability including big data decision-making ability and big data control ability directly, and mediates the relationship between supervisor's knowledge leadership and R&D team's big data application ability including big data decision-making ability and big data control ability significantly.

Keywords: Knowledge Leadership · AI Technology Adoption · Big Data Application Ability

1 Introduction

With the new round of technological revolution, the digital economy with new information technology as the core is booming, constantly giving birth to new industries, and has become a new engine for China's economic development [1]. Hence, for enterprises in the era of digital economy, in order to catch up with the trend of digital economy, it is very important to use data reasonably. Data has replaced traditional production factors such as land, labor and capital, and has become a brand new production factor [2].

Tao et al. pointed out that the essence of big data application is to realize value creation through big data, that is, to use relevant methods and tools to analyze stored big data, so as to provide support for R&D, production, service, management and decision-making [3]. Bharadwaj et al. defined big data application ability as the capability of an enterprise to use big data technology to capture, store, clean and transform massive amounts of data by integrating internal and external resources [4]. Wamba et al. defined it from perspective of IT capabilities; it is believed that big data application ability is the extension of IT capabilities [5].

However, the current research on big data application ability is still in its infancy, mainly focusing on the impact of big data applications on specific operational practices and corporate performance [6], and most empirical studies regard big data application ability as an antecedent variable. Few studies take big data application ability as outcome factor, and study its influencing factors from the perspective of knowledge and team management.

Therefore, this paper takes 113 R&D teams from 42 enterprises in Guangdong as the research samples to understand whether and how the R&D team supervisor's knowledge leadership improves R&D team's big data application ability through enhancing AI technology adoption, and provides enterprises new approaches to adapt to the digital economy era.

2 Literatures Review and Research Hypotheses

Skyrme first proposed the concept of knowledge leadership, and believed that knowledge leadership can deeply understand knowledge workers and provide high support for the knowledge behavior of knowledge work [7]. Based on previous research, Vitala divided knowledge leadership into four dimensions: learning orientation, creating an atmosphere that supports learning, supporting individual and team-level learning, and playing a role model, providing tools for the measurement of knowledge leadership [8]. Moreover, many scholars agree that knowledge leadership can effectively promote the acquisition, absorption, transformation and application of internal and external knowledge by team members [9, 10]. That is to say, the knowledge leadership implemented by the head of the R&D team can create a good atmosphere for knowledge sharing and acquisition. After the relevant data knowledge is circulated, the knowledge base of each member of the team is enriched, and with the support of sufficient knowledge, they can quickly got help to improve the ability of big data applications including big data decision-making ability and big data control ability of the AI R&D team. Based on this, this paper proposes the following research hypotheses:

H1a: Knowledge leadership is positively related to R&D team's big data decision-making ability.

H1b: Knowledge leadership is positively related to R&D team's big data control ability.

The connotation understanding of AI technology adoption should be based on the understanding of AI technology and technology adoption. AI technology is a technology that can correctly interpret external data, learn from it, and flexibly use the learned content to achieve specific goals and tasks [11]. Technology adoption originated from related research on information technology adoption, Cheung et al. define it as the process by which an individual or organization uses a technology purposefully [12]. On this basis, Li and Tao defined the AI technology adoption from the organizational level and the individual level, and believed that AI technology adoption at the organizational level means that the organization realizes the advantages of AI technology and begins to obtain resources [13]. The knowledge leadership method adopted by the R&D team leader can reflect the emphasis on knowledge and technology, and at the same time pass this awareness to many members of the team, and the AI related knowledge circulating in the team is just the required resource support. Based on this, this paper proposes the following hypotheses:

H2: Knowledge leadership is positively related to AI technology adoption.

Information technology can be divided into computer technology, communication technology and sensor technology, and the most popular computer technology also includes a branch of technology closely related to big data, namely AI technology [14]. In other words, the relationship between AI and big data is very close. Specifically, with the rapid application and popularization of AI, algorithms such as deep learning and reinforcement learning are continuously optimized. Algorithms make a large amount of data valuable, and also help the R&D team to improve their big data application ability. Secondly, AI intelligently promotes the deepening of big data applications. In the industry, AI is inseparable from big data, and many applications of big data can be attributed to AI. Based on this, this paper proposes the following hypotheses:

H3a: AI technology adoption is positively related to R&D team's big data decision-making ability.

H3b: AI technology adoption is positively related to R&D team's big data control ability.

Combined by the proposes of H1a through H3b, and the mediating effect principle of Baron and Kenny [15], this paper proposes the following hypotheses:

H4a: AI technology adoption mediates the relationship between knowledge leadership and R&D team's big data decision-making ability.

H4b: AI technology adoption mediates the relationship between knowledge leadership and R&D team's big data control ability.

3   Research Design

3.1   Research Framework

According to literature review, the research framework is presented in Fig. 1.

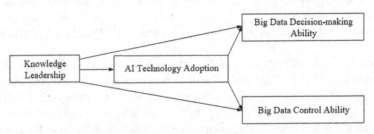

Fig. 1. The research framework

3.2 Measurement

A five-point Likert scale was used for empirical study in this paper. The measuring scale of knowledge leadership (KL) was used from Yang and You which had 5 items [16]. The measuring scale of AI technology adoption (AITA) was used from Davis which had 3 items [17]. The measuring scale of big data application ability (BDAA) was development from Xu et al. which had 2 dimensions including big data decision-making ability (BDDA) and big data control ability (BDCA) with 3 items respectively [6].

3.3 Sampling

The research samples are 113 AI product R&D teams from 42 enterprises in Guangdong Province of China. We sent out 150 questionnaires to 150 AI product R&D teams and got 124 returned with 113 were valid. The questionnaire recovery rate is 75.3%. Among them, there are 16 AI product teams in education, 9 AI product teams in retail, 12 AI product teams in security, 11 AI product teams in finance, 11 AI product teams in medical, 14 AI product teams in transportation, 31 AI product teams in industrial robot, and 9 AI product teams in others. Most of the AI R&D team supervisors are well educated with master and doctoral degree (83.2%).

4 Data Analysis

4.1 Reliability and Validity Analysis

Cronbach's α test was done by SPSS19.0 to guarantee the reliability of measuring scale. The test results was presented in Table 1 and indicated that all Cronbach's α value were higher than the standard value of 0.7, suggesting that the measuring scales of knowledge leadership, AI technology adoption, big data decision-making ability and big data control ability have good reliability.

Table 1. Coefficient of Cronbach's α

Variables	α value
Knowledge leadership	0.81
AI technology adoption	0.81
Big data decision-making ability	0.89
Big data control ability	0.90

And the validity test of knowledge leadership, AI technology adoption, big data decision-making ability and big data control ability was used CFA method. The test results showed in Table 2 indicated that the four-factor model fitness was considerably better than any of the alternative models, suggesting that all the scales of knowledge leadership, AI technology adoption, big data decision-making ability and big data control ability have good validity.

Table 2. CFA Results for validity analyzing

Model	Factors	CFI	TLI	RMSEA	$\chi 2/df$
Four-factor	KL, AITA, BDDA, BDCA	0.977	0.970	0.049	1.274
Three-factor -1	KL, AITA + BDDA, BDCA	0.885	0.859	0.108	2.296
Three-factor -2	KL + AITA, BDDA, BDCA	0.877	0.849	0.111	2.388
Three-factor -3	KL + BDCA, AITA, BDDA	0.779	0.728	0.149	3.502
One-factor	KL + AITA + BDDA + BDCA	0.582	0.506	0.201	5.546

4.2 Test of Overall Theoretical Model

Chen & Zhou believed that the overall model fitness of SEM should be reported from 3 aspects including absolute fitness, asymptotic fitness and summarized fitness [18]. Table 3 presented analyzing results of the direct and indirect SEM fitness. It can be seen that most of the indicators were at the accepted level.

Table 3. The overall model fitness results of direct and indirect SEM

Overall model fitness		Ideal criteria	Accepted criteria	Direct SEM	Indirect SEM
Absolute fitness	GFI	≥0.90	≥0.80	0.924	0.909
	RMR	≤0.05	≤0.08	0.087	0.040
	RMSEA	≤0.08	≤1.00	0.057	0.049
Asymptotic fitness	AGFI	≥0.90	≥0.80	0.879	0.867
	RFI	≥0.90	≥0.80	0.887	0.875
	NFI	≥0.90	≥0.80	0.914	0.901
	CFI	≥0.90	≥0.80	0.975	0.977
Summarized fitness	$\chi 2/df$	1.00 ~ 2.00	2.00 ~ 3.00	1.364	1.273
	PNFI	≥0.50	≥0.50	0.698	0.713
	PGFI	≥0.50	≥0.50	0.588	0.623
	AIC	<Satu. AIC (157)	<Indp. AIC (210)	687.146	956.038

4.3 Test of Hypothesis

Test results of hypothesis sum up from direct and indirect SEM model can be seen in Table 4. In this paper, H1a, H1b, H2, H3a, H3b, H4a and H4b were supported.

Table 4. Path coefficient and hypothesis test results

Paths	Estimate	P-value	Hyp	Result
KL → BDDA	0.372**	0.002	H1a	√
KL → BDCA	0.322**	0.005	H1b	√
KL → AITA	0.627**	0.000	H2	√
AITA → BDDA	0.768**	0.000	H3a	√
AITA → BDCA	0.745**	0.000	H3b	√

Notes: * Significant at P < 0.05; ** Significant at P < 0.01;

The direct and indirect SEM model with path coefficient can be seen in Fig. 2 and Fig. 3.

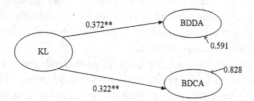

Fig. 2. The direct model with path coefficient

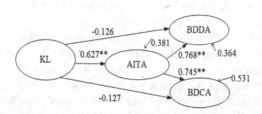

Fig. 3. The indirect model with path coefficient

The results in Fig. 2 and Fig. 3 suggested that when the direct SEM model was added with AI technology adoption, the direct effect of knowledge leadership on R&D team's big data application ability including big data decision-making ability and big data control ability became insignificant. According to the theory of Baron and Kenny [15], it suggested that AI technology adoption was likely to play mediating role between knowledge leadership and R&D team's big data application ability including big data decision-making ability and big data control ability.

In order to test the mediating effect, we used bootstrap methods recommended by Hayes to make further analysis [19]. Bootstrapping results in Table 5 showed that the indirect effect of AI technology adoption on big data decision-making ability and big data control ability were 0.459 and 0.410, between 95% confident interval of [0.321, 0.706] and [0.235, 0.587]. As 95% confident interval of AI technology adoption on big data decision-making ability and big data control ability both include no zero, it showed that the indirect effect of AI technology adoption were significant. Thus, H4a and H4b were supported.

Table 5. Bootstrap testing results for the mediating effect of AI knowledge transfer

Direct path	Indirect path	Mediating effect	95% confident interval
KL → BDDA	KL → AITA → BDDA	0.459	[0.321, 0.706]
KL → BDCA	KL → AITA → BDCA	0.410	[0.235, 0.587]

5   Conclusions and Discussion

This paper studies how R&D team supervisor's knowledge leadership can help increasing R&D team's big data application ability through improving AI technology adoption with samples of 113 AI product R&D teams from 42 in Guangdong Province. The conclusions have theoretical and practical significance.

First of all, this study confirmed that knowledge leadership was a variable with significant predictive power. It will significantly improve R&D team's big data application ability, and it will help the R&D team realize the important role of big data application and take action to obtain resources. Therefore, in order to better apply big data to create value for enterprises, personnel with knowledge leadership style should be selected as the supervisor of the R&D team as much as possible to meet the requirements of technical managers in the era of digital economy.

Second, this study confirmed that the AI technology adoption by the R&D team will significantly improve the big data application ability. This showed that through the extensive application of AI technology in the R&D team, the entire R&D team has a better understanding of AI technology and is more skilled in using it, so the big data application ability of the entire R&D team will be stronger. Therefore, enterprises should build a harmonious atmosphere for knowledge sharing, promote the effective dissemination of AI-related technical knowledge within the R&D team, and be actively adopted by team members. In addition, an effective knowledge transfer management mechanism can also help AI technology to be better adopted and promote the big data application ability of R&D teams.

Finally, the empirical research in this paper showed that AI technology adoption played a significant mediating role in the relationship between R&D team supervisor's knowledge leadership and big data application ability including big data decision-making ability and big data control ability. This research result revealed the "black box" between the R&D team's knowledge leadership and big data application ability, indicating that knowledge leadership can help R&D teams better adopt AI technology to improve the R&D team's big data application ability including big data decision-making ability and big data control ability. This conclusion was of great significance for our in-depth understanding of the positive process of knowledge leadership, and it also provided a reliable path for improving the big data application ability.

Acknowledgments. This work was supported by Guangdong Soft Science Project (Grant No. 2020A1010020045), Innovative Team Project of Guangdong Universities (Grant No. 2019WCXTD008), Guangzhou Science & Technology Plan Project (Grant No. 202102080243), and Guangdong Provincial Philosophy and Social Science Project (Grant No. GD23YGL10).

References

1. Gregory, V.: Understanding digital transformation: a review and a research agenda. J. Strat. Inf. Syst. **28**(2), 118–144 (2019)
2. Xu, X.C., Zhang, M.H.: Research on the measurement and calculation of China's digital economy-based on the perspective of international comparison. China Ind. Econ. **5**, 23–41 (2000)
3. Tao, X.L., Liu, S., Zhong, Y.R., et al.: The co-evolution of big data application and enterprise open innovation-a comparative case study based on grounded theory. Sci. Technol. Prog. Countermeasures **38**(5), 69–78 (2021)
4. Bharadwaj, A., Sawy, O., Pavlou, P.A., et al.: Digital business strategy: toward a next generation of insights. MIS Q. **37**(2), 471–482 (2013)
5. Wamba, S.F., Akter, S., Edwards, A., et al.: How 'big data' can make big impact: findings from a systematic review and a longitudinal case study. Int. J. Prod. Econ. **165**, 234–246 (2015)
6. Xu, F., Tian, M., Xu, G.H.: Research on the impact of big data application ability on enterprise innovation performance-the intermediary effect of supply chain collaboration and the moderating effect of strategic matching. Macroecon. Res. **3**, 101–119 (2020)
7. Skyrme, D.: Developing a Knowledge Strategy: From Management to Leadership. MIT Press, Cambridge (2000)
8. Vitala, R.: Towards knowledge leadership. Leadersh. Org. Dev. J. **25**(6), 528–544 (2004)
9. Yang, Y., You, D.M.: Measuring and testing the content structure of enterprise knowledge leadership. Stat. Decis. Mak. **22**, 84–87 (2013)
10. Zhou, J.M., Chen, M., Liu, Y.F.: Analysis on the relationship between knowledge leadership, team knowledge sharing and product innovation performance. Enterp. Econ. **9**, 120–125 (2015)
11. Kaplan, A., Haenlein, M.: Siri, Siri, in my hand: who's the fairest in the land? On the interpretations, illustrations, and implications of artificial intelligence. Bus. Horiz. **62**(1), 15–25 (2019)
12. Cheung, C.M.K., Lee, M.K.O., Rabjohn, N.: The impact of electronic word-of-mouth- the adoption of online opinions in online customer communities. Internet Res. **18**(3), 229–247 (2008)
13. Li, Y.P., Tao, N.N.: Multi-level dynamic impact model of employee artificial intelligence technology adoption: a literature review. China Hum. Resour. Dev. **39**(1), 35–56 (2022)
14. Xu, Y.J., Wang, P.: Does big data mean big wisdom also on 'Green Artificial Intelligence' as a new direction of information technology development. Acad. Res. **10**, 28–35 (2016)
15. Baron, R.M., Kenny, D.A.: The moderator-mediator variable distinction in social psychological research: conceptual, strategic, and statistical considerations. J. Pers. Soc. Psychol. **51**(6), 1173–1182 (1986)
16. Yang, Yi., You, D.M.: Measurement and inspection of enterprise knowledge leadership content structure. Stat. Decis. **22**, 86–89 (2013)
17. Davis, F.D.: Perceived usefulness, perceived ease of use, and user acceptance of information technology. MIS Q. **13**(3), 319–340 (1989)

18. Chen, M., Zhou, J.M.: The impact of enterprise culture and knowledge integration mechanism on knowledge transfer performance among enterprises. Stud. Sci. Sci. **4**, 102–109 (2009)
19. Hayes, A.F.: An Introduction to Mediation, Moderation and Conditional Process Analysis: A Regression-Based Approach. Guilford Press, New York (2013)

RFLSem: A Lightweight Model for Textual Sentiment Analysis

Bo Yang[1,2], Jiayi Dang[1], Huai Liu[3], and Zhi Jin[4,5(✉)]

[1] School of Information Science, Beijing Forestry University, Beijing, China
yangbo@bjfu.edu.cn
[2] Engineering Research Center
for Forestry Oriented Intelligent Information Processing, National Forestry
and Grassland Administration, Beijing 100083, China
[3] Department of Computer Science and Software Engineering,
Swinburne University of Technology, Hawthorn VIC 3122, Australia
hliu@swin.edu.au
[4] Key Laboratory of High Confidence Software Technologies,
Peking University, Ministry of Education, Beijing 100871, China
[5] Institute of Software, School of Computer Science, Peking University,
Beijing 100871, China
zhijin@pku.edu.cn

Abstract. In the current Internet age, lots of emotions are being expressed and recorded in various recommender systems, including the public reviews of movies and restaurants as well as those on social media such as Twitter and Weibo. Accordingly, sentiment analysis has become a main research topic in the WWW community. Currently, deep learning (DL)-based sentiment analysis is the most promising research trend in this context. However, DL-based sentiment analysis methods are still confronted with great challenges, such as controversial robustness and the difficulty in reproducing in the face of the analysis of sentiment classification and sentiment score. In this paper, we propose RFLSem, a text-based lightweight sentiment analysis model that uniformly considers the difference between sentiment classification and sentiment score, the robustness of the sentiment analysis model, and the reproducibility problem in the sentiment analysis process. Large-scale experiments have been conducted on script datasets in both Chinese and English, including Chinese and English screenplay datasets as well as IMDB and SST datasets. The experimental results demonstrate that RFLSem can achieve better results than state-of-the-art sentiment analysis techniques.

Keywords: Sentiment Analysis · Recommender Systems · Pre-trained Model · Deep Learning

1 Introduction

Sentiment analysis has been widely used in human daily lives. For example, on Amazon, Tmall, and Taobao, there will be user reviews, and the system will analyze the review information with user emotions to further recommend products. Therefore, how to accurately perform sentiment analysis is valuable research work in recommender systems.

Currently, there are three main categories of methods for sentiment analysis, including the traditional approaches based on sentiment dictionary, machine learning (ML)-based techniques, and deep learning (DL)-based methods. The method based on traditional sentiment analysis is the classification of text sentiment based on the emotion dictionary, which carries out the simplest simulation through human memory and judgment. For example, Han et al. [6] used a SentiWordNet-based sentiment classifier to score the dataset and extracted some emotional words in positive and negative comments according to the sentiment score to train and generate domain sentiment dictionaries. Fiaidhi et al. [5] categorized text using two sentiment dictionaries, including Opinion Lexicon and Dadvar Lexicon. Chakravarthi et al. [3] To overcome the limitations of a single-language dictionary, created a gold-standard Tamil-English encoded mixed, emotionally annotated corpus containing 15,744 review articles from YouTube.

ML-based techniques first use the data with sentiment labels to train an emotion classifier and then predict the affective tendency of new sentences in the test set. Uddin et al. [26] developed Sentisead, a surveillance tool that uses polar labels and word packs as features. Huq et al. [7] used K-Nearest Neighbor (KNN) and SVM to identify the emotional polarity of Twitter text.

DL-based methods are mainly based on deep neural networks, the most representative of which are: Convolutional Neural Networks (CNN), Recurrent Neural Networks (RNN), long short-term memory (LSTM), etc. For instance, Ouyang et al. [17] proposed a structure based on Word2vec recommended by Google and used it to build a suitable CNN framework through sentiment analysis. Liu et al. [13] proposed a Roberta model with better performance using dynamic masking. Zhang et al. [32] introduced the ERNIE2.0 model and adopt the concept of continuous multi-task learning, and added a series of tasks with a granularity from coarse to fine (which can be considered as different loss functions). In addition, Onan [15] combined the LSTM with the notation based on the GloVe word embedding scheme to achieve the highest prediction performance on the MOOC review dataset, with a classification accuracy of 95.80%.

However, it is difficult to obtain the semantics existing between sentiment data based on traditional sentiment dictionaries and ML-based sentiment analysis methods. In the DL-based methods, there are a lack of detailed analysis of the downstream tasks of sentiment analysis, and the current better sentiment analysis method is generally to directly use the pre-trained model and then use the classification layer to process it. However, when the downstream task expects not only the result of sentiment classification but also a certain sentiment score, the use of the original method will bring a large score error. In addition, for the general pre-training model because of the randomness of the parameters during training, the model trained in the general domain is sometimes difficult to reproduce when it is specifically applied to downstream tasks. In addition, the robustness of the model in the process of using the pre-training model is also a problem to consider.

To this end, we propose a lightweight model, namely RFLSem, which mainly uses random seed, FGM confrontation, and linear layer to further improve the performance of Sentiment analysis. The contribution of the paper is three-fold, as summarised in the following:

- A lightweight sentiment analysis model RFLSem is proposed, which not only makes use of the good performance of the pre-trained model, but also performs optimized strategy in three aspects: random seed, FGM confrontation, and linear layer.
- RFLSem and a variety of typical methods are not only applied to English datasets, but also to Chinese datasets. RFLSem achieved good results on datasets in both languages.
- The proposed RFLSem model is implemented and evaluated on 4 datasers and 12 classical methods. The experimental result shows that our approach can obtain higher performance than state-of-art techniques.

The rest of this paper is organised as follows. RFLSem is described in Sect. 2. Section 3 presents the experiments for evaluating RFLSem, the results of which are reported in Sect. 4. Section 5 presents the related work. Finally, we conclude this paper in Sect. 6.

2 Methodology

2.1 RFLSem Model

The overall network structure of the RFLSem model is shown in Fig. 1. The model includes six parts: input, data encoding, FGM adversarial, transformer with random seed added, and linear output.

Firstly, the model performs word segmentation processing on the training set of the data. The model then vectorizes the data after the participle. Next, to increase the robustness of the model, we add FGM adversarial training to the model. Secondly, we will group the data (max_len = 256, batchsize = 16), and each record of each set of data will learn through the 12-layer Transformer Encoder in turn to obtain the classification result vector.

Finally, we add a linear regression layer to transform the classification task into a linear regression task. For the continuous values of the output, we classify it by determining the maximum component of the fitted output. To realize the reproducibility of model data and reduce the randomness of the algorithm, we add random seeds for fixation.

2.2 Data Encoder with FGM

The input mechanism of the model in the experiment is shown in Part A in Fig. 1. The input vector is summed by three different Embeddings, including text vectors, text vectors, and position vectors, and uses them as input to a pattern. Specifically, English data require a subdivision of English words into smaller semantic units. For example: divide words into straw and berries. However, in terms of Chinese, we have not yet segmented the input text, and only treat individual words as the basic unit of text.

For the input text $X(x_i|i = 1, 2..., T)$, the corresponding classification result is Z. We pass the word through the tokenizer of the model. Then, we add FGM for data confrontation, introduce noise training samples, and increase perturbation to the samples. The calculation formula is as follows:

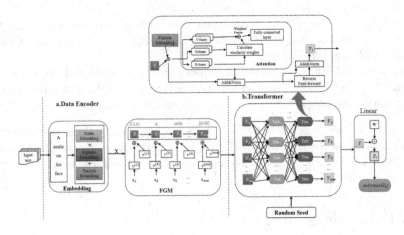

Fig. 1. The RFLSem model

$$g = \nabla_x L(\theta, x, y) \tag{1}$$

$$r_{adv} = \varepsilon \bullet g/\|g\|_2 \tag{2}$$

$$x_{adv} = x + r_{adv} \tag{3}$$

where ε is hyperparameter, the default value is 1.0.

2.3   Transformer with Random Seed

The RFLSem model uses a transformer structure, in which the main body is stacked with 12 Transformer Encoder structures. Each Transformer Encoder consists of a multi-headed self-attention mechanism layer and a forward fully linked layer. Transformer Encoder adds three more operations on top of Multi-head Self-Attention, namely Residual Connection, Layer Normalization, and Linear Transformation. The Residual Connection directly adds the inputs and outputs of the model group to the final output. In this way, the network will be much simpler. Layer normalization uses the 0-mean-1 variance method to normalize a certain layer of neural network nodes. To improve the expressiveness of the overall model, a linear transformation is required to perform two linear transformations on the semantic vector of each word. Therefore, the converted vector is the same length as the original vector.

The multi-head attention mechanism layer maps Q, K, V, and other information through the parameter matrix, and then performs a self-attention operation. Eventually, combine this data into a complete link layer. In this model, the weighting of each value is calculated by the similarity function of the query and corresponding key. The mathematical calculation formula corresponds as follows:

$$Attention(Q, K, V) = \text{softmax}(\frac{QK^T}{\sqrt{d_K}}V) \tag{4}$$

The multi-head self-attention layer is to map the Q, K, and V parameters of a single layer through the parameter matrix accordingly, and then does self-attention. Then, the results are spliced and finally output through a fully connected layer. The mathematical calculation formula corresponds as follows:

$$MultiHead(Q, K, V) = \text{Concat}(head_1, \ldots, head_h)\, W^O \tag{5}$$

$$head_i = \text{Attention}\left(QW_i^Q, KW_i^K, VW_i^V\right) \tag{6}$$

where $W_i^Q \in R^{d_{model} \times d_Q}, W_i^K \in R^{d_{model} \times d_K}, W_i^V \in R^{d_{model} \times d_V}, W_i^O \in R^{d_{model} \times h d_V}$

The feedforward fully connected layer module consists of two linear transformation modules, with a Relu activation function in the middle, and the corresponding mathematical formula form is as follows:

$$FFN(x) = \max(0, xW_1 + b_1)\, W_2 + b_2 \tag{7}$$

For each random parameter in the model, we use the linear congruence method to generate random seeds, and the linear congruence method (LCG) is used to generate pseudo-random numbers. The formula for generating LCG is:

$$RandSeed = (A * RandSeed + B) \tag{8}$$

The most important of the linear congruence method is three integers, the multiplier A, the delta B, and the modulus M. Where A, B, and M are constants set by the generator. The maximum period of LCG is set to M (generally less than M). And, A, B, M meet the following setting conditions: B and M comatter; Any prime factor of M is divisible by A-1; If M is a multiple of 4, then so is A-1; Both A and B are positive integers smaller than M.

2.4 Adding Linear Layer

The output of the model body is added to the previous linear layer for regression calculation. The purpose of this operation is to transform the classification task into a linear regression task, that is, logical classification. For continuous values of the output, we classify by determining the maximum component of the fitted output. This can make it convenient to obtain the sentiment value of specific sentiment classification according to the specific requirements of downstream tasks. In addition, we add the Dropout function to prevent overfitting, and the linear regression calculation formula is as follows:

$$z_i = y_i \bullet w + b \tag{9}$$

where y_i is the vector output of the model. Finally, we can calculate the classification result by the following formula.

$$Z_i = \text{softmax}\,(z_i) \tag{10}$$

3 Experiments

3.1 Research Questions

Our experiments were particularly designed to answer the following four research questions:

- **RQ1:** Is RFLSem more effective than the existing traditional methods such as: GRU, RNN, LSTM, etc.?
- **RQ2:** Is RFLSem more effective than existing typical pre-trained models?
- **RQ3:** How effective RFLSem compares to typical pre-trained models after optimization?
- **RQ4:** How effective it is for the three core model components in RFLSem?

3.2 Subjects Under Study

The experiment uses four datasets, which as shown in Table 1. They are the Chinese dataset[1] (CData), English dataset[2] (EData), IMDB dataset[3] and Stanford Sentiment Treebank[4] (SST).

The Chinese dataset is six classification data of love, happiness, shock, anger, fear, and sorrow, including a training set of 36782 data and a test set of 21376 records. The English dataset comes from the open source dataset on the Kaggle platform, each record describes the words of a character, and the sentiment is classified into two categories, 0 represents negative emotions, 1 represents positive emotions, and contains a training set of 40000 data and a test set of 20000 records.

The IMDB dataset is a film review dataset containing 5043 movies with 28 different columns, each column describing different information about the movie, and each record representing a film review. In the experiment, we only used the review and sentiment columns in it, the training set containing 40,000 data, and the test set with 10,000 records.

SST is a standard sentiment dataset, used for sentiment classification, where each node of the sentence analysis tree has fine-grained sentiment annotations. The sentiment values correspond to the categories: [0, 0.2], (0.2, 0.4], (0.4, 0.6], (0.6, 0.8], (0.8, 1.0] correspond to five categories of emotions, which we process and divide into five results: 0, 1, 2, 3, and 4. The training set contains 8454 pieces of data and the test set of 2200 records.

---

[1] https://www.datafountain.cn/competitions/518.
[2] https://www.kaggle.com/datasets/lowoncuties/czech-movie-review-csfd.
[3] https://www.kaggle.com/datasets/lakshmi25npathi/imdb-dataset-of-50k-movie-reviews.
[4] https://nlp.stanford.edu/sentiment/code.htm.

Table 1. Statistics of the dataset

Name	Training set	Testing set	Categories
CData	36782	21376	6
EData	40000	20000	2
IMDB	40000	10000	2
SST	8454	2200	5

3.3 Variables

Independent Variables – Methods Under Comparison. The independent variable in our study is mainly about the methods to be evaluated and compared. Our proposed approach, by nature, was selected in the study. As discussed above, two types of connected graphs (Noun-based and Verb-based) are used in this study. Thus, two variants of our approach, namely RFLSem-Noun and RFLSem-Verb, would be evaluated in the experiments.

For comparison, we also chose 12 baseline techniques (six for RQ1 and six for RQ2), as described in the following. For RQ1, we selected six traditional sentiment analysis tools StandfordCoreNLP, Sentistrength, GRU, CNN, FNN, and Lstm+textcnn.

For RQ2, we compare the typical pre-trained models BERT[5], Roberta[6], Albert[7], XLNet[8], ERNIE[9] and GPT[10]

For RQ3, we apply the model optimization method to other pre-trained models for comparative experiments.

For RQ4, the three optimization strategies (OS) are applied separately to the model for optimization, and the optimized effect is observed.

Dependent Variables – Evaluation Metrics. For RQ1 and RQ4, we chose the *Precision, Recall, RSME* [27], *macro-F1* [16] and *micro-F1* [12] to evaluate the prediction result on test sets. Assuming a task has K classes. For a binary classification task, the *F1-score* (F1) is defined as follow:

$$F1\text{-}score = \frac{2 * precision * recall}{precision + recall} \qquad (11)$$

where $precision = \frac{TP}{TP+FP}$ and $recall = \frac{TP}{TP+FN}$, TP denotes the true positive, FP represents the false positive, and FN refers to false negative.

---

[5] https://huggingface.co/bert-base-cased/tree/main.
[6] https://huggingface.co/Roberta-base.
[7] https://huggingface.co/Albert-base-v1.
[8] https://huggingface.co/xlnet-base-cased.
[9] https://huggingface.co/nghuyong/ernie-2.0-base-en.
[10] https://huggingface.co/gpt2.

A multi-label classification task can be considered as several binary classification tasks on different labels. Based on that, assuming the task has K classes, the *macro-F1* can be defined as follow:

$$Macro\text{-}F1 = \frac{1}{K} \sum_{i=1}^{K} F1\text{-}score_i. \tag{12}$$

micro-F1 can be defined as follow, First calculate the total Precision and Recall of all categories:

$$Precision_{\text{micro}} = \frac{\sum_{i=1}^{n} \text{TP}_i}{\sum_{i=1}^{n} \text{TP}_i + \sum_{i=1}^{n} \text{FP}_i}. \tag{13}$$

$$Recall_{\text{micro}} = \frac{\sum_{i=1}^{n} \text{TP}_i}{\sum_{i=1}^{n} \text{TP}_i + \sum_{i=1}^{n} \text{FN}_i}. \tag{14}$$

$$Micro\text{-}F1 = 2 \cdot \frac{Precision_{micro} \cdot Recall_{micro}}{Precision_{micro} + Recall_{micro}}. \tag{15}$$

RMSE is the standard deviation of the residuals (prediction errors), which is a measure of how spread out these residuals are.

$$RMSE = \sqrt{\frac{\sum_{i-1}^{n} \sum_{j-1}^{n} \left(y_{i,j} - x_{i,j}\right)^2}{n}} \tag{16}$$

3.4   Parameter Settings

We conducted a comparative analysis and applied uniform epoch and learning rate parameters in RQ1 and RQ2. The epoch selected here is 4, and the learning rate is 2e−5.

4   Results and Analyses

4.1   RQ1 – Comparison with Typical Sentiment Analysis Techniques

We reproduced the six typical sentiment analysis techniques according to their original algorithm. The comparison results with our methods on Macro-F1, Micro-F1, RSME, Precision, and Recall are summarised in Table 2. It is clearly shown that RFLSem outperformed the existing typical sentiment analysis techniques in all data sets.

To further measure the magnitude of performance improvement, we analyzed the results. From the results of Table 2, we can see that the effect of the RFLSem sentiment analysis method is significantly higher than that of other traditional sentiment analysis methods. Stanford CoreNLP mainly relies on sentence structure to construct the representation of the entire sentence, performs sentiment analysis according to the sentence grammar tree, and does not integrate contextual knowledge. SentiStrength is about looking at words in isolation, giving

Table 2. Comparison with typical sentiment analysis techniques

Data	Approach	Macro-F1	Micro-F1	RSME	Precision	Recall
Movie-ch	Stanford CoreNLP	–	–	–	–	–
	SentiStrength	–	–	–	–	–
	LSTM+TextCNN	0.1421	0.7430	0.8082	0.1238	0.1667
	GRU	0.1421	0.6333	0.8088	0.1520	0.1430
	RNN	0.2402	0.7431	0.8081	0.1521	0.1433
	FNN	0.1421	0.6335	0.8083	0.1522	0.1431
	RFLSem	0.7758	0.9247	0.3553	0.8821	0.8745
Movie-en	Stanford CoreNLP	0.3333	0.3333	0.7071	0.2500	0.5000
	SentiStrength	0.6005	0.6005	0.6098	0.6768	0.6281
	LSTM+TextCNN	0.4808	0.4808	0.7078	0.4989	0.4990
	GRU	0.4920	0.4920	0.7071	0.4990	0.5001
	RNN	0.4921	0.4921	0.7070	0.5000	0.5001
	FNN	0.4806	0.4806	0.7080	0.4986	0.4988
	RFLSem	0.9620	0.9620	0.1380	0.9648	0.9549
IMDB	Stanford CoreNLP	0.3330	0.3330	0.7076	0.2496	0.5000
	SentiStrength	0.4702	0.4702	0.7026	0.5093	0.5068
	LSTM+TextCNN	0.4914	0.4914	0.7075	0.4992	0.4993
	GRU	0.5006	0.5006	0.7053	0.5027	0.5026
	RNN	0.4973	0.4973	0.7076	0.4992	0.4993
	FNN	0.4954	0.4954	0.7089	0.4974	0.4974
	RFLSem	0.9437	0.9437	0.1300	0.9438	0.9437
SST	Stanford CoreNLP	–	–	–	–	–
	SentiStrength	–	–	–	–	–
	LSTM+TextCNN	0.1676	0.2034	0.8250	0.1429	0.2061
	GRU	0.1720	0.1981	0.9300	0.1579	0.1967
	RNN	0.1275	0.1666	0.8666	0.0971	0.1872
	FNN	0.1721	0.1996	0.7488	0.1979	0.1984
	RFLSem	0.5457	0.5512	0.7567	0.5435	0.5530

positive points for positive words and negative points for negative words, and then summarizing those points, accumulating the score to judge sentence-level emotions. In this way, the order of words will be ignored and the relationship information between words will be lost. GRU, CNN, FNN, and LSTM+TextCNN all use the Bert model as a tokenizer, and then stitch on each neural network, because these traditional neural networks rely on the support of numerous training texts on the one hand, and on the other hand, the model needs to train itself, so the evaluation index score effect is not as good as the pre-training model.

In conclusion, our approach significantly improves the capability of sentiment analysis tasks compared with typical ML-based methods and DL-based methods.

4.2   RQ2 – Comparison with Classical Pre-trained Models

The experimental results of RQ2 are shown in Table 3. It can be observed from Table 3 that our approach normally achieved the best effectiveness for most data sets.

The RFLSem model structure is relatively close to BERT, Roberta, and Albert. However, compared to the models of BERT, Roberta, and Albert, RFLSem adds a linear layer that transforms the classification problem into a logical classification problem. In addition, in the process of data training, random seed and FGM confrontation are added to enhance the robustness of data and reduce the influence of data disturbance on model training.

The XLNet model is more suitable for the analysis of long texts. When the amount of data is small and the sentences involved in sentiment analysis are short, the performance of the model has not been fully reflected.

The GPT model is different from the BERT, Roberta, and ALBERT model structures, which use the transformer's Decoder structure to shield the content behind the word. In this way, for the prediction information, the GPT model only considers one-way information, so the prediction effect is reduced.

The ERNIE model enables the model to learn the semantic representation of complete concepts by masking semantic units such as words and entities. Compared with BERT learning the original language signal, ERNIE directly models the prior semantic knowledge unit, which enhances the semantic representation ability of the model. The training corpus of ERNIE introduces multi-source data knowledge. However, ERNIE uses knowledge entities as the mask granularity, which is equivalent to forcibly introducing knowledge priors. There are limitations in partially open entity domains.

It is worth noting that the experimental results show that RFLSem is higher than ERNIE and XLNet in the indicators of RMSE. RMSE is mainly related to training error, and in the process of text sentiment analysis, it is mainly to understand a semantic relationship in context and focus on understanding the specific meaning of phrases, so this leads to a higher RMSE value of RFLSem than ERNIE and XLNet.

From the comparison results, we can observe that for all four datasets, our approach had higher performance than the six classical pre-trained models.

4.3   RQ3 – Comparison with the Optimized Pre-trained Models

The experimental results of RQ3 are shown in Table 4. It can be seen from Table 4 that RFLSem has the best effect in the process of model optimization of each pre-trained model. This is due to the sentiment analysis of the script, which must be very dependent on the context. ERNIE can make the model more general by merging masks and can learn the dependencies of knowledge and the dependencies of the longer sense. More improvements in the Albert model are biased towards NSP tasks, while in sentiment analysis tasks, NSP tasks are not used much.

We can find that the overall indicator of the performance of the English dataset will be better than the Chinese. This is because English vocabulary is better trained on a large corpus. However, our model does not segment Chinese input, and only treats a single word as the basic unit of text. Moreover, the selected English data set is mostly short comments and sentiment classification for a certain aspect, a single sentence is a learning unit, and the upper and lower records have no emotional connection and impact. The Chinese dataset is a script dataset, and the upper and lower sentences are mostly complete learning units, and even in the text across the drama, there is still an emotional connection and impact. There is a strong context and connection between the scenes, so the evaluation results are quite different. Moreover, Chinese the complexity of grammar and semantics, to a certain extent, increases the difficulty of sentiment analysis.

In conclusion, our approach had higher performance than the six optimized pre-trained models.

Table 3. Comparison with typical sentiment analysis techniques

Data	Approach	Macro-F1	Micro-F1	RSME	Precision	Recall
Movie-ch	BERT	0.7641	0.9123	0.4026	0.8130	0.8201
	Roberta	0.7668	0.9210	0.4193	0.8746	0.8700
	Albert	0.7533	0.9110	0.4008	0.8004	0.8155
	XLNet	0.7610	0.9092	0.4102	0.8655	0.8532
	ERNIE	0.7644	0.9100	0.3975	0.8337	0.8320
	GPT	0.6806	0.8687	0.4506	0.8034	0.8142
	RFLSem	0.7758	0.9247	0.3553	0.8821	0.8745
Movie-en	BERT	0.9375	0.9375	0.1455	0.9425	0.9422
	Roberta	0.9515	0.9515	0.1331	0.9484	0.9483
	Albert	0.9305	0.9305	0.2064	0.9300	0.9300
	XLNet	0.9508	0.9508	0.1361	0.9475	0.9469
	ERNIE	0.9211	0.9211	0.2238	0.9213	0.9245
	GPT	0.8677	0.8677	0.4015	0.8550	0.8810
	RFLSem	0.9620	0.9620	0.1380	0.9648	0.9549
IMDB	BERT	0.9121	0.9121	0.3267	09154	0.9122
	Roberta	0.9108	0.9108	0.2346	0.9122	0.9108
	Albert	0.9108	0.9108	0.4113	0.9122	0.9108
	XLNet	0.9322	0.9322	0.2675	0.9322	0.9322
	ERNIE	0.9209	0.9209	0.3841	0.8011	0.8045
	GPT	0.8002	0.8002	0.4769	0.8019	0.7986
	RFLSem	0.9437	0.9437	0.1300	0.9438	0.9437
SST	BERT	0.4951	0.5087	0.7436	0.5212	0.4933
	Roberta	0.5360	0.5568	0.7391	0.5380	0.5069
	Albert	0.4493	0.4627	0.8970	0.4751	0.4542
	XLNet	0.5077	0.5127	0.7647	0.5208	0.5135
	ERNIE	0.5124	0.5200	0.7344	0.5289	0.5011
	GPT	0.4123	0.4211	0.7955	0.5016	0.5108
	RFLSem	0.5457	0.5512	0.7567	0.5435	0.5530

4.4 RQ4 – Ablation Study About Optimized Strategies

The experimental results of RQ4 are shown in Table 5, which shows the results of the step-by-step verification of the optimization strategy involved in the RFLSem model. In the table, Linear means that only the linear regression layer is added, LCG means that only random seeds are added, and FGM means that only FGM adversarial training is added.

From Table 5, we can see that the optimization effect is not particularly obvious with LCG. The reason is that the role of LCG is not to optimize and improve the evaluation index of the model, which can make it reproducible each time the initial parameters are randomized. The addition of a linear regression layer and FGM adversarial training improved the effect of the model to a small extent. The linear regression layer is added to transform the classification task into a linear regression task, that is, logical classification and the continuous value of the

Table 4. Comparison with the optimized pre-trained models

Data	Approach	Macro-F1	Micro-F1	RSME	Precision	Recall
Movie-ch	BERT	0.7755	0.9247	0.3872	0.8744	0.8732
	Albert	0.7587	0.9180	0.3945	0.8634	0.8501
	XLNet	0.7623	0.9210	0.3839	0.8709	0.8712
	ERNIE	0.7674	0.9215	0.3698	0.8655	0.8439
	GPT	0.7541	0.8791	0.4002	0.8554	0.8530
	RFLSem	0.7758	0.9247	0.3553	0.8821	0.8745
Movie-en	BERT	0.9394	0.9393	0.1459	0.9531	0.9514
	Albert	0.9349	0.9349	0.2171	0.9448	0.9502
	XLNet	0.9523	0.9523	0.1356	0.9527	0.9533
	ERNIE	0.9201	0.9201	0.2310	0.9438	0.9367
	GPT	0.8006	0.9015	0.3901	0.8590	0.8921
	RFLSem	0.9620	0.9620	0.1380	0.9648	0.9549
IMDB	BERT	0.9190	0.9190	0.1386	0.9200	0.9198
	Albert	0.9046	0.9046	0.1329	0.9062	0.9047
	XLNet	0.9303	0.9303	0.1262	0.9306	0.9303
	ERNIE	0.9289	0.9289	0.1400	0.9114	0.9120
	GPT	0.8853	0.8853	0.3901	0.8590	0.8921
	RFLSem	0.9437	0.9437	0.1300	0.9438	0.9437
SST	BERT	0.4992	0.5089	0.7438	0.5139	0.4948
	Albert	0.4634	0.4786	0.7733	0.4787	0.4598
	XLNet	0.5288	0.5310	0.7678	0.5242	0.5493
	ERNIE	0.5310	0.5324	0.7723	0.5279	0.5489
	GPT	0.5273	0.5301	0.7810	0.4689	0.5105
	RFLSem	0.5457	0.5512	0.79	0.5435	0.5530

Table 5. Comparison results of different optimized strategies

OS	MacroF1	MicroF1	RSME	Precision	Recall
Linear	0.9344	0.9344	0.1365	0.9355	0.9344
LCG	0.9161	0.9161	0.1300	0.9161	0.9161
FGM	0.9225	0.9325	0.1346	0.9224	0.9225
RFLSem	0.9437	0.9437	0.1300	0.9438	0.9437

output is classified by determining the maximum component of the fitted output. Compared with the direct output of classification result vectors, the accuracy is improved. FGM adversarial training is added and noise training is introduced to regularize the parameters of the model. This enhances the robustness and generalization ability of the model and improves the application performance of the model.

In conclusion, the three optimization strategies adopted by RFLSem have positive effects on the results of sentiment analysis.

5 Related Work

There are many studies on the emotional classification of traditional approaches based on sentiment dictionaries. For example, Subasic et al. [24] have completed the determination of the emotional polarity of words based on artificially constructed emotional polarity dictionaries. et al. [11] propose a method that can take into account the contextual polarity of each emotional word. et al. [30] designed and used Weibo emotional words to extend the basic emotional dictionary. Then, they applied the fusion dictionary to analyze the online comment text. In the end, they verified the effectiveness of the sentiment analysis technique based on the microblog dictionary through experiments.

Many researchers have proposed ML-based methods. For example, Kennedy et al. [1] proposed the Unigram hybrid model, which extended the domain-specific sentiment dictionary to extract sentiment classification features more efficiently. Wawre et al. [28] compared and analyzed two machine learning methods, SVM and Naive Bayes (NB). Huq et al. [7] used K-Nearest Neighbor (KNN) and SVM to identify the emotional polarity of Twitter text, and classified the sentiment label by principal component analysis in SVM, because of the few experimental dimensions, the hyperplane of SVM is difficult to determine, so the classification effect of KNN algorithm is better than that of SVM when classifying positive and negative emotions.

Kaur et al. [10]. Jin et al. [9] combined the training methods of text vectors (Word2vec Doc2veC TF-IDF model) and machine classification models for classification. Iqbal et al. [8] propose an integrated framework that can narrow the difference between dictionary-based and machine learning, and improve accuracy and scalability.

ML-based methods are superior to the traditional approaches based on sentiment dictionaries, but it requires a lot of feature processing, and due to the massive amount of text information in the network, it cannot be extracted manually. Therefore, the researchers turned their attention to DL-based methods.

DL can help obtain in-depth semantic information in the emotion, the DL-based methods have become the most promising research trend in this context. Socher et al. [23] introduced a recursive autoencoder-based model for sentiment analysis of film evaluation, which was more obvious than traditional methods. Bengio et al. [2] proposed a single-neuron network sentiment analysis method based on input, hidden, and output based on a three-layer forward neural network.

Generally speaking, it is a network trained and preserved by a large amount of data, that is, a model created by predecessors to solve similar problems, we directly start from this model when we encounter new problems, and can achieve better sentiment classification results applied to specific downstream tasks by fine-tuning in all aspects on the basis of the pre-training model.

Currently, a variety of pre-training modes are widely used, and the pre-training mode is a model trained by an existing data set. Dai et al. [4] proposed semi-supervised sequence learning, which is an improved recurrent neural network based on language models and sequence self-coding. Ramachandran et al. [21] extend the previous study and propose that the accuracy of the Seq2Seq [25] model can be improved through pre-training. This method proves that this method is also effective for the Seq2Seq model by adjusting a small number of monitored data under a large number of unsupervised conditions. Peters et al. [18] proposed a text-based fusion context expression method and experimented with some typical tasks, and achieved good results. The language model GPT (Generative PreTraining) published by [20] is based on the Transformer structure. The first thing it has to do is unsupervised pre-training of a large number of corpora, and then use the model obtained in the previous step. Next, fine-tune specific tasks. Then, monitor it to a smaller extent. Finally, we can get the model. Pota et al. [19] propose a sentiment analysis method for Twitter, they take into account some noise present in spotting and emojis that may affect sentiment analysis. In addition, they analyzed tweets in both English and Italian using the BERT model. Nugroho et al. [14] propose a BERT-based model for transfer learning, and the dataset is based on Indonesian user reviews of the top ten best apps in Google Play websites in 2020. Zhang et al. [31] analyzed the sentiment in online course reviews, and they believed that accurate analysis of sentiment in online course reviews was helpful to understand learners' emotional changes and improve course quality.

Sarangi et al. [22] propose a BERT-based encoder that combines syntax and pre-trained embeddings with BERT embeddings through a tandem mechanism. Based on this method, the sentiment in the structured text is analyzed. Wu et al. [29] Aspect-based sentiment analysis (ABSA) and goal-based sentiment analysis (TABSA) allow for more fine-grained inferences about sentiment from the same text based on context. For example, for a given text, you can have different goals (e.g., neighborhood) and different aspects (e.g., price or security) to analyze the sentiment associated with each target domain aspect. In addition, Wu et al. [29] add context to the self-attention mechanism and propose a context-guided BERT model (CG-BERT) to improve the performance of sentiment analysis.

6 Conclusion

In this paper, we proposed an model, namely RFLSem, for analyzing sentiment both the Chinese dataset and English dataset. The source code was developed to implement the RFLSem. Experiments showed that RFLSem had higher precision, recall, Macro-F1, Micro-F1 than state-of-art techniques. In addition, RFLSem could deliver fast analyzing sentiment and achieve high F1-score in practice.

However, considering the complexity of sentiment analysis of text data, we will closely combine key research with downstream tasks, design more targeted methods, and continue to improve the sentiment analysis model. In addition, we will try to find a better way to consider the contextual relationship and improve the sentiment analysis ability of the model.

References

1. Bandhakavi, A., Wiratunga, N., Padmanabhan, D., Massie, S.: Lexicon based feature extraction for emotion text classification. Pattern Recognit. Lett. **93**, 133–142 (2017)
2. Bengio, Y., Ducharme, R., Vincent, P., Janvin, C.: A neural probabilistic language model. J. Mach. Learn. Res. (2003)
3. Chakravarthi, B.R., Muralidaran, V., Priyadharshini, R., McCrae, J.P.: Corpus creation for sentiment analysis in code-mixed Tamil-English text. In: Workshop on Spoken Language Technologies for Under-resourced Languages (2020)
4. Dai, A.M., Le, Q.V.: Semi-supervised sequence learning. In: NIPS (2015)
5. Fiaidhi, J., Mohammed, O., Mohammed, S., Fong, S.J., Hoon Kim, T.: Opinion mining over twitterspace: classifying tweets programmatically using the r approach. Seventh International Conference on Digital Information Management (ICDIM 2012), pp. 313–319 (2012)
6. Han, H., Zhang, J., Yang, J., Shen, Y., Zhang, Y.: Generate domain-specific sentiment lexicon for review sentiment analysis. Multimed. Tools Appl. **77**(16), 21265–21280 (2018). https://doi.org/10.1007/s11042-017-5529-5
7. Huq, M.R., Ali, A., Rahman, A.: Sentiment analysis on Twitter data using KNN and SVM. Int. J. Adv. Comput. Sci. Appl. **8** (2017)
8. Iqbal, F., et al.: A hybrid framework for sentiment analysis using genetic algorithm based feature reduction. IEEE Access **7**, 14637–14652 (2019)
9. Jin, X., Xu, Y.: Research on the sentiment analysis based on machine learning and feature extraction algorithm. In: 2019 IEEE 10th International Conference on Software Engineering and Service Science (ICSESS), pp. 366–369 (2019)
10. Kaur, S., Sikka, G., Awasthi, L.K.: Sentiment analysis approach based on n-gram and KNN classifier. In: 2018 First International Conference on Secure Cyber Computing and Communication (ICSCCC), pp. 1–4 (2018)

11. Kennedy, A., Inkpen, D.: Sentiment classification of movie reviews using contextual valence shifters. Comput. Intell. **22** (2006)
12. Lipton, Z.C., Elkan, C.P., Narayanaswamy, B.: Optimal thresholding of classifiers to maximize f1 measure. In: Machine Learning and Knowledge Discovery in Databases: European Conference, ECML PKDD ... : Proceedings. ECML PKDD, vol. 8725, pp. 225–239 (2014)
13. Liu, Y., et al.: RoBERTa: a robustly optimized BERT pretraining approach. arXiv abs/1907.11692 (2019)
14. Nugroho, K.S., Sukmadewa, A.Y., HaftittahWuswilahaken, D., Bachtiar, F.A., Yudistira, N.: BERT fine-tuning for sentiment analysis on Indonesian mobile apps reviews. In: 6th International Conference on Sustainable Information Engineering and Technology 2021 (2021)
15. Onan, A.: Sentiment analysis on massive open online course evaluations: a text mining and deep learning approach. Comput. Appl. Eng. Educ. **29**, 572–589 (2020)
16. Opitz, J., Burst, S.: Macro f1 and macro f1. arXiv abs/1911.03347 (2019)
17. Ouyang, X., Zhou, P., Li, C.H., Liu, L.: Sentiment analysis using convolutional neural network. In: 2015 IEEE International Conference on Computer and Information Technology; Ubiquitous Computing and Communications; Dependable, Autonomic and Secure Computing; Pervasive Intelligence and Computing, pp. pp. 2359–2364 (2015)
18. Peters, M.E., et al.: Deep contextualized word representations. In: North American Chapter of the Association for Computational Linguistics (2018)
19. Pota, M., Ventura, M., Fujita, H., Esposito, M.: Multilingual evaluation of preprocessing for BERT-based sentiment analysis of tweets. Expert Syst. Appl. **181**, 115119 (2021)
20. Radford, A., Narasimhan, K.: Improving language understanding by generative pre-training (2018)
21. Ramachandran, P., Liu, P.J., Le, Q.V.: Unsupervised pretraining for sequence to sequence learning. In: Conference on Empirical Methods in Natural Language Processing (2016)
22. Sarangi, P., Ganesan, S., Arora, P., Joshi, S.R.: Amex AI labs at SemEval-2022 task 10: contextualized fine-tuning of BERT for structured sentiment analysis. In: SEMEVAL (2022)
23. Socher, R., Lin, C.C.Y., Ng, A., Manning, C.D.: Parsing natural scenes and natural language with recursive neural networks. In: International Conference on Machine Learning (2011)
24. Subasic, P., Huettner, A.K.: Affect analysis of text using fuzzy semantic typing. In: Ninth IEEE International Conference on Fuzzy Systems. FUZZ- IEEE 2000 (Cat. No.00CH37063), vol. 2, pp. 647–652 (2000)
25. Sutskever, I., Vinyals, O., Le, Q.V.: Sequence to sequence learning with neural networks. In: NIPS (2014)
26. Uddin, G., Guéhénuc, Y.G., Khomh, F., Roy, C.K.: An empirical study of the effectiveness of an ensemble of stand-alone sentiment detection tools for software engineering datasets. ACM Trans. Softw. Eng. Methodol. (TOSEM) **31**, 1–38 (2021)
27. Wang, Z., Bovik, A.C.: Mean squared error: love it or leave it? A new look at signal fidelity measures. IEEE Sig. Process. Mag. **26**, 98–117 (2009)
28. Wawre, S.V., Deshmukh, S.N.: Sentiment classification using machine learning techniques (2016)
29. Wu, Z., Ong, D.C.: Context-guided BERT for targeted aspect-based sentiment analysis. arXiv abs/2010.07523 (2020)

30. Yan, H., Peng, X.F., Zhu, X.W.: Research on sentiment analysis and abnormal feature extraction technology based on comments data. In: Proceedings of the 2019 International Conference on Electronical, Mechanical and Materials Engineering (ICE2ME 2019) (2019)
31. Zhang, H., Dong, J., Min, L., Bi, P.: A BERT fine-tuning model for targeted sentiment analysis of Chinese online course reviews. Int. J. Artif. Intell. Tools **29**, 2040018:1–2040018:23 (2020)
32. Zhang, Z., Han, X., Liu, Z., Jiang, X., Sun, M., Liu, Q.: Ernie: enhanced language representation with informative entities. In: Annual Meeting of the Association for Computational Linguistics (2019)

Author Index

A
Annisa, Annisa 35

B
Bi, Ke 366

C
Cao, Yang 35
Chen, Enhong 151
Chen, Gangbin 291
Chen, Guibin 250
Chen, Hao 99
Chen, Lei 279, 430
Chen, Nanxi 387
Chen, Yulong 99
Cheng, Debo 35, 418
Cheng, Junwei 291
Cheng, Shuang 189
Cong, Shan 356
Cui, Xu 343

D
Dang, Jiayi 451
Ding, Ningpei 418

F
Fan, Chenyou 3
Fang, Quntian 318
Feng, Zaiwen 418

G
Gong, Lu 197, 211, 304
Guo, Ping 140

H
Han, Liangzhe 112
Han, Sheng 267
He, Chaobo 291
He, Dongxiao 56
He, Ping 442

He, Shanshan 242
Hu, Biao 318
Hu, Minghao 318
Hu, Xinyu 12
Hu, Yue 124, 140
Huang, Cheng 175
Huang, Heyan 124, 140
Huang, Weichun 12
Huang, Yuxiao 56
Huang, Zhen 318
Huo, Cuiying 56

J
Ji, Yucheng 163
Jiang, Shuai 35
Jin, Di 56
Jin, Zhi 451

L
Lai, Yutao 279
Li, Chen 35
Li, Dongsheng 318
Li, Fei 366
Li, Haonan 343
Li, Hongli 366
Li, Mingkang 197, 211, 304
Li, Mingyong 163
Li, Tianpeng 403
Li, Wei 366
Li, Xiang 163
Li, Xiangxia 242
Li, Xiaoxia 418
Li, Yu 343
Li, Zhaokui 366
Liang, Wanying 291
Lin, Youfang 267
Ling, Tongtao 279
Liu, Bo 69
Liu, Hai-Lin 279, 430
Liu, Huai 451
Liu, Jiayong 175

Z. Jin et al. (Eds.): KSEM 2023, LNAI 14120, pp. 469–471, 2023.
https://doi.org/10.1007/978-3-031-40292-0

Printed in the United States
by Baker & Taylor Publisher Services